58·08

Real World

Adobe GoLive 5

by

Jeff Carlson

Glenn Fleishman

with

Neil Robertson

Agen Schmitz

☽   ☽

From equinox to equinox, for Lynn D. and Kimberly

Real World Adobe GoLive 5

By Jeff Carlson and Glenn Fleishman
With Neil Robertson and Agen Schmitz

Copyright © 2001 by Jeff Carlson and Glenn Fleishman

Peachpit Press

1249 Eighth Street
Berkeley, CA 94710
510/524-2178 or 800/283-9444 (voice)
510/524-2221 (fax)

Find us on the World Wide Web at: http://www.peachpit.com
Peachpit Press is a division of Addison Wesley Longman

Real World Adobe GoLive 5 is published in association with Adobe Press.

For resources mentioned in this book, see: http://www.realworldgolive.com

Editor: Marty Cortinas
Production Coordinators: Lisa Brazieal, Connie Jeung-Mills
Copy Editors: Toby Malina, Don Sellers
Proofreaders: Charles Fleishman, Liane Thomas
Interior design: Jeff Carlson
Graphics production: Carl Juarez, Jeff Tolbert
Compositor: Owen Wolfson
Cover design: Gee + Chung Design
Cover illustration: Jeff Brice
Indexer: Kari Kells

Colophon

This book was written in Microsoft Word 98, and created using Adobe Photoshop 5.5, Adobe Illustrator 8 & 9, Adobe LiveMotion 1, Adobe GoLive 5 (of course), Equilibrium DeBabelizer 3 (Mac), Exposure Pro (Mac), HyperSnapX (Windows), and QuarkXPress 4.11—with a liberal use of Qualcomm Eudora, Timbuktu Pro, and AppleShare IP—on a variety of computers, including a generic Pentium II, Connectix Virtual PC 3, two PowerBook 400 Mhz 1999 Series G3s, iMacs, and a G4 Cube. The fonts used are Adobe Minion and Formata.

ISBN 0-201-70406-4

9 8 7 6 5 4 3 2 1

Printed and bound in the United States of America

Foreword

By John Kranz, senior product manager, Adobe GoLive

The complexities underlying Web design grow with nearly the same exponential speed as the Web itself. What was initially simply the need to author static information on the Web is now frowned upon in most Web design circles as yesterday's brochureware.

Many of today's common productivity tools, down to the level of a word processor, provide a convenient "Export to HTML" feature to meet the need for Web authorship. But is this really the road best traveled towards effective Web design?

The focus of successful Web sites transcends design itself, and goes well beyond simple HTML conversion of documents, focusing on dynamic information, tailored for the individual visitor, updated continuously. This, after all, is what creates a "sticky" site: one to which a customer will return again and again. Just as one can't judge a good book by its cover, a well-designed Web site must extend beyond simple layout and design to encompass sound architecture and the added value that results from presenting in an engaging manner.

How does Adobe GoLive 5 help one create a compelling Web site in today's complex, dynamic Web design equation?

Hats, and Hands, Off

Web designers find themselves wearing many hats nowadays. Whether you're designing your first Web site on your own, or are part of a professional workgroup, it's imperative that the tools at your disposal meet not only your requirements, but also those of your collaborators.

This was one of the mandates behind our 360Code feature with the 5.0 release. This feature ensures that the graphic design work accomplished by one person could be created without altering the source code that may have been entered by a programmer. While this effort required rearchitecting GoLive itself to no longer "mess with code," the fruits of this labor now empower the graphic professional and hand-coder to work harmoniously side-by-side without causing any compromise in their collective efforts.

A Web design tool must also be extremely flexible: enough to meet your needs while it grows in power to match the quickening complexity of Web design itself. Designers (and clients) embrace the latest Web technologies, such as SWF (Flash) and QuickTime, while at the same time trying to honor Web standards established by the W3C (World Wide Web Consortium, www.w3c.org), including XML and XHTML. This flexibility must also know no bounds in addressing customer needs, which is the motivating factor behind the robust GoLive SDK and JavaScript Debugger application built into GoLive so developers can add new levels of functionality to the product. Several new and exciting GoLive Extensions have already been introduced by Adobe in partnership with key associates, and are available for downloading from adobe.com.

Towards this end, Adobe GoLive 5 has developed into a Swiss Army knife of sorts, offering a multiplicity of powerful authoring and site management features. In fact, I commonly refer to GoLive as being many applications in one, sporting a robust cafeteria style of services to choose from depending upon the type of design work you're carrying out. Simply look at the QuickTime editing tools or the new Site Design feature as clear examples.

Putting Tools to Use

The breadth of these features and how best to present them is the greatest challenge confronting the authors of *Real World Adobe GoLive 5*. Jeff Carlson and Glenn Fleishman have answered this challenge by not only covering the countless features included, but by masterfully introducing features involved, from the simplest to most advanced tasks, in a readable, digestible, and engaging format.

The authors could have easily become lost by simply focusing on various tips and tricks (enough to fill the pages of a separate book) rather than meaningful tasks—the "bigger picture." But, instead, they have followed the integrated design approach Adobe has pursued in creating a tool that gracefully provides a range of tools that allow simple layout all the way to the most advanced site and programming options available.

I guess you could say I'm one of Jeff's and Glenn's biggest fans, or I'm simply out to embarrass them as much as possible. I've witnessed firsthand the countless hours they have invested in this work—dating originally to our previous release of GoLive 4—in compiling this exhaustive resource to literally guide you through the many new features offered in GoLive 5.

Most importantly, rather than simply telling you the GoLive story, they have both been proactively engaged in it, providing valuable feedback and direction throughout the development and testing of this product—down to many email exchanges with our product management and development team. I mention this to simply spotlight and recognize the wealth of knowledge and insight the authors bring to this work, which you will undoubtedly recognize from the opening pages.

While inspiration is perhaps one of the single most important ingredients to successful Web design, and life itself, people often need a guide to help them channel their energies in the most productive and focused manner possible. This is the most lasting impression this book will leave on many, as the authors manage the burden of introducing you to the multiple new, exciting features of Adobe GoLive 5 that will turn your design inspirations into reality much quicker and easier than you could have imagined.

In closing, there is also the promise of what tomorrow brings, and tomorrow will bring future versions and enhancements to Adobe GoLive. Towards this end, I encourage readers to submit their product feature wishlist requests to <golivewishlist@adobe.com>, as one of my primary roles in the organization is to put on my listening cap and make sure your wishes are not only heard, but acted upon in future product releases.

—September 2000

Preface

Wwwwwl cnnn!
— *The Tin Woodsman from "The Wizard of Oz"*

Of course, we adore GoLive. We've spent countless hours working with it. We wrote a book about it. But GoLive 4, despite having huge improvements over its predecessor, CyberStudio 3, still had creaky joints and missing bolts. We'd poke at it some times and hear that squeak emerge, "Wwwwl cnnn! Wwwwwl cnn!" We finally figured out (like Dorothy) that the program was saying, "Oil can!"

To painfully extend the metaphor, the Adobe GoLive product managers and engineers supplied the grease that turned GoLive 4 into the well-oiled machine of GoLive 5. (And, yes, it does have a heart and brain, but we're wondering how it will exhibit courage.)

So many of the features that had caused us trouble in version 4 were fixed, improved, or replaced with better ones. That doesn't make good copy, of course, nor does it lend itself particularly well to writing a book update. For example: "In GoLive 4, you had to press Enter or Tab to make the program accept the text. In GoLive 5…you don't." "In GoLive 4, you couldn't apply external Cascading Style Sheets to more than one file at once. In GoLive 5…you can."

You get our point.

We tried to avoid the trap in this second edition of *Real World Adobe GoLive* of sounding like a squeaky wheel (yes, gotta strain that metaphor). The first edition covered versions 4.0 and 4.0.1, and was written just after Adobe acquired GoLive, Inc., a German-based firm that had shepherded a product then known as GoLive CyberStudio through three major revisions.

This 5.0 release came almost 18 months after 4.0's Macintosh release and a year after the Windows 4.0 release. In that time, Adobe truly did survey and listen to its users, and even convened a panel of GoLive experts early enough in the 5.0 revision process to garner input on revisions and new features.

The final product is pretty terrific. We liked versions 2, 3, and 4 of GoLive, but 5 is starting to feel, well, mature. It's got most of the features we need for day-to-day purposes, and a lot of extras packed in that help us out when we try something new.

Even better, version 5 cleaned up its act. There were plenty of small annoyances and a few not-quite-there features (like the Table Inspector's Hidden tab) that teased us without pleasing us. But now GoLive 5 is up to snuff and works as expected. (We even figured out how to use URL Mapping, which baffled us in all previous versions.)

Throughout the book, you'll see notes and sidebars that help those of you using GoLive 4 make a smoother transition into GoLive 5. In many instances, we provide an explanation for where to find something that's been moved, renamed, or revamped.

Real World Means Real World

Our focus is and always has been on production: taking design ideas and turning them into practical expressions of page structure and HTML code. This book tries to advise you on using GoLive for that kind of production work, whether you're modifying a few pages every couple of days, or running a 10,000-page site with shared navigational elements.

If you want to know how to use GoLive from the ground up and create world-class pages that work across all browsers, and make best use of the built-in features of GoLive, buy this book (if you're just browsing), or read it from cover to cover (if you've already purchased it).

If you're looking for a book on graphic design or designing on the Web, this isn't it. This also isn't an HTML introduction that advises you on the content and values of each tag (though you'll find that we do cover many tags in detail as they relate to GoLive features). We eschew general discussions of aesthetic principles and encyclopedic coverage of coding in favor of production-oriented advice and tips. For instance, we explain how to get around some limitations in the underlying HTML to achieve a purpose; we also explain why certain design ideas may work better as expressed in HTML than others. (See our Web site at http://realworldgolive.com/ for recommendations on complementary books that are intended for both HTML and Web design beginners, or those interested in that approach to GoLive or other subjects.)

Why Not Use WordPad or SimpleText?

GoLive rarely squeezes HTML's round pegs into a browser's square holes. With the exception of a kludge popularized by other visual editors and that is truly demanded by users—layout grids—GoLive structures itself around HTML instead of pushing HTML around to achieve dubious results.

The novice Web designer or production person can fire up GoLive and know, with some certainty, that the pages he or she produces won't cause most browsers to react with horror; part of the function of this book is to help you avoid the situations in which a browser (and by extension, a client or employer) might break out in a rash.

The advanced HTML coder has probably already realized that the profusion of acronyms—XML, XHTML, CSS, DHTML—has overwhelmed his or her ability to create complex documents and manage all the content in them. GoLive provides advanced management tools that offer consistent control over the most disparate elements on a page or across a site without a commensurate amount of work.

On its face, GoLive seems like a vast, fractal Swiss Army knife, with every attachment you unhinge revealing subattachments on to infinity. If you glance through the manual and palettes, and click buttons that look like little footballs, stairs, and grids, you might think you've bitten off more than you can chew. But don't rely on first impressions.

The GoLive Way

When you scratch the surface, GoLive has a relatively consistent approach to handling a huge number of complex tasks without making you manage them individually.

Many programs allow you to create simple objects from a toolbar. You select shapes or tools from a palette and then draw or place objects on a page which you can then modify via menus or modal dialog boxes. (GoLive has a toolbar, but it's used almost entirely to manipulate objects; it only creates a limited number of GoLive objects.)

The GoLive way is to figure out the kind of object you need (a floating box, an image, a QuickTime object), drag it onto an open page, and then use a floating palette—the Inspector—to set its values. That's the whole secret. It can be initially baffling. The first time Glenn used the program, he literally couldn't figure out how to get started when faced with a blank window. (He did learn how, we promise.)

You can use GoLive your entire life and never once look at a line of code or modify any HTML. The flip side is that wireheads who use some of GoLive's site-management, editing, and repeating-element features might spend a lot of their time in HTML source and outline views. It's up to you, and the program sings like a songbird either way.

GoLive can work for you in a multitude of ways because it simplifies and centralizes all the problems of managing sites. If you're creating a few pages that aren't much linked together, GoLive is a glorified page editor. But the powerful features it includes for creating rich content on a page—integrating style sheets, dynamic motion, prefabricated scripts, and good ol'-fashioned HTML—couple mightily with the tools for creating small and large consistent Web sites that are a snap to expand and update.

The best part of using GoLive, and the best part of writing this book, is that although it isn't all things to all people, it certainly is most things to many people. Most users find themselves deep into the program within a short time, whether they're using it to work on a single page or a large site.

Who's This Book For?

We wrote this book with three types of users in mind:

The slightly experienced beginner. We define this kind of person as someone who has learned a bit about the Web, used one or more programs, and has some kind of concept of how it all fits together. You don't need to be able to sit down at the keyboard and write pages from scratch, but being able to decipher HTML or just having some familiarity with conventions will help tremendously. (See the next section if you rank yourself below this level.)

If you've just started using GoLive, or have spent some time with it and are trying to sort out the many, many features in the program, *Real World Adobe GoLive 5* offers Part 1, *GoLive Basics*. This part of the book provides a comprehensive overview of all the features, palettes, preferences, and interface approaches used in the program. Consider it a ramp-up guide to beginning to use the software.

The next two parts, *Pages* and *Sites*, focus on the nitty-gritty of production and working within and outside of GoLive's constraints.

The *Advanced* part is the icing on the cake: a section devoted to the extra goodies that you'll want to get to in time.

The intermediate user. Before starting on the first edition of this book, we categorized ourselves between intermediate and advanced GoLive users; by the time we had finished, after months of hard work pushing and pulling the program, we called ourselves "advanced." To paraphrase Keanu Reeves's eloquence in *The Matrix*, "We know kung-fu." (Your reply should be: "Show me.") We want to transfer that acquisition of knowledge to the intermediate user who needs to get more out of the program, but has reached a plateau in the learning curve.

The *GoLive Basics* part of the book offers a good reference guide to features when you just can't find that one Inspector tab (out of at least 100) that you need to accomplish a task; or you're mystified about where a given preference might live (just ask us about how to set the line break preference!).

The real meat for intermediate users is *Pages* and *Sites*, as we've ferreted out all the day-to-day, real-world tricks and techniques you need to accomplish your specific tasks. We also cover all the options, basics, and extras of tools to visually edit and manage pages and sites.

Part 4, *Advanced*, is where you, as an intermediate user, can really leap ahead. You might be interested, for example, in using JavaScript. Although the *JavaScript* chapter doesn't teach you how to code that language—we offer some recommendations on where to learn—it does get you quickly up to speed on how to use GoLive to carry out your codes. The same is true for DHTML, Cascading Style Sheets (CSS), and other advanced topics.

The advanced user. For a program as vast and deep as GoLive, we find ourselves often wishing for a reference that tells us everything about the program, even the fiddly little bits like editing the XML source file that contains all the special characters.

Well, friends, this book serves that purpose. The *GoLive Basics* part of the book can serve as a reference for you, just as for an intermediate user, in quickly getting the correct value, method, or location for a given task. It also can be a great visual reference for plotting a plan of attack for a given project. Making sure GoLive has a particular feature can save some time.

The *Pages* and *Sites* sections might be more of a review than a primer for an advanced user, but we've tried to include as much detail and advice as possible for achieving best results, or for learning new tips to improve your workflow. A review of selected chapters might help you eke out even more efficiency.

The *Advanced* part of the book is aimed at helping those users who already know the basics of a protocol GoLive supports, like DHTML or XML, to quickly use those features with GoLive's tools; or to bypass GoLive's tools with knowledge of how GoLive interacts with hand coding.

Starting Out from Scratch

If you've never touched the underlying HTML of a Web page, never used a graphical page editor, and never worked on a Web site in any capacity, our book makes a number of assumptions that might leave you frustrated. How's that for honesty?

Although our book is the source of all that is good and true, you should get another book or three (recommended on our Web site at http://realworld-golive.com) that can start you down the path. You don't need to go very far in your other studies, but we don't recommend diving in feet-first without getting acclimated to the water first.

How This Book Is Structured

Real World Adobe GoLive 5 is broken into four parts:

GoLive Basics. This section covers all the details that make up GoLive. We start with a quick overview of using all the features in the program to build a page and then a site. We proceed to cover all the myriad appearances of the attribute-examining, many-tabbed Inspector palette, and then on to the palettes and parts of the interface that allow you to modify or insert elements. Next, we cover where all the settings and preferences live in GoLive, what they control, and how to "detail" your program (like a racing car) to match your needs.

Pages. GoLive has a fully integrated visual page editor that allows you to drag and drop elements onto a page, format text, add colors, and control tables, frames, and other structured elements. This part of the book fully delves into each area in turn. We start with an overview, and then proceed through the Layout Editor, the Head section, text and fonts, images, color, tables, layout grids, frames, floating boxes, and forms. The section also looks at editing HTML source code and incorporating various media elements (such as QuickTime editing, Flash and PDF URL management, and using browser plug-ins in GoLive to simulate browser behavior). We then finish with a round-up of other page-related features that don't fit neatly into any of those categories.

Sites. GoLive shines at site management, which includes tracking content across a site—such as images, links, and colors—and correctly uploading new files to a remote Web server. This part walks through the overall organization of the Site window, in which site management is focused in GoLive, and then into individual tabs and subjects. We cover prototyping and building new sites and site sections using the stupendous (and new) site design feature; handling sitewide font sets and colors through the Font Sets and Colors tabs; and uploading, downloading, and synchronizing content through built-in FTP (File Transfer Protocol) and WebDAV support.

This part finishes up with a chapter on the popular subject of importing an existing site created by hand or in another application. (This is probably the number-one how-to query from readers and GoLive users.)

Advanced. It's always a judgment call when talking about what's "advanced" and what's not. We bit the bullet and grouped all the newer and browser-dependent parts of GoLive—which were complex enough to require a real grounding in knowledge found outside the scope of this book—into the *Advanced* section.

This includes the JavaScript scripting language; DHTML (Dynamic HTML), which we opted to split into the two discrete parts that GoLive has defined: animation and pre-defined Actions; Cascading Style Sheets for controlling text ranges and text blocks; Dynamic Link, a new tool for hooking GoLive into certain databases to feed live content out on Web pages; and Web Settings, which is a many-tabbed dialog box acting as a kind of GoLive command and control center for all the assumptions about global HTML behavior, HTML tags and attributes, browser simulations, CSS, and file mapping.

Appendixes. But wait, there's more! In Appendix A, we offer up Macintosh-specific issues and extras: a few things that are found only in the Macintosh version of GoLive, including AppleScript support and Apple ColorSync color management.

Ditto, we cover Windows issues and special features in Appendix B, such as…well, precious little. The Macintosh extras are really Apple add-ons that GoLive supports, not GoLive add-ons. The Windows version is pretty much plain vanilla bean.

How to Read This Book

No, this isn't a trick headline: we really do have recommendations. There's too much structured content in this book for a straight-through reading; many features aren't relevant to all users. Our recommendations for getting the most of this book:

- **Scan it first.** Glance through the whole thing to find out where we've put everything and why. The structure above helps, and you can, of course, use the table of contents and index. But it's a big book, and we want you to know the lay of the land.

- **Answer your pressing questions.** Are there subjects you just don't understand? Features that drive you nuts? Parts of the program you adore and want to know more about? Check out the index, and look up those parts of the book.

- **Find the right chapter.** We've tried to structure this real-world book around themes and subjects that we focus on in our professional work on the Web, and that people have told us they use in their working methods.

- **Read the whole thing.** If you can't restrain yourself, stay up til 5 a.m. and read the book cover-to-cover. Once you're done, pop it in the shredder and fill a pillowcase with it. You'll sleep like a baby.

More Knowledge than Fits in Print

We've created a Web site at http://realworldgolive.com that's more than marketing (though we admit to a little of that; it *is* the Web, after all). Use it as a real resource for getting answers to your pressing questions and sharing information with other users, as well as the authors and contributors to this book.

The site contains updates to the book, fixes to errata (we freely admit that we lack infallibility), references to online resources, excerpts or the entire text of articles written by us on GoLive specifics, advanced advice on using the program, and news about GoLive developments.

You can also participate in an active, moderated, archived forum on GoLive that will provide a way for you (and hundreds of readers already subscribed) to get some real answers to some real stumpers.

All the examples noted in the book can be found at the site, as well; this is especially useful with some of the tutorial material in the *Advanced* part of the book.

Of course, you can also buy the book from the site—but, wait...you've already bought the book, haven't you? (If not, support your authors and booksellers by spending your hard-earned money to share our hard-earned knowledge.)

What's Different in the Second Edition

This second edition of *Real World Adobe GoLive* covers GoLive 5 from start to finish, but we do mention important new features or differences in the program from GoLive 4.0 or 4.0.1 to 5. If you've used previous versions of GoLive, look for the section at the start of many chapters that summarizes all the new features in GoLive 5 for that subject, if any.

Generally, we fixed errors, rewrote sections that needed revision, wrote entirely new chapters about subjects that didn't exist in GoLive 4 or that we felt needed more coverage than we originally provided. Fundamentally, the approach to the book is the same. Technically, somewhere between 10 percent and 100 percent of each chapter is new, with the typical case being about a third new material, and two-thirds updated.

We listened to our Windows readers who felt the book didn't cover their issues thoroughly enough. You'll notice more screen captures from the Windows version of Adobe GoLive in this edition, but at the same time Adobe eliminated virtually all of the differences between the Macintosh and Windows versions of the program.

Our Relationship with Adobe

Although this is an Adobe Press book, it's also a Peachpit Press book. This may be confusing to some readers not intimate with the book industry. We're proud and happy to have the Adobe banner over this title, and they provided technical resources and feedback on drafts of this book. However, they aren't responsible for errors, omissions, statements of opinion, or the current color of our unruly hair.

But, more importantly, Adobe didn't direct or change the content of this book. Because this is a Real World book, we state our opinions and results of our research quite clearly; this book is not the product of a marketing department, nor do we pull punches about things that don't work. At the same time, we're just as positive about what does work; we love this program. This Real World book doesn't give you a tour through the program's menus (though by the end you'll know what each one does). Rather, it shares the knowledge we've gained from our own use of GoLive and that of designers working with it every day in the field.

Conventions Used in This Book

We believe in making text contextually self-explanatory, and have tried to keep fonts, formatting, and special dingbats to a minimum. However, a few conventions are worth highlighting.

Because this book covers both Macintosh and Windows versions of Adobe GoLive, we've made a lot of effort to be as inclusive of both platforms as possible. The screen captures you see throughout the book were made fairly arbitrarily on either platform to emphasize how similar they are. However, whenever something is significantly different between the display in the two platforms, we've included platform-specific screen captures.

Similarly, whenever a key command or menu item is specific to a platform, in the text you see a note such as, "To bring up the contextual menu, Control-click on the Mac or right-click under Windows." At the same time, we didn't go overboard. GoLive is full of keyboard shortcuts and contextual menus that speed up access to its controls, but we don't note every one. In general, if it took longer to mention all the alternate methods of accessing a feature than to actually describe it, we opted for brevity.

TIP:
Read the
Tips!

Tips appear called-out in the margins (as this one is), and generally contain real-world advice, ideas on tweaking settings, or slightly extraneous bits of knowledge that you might enjoy.

NEW IN 5:
New
Features

Items marked with this tag have attention brought to them particularly for users of GoLive 4 who might find the change noteworthy or perplexing.

Code samples are marked in the Courier font to indicate something you can type in:

```
.foobar { text-size: 1000 px }
```

Humor is not specially marked throughout, and you need to apply a special irony filter to your optical input in order to recognize it. (Sarcasm is strictly avoided. Yeah, right.)

Our Team

We couldn't have written this book without the help of some very fine people who shaped the book with their work and advice.

Contributing Writers

Agen "Eggsy" Schmitz (now his real name) was the primary writer of the GoLive Basics part of the book, as well as Chapter 17, *Media* and Chapter 32, *Languages and Scripting*. He started with conference editorial planning, and moved to a "large, unnamed Redmond, WA-based company." After a freelance stint, he now works for a small, Seattle-based company; let's say "a river runs through" its name.

Neil "Super Dooper Action Scooper" Robertson did the primary work on the *JavaScript*, *Animation*, *Actions*, and *Dynamic Link* chapters. Neil is a multimedia and Web designer and producer, having created Web sites back in the days when people asked, "What's a Web site?" He works as a senior multimedia designer and programmer at Phinney-Bischoff Design House.

Neil and Agen performed these tasks for both the first and second editions of this book, and we are indebted to them for the time they put into their work.

Editing, Composition, and Indexing

Forget the myth that a book goes directly from author to press. The reason our book is filled with updated screen shots and absent many typographical errors is that we assembled a crack team of professionals.

Don Sellers, Toby Malina, Liane Thomas, and Charles Fleishman copyedited and proofread the book in various stages of production, and caught those really dumb mistakes that are bound to happen when you're trying to discern features at 2:30 a.m.

Carl Juarez saved us hours of work by updating screen shots of elements whose features didn't change between GoLive 4 and 5, but whose appearance under the new user interface did.

Jeff Tolbert, in addition to putting up with our strange humor and 10:00 a.m. lunch cravings, designed the section title pages.

Owen Wolfson took on the huge task of composing the book, and if it weren't for his speed and quality, we'd still be working. The amount of pain and suffering he saved us is equal to the degree of aplomb with which he carried out his duties.

And finally, Kari Kells created the index, and reinforced our belief that no book should be published without the skills of a professional indexer.

Acknowledgements

Peachpit Press is an author's dream. Supportive and intelligent editors, a great production team, PR and marketing folks who return email promptly and enjoy hearing ideas from authors, and an understanding of, shall we say, the creative mind that doesn't always, ahem, conform to the idea that a month has only 31 days maximum, or that a "week" is the same thing in every culture.

Peachpit has made this book possible in so many ways from the get-go, endorsing our approach to this book, and giving us the variety of encouragement, feedback, and kicks in the tuchis necessary for any good tome.

Glenn was able to convey his early excitement about GoLive to Nancy Aldrich-Ruenzel, Peachpit's publisher, who thought a *Real World* title on GoLive would find a broad audience. (She was right!)

We've worked with three editors across two editions as editors moved around the world and onto other projects: Corbin Collins and Marty Cortinas gave us sanity checks on the first edition (with a boost from Marjorie Baer); Marty was also our second edition editor, who helped speed the book to completion through excellent feedback.

We confessed our undying affection and adoration of Amy Changar in the first edition of the book. Her timely suggestions and advice go beyond production, and for this edition, we're announcing the Shrine of Amy, to which we bow in supplication whenever deadlines loom. Amy changed firms as we moved into production on the book, replaced by Lisa Brazieal who filled big tennis shoes with great aplomb and good work.

Many, many, many people at Adobe Systems made our job as authors so much vastly easier. John Kranz, first and foremost, the senior product manager of Adobe GoLive (and author of our foreword) helped us—and a host of our colleague authors working on other titles—get precisely the kind of access and allowed us the kind of feedback that we think benefits the readers of our respective books and the users of the software. Early and frequent access to beta releases and engineers helped us scout out the details that make GoLive a real powerhouse for design and production. (It also allowed us to moan about small details in the interface which, remarkably, they changed due to the various beta testers' feedback! Hurray, Adobe!)

The multitude of others at Adobe Systems includes Daniel Brown (now working on LiveMotion), Matt Ridley (the god of Actions), Sean Hiss (our trade show friend and a constant source of good feedback from real users), and Adam Pratt and Lisa Grillo (who liked the product so much, they joined the company—honestly). Thanks to the engineers for enjoyable exchanges in English and German by email and phone, including Jens Neffe, Lars Peters, and Lance Lewis.

URL Mappings frankly always baffled us until Rob Keniger posted a concise and clear explanation on the beta testers mailing list. This opened our eyes to how to use it (period) and use it well. Thanks, Rob!

Jeff and Glenn (that's us) share a small and tidy office in a lovely part of Seattle with a bunch of fellow procrastinators and caffeine imbibers. (Some abstain.) Ole Kvern is our guru, Brett Baker is our sensei, David Blatner is our rabbi, and Agen Schmitz is our father confessor. Toby Malina is our Mars Explorer. Our newest colleagues Steve Roth (have PowerBook and Hamlet, will travel) and Jeff Tolbert (the Tuesday night movie maven) were great moral supporters, too.

And, not quite most importantly, but certainly utmost in our minds at this writing, we thank the La Pavoni espresso machine in our office (under the direction of Ole Kvern) for keeping us awake when we thought we lacked the consciousness for writing just…one…more…word.

From Glenn: "Jeff's a kick in the pants (literally, ow!) and a lot of fun to work with. It's great to have an officemate and co-author so cheery and ready to keep on working through the fast pace of revision crunch. My parents and grandparents continue, as always, to lend me the kind of support that only they can do to keep me living a happy life, and producing endless quantities of prose. My partner, my love, Lynn D. Warner, makes this work meaningful, and she's a lot of fun to come home to at the end of the day—unless I'm home first, in which case I say, 'Honey, you're home!'"

From Jeff: "During the first edition of this book, people told us that writing a 700-plus-page book about Adobe GoLive would drive us insane, and, of course, they were correct—for both editions. Despite some nights of sleep-deprived hallucinations and numerous discussions of whether Inspector should be capitalized, the project concluded—and there's still some sanity left. This is entirely due to the patience and generosity of my wife Kimberly, my parents and extended parents Larry & Janet and Susan & Ron, and the folks who were kind enough to ask how the project was going and make coffee when it was most needed. Oh, and there's that Glenn fellow, who is entirely responsible for making this book happen in the first place; who protected our interests when people posted way-off negative comments about the book online ('I can't believe this book has so many words…'); and who has been an excellent co-author and good friend."

Overview

Table of Contents

CHAPTER 21
Files, Folders, and Links 591

CHAPTER 24

Importing a Site **719**

PART 4

Advanced **741**

CHAPTER 25

Advanced Features **743**

CHAPTER 29
Cascading Style Sheets 827

CHAPTER 30
Dynamic Link 863

CHAPTER 31
Web Settings 885

GoLive
Basics
PART 1

CHAPTER 1

Getting Started

Falling in love with a program isn't like falling in love with a person. A person has likes and dislikes, quirks and charms. A program is a bundle of bits structured to perform specific tasks repetitively and identically. But as you may wind up spending more time with programs than your beloved and friends, perhaps you should learn to love GoLive, just a wee bit.

GoLive is a big, sprawling, husky-voiced program that likes to plop down on your sofa, open a bag of chips, and watch football on the picture-in-a-picture while flipping the dial to watch other programs. At the same time, it's a smart, big-hearted program with a great deal of potential just waiting to be tapped.

It's all about becoming familiar with its way of doing things. The so-called experts say you can't really change your partner into what you want; and the same is true with GoLive. It is what it is, just like any program, and you have to learn to think a bit like it does to fully evolve your working relationship.

This part of the book provides an overall guide to the program, walking you through each section of the program so you can become comfortable with its conventions and its interface.

When reading other parts of the book, feel free to refer to these first chapters to get visual explanations of given interfaces or palettes. But our goal is to get you started quickly so you can learn how to accomplish your given tasks.

This chapter walks briskly through the whole process of using GoLive, so you can see every major feature of the program; the next three chapters in this section focus on individual areas and parts of the interface.

Installing GoLive

If you haven't installed GoLive yet, whip that CD out of its slipcase and stick it in your computer's CD-ROM drive. Double-click the Adobe GoLive 5.0 installer icon and continue through the initial screens (the last-minute release notes and software license).

TIP:
Prepping Your System

On the Mac, you need, at a minimum, Mac OS 8.6 with 48 MB of RAM available for the program; realistically, that means having at least 96 MB of real RAM (not virtual or RAMDouble'd).

Under Windows, you need to run Windows 98 or NT or later (such as Windows ME or 2000) with 48 MB of RAM set aside for Windows 98 or 64 MB for NT. Since you can't assign RAM to specific applications under Windows, this means that you need 96 MB for Windows 98 or 128 MB for Windows NT, 2000, or ME installed on your machine for minimally acceptable performance.

TIP:
Allocate Memory Before Starting (Mac)

Making large-scale changes to sites of more than a hundred pages or so can require extra memory. The Mac OS doesn't automatically allocate space to programs on demand, so before you start, find GoLive's application icon, and then either select Get Info from the File menu or press Command-I. Select Memory from the Show popup menu.

Add 5,000K to 10,000K to both the Preferred and Minimum memory fields. We recommend starting with at least 48,000K (48 MB) for both fields and going up from there if you still have memory problems.

TIP:
Virtual Memory

You can turn virtual memory on in both the Macintosh and Windows systems, providing you with additional available memory for programs. However, this slows down overall system performance because virtual memory involves reading and writing from the hard disk. (For details on turning virtual memory on or tweaking memory values, see http://realworldgolive.com/vm.html.)

On the Mac, you can choose between Easy Install (which installs all components) or Custom Install (which allows you to choose individual pieces from a short list). With the Windows installer, choose between Complete, Compact (which installs just the bare necessities), and Custom (see Figure 1-1).

TIP:
Uninstalling (Windows)

Windows installers scatter files all over the place, into the system's registry, and often into system folders. So when you want to remove a program, it's important to use the uninstaller that comes with it. Running the installer for GoLive with the program already loaded allows you to remove all of its components; we know running an installer to uninstall is an oxymoron. This can help on occasion when you are having problems with GoLive or your system: run the uninstall and then reinstall. This can clean out corrupted files or other garbage.

Figure 1-1
Windows
installation
choices

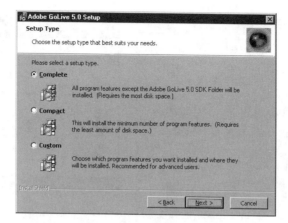

GoLive 5 also installs the Adobe SVG Viewer plug-in (which enables you to view vector-based SVG—scalable vector graphics—files) into browser plug-in folders found on your system. On the Windows side, you're given more of a choice for installation of SVG items (see Figure 1-2); the Mac installer just plows ahead and installs it into every browser on your local hard drive with no choice offered.

Figure 1-2
Windows SVG
installation

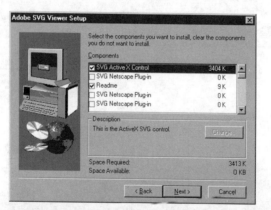

All installed parts are placed within an Adobe GoLive 5.0 folder in the specified directory on the Mac; the Windows installer places the program folder, by default, within an Adobe folder in the Program Files directory (see Figure 1-3). Here you find the GoLive application and a bevy of folders, containing modules (pieces of the program, such as WebObjects, PNG Support, and more), imported images (which GoLive can render and display on the fly), browser plug-ins (to view Shockwave, RealAudio, and other media within GoLive), and the new Dynamic Link feature.

Figure 1-3
Installed
components:
Mac and
Windows

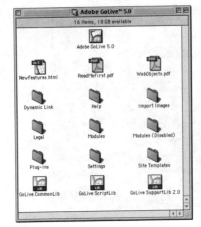 

Opening GoLive

Launch GoLive for the first time and you might start plotting to finally buy
that cinema-sized monitor you've always dreamt of (see Figures 1-4 and 1-5).

Figure 1-4
Macintosh
GoLive
first look

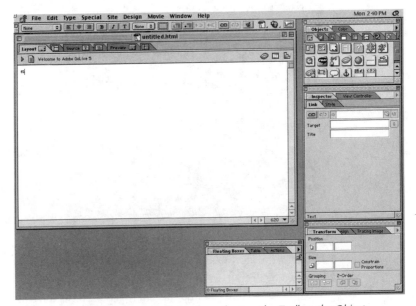

*GoLive's essential elements, clockwise from the top: the Toolbar, the Objects
palette, the Inspector palette, the Transform palette, the Floating Boxes palette,
and the Document window.*

Figure 1-5
Windows
GoLive first
look

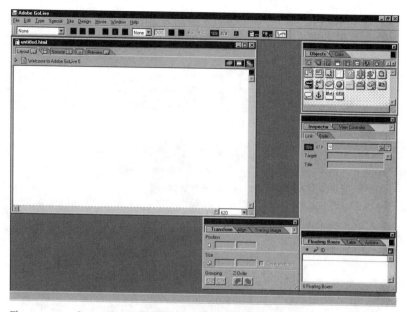

The same configuration under Windows as the Mac

At the top of the screen is the Toolbar, which changes contextually to fit a variety of tasks (see Figure 1-6). You see the Text toolbar while carrying out most tasks in the Document window's Layout Editor, but other toolbars appear from time to time, including the Layout Grid, CSS, and Site toolbars.

Figure 1-6
Three toolbars

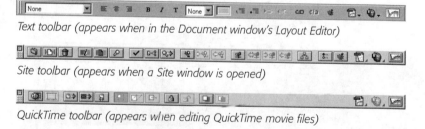

Text toolbar (appears when in the Document window's Layout Editor)

Site toolbar (appears when a Site window is opened)

QuickTime toolbar (appears when editing QuickTime movie files)

Below the Toolbar rests the Document window, where you build your page, as well as edit its underlying HTML, create frames, and simulate a preview in different browsers. It includes the Layout Editor (the WYSIWYG heart of GoLive's page design engine), the Frame Editor (for creating framed pages), the HTML Source Editor (where you can monitor and edit your page's underlying code), the HTML Outline Editor (which provides a structured view of your source code), and Layout Preview (which simulates how a browser

displays your page); see Figure 1-7. On the Mac, you also find a Frame
Preview tab for viewing framed pages; Windows users need only use Layout
Preview to see frames.

Figure 1-7
Document
window tabs

Mac Document window

Windows Document window

But what really grabs your attention is the astounding number of floating
palettes, which are organized into six palette groups: Objects/Color,
Inspector/View Controller, Transform/Align/Tracing Image, Floating
Boxes/Table/Actions, In & Out Links/Site Navigator/Source Code/JavaScript
Shell, and Markup Tree/History (see Figure 1-8).

Figure 1-8
Palette groups

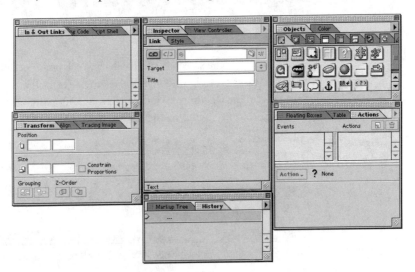

If you're familiar with any desktop-publishing or graphics program, the
idea of floating palettes isn't new. However, in an effort to standardize interface features across its line, Adobe has taken a cue from Photoshop and
Illustrator (where palettes provide decentralized control over an open document and can be closed depending on need) and grown GoLive 5's total to 16
from just a few in the previous version. The most essential palettes include:

- **The Objects palette.** This palette contains the arsenal of HTML elements (from table and image to form and Head section tags), extras such as prefabricated JavaScript items, and site objects such as color and font set references (see Figure 1-9).

Figure 1-9
Two Objects palette tabs

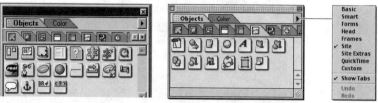

The Basic Tab   *The Head Tab*

NEW IN 5:
TEFKTP

The Objects palette replaces The Entity Formerly Known as The Palette (TEFKTP), which in GoLive 4 was also known by the redundant moniker of Palette palette.

TIP:
ToolTips Aid Memory

To make it easier to figure out the purpose of the sometimes obscure icons that GoLive uses in its Toolbar and palettes, turn on ToolTips. Doing so causes an item's name to pop up when you hover over the item for more than a few seconds. On the Macintosh, select Show Tooltips from the Help menu; under Windows, the ToolTips appear automatically.

In the Objects palette, the icon names show up at the bottom of the palette whenever you move your cursor above any item.

- **The Color palette.** By default, the Color palette is paired in the same group as the Objects palette and features a number of ways of finding and adding color to HTML elements—from RGB and CMYK sliders to a Web-safe color list (see Figure 1-10).

Figure 1-10
Two Color palette tabs

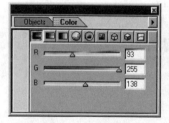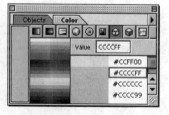

- **The Inspector palette.** This control panel contextually changes to allow modification of attributes to objects dropped into your page from the Objects palette (see Figure 1-11). For example, after dragging the Image icon into a page, the Inspector becomes the Image Inspector; you can assign the image's source file, link it to another page, and configure an imagemap within its three tabs.

Figure 1-11
Two Inspector
palettes

- **The View Controller.** This palette is paired with the Inspector, and lets you configure what gets displayed in a variety of GoLive windows, from the Document window to the new Design Window, within which you can prototype new sites or subsections (see Figure 1-12).

You can close a palette by clicking the close box in the upper left (Mac) or upper right (Windows) corner; alternately, you can choose a checked palette name from the Window menu to close it or choose an unchecked palette to open or make it active.

Figure 1-12
View
Controller

NEW IN 5:
Goodbye
View Menu
(Windows)

GoLive 4 for Windows had a View menu under which you found many palettes and other items. GoLive 5 brought the Macintosh and Windows versions into sync, so that you no longer are, paradoxically, looking for the Window menu on the Mac, and the View menu under Windows; both platforms put all palettes under the Window menu.

TIP:
Closing Groups

Selecting a checked palette name from the Window menu to close it also closes all palettes that are included in the group.

You also can control the display of palettes (and the Toolbar) by pressing the keyboard shortcuts in Table 1-1.

Table 1-1
Palette keyboard shortcuts

Palette	Keystroke*
Toolbar	0
Inspector	1
Objects	2
Color	3
JavaScript Shell	4
Site Navigator	5
Table	6
History	7
Align	8
View Controller	9

* On the Mac, add the Command key; under Windows, add the Control key.

TIP:
Custom Keystrokes

GoLive 5 allows you to configure your own sets of keyboard shortcuts (by choosing Keyboard Shortcuts from the Edit menu, or pressing Shift-Alt-Control-K on Windows or Command-Option-Shift-K on the Mac).

TIP:
Reset Palettes

To return palettes to GoLive's default state (which is what you see when you first open the program), choose Reset Palettes from the Window menu.

TIP:
Hide All Palettes

GoLive 5 also allows you to hide all palettes: press Control-J under Windows, or Control-Tab on the Mac.

Move a palette out of a group by dragging its title tab to a location away from its group; conversely, create your own groups by dragging a palette's title tab and docking it with an open group.

For more information on the wonderful world of the Inspector palette, see Chapter 2, *The Inspector*. The Toolbar and all things palette-oriented are covered in Chapter 3, *Palettes and Parts*.

Managing Windows & Palettes

As you work with GoLive, your view of the program can become cluttered with a dizzying amount of windows, palettes, Inspectors, and controllers (see Figure 1-13). However, GoLive provides a set of options to optimize and manage all the items on your display.

Managing on the Mac. On the Mac, you can minimize GoLive's palettes by Control-clicking the title bar of one or more palette groups. Control-Shift-clicking minimizes all open groups. GoLive minimizes palettes by turning them into a sideways window showing all tabs in the group along the right side of your screen (see Figure 1-14).

Any palette can be maximized back to its original form by clicking the bar; Control-Shift-clicking any bar restores all palettes.

If you Control-click a Document or Site window, its minimized tab appears at the bottom of the screen, and, unlike the palette tabs, these can be clicked and dragged to another position.

You can also click the Windowshade box on the far right of any window or palette; or double-click the title bar if you've checked the Double-Click Title Bar option in the Appearance control panel. This "rolls up" the window, minimizing it to just a title. Unroll the window by clicking the Windowshade box again, or double-clicking the title bar.

NEW IN 5: **No Click** **and Drag**	Unfortunately, you can't position the minimized tabs by clicking and dragging as you could in GoLive 4.
NEW IN 5: **GoLive 4** **Leftovers**	Control-clicking the Toolbar or the DHTML Timeline editor (which opens after clicking the filmstrip icon in the Document window's Layout Editor) minimizes the item to a square tab with an icon resting along the right side of the screen (see Figure 1-14).

Figure 1-13
Welcome to
the jungle

Figure 1-14
Minimizing
Mac windows

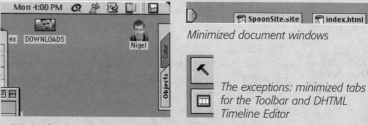

Minimized document windows

The exceptions: minimized tabs for the Toolbar and DHTML Timeline Editor

Minimized palettes

As you drag palettes around the screen, notice that they tend to snap into place near each other to make them organize more neatly.

Minimizing problems with multiple resolutions. GoLive keeps track of where on the screen you minimized palettes the last time you did so, even if you're no longer viewing the screen at that same resolution. Minimized items stick to the border of the screen they're assigned, while palettes that might be floating off the screen get repositioned automatically. In addition, you can return all palettes to their default positions by choosing Reset Palettes from the Window menu.

Managing under Windows. As with the Mac, you can drag palettes near another and have their borders snap together without docking (see Figure 1-15); you can also drag the Toolbar out of its docked position at the top of the GoLive window.

You can choose Hide Palettes from the Window menu (or press Control-J) to give yourself a break from all the clutter, as well as choose Reset Palettes if things get too out of hand. Or, Control-Shift-click any palette group's titlebar to minimize them all to the right of the screen as little bars, just as on

the Mac. You can then click any of those bars and restore the palette, or Control-Shift-click to restore all palettes.

GoLive resolution. We've noted that GoLive was designed with at least a 1,024-by-768-pixel window in mind. It's hard to display your HTML page and a couple palettes, along with the toolbar, without having a lot of overlaps at lower resolutions. If you're going to be dedicating more than 10 hours a week to using GoLive,

Figure 1-15
Minimizing
Windows
windows

Managing Windows & Palettes *continued*

we recommend getting at least a 17-inch monitor, if not a 19-inch one. Prices at this writing are as low as $540 for a high-quality 19-inch Sony Trinitron monitor with lots of bells and whistles.

NEW IN 5: Abandoned Docks	GoLive 5 abandons version 4's frustrating palette docking scheme, which seemed very promising at first. If you double-clicked a palette's title bar, the palette would snap to the right border of the application and fill the window's height with a gray column. If you double-clicked subsequent palettes (or dropped them anywhere near the gray column) you could create a docking set. However, palettes seemed to get lost pretty easily as the column filled up and it was rather difficult to undock them.
NEW IN 5: Resolution Changes Resolved	In GoLive 4, items could be lost off the edge of a screen if you switched resolutions on your monitor, such as when, after working at a high resolution on an external monitor, you switched to a PowerBook's lower resolution on the road. Palettes could be lost in resolution limbo—and it only got worse if you had minimized any palettes. Your only solution was to close GoLive and trash the system preferences.

Getting Started: Step by Step

Now that you've opened GoLive and looked under the hood, it's time to take it out for a spin. In this introductory chapter, we cover the day-to-day tasks you will perform with GoLive: creating a site, designing a page, and publishing to the Web. Along the way, we introduce you to the program's basic concepts, from dragging and dropping HTML objects to configuring elements via the menagerie of palettes and windows to understanding the basics in GoLive site management.

Creating a New Site

When you first open the program, you're greeted by the Document window, which is a new, untitled Web page. On this page, you can mix and match HTML items from the Objects palette and add references to images and plug-in media.

But before we can let our right-brain creativity flow, we need to satisfy our left-brain logic by applying one of GoLive's strongest features: site management. By creating a GoLive site document that encapsulates all your files—pages, media, style sheets, and more—you let GoLive take over a lot of tedious work, from managing links to updating references when pages get moved. On top of that, you get a lot of GoLive bonuses, including storage areas for site-specific colors and font sets, frequently used external links, and the ability to transfer and synchronize your site to an outside Web server using FTP.

Creating a new site is easy. From the File menu's New Site submenu, choose Blank or press Command-Option-N (Mac) or Control-Alt-N (Windows). In the Create New Site dialog box that opens, enter a name in the Site Name field, and then navigate to the directory location where you want to place this site (see Figure 1-16). (Under Windows, you can type the directory path or click the Browse button to navigate.) Select the folder where you want to place the site and click Choose on the Mac or OK on Windows. If Create Folder is checked, an additional folder is created within the selected folder; if you don't want to add another directory level, uncheck this option.

Figure 1-16
Create New
Site dialog
boxes

A new site document opens in the Site window with a single page titled index.html listed in bold under the Files tab. The Files tab is where you build the physical structure—pages, images, etc.—of your site (see Figure 1-17). The other tabs in the Site window (External, Designs, Colors, Font Sets, and Custom) are essentially libraries (such as for holding references to all external links from your site).

Figure 1-17
Site window
open to Files
tab

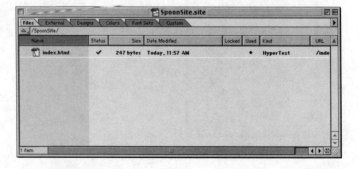

Go to your Desktop and drill down to the directory location you specified for this site so you can see what GoLive has left for you (see Figure 1-18). You see a GoLive site file with the specified name, followed by a .site extension, which acts as a database for your site, tracking link relationships between files. (GoLive automatically creates a backup of this file every time you save it from the File menu or quit the program.) You also find two folders: one with the name you specified for the site (this is where you store your pages and media files) and one with that same name and a .data extension (this is where you store files such as stationery and component files).

Figure 1-18
Site's contents
on the
Desktop

TIP:
**Importing
a Site**

You can create a site using existing files by using the Import from Folder item under the New Site submenu. For details and strategies for importing older or complex sites, see Chapter 24, *Importing a Site*.

File Information

Back in the GoLive site document, selecting the index.html file opens up the File Inspector (see Figure 1-19). If you don't have the Inspector palette open, select it from the Window menu or press Command/Control-1. The File tab provides file information (size and creation and modification dates); you can also change the file's name.

Figure 1-19
File Inspector

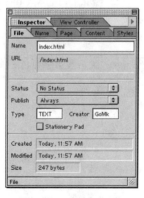

TIP:
Default
Home Page

When creating a blank site, GoLive defaults to naming the home page index.html. To change this default, go to Preferences under the Edit menu (or press Command/Control-Y). From the Site pane, you can modify the default home page name as well as the HTML file extension that applies to all new files (.html by default).

In the Files tab, you can also view the basic file information listed in the site document under columns corresponding to file characteristics, like modification date and time. To change the column view, open the View Controller (by selecting it from the Window menu or clicking on its title tab), and select items from the Show Columns popup menu (see Figure 1-20).

Figure 1-20
View
Controller with
Site document
open

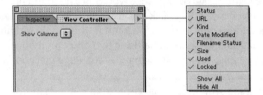

You can determine under what circumstances a file gets uploaded to a Web server by choosing the appropriate option from the Publish menu: Always (the GoLive default), Never, or If Referenced. Choosing If Referenced uploads a file only if another page in the site higher in the navigational hierarchy links to it.

Clicking the File Inspector's Page tab allows you to type a title that appears in the Web browser's title bar (see Figure 1-21); by default, GoLive toots its own horn with "Welcome to Adobe GoLive 5." To enter a new title, select the current text and type a new title.

The Home Page box is automatically checked (and grayed out) since this is the first file that's been added to the site. After more files have been added to the site document, you can choose another file as the site's home page by bringing up the File Inspector for that page and checking Home Page.

Figure 1-21
File Inspector's
Page tab

NEW IN 5:
Many Happy Returns

In GoLive 4, you had to accept any edits made to an Inspector palette field by pressing Return (Mac only), Enter, or Tab; a carriage-return icon appeared to remind you. GoLive 5 automatically accepts edits. All you need to do is click elsewhere (in the Inspector, on another palette, or back within the Site or Document window) to save the edit. You can also still press Return, Enter, or Tab without being charged extra for the privilege.

NEW IN 5:
Return, O Return

If you miss the GoLive 4 carriage return icon (or just want to feel old school), you can bring it back by checking Direct Input for Text Fields under the General pane's User Interface settings in Preferences.

TIP:
Many Roads on Same Path

You'll soon find out that GoLive provides a number of different routes for accomplishing the same tasks. For instance, you don't need to change the file name using the Inspector; simply click the file name in the Site window and wait a second for the name to be highlighted and editable. Additionally, you can modify the page's browser bar title using two other methods once you open up the page for editing; see the "Designing a Web Page" section for details.

TIP:
It's in the Context

If you select a file and bring up its contextual menu (Control-click on the Mac, right-click in Windows), you have access to a range of options at your fingertips, including opening a GoLive document in a specific mode (such as the HTML Source Editor instead of the Layout Editor), opening an image file in its source application, and opening the file's location in the Macintosh Finder or Windows Explorer (see Figure 1-22).

Figure 1-22
Contextual menu

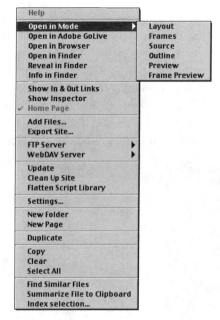

Adding Files to a Site

You have a few options for adding images, HTML pages, and other files to the site.

- Outside of GoLive, drag and drop files from any hard drive or network volume into your site folder. However, these files don't immediately appear in the Site window when you return to GoLive. To refresh this display, click the Update button on the Site toolbar, choose Rescan from the Site menu, choose Update from the contextual menu, or press Command-Shift-U on the Mac or F5 on Windows.

- With the site document open, select a file from your desktop and drag it into the Files tab. The original file remains and a copy is added to the site document.

- To add a large number of files (even from different directory locations), choose Add Files from the Site menu's Finder (Mac) or Explorer (Windows) submenu. This opens the Add to Site dialog, in which you can navigate to files in the top pane and add them to the bottom list pane (see Figure 1-23). When finished, click Done to import copies of the original files into your site document.

Figure 1-23
Adding files to
a site

TIP:
Adding Folders

To add folders to the Files tab of the Site window, simply select the directory level—click within the root of your site or open another folder to descend another directory level—and click the Folder icon from the Site toolbar.

See Chapter 2, *The Inspector*, for complete details on the File Inspector. See Chapter 4, *Preferences and Customizing* to learn about setting up the Encoding and Status fields. For more on sites, see Chapter 19, *Site Management*, Chapter 23, *Synchronizing Sites*, and Chapter 24, *Importing a Site*.

Designing a Web Page

In the Site window's Files tab, double click index.html; alternately, select it and choose Open from the File menu or press Command/Control-O.

GoLive on the Macintosh also maintains a list of recently accessed files, and assigns three keyboard shortcuts to the most recently accessed files according to three file types: Command-1 for HTML documents, Command-2 for site documents, and Command-3 for other materials such as text files or QuickTime movies (see Figure 1-24).

Figure 1-24
Recent files Mac keyboard shortcuts

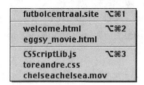

If you want to add more pages to your site, choose one of the following options.

- Choose New from the File menu to open a blank HTML document. When you're ready to save the page into your site, choose Save from the File menu and use the popup menu to navigate to the root folder of your site (see Figure 1-25).

Figure 1-25
Saving new document

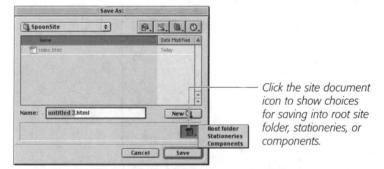

Click the site document icon to show choices for saving into root site folder, stationeries, or components.

- Open the Site tab of the Objects palette and drag the Generic Page icon into the Files tab of the site document (see Figure 1-26). Its name is highlighted and selected, allowing you to enter a name; by default, the file is named untitled.html. A yellow yield icon appears in the Files tab's Status column to indicate that the document is empty.
- You can also add a blank page by choosing Page from the Site menu's New submenu or choosing New Page from the contextual menu in the Site window with no item selected or under the cursor.

Figure 1-26
Adding new page from Objects palette

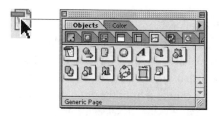

With the blank canvas of the Document window open, you can start by adding a page title if you hadn't already done so using the Inspector palette. Click anywhere within the Page Title field, located to the right of the Page icon at the top left of the Document window. The entire title becomes highlighted and editable and the Inspector palette changes to the File Inspector. When finished typing, click elsewhere to accept the new name.

Page Settings

To set up the basic properties for your page—the attributes of the Body tab—click the Page icon to open the Page Inspector. Here, you can modify a page's title (in yet another way), text colors, background colors and images, and ColorSync profiles, as well as how GoLive handles JavaScript and color management within the page.

On the Mac, you can press Tab to automatically select the Page icon and open the Inspector palette (if it's the active palette in its group). If your cursor is within a table, however, you only tab to the next table cell.

Page title. To modify a page title using the Page Inspector (and this isn't the last time we mention this), select the Page tab, then click within the Title field. Enter your new title.

Text colors. The Text Colors section allows you to change the color of a page's body text and links. The section is made up of four items—Text, Link, Active Link (the color that appears when a link is being clicked), and Visited Link—each with a color field and a checkbox (see Figure 1-27). GoLive defaults to show standard HTML text colors for these items, such as blue for links, with the items unchecked.

Figure 1-27
Modifying text and link colors

To modify the colors, click one of the color fields (its border turns from white to black) to display the Color palette. The Color palette features nine tabs, each of which offers you a different method of searching for a desired color—from RGB and CMYK sliders to an HSV wheel.

Click the Color palette's Web Color List tab, which features a list of "browser-safe" colors that are a part of the system color palettes for both Windows and Macs; or, choose it from the popout menu in the Color palette's top right corner (see Figure 1-28). To select a color, click a swatch in the color box with the eyedropper cursor icon, or click a color from the list, which also displays its hexadecimal value. A preview of the color appears in the preview pane at the left of the palette.

Figure 1-28
Color palette's
popout list

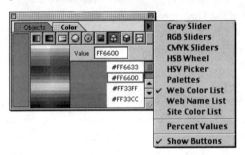

Because you clicked a color field in the Page Inspector (and made it active), selecting a color automatically adds it to the field and checks its box to make it active on the page. To search colors without automatically adding them to a field, simply click the field a second time to return its black border to white (and thus making it inactive).

To add color to an inactive field, find a color from a selected tab and click to view it in the preview pane. Place your cursor over the preview pane (or over the color swatch in the list, to the left of the color's name), hold down your mouse button, and drag a small color swatch to the Page Inspector. Drop the color sample over the Text Colors Link field.

If you uncheck any of the Text Colors boxes, the color you chose for that field remains visible, but it is not active for that attribute.

NEW IN 5:
**Lots o'
Undoing**

GoLive 4 featured only one level of undo (Command-Z on the Mac or Control-Z under Windows), and sometimes it didn't even reach that. For example, if you added a color swatch to a color field, you couldn't undo it; you could only uncheck it to make it inactive. However, GoLive 5 offers multiple levels of undo, which can be easily viewed using the History palette (press Command/Control-7 to open it); see Figure 1-29.

Simply click on a previous state within the history list to revert to that previous state. You can move back and forth between states by clicking through the list (up to 20 levels by default). Pressing Command/Control-Z moves backward (undo) and Shift-Command (Mac) or Shift-Control (Windows) moves forward (redo). For details on using this palette, see Chapter 3, *Palettes and Parts*.

Figure 1-29
History palette

Background. In the Background section of the Page tab, you can choose a color for your page as well as a tiled image. To select a color, repeat the steps taken in the Text Colors section above; by default, white (or #FFFFFF) is added. To place an image, check the box to the left of the Image field, making the field active and inserting an "(Empty Reference!)" reminder (see Figure 1-30).

Figure 1-30
Modifying
background
color and
image

TIP:
**Older
Browser
Workaround**

Ancient browsers don't display a background image, although some of them display a background color. If you select both a color and an image, browsers that can show a background do; others display the color. Also, if your background image is large or takes time to load, the background color shows up while the image is loading.

TIP:
**Dragging
Background
Color**

If you just want to change the background color and you don't want to mess around with the Page Inspector, simply drag a color swatch from the Color palette onto the Page icon and the color is added. This trick also works with background images: just drag an image file from a window in the Desktop or a Site window and drop it onto the Page icon.

If you know the directory path of your desired image, type it in the Image field. To browse your hard drive, click the folder icon to the right of the field, navigate to the file using the Open dialog, and then click Open to add the link reference to the Image field (see Figure 1-31). GoLive lets you import Web-friendly image formats like JPEG, GIF, and PNG; other formats are converted by the Save for Web feature, which is detailed in Chapter 9, *Images*. The selected image is then tiled to fill the background of your page.

Figure 1-31
Adding image
by browsing

A second option is to use the squiggly Point & Shoot button to the left of the Image field, which allows you to visually link items in a page on a site to other pages and files in the same or other Site windows. (This is listed as "Fetch URL" in the ToolTip that appears over the button.)

Clicking the Point & Shoot button and holding the mouse button down drags a rope-like connector originating at the button. Drag the rope to an image file housed inside your Site window and the name of the file appears in the Image field (see Figure 1-32). Release your mouse button to accept this link; the Point & Shoot rope disappears, and your selected image tiles across the page (see Figure 1-33).

If you release your mouse button over anything that GoLive doesn't accept as an end point for this link—such as blank space in the site document or a color reference in the Site window—the rope snaps back and disappears.

Figure 1-32
Adding image
using Point &
Shoot

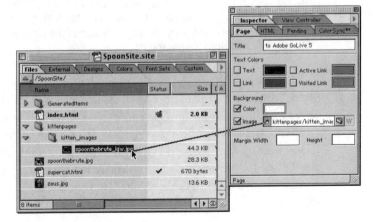

Figure 1-33
Tiled
background
image

To delete a background image, simply uncheck the Image checkbox. The name of the image file is immediately deleted from the Image field. Should you change your mind and check Image to return the background image, you are met with the "(Empty Reference!)" reminder again.

See Chapter 2, *The Inspector* for more on the Page Inspector's tabs. For in-depth coverage of the Color palette and use of color on the Web, see Chapter 3, *Palettes and Parts*, and Chapter 10, *Color*. Also see Chapter 9, *Images*.

Text

When designing or editing a page, you see a lot of the Text toolbar, which allows you to control attributes of HTML text from paragraph style to setting bold and italic, from creating lists to linking text and objects.

As is the case with much about GoLive, the Toolbar is but one path of many you can choose to walk. If you love menus, many of these formatting controls can also be accessed through the Type menu or the contextual menu, while those who let their fingers do the walking can accomplish the same feats via keyboard shortcuts.

NEW IN 5:
Consolidated
Controls

In GoLive 4, the controls found in the Type menu were spread across two menus: Format and Style. Now they're grouped under the Type menu.

When you place your cursor within the main area of the Document window, the Text Inspector becomes active (see Figure 1-34). The Link tab duplicates the New Link button from the Text toolbar, but also adds fields for specifying the URL, the link's target (if you're working in a frames-based site, or want to open a second window with a link), and title (a ToolTip-style box that appears when your viewer mouses over the link in Internet Explorer).

Figure 1-34
Text Inspector

TIP:
Support for Target

Though the Target attribute is a part of the standard HTML 4 specification, only Microsoft Internet Explorer 5 and later for Windows and version 4.5 and later for the Mac support it.

Several other flavors of the contextual Toolbar are introduced in this chapter, but the complete assortment (from Text and Site to Outline and Layout Grid) is detailed in Chapter 3, *Palettes and Parts*. For details on the Text Inspector and using the Style tab for applying Cascading Style Sheets styles, see Chapter 2, *The Inspector*, and Chapter 29, *Cascading Style Sheets*.

Point & Shoot

You find the Point & Shoot feature associated with any Inspector field that requires a URL reference; the collected set of navigation tools, including Browse, Edit URL, and Absolute Link, are known as the "URL Getter." They appear when you want to link to another page, to a style sheet, or to an image or media file.

Although it can require a bit of dexterity to navigate among a number of open GoLive windows, Point & Shoot is a pretty nifty and useful feature. (And we're still entertained by the animated snapped-back rope.) There is, however, one requirement for using Point & Shoot: you must have a site document open.

For instance, if you tried to grab an image from your desktop using the Point & Shoot button, you only get a snapped-back rope. GoLive only allows you to link to files that are collected within an open Site window—just another reminder that GoLive's true power is

fully unleashed when working with its site-management features.

Keyboard dragging. If you Command-drag (Mac) or Alt-drag (Windows) while hovering over an item (an image, an existing link, selected text), a squiggly Point & Shoot curl appears beneath your cursor. You can use it to bypass the Inspector's button and drag your Point & Shoot rope to the desired location.

Accessing files in a Site window. When first confronted with the notion of Point & Shoot, you might (logically) think that you have to manually open folders within the Site window to the desired directory location before pointing can begin. However, when you drag an item onto a folder with the Point & Shoot rope, it springs open to the lower level.

To access files in a directory location below the one currently displayed in the Files tab, drag your mouse over the folder. After a few seconds' delay, the Files tab fills with the folder's contents. If you want to go up a level, drag your mouse over the Path icon at the top-left of the Files tab.

If you find it difficult to maneuver through all your open windows, here's a little trick to help you get to the Site window: direct your Point & Shoot rope to the Select Window button in the Toolbar. GoLive switches to the Site window while keeping your Point & Shoot rope active, letting you drag through your site's files.

Clicking the Toolbar's Select Window button also switches you from one window to the other (i.e., from document to site). However, to switch from document to document, click the down arrow to the right of the icon to display the Toggle Between Windows popup menu.

Creating anchors. If you want to link to a specific point on the same or another page, drag the Point & Shoot button to that point in the open document. Releasing the mouse button creates an anchor tag placeholder, and enters a generic name in the Inspector's URL field. If you create this anchor on another page, the page's file name is placed before the anchor's pound sign (#).

To edit the anchor's name, go to the page where the anchor resides and select it; the cursor turns into a selection arrow when mousing over an anchor icon. In the Anchor Inspector, type your anchor's new name in the Name field. GoLive asks if you wish to update all project files referencing this anchor; click the Update button to change the link reference on the original page (see Figure 1-35).

It's very important that you edit the anchor using the Anchor Inspector. If you were to edit the anchor's name from its reference point using the URL field of the Text Inspector's Link tab, the anchor in the URL reference would change its name, but the anchor that's referencing it would still have the generic, numeric name.

TIP: Spring Forward	Spring-loaded Folders must be checked in the Site pane of Preferences; if unchecked, directory folders just expand open as they would in the Finder or Windows Explorer.
TIP: Point & Shoot to Anchors	You can use Point & Shoot to create links to anchors that already exist within a page without having to open the document. Point & Shoot at the gray triangle to the left of the document in the Site window until it opens to display anchors; then point to a listed anchor.

Figure 1-35
Updating an anchor

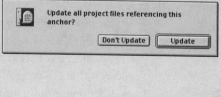

Fonts

GoLive doesn't specify a font by default for a page's text; instead, the page uses the font specified in your viewer's browser (which can, itself, be a default or chosen by the user). GoLive, however, makes it quite easy to create font sets that you can use to format page text, and in fact comes with three built-in sets: Times New Roman, Arial, and Courier New.

Each font set includes the named primary font choice, as well as additional font choices for viewers whose computers do not have the first choice or choices available (see Table 1-2).

Table 1-2
Font sets

Font Set	Font Attributes
Times New Roman	<font face="Times New Roman,Georgia,Times">
Arial	<font face="Arial,Helvetica,Geneva,Swiss, SunSans-Regular">
Courier	<font face="Courier New,Courier,Monaco">

You can make changes to existing font sets or create new sets through the Font Set Editor (see Figure 1-36), which is opened by pressing Command-Option-F (Mac) or Control-Alt-F (Windows), or selecting Edit Font Sets from the Font submenu of the Type menu.

Figure 1-36
Font Set Editor

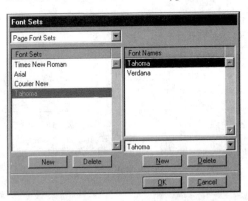

Select the Page icon in the left menu (Mac) or select Page Font Sets from the top menu (Windows) to work on sets for the open page.

Click the New button beneath the Font Sets pane and New Font Name appears within this pane and the adjacent Font Names pane. To name the font set, either type a font name in the field below the Font Names pane (Mac), select a font in the Font Names pane (Windows), or select a font from the popup list to the right of the field. The selected font appears in the Font Names list, as well as the name of the Font Set.

Selecting the Default icon and creating a font set adds it to GoLive's list of built-in sets. However, you must quit GoLive and reopen it for this font set to become active in the list.

If you don't have a font you want loaded on your system, and you're a Mac GoLive user, you can type a font name in the Font Names field.

To add fonts to a Font Set, click the New button below the Font Names pane, then type the name or select a font from the popup list. When finished, click OK. You can check to see that the font set now has been added to the page's Font Set list under the Font submenu. To apply a font set, select a range of text in the Layout Editor then select a set from the Font submenu.

For more information, see Chapter 8, *Text and Fonts*.

If you wanted to set the default font for your page, the first place you might look would be Preferences. Selecting the Fonts pane brings up the Fonts list box with attributes for Western font encodings, and includes settings for Proportional and Monospaced, as well as the Cascading Style Sheets attributes Serif, Sans Serif, Cursive, and Fantasy Fonts (see Figure 1-37).

However, changing the default font in Preferences (by choosing an available font such as Verdana from the popup list at the bottom of the Fonts list box) only changes the viewable font within GoLive's Layout Editor; even then it only changes text for the selected language encoding group—in this case, Western.

Figure 1-37
Font
Preferences

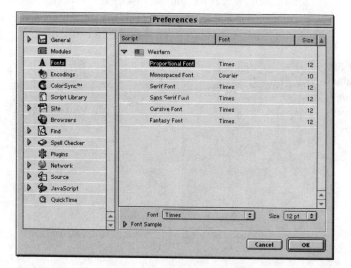

Tables

Here's your first encounter with GoLive's drag-and-drop, WYSIWYG interface. Open the Objects palette. From the Basic tab, click the Table icon and drag it into the Layout Editor of an open Document window (see Figure 1-38).

Figure 1-38
Adding a table

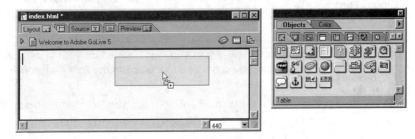

TIP:
Dragging Items for Placement

Dragging and dropping HTML objects allows you to position them on your page more precisely. However, if you place your cursor at your desired entry point, double-clicking an object icon automatically places the item at that spot.

GoLive places a three-row-by-three-column table that's 180 pixels wide. You modify the attributes within the Table Inspector, starting with the Table tab, where you make adjustments to the number of rows and columns, overall width, border appearance, and the table alignment (see Figure 1-39).

Enter values into the Rows and Columns fields to change the makeup of the table. Alternatively, select an individual cell by clicking its bottom or right-hand border or using the Table palette's proxy or stand-in for selection, and then click the Add Row/Column or Delete Row/Column buttons that appear in the Cell tab; added rows appear above the selected row, while added columns come in to the left (also see Figure 1-39).

Figure 1-39
Table Inspector's Table and Cell tabs

NEW IN 5:
Table
Palette

The Table palette is a welcome addition allowing, among other things, for the simple selection of one or more cells, rows, or columns through a proxy that represents the currently active table. Choosing items in the Table palette selects them for manipulation in the Layout Editor.

You can alter the dimensions of the entire table by entering values into the Width and Height fields. In the popup menu to the right of the Width field, Pixel is the default measurement (Auto is selected by default for Height). If you select Percent, the table calculates its width based on the size of the browser window. If you select Auto at this point with no cell contents, your table gets scrunched up into almost nothing. Remember, a table with no assigned width conforms only to the width of its contents.

TIP:
Dragging
Dimensions

With Pixel selected as your Width measurement, place your cursor over the right outside border of the table (see Figure 1-40). It transmogrifies into a blue two-way arrow, showing that the width can be changed by dragging. Click the border and drag; the measurement in the Width field changes. To change the width of a table's columns, press Option (Mac) or Alt (Windows) with the cursor over an interior border and drag: a light-blue two-way arrow appears.

If Percent is selected, you can't automatically drag the outside border of your table; you need to press Option (Mac) or Alt (Windows) to bring up the blue two-way arrow. However, Option/Alt-clicking and dragging the width of the table changes the measurement from Percent back to Pixel.

Finally, you can Control-Option-drag (Mac) or Control-Alt-drag (Windows) either the exterior or interior borders to make the table resize dynamically.

Figure 1-40
Dragging width
of entire table

To add a background color for the entire table, drag a color swatch from the Color palette into the Color field; or, select the Color field, and then select a color from the Color palette to add it automatically. You can also add a background image to a table, which, if not transparent, overlays the background color. Finally, you can set background colors and images for individual cells (via the Cell tab of the Table Inspector) and background color for a row (on the Row tab).

TIP:
Empty Cell
Syndrome

If you set a background color and do not place either text or an HTML element into a table cell, the color does not show up in GoLive or in most browsers. To make the color viewable, place your cursor into the cell and press Option-spacebar (Mac only) to create a non-breaking space.

With one or more cells selected, you can also bring up the contextual menu and choose Insert   (which is the HTML code for a non-breaking space). This is most helpful when you need to fill many cells at once.

The Alignment menu shows Default (by default), in which case the table is regarded as just another inline object. Although you can include text or other objects on the same line, they appear even with the table's baseline. Choosing Left or Right allows you to flow text around the table. For this example, since we're creating a layout structure for the page, we choose Default.

You can set the alignment of an individual cell's contents by selecting a cell, clicking the Table Inspector's Cell tab, and choosing options from the Vertical and Horizontal Alignment menus. (With a cell selected, you can also set the alignment for all cells within a row by using the same menus on the Row tab.) From the Cell tab, you can also set row and column spanning as well as set the height (which affects the entire row) and width (affecting the entire column).

See Chapter 11, *Tables*, for more on configuring tables and using the Table palette.

Images

To bring images into your page, open the Objects palette to display the Basic tab and drag the Image icon into the Layout Editor, or double click the icon to place the image tag at your text insertion point. The Inspector palette changes to the Image Inspector and opens to the Basic tab. Specify an image using either the Source field's Point & Shoot or Browse buttons or by typing the path and file name.

TIP:
Dragging in Images

You can also drag an image file (in GIF, JPEG, or PNG format) from your site document and place it anywhere within the GoLive document (see Figure 1-41).

Figure 1-41
Adding image file by dragging

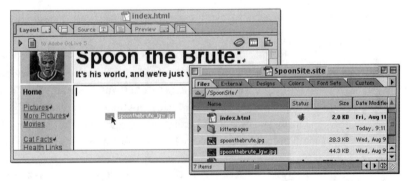

Select image file from site document and drag into open Document window.

Once the image is placed, the Width and Height fields are automatically filled in with the image's actual pixel dimensions. If you're not happy with the size of an image, it's best to modify its dimensions in an image editing program (like Photoshop). Otherwise, if you modify the Width and Height measurements in pixels, your image looks scrunched, stretched, or pixelated. If you're comfortable with those results (or if you're just making rough layouts where image quality isn't important), you can also modify the size of an image by dragging the blue resizing handles that appear in the corner and bottom and left borders of the image.

TIP:
Dynamic
Resize

On both Mac and Windows, if you Control-drag any of the resizing handles, the image displays dynamically as it's resized. Shift-dragging the corner box resizes the image proportionally, while Control-Shift-dragging the corner box proportionally resizes before your very eyes.

If you modify the size of an image from its actual dimensions, a resize warning icon appears on your image indicating that the icon might not display at its optimal resolution (see Figure 1-42). To return to the original dimensions, click the image resize warning button in the Image Inspector to reset both measurements. You can also individually select Image from the Width and Height popup menus.

NEW IN 5:
Smart
Resizing

GoLive 5 introduces Smart Objects to the imaging mix, which provides a method of linking native Photoshop, Illustrator, and LiveMotion files to your page. A Web-ready version is stored on the page itself, but when you resize the Photoshop or Illustrator object, GoLive builds a new image using the rendering capabilities of the original application (LiveMotion files are composed of vector data, and are dynamically resized by the browser). The result is a smooth, high-quality image every time.

Figure 1-42
Modifying
image
dimensions via
the Image
Inspector

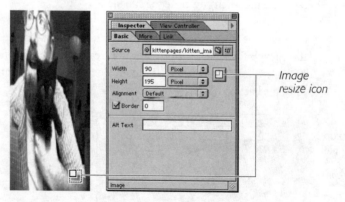

If you select Percent from the measurement popup menus, the image bases its size on the area where the image is placed (either the page as a whole or a table cell); choosing Percent makes the blue resizing handles disappear.

NEW IN 5:
Zero Border
by Default

GoLive 5 has corrected one of the biggest annoyances of the previous version: a Border value of zero is set by default, thus ensuring that no ugly blue border is added to linked images when viewed in a browser.

If you have a fairly sizeable image that might take a while to download in a browser, GoLive can automatically create a low-resolution placeholder image that loads first. On the More tab, check Low, and then click the Generate button to create a GIF file. The new file keeps the name of the original image, but adds ".ls" to the end. The More tab also enables you to create an image map or use an image as a form button.

TIP:
Changing
Lowsource
Type

GoLive can generate low-resolution JPEG files in addition to black-and-white GIFs as lowsource images, or ask you for your preference on an image by image basis. See Chapter 4, *Preferences and Customizing*, for more on setting this preference.

For more information, see Chapter 9, *Images*. For details on the Image Inspector, see "Document Layout Inspectors" in Chapter 2, *The Inspector*.

Managing a Site

After adding and designing pages, take a minute to work at the site level. Like any document you work with, it's a good idea to occasionally save your site file by choosing Save from the File menu with the Site window frontmost. GoLive saves you (no pun intended) some extra work by automatically saving the database file when you close the site file.

Additionally, if you should (heaven forbid) crash before either saving or closing a site file, you can return to the previously saved site state by opening the backup file which is automatically created in the same folder as your site document (see Figure 1-43). If the site document is closed and saved successfully, the backup file is deleted.

Figure 1-43
Site backup
file

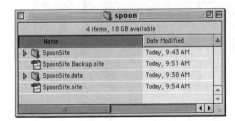

Updating Site References

If you have suffered a crash and, upon reopening your site document, find that files you added recently aren't appearing (or deleted files mysteriously are), synchronize the Site window display with the site database by choosing Rescan from the Site menu or clicking the Update button from the Site toolbar.

In addition, if you open one of the site library tabs, such as External, and click the Update button, all references that have been added to pages since the last update are added to the list. Selecting a reference brings up its Inspector, from which you can modify its name and, depending on the reference, change its URL, color, or font set contents.

TIP:
Blank References

To add new, blank references to these tabs, open the Site tab on the Objects palette to find icons for external and email links, colors, and font sets—as well as reference-specific folders.

TIP:
Color References

Color references found in the site document's Colors tab also appear in the Color palette's Site Color List.

Moving Files

Remember moving files from one directory location to another, and then having to manually edit the source code of every page that referenced those files? Thanks to the site file's database, file movement is tracked and GoLive tells you which files need to be updated (see Figure 1-44). Even better: it then updates them for you. Drag files to any other location in the Files tab, and the Move Files dialog box appears Check individual files to be updated to point to the new locations of the files you're moving, or check the top box to select all. To see the folders under which the pages are organized, check Show Folder Structure.

Figure 1-44
Move Files
dialog box

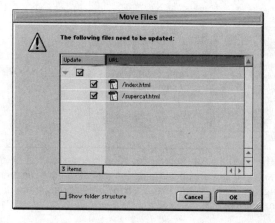

Deleting Files

To delete files, folders, and references from your site document, select an item and click the Trash button from the Site toolbar. You're met with a dialog asking you to confirm the deletion (see Figure 1-45).

By default, deleted files are not automatically sent to the system Trash (Mac) or Recycle Bin (Windows), but are instead stored in a Site Trash folder found in the Site Extras section.

Figure 1-45
Confirming
deleted files

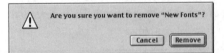

On Mac, click Remove; under Windows, click Yes.

TIP:
**Viewing the
Site
Window's
Right Half**

To view the Extras tab (among others), click the two-way arrow button at the bottom of the site document. The Site window divides in half to display the Extras section, which includes folders for Components, Designs, Site Trash, and Stationeries (see Figure 1-46). (These folders are housed on your hard drive in the site's data folder.) It also displays tabs for FTP, WebDAV, and Errors.

Figure 1-46
Opening Site
Extras area

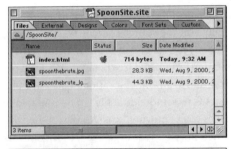

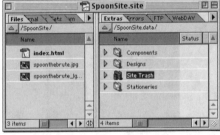

TIP:
**Axe the
Asking**

Under the Site pane of Preferences (Command-Y on the Mac, Control-Y under Windows), you can uncheck the option for Ask Before Deleting Objects, as well as change the way deleted files are handled (sending them directly to the Trash folder or Recycle Bin).

To move files to your system trash, Control-click (Mac) or right-click (Windows) the Site Trash folder to bring up the contextual menu and choose Empty Trash; alternatively, select files within the folder and click the toolbar's Trash button. If you need to repatriate a file marked for trash back to the active site, select it from the Site Trash folder and drag it back into the Files tab.

Site Extras: Stationery and Components

GoLive's site management features include the ability to create template pages for commonly used designs (Stationeries) and slices of HTML that can be embedded into other HTML pages (Components).

Stationeries. Creating Stationery files is simple. After you finish preparing the design of a template page, use Save As to locate it in the Extras tab's Stationeries folder. Click the special popup button in the Save As dialog box. Or, you can drag existing pages from the Files tab into the Stationeries folder.

GoLive automatically treats pages placed into the Stationeries folder as templates. Double-clicking a page brings up a dialog box that asks whether you want to create a new page from the selected template or modify the existing template file (see Figure 1-47).

On the Mac, click the Create button to open a new page based on this template file. Oddly, in Windows, you must click No to create a new file.

Figure 1-47
Opening a template file

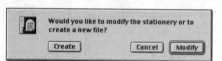 

On the Mac, click Modify to edit template file, or click Create to start a new page based on the template.

Under Windows, click Yes to edit template file, or click No to start a new page based on the template.

TIP:
Visualizing Stationery

On the Mac, the file's icon turns into a stationery pad icon and, if you select the file and view the File Inspector, the Stationery Pad checkbox is marked. Unfortunately, you don't get either of these visual cues in Windows. However, because the page is stored in the Stationeries folder, the page acts accordingly.

Components. The ability to swap slices of HTML (from images to plug-in media to text that needs to be updated frequently) in and out of pages is a dandy feature. But here's something even cooler: if you make an edit within a Component, the change is automatically updated in all pages that includes the Component. Ausgezeichnet!

To create a Component, add and configure your HTML elements, and then, before saving, click the Page icon and bring up the Page Inspector's HTML tab. Click the Component button to set up the page as a Component (see Figure 1-48). When you save the page, store it in the Components folder.

Figure 1-48
Setting up a
Component file

To include a Component in another GoLive page, open the Objects palette to the Smart tab and drag a Component icon into your page. A blank, rectangular placeholder is added to the page and the Component Inspector opens. Navigate to your desired component using the Page field's URL Getter (see Figure 1-49).

Figure 1-49
Adding a
Component to
a page

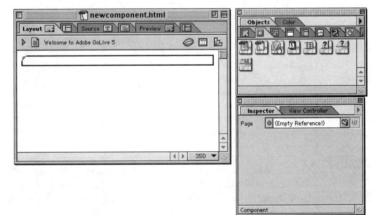

TIP:
Site Extras
Tab

Component and Stationery are also listed in the Site Extras tab of the Objects palette; use the popup menu at the bottom of the palette to switch between components and stationery pads, as well as custom HTML objects (see Figure 1-50). To add a component to a page, drag a Component icon from the Objects palette (bypassing the need to first add a Component placeholder from the Smart tab). Adding Stationery to a site is just as easy—drag it from the palette to the desired directory location.

Figure 1-50
Objects
palette's Site
Extras tab

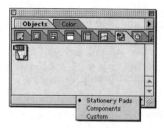

Click the popup menu at the bottom of palette to choose between Stationery pads, Components, and custom-saved items.

See Chapter 21, *Files, Folders, and Links*, for details on using Stationery and Component files and customized HTML objects. See Chapter 20, *Prototyping and Mapping*, for details on using GoLive 5's new Design feature. Also see Chapter 28, *Actions*, to learn more about the JavaScripts included in GoLive.

Uploading to a Server

After all this work, you want your site to be seen by the world. Working through the Site window, you can post all or a selection of your pages. With the Site window open, click the Site Settings button on the Toolbar, which opens the Site Settings dialog box.

GoLive opens to the General section, which shows an inactive field with the title of your home page. (If you need to choose a different home page, use the Point & Shoot button and drag the rope to a file within the open Site window.) Clicking the FTP & WebDAV Server pane shows you the settings for storing files on your Web server via FTP and WebDAV (see Figure 1-51).

Figure 1-51
Configuring
Site Settings
server
information

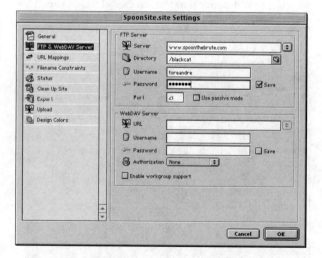

TIP:
WebDAV for
Workgroups

WebDAV is a great new standard intended for workgroups, but useful for everyone. It allows files to be checked in and out via its interface so that many people can work from the same set of files without worrying about who owns the latest version. See more about this in Chapter 23, *Synchronizing Sites*; the example below is using the more common FTP file service.

Under FTP Server, type the server address in the Server field. Clicking the popout button to the right and selecting Add Current Server adds this address to a program-wide list of FTP servers. If needed, you can specify a directory path in the Directory field; or, when connected to your server, you can click the Browse button to select a path. Type in your username and password. If you want GoLive to remember your password, check the Save box. (Otherwise, you are asked to type your password each time you connect—which can be good for security reasons.)

In the Upload pane, you can choose the defaults for what GoLive tries to upload to your site (see Figure 1-52). Checking the Honor Publish State of Folders and Files boxes causes GoLive to use the individual file settings that you configured using the Publish popup menu on the File Inspector. If you uncheck either of these boxes, GoLive uses a complex set of criteria to decide which files to upload.

Click OK to accept your changes. Back on the Site toolbar, click the FTP Server Connect button to access your server. This automatically opens the Site window's FTP tab if it's not already open, and turns the Toolbar gray while connecting. Once connected, you see the directory structure of your Web server. You also notice that the directory level of your server address has been placed in the FTP pane.

Figure 1-52
Configuring
Site Settings
Upload
preferences

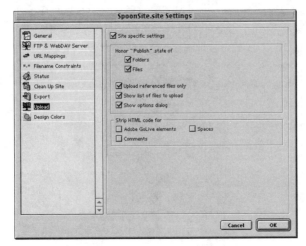

Next, click the Upload to Server button on the Toolbar. GoLive presents you with the Upload Options dialog box, which shows the options you chose or the defaults for the Upload pane of Site Settings (see Figure 1-53).

Figure 1-53
Site Settings
upload options

Checking Show List of Files to Upload brings up the Upload Site dialog, enabling you to manually select files to upload.

If you leave the Show List of Files to Upload checkbox marked, you get the Upload Site dialog box, where you can leave all files selected in your site to upload, or choose to uncheck individual files (see Figure 1-53, above). Click OK to begin transferring your files from your hard drive to your Web site. If you've selected all the files from your site, the FTP pane should mirror the file structure in your files list when finished.

Now that you're finished, click the FTP Server connect/disconnect button again—the status bar at the bottom of the FTP tab changes from connected to disconnected—and check your handiwork in a Web browser.

For more information, see Chapter 23, *Synchronizing Sites*.

Big Picture Workout

Now that you've seen the big picture of GoLive from creating pages to uploading a site, and gotten a good brain and mouse workout, we can move on to more details of how the program works. We start with the many Inspector palettes, continue into identifying parts, and finish with setting preferences.

CHAPTER 2

The Inspector

Inspector Clouseau:	Does yer dewg bite?
Inn Keeper:	No.
Inspector Clouseau:	Nice doggy. (Bends down to pet a dachshund; it snarls and bites him.) I thought you said yer dewg did not bite!
Inn Keeper:	Zat . . . iz not my dog!

—Scene from *The Pink Panther Strikes Again* (United Artists, 1976)

The shifting nature of GoLive's contextual Inspector palette is wonderful: it gives you the tools you need to complete most HTML tasks in one centralized location. It ranges from controlling the attributes for a single tag of HTML code to creating a CSS style to helping you command and control the management of your site. But despite its simple power, trying to understand how to use dozens of Inspectors can come back to bite you when you're faced with an unfamiliar set of options and menus.

Inspector Basics

In the real world, Inspectors are often investigators with an uncanny eye for detail; in GoLive, the Inspector is the tool used to narrow your focus on whatever item is currently selected (see Figure 2-1). With the item's Inspector visible, you can control nearly all its settings. Initially, the majority of Inspectors—save for a few exceptions, such as the View Controller—are displayed when an icon is placed onto a page or into a Site window from the Objects palette. Just to make sure we have all our bases covered before jumping in with both feet, here's a quick refresher on working with Objects palette icons.

Figure 2-1
A small
sampling of
palettes and
Inspectors

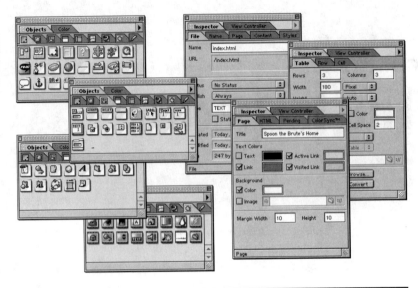

NEW IN 5:
View
Controller
and
Inspector
Palette

In GoLive 4, the View Controller sometimes appeared as an Inspector palette, sometimes was invoked by clicking an eyeball icon, and sometimes was a dialog box. In GoLive 5, the View Controller is a standalone palette, so you can view the contextual Inspector palette and the View Controller at the same time. Nonetheless, we're covering them both in this chapter under the rubric of "Inspector" because so much of what they control is contextually linked.

TIP:
Naming the
Inspector

An Inspector's name shows up in the lower-left corner of the Inspector palette. (In GoLive 4, it was in the palette's title bar.)

- Icons can be dragged from an Objects palette tab to a specific spot in the appropriate work space, such as the Layout Editor's body section for any of the Basic tab's icons. If you double-click most icons in the Objects palette, GoLive inserts the corresponding object at the current text-insertion point.

- When you place an HTML tag icon into the Layout Editor, GoLive inserts a placeholder icon; this often remains a generic icon until you configure its attributes, such as specifying an image's source file. Some placeholders, like anchors or comments, don't change appearance based on their contents; they're only there to show that you've added one of these items. To edit the attributes for a placeholder, select it in the Document window, which displays the Inspector that corresponds with its function.

Palette-centric information can be found in Chapter 3, *Palettes and Parts*, but you can also find references to the Object palette's icons that partner with the individual Inspectors in this chapter.

Common Attributes

While each Inspector typically handles a single HTML tag or site-based object, many of the controls recur in each Inspector palette. This is because HTML tags share a limited set of specifiers; the properties, or attributes, of HTML tags often include a URL or file location, a color name, or plain text. (This topic is discussed in more depth in Chapter 31, *Web Settings*.) The following are some of the controls you run into most frequently.

URL Getter (also known as Source, URL, File, and Base). When you need to define the path to a reference page or the source file for an image file, multimedia plug-in, or Java applet, GoLive provides the URL Getter. This is their official name for this set of fields and buttons that allow you to choose or type in a URL or path. The default on creating a new link is a text-input field with "(Empty Reference!)" placed into it to remind you to grab the necessary file (see Figure 2-2). If you don't replace this text, "(Empty Reference!)" is literally inserted into your page.

Figure 2-2
Source
attribute

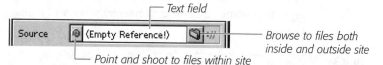

You have four choices for entering or selecting the reference in the URL Getter:

- Type the file name and directory location directly into the text field.
- Use the Point & Shoot button's lasso to rope that dogie…er, file. Remember, Point & Shoot works only in conjunction with files placed into site documents, or other open windows.
- Click the Browse button to navigate through your hard drive's file directory to the source file.
- Option-click (Mac) or Alt-click (Windows) the Browse button to access the Edit URL dialog box, in which you can enter or edit longer URLs.

In addition, click the Absolute Link button to use a full directory path from the root of the directory to the individual file instead of GoLive's relative default.

Target. If defining a link to another page, you are also given the choice of opening that link within another frame or in another window (see Figure 2-3). The standard four targets are:

- **_top** loads the link into the full body of a window that replaces your current frameset.

- **_parent** loads the link into the parent frame within a frame set.

- **_self** loads the link into the same frame as the selected link.

- **_blank** loads the link in a new blank window.

Figure 2-3
Target attribute

If you're building a framed page and name the individual frames, those names also appear in the Target popup menu.

Title. Another attribute associated with links is Title, which acts like the Img (image) tag's Alt attribute. Text added to this field shows up in a balloon or Tooltip (depending on the browser) when you mouse over the link (see Figure 2-4).

Figure 2-4
Title attribute

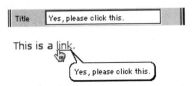

TIP:
Working
Title

The Title attribute only works on Windows Internet Explorer 4 and above, Windows Netscape Communicator 4 and above, and Mac Internet Explorer 4.5 and above.

Color. You can set a background color (for a page or a table cell) by dragging a color swatch from the Color palette into an Inspector's Color field (see Figure 2-5). This changes the field to the new color and the corresponding box becomes checked. If a Color box is unchecked, the previous color remains within the field but does not show up in the page.

Figure 2-5
Color attribute

Alignment (also Align). To set the alignment of an object—such as an image file or media plug-in—choose one of the following (see Figure 2-6).

- **Top:** aligns the top of the object with the top of the largest item in a line.

- **Middle:** aligns the middle of the object with the text baseline.

- **Bottom:** aligns the bottom of the object with the text baseline; this does the same as Baseline, below.

- **Left:** places the object at the left margin; for most objects, like images or whole tables, this flows text around its right side.

- **Text Top:** aligns the object's top with the top of the text in the current line.

- **Abs Middle:** aligns the object's middle with the middle of the current line.

- **Baseline:** aligns the bottom of the object with the text baseline.

- **Abs Bottom:** aligns the object's bottom with the bottom of the current line.

Note that other elements (such as tables and marquees) have a different set of options in their Align or Alignment popup menus.

Figure 2-6
Align attribute

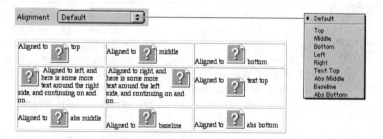

Document Layout Inspectors

The Inspectors in this section appear when you add or edit page-based elements in the Layout Editor's body section. (Form elements, which are also placed into the body section, are a different breed unto themselves; we cover them in "Forms Inspectors," later in this chapter.)

Page Inspector

The Page Inspector is used to set up the basic attributes of an individual page, from page title and link colors to whether a color profile is used (see Figure 2-7). While in the Layout Editor, click the Page icon in the upper left corner of the document window.

Figure 2-7
Page
Inspector's
Page tab

Page Tab

In the Title field, you can type a descriptive title that appears in a browser's top title bar. GoLive defaults to "Welcome to Adobe GoLive 5", so be sure to remember to change the title to reflect your page.

TIP:
We Know You Love GoLive, but…

Because GoLive prefills the Page Title field, many people completely forget to change the title, or may not have realized they could or should. If you search on just the title of a page containing the word "golive" on AltaVista (by entering "title:golive" without quotes), you can see how many colleagues never made this change. A recent search brought up 193,880 pages (up from 50,000 pages, searched for in the last edition of this book). It's also interesting to note the search results include pages documenting the entire lifespan of GoLive, from its CyberStudio GoLive roots to GoLive 5.

TIP:
Templates for Titles

You can avoid the page title problem by creating a simple template that GoLive opens as a default whenever it creates a new, blank page. Open the Preferences dialog box, and make this selection under the General pane, where you can choose a template to open.

TIP:
Adding Descriptions to Page Titles

According to friends who specialize in promoting Web sites and understanding search engines, the text that appears in a page's title (in the Title tag set by GoLive's Page Title field) appears to be the most heavily weighted information that most search engines index. To get your site noticed, consider adding a longer description of your site in addition to the name of the individual page. GoLive doesn't seem to limit the number of characters within the Page Title field, so you can write as long a description as you want. However, long page titles don't always fit within a Web browser's title bar, and could look a little messy.

The Text Colors section allows you to set colors for body text, standard link text, active links, and visited links. To change one of these settings, select the Color palette from the Window menu, or click a color field. Choose a color from the Color palette and drag a swatch from the Preview pane to the desired color field.

You can also set a background color or image to appear behind your page's text and images. For a refresher on using background images, consult Chapter 1, *Getting Started*.

GoLive 5 now includes fields for Margin Width and Height, which allow you to add space from the top and left edges of a page. But because of differences in attributes for this feature (IE uses Leftmargin and Topmargin, while Netscape uses Marginwidth and Marginheight), GoLive cleverly includes both sets in the body tag. Here's an example of placing 20 pixels of width from the left and 40 pixels from the top.

```
<body leftmargin="20" marginwidth="20" topmargin="40"
marginheight="40">
```

HTML Tab

If you don't want your page to automatically include such basic tags as Html, Head, Title, or Body—for instance, if you were planning on bringing in customized HTML fragments later—you can uncheck these options on the Page Inspector's HTML tab (see Figure 2-8).

Figure 2-8
Page
Inspector's
HTML tab

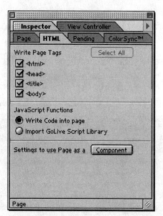

If one or more of the tags are unchecked, you can reset them all to be checked by clicking the Select All button.

The JavaScript Functions options correspond to GoLive's Actions: prefabricated JavaScript code that allows you to accomplish sophisticated tasks without hand coding. GoLive defaults to Write Code into Page, which includes all necessary JavaScript code in the individual HTML page. If you're creating a site, however, select Import GoLive Script Library, which creates a separate file containing all the necessary code for all Actions; your HTML page refers to this file, and a browser loads it separately. For the full details, see Chapter 28, *Actions.*

If you choose Import GoLive Script Library, the Component button becomes depressed and inactive—but don't feel sorry for it. This is just GoLive's way of denoting that this file is ready for use as a Component file, which requires any scripting (your own or from GoLive's built-in actions) to be written to the script library file. To learn more about using Components, see Chapter 21, *Files, Folders, and Links.*

TIP:
Components and Basic Tags

Because of the way GoLive inserts Components, it wants you to include all the basic tags like Html, Head, etc., even though it removes them. By including these tags, GoLive lets you turn a normal HTML page into a Component. The HTML page can be edited just like any other in GoLive, which wouldn't be true if it were missing all the basic structure tags.

Pending Tab

GoLive 5 offers you more advanced options for prototyping and creating sites with the Design window and Navigation and Links views. If you create pages or links through these means, you wind up with a heap of HTML files but a paucity of actual links.

However, you can keep track of which pages still need to be linked via the Page Inspector's Pending tab, which lists all the files within a site (both HTML and assorted media) that are associated with or linked from an individual page (see Figure 2-9).

Figure 2-9
Page
Inspector's
Pending tab

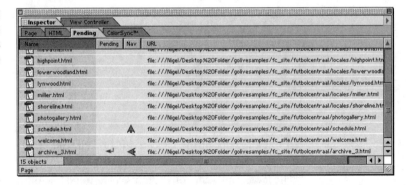

If a page is marked with a blue carriage-return icon in the Pending column, that page has been created within a design in the Design tab of the Site window, but the page you're examining doesn't yet link to that new page. The green arrows in the Nav column (pointing up, down, left, and right) indicate hierarchical direction in relation to the current page. (For more on these matters, see Chapter 20, *Prototyping and Mapping*.)

The Pending tab also lists the files' directory location under the URL column (which is quite helpful when you have a plethora of "default.html" files). The Pending tab is blank unless a page is part of a site.

ColorSync Tab (Mac)

On the Macintosh, GoLive applies Apple's ColorSync color-matching capabilities by default to all JPEG images collected on a page. The ColorSync tab lets you change GoLive's default settings (see Figure 2-10). You can select an external color profile by clicking the Profile radio button and either using the Point & Shoot button or clicking the Browse button to select the profile. You can also choose not to use any color profile; this is wise, as the integration of ColorSync color-management into browsers is currently limited to Explorer 4.0 and later on the Mac.

Figure 2-10
Page
Inspector's
ColorSync tab

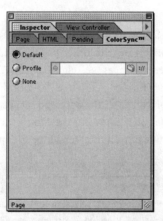

If you choose an external color profile, be sure to check that it gets uploaded to your Web site, as GoLive's link parser does not monitor color profiles. See Chapter 9, *Images*, for more on ColorSync.

Text Inspector

The Text Inspector, the Inspector palette you see the most, lets the Text toolbar handle the main text-formatting duties, and instead concentrates on creating links and assigning CSS styles. To get to the Text Inspector, place your cursor in any piece of text or blank space in the body section of the Document window or make any selection in that window (see Figure 2-11).

Figure 2-11
Selecting text in the Document window

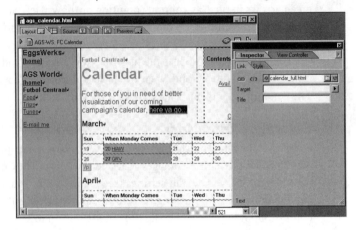

NEW IN 5:   The Actions tab found in the Text Inspector in GoLive 4 has now become the stand-alone Actions palette in GoLive 5.

Link Tab

Using the Link tab, you build the interconnecting framework of your Web site, linking items on the current page to other pages within your site, or to external Web pages and other resources (see Figure 2-12). After selecting text and creating a new link, an "(Empty Reference!)" reminder appears in the URL Getter. At this point, you can enter the path and file, use the Browse button to navigate to the file, Point & Shoot to the file in the Site window, or Option- or Alt-click the Browse button to enter a longer name.

Our Favorite Keyboard Shortcuts

GoLive really, really wants you to use its Point & Shoot feature, which certainly isn't a bad desire. It might take a little practice to get used to, but it's handy. However, GoLive's relentless focus on driving you to use this feature comes at a sacrifice of better support for editing URLs by hand.

However, you can take advantage of a set of keyboard shortcuts. Pressing Command-comma on the Mac jumps your text-insertion point from a linked text selection to the Text Inspector's URL field. Pressing Command-semicolon returns the insertion point back to the text selection in the Document window.

If the URL exceeds the width of the Inspector palette, resize the window, or Option- or Alt-click the Browse button (which changes to the pencil icon) to bring up the Edit URL dialog box.

Figure 2-12
Text Inspector's
Link tab

TIP:

**Creating a
Text Link**

GoLive offers several ways to create a text link. After selecting text you can: press Command-L (Mac) or Control-L (Windows), click the New Link button in the Text toolbar, select New Link from the Special menu, or click the Link button in the Text Inspector.

Style Tab

If you've set CSS styles for a page, they are listed in the Style tab, and may be set for different selections on a page by checking one or more of the boxes to the right of the style name with an appropriate text selection or insertion point (see Figure 2-13). The columns Inline, Par, Div, and Area correspond, respectively, to ranges of selected text, paragraphs in a selection (individually set), paragraphs in a selection (collectively grouped), and the entire body of the page or the contents of a table cell.

For instance, suppose we set up a style called "sheridan" (serve the One) that turns text purple and increases its size to 16 pt. If we only want a few

Figure 2-13
Text Inspector's
Style tab

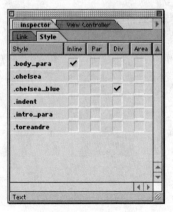

words to reflect this style, we select that range and then check the Inline column's box. (Notice that a green plus sign appears next to your cursor when it floats over an unchecked box, while a red minus sign appears when you mouse over a checked box.) Inline styles can only include items that affect type, not paragraph (also called "block") borders, backgrounds, or spacing.

If you want to set each paragraph in a selection to a style, check the box in the Par column. To apply a style around a selection, check the Div column, which creates a division (or Div) container around the selected paragraphs. (This works for borders, as one example, where you would want to differentiate between putting a border around each individual paragraph or around a whole set of paragraphs.)

Depending on where the text-insertion point is, checking the Area column's box applies a style to one of two places. If you're in a table cell, Area applies it just to that cell (via its TD tag). If you're elsewhere on a page, it affects the entire body section through the Body tag.

For more on Cascading Style Sheets, see Chapter 29, *Cascading Style Sheets*.

Image Inspector

Bringing an image into a GoLive document, either by dragging an image file from your hard drive or dragging the Image icon from the Object palette's Basic tab, calls up the Image Inspector.

Basic Tab

If you use the Objects palette's Image icon, you can set the source of your image in the Basic tab using the URL Getter (see Figure 2-14).

Figure 2-14
Image
Inspector's
Basic tab

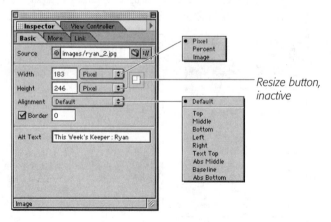

Resize button,
inactive

Width and Height. The Width and Height fields are automatically filled in with the actual pixel dimensions of the image. You can choose a measurement unit through the field's menus if you want to change the image's actual dimensions. For instance, choosing Percent calculates an image's height or width based on the current size of the browser window. This is not recommended, as it could dramatically resize an image depending on the user's browser window size. Also, keep in mind that resizing an image on a Web page doesn't resample it for that size, so the image quality will suffer.

If you want to change the dimensions of an image, type a number in the Width and/or Height fields, or click and drag one of the image's resize handles. A resize warning icon appears within your image reminding you that the current size doesn't match the original, and the resize warning button on the Image Inspector becomes active (see Figure 2-15). If you want to return to the image's original width and height dimensions, click the resize button.

Figure 2-15
Image resize
warning

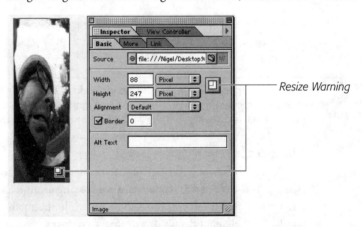

Resize Warning

Specifying the width and height of images helps Web browsers render pages faster. If a browser knows how much space to reserve for the images it's receiving, it can flow text around that space first, giving your viewer something to read while waiting for everything else to appear. GoLive automatically imports an image's dimensions, so this really is a no-brainer.

You can proportionally alter an image's size by Shift-dragging the lower-right corner handle. Adding Control (Mac and Windows) allows you to dynamically view the image resizing and the current pixel dimensions in the Image Inspector. However, if you enter, say, a larger value in the Width field, then change the Height menu to Image, you achieve the same proportional resize.

Alignment. Below the Width and Height fields, you can choose the image's alignment on the page from the Alignment menu.

Border. To create a (usually ugly) border around an image, especially when adding a link to it, enter a value in this box (not that we have an opinion, mind you). It's checked by default and set to zero, which removes the border. You can enter other values as well. Unchecking it allows a browser to use its internal default, which is usually a single pixel.

NEW IN 5:
Goodbye
Blue Border

Adobe has fixed one of GoLive 4's biggest little annoyances with the simple addition of a checkmark. The Border field always defaulted to zero, but you had to manually check this option to remove the border any time a link was added. (Or you had to go under the hood into the old Web Database—now Web Settings dialog box—and make this setting an absolute value.) But now GoLive 5 defaults to a checked border of zero, so you never again have to worry about the ugly blue border that appears around a linked image in a browser—unless of course you really want it. If so, just enter a value other than zero. Also, if you uncheck Border with a linked image, the border returns by default.

Alt Text. Alt Text appears in a browser if a user has chosen not to load images. It can also appear while images load in some browsers, or if a user has the not-entirely-rare lynx text-only browser.

TIP:
Alt Text
vs. Title

Alt Text also appears as a yellow Tooltip in Windows Internet Explorer as you move your mouse over an image. If you add text in the Title field, that attribute overrides the Alt Text Tooltip, but the Alt Text still shows up if images are turned off.

More Tab

The More tab sports miscellaneous items that don't fit into other categories (see Figure 2-16). In this tab you control spacing around an image, set an alternate low-resolution image to show up while the main image loads, and handle form element details if your image is a form.

Figure 2-16
Image
Inspector's
More tab

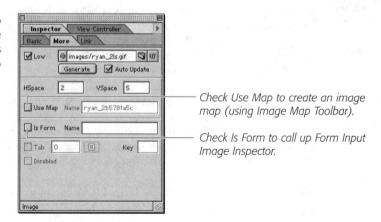

Check Use Map to create an image map (using Image Map Toolbar).

Check Is Form to call up Form Input Image Inspector.

Lowsource. If you have a fairly large image that could take a while to load into a browser, specify a low-resolution image in Lowsource. This image should be (or could be) identical in resolution to the larger image but with a lower bit depth or higher compression ratio, making it smaller in total bytes. (Some artistic uses of lowsource include adding a different image or one with different specifications so that the user gets an interesting first blast, and then the actual image.)

To add a lowsource image, check the Low box and navigate to an existing lowsource image; or, click the Generate button to have GoLive create a compressed black-and-white image for you. Checking the Auto Update option then updates the lowsource file each time the original image is modified.

Hspace and Vspace. Adding a value to the Hspace (horizontal space) field adds that number of pixels to the left and right sides of an image, while a Vspace (vertical space) value adds pixel space to the top and bottom.

Use Map. Check this option to create an imagemap, where you can specify different regions of an image to link to different pages. Type a unique name to identify this imagemap—especially useful if the imagemap is included in any scripting. By default, GoLive adds "MapName" followed by a random string of numerals and characters.

TIP:
Image Map Icon

A small yellow M appears to the right of the image, denoting the Map tag, a required element for client-side image maps. However, if you decide not to create an image map and uncheck Use Map, the yellow M doesn't disappear. You have to manually select the M icon and delete it.

NEW IN 5:
Change of Address

In GoLive 4, the Image Inspector had an entire tab devoted to creating imagemaps. The selection functionality of this tab has been transferred to the Image Map toolbar, discussed in Chapter 3, *Palettes and Parts*, while you link map regions in the new Map Area Inspector (discussed in the next section).

Is Form. If the Is Form option is checked, the image becomes a clickable form button and the Inspector name changes to the Form Image Inspector. Meanwhile, the Use Map field becomes inactive. The form options for the More tab are covered later in this chapter in "Form Inspectors," and in Chapter 15, *Forms*.

NEW IN 5:
Retaining Imagemap Settings

If you unchecked the Use Map button, checked the Is Form button, then changed your mind and reverted your checkboxes in GoLive 4, the program erased all your imagemap settings. GoLive 5 appears to be friendlier. Once you create an imagemap, it inserts the information in the HTML as a client-side imagemap (discussed in Chapter 9, *Images*). If you uncheck Use Map, it retains the name and keeps the HTML intact. This allows you to recheck it without any loss.

Link Tab

Creating links for text or images reminds you that GoLive offers many ways to get there from here (see Figure 2-17).

Figure 2-17
Image
Inspector's
Link tab

After creating a link, GoLive displays images with a border set to zero. Return to the Basic tab to uncheck the Border box to use the browser default, or to set this to another value.

For more information on the Title and Target fields, refer back to "Common Attributes," at the beginning of this chapter.

ColorSync (Mac). A true multi-tasker, the Link tab also includes the ColorSync options that were available in the Page Inspector. Choose the default ColorSync profile, or specify a profile for this image.

Map Area Inspector

If you do create an imagemap by checking Use Map on the Image Inspector's More tab, this Inspector appears after you create or select a region within the map using the Map Area toolbar (see Figure 2-18).

Add a destination URL to a region in the URL field via normal linking options, and add information to the Target, Title, and Alt fields as necessary or desired. If the region link is to be part of a form, check Tab under Focus to assign this item's slot in the tabbing order.

Figure 2-18
Map Area
Inspector

Table Inspector

Tables have become a staple of any HTML page, from simple and logical presentations of data to elaborate layout schemes that are invisible to the viewer. But wrapping your brain around hard-coding TD and TR tags with precise pixel measurements seems a bit daunting. Generating tables with GoLive's Table Inspector can put you at ease immediately; it is one of the program's stellar performers.

To open the Table Inspector, drag the Table icon from the Objects palette's Basic tab; or, select an existing table by clicking its top or left border (you can tell you're on top of it when the cursor changes to an object selection cursor, indicated by a small box next to the cursor). You can also click the right border; hovering over it turns the cursor into a two-way arrow (used to increase the width of the table). Both these actions open the Table Inspector to the Table tab. Clicking within the table (with a pointer) selects an individual cell and still opens the Table Inspector, but places you in the Cell tab.

NEW IN 5:
I Move to
Table That

Selection is one of the hardest tasks associated with tables, and GoLive 5 has added a new Table palette to simplify selection. This palette allows you to select one or more cells using a schematic proxy—that is, an outline of the table without any contents. The selection you make on the outline affect the table on the HTML page. In addition, you can now sort information in table rows as well as apply or capture background colors as table styles. For more information on the Table palette, see Chapter 3, *Palettes and Parts*. For all other things table-related, see Chapter 11, *Tables*.

NEW IN 5:
No More
Hiding

The Hidden tab of GoLive 4's Table Inspector turned into the fully functional Table palette in GoLive 5, so it's gone, gone, gone, daddy-o.

Table Tab

If you've dragged a table placeholder from the Objects palette, GoLive drops in a default table that's 180 pixels wide, includes three columns and three rows, and features a 1-pixel border. The Table Inspector's Table tab is where you can edit these attributes, as well as row height, alignment of the table on the page, border size, background color, and cell spacing and cell padding (see Figure 2-19).

Figure 2-19
Table
Inspector's
Table Tab

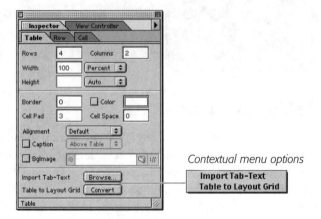

Contextual menu options

Alignment. This refers to how the table is placed on the page; at its default setting, text doesn't wrap around the table. If you choose Left, text wraps to the right; choose Right and text wraps to the left.

TIP:
**Center-
Aligning
a Table**

Even though HTML specifications allow you to center-align a table within the Table tag's attributes, GoLive doesn't offer this option. (GoLive prefers to center items using the Div tag.) To center-align a table, select the entire table and click the Align Center button from the Text toolbar.

Caption. To add a title to your table, check Caption and a row is placed above or below your table. GoLive defaults to centered text within the caption, but you can select the text and align it either left or right. However, this new alignment shows up only in Netscape's browsers; Internet Explorer continues to center the text.

Background image. You can add a background image to your table, which is much like adding a background image to your page. Check BgImage, then select your image file. A tiling effect occurs if the table is larger than the image; if the table is smaller, the image is cut off and not proportionally fit into the table.

Converting text to table. You can import text into a table from a standalone text file (.txt under Windows or set to the text file type on the Mac). Each field in the text file must be separated or delimited by a tab, space, semicolon, or comma, but you can only choose one of these delimiters per file. Drag a table placeholder into your page, click the Browse button to the right of Import Table Text, navigate to the text file, select the delimiter from the popup menu (it defaults to Tab), and press Return or Enter. The default placeholder modifies itself to conform to the number of columns needed to represent the fields in the first line and the number of rows equal to the number of lines of text. (We cover this in more depth in Chapter 11, *Tables*.)

Converting table to grid. Clicking the Table to Layout Grid Convert button transmogrifies your table into...another table, but one that doesn't seem like a table. For information on layout grids, see "Layout Grid Inspector," later in this chapter. Note that the layout grid removes any background image.

Cell Tab

Clicking on a cell within a table opens the Table Inspector to the Cell tab (see Figure 2-20). To select an individual cell, click its bottom or right border with the arrow cursor; Shift-click to select multiple cells. You can also choose individual cells one or more at a time from the Table palette.

Figure 2-20
Table
Inspector's
Cell Tab

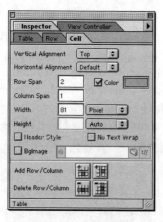

In the Cell tab, you can:

- Choose alignment of text and objects within the cell using the Vertical and Horizontal Alignment menus.

- Span across a number of columns and/or down a number of rows.

- Set the background color for individual cells.

- Set width and height in pixels, as an automatic resize (Auto), or in percentages.

If you select a cell and change its Width measurement, that measurement is applied to all other cells within that column; a change to its Height applies to all cells within that row.

Checking Header Style changes the source code of the cell to the HTML tag for table headers; this changes the preview for the text in that cell to bold, simulating how most browsers treat table headers. Checking No Text Wrap adds a Nowrap attribute to the table cell tag, which prevents text from wrapping in a table cell depending on the browser.

As in the Table tab, you can specify a background image, but one that displays only within a selected cell. If you select multiple cells, then add a background image, the image gets placed into each cell and doesn't span in adjoining cells.

TIP:
Active Fields

With multiple cells selected, the Row Span, Column Span, Width, and Height fields become inactive. However, with Width and Height, simply choose Pixel or Percentage from the popup menu to make the field active (a simple but great fix to a frustrating bug in GoLive 4). If the selected cells have the same width or height, the value is placed into the field; however, if the values are different, the field is left blank.

To add or delete columns or rows, select a cell, then click the appropriate button in the Cell tab. A new row appears above the selected cell's row, while a new column appears to the left of the selected cell's column. The new table items pick up the table attributes of the selected column or row (including cell alignment and row height). However, a cell that spans multiple rows or columns produces a row or column formatted with all the original cells. In addition, any text formatting from the selected cell's row or column is not carried over.

Row Tab

The Table Inspector's Row tab allows you to change many of the same attributes found on the Cell tab, including background color, row height, and alignment of objects and text within table cells (see Figure 2-21). However, modifying attributes on the Row tab applies those changes across an entire row.

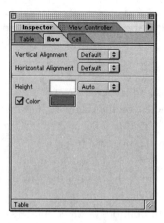

Figure 2-21
Table
Inspector's
Row Tab

Layout Grids

At first glance, GoLive's layout grid looks a little wacky, letting you place objects and boxes of text any ol' place you want on a grid and have the placement appear accurately within a browser. If you're familiar with HTML, you know it just doesn't do that...does it? A quick look at the source code, though, reveals that the layout grid is actually a complex HTML table, to which you can add the full range of HTML objects.

Layout Grid Inspector

On first placing a layout grid on a page (by dragging it over or double-clicking the Layout Grid icon in the Objects palette's Basic tab), the Inspector palette becomes the Layout Grid Inspector (see Figure 2-22). The Toolbar changes as well, but its fields are inactive. Once an object is selected, the fields and buttons come to life, allowing you to modify position and alignment within the grid, and size of the object.

Figure 2-22
Layout Grid
Inspector

TIP:
Palette
Transformation

The Transform and Align palettes also duplicate information found in the Layout Grid toolbar. For more on the toolbar and the palettes, see Chapter 3, *Palettes and Parts*.

GoLive defaults to placing a square grid measuring 201 by 201 pixels. You can use one of the three handles (on the right and bottom borders and bottom right corner) to drag the grid to your desired size, or you can use the Width and Height fields in the Layout Grid Inspector.

Optimize. The Optimize button to the right of these fields is grayed out and remains so until objects are placed onto the grid. Once active, clicking Optimize shrinks the right and bottom borders to be flush with the outermost borders of the objects contained within the grid.

Grid size. The default grid size is 16 pixels by 16 pixels, but this can be changed for either Horizontal or Vertical measurements to produce smaller or larger grid patterns. If you want to view your layout without the background pattern or, say, only utilize vertical guides, uncheck Visible. In addition, if you're a free spirit and don't want your objects to automatically conform to being placed according to the grid pattern, you can uncheck Snap.

Background color. You can drag a color swatch to the Background color field to fill your grid with color.

TIP:
Moving
Text Boxes
One Pixel
(or More)
at a Time

When Snap is checked for either or both Horizontal or Vertical Grids, you can hold down Option (Mac) or Control-Alt (Windows) and use the arrow keys to move a selected object one pixel at a time, or press an arrow key by itself to move the object one full grid box at a time. However, unchecking either of the Horizontal or Vertical snap options simply reverses the keyboarding: Option or Control-Alt moves by grid increments while just the arrow key moves items pixel by pixel.

Layout Text Box Inspector

To add text within a layout grid, you must first drag in a Layout Text Box from the Objects palette's Basic tab, which brings up the Layout Text Box Inspector (see Figure 2-23). If you're selecting an existing text box, be sure to click on its outside border, indicated by the object selection cursor.

Check Color and drag a color swatch in from the Color palette to add a background color to the text box. If Allow Content Overflow is checked, the dimensions of the box are locked; a plus sign appears in the bottom-left corner of a text box if text flows beyond the locked dimensions. If you want the box to grow with the text that's added, keep this option unchecked.

Figure 2-23
Layout Text
Box Inspector

NEW IN 5:
Multiselection
Inspector

This GoLive 4 Inspector has been moved in its entirety to the Align palette, which makes it easier to use alongside other controls; see Chapter 3, *Palettes and Parts*, for details.

Floating Box Inspector

Floating boxes could be the biggest thing in HTML since…tables!? That's right, tables. Remember when the Table tag and its ability to provide a rather complex layout scheme for your page seemed fresh, exciting, and downright cutting edge? A better question these days might be, "When don't you use tables?"

The floating box itself is a pretty handy way to create complex and dynamic layouts for version 4.0 and later browsers by dividing up sections of a page into rectangular segments using the division (Div) tag and a Cascading Style Sheet definition. The ins and outs of floating boxes are discussed at length in Chapter 14, *Floating Boxes*, as well as Chapter 27, *Animation*, but here's how to set up the basic elements.

Drag the Floating Box icon from the Objects palette into the Layout Editor and a floating box placeholder appears with a tiny yellow box labeled "SB". The 100-by-100-pixel empty box includes a number in its bottom-right corner indicating the order it was inserted into a page (see Figure 2-24). Placing your mouse over the box boundary lines turns the cursor into a sideways grabber hand.

Dragging the box around the page changes its absolute x/y coordinates (as evidenced by the changing Left and Top values in the Floating Box Inspector), but the yellow floating box marker remains in the same position.

Figure 2-24
Floating box
on page

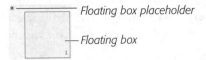

Floating box placeholder

Floating box

You can add HTML items to your floating box just as you would to the rest of your page, or within a layout grid or table cell. Drag in and configure images, Java applets, horizontal rules, and so on.

Name. In the Floating Box Inspector, enter a Name to identify a box; by default, GoLive enters "layer" followed by a number.

Left and Top. To set how far the box sits from the left border of the browser window, type a pixel value in the Left field, then type a value in the Top field to place the box x number of pixels from the top of the window.

Depth. The stacking order over overlapping floating boxes is set by entering a value in the Depth field. A floating box with a higher number is placed on top of the heap, while the box with the lowest number is placed on the bottom.

Width and Height. Enter values in the Width and Height fields to modify the size of a box. (You can also click one of the blue handles within the floating box placeholder in the Document window and drag.) Choose Pixel for an absolute measurement, Percent for a measurement relative to the size of the browser window, or Auto to fit the content that's placed into the box.

Background. To add a background color to the box, drag a swatch from the Color palette into the Color field. If you click the swatch in the Inspector, the border fills in and any color you choose in the Color palette changes the background of the floating box without you having to drag the color into the swatch. To add a background image, check BGImage and type the image file's URL; or navigate to it using Point & Shoot or the Browse button.

Animation. The Floating Box Inspector's Animation controls set the shape of an animation path (such as Linear, Curve, or Random), and the color for the keyframe icon in the Timeline Editor, where an animation is configured. Clicking the Record button allows you to set the path of an animation by dragging the floating box to desired points within the Document window. For more on creating floating box animations, see Chapter 27, *Animation*.

Line Inspector

A horizontal rule is one of the few graphical elements that is generated by a browser without needing to load an image. To open the Line Inspector, double-click the horizontal Line icon in the Objects palette, drag it onto the page, or select an existing rule (see Figure 2-25).

Figure 2-25
Line Inspector

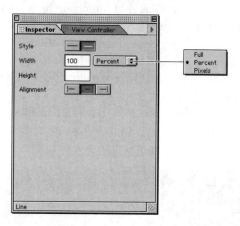

Style. Choose between a solid bar (the left button) or the default shaded, three-dimensional line (the right button).

Width. GoLive defaults to Full, which spans the entire width of the area the rule occupies. Choosing either Percent or Pixels makes the Width field active, allowing you to enter a specific measurement.

Height. Here you can enter the Size attribute, which determines the rule's height in pixels. If this field is left blank, the line defaults to a height of 2 pixels.

Alignment. If you've specified a width measurement, you can choose an alignment (left, center, or right).

TIP:
Color Rules

You can't add color to a horizontal rule—it's either black or embossed according to HTML 4 specifications. However, if you choose a solid bar (the Noshade attribute) and manually add a color attribute in either the HTML Source Editor or HTML Outline Editor, then preview in Internet Explorer 4 and higher (both Windows and Mac), you see the color applied.

Spacer Inspector

If you're producing Web pages for an audience that primarily uses Netscape (version 3 or later), you can add white space to a page using the Spacer tag, thus avoiding the inclusion of transparent GIFs to separate items on a page. Otherwise, you may want to avoid using the tag, as it is ignored by all flavors of Internet Explorer (which is the vastly dominant browser currently in use).

After dragging the Horizontal Spacer icon from the Objects palette, you can configure the size of the blank space in one of three ways in the Spacer Inspector (see Figure 2-26): horizontally (which opens the Width field), vertically (which opens the Height field), or as a block (which allows you to edit its Width, Height, and alignment).

You can also select the Spacer icon in the Document window and drag a blue handle to your desired size. Control-dragging dynamically resizes both the Spacer icon as well as any surrounding text or images.

Figure 2-26
Spacer
Inspector

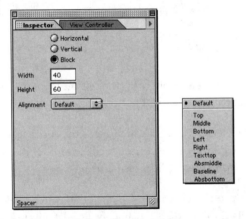

Body Script and JavaScript Inspectors

To start writing JavaScript, you need to choose whether to use a body script or a head script; consult Chapter 26, *JavaScript*, on making that choice. (Generally, you opt for scripts that appear in the Head section.)

If a body script is right for you, drag the JavaScript icon from the Objects palette's Basic tab onto your page. This calls up the Body Script Inspector (see Figure 2-27). (If you drag the Script icon from the Objects palette's Head tab into the Document window's head section, GoLive instead brings up an identical Inspector named Head Script Inspector.)

Type a unique identifier in the Name field. Choose browser compatibility from the Language popup menu, which then supplies the appropriate version of JavaScript in the field below (see Table 2-1).

Figure 2-27
Body Script
Inspector

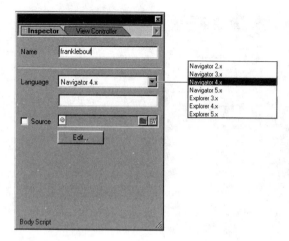

Table 2-1	**Browser Version**	**JavaScript Version**
JavaScript	Navigator 2.x	JavaScript (the original version)
Languages	Navigator 3.x	JavaScript 1.1
	Navigator 4.x	JavaScript 1.2
	Explorer 3.x and 4.x	JScript

If you have a text file with JavaScript code already prepared, check Source and enter the the file's name and directory location or navigate to the file. However, if you still need to type in the script, click the Edit button to open the JavaScript Editor, where the name you entered in the InspectorName field is also displayed in the script name popup menu.

TIP:
Opening the
JavaScript
Editor

In grand GoLive tradition, you have a number of options at the tips of your fingers to open the JavaScript Editor: click the coffee bean icon in the top-right corner of the Document window, click the Edit button in either the Head or Body Script Inspector, or double-click the placeholder icon in the Layout Editor.

Opening the JavaScript Editor also brings up the JavaScript Inspector. The Script tab mirrors the information found in the Body Script Inspector (name, language, source), but adds the Functions field, which lists all JavaScript functions found in an individual script (see Figure 2-28). Select an item from the Functions list and it becomes highlighted in the JavaScript Editor.

To add an event to your script, select from the list of available functions found under the Events tab and drag the item into the JavaScript Editor (see Figure 2-29). The function appears both in code in the JavaScript Editor, as well

Figure 2-28
JavaScript
Inspector's
Script tab

Figure 2-29
JavaScript
Inspector's
Events tab

as in the Event Code text box at the bottom of the JavaScript Inspector's Events tab. Notice that a description of the function appears to the right of the Event Code heading, and the selected function's icon now appears as active in the list.

Functions that are added to a script are summarized in the Functions field of the Script tab. Selecting an item from this list highlights the code in the JavaScript Editor.

TIP:
Editing
JavaScript
Functions

Adding a function to the JavaScript Editor allows you to edit its code in the Event Code field. Drag a function into the Editor, then make your edits or additions to the code. Select that function and drag it again into the Editor, and your edits appear in your script. Also, if you return to a function that has already been added (showing as active), selecting it adds a pen to the script icon, denoting that it is now editable.

To add objects and methods to the functions of your script, click the Objects tab, select from the list of available objects, then drag it to the desired point in the script (see Figure 2-30).

Figure 2-30
JavaScript
Inspector's
Objects tab

Marquee Inspector

To create a scrolling text message (which acts like a stock ticker), drag the Marquee icon in from the Objects palette's Basic tab (see Figure 2-31). The Marquee tag that creates the scrolling information only works with Internet Explorer; you get just text—no scrolling and no background color—when viewed in Netscape Navigator.

Figure 2-31
Marquee
Inspector's
Basic tab

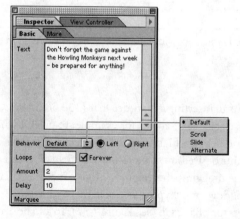

Basic Tab

After adding your message to the Text field, you can configure how the marquee scrolls with the Behavior menu.

- Scroll causes text to continually move across the marquee area. (Default is the same as Scroll.)

- Slide scrolls text into the marquee area, then holds it onscreen. If this option is selected, make sure the text fits into the marquee box; otherwise, your message could be cut off.

- Alternate scrolls text first left and then right across the marquee area. (The Left and Right radio buttons become inactive with this option.)

By default, the marquee's message repeats endlessly in browsers (even with Forever unchecked, the feature that's supposed to control the limits of forever). If you enter a value in the Loops field, the marquee repeats that number of times. (These two options are inactive when Slide is chosen since the message is kept in the marquee box once it hits the screen.) Once the number of loops have completed, the marquee box remains blank. Entering a value of 0 (zero) automatically checks Forever.

To alter the scrolling speed, type a value in the Amount field. To set a delay between repetitions, enter a value in the Delay field. Choose to begin your text scrolling from either the left or right by clicking one of the Direction buttons.

TIP:
Setting Amount and Delay to Nil

GoLive defaults to entering no values in either the Amount or Delay fields. This can look a little choppy, though, so it's advisable to enter a value. However, if after experimenting with Amount values you delete the value, no text shows up in the marquee box.

TIP:
Speeding up the Scroll

If the marquee is too pokey for you, enter a negative value in the Delay field to speed it up.

More Tab

GoLive defaults to inserting a marquee that's 150 pixels wide, while the height adjusts to the selected text setting; for example, 14 pixels high for plain text set to a size of 3, or 28 pixels high for heading 1 text set to a size of 3.

Type in your desired message in the Text field. You can adjust the width and height by dragging the handles of the marquee placeholder in the Document window, or by typing values in the Width and Height fields in the Marquee Inspector's Basic tab (see Figure 2-32). To add horizontal and vertical space surrounding the marquee, enter values in the HSpace and VSpace fields.

Figure 2-32
Marquee
Inspector's
More tab

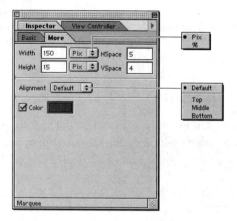

If the marquee is placed within the flow of text, you can configure its placement (Default, Top, Middle, and Bottom) using the Align menu. To add a background color, drag a color swatch into the Color field.

Comment Inspector

A helpful tool for any Web publisher is the comment tag, which in HTML starts with <!-- and ends with -->. For example:

```
<!-- page layout table begins here -->
```

Any text or additional code that is placed within this tag container does not show up in a Web browser, though it is visible in the page's source code. This is perfect for adding reminders or placing page items or links that need to be added at a later date. Some scripting languages or techniques, like SSI (Server-Side Include), require special code placed in comments.

The Comment Inspector appears when the Comment icon is dragged from the Objects palette, or an existing Comment icon is selected on a page (see Figure 2-33). To add a comment's content, click within the notepad-like field and type away.

Figure 2-33
Comment
Inspector

TIP:
Your
Comment
Here

GoLive 5 handily—or awkwardly, depending on your point of view—adds a "your comment here" reminder to the Comment Inspector. You need to select the text and delete unless you want to include this with your comment.

Anchor Inspector

An anchor allows you to create a hyperlink to a specific point on another page, or to a designated position within the currently viewed document (see Figure 2-34). For a refresher on creating anchors, see Chapter 1, *Getting Started*.

Figure 2-34
Anchor
Inspector

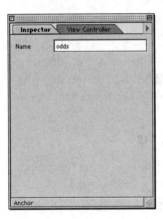

TIP:
Anchor
Keyboard
Shortcut

In addition to dragging the Anchor icon in from the Objects palette or using Point & Shoot, you can also Command-Option-click (Mac) or Alt-click (Windows) within the text of an unselected text link (i.e., a text link that's not highlighted). This action adds an Anchor icon to the left of the word; you can drag that to your desired location. In addition, the word within which you clicked appears in the Anchor Inspector's Name field between "Anchor" and the number GoLive automatically assigns.

Line Break Inspector

In HTML, a line break (the BR tag) is a way to begin a new line without inserting any extra space between lines (which the P tag does). In GoLive, the easiest way to add a line break is pressing Shift-Return (Mac) or Shift-Enter (Windows) with your cursor placed at the appropriate point in the body section of the HTML page. You can also drag the Line Break icon from the Objects palette into the page, although this is somewhat awkward. If you create a line break via the keyboard, the Line Break Inspector doesn't appear unless you select the icon on the page (see Figure 2-35).

Figure 2-35
Line Break
Inspector

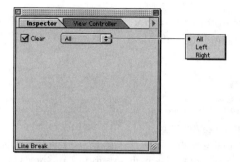

The Clear attribute works in conjunction with images only. If Clear is checked, you can choose All, Left, or Right from the Clear menu. Selecting either Left or Right stops the flow of text around an image until there are no more images aligned to either respective margin. Selecting All stops the flow of text around an image until there are no images aligned to either margin.

Tag Inspector

If you're adding code to a page other than standard HTML objects (such as XML tags), you use the Tag Inspector. Drag the icon from the Objects palette into your page, and a placeholder with a "noedit" tag and closing tag (with only a forward slash) appears (see Figure 2-36).

Figure 2-36
Tag Inspector

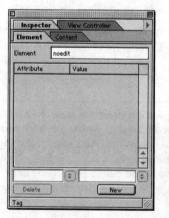

In the Element tab, enter the tag's name in the Element field. To add attributes, click the New button, type an attribute name in the Attribute field and its value in the Value field; repeat until you've had your fill of attributes. To get rid of an attribute, select it from the list and click the Delete button.

In the Content tab, add your desired text to the Content field; notice, however, it doesn't readily show up in your page. To add the text to your page, click one of the other tabs in the Document window, then return to the Layout Editor to find your added text.

Head Inspectors

The Head section of an HTML page contains tags that describe the page to the viewer and search engines; these tags also identify foreign scripts, target frame or window destinations after a link is clicked, and handle other miscellany.

Head tags, the icons of which are found in the Head Section of the Objects palette, can only be placed within the Head section of the Document window. GoLive defaults to placing three Head icons into the Head section with the following code:

- `<META HTTP-EQUIV="content-type"content="text/html;charset=iso-8859-1">` identifies the character set used in the page, which can be changed in Preferences (see Chapter 4, *Preferences and Customizing*).

- `<META NAME="generator" content="Adobe GoLive 5">` identifies GoLive as the creator of this page, which can be turned off in the General panel in Preferences under the Edit menu.

- `<TITLE>`Welcome to Adobe GoLive 5`</TITLE>` (the default text) appears in a browser's titlebar; change the title by clicking and editing the field to the right of the Page icon, or editing the Title field in the Page Inspector.

To add more tags, click the Head Section toggle triangle to open this area. Alternately, drag a Head tag icon from the Objects palette and hold it over the triangle; after a second or so, the Head section opens up, allowing you to place the icon.

TIP:
Head Section's Title Icon

The Title icon in the Head section does not have an accompanying Objects palette icon; the title is modified either via the Page Inspector or by entering text into the title field to the right of the Page icon in the Layout Editor. If you delete the Title icon in the Head section, both the Page Inspector and the title field become blank. However, if you delete all title text from either of these locations, the Title icon remains in the Head section (and exists in your source code as <TITLE></TITLE>).

Meta Tags

The workhorse of the head section, the Meta tag, lets you embed invisible information about your page, such as the author's name, keywords, and a description of the page's content. You can also control a page's refresh rate (for updating live information) or jump to a new destination after a set amount of time viewing the page.

GoLive offers a generic Meta Inspector for most of the settings you can apply to a page, but it also offers the Keywords Inspector and the Refresh Inspector for managing those two specific tasks.

Meta Inspector

To add a Meta tag, drag its icon from the Objects palette's Head tab to the Document window's Head section; this brings up the Meta Inspector (see Figure 2-37). The Meta Inspector has a popup menu from which you can select either of the Meta tag's two attributes: Name and HTTP-Equivalent. Name is used for ordinary information, like an author's name, while HTTP-Equivalent (or HTTP-Equiv, as it's named in the underlying HTML) can be used to insert values that are normally traded between a server and browser, such as a cookie setting or an expiration date for the page.

Figure 2-37
Meta Inspector

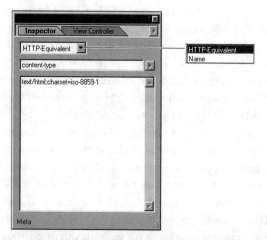

The popup button to the right of the top field is inactive, so you don't have a list of attributes to choose from. See Chapter 7, *Head Section*, for more details.

In the Content field, type the value that corresponds with the attribute. A page can have an unlimited number of Meta tags.

Keywords Inspector

The Keywords Inspector lets you view, add, or edit a list of keywords describing your page's content (see Figure 2-38). For details on choosing keywords, see Chapter 7, *Head Section*.

Figure 2-38
Keywords
Inspector

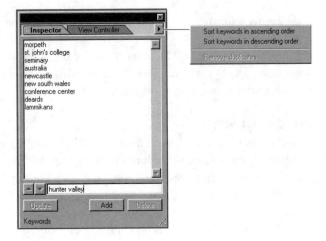

To add keywords to a page, drag the Keyword icon into the Document window's Head section, click within the text field, type a word or phrase and press Return or Enter, or click the Add button. Additional items are added into the list alphabetically. To delete an item, select it from the list and click the Delete button. To edit an existing item, select it from the list, make your edits, then click the Update button.

Shift-click on items to select consecutively; for example, shift-clicking the top and bottom items in a list selects all items. To select noncontiguous items, Command-click (Mac) or Control-click (Windows).

To move items up or down the list, make a selection and click the up or down arrows. If you want to view the list in alphabetical or reverse alphabetical order, select Sort Keywords in Ascending Order or Sort Keywords in Descending Order, respectively, from the popup menu at the top-right corner of the Inspector.

GoLive is smart enough to know what's already in the list, so if you type a keyword that's already been added both the Update and Add buttons are inactive. However, if you are working with an imported page, you can select Remove Duplicates from the Inspector's popout menu to do some quick editing.

TIP:
Adding Keywords from Text

As you add or edit content in the Layout Editor, select a word or range of words and press Command-K (Mac) or Control-K (Windows) to add the selection to the keywords list, or choose Add to Keywords from the Special menu.

TIP:
Updating Keywords

If you select an existing list item and edit it, you must click the Update button; pressing Return adds a new keyword item to the list.

Now here's an interesting "feature": if you first select an item residing at the bottom of the alphabetical list (either in normal order or reversed), then select additional items above it using either Shift or Command/Control, the Update button becomes active. Clicking the Update button copies the item from the list's bottom to the top selected item (leaving all items in between unchanged). This seems to be a bug from GoLive 4 that still hasn't been corrected.

Refresh Inspector

Another member of the Meta tag family, the HTTP-Equivalent "Refresh" setting (as represented by the Refresh icon from the Objects palette's Head tab) allows you to control how often a page's content is refreshed. This could be useful for a page publishing minute-by-minute soccer scores or showing current traffic conditions. This same tag can be used to redirect a user's browser to another page after an automatic delay; this feature often gets used for introductory splash pages or for taking users to a new page after informing them that the original page they were trying to reach has moved.

In the Delay field of the Refresh Inspector, type a value in seconds for the refresh interval (see Figure 2-39). If you want to redirect the user to another page, click the Target URL radio button and type the file destination, or navigate to the file either using Point & Shoot or the Browse button. (By default, Target This Document is selected.)

Figure 2-39
Refresh
Inspector

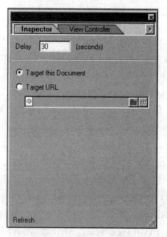

Link Inspector

The Link feature allows you to link to other related resources, from style sheets to Web-formatted fonts, as well as define relationships to other pages within your site. This latter functionality can help with usability/accessibility issues, such as setting up a linear navigation system (next page, previous page) or sending visitors with limited HTML capabilities (i.e., text readers for the blind don't deal with tables well) to an alternate, more accessible, page.

NEW IN 5:
**An End
to Link
Madness**

GoLive 4 featured a Link Inspector that configured the Head section Link object as well as a Link Inspector that visually tracked incoming and outgoing links to a file. GoLive 5 has renamed the latter item the In & Out Links palette—slightly awkward, but a little less confusing.

Drag the Link icon from the Objects palette's Head tab into the Layout Editor's Head section; this brings up the Link Inspector (see Figure 2-40).

Figure 2-40
Link Inspector

Select a linked document or page using the URL Getter. Type a brief descriptive title of the file that is referenced in the Title field (if pointing visitors to an alternate file). You can also provide a unique name for the link, which can be helpful if referenced within a script (though this attribute doesn't seem to be a part of the official HTML spec published by the World Wide Web Consortium). You can skip the URN (Uniform Resource Number) field, as that isn't supported, as well as the Methods field, which is rarely used. You can enter values into the Rel attribute field to indicate the type of relationship this page has with the referenced file (including Next, Prev, Stylesheet, Appendix, and more). Values entered into the Rev field indicate a reverse relationship to a file that is linking to the current page. Unfortunately, the popup menus for these fields are inactive in the GoLive 5 release (a carryover from GoLive 4); if you want to access these attributes you either have to type them from memory in the Link Inspector's fields or use the HTML Source Editor. For more details, see Chapter 7, *Head Section*.

TIP:
**More about
Links**

To learn more about using the Link tag, refer to the W3C specifications (http://www.w3.org/TR/REC-html40/struct/links.html#h-12.3). Also, Web Techniques has an introduction on designing for the Web with accessibility issues in mind (Web Accessibility with HTML 4.0, http://www.webtechniques.com/archives/1999/12/desi/).

TIP:
Linking to
CSS Files

As mentioned above, the Link tag is also used to link to external CSS files. You could configure the style sheet link using the Link Inspector, but an easier way is using the Style Sheet editor. After linking to the CSS file, click one of the other tabs in the Document window, then return to the Layout Editor; you find an external CSS file icon placed into the Head section. Clicking this brings up the External Style Sheet Inspector, which is covered later in this chapter.

IsIndex Inspector

The IsIndex feature dates back to Web antediluvian times when Web sites had only primitive tools. The Isindex tag designated a page searchable while simultaneously inserting a search field at the top of a page.

The IsIndex Inspector features one field—Prompt—which, when filled in, places the text to the left of a search field (see Figure 2-41). When a user types in text and presses Return, a new URL forms with the address of the current page, followed by a question mark and the keywords entered into the field (each separated by a plus sign).

Figure 2-41
IsIndex
Inspector

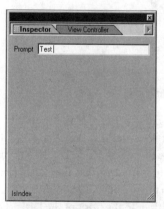

GoLive—and the rest of the world—considers this tag obsolete, and the program doesn't preview it; you must preview the page in an external browser.

Base Inspector

Links and media file sources are typically written in code as relative to the current page. For example, if you're linking to an item at the same directory level, you only need to include the file name (i.e., "eggsy.gif"); if linking to a directory one level above, you'd type the HTML shorthand for moving up a level and include the directory name (i.e., "../gifs/eggsy.gif"). See the "It's All

Relative" sidebar in Chapter 7, *Head Section*, for a discussion of relative and absolute linking.

Using the Base tag, you can specify a URL that substitutes for the current page's location as the base on which to add or navigate any relative links on the page, including image and file references.

After dragging in the Base tag icon from the Objects palette's Head section, the Base Inspector appears (see Figure 2-42). Check the Base box and either enter the URL you want used as the page's base address or navigate to it. You can also designate a destination frame or window for all hyperlinks using the Target popup menu.

Figure 2-42
Base Inspector

Checking the Absolute Link button applies the absolute directory path to the item in the Base field if it's a local file (i.e., "file://YMO/welcome.html"); this applies to both the Base Inspector and to the underlying source code.

GoLive has two other kinds of identifiers that it appears to use for its own purposes, but which we can't figure out. Checking Write Base Always Absolute adds a GoLive-specific identifier to the front of the URL: "GLCSabs:" If you've also pressed the Absolute Link button to its above right, it uses "GLCSrel:". GoLive doesn't show this identifier in the Base field, but it does insert it in the underlying HTML.

TIP:
Absolutely
Yes! Or No!

Once you have clicked the Absolute Link button and checked Write Base Always Absolute checkbox, go to the Source Editor to check on the code—it seems fine. However, upon return to the Layout Editor, the Write Base... checkbox is no longer checked. Back to the Source Editor produces code without the GLCSabs reference. But clicking back to the Layout Editor shows the Write Base... checkbox checked again. Oy vay. If you are configuring the Base tag, it would be best to do it last, then close and save your file to avoid this confusing dance.

Tag and End Tag Inspectors

See the description for the Tag and End Tag Inspectors in "Document Layout Inspector," earlier in this chapter.

Comment Inspector

See comments about the Comment Inspector in "Document Layout Inspector," earlier in this chapter.

Head Script Inspector

If you want to add a script to a page's Head section, drag the Script tag icon in from the Objects palette. This calls up the Head Script Inspector, which is virtually the same Inspector as the Body Script Inspector (see description in "Document Layout Inspector," earlier in this chapter), save for the name.

Frame Inspectors

When viewing a page in the Frame Editor (after placing a frameset from the Objects palette's Frame tab), you run across two Inspectors that control the behavior of framesets and individual frames.

Frame Set Inspector

The Frame Set Inspector appears immediately following the placement of a Frameset icon from the Objects palette, or when you click on the border between two frames (see Figure 2-43). When a frameset is first inserted, the entire set is

Figure 2-43
Frame Set
Inspector

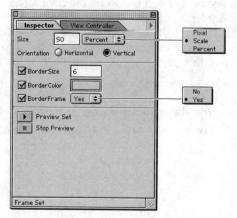

selected (indicated by an orange line surrounding all its frames), and any changes made on the Frame Set Inspector affect the entire set.

If you click on a frame border that divides several frames of the same orientation (either horizontal or vertical), GoLive places a colored boundary around those frames, and any modifications to the Frame Set Inspector affects just those frames.

Sizing. You can set the size of two or more selected frames nested within a larger frameset. (If the entire frameset is selected, Size is inactive.) Choosing the default Scale automatically resizes the selected frames when a viewer alters a browser's size. Choosing Pixel sets an absolute measurement, while choosing Percent proportionally resizes based on the size of the browser window.

Orientation. A frameset's Orientation is set to either Horizontal or Vertical depending upon the way it sits within the frame layout. If you click the other radio button, your frameset flips to this orientation.

TIP:
Mixing Up Framesets

If you have three or more frames on your page, you can rearrange how the frameset lays out by clicking one border and changing its Orientation, then clicking another border and changing its setting, and so on, and so on…

Border properties. Check BorderSize and enter a value in the field to the right to change its width; if checked, GoLive sets it by default to six pixels. To change the border's color, drag a swatch from the Color palette to the BorderColor field; GoLive sets it to gray by default. Checking BorderFrame outlines the frame with a thin, gray border; the default setting, when checked, is Yes.

TIP:
Frame Colors

While you have to individually select each frame divider to modify border size and frame, you need only select one to set the color for all borders. The color chosen for that border bleeds into all other borders that do not have a color value assigned. Also note that, unlike the color fields in the Table Inspector, colors cannot be dragged into the unchecked BorderColor field and have the color accepted; you must first check the option to make it active, then drag in your desired color.

Preview. To preview the frameset on the Mac without using the Frame Preview, click the Preview Set button. To return to the file icon view, click the Stop Preview button.

Frame Inspector

To begin setting the attributes of an individual frame, click anywhere within a frame except on the divider. You can set the measurement for a frame in the Frame Inspector by choosing either Pixel or Percent from the Size popup menu, then entering a value into its field (see Figure 2-44).

Figure 2-44
Frame
Inspector

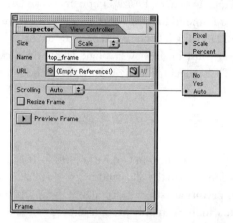

A frame's width is modified if its orientation—found in the Frame Set Inspector—is set to Horizontal, and its height is modified if a Vertical orientation is chosen. As with the Frame Set Inspector, if a frame's size is set to Scale, it sizes automatically when resized in a viewer's browser.

Choosing Pixel sets an absolute measurement that isn't resized, while choosing Percent proportionally resizes the frame relative to the overall width and height of the frameset. (You can also resize frames the old-fashioned way by dragging the frame divider.)

TIP:
Framing
Size

A frameset with multiple frames within an orientation (vertical or horizontal) specifies one frame's Size to Scale, while the others are set to an absolute pixel size. This takes some of the burden off browsers when doing the math to accommodate different window sizes.

To specify the contents of a frame, enter the file name in the URL field, or navigate to the file. (You can also Command/Control-drag from the frame's file icon to a file within a Site window.) The question-mark file icon turns into a GoLive file icon, and the file name and directory information appear below. Next, give this frame a unique title in the Name field, which then appears above the file icon; this is used to manage links between frames.

In the Scrolling menu, you can choose the default Auto option, which places a scroll bar (either vertical or horizontal) where text overflows the boundaries of the frame. If you choose Yes, a scroll bar is placed whether or not there is overflowing content, while choosing No does not produce a scroll bar even if content overflows.

GoLive defaults to leaving Resize Frame unchecked. If this is checked, a user can resize a frame in browsers that support this feature by dragging a frame border and moving it left or right, or up or down.

On the Mac, you can preview a single frame by clicking the Preview Frame button. Click it again to turn off previewing and return to the file icon view.

Site Inspectors

The site-management features in GoLive are less focused on Inspectors and more on the various tabs in the Site window, in which all management is centralized. The Inspectors are still important, but many attributes and relationships in the Site window can only be, or also be, modified through dragging and dropping, or selecting an object and editing it directly.

The Site window is organized into six tabs: Files, External, Designs, Colors, Font Sets, and Custom. These tabs handle, respectively, HTML and media files, external Web links and email addresses, site prototyping and mapping, sitewide color usage, sitewide font set usage, and customized HTML objects. Each tab has its own set of Inspectors that correspond to the kinds of objects stored in the tab.

File Inspector

The File Inspector helps you configure and view document basics, from static information such as creation date, to editable fields, including name, title, and "publish state." To invoke the File Inspector, select a file—any file—in the Files tab or within the Navigation View or Links View.

File Tab

In the File Inspector's File tab, GoLive puts much of the same information you'd find in the Macintosh Finder or Windows Explorer, such as file type and creator (Mac only), creation and modification dates, and file size (see Figure 2-45). It also shows the file's location within the site in URL format.

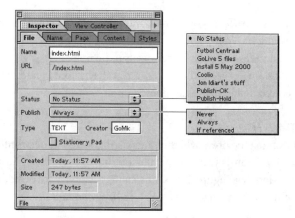

Figure 2-45
File Inspector's
File tab

Name. You can modify a file's name by editing within the Name field. If the file is referenced by others in the site, the Rename File dialog box appears and asks you whether you want GoLive to update all links with this new name. Check all boxes to the left of the file name that apply, then press Return.

Stationery. If you want to use a page as a template for designing other pages, check the Stationery Pad box. The file then opens as an untitled GoLive document. (If you check Stationery for a media file, it opens in the application that created it, such as Acrobat or Photoshop, and sports a "1" after its name.)

TIP:
Setting
Stationery

If you select a file within the Stationeries folder in the Extras tab, Stationery Pad is checked by default.

Status. The Status popup menu mirrors the Label color and title designations in the Macintosh Finder. Under Windows, it includes the standard labels that you would find on a Macintosh. See Chapter 21, *Files, Folders, and Links*, for a more detailed discussion of this setting.

NEW IN 5:
No Label

The Macintosh version of GoLive 4 had a Macintosh-specific setting for changing the Finder Label of a file. This would affect the file on the Desktop. GoLive 5 switched entirely to the Status setting which is cross-platform compatible when you transfer site files between Macintosh and Windows versions of GoLive.

Publish state. In the Publish popup menu, choose a "state" for the document that controls how it interacts with GoLive's FTP synchronization feature. When you upload files via FTP using any of GoLive's synchronization options, you're presented with a dialog box in which you can ask GoLive to observe the Publish state of files and folders. Setting a file to Never prevents its upload, Always forces its upload, and If Referenced checks first to see if the file is linked by a Web page before uploading it. For folders, Never prevents its creation unless a nested folder needs to be uploaded, Always creates the folder if it doesn't exist on the server, and If Referenced creates it if any files inside it are needed and the folder doesn't exist.

Name Tab

The Name tab shows whether an existing file or folder conforms to the filename constraints you may or may not have set as an application setting or a site setting (see Figure 2-46). The subject is pretty involved, and we devote a lot of ink to it in Chapter 21, *Files, Folders, and Links.*

Figure 2-46
File Inspector's
Name tab

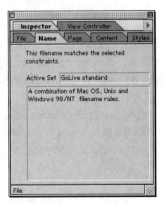

Page Tab

The Page tab appears in the File Inspector when an HTML document is selected (see Figure 2-47). You can modify a page's title just like you can in the Layout Editor via the Page Inspector, as well as view its encoding language.

Figure 2-47
File Inspector's
Page tab

The language encoding for a page appears in this tab, even though you cannot modify it here. (See Chapter 4, *Preferences and Customizing*.)

If you are viewing a page designated as the root page or home page for the entire site, Home Page is checked and inaccessible. To designate another page as the root, select that file, click the File Inspector's Page tab, and check Home Page. That causes the file's Home Page box to become checked and inaccessible, while simultaneously unchecking the previously marked home page.

You can also designate a home page through the rather lonely General area of the Site Settings (it's the only control in that section).

Content Tab

Click the Content tab, and a thumbnail preview appears of the selected item if it's an HTML page or an image (see Figure 2-48). If the image is animated, it previews the animation in the Content tab.

Figure 2-48
File Inspector's
Content tab

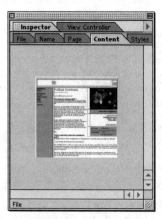

If you select a QuickTime file, the QuickTime playback bar appears at the bottom, allowing you to preview the movie or sound file directly in the Inspector. (A Pan button allows you to move the movie around.) Additionally, a popup menu enables you to play the movie once, repeat, or play backwards after it's played once; however as of this writing, these options don't seem to work.

You can also preview other media files, like Acrobat PDFs and Shockwave and Flash files, as long as you place their respective browser plug-ins into the GoLive plug-in folder. See Chapter 17, *Media*.

But wait—the Content tab isn't just for previewing! Click the thumbnail, drag it into an open document, and—voilà—it's placed into the file with the correct file reference. You can also drag the thumbnail to another open Site window. If you drag the image into another folder within the site where the image already resides, a copy of the image is placed into that folder. This isn't usually advisable, as there's more chance that GoLive could get confused and break links in existing pages.

TIP:
**Turning On
Content
Preview**

If you imported files into a site, the Content tab probably isn't working for you with HTML files; they only preview once you've edited a file, saved, and closed it. If you're dead set on getting the Content preview working, open a file, add a space and delete it, save the file and close it, then return to the Site window and select the file to see your handiwork. An easier, but more expansive option is to use the Create Thumbnails command to make these previews for every dang file in the site. Hold down Command-Option (Mac) or Control-Alt (Windows) and select the Site menu; the menu item only appears with those keys held down.

TIP:
**Dragging
QuickTime
Images**

Select a QuickTime movie file from the Site window, scan through the frames to find a desired image, then drag it into an open document. The Save for Web dialog opens, enabling you to save the dragged item as an image file. Choose the file type and configure its compression and other appropriate settings, then click OK. A Specify Target File dialog opens, allowing you to name the file and save it into your desired location; GoLive assigns "DragDrop" as the generic file name. Click OK, and the image appears in the open document.

This functionality replaces how GoLive 4 handled dragged selections (from QuickTime or from external image editors), which placed them into an import folder location set in Preferences. To learn more about the Save for Web feature, see Chapter 9, *Images*.

Styles Tab

Links to external style sheets are listed in the Styles tab (styles that are stored within the document are not listed); you can also link to a style sheet document via the URL Getter (see Figure 2-49). Click the Add button to add it to the list.

Figure 2-49
File Inspector's
Styles tab

Alternately, click the popup menu to the right of the field to find a list of .css files found within your site; select an item to populate the field, then click Add.

TIP:
Opening
Style Sheets

Double-clicking a CSS file icon in the Styles tab opens the file in the Style Sheet editor, enabling you to edit or add new styles.

Folder Inspector

Selecting a folder in the Files tab brings up the Folder Inspector, which is a truncated version of the File Inspector (see Figure 2-50). Here you find most of the same information found on that Inspector's File tab, including name, location in the site, status, publish state, and creation and modification dates. You can also see the Name tab for filename constraints as they apply to folders.

Figure 2-50
Folder
Inspector

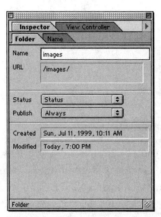

TIP:
Selecting
Folders from
Right Pane

If you select a folder from the Extra tab in the right pane of the Site window, all editable fields and popup menus are rendered inactive.

Reference Inspector

GoLive gathers all external Web addresses and email addresses used in a site and organizes them in the External tab whenever you import a site, add URLs and addresses via GoLive, or select Get References Used from the Site menu. These items appear in the External tab alongside ones you create from scratch by dragging or double-clicking the URL or Address icon from the Site tab of the Objects palette.

After creating a new address or URL, you must type a name in the high-lighted field of the file icon and press Return or Enter to accept the edit before the Reference Inspector comes up (see Figure 2-51). Once it does appear, you can make further edits in the Name field and type in its URL for external Web links. If you have an especially long URL, you might want to modify it by using the Edit button, which opens the Edit URL dialog box.

Email addresses are automatically given a "mailto:" prefix if this option is selected in Preferences under the General pane's URL Handling settings.

Figure 2-51
Reference
Inspector

Site Design Inspectors

With GoLive 5, you can prototype a site using the new Design feature. References to the designs you create are stored in the Designs tab of the Site window. Create a new design by choosing New Design from the contextual menu; if you've already created a design, select it from the list. The Site Design Inspector opens, displaying creation and modification dates and allowing you to change its name (see Figure 2-52). Not much there; but with new features come new Inspectors…

Figure 2-52
Site Design
Inspector

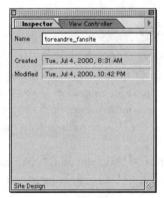

Page Inspector

It's best to designate a page within a desired directory location that acts as your anchor when you finish the design prototype and submit live pages into your site. If no anchor page is designated, the submitted pages are placed at the root level of your site, and things can get a little messy.

To add an anchor, select a page currently residing within your site and drag its file icon into the Design window's Design tab. A rectangular reference is added, with the name of the file in italics to denote that it is an alias/shortcut; the icon also receives a Point & Shoot button and an anchor icon below its lower right corner (see Figure 2-53). (You can change how GoLive displays pages and section icons via the Design View Controller; see Chapter 3, *Palettes and Parts*, for more information.)

The Page Inspector appears, enabling you to add a unique name to this design object, and modify its file name and HTML title (see Figure 2-54).

TIP:
When Page Inspectors Aren't Page Inspectors

Obviously, this Page Inspector isn't the Page Inspector that appears when you open a GoLive HTML page and click the Layout Editor's page icon to configure title, link colors, etc., which is covered in the earlier "Document Layout Inspectors" section. But with this many Inspectors, can you blame the engineers for being tapped out of creative Inspector names?

Figure 2-53
Anchor object

Figure 2-54
Site Design
Page Inspector

You can create additional pages for the site design by selecting the anchor page and choosing New Page from the Design menu (or choosing New Page from the contextual menu). New pages display their file names in roman text (not italics), do not include the anchor icon, and feature the same fields in the Page Inspector.

Section Inspector

Drag a Design Section icon from the Objects palette's Site tab into an open Design window to create a subtree hierarchy of additional design pages. The section object that appears in the Design window is the top page of this sub-tree, and new pages can be added below it (child pages) and at the same hier-archical level (sibling pages).

The Section Inspector actually opens to the Section tab first, enabling you to assign a filename to newly created child pages in the New Filename field (see Figure 2-55). For instance, if you enter "welcome.html", child pages added later are named "welcome1.html", "welcome2.html", and so on. Provide a target subdirectory for child pages in the Folder field. If you have Stationery files stored in your site's Stationeries folder, you can choose to assign one of those templates to this section with the Use Section popup menu.

To create pages via the Section Inspector, first use the two popup menus to configure how links behave from the Parent (the currently selected Section object) and between the various Sibling pages that are generated. Enter a value in the Count field for the number of child/sibling pages to create within this section, then click the Create New Pages button.

Figure 2-55
Section Inspector's Section tab

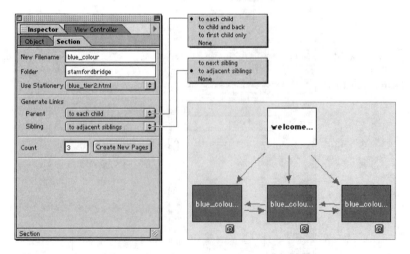

On the Object tab, enter a unique identifier for this page in the Name field and modify the Filename and Page Title fields as necessary (see Figure 2-56).

Figure 2-56
Section
Inspector's
Object tab

Group Inspector

Drag a Design Group icon from the Objects palette's Site tab to create a grouping unit that houses individual design sections and pages (which can be dragged into the group window).

In the Group Inspector, add a name to the group, or modify its color (see Figure 2-57). Uncheck the Display Title Bar option to hide the group's name. If Auto Resize is left checked, the group grows and shrinks depending on what is placed into the group.

Figure 2-57
Site Design
Group
Inspector

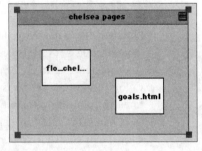

Annotation Inspector

Adding an Annotation icon to the design window (the yellow note icon) brings up the Annotation Inspector, where you can type a title in the Subject field and your note in the Text field (see Figure 2-58). (This Inspector also appears if you select a note from the Design window's Annotations tab list.) If you want to display the Subject and Text near the note icon, check those options at the bottom of the Inspector. The Position popup menu allows you to place these items above, below, to the right, or to the left of the note icon.

For details on using the Design feature, see Chapter 20, *Prototyping and Mapping*.

Figure 2-58
Annotation
Inspector

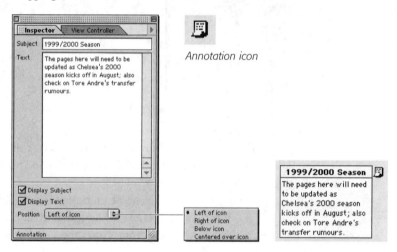

Annotation icon

Color Inspector

GoLive collects references to colors used anywhere in your site in the Colors tab; selecting Get Colors Used from the Site menu reparses the site and adds color references. Alternately, you can create new color entries by dragging the Color icon from the Objects palette's Site tab. A new color requires a name before the Color Inspector appears (see Figure 2-59).

Change the color's title in the Name field, and modify the color by dragging a color swatch from the Color palette into the Color Field. Double-clicking a color (either its swatch or any part of its name or attributes) opens the color in the Color palette's preview pane.

TIP:
Cluing in
on Colors

If you freshly import a site or reparse a site to get recently added colors, you find a heap of untitled color references. To start investigating where these colors are coming from, select a color swatch from the Color tab list, then click the In

& Out Links palette button to see where the color reference originates. You can do this trick with any of the other Site Extras references.

Figure 2-59
Color Inspector

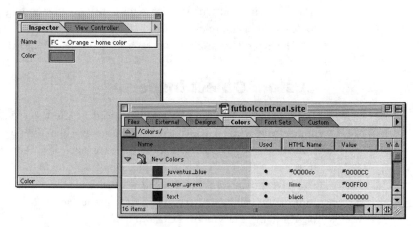

Font Set Inspector

To create a site-specific font set, drag the Font Set icon from the Objects palette's Site tab into the Site window's Font Sets tab; GoLive also gathers font sets used in a site when you select Get Font Sets Used from the Site menu. Give your set a name by typing a title in the Name field in the Font Set Inspector (see Figure 2-60).

Figure 2-60
Font Set
Inspector

Select "New Font" from the Font Names list, then click the menu to the right of the text field at the bottom of the Inspector to see a list of your active system fonts. Selecting a font from the list places the font name in both the text field and in the Font Names list. You can also enter a name from scratch to add it to the font set.

Click the New button to add additional fonts to this set; to do away with an individual font, select it and click the Delete button or select Clear from the Edit menu. You can't reorder items in this list after adding them; you have to delete them and re-enter them in the preferred order.

The font set list displays each set using a preview of the first font's typeface.

Custom Object Inspector

With GoLive 5, you can now add site-specific custom HTML objects (which appear only with an associated Site document when it's open). To add a custom HTML object (such as a commonly used table layout or an image), select it in a page then drag it to the Objects palette's Site Extras tab (making sure you have the Custom section open, accessible via the popup menu at the bottom of the palette). Alternatively, drag a selected HTML object from your page into the Site window's Custom tab.

References to these site-specific custom objects are stored in both the Site Extras tab and the Site window's Custom tab; icons in the latter location resemble Mac clipping file icons. Select an object to open the Custom Object Inspector, where you can modify its name as well as view and modify its source code (see Figure 2-61).

Figure 2-61
Custom Object
Inspector

TIP:
Remember
Your Name

If your Site window is open to the Custom tab when you drag an HTML object from your page into the Site Extras tab of the Objects palette, GoLive switches to the Site window and prompts you to add a name to the object in the Custom tab. If any other tab in the Site window is open, this doesn't occur.

Group Inspectors

Although sounding more like some cabal of oversight committees, GoLive's Group Inspectors centralize the attributes for working with external links, colors, and font sets within a site.

Group Inspector

Drag either the URL Group or Address Group icon from the Objects palette's Site tab into the External tab to create a folder where you can collect references to sites and email addresses. The Group Inspector allows you to modify the title of the folder, as well as assign one of four folder types: URLs, Addresses, New URLs, and New Addresses (see Figure 2-62). If you've just imported a site, GoLive carefully separates the two groups into New URLs and New Addresses folders.

Figure 2-62
Group
Inspector

	TIP:
Links and Addresses, Living Together	It really doesn't matter which folder you choose from the Group Inspector to house your email or external links—URLs live just fine in Address Groups, and Addresses are dandy in URL Groups. The Group Inspector only manages what icon is displayed and has no bearing on functionality.

	TIP:
Everyone Needs an Editor	The Objects palette's Site tab holds the Font Set Group icon, but you open the Font Set Group Inspector.

Color and Font Set Group Inspector

The Color and Font Set Group Inspectors win the award (again) for most redundant items in the GoLive pantheon of palettes and Inspectors (see Figure 2-63). Selecting a folder within either the Colors or Font Sets tabs of the Site window (or inserting that tab's group icon from the Objects palette into the tab) brings up the Color or Font Set Group Inspector. Each of these two Inspectors contain just one field—Name—which you could easily change by selecting the object in the Site window and typing your edits.

Figure 2-63
Color and Font
Set Group
Inspectors

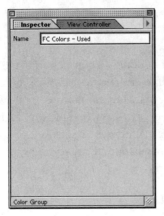 

Error Inspector

The dreaded green bug to the right of a file in the Files tab's Status column indicates bad links on that page. To see a list of errors, click the Error tab in the second pane of the Site window. On the Mac, click the two-way arrow button at the bottom of the window.

Unfortunately, the Error Inspector doesn't provide a lot of information; the only field included with the Inspector is a URL field with the usual Point & Shoot and Browse buttons to navigate to a solution (see Figure 2-64). And the Inspector doesn't tell you what file this error appears in.

Figure 2-64
Error Inspector

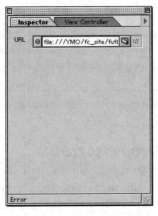

To get to the heart of the matter, select the error item, then click the In & Out Links button on the Toolbar to open that palette. The source of this link angst is identified, and you can go ahead and make the proper adjustment through the Error Inspector or via the Point & Shoot button in the In & Out Links palette.

FTP File and Folder Inspectors

Once you've uploaded your site to a Web server, you can view file information, change a file or folder's name, examine links (symbolic links, aliases, or shortcuts) to other files, and set up access permissions via Inspectors.

TIP:
Connect First

Connect to your remote FTP server before following any of the directions below; if you don't yet have this set up, consult Chapter 23, *Synchronizing Sites*, to get everything in place.

FTP Folder Inspector

When you select a folder from the FTP tab, the FTP Folder Inspector comes up (see Figure 2-65). If you want to change the title of a folder, type it in the Name field, making sure to press tab, Return or Enter to accept the edit (there is no carriage return icon to remind you).

Figure 2-65
FTP Folder
Inspector

The fields below the name are informational only, displaying the URL for the FTP site and the date when the folder was last updated with a new file. The datestamps of files or other folders that reside within the directory don't affect the datestamp on the FTP Folder Inspector when they are updated.

In the Rights section, you can view and change the access permission, or rights, to the folder in three categories: read, write, and execute. Permissions can be set for the owner of a folder, others in an associated work group, or everyone else in the world; the owner and group have to be set by the system administrator. When you change a checkbox's state, the Set Rights button becomes active and must be clicked to apply the change.

TIP:
Owner
Permissions

If Execute is unchecked for Owner, you can't even open a folder by clicking its toggle arrow; you only get an error message saying permission is denied. To change permissions to reflect Execute for Owner, select the folder and check the option. Execute must be set for Group or Other only if the group or world at large also has write permission to modify items in the folder or upload new items to it.

Checking Recursive applies all the permissions you've set for the folder to every item underneath the folder, including all nested folders and files.

FTP File Inspector

The FTP File Inspector mirrors the FTP Folder Inspector's items, save for the Recursive option and the addition of a Size field (see Figure 2-66).

To set a level of access for an individual file, select the item's icon in the FTP tab, then check or uncheck your desired options in the FTP File Inspector.

Figure 2-66
FTP File
Inspector

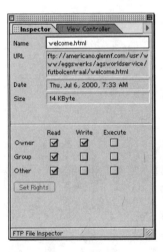

FTP Link Inspector

GoLive also has an almost identical Inspector that works only with links to other files (see Figure 2-67). Under Windows, these links are called "shortcuts" and on the Mac they're "aliases." In both cases, the file icons have italic type and an arrow symbol to indicate they point to another file; the FTP Link Inspector shows both the pointer's location and the destination's location.

Under Unix, these links are called "symbolic links," and they cannot be modified via GoLive. The subject gets dense pretty quickly; for an in-depth discussion, see Chapter 23, *Synchronizing Sites*.

Figure 2-67
FTP Link
Inspector

Smart Objects

GoLive collects a number of cool tricks that can be inserted into pages from the Objects palette's Smart tab, including automatic browser switching and effects such as timestamps and datestamps and URL popup menus. (These are discussed in the context of GoLive Actions in Chapter 28, *Actions*.)

Live Image Inspector

By enabling the Smart Links module in Preferences, you can import a whole range of image file formats from Illustrator, LiveMotion, and Photoshop (including TIFF, PSD, PICT, BMP, and TARGA) into GoLive and save them into Web-friendly formats (i.e., GIF, JPEG, and PNG). But it's more than just a conversion utility.

Start by dragging the Smart Photoshop icon from the Objects palette's Smart tab into a page; a very colorful placeholder icon appears in the page.

TIP:
Missing
Smart Icons?

GoLive only activates Smart Objects for programs that are installed on your hard disk. So if you don't own a copy of LiveMotion, for example, the Smart LiveMotion icon doesn't appear.

Basic Tab

Navigate to your desired file (for our purposes, we're bringing in a Photoshop file) using the usual methods from the Source field. Choosing a file brings up the Save for Web dialog, from which you can modify the settings for your optimized, Web-friendly image. When configured, click OK to bring up the Save dialog, then save the image into a desired directory location (see Figure 2-68).

Figure 2-68
Live Image
Inspector's
Basic tab

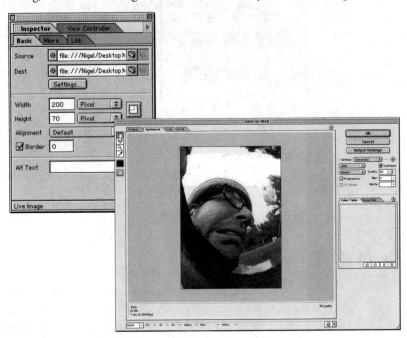

TIP:
Drag for Web

If you dragged an image file directly into the page, the Save for Web dialog opens up automatically.

The image appears in your page, and the location of the optimized file is entered into the Dest field. Clicking the Settings button opens the Save for Web dialog again, from which you can make further tweaks to the optimized image.

TIP:
Double-click to Creator

Double-clicking an image in the page opens the file in the program that originally created it (i.e., Photoshop).

Like any other image you bring into an HTML page, it's best to determine an image's dimensions in the program that created the image. However, if you change the Width or Height dimensions with a Smart Photoshop or Smart Illustrator object (either by entering a value in one of the fields or dragging an image handle), GoLive references the original source file to resize the Web image. Thus, resized Smart Photoshop objects look moderately cleaner and less pixelated than not-so-smart images after resizing in GoLive (see Figure 2-69).

If you do change the dimensions of a Smart Photoshop object, the Reset button becomes active in the Basic tab (but doesn't appear within the image, as it does with an Image object). Click it to return the image to the original dimensions.

Figure 2-69
Comparing
resized images

Smart Photoshop object   *Image object*

More and Link Tabs

The options found on these tabs include the same functionality as the Image Inspector's More and Link tabs (which are covered in the "Document Layout Inspectors" section).

See Chapter 9, *Images*, for much more on configuring Smart Objects and using the new Save for Web feature.

Component Inspector

If you create a wide range of pages that need to have the same item updated frequently, consider using GoLive's centrally-managed Component feature, a Smart Object placed onto a page that references a snippet of HTML saved as another page elsewhere. Components are discussed further in Chapter 21, *Files, Folders, and Links*.

The simple Component Inspector has a single function: it allows you to specify the source of the Component you've dragged onto a page or want to modify (see Figure 2-70).

Figure 2-70
Component
Inspector

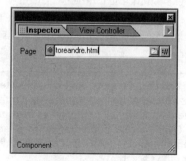

Rollover Inspector

GoLive provides an easy method of setting up rollovers—images that change when the mouse is rolled over them—via the Rollover object. Drag the Rollover icon from the Smart tab of the Objects palette into the body section of the Layout Editor to reveal the Rollover Inspector.

NEW IN 5:
No Longer
Button Image

GoLive 5's Rollover object functions the same as GoLive 4's Button Image, only with a more understandable name.

In the Name field, enter a unique identifier for the button (see Figure 2-71). By default, GoLive names the object "button"; additional rollovers added to the page are named "button2" and so on if the first item is not named. Select the Main icon and specify the image file you want to display without any mouse action when the page loads. A preview of the image replaces the Main icon, while the checkbox to the left of the field is inactive (and stays that way, since the main image has to be displayed).

Figure 2-71
Rollover
Inspector

Select the Over icon to swap in another image when a viewer's mouse passes over the image area; check the box to the left of the field below and navigate to the desired file. Do the same for the Click icon, which displays another image when a viewer clicks the object. (You can choose to apply just one or the other option.) In the Layout Editor, the main image is displayed in the button image placeholder.

TIP:
Dragging
and
Dropping
Rollover
Images

GoLive allows you to drag and drop images from either the Site window or your hard drive into the Rollover placeholder icon. For the Main image, drag a file as you would any other, where a thumbnail of the image is displayed in place of the Main icon. To add an Over image, Option-drag on the Mac or Control-drag under Windows. Shift-Option-dragging (Mac) and Control-Shift-dragging (Windows) assigns an image to the Click item.

TIP:
Resizing Rollover Images

Dragging images into the Rollover placeholders, instead of using Point & Shoot, sizes the image according to the dimensions of the placeholder. To return the image to its actual dimensions, click the Image Resize button to the right of the three image previews in the Inspector. (An inactive button means that the image is just fine.)

Also, if either the Over or Click option is unchecked but selected, the Image Resize button is active, and clicking it makes the placeholder return to its small default size. To fix this, select one of the images that's already placed and click Resize to bring back the true dimensions.

Check Status to enter a message that displays at the bottom of a browser window in the Status field when you mouse over the Main image.

TIP:
GoLive Knows Best

When the Rollover Inspector opens, you notice the URL field is checked and includes a pound sign (#) in the field. If you decide you don't want to link this item and uncheck URL, then come back to the rollover later, you find URL checked again with the pound sign placed back in the field. GoLive knows that this rollover effect requires it to be linked, and keeps URL checked.

Modified Date Inspector

To add a datestamp and/or timestamp to your page, which shows viewers the last time a page was updated, drag the Modified Date icon from the Smart tab of the Objects palette into the body section of the Layout Editor. The time and date is read from your computer's built-in clock; the information is updated each time the file is saved.

From the Modified Date Inspector, choose the language format of how the date and time are written from the Format popup menu (a great way to learn some basics of another language), then choose the time and date style to be displayed (see Figure 2-72).

Figure 2-72
Modified Date Inspector

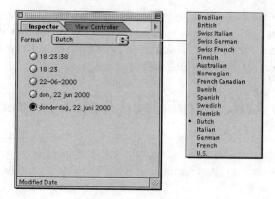

URL Popup Inspector

To give your viewers easy access to other pages in your site without cluttering the page landscape with a lot of links, use the URL Popup object to create a popup menu that, when an item is selected, jumps to that designated page. To create this effect, drag the URL Popup icon into the main body section of the Layout Editor; this brings up the URL Popup Inspector (see Figure 2-73).

Figure 2-73
URL Popup
Inspector

The top item in the list pane is the popup menu's label, the item that viewers see first before clicking to reveal the menu's items. GoLive defaults to placing Choose in the Label field, but you can type another message in the list to entice your viewers.

Select the next item (by default, a link to Adobe) and enter a description of your first link in the Label field. In the URL field, type a link destination or navigate to it using the usual methods. If you want to specify a target frame or browser window, choose or enter your destination window, method, or frame in the Target field.

To add a new list item, click the New button; or, click the Duplicate button. To reposition an item within the list, select it and click the up or down arrow to the left of the list scrollbar. Note that you can't reposition the top item in the list, nor can you link it to a page.

Body Action and Head Action Inspectors

Most Actions are triggered when the viewer does something, like clicking a link. To start an Action automatically, use the Body Action and Head Action icons. Dragging a Head Action icon to the Document window's Head section, or dragging the Body Action icon into the body section, inserts an Action placeholder that isn't attached to a text, image, or other hyperlink.

If you place a Head Action, you can choose to trigger the Action as the page loads or as the viewer leaves the page. To determine the trigger for a Head item, select an item from the Exec. popup menu of the Action Inspector (see Figure 2-4). Be sure to add a unique identifier in the Name field. If you place a Body Action in the body of a page, the browser triggers that effect once the page load reaches the Action's position on the page as it parses.

For more information on setting up Actions, see the Action Inspector section earlier in this chapter. For more on Actions in general, see Chapter 28, *Actions*.

Figure 2-74
Body and
Head Action
Inspectors

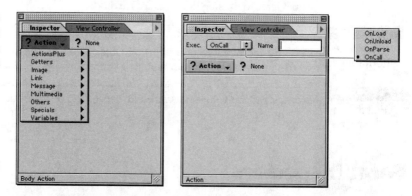

Browser Switch Inspector

To send viewers with an incompatible browser to an alternate page with compatible content, drag the Browser Switch icon from the Objects palette into the Document window's Head section; this brings up the Browser Switch Inspector (see Figure 2-75).

Figure 2-75
Browser
Switch
Inspector

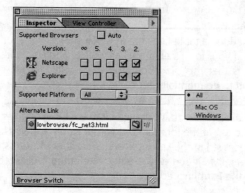

If you want GoLive to determine browser compatibility, leave Auto checked. GoLive then checks the appropriate items for the browsers listed below based on the content of your page. For instance, only the 4.0 and 5.0 browsers are checked if you've included Cascading Style Sheets; in the case of viewers with version 3.0 browsers or lower, you would want to send them to an alternate page.

To determine your own options, uncheck Auto and check the browser versions that are compatible for your page. In the Supported Platform popup menu, select All, or choose between Windows and Mac OS.

In the Alternate Link field, type a destination URL for the alternate page or navigate to it using the standard methods.

TIP:
Multiple Alternatives

After configuring one Browser Switch for a particular platform, drag another icon into the head section from the Objects palette and set up an alternate switch for the other platform.

TIP:
Watch the Switch

Browser switching does not work with version 2.0 browsers or Internet Explorer 3.01 for the Mac.

Form Inspectors

Working with forms in GoLive is the subject of Chapter 15, *Forms*, so here we just want to touch on the basics of inserting a form into your page and give you a feel for the different Inspectors that you'll encounter.

Form Inspector

Every form starts with the Form tag, which is inserted by dragging the Form icon into the Layout Editor from the Forms tab of the Objects palette.

NEW IN 5:
New Form Placeholder

GoLive 5 has added a table-like area as a placeholder for your form, where you can place all of your form's elements as well as add text. The best thing about this, though, is that this placeholder automatically adds a closing Form tag, which you had to do manually in GoLive 4.

TIP:
Space— The Form Frontier

The Form tag placeholder that's dragged into your page makes it look like space is added at the top of the form area. This space only appears in GoLive's Layout Editor; when viewed in the Layout Preview or other browsers, the space disappears. However, it's a good way to select the entire form section of your page and bring up the Form Inspector.

You can still drag form elements into your page without starting with the Form object. However, they aren't associated with a form's Post or Get methods and information from these form objects aren't transmitted anywhere.

In the Form Inspector, type a unique name for this form in the Name field (see Figure 2-76). In the Action field, checked by default, set the destination file name and directory location of the CGI script that processes the information on the server when the form is submitted. (If you don't have a CGI set up, contact your system administrator who needs to configure it on the Web server.) Set a target frame or window using the Target popup menu.

Figure 2-76
Form Inspector

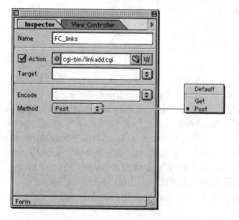

If you're requesting the user to upload a file (a rare request), choose a setting from the Encode popup menu. Normal forms use "application/x-www-form-urlencoded", while file uploading uses "multipart/form-data". A system administrator would tell you if you need to use any other value for that attribute.

Choose the way your information is sent from the Method menu: Get (GoLive's default) specifies that all the data is sent as part of a URL. However, the Post method, which sends the data in a less public manner, is a better option. Default omits a Method from the Form tag, but browsers default to Get.

If you are sending form data to an email address, type "text/plain" in the Encode field and select the Post from the Method menu.

Focus. You might notice that most Form Inspectors include much of the same information, but the Focus settings might be most mysterious. These features are all part of the HTML 4.0 specification, which no browser has fully implemented yet. Some of the 4.0 and later browsers support a few of these features, but it's not safe to rely on any them.

The items you find in the Focus area include Tab, Key, Readonly, Selected, and Disabled (see Figure 2-77). The Tab checkbox, if selected, allows you to set an order by which pressing the Tab key advances the text-insertion point from element to element in a form. You can click the button next to the Tab field and then click fields one at a time to set order. The Key field lets you select a keyboard shortcut for a user to type to jump to that field. Readonly and Disabled are modifiers which either render text fields uneditable or dimmed back. Selected marks either a checkbox or radio button by default.

For more information on setting up the Focus section, see Chapter 15, *Forms*.

Figure 2-77
**Form
Inspectors'
Focus Section**

TIP:
**Keeping
Focus**

Here are a few things to keep in mind when configuring Focus area items (thanks to Elizabeth Castro, author of the invaluable *HTML 4 for the World Wide Web: Visual QuickStart Guide*). If you set a tab order for form elements, remember that the first time a user hits the Tab key, the browser's Address field is activated first (even if the toolbar is hidden). Remember that keyboard shortcuts you set for your form override the browser's built-in shortcuts; also, the Windows Alt key is a better choice than Control, as the latter manages the main keyboard functionality. But what about the Mac's Command key? Sorry, form keyboard settings currently work only with Windows browsers.

Form Button Inspector

The Form Button Inspector actually appears for three types of buttons found in the Forms tab of the Objects palette: the Submit Button, the Reset Button, and the customizable Button (see Figure 2-78). The differences among these three are subtler than appearances imply. There are really three settings and two kinds of buttons masquerading as three settings and three icons.

Dragging the Submit or Reset button from the Forms tab of the Objects palette creates one kind of button, a standard HTML button that can be set to submit a page to a server for processing, reset its contents (erasing all entered values), or trigger a JavaScript (the Normal setting).

The other kind of button—really an HTML 4.0 Button tag behind the scenes—is created by dragging the Button icon from the Objects palette. This button defaults to the Normal setting, and looks like any ol' button when only text is added to it However, it's substantively different, as you can include any HTML element within the button, including tables, form elements, images, and so on. Selecting within the button text allows you to edit it and paste items into it.

Figure 2-78
Form Button
Inspector

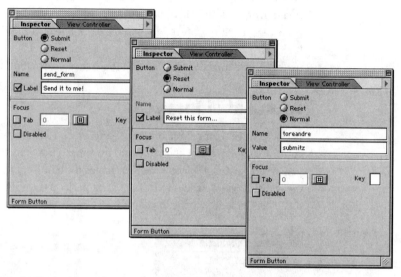

Submit. A viewer presses the Submit button when he or she is ready to send the form's data to the server for processing. Enter a name for the form object, then enter the wording you want to appear in the button by checking the Label and typing in the field. If unchecked, GoLive leaves that value empty but previews it as Submit.

Reset. To enable a viewer to clear a form's data and start entering it again from scratch, insert a Reset button. The Name field is inactive, as HTML doe not send a name for this button to the server. Use the Label field to customize the button's wording. If unchecked, GoLive leaves the value empty, but previews it as Reset.

Normal. The Normal setting creates a button—standard or advanced button variety—that has no action associated with it. You can create a JavaScript that has, as its trigger, a user clicking, mousing over, or otherwise manipulating this button. As with the other two Inspectors, enter a name for the form object.

TIP:
Changing
Button
Types

Any type of button can be changed to be a Submit, Reset, or Normal button. If you want a Normal button that has rounded corners, drag a Submit or Reset Button icon onto the page, then use the Button Inspector to change it to Normal. Likewise, if you want an advanced Submit button with rich HTML content in it, drag a Button icon to the document and then click Submit in the Inspector.

Form Image Inspector

To add an image to your form as, say, a customized button, drag the Input Image icon into the Layout Editor. Or, select an image already placed into your page, click the More tab, and check Is Form in the Form section. The Image Inspector then changes its title to Form Image Inspector, keeping all its typical image controls while adding the Focus information to the More tab.

Form Label Inspector

For HTML 4.0-compatible browsers, you can add a descriptive label to a form control (such as a checkbox or radio button). Drag the Label icon into your page to add a "Label" placeholder. To change the name of the Label, click within the text and type your desired name. Click back on the outside border to select the Label element to bring the Form Label Inspector back up (see Figure 2-79).

Figure 2-79
Form Label
Inspector

Under the Reference field, use the Point & Shoot button to select a form element on the page, which adds an ID name/number to the field; you can also Command-drag (Mac) or Control-drag (Windows) to a form element. This adds a randomly generated number to the end of the form name pointed to, as well as a preceding "ID" label; modify this to something more applicable. To show which form element is associated with this label, click the Show button to display a pointer to the element.

Form Text Field and Password Inspectors

To add a one-line text field to your form, drag the Text Field icon from the Objects palette; to create a text field that hides characters as they're typed (i.e., "••••••"), drag the Password icon into your form.

The Is Password Field option is checked when you drag a Password icon to the Document window. Check this field to turn a text field into a Password field and vice-versa (see Figure 2-80).

Figure 2-80
Form Text Field
and Password
Inspectors

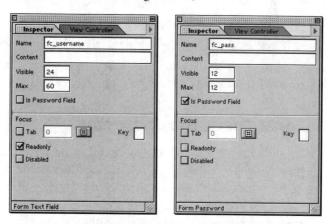

Type a unique name in the Name field. You can prefill a form field by entering text in the Inspector's Content field. You can control the width of the field (in characters) by entering a value in Visible, and the maximum number of characters allowed in the Max field.

Form Text Area Inspector

To add an area on your page where viewers can type multiple lines of text, drag the Text Area icon from the Objects palette and type a unique identifier in the Name field (see Figure 2-81). In the Row field, type a value to determine the height in rows of text; in the Columns field, type a value to set its width in number of characters.

Figure 2-81
Form Text Area
Inspector

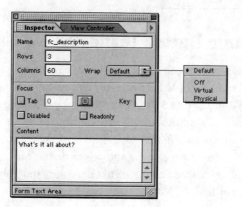

Word wrapping in the text field is turned on by default in the Wrap popup menu; you can also select one of the following options:

- **Off:** stops text from wrapping; lines are sent exactly as typed.
- **Virtual:** displays word-wrapping, but the breaks aren't sent to the server.
- **Physical:** displays word-wrapping, and the breaks are sent to the server.

If you want to add sample text that your viewer can overwrite, type that content in the Content text field at the bottom of the Inspector.

Form Check Box Inspector

To add a checkbox within a form, drag the Check Box icon into your page from the Objects palette. Type a unique identifier for the range of checkboxes in the Name field, then add a specific value for each added checkbox to the Value field (see Figure 2-82). Check Selected under the Focus area to mark a checkbox by default; you can have more than one checkbox marked.

Figure 2-82
Form Check
Box Inspector

Form Radio Button Inspector

Drag the Radio Button icon from the Objects palette onto a page, and assign an individual value in the Value field (see Figure 2-83). The Group field acts as the Name field in the Check Box Inspector; type a unique identifier for the entire range of radio buttons being added to the page. Then, enter specific values for each radio button in the Value field. If you have more than one group of radio buttons on a page, select the group name from the popup menu. Check Selected under the Focus area to select one (and only one) radio button to turn on by default.

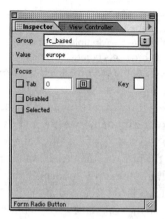

Figure 2-83
Form Radio
Button
Inspector

Form Popup and Form List Box Inspectors

Adding the List Box icon into your page creates a scrolling list that offers multiple options for your viewer to select from; adding the Popup icon accomplishes the same effect but with a popup menu. To switch between the two Inspectors, check Multiple Selection to change to a List Box from a Popup, or vice versa (see Figure 2-84). Additionally, changing the value in the Rows field to 2 or more changes a Popup to a List Box.

Figure 2-84
Form Popup
and List Box
Inspectors

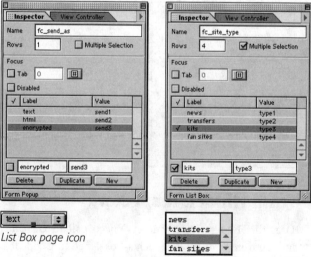

List Box page icon

Popup page icon

TIP:
Changing
List Types

To create a one-row list box in some browsers, check Multiple Selection and type a value of 1 in the Row field. If you leave Multiple Selection unchecked, but type a Row value greater than 1, some browsers create a list box, others create a popup menu, and some list the contents of the box on a single line. Use at your own risk.

GoLive defaults to placing three numerical items in the list area. To add your own value, select one of the list items to activate the text input fields at the bottom of the Inspector. In the first field (the Label column), type the label you want to appear in the browser, then type a value in the second field (under Value) which gets sent to the server to identify that option. A checkmark to the left of the Label text field specifies that item as initially displayed as the selection, either shown in the popup menu or highlighted in the list box.

Form File Inspector

To add a file-selection field to your form, which allows viewers to locate and upload files to your server, drag the File Browser icon from the Objects palette. In the Name field, enter the name of the field (see Figure 2-85). In the Visible field, type a number that determines the field's width on your page.

Figure 2-85
Form File
Inspector

Form Hidden Inspector

Drag the Hidden icon from the Objects palette to create an input tag that is hidden from your viewer (such as for generating code for fields in your form via a script). Type a unique identifier in the Name field and a descriptor in the Value field (see Figure 2-86). Check Disabled to turn this element off until an event triggers it (such as filling out all required fields).

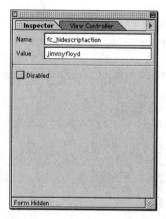

Figure 2-86
Form Hidden
Inspector

Form Keygen Inspector

Adding a Keygen icon to your page inserts a key generator tag that is used with certificate-management systems. (Chapter 15, *Forms*, talks more about generating keys). Type a unique identifier in the Name field, then type a security level in the Challenge field (see Figure 2-87).

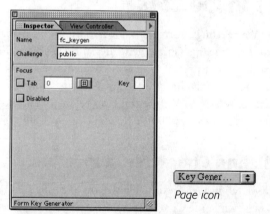

Figure 2-87
Form Keygen
Inspector

Page icon

Form Fieldset Inspector

In HTML 4.0-compatible browsers, you can visually group a set of form elements using a fieldset, which is a box that surrounds a set of form elements. After dragging the Fieldset icon into the Layout Editor, you can add a title to the group by selecting the word "Legend" on the page and typing your desired descriptor.

To align the legend along the top of the boundary box, select an option from the Alignment popup menu, or uncheck Legend to turn it off (see Figure 2-88). Now you're ready to start adding content to this box by typing text and dragging form elements in from the Objects palette.

Figure 2-88
Form Fieldset
Inspector

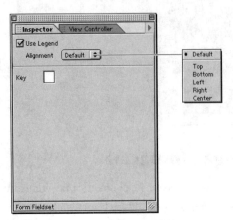

Web Settings Inspectors

GoLive's Web Settings (formerly known as the Web Database) is the control center for the code that GoLive generates, from HTML to XML to Cascading Style Sheets. This aspect of GoLive is covered in depth in Chapter 31, *Web Settings*, but the individual Inspectors associated with Web Settings are offered here for reference. Web Settings can be invoked through the Edit menu, or by pressing Command-Shift-Y (Mac) or Control-Shift-Y (Windows).

HTML and Character Inspectors

The HTML tab in Web Settings allows you to configure the entire library of HTML tags, while the Characters tab lets you control encoding for special characters (see Figure 2-89).

Both tabs are viewed in a hierarchical file structure, with each level corresponding to a specific Inspector (see Figure 2-89). The HTML tab's default view groups tags into thematic folders. For instance, the Master Container folder collects the Html, Head, and Body tags, and their associated attributes, while the Head Section folder collects all tags that can be inserted into the Head container tag.

Figure 2-89
Web Settings
HTML and
Character
structures

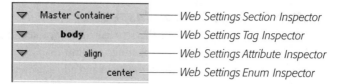

HTML tab

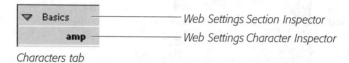

Characters tab

TIP:

Flat Viewing

To view items in the HTML and Characters tabs in a flat, alphabetical view, open the View Controller and select Flat (see Figure 2-90). Alternately, bring up the contextual menu and choose Flat Structure from the View item. In GoLive 4, view was controlled via the WebDB Inspector.

Figure 2-90
Web Settings
View
Controller

Click the top section level in this structured view to view the Web Settings Section Inspector. Clicking the next level down (the Body tag, which appears in bold) brings up the Web Settings Element Inspector. Expanding a tag and selecting an item below it calls up the Web Settings Attribute Inspector; to define an attribute's values (or enumerations), select an item below the attribute to bring up the Web Settings Enum Inspector.

The Characters tab features two Inspectors: the Web Settings Section Inspector (when in the structured view) and the Web Settings Entity Inspector (which allows you to set characteristics for individual characters).

Web Settings Section Inspector

When viewing either tab in the structured view, select one of the section headings to bring up the Web Settings Section Inspector (see Figure 2-91). You can modify its title in the Name field and add comments in the appropriately named Comment field.

Figure 2-91
Web Settings
Section
Inspector

Web Settings Element Inspector

Selecting an HTML tag (displayed in bold face) brings up the Web Settings Element Inspector.

Basic. The Basic tab displays the tag's name in the Tag Name field and a description of its function in the Comment field (see Figure 2-92). The Structure popup menu details the structural information about a tag; for instance, Block creates a block-level tag that can contain other tags (such as the Body tag), while Inline Invisible creates a tag that influences the visual content of HTML but that isn't visible itself (such as the Bold tag).

Figure 2-92
Web Settings
Element
Inspector's
Basic tab

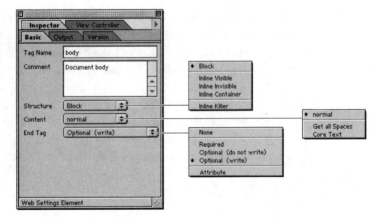

The Content popup menu displays how a tag's content is viewed in the HTML Source Editor; for instance, Normal indicates that content is displayed using line breaks, tabs, and spaces.

The End Tag popup menu controls whether an end tag is required. Select Required to have GoLive write and read an end tag. If an end tag is optional, select Optional (Do Not Write) to have GoLive not add it to your code or Optional (Write) to have GoLive write it anyway.

Output. The Web Settings Element Inspector's Output tab allows you to control formatting of source code (see Figure 2-93) in the HTML Source Editor. The Outside popup menu configures the vertical spacing between the tag and other elements above and below it, while the Inside popup menu configures vertical spacing of interior content between the start and end tags. Check Indent Content to add space horizontally before the beginning of a tag.

Figure 2-93
Web Settings
Element
Inspector's
Output tab

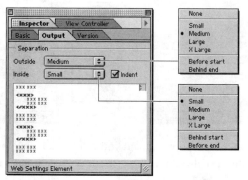

Version. The Version tab indicates which browser or HTML versions display this tag, in order to flag errors by version with the HTML Source Editor's Check Syntax feature (see Figure 2-94). Checking Can Have Any Attribute

Figure 2-94
Web Settings
Element
Inspector's
Version tab

prevents the syntax checker from flagging attributes assigned to a tag that aren't listed in the Web Settings list of attributes for that tag.

Web Settings Attribute Inspector

Click the toggle arrow to the left of a tag to reveal a list of its available attributes, then select one to bring up the Web Settings Attribute Inspector (see Figure 2-95). Again, the name of the attribute and a brief description of its function are displayed. The Attribute Is popup menu displays whether the tag requires its inclusion or is optional.

Figure 2-95
Web Settings
Attribute
Inspector

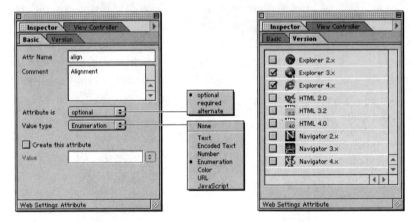

The Value Type popup menu indicates what kind of content the attribute's value can have (such as Number for numerical values only, or Enumeration for multiple options).

Check Create This Attribute to force GoLive to write the attribute even if it's empty; if you enter a value or choose it from the popup menu, GoLive inserts the value as the default for the attribute.

The Version tab is identical to the Web Settings Element Inspector; in this case, it controls whether the Check Syntax feature flags attributes as available for a given browser version or HTML specification.

Web Settings Enum Inspector

If an HTML attribute includes a toggle arrow to its left, click it to reveal a list of predefined values, or enumerations, associated with it; selecting one brings up the Web Settings Enum Inspector (see Figure 2-96). The value's name is listed in the Enum Name field, while a brief description may be displayed in the Comment field. Click the Version tab to see which browser versions support this particular value.

Figure 2-96
Web Settings
Enum
Inspector

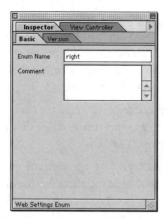 

Web Settings Entity Inspector

On the Web Settings Characters tab, select a character (listed in bold) to bring up the Web Settings Entity Character Inspector (see Figure 2-97). The name is listed in the active Name field, while its HTML equivalent is listed in the inactive field to its right. A brief description of the character is included in the Comment field.

Figure 2-97
Web Settings
Entity
Inspector

The ISO fields display the character's ISO decimal and hexadecimal (base 16) code, while the Mac fields (which display on both Windows and Mac) display the numeric and byte codes for Mac OS encodings, as well as the local symbol for that character.

Check Write to create a value that gets written for this character that's different from the name. We haven't yet seen an instance of this, but it must crop up from time to time.

A large preview of the character is rendered at the bottom of the Inspector.

Cascading Style Sheet Inspectors

Cascading Style Sheets (CSS) can control the typeface characteristics, position, border, and other attributes of a selection or block of text in an HTML document. However, GoLive has two distinct ways to access and use CSS.

- In the Style Sheet Editor, accessed by clicking the stairstepped icon in the Layout Editor, you can create and define styles that you apply to text ranges and paragraphs in an HTML file.

- In the CSS tab of Web Settings, you can examine and create browser-specifc CSS sets. These sets include specifications for individual styles, as well as specs for HTML tags (see Figure 2-98), which are then used by GoLive to simulate the previews of different browsers on different platforms in the Layout Preview. (This tab also affects which browsers show up in the Version tab of the Web Settings Inspectors for tags, attributes, and enumerations, for configuring the HTML Source Editor's syntax checking.)

Figure 2-98
Viewing HTML
properties

Specifications for individual HTML tags can be found in the CSS tab of Web settings, such as the H1 tag.

Both the Style Sheet Editor and the CSS tab use the same Inspectors for creating or changing individual styles.A style is a collection of characteristics that controls the display of a selection and manages all instances of that style, so making a modification to a style changes the appearance of all selections to which that style was assigned.

There are a few Inspectors specific to the CSS tab and the Style Sheet Editor that are broken out below; the CSS Selector Inspector is common to both.

Web Settings CSS Tab

In the CSS tab of Web Settings, select a style sheet grouping (such as the Mac version of Internet Explorer 5.0). The Root Style Sheet Inspector that comes

up has all its fields dimmed because the built-in browser sets GoLive provides
are locked and cannot be modified. You can create new sets by selecting an existing set and clicking the Duplicate button in the CSS toolbar; this creates a
new set with a pencil icon to the right, signifying that you can modify the set.

TIP:
**Clowning
Around**

If you duplicate a set, then give it a name that doesn't begin with "Adobe",
"Explorer", or "Navigator", the icon to the left of the name changes to a clown
icon after you quit GoLive, then return to the program later (see Figure 2-99).
But don't worry—it's only an icon, not a reflection on your CSS writing abilities.
For more information on using Web Settings, see Chapter 3, *Palettes and Parts*.

Figure 2-99
Non-Netscape/
IE set icon

Icon

Root Style Sheet Inspector. The Root Style Sheet Inspector displays general
information about the set on the Basic tab (including name and operating system), as well as a Comment text field for a brief description (see Figure 2-100).

Figure 2-100
Root Style
Sheet
Inspector

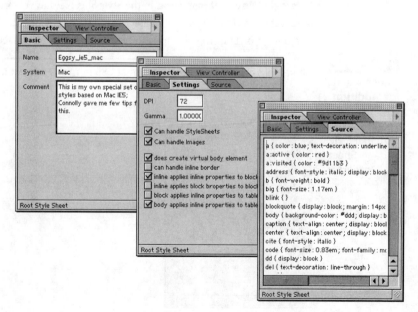

The Settings tab displays the assigned screen resolution for the selected system, which controls how it previews pixel-based settings in the CSS Selector Inspector, as well as Gamma settings. The first two checkboxes indicate whether or not it can handle style sheets and images. The checkboxes below determine how styles are applied as well as whether or not a virtual body element is created.

The Source tab lists the selectors and properties for every tag within a browser-specific set. If you are working with an editable set, you can make modifications to styles here rather than going through the CSS Selector Inspector.

TIP:
Edits Aren't
Saved

Despite the locked status of a built-in style, you might be tempted to edit styles in the Root Style Sheet Inspector's Source tab, as it seems you can select, type, and make modifications. However, any changes made to a locked style are not saved by GoLive after you close Web Settings.

Style Sheets Editor

The Style Sheets Editor appears when you click the stairstepped icon in the Layout Editor. It's discussed in depth in Chapter 29, *Cascading Style Sheets*. Selecting any style in the editor brings up the CSS Selector Inspector, discussed below. The one Inspector unique to the editor handles externally-linked style sheets.

External Style Sheet Inspector. In the Style Sheets Editor, click an External style sheet reference (a file icon) or create a new item by clicking the New Style Sheet File button or Duplicate buttons in the Style Sheet toolbar (see Figure 2-101).

TIP:
Contextual
Addition

Alternately, choose Add Link to External CSS from the contextual menu.

Figure 2-101
External Style
Sheet
Inspector

Modify or enter a new style sheet location using the URL field's tools. If Relation or Media aren't filled in, type "stylesheet" and "screen" respectively. Add a brief description in the Title field. Click the Open button to open the style sheet document for editing, and click either directional arrow buttons to move the item up or down in the list to change the cascading order.

Internal Style Sheet Inspector. Clicking a folder containing internal styles (those that are specific to a page) brings up the Internal Style Sheet Inspector (see Figure 2-102). The Type field should automatically fill in with "text/css," while the Media field is blank, allowing you to specify it yourself. There's also an Edit button, but this seems to be inactive.

Figure 2-102
Internal Style
Sheet
Inspector

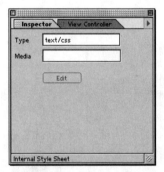

CSS Selector Inspector. To view or edit the attributes of a specific style in either the Style Sheet Editor or the CSS tab of Web Settings, select a style name (in bold) listed underneath the style sheet group, which brings up the eight-tab CSS Selector Inspector.

The following illustrations, Figures 2-103 to 2-110, show an example of setting up a new style using each of the eight tabs.

Figure 2-103
CSS Selector
Inspector's
Basic tab

Figure 2-104
CSS Selector
Inspector's
Font Properties
tab

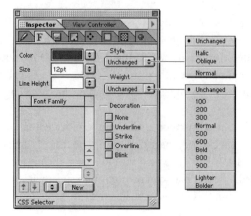

Figure 2-105
CSS Selector
Inspector's Text
Properties tab

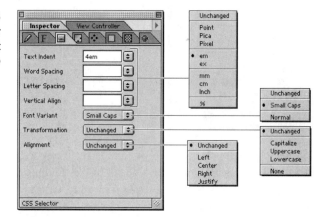

Figure 2-106
CSS Selector
Inspector's Box
Properties tab

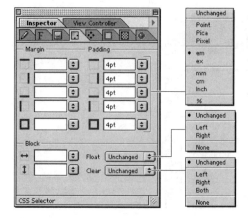

Figure 2-107
CSS Selector
Inspector's
Positioning
Properties tab

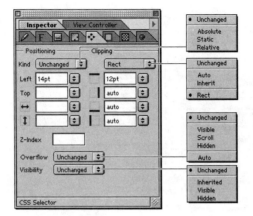

Figure 2-108
CSS Selector
Inspector's
Border
Properties tab

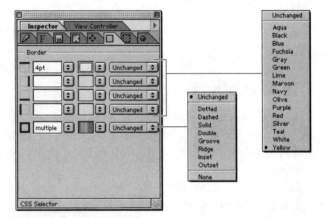

Figure 2-109
CSS Selector
Inspector's
Background
Properties tab

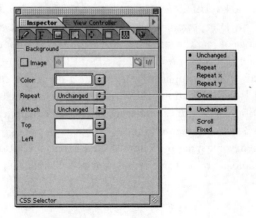

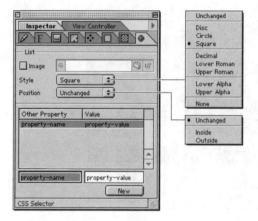

Figure 2-110
CSS Selector
Inspector's List
and Other
Properties tab

XML Inspectors

Not to delay the fun, but all things XML are covered in Chapter 32, *Languages and Scripting.*

File Mappings

To view and edit files not directly supported by GoLive—like media files that require plug-ins, such as MP3 audio or RealVideo files—open the File Mappings tab in Web Settings. In GoLive 4, this functionality was handled through Preferences.

By default, GoLive collects file formats into thematic folders (such as Application, Image, etc.); you can view the list in alphabetical order by choosing Flat in the View Controller. Select a file format suffix (or extension, displayed in bold) to bring up the File Info Extension Inspector, which lists the MIME type and kind of file as well as file type and file creator (originating application). The Basic popup menu allows you to choose between Binary File, Text, or a range of markup languages, while the Transfer popup menu allows you to configure how the file is configured for FTP (see Figure 2-111).

To specify a native application to handle a file (from either Default or GoLive), click the Application field's Browse button to bring up an Open dialog box, within which you can navigate to the desired application. To delete the program, click the Clear button.

To add a new file mapping, click the New Extension button from the File Mappings toolbar, or select an existing item and click the Duplicate button.

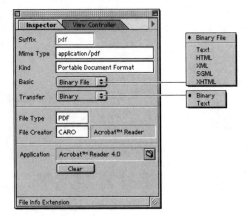

Figure 2-111
File Info
Extension
Inspector

Zat is Not My Dog!

The Inspector palette is powerful, multifaceted, deep, and omnipresent. However, you should now have a grasp on its many manifestations; now you can take this information and control more of GoLive's inner workings.

In the next chapter, we move on to the rest of the pieces that make GoLive tick: *Palettes and Parts*, covering the other things that float, click, and slide.

CHAPTER 3

Palettes and Parts

After the first two chapters, your head might be swimming a bit from everything that's been thrown at you. This chapter turns down the volume a little, giving you a visual reference guide to the supporting parts and pieces that make GoLive's engine hum along. Here's what's covered:

- Palettes, palettes everywhere... GoLive 5 has exploded with palettes that control layout grids and text boxes, preview source code, store table designs, and more. Each palette is covered here, starting with the Objects palette (formerly just "The Palette" in GoLive 4), which houses HTML tag objects, site references, and QuickTime tracks. (The one palette that isn't covered here is the View Controller, which, believe it or not, controls the view of a selected window or editor. Both its concept and its execution are simple enough—though with enough quirks to keep you interested—and we'll call it out when it comes up.)

- The various flavors of the contextual Toolbar are covered, with references to each button's function, and what causes each Toolbar to appear.

- While the nine tabs of the Color Palette are covered extensively in Chapter 10, Color, each tab of the Color palette is referenced here.

- And finally, get an introduction to the editors and windows that control GoLive's advanced features, including the JavaScript Editor, Timeline Editor, Track Editor, and Style Sheet Editor.

Palettes

In addition to the growth in numbers, GoLive 5 added palette docking, just like in Photoshop and other graphics programs. This minimizes the screen real estate they take up. When GoLive is first opened, groups A, B, C, and D (from

Table 3-1 below) appear by default. Click a tab within a palette group to bring that tab to the front of the group and make it active.

TIP:
**Reset
Palettes**

Choosing Reset Palettes from the Window menu opens the above-mentioned palette groups and returns them to their default locations.

What's New in 5

As if you didn't have reason enough to invest in a 19-inch monitor, along comes GoLive 5 with a 320% increase in palettes from the original five in GoLive 4. Table 3-1 shows the original GoLive 4 palette items, their counterparts in GoLive 5, and keyboard shortcuts (if available).

Table 3-1
Palette comparison

	GoLive 5 Palettes	GoLive 4	Group Shortcuts*
A	Palette, Color Palette**	Objects Color	2 3
B	Inspector Layout View Controller Dynamic Link***	Inspector View Controller	1 9
C	Transform Tracing Image	Align	8
D	Floating Box Controller	Floating Boxes Table Actions	6
E	Link Inspector	In & Out Links Site Navigator Source Code	5
F	Markup Tree	History	7 or Control-Alt-Shift-Z (Windows only)

* Press Command on the Mac or Control on the PC plus the number, except as noted.

** Yes, the name of the palette was Color Palette, making it the Color Palette palette. We all know what it means, but us writerly types find ourselves making these types of word comparisons. Thanks for indulging us.

*** For the Dynamic Link palette to be available, you must activate the eponymous module in the Modules pane of Preferences. For more on Dynamic Link, see the Modules section in Chapter 4, *Preferences and Customizing*, and Chapter 30, *Dynamic Link*.

This structure, however, is flexible. To view a palette on its own, tear it away from its group by clicking the palette's title tab and dragging it out of the group. To dock it with its default group (or add it to another group), click and drag the title tab and drop it onto a group palette; an outline appears within the group palette to show that it's ready to accept visitors.

TIP:
Dragging Top Bar

If you click and drag the bar at the top of the palette, you only move its positioning and can't drop it onto another palette group.

TIP:
Dropping In

When one palette is dropped onto another, its title tab appears at the end of the list. You can't change the order of tabs unless you drag all tabs out of the group, then drag and drop palettes in the order you desire.

TIP:
Super Palette

Yes, it is possible to make one gigantic super palette—but this isn't recommended for the claustrophobic (see Figure 3-1).

Figure 3-1
Palettus
Gigantus

When a palette is selected, a checkmark appears next to it in the Window menu. If you drag a palette out of its original grouping, the grouped list doesn't change in the Window menu, and it's possible to have all members of a group selected and checked in the menu.

To hide a palette that's included in a group, click one of the other tabs in the group. To close a palette (either individual or group), click the close box in the upper left (Mac) or upper right (Windows) corner of the palette bar. Pressing Command-W (Mac) or Control-W (Windows) closes open files and does not affect palettes. Selecting a checkmarked palette from the Window menu also closes it.

TIP:
Close Whole Group

If you select a checked palette from the Window menu, and the palette is included within a group, the entire group palette is closed.

TIP:
Palette Menu Shortcut Reminders

Speaking of the Window menu, both Windows and Mac versions include handy references to the various palette keyboard shortcuts.

TIP:
Hide or Minimize All Palettes

Sometimes you want to temporarily hide all of the palettes to view a large Web page. On the Mac, type Control-tab to make them disappear; under Windows, the combination is Control-J. To move a palette out of the way without removing it from the screen entirely, Control-click its title bar: its group snaps to the right side of the screen, displaying only the tab titles vertically. Shift-Control-click minimizes all palettes. To get them back, just click or Shift click their tab titles.

Popout menu. A button appears at the top right corner of a palette, which displays a popout menu with items specific to a selected palette (see Figure 3-2). For instance, the Objects and Color palettes list their individual tabs, while the Tracing Image palette lets you position an image or crop a section. For those palettes where there is no popout menu functionality, the popout button remains inactive.

Figure 3-2
Examples of palette popout menus

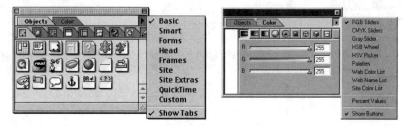

Resizing. To change the size of a palette, click and hold its bottom right corner and drag to your desired size. Under Windows, you can also use any of the palette's outside edges to resize it. If you click on another palette tab within a group, that palette loses the dimensions you just dragged; GoLive remembers the last size the selected palette was displayed at and returns to those dimensions.

Docking. To keep everything in order, overlapped palettes snap to the border of another palette. You can overlap palettes if you want (just continue dragging to a desired point), but GoLive's first inclination is to dock palettes into a larger entity. For more on docking and minimizing palettes, see the "Managing Windows & Palettes" section in Chapter 1, *Getting Started*.

Objects

The Objects palette is the WYSIWYG heart of GoLive (see Figure 3-3). While seeming a little cumbersome at first—especially for those of us who pine for keyboard shortcuts—dragging and dropping tag icons onto a page quickly becomes second nature.

Figure 3-3
Objects palette

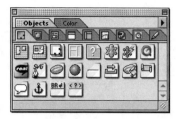

You can access each tab of the Objects palette by clicking on each tab. Alternatively, you can click the popout menu at the top right and select a tab name. To save yourself some screen real estate, deselect Show Tabs to get rid of the tab icons—though frankly, you're not saving much and it is much easier to click from tab to tab rather than having to use the menu each time.

The Undo and Redo items work in conjunction with HTML objects dragged into the Custom tab (or the Custom section of the Site Extras tab).

The Basic Tab

If you're designing pages, you spend most of your GoLive time with the Objects palette's Basic tab open. In it, you find an arsenal of the most often used page layout placeholder items (see Table 3-2). These can be inserted by dragging and dropping or by double-clicking the icon with the Layout Editor active. You can drag and drop icons into the HTML Source Editor and HTML Outline Editor, but double-clicking fails.

NEW IN 5:
Plug-in
Additions

GoLive 5 has added a few specific plug-in items to the Basic tab (to supplement the lonely, catch-all plug-in item from GoLive 4) and replaced the ActiveX item with the Object item. Also, the Tag item now creates its own closing tag, thereby doing away with the End Tag item.

The Smart Tab

You can find the whole range of GoLive's special Actions and Action-like objects (including the Component icon, which isn't specifically an Action, but it's more than just a regular object) collected under this tab, from a date and time stamp to a URL list popup menu. See Table 3-3 for a list of Smart items and where in the Layout Editor they can be placed (either in the Head or body section). For more information, see Chapter 28, *Actions*.

TIP:
Double-Click
to Insert
Body Smart
Icons

You can double-click the Smart icons that go into the body section of the Layout Editor, but to add the Head Action and Browser Switch icons into the Head section you have to first toggle the Head section open and then double click.

Table 3-2
Basic tab icons

Basic Tab Icon	Icon Name	Tag
	Layout Grid	table
	Layout Text Box	td
	Floating Box	div
	Table	table
	Image	img
	Plug-in	embed
	Flash (SWF or Shockwave)	object type="application/x-shock-wave-flash"
	QuickTime	embed type="video/quicktime"
	Real (RealMedia)	embed type="audio/x-pn-realau-dio-plugin"
	SVG	embed type="image/svg-xml"
	Java Applet	applet
	Object	object
	Line	hr
	Horizontal Spacer	spacer
	JavaScript	script
	Marquee	marquee
	Comment	<!-- -->
	Anchor	a
	Line Break	br
	Tag	noedit

Table 3-3	Smart Tab Icon	Icon Name	Head or Body?
Smart tab icons		Smart Photoshop	Body
		Smart Illustrator	Body
		Smart LiveMotion	Body
		Component	Body
		Rollover	Body
		Modified Date	Body
		URL Popup	Body
		Body Action	Body
		Head Action	Head
		Browser Switch	Head

The Forms Tab

Like the tag icons from the Basic tab, you can insert Forms tags into either the Layout Editor or HTML Source Editor (see Table 3-4 for the complete list).

NEW IN 5:
Form Objects

The biggest change for GoLive 5 is the creation of a Form object, which groups all form elements in a bordered box and automatically inserts a closing Form tag (hence, no End Tag icon from GoLive 4). For details on configuring forms in GoLive, see Chapter 15, *Forms*.

Table 3-4	Forms Tab Icon	Icon Name	Tag
Forms tab icons (continued on next page)		Form	form
		Submit Button	input type="submit"
		Reset Button	input type="reset"
		Button	button type="button"
		Form Input Image	input type="image"
		Label	label
		Text Field	input type="text"
		Password	input type="password"

Table 3-4	Forms Tab Icon	Icon Name	Tag
Forms tab icons *(continued)*		Text Area	textarea
		Check Box	input type="checkbox"
		Radio Button	input type="radio"
		Popup	select
		List Box	select multiple
		File Browser	input type="file"
		Hidden	input type="hidden"
		Key Generator	keygen
		Fieldset	fieldset

The Head Tab

The icons found in the Objects palette's Head tab help you control the background workings of a page, from keywords and description of the page to refresh rate and scripts you can create to, say, sniff for the version of a browser viewing the page (see Table 3-5). These icons can only be placed into the Head section of the Document window's Layout Editor. For more details, see Chapter 7, *Head Section*.

Table 3-5	Head Tab Icon	Icon Name	Tag
Head tab icons		IsIndex	isindex
		Base	base
		Keywords	meta name="keywords"
		Link	link
		Meta	meta name="generic"
		Refresh	meta http-equiv="refresh"
		Tag	noedit
		Comment	<!-- -->
		Script	script

The Frames Tab

The Objects palette's Frames tab diverges slightly from the way the previous three tabs work. Rather than dragging icons that represent HTML tags into a page, you drag icon representations of frame layouts into the Document window's Frame Editor.

TIP:
No Insertion
Shortcut

You cannot double-click a Frameset icon to place it within the Frame Editor; it must be dragged in.

See Figure 3-4 for a visual representation of all the layout options you have at your disposal. Sections with a frame icon that are tinged with purple are given a specific pixel size, while sections in blue are set to scale according to the size of the browser window. For everything you ever wanted to know about frames (and a little more), see Chapter 13, *Frames*.

The Site Tab

Taking a break from the Document window, we move to the basic controls for the Site window, which let you group files and collections of color references and external Web and email references. You can either drag or double-click these icons to place them into their appropriate Site window tabs (listed in Table 3-6). If you try to add an icon to a tab where it doesn't belong, it either returns to the Objects palette (if dragged) or an error sounds (if double clicked).

For more information, see Part 3, *Sites*, especially Chapter 21, *Files, Folders, and Links*, and Chapter 22, *Sitewide Sets*.

NEW IN 5:
Design Icons

GoLive 5 added three new icons that deal with the new Design feature available for sites, and which can only be placed into an open design window.

TIP:
Inserting
Blank Pages
in the Files
tab

With the Files tab of a Site window open, double-clicking the Generic Page icon places a blank HTML file (titled "untitled.html" and marked with the under construction status icon) at the directory level you currently have selected; if no directory is selected, it creates the folder named in Preferences's Site pane for new items and places it there. If you have a folder selected, the file is placed at that directory level. (Also, if the folder is closed, GoLive opens it to reveal the new file.) This also works if you have the Site window open to the Extras tab and that part of the window is active.

Figure 3-4
Frames tab
icons and
examples

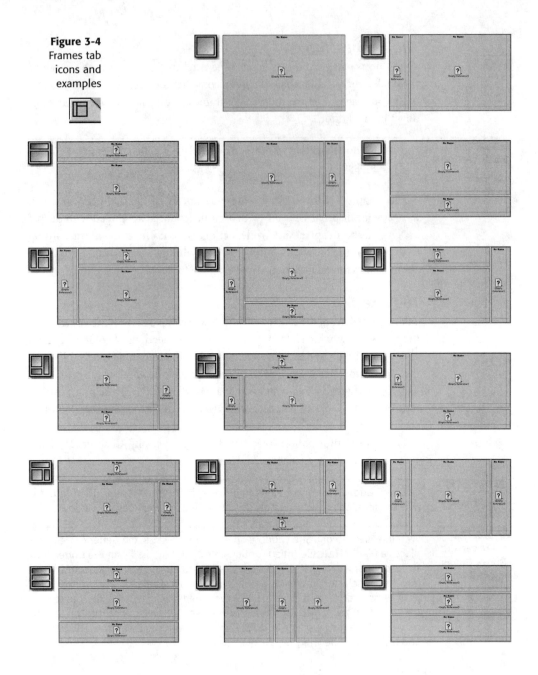

Table 3-6	Site Tab Icon	Icon Name
Site tab icons		Generic Page
		URL
		Address
		Color
		Font Set
		Folder
		URL Group
		Address Group
		Color Group
		Font Set Group
		Design Section
		Design Group
		Design Annotation

The Site Extras Tab and Custom Tab

The Objects palette's Site Extras tab is three-tiered. You can find your collection of HTML Stationery files and GoLive Components, both of which can also be accessed by opening up the split pane view of the Site window (see Figure 3-5). If you're confused as to what the difference is between these two items, here's a quick refresher:

Figure 3-5
Site window's
Extras tab

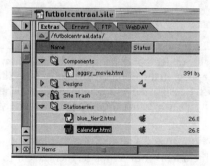

- Stationery files are template pages that allow you to create a consistent layout for use throughout your site. When you open a Stationery file from the Stationeries folder in the right pane's Extras tab, you are prompted to open either the original file for editing, or create a new, unnamed page using that file's contents.

- Components are HTML source files that include one item (such as an image) or a collection of HTML code (such as a complex table), which can then be inserted into individual pages. If a Component is modified, all pages including that Component are automatically updated.

Additionally, GoLive enables you to save commonly used HTML objects in Custom areas. This includes everything from images and plug-in media files to customized tables to layout grids to line breaks (essentially anything inserted into a page from the Objects palette). GoLive 4 provided the Custom tab for this collection, but GoLive 5 adds a site-specific Custom section to the Site Extras tab. Objects added to the Custom tab are always available, while those that are added to the Custom section of the Site Extras tab are associated with a specific Site document and are available only when that Site is open.

Switch between the Stationery Pads, Components, and Custom views via the popup menu at the bottom of the Objects palette (see Figure 3-6).

Figure 3-6
Object
palette's Site
Extras tab

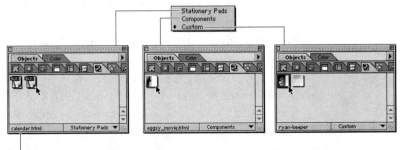

Hold your cursor over a file to display its name in the text field at the bottom of the Objects palette.

TIP:
What You
See

Files in the Components folder that don't have a .html or .htm extension (such as a .txt file) will not appear in the Components view of the Site Extras tab. And on the Mac, if a file isn't designated as a Stationery file (unchecked on the File Inspector's File tab), its file icon won't show up with Stationery Pads selected.

Stationery Pads section. To add a new Stationery file, configure the page elements you want to include in your template, then save it to the Stationeries folder in your site document. You can do this easily by selecting Stationeries from the site document button in the Save dialog box, found only when you have a Site window open (see Figure 3-7). HTML files added to this folder are automatically treated as Stationery files. After saving a file to this folder, its file icon appears in the Site Extras Stationeries section.

Figure 3-7
Save dialog's
site document
button

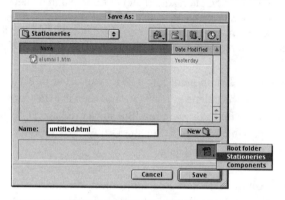

TIP:
Creating
Stationery
(Mac)

You don't have to place HTML files in the Stationeries folder to create a Stationery file. Select any HTML file within your site, then check Stationery Pad on the File tab of the File Inspector.

To add a new page to your site based on a Stationery file, drag its file icon from the Site Extras tab into a desired folder in the Site window, and then type a name in the file's highlighted name area. Dragging a file icon from the Stationeries folder in the Extras tab also adds a copy of the template.

Components section. To add a Component, configure your desired HTML, and then save it to the Components folder in your site document (as you did with the Stationery file). After saving a file to this folder, its file icon is added in the Site Extras Components section.

TIP:
What a Drag
(and Drop)

You cannot double-click Components to insert them on a page. You have to drag a Component from the Objects palette onto a page. Stationery can't be double-clicked here to open a new version; you can only drag Stationery icons into the Files or Design tabs.

TIP:
Modifying
Templates

To modify an existing Stationery or Component file, you must open it from within a document or the Site window's Extras tab (or wherever you may have it stored within your site); you cannot double-click the Objects palette icon.

TIP:
Adding
Thumbnail
Previews

After files are saved or dragged into either the Stationeries or Components folders, generic file icons are added to their respective section in the Site Extras tab. (You can tell the name of a file by placing your mouse over an icon; its name appears at the bottom of the Objects palette.) However, you can change this icon to a thumbnail shot of the file's content by opening the file from the Site window, modifying it (even just adding a space and deleting it), and saving it. The icon immediately changes in the Objects palette. You can also hold down the Command and Option keys (Mac) or Control and Alt keys (Windows) when clicking on the Site menu, then select Create Thumbnails (which is normally the Rescan command when the keys aren't held down). One small word of caution, however: creating thumbnails can dramatically increase the size of your site file.

To insert a Component into a page, you could insert a Component icon from the Objects palette's Smart tab, and then use the Component Inspector to link to a file in the Site window. But since you have this collection of files in the Components section of the Site Extras tab, simply drag a Component's icon into an open HTML page.

Custom Objects. To add a custom object, configure your HTML element, then select it and drag it to either the Custom tab or the Custom section of the Site Extras tab. A new icon with a thumbnail of the element is added. GoLive doesn't allow you to drag files directly from the Site window into either Custom area.

TIP:
A Clip Here,
a Clip There

If you drag a file (page, image, CSS style sheet, etc.) from a Site window into either Custom area, a clipping reference to that file is created (with a generic text clipping icon). If you place this clipping item into a page, an absolute reference to that item on your hard drive is added.

Place your cursor over the thumbnail and GoLive displays "untitled snippet" in the lower left corner of the Objects palette. To give the object a name, double-click the thumbnail to bring up the Palette Item Editor; type the object's name in the Item Name field and click OK (see Figure 3-8). The object in the Custom tab references the file originally referenced in the page that the object was dragged from (got that?), so it doesn't need to be placed into a special folder (á la Components).

Figure 3-8
Naming
custom objects

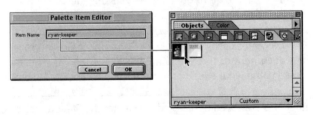

Double-click an icon in the Custom tab (or Custom view of the Site Extras tab) to bring up the Palette Item Editor, where you can name the item.

So, you're probably wondering to yourself, how is this really different from a Component? Custom objects don't automatically update themselves wherever they appear in a site when they're modified; Components do. To update custom objects, you have to open every page on which they appear, make any change, and save them.

You can select and drag a range of text—even formatted text—into one of the Custom areas (the icon that shows up looks like a text clipping icon, but instead shows the opening and closing brackets of an HTML tag). However, when you add a Custom text object to a page, you often get an extra paragraph added before the inserted text. If you place your cursor at the point of this extra paragraph and press Delete, you erase any included formatting. A better, though more roundabout, way is to add a Custom text object to the Layout Editor, then switch views (such as to the HTML Source Editor); upon return to the Layout Editor, the extra line is deleted.

For more information, see the "Smart" section in Chapter 2, *The Inspector*, for details on the Component Inspector. See Chapter 21, *Files, Folders, and Links*, for further details on creating and managing Stationery and Component files.

The QuickTime Tab

To add tracks to QuickTime movie and sound files, from music and sound to text and links, drag a QuickTime Track icon into the Timeline Editor (no double-clicking). The track appears at the bottom of the track list on the left side of the editor.

For more information on editing QuickTime files, see Chapter 17, *Media*.

GoLive 5 has added several new track items, including MPEG, SWF, and Streaming tracks.

Table 3-7
QuickTime tab
icons

QuickTime Tab Icon	Icon Name
	Video Track
	Picture Track
	Generic Filter Track
	One Source Filter Track
	Two Source Filter Track

QuickTime Tab Icon	Icon Name
	MPEG Track
	Sprite Track
	SWF Track
	3D Track
	HREF Track
	Chapter Track
	Text Track
	Sound Track
	MIDI (Music) Track
	Streaming Track
	Folder Track

Color

Select Color from the Window menu to activate the Color palette, from which you can select colors and shades of gray to add to items on your page, including text, table cells, and page backgrounds. To add color to an item, select a color from one of the Color palette's tabs and drag a color swatch from the Preview Pane to the desired location, such as highlighted text on a page, a color field on an Inspector, or the Text Color field on the Text toolbar.

You have nine tabs to choose colors from, each of which allows you to manipulate, select, and store colors just a little differently.

Color Palette Basics

You can move from one tab to another by clicking tabs, or select the name of the tab from the Palette popout menu. The first five tabs (Grayscale, RGB, CMYK, HSB, and HSV tabs; the order varies by platform) allow you to manipulate sliders, pinpoint colors from a wheel/square, or type in values to come up with color combinations (see Figure 3-9). If you select Percent Values from the palette's popout menu, you switch from a numeric range of 256 color steps to a percentage range.

Figure 3-9
Color palette
controls

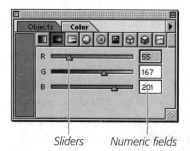
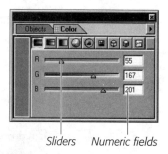

Sliders   *Numeric fields*   *Sliders*   *Numeric fields*

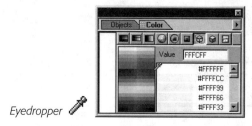

Eyedropper

TIP:
Button Up

If you deselect Show Buttons from the popout menu, the various Color tabs disappear. Frankly, it's far easier to move between the sections of the Color palette by clicking tabs than using the popout menu (and you don't save much screen real estate), so we recommend keeping Show Buttons selected.

On the Palettes tab, you can select from a fixed set of 256 system colors using an eyedropper cursor icon. The Web Color List tab allows you to use the eyedropper, as well as choose from a list of Web-safe colors, which include a color swatch and hexadecimal value. The Web Name List tab drops the palette scheme and allows you to choose from a list of colors with associated names either by name or hex value.

Of course, each tab within the Color palette is a little different, offering you a slightly different measure of access to finding just the right color.

- The Grayscale tab allows you to select a shade of gray (see Figure 3-10).

Figure 3-10
Grayscale tab

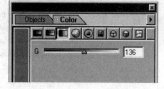

TIP:
Color Your
World

After you click the Grayscale tab, the Preview Pane still displays the last color selected from one of the other tabs. To turn that color gray, simply click the slider without moving it.

- The RGB Sliders tab allows you to select a color from the red, green, and blue values (see Figure 3-9).

- The CMYK Sliders tab allows you to select a color by adjusting the values for cyan, magenta, yellow, and black (see Figure 3-11).

- The Palettes tab displays five different fixed system color profiles: 256 colors, 16 colors, 16 grays, desktop colors, and a custom palette of colors that you can drop into the 36 available spots (see Figure 3-12).

Figure 3-11
CMYK Sliders tab

Figure 3-12
Palettes tab

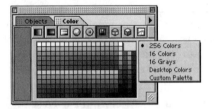

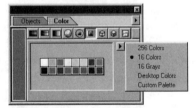

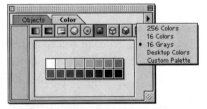

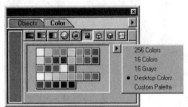

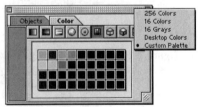

The 34 desktop colors reflect the colors available to the operating system and do not change to reflect different colors chosen for the background desktop.

To add colors to the custom palette, find a color via one of the other Color palette tabs (such as the RGB Sliders tab), return to the Palette tab's custom palette, and drag a swatch from the Preview Pane to one of the custom squares.

TIP:

Sample with Eyedropper

On the Palettes and Web Color List tabs, place your cursor over a color grid to turn your mouse pointer into an eyedropper. Click and hold your mouse, then move it about the screen. The Preview Pane displays any color the eyedropper touches, even items outside of GoLive. To keep a color, select the Custom Palette in the Palettes popup menu and drag a color swatch from the Preview Pane into one of the palette's squares.

- The HSV Picker tab allows you to set hue, saturation, and value independently. Set the hue in the outer ring, then set the saturation and value by selecting a point in the interior color square (see Figure 3-13).

- The HSB Wheel tab's color wheel allows you to choose from any color currently available to you from your video hardware. It also includes a Brightness control slider and value input field (see Figure 3-14).

- The Web Color List tab provides 216 cross-platform, browser-safe colors that don't dither. The Value field displays each color's hexadecimal value (see Figure 3-15).

Figure 3-13
HSV Picker tab

Figure 3-14
HSB Wheel tab

Figure 3-15
Web Color List tab

- The Web Name List tab displays a collection of colors that can be specified by name, but not all of which are fully browser-safe (see Figure 3-16).

- The Site Color List tab displays the colors collected in the Site window's Colors tab. You must have a Site window open to view its colors (see Figure 3-17).

Figure 3-16
Web Name List
tab

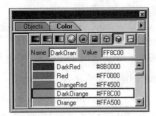

Figure 3-17
Site Color tab

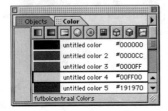

For more information, see Chapter 10, *Color*. For details on collecting the colors used by a site, see Chapter 22, *Sitewide Sets*.

Dynamic Link

This palette is closely integrated with the advanced functionality of creating dynamic ASP pages, and is covered extensively in Chapter 30, *Dynamic Link*.

Transform and Align

These two palettes work in conjunction with layout grids and text boxes, and are covered under the Layout Grid Toolbar later in this chapter.

Tracing Image

Using the Tracing Image palette, you can create your page's layout based on a schematic saved as an image file (see Figure 3-18). Check Source, and then navigate to the image file using the Point & Shoot or Browse buttons. You can import the standard Web image formats, as well as Photoshop /PSD (provided they are RGB and 8-bit), TIFF, BMP (Windows), PICT (Mac), PCX, TARGA, etc.

Figure 3-18
Tracing Image
palette

TIP:
Tracing
Source Code

Placing a tracing image in a page adds the Tracingsrc attribute to the Body tag. When viewed in an external browser, this image does not display.

TIP:
Sizing to
Dimensions

After adding a tracing image, choose Tracing Image from the Layout Editor's Window Size popup menu to change the size of the Document window to the dimensions of the tracing image.

The image appears dimmed in the page to 50 percent opacity (by default); you can change how dimmed the image displays via the Opacity slider. By default, the image displays starting at the top left corner of the Layout Editor; to adjust its positioning, add horizontal (first field) and vertical (second field) values. To manually adjust the positioning, click the Move Image Tool (the grabber hand) button, then select the image and move it to a desired location.

Click the Crop Tool button, and then select a rectangular area of the tracing image. Clicking the Cut Out button (or selecting Cut Out from the palette's popout menu) opens the Save for Web dialog, allowing you to save the image in a Web-friendly format. The saved image is then placed into a floating box, which you can precisely place on the page by clicking and dragging or using the Floating Box Inspector.

The palette's popout menu also allows you to automatically reset the tracing image to a zero horizontal and zero vertical position, as well as align the image with any selected page element.

Floating Boxes

Speaking of floating boxes, you can manage multiple, overlapping floating boxes within a page using the Floating Boxes palette (called the Floating Box Controller in GoLive 4).

Each floating box is listed with the name assigned to it in the Floating Box Inspector. Click a name in the list to make that floating box the active item on the page (see Figure 3-19).

Figure 3-19
Floating Boxes
palette

Click the Eye icon to make the floating box invisible in the Layout Editor preview. If you use another view in the Document window, then return to the Layout Editor, any floating box that was made invisible becomes visible again.

Clicking the Pencil icon locks a floating box, leaving it visible on the page but not selectable. To unlock it, simply click the floating box's name in the palette.

TIP:
Selecting Placeholder Icon

You can also click the floating box placeholder icon (the small yellow box marked SB) to activate the Floating Box Inspector, from which you can make modifications to the box.

TIP:
Locking and Visibility

Control-click a Pencil icon to lock/unlock all floating boxes, and Control-click an Eye icon to toggle all floating boxes between visibility and invisibility.

From the palette's popout menu, selecting Convert to Layout Grid opens a new GoLive page with the floating boxes placed within a layout grid. Any content not placed within a floating box is not converted. Clicking Floating Box Grid Settings let you add an invisible layout grid to the current page (see Figure 3-20). This grid doesn't get added to your source code. From the dialog box that opens, adjust the horizontal and vertical grid measurements, and configure whether floating boxes snap to position and if the layout grid is visible as you manually move floating boxes (using the grabber hand). If Prevent Overlapping is checked, a buffer of about 10 pixels keeps floating boxes apart.

For more information, see Chapter 14, *Floating Boxes*.

Figure 3-20
Floating Box
Grid Settings
dialog

Table

The Table palette enables you to easily make selections (from individual cells to entire rows and columns), as well as sort content and apply preformatted and saved styles.

The Select tab shows a schematic of a selected table; if no table is selected in the Layout Editor, the palette is blank. To select an individual cell, place your cursor over a desired cell and click; the cell becomes highlighted in the palette as well as in the Layout Editor. Additionally, a blue line appears above the table schematic to indicate the selected cell's column and to the left to indicate the cell's row. To select an entire row or column, place your cursor above the table or to the left respectively (which brings up a lighter colored diagonal pointer) and click (see Figure 3-21). If you place your cursor along the right edge of, or below, the table schematic and then click, you select the entire table.

Figure 3-21
Selecting cells
and rows

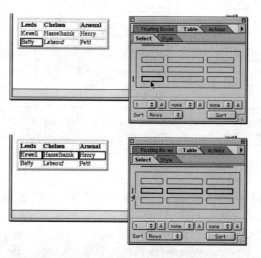

To make multiple selections—either cell by cell or multiple rows or columns—just add the Shift key.

The popup menus at the bottom of the Select tab enable you to configure sorting within the table. From the Sort popup menu, select whether you want to sort rows or columns. If you chose Rows from the Sort popup menu, the number of columns within your table appears in the first popup above; select the primary column to sort by (1 to select the first column, 2 to select the second, and so on). If you chose Columns, the number of rows appears in the popup, and you choose the primary row to sort by. The second and third popup menus allow you to sort by two other row/column criteria. The triangular buttons to the right of each of the popup menus allow you to sort by ascending or descending order. When your sorting criteria is set, click the Sort button.

On the Style tab, GoLive provides a number of predefined styles for table background colors. Choose a style from the popup menu, then click the Apply button or click the Clear button to return the table to its tabula rasa (er…blank) state (see Figure 3-22). If you had colored any cells previously, then applied a style and cleared it, the previous colors aren't displayed.

Figure 3-22
Applying styles
with Table
palette

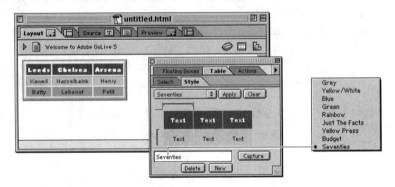

TIP:
Undoing a
Style

If you have any pre-colored cells in a table, then apply a style and clear it, the table indeed returns to a completely blank table and your previously set colors are voided. However, you can always use the History palette to return to a previous state.

To add a new style, configure your table's colors, click the New button, add a descriptive name, then click the Capture button. If you click the Capture button with one of the predefined styles chosen from the popup menu, the newly captured style overwrites it. To get rid of a style, select it from the popup and click the Delete button.

For more information, see Chapter 11, *Tables*.

Actions

GoLive Actions are prefabricated sets of code that you can combine to set up complex sets of actions attached to text, buttons, and animations. Actions can preload images, add sounds, dynamically change the content of images, open links in new browser windows, and other functionality. GoLive 5 breaks Actions out of a number of GoLive 4 Inspectors (including Text and Image) and gives them their own palette.

TIP:
**GoLive
Actions vs.
Photoshop
Actions**

GoLive Actions shouldn't be mistaken for the kin of Photoshop Actions, which are a series of recorded image-editing steps. While GoLive does not currently allow you to record sequences like in Photoshop or CE Software's QuicKeys, GoLive's History palette does at least give you a map of what modifications you've been making within a page.

To create an Action, create a link or click inside any range of text that has a link applied; the link can be empty—or set to the default "(Empty Reference!)"—without causing any problems running the Action. Next, click the Actions palette. In the Events pane of the palette, select a trigger, or a method by which the Action gets invoked by the user (see Table 3-8).

Table 3-8
Event and
Actions

Event Trigger	User Action
Mouse Click	User clicks an item
Mouse Enter	User moves cursor into item's area (mouseover)
Mouse Exit	User moves cursor out of item's area
Double Click	User clicks item twice in rapid succession
Mouse Down	User holds down mouse button over item
Mouse Up	User releases mouse button over item
Key Down*	User presses any key
Key Press*	User presses any key
Key Up	User releases any key

* Key Down and Key Press are effectively the same; but, ideally, Key Down would capture an event only while the key is depressed.

After selecting an event, click the New Action (notepad) button above the Actions pane, where a new Action titled "None" preceded by a question mark appears. A dot also appears to the left of the event name to indicate that an Action has been assigned to it.

Click the Action button below the Events pane to select from the list of Actions, and fill in the necessary information for that Action in the lower half of the palette (see Figure 3-23).

To add another Action associated with this item, click the New Action button again. To delete an Action, select it in the Actions pane and click the Delete Action (trash can) button.

For more information, see Chapter 28, *Actions*.

Figure 3-23
Adding an
Action

When a viewer clicks this link, an alert
window opens displaying text that you
specify in the Action palette.

In & Out Links

The In & Out Links palette reveals the relationship among a selected page,
incoming links (all the media and pages that point to the selected page), and
outgoing links (graphics, URLs, email addresses, and other pages the selected
page includes or points to); see Figure 3-24.

Figure 3-24
In & Out Links
palette

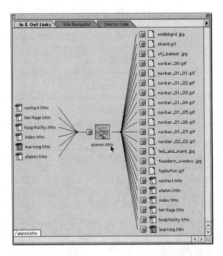

The In & Out Links palette was the confusingly named Link Inspector in GoLive 4.
There was another Inspector with the same name, and it wasn't really an
Inspector, either. The new name is a bit clunky, but it's accurate, and it's a stand-
alone palette that can't be confused with any other GoLive feature.

It can also show which font sets, colors, external links (URLs), and email
addresses are used on which pages (see Figure 3-25). If the item is a Web

page—or an Acrobat PDF, QuickTime movie, or Flash animation with embedded URLs—the In & Out Links palette shows all outbound links. You can select any page or item in any of the Site window's tabs, including any item in a design or in the Navigation or Links Views.

Figure 3-25
Viewing usage
of email
reference

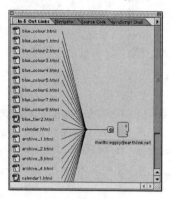

You can use the Point & Shoot button to relink all the inbound links pointing to the selected item to any other item in its category. In Figure 3-26, for example, you could relink "mailto:franklebeouf@hotmail.com" by using Point & Shoot to select "mailto:pele@footie.br". You can also link to objects that are not in the same tab, like replacing a link to an email address with an HTML file.

Figure 3-26
Changing
references
with In & Out
Links

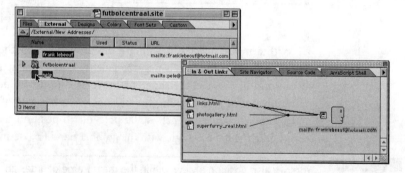

Click the palette popout menu to access the In & Out Links Palette Options dialog (see Figure 3-27). Choose whether to show inbound or outbound links or both, and filter which outbound links are showing. Checking Icon Instead of Thumbnail displays the Finder icon (on the Mac) or a default icon (under Windows) instead of a Web page thumbnail. The URL at Bottom checkbox toggles the display of the item's location on the site.

Figure 3-27
In & Out Links
Palette
Options

The Print option in the popout menu allows you to print the currently displayed set of relationships.

Site Navigator

The Site Navigator palette works in conjunction with design windows and Navigation and Links Views. It ontrols the view of a large, unwieldy collection of files much like the Navigator palette in Photoshop (see Figure 3-28).

Figure 3-28
Site Navigator
palette

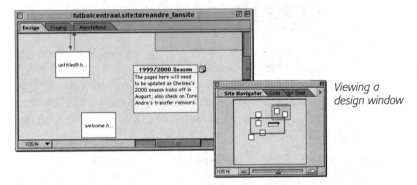

Viewing a design window

With a frame selected in either a design window or the Navigation or Links View, open the Site Navigator palette. Enter a value as a percentage to zoom in or out, use the slider, or move up and down incrementally (10 percent at a time) by clicking the buttons on either side of the slider. The maximum size you can reach is 500 percent. To position the view within a frame, drag the red rectangle with the grabber hand to a desired location.

TIP:
Panoramic Viewing

You can also position a view within the main frame of a design window and the Navigation or Links Views by using the Panorama frame, though you must use the Site Navigator to modify the view's zoom percentage.

Source Code

If you like to see what's happening in the background of your HTML page as you add objects, open the Source Code palette (see Figure 3-29). It displays every addition, every added attribute and value pair, and all the text you type as it happens. It also offers a handy way of directly editing the code, rather than switching between the Layout Editor and HTML Source Editor in the Document window.

Figure 3-29
Source Code
palette

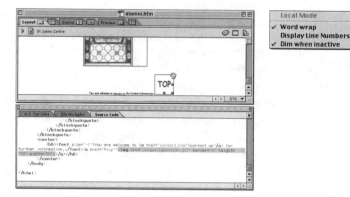

Code appears dimmed or grayed out if the active cursor isn't within the palette; click within the Source Code palette to make it active and start editing. (You can also uncheck Dim When Inactive from the palette's popout menu.) To make edits in the Source Code palette appear in the Layout Editor, click back anywhere in the Layout Editor.

TIP:
Formatting in the Palette

While the color, font, and indentation choices that you set up in the Source pane of Preferences display in the Source Code palette, word wrapping and line numbering do not show up by default. You can choose to set these options separately via the palette's popout menu.

Markup Tree

An additional view into the background of your page's source code is the Markup Tree palette, which lets you navigate through a hierarchical view of a page's code elements (see Figure 3-30). This palette works alongside the Layout Editor, Outline Editor, and Preview tabs in the Document window.

Figure 3-30
Markup Tree
palette

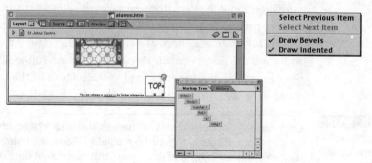

Place your cursor within a range of text or select an HTML element from either the Layout Editor or Preview tab, or select an element from the Outline Editor. The palette displays the structure of the page starting from the top (the Html tag) and ending with your selection.

Alternatively, you can use your arrow keys to move within the Layout and HTML Outline Editors to view individual elements. This can be done within Preview as well, though your cursor isn't visible.

If you select an element from the Markup Tree palette, the element is also selected in the Document window. Within the Markup Tree's hierarchy, you can only step up to the top of the hierarchy (i.e., if you select a Table tag, its TR and TD elements aren't displayed, but you can select any other element that contains the Table tag, such as the Body or another Table).

From the palette's popout menu, you can choose Select Previous Item to return to the last element that was selected. Going back to a previous item also makes Select Next Item active so that you can return to the first element. Choosing Draw Bevels displays elements as buttons, while choosing Draw Indented displays a more visually hierarchical structure (see Figure 3-31).

Figure 3-31
Changing
views in
Markup Tree
palette

 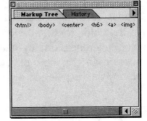

History

The History palette records actions taken in GoLive and allows you to revert to many previous states. It's really a multiple-level Undo/Redo with more information about the steps that were taken; it's almost identical to Photoshop's History palette. The History palette works with the Layout, HTML Source, and HTML Outline Editors, as well as the Design tab of the Site window. As you work, the History palette records each action (up to 20 by default). The most recent modification is found at the bottom of the list, and the active state is indicated with a tab arrow on the left side of the list.

Command-Z/Control-Z removes changes made to a page, and takes you step-by-step back through the History palette. Command-Shift-Z/Control-Shift-Z recreates your changes and steps you forward through the list.

TIP:
Reverting to
Original

To return to the original state of a document (from when it was last opened), choose Revert to Saved from the File menu.

Click a level in the history above your current state to revert to that previous state. All levels below a selected state become inactive, and the page displays the state it was in at that point in the editing process (see Figure 3-32). If you select a previous state in the history, then make a modification to the page, the inactive items below are wiped out and replaced by the new changes. Click the top-most level (marked with the ellipsis) to return to the original state of the document if less than 20 modifications have been made; if more than 20 modifications have been made, clicking this item brings you back to the document's state 20 changes from the most recent edit.

Figure 3-32
Stepping
through the
History palette

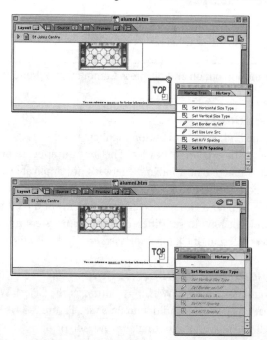

TIP:
One Tab to
Another

Beware of clicking from one editing view to another—like Layout Editor to HTML Source Editor—when monitoring your editing history: the History palette clears itself with each move and the recording of modifications starts over.

Click the palette popout menu to clear the recorded history. Choosing History Options brings up a dialog where you can specify the number of actions recorded by the Palette (see Figure 3-33).

The Toolbar

Like the Inspector, GoLive's Toolbar contextually changes to fit the task at hand. But you can breathe a sigh of relief, as it doesn't have quite as many flavors as the Inspector does.

Toolbar Basics

While each Toolbar offers a range of different attributes you can tweak, a few items appear on every Toolbar.

TIP:
Toggling Toolbar

To toggle the Toolbar on and off, press Command/Control-0 (zero).

Link Warnings

Clicking the Link Warnings button highlights broken text and image links on your page with a colored border. This button appears on every Toolbar, though it is inactive on toolbars where it's not applicable (such as the Web Settings and Stylesheet toolbars). The Link Warnings icon only becomes active on the Site Toolbar if GoLive detects errors in any of the site's pages.

To find out how to set different link warnings colors, see the "General Preferences" section of Chapter 4, *Preferences and Customizing*.

Document/Site Window Toggle

To the right of the Link Warnings button is the Select Window toggle, a popup list of open sites and documents (see Figure 3-34). This works especially well when you have both a Site and one or more Document windows open. With the Document window frontmost, the button shows a site icon; click it to switch directly to the open site file. To return to the last active document, click the button again, which now displays a document icon.

TIP:
Rotating through Windows

If you have multiple Document windows open and no Site window, you can click the toggle icon to scroll through the open documents. (This also works if you have multiple Site windows open, and no Document windows.) However, if you open a Site window, you return to only toggling between the Site window and the last active Document window.

Figure 3-34
Document/Site
window toggle

Document icon

Site icon

*Site files appear at the bottom of the
list on the Mac (left), but at the top
of the list in Windows (right).*

To view a list of all open files, click and hold the triangle to the right of the icon to display a popup menu with a list of sites and documents (including pages, media files, text files, and external style sheets).

Show in Browser Button

For a true representation of how your pages behave in various browsers, it's wise to go ahead and view them in those browsers, rather than just relying on the Document window's Layout Preview. The Show in Browser button loads a temporary version of your page into the browser you select.

TIP:
**Identical in
Windows**

GoLive for Windows uses Internet Explorer to preview pages, so Layout Preview and Internet Explorer should show an identical display.

To set up this feature, first select the Browsers pane in Preferences to gather a list of browsers found on your hard drive, and then check the browser you use most to preview your page designs to assign it as your default browser.

TIP:
**Setting up
Browsers**

If you haven't set up a preview browser (or list of browsers) in Preferences, GoLive reminds you that this information is missing (see Figure 3-35). Click the Specify button and GoLive automatically opens Preferences. Find the browsers on your system, choose your default, then click OK; the browser(s) selected as default opens and previews your page.

Figure 3-35
Specify
Browser
warning

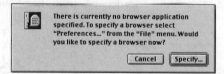

If you want to view the page in other browsers within your list besides the default, click and hold the small triangle to the right of the icon to bring up a popup menu with that list (see Figure 3-36).

The Show in Browser icon takes on the appearance of the browser icon selected as default (such as the Internet Explorer icon). If multiple browsers are selected, GoLive mixes them into an icon mélange.

Figure 3-36
Show in
Browser
buttons

If, like most of us, you're a bipolar Web designer who needs to check code in both Navigator and Internet Explorer, you can rest at ease and check multiple browsers as your default. When the Browser Switch button is clicked, your page opens in both Navigator and Explorer (each browser can have only one release of itself open at a time—i.e, you can't open a page in both Netscape version 4 and version 4.7).

For more on configuring browser sets, see the "Browser Sets" section of Chapter 4, *Preferences and Customizing.*

Adobe Online Button

To connect directly to the Adobe Web site to download GoLive updates as well as "tips, solutions, support, and more," click this button at the far right of every Toolbar. Click the Refresh button to connect, and click the Preferences button to configure your connection. The bookmark icon to the right of the URL field finds links to other useful Adobe pages.

Adobe Online preferences are also covered in Chapter 4, *Preferences and Customizing.*

Text Toolbar

If you work at all with creating or editing pages in GoLive, you see a lot of the Text toolbar. Through it, you can control both the way text looks and the way paragraphs with text and objects act (see Figure 3-37).

Placing your cursor within a paragraph (in HTML, that's all text within a P container tag) and choosing a header style from the popup menu formats

Figure 3-37
Text Toolbar

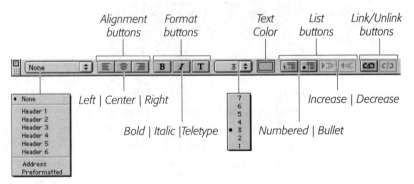

an entire paragraph as that style. Selecting Address adds italics to the paragraph, while selecting Preformatted formats the paragraph in a monospaced font and maintains spacing and line breaks (perfect for your collection of ASCII art). You can also select alignment (left, center, and right) and assign a list style (numbered or bulleted).

Selecting a word or range of text, you can assign basic formatting (bold, italic, and teletype), choose an absolute (1 through 7) or relative (–7 to –1 and +1 to +7) HTML text size, as well as add color. You can also designate a link (or take the link designation away).

For more information, see Chapter 8, *Text and Fonts*.

TIP:
Changing the Level

If you want to indent a paragraph or object without adding a list style, select Increase Block Indent from the Alignment submenu of the Type menu or contextual menu. Conversely, use Decrease Block Indent to reverse the indent.

Layout Grid Toolbar and Associated Palettes

If you add a layout grid to a page while in the Layout Editor, GoLive brings up the Layout Grid toolbar once the grid is selected. However, everything within the Toolbar is inactive until you add either a Layout Text Box or an object to the grid.

For example, place a layout grid onto a page, then drag an Image icon into the grid. The first two fields display its position within the grid structure (32 pixels from the left and 16 pixels from the top), while the second two fields display the object's dimensions (32 by 32 pixels). In addition to the Toolbar, this positioning information is also found in the Transform palette, where you can also check Constrain Proportions to make any dragged modification to the element proportional (see Figure 3-38).

Figure 3-38
Working with layout grids

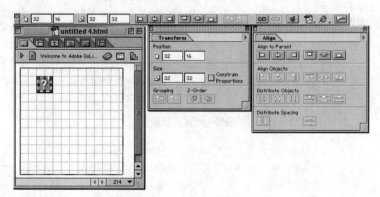

To move an object around the grid, either drag it or use the Toolbar's horizontal and vertical positioning buttons. In addition, you can move an object one grid square at a time by pressing your arrow keys. The positioning buttons are also found on the Align palette.

Add another item to the grid, select the two objects, and move them about as described above. The Group button becomes active in the Toolbar and the Transform palette (the objects default to ungrouped); clicking it makes GoLive collect the objects as one group. The total dimensions of the group appear in the height and width fields. This also brings up the Group Inspector, which allows you to choose to keep the contents of this group locked or unlocked. If you choose to lock the items, you can't configure the attributes of each object. However, by choosing unlocked, you can manipulate the group's items individually while still being able to move the group around the grid as one (see Figure 3-39).

Figure 3-39
Group
Inspector

— Locked

If you click the Ungroup button (or didn't click the Group button to begin with), the Align palette's Align Objects buttons become active. If you select three or more items (without grouping them), the Distribute Objects and Distribute Spacing buttons become active.

If you include an image with an image map in a layout grid, you can control the stacking order of the map sections using the Z-Order buttons in the Transform palette.

TIP:
Duplicity of
Redundant
Repetition

GoLive's duplicity shines through with the Layout Grid Toolbar and Align and Transform palettes. If you have added a floating box to your page, select it; notice that you can control positioning and alignment on the page for the floating box using these layout grid tools.

For details on using layout grids and the Transform and Align palettes, see Chapter 12, *Layout Grids*. For more on image maps, see Chapter 9, *Images*.

Image Map Toolbar

Speaking of image maps, if you've used GoLive 4 you might be a little confused as to where the Site Map tab of the Image Inspector went: it became its own Toolbar (see Figure 3-40). To create an image map and bring up the Image Map toolbar, check Use Map on the More tab of the Image Inspector.

Figure 3-40
Image Map
toolbar

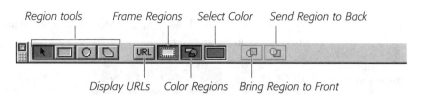

Region tools   Frame Regions   Select Color   Send Region to Back

Display URLs   Color Regions   Bring Region to Front

On the Toolbar, you find selection shapes, formatting buttons (to change region colors, add outline, and display URLs), and the Bring to Front/Send to Back buttons. Again, for much more on image maps, see Chapter 9, *Images*.

Region tools. To select an area of your image to map, click one of the Region tools (rectangle, circle, or polygon) and drag the shape to cover the desired area. Choosing the polygon tool allows you to click from point to point to create a shape within your image; if you later want to edit the points you've created, double-click the shape with the selection tool (the first button with the arrow pointer), then manipulate the points individually. Shift-click to select multiple map elements within an image.

Display region tools. The next four buttons control how an imagemap displays on a GoLive page. Clicking the Display URLs button toggles the display of the destination URL for each mapped area. Clicking the Frame Regions button turns on or off a border around each area. The Color Regions button toggles whether areas are filled with colors or not; you can drag a color swatch from the Color palette to the Color Select button to change that fill. If you have overlapping map regions, you can use the Bring Region to Front/Back buttons to determine their stacking order.

See the "Map Area Inspector" section in Chapter 2, *The Inspector*, for more on configuring links for individual regions.

Outline Editor Toolbar

In the Document window, clicking the Outline tab opens the HTML Outline Editor, which in turn brings up the Outline toolbar. The Outline toolbar isn't essential for working in the HTML Outline Editor (as you can drag in tag icons from the Palette), but it can be helpful.

From the Toolbar, you can add new tags and new attributes to existing tags, as well as add new containers for text and comments (see Figure 3-41). Click the New Generic Element button to add a non-HTML tag, such as those used for Active Server Pages (ASP), Extensible Markup Language (XML), or Standard Generalized Markup Language (SGML); the container tag's popup menu allows you to choose from these three options, as well as Unknown. The

Toggle Binary button allows you to select whether a tag stands on its own (unary) or requires an end tag (binary).

Figure 3-41
Outline toolbar

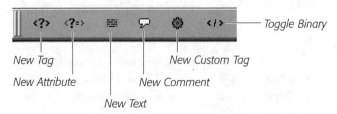

Toggle Binary

New Tag

New Custom Tag

New Attribute

New Comment

New Text

Site Toolbar

The Site toolbar allows you to do basic maintenance, like adding folders to and deleting items from your site, displaying Mac file information or Windows properties, and opening GoLive's Find dialog box (see Figure 3-42). You can refresh the site to show any files recently saved into the site folder by clicking the Update button (checkmark). You can also open the In & Out Links palette to view which files are linked to and referenced from a page, and change link references to a page by clicking the Change References button.

TIP: Contextual Shortcuts	GoLive provides many of the Site toolbar's controls at the click of a mouse via a contextual menu (right-clicking in Windows and Control-clicking on the Mac).

Figure 3-42
Site toolbar

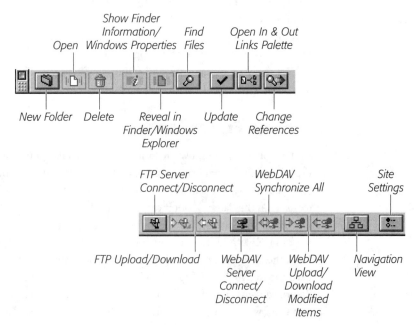

Show Finder
Information/   Find   Open In & Out
Open   Windows Properties   Files   Links Palette

New Folder   Delete   Reveal in   Update   Change
                        Finder/Windows   References
                        Explorer

FTP Server   WebDAV   Site
Connect/Disconnect   Synchronize All   Settings

FTP Upload/Download   WebDAV   WebDAV   Navigation
                      Server   Upload/   View
                      Connect/   Download
                      Disconnect   Modified
                                    Items

When you're ready to transfer files to your Web server, click the Site Settings button to enter your FTP information, then click the FTP Server Connect button to open up the FTP location. To upload your site from your hard drive, click the Incremental Upload button, or click Incremental Download if you've made changes on the server and need to update the files stored on your hard drive.

To use the new WebDAV feature, first enter your WebDAV server information in Site Settings, then click the WebDAV Server Connect button to hook up to the server. Once connected, you can synchronize your local files with those on the WebDAV server, and upload or download modified files.

Click the Navigation View button to open a graphical view of a site's navigational hierarchy (kind of like the In & Out Links palette on steroids).

For more information, see Chapter 19, *Site Management*.

Navigation View Toolbar

Since we're on the subject, once you open the Navigation View, the Toolbar changes slightly. The first six buttons remain, though the New Folder button remains inactive. The new buttons that follow allow you to add new blank pages when in the Navigation tab, including new Next and Previous pages and new Child and Parent pages (see Figure 3-43). These buttons are not active in the Links tab.

Figure 3-43
Navigation
View toolbar

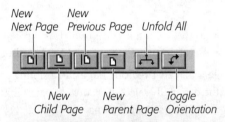

New Next Page *New Previous Page* *Unfold All*

New Child Page *New Parent Page* *Toggle Orientation*

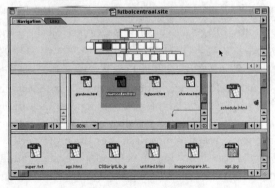

Select a parent page that leads to a group of child pages (indicated by a stacked file icon, as well as a plus sign below the icon), and then click the Unfold All button to open everything. To change from horizontal to vertical orientation, click the Toggle Orientation button.

For more information, see Chapter 19, *Site Management*.

TIP:
More Navigation Help

While in either tab of the Navigation View, you can control what you're seeing via the Site Navigator palette, in addition to the Panorama pane (which can be selected using the View Controller).

Design Toolbar

Opening a design window in the Designs tab brings up the Design toolbar, from which you can add pages to sections and make a design go live—that is, move the placeholder sections and pages into a real site document (see Figure 3-44).

Figure 3-44
Design toolbar

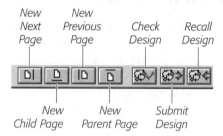

New Next Page   New Previous Page   Check Design   Recall Design

New Child Page   New Parent Page   Submit Design

To add new pages to a design section (which is typically the page at the top of a subsection hierarchy), click one of the New Page buttons:

• **New Next Page** and **New Previous Page** add a sibling page (a page at the same level of the originally selected section or page) that precedes or follows the current page or sequence of pages.

• **New Child Page** adds a page one level below the selected section or page.

• **New Parent Page** adds a parent page one level above the selected section or page. If the selected item already had a parent, the new parent page is inserted between the original parent and the selected item.

Each of the New Page buttons creates items that are linked both ways (from the original item to the new page, and to the original item from the new page) unless you change defaults via the Section or Page Inspector.

When you're ready to move a site design's prototyped sections and pages to a live site (or a subsection of an already live site), you first want to make sure that at least one of the design's pages is connected to an anchor page that's part of the current site (if any), as well as ensure that there no associated errors are present.

Open a design window to the Staging tab and click the Check Design button. If a checkmark appears in the Check column, no worries, mate. However, if you find any other icon or message in this column, you need to fix the error before submitting the design.

When you're ready to release a site or subsection design, click the Submit Design button to move pages from the Staging tab's Design Pages folder to the Live Pages folder. While that doesn't sound too momentous, the pages are also added to a previously designated target folder and appear as pages within the Files tab of the Site document.

<table>
<tr><td>TIP:
Preferred Target Folder</td><td>If no target folder is specified, the design's pages are placed into a generically named folder ("NewFiles" by default). To change the name of this folder for newly generated files, specify one in the Site section of Preferences (see Chapter 4, Preferences and Customizing, for details).</td></tr>
</table>

To undo this move into the live section of a Site document, click the Recall Design button. Pages that were placed into the target folder are removed (though the target folder, or default generated folder, remains), and pages return from the Live Pages folder to the Design Pages folder in the design window's Staging tab.

For much more on the Design feature, see Chapter 20, *Prototyping and Mapping*.

Web Settings Toolbar

Open Web Settings (Command-Shift-Y on the Mac or Control-Shift-Y under Windows) and click the HTML tab to bring up the Web Settings toolbar (see Figure 3-45). (An inactive Text toolbar appears when the Global tab is selected.) With nothing selected, you can click the New Section button to add another section folder or click the New Element button. Once you create a new tag or select a tag from the list, you can add new attributes to tags, and new values to attributes (using the New Enum button). You can also select a tag and copy it (using the Duplicate button), then go in and modify it.

Under the Characters tab, only the New Character (the ampersand icon) and Duplicate buttons are active—which is fine, since that's all you need. (The ToolTip for New Character reads New Enumeration, which is incorrect.)

For more information, see Chapter 31, *Web Settings*.

Figure 3-45
Web Settings
toolbar

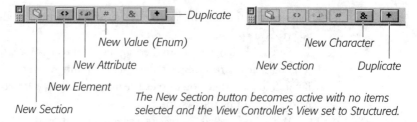

—Duplicate

New Value (Enum)

New Attribute

New Element

New Section

New Character

New Section   Duplicate

The New Section button becomes active with no items
selected and the View Controller's View set to Structured.

Style Sheet Toolbar

To add Cascading Style Sheets to a page, click the stairstepped icon in the
Document window's Layout Editor. The Style Sheet Editor opens, and the
Toolbar changes to the Style Sheet toolbar. This Toolbar also appears when
you open the CSS tab of Web Settings.

Through the Toolbar, you can add classes, tags, and IDs specific to an active
page, or link to an outside style sheet (see Figure 3-46).

Figure 3-46
Style Sheet
toolbar

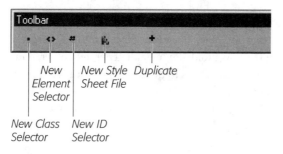

New   New Style   Duplicate
Element   Sheet File
Selector

New Class   New ID
Selector   Selector

You can't delete an item from the Style Sheet list via the Toolbar. To delete a
class, tag, or ID, select it then choose Clear (Mac) or Delete (Windows) from the
Edit Menu, or choose this option from the contextual menu.

See "Style Sheet Editor" later in this chapter for more details on adding
style sheets to a page. For more on configuring CSS in GoLive, see Chapter 29,
Cascading Style Sheets, and Chapter 31, *Web Settings*.

File Mappings Toolbar

Rounding out the Web Settings toolbar collection is the File Mappings toolbar
(see Figure 3-47). File Mappings is where you configure what applications
open specified file types when double-clicked in GoLive. However, this isn't

the most robust of toolbars—click the New Extension button to add a new Mime type, or select an existing Mime type and click the Duplicate button. The rest of the work is done via the File Info Extension Inspector (which is detailed in the Web Settings section of Chapter 2, *The Inspector*).

Figure 3-47
File Mappings
toolbar

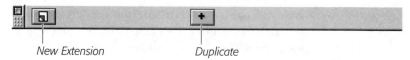

New Extension   *Duplicate*

QuickTime Toolbar

When you open a QuickTime file (by double-clicking the file in the Site window or double-clicking a plug-in icon where the file is placed within an individual page), the file is opened in the QuickTime Movie Viewer and its attending QuickTime toolbar appears (see Figure 3-48).

Figure 3-48
QuickTime
toolbar

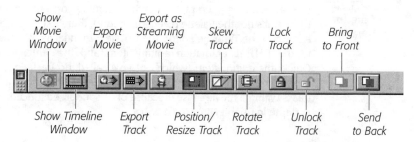

You can click the Export Movie and Export as Streaming Movie buttons to save the file into either of these formats. To edit individual tracks within a movie, click the Show Timeline Window button. A separate timeline editor opens up showing the tracks that currently make up the movie. Select an individual track and click the Export Track button to save only that track (such as just the sound from a movie).

Select a track and click the Bring to Front or Send to Back buttons to reposition it. To lock a track (to prevent it from being accidentally edited, perhaps), select it and click the Lock Track button, or click the Unlock Track button to release a track for editing. You can also resize, skew, and rotate individual tracks.

See Chapter 17, *Media*, for more on editing QuickTime movies, including various media tracks.

Advanced Feature Editors

Three of GoLive's advanced features—Cascading Style Sheets, Dynamic HTML (DHTML) animation, and JavaScript—are handled largely through three separate windows (with the help, of course, of several different Inspectors). The Style Sheets (CSS), Timeline (DHTML), and JavaScript Editors are accessed by clicking one of the three icons in the top-right corner of the Document window's Layout Editor, (see Figure 3-49).

Figure 3-49
Editor icons

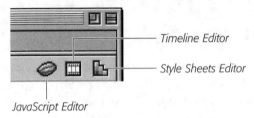

Timeline Editor

Style Sheets Editor

JavaScript Editor

TIP:
Time for
Timeline

Despite Adobe's attempts to get their naming conventions into better shape (notice, it's not the Palette palette anymore), there's still a bit of confusion hovering over the Timeline Editor. The GoLive 5 manual assigns the Timeline Editor to the DHTML animation editing item and the Timeline Window to the QuickTime editing item (which GoLive 4 called the Track Editor). For this book, we continue to refer to the QuickTime Timeline Editor (since it is indeed editing tracks within a movie). Also, because of its specialized functionality, it is covered in depth in Chapter 17, *Media*.

JavaScript Editor

To add a new piece of JavaScript to a page, drag a script tag icon in from the Objects palette to either the Head section or body of a page, type a name to identify it in the Name field of either the Head Script or Body Script Inspector, and then select the appropriate version of JavaScript from the Language popup menu. Clicking the Edit button opens the JavaScript Editor in a new window, which is where you type your script or add events and objects from the JavaScript Inspector (see Figure 3-50).

Alternatively, you can click the coffee bean JavaScript icon to open up the JavaScript Editor. If you open the editor by clicking the icon without first adding either a Head Script or Body Script tag icon to your page, you are met with a blank, inactive JavaScript Editor. To start a script, click the New Script Item button. By default, new scripts created this way are placed into the HTML Head section. If you did want to make sure your script was placed within the HTML Body section, be sure to drag in a JavaScript icon from the Objects palette.

Figure 3-50
JavaScript
Editor

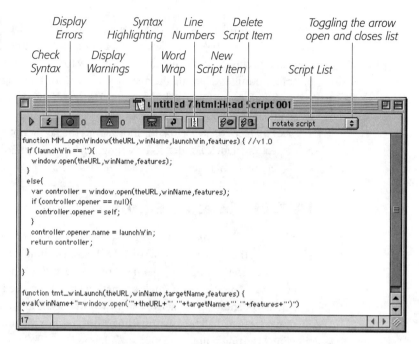

Move between different scripts in your page by clicking the Select Script menu and selecting an item. If you haven't labeled a script—using the Name field in either the Body Script or Head Script Inspectors—GoLive applies generic numeric names to your script, like Head Script 001, Body Script 001, and Body Script 002.

TIP:
Another
Opening

You can also open the JavaScript Editor by double-clicking either a Head Script or Body Script icon in the Layout Editor.

As with the Document window's HTML Source Editor, you can also configure the way GoLive displays code in the JavaScript Editor via the supplementary Toolbar found at the top of the editor. GoLive defaults to coloring different parts of JavaScript (such as keywords, symbols, and operators). To turn off the colors and just display black text, click the Syntax Highlighting button. If you have long lines of code that run off the right side of the Editor, click the Soft Wrap button to wrap lines within the boundary of the editor window. To add numbers to each line of code, click the Line Number button. You can specify the colors for parts of code in the JavaScript item in Preferences, as well as specify font, indent, and printing settings.

To check for errors and warnings of bad syntax within your code, click the Check Syntax button (the one with the lightning bolt), or press Command-K

(Mac) or Control-K (Windows). If errors exist in your script, the error log section is opened below the JavaScript Editor toolbar; this area can also be opened and closed by clicking the toggle arrow to the left of the Check Syntax button. A number denoting the quantity of errors or warnings appears to the right of their respective Toolbar buttons. However, no errors or warnings are listed unless those buttons are depressed.

See Chapter 26, *JavaScript*, for more about the JavaScript Editor and related Inspector palettes. For details on configuring JavaScript Editor preferences, see its section in Chapter 4, *Preferences and Customizing*.

DHTML Timeline Editor

To add DHTML animations to your page, you must first add a Floating Box placeholder, then place any kind of HTML content in it. Click the film strip icon in the top right of the Layout Editor to open the Timeline Editor (see Figure 3-51). This displays a single animation track (denoted by the number 1 and an arrow showing the active track) within a scene and a single keyframe (denoted by the small box surrounding a dot) within the track, placed at the timeline's starting point.

Figure 3-51
Opening the
DHTML
Timeline Editor

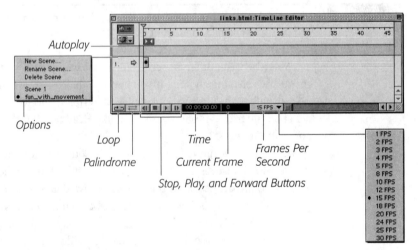

As you've probably picked up, the Timeline Editor uses the metaphor of a film-editing program for its various parts, which break down into three main parts:

- A track is one floating box, which can then be broken down into individual scenes. A page can have multiple floating boxes, and thus multiple tracks.

- You can assign multiple scenes to a track. Each scene's animation is dependent upon hitting certain points on a page at specific lengths of time; these are called keyframes.

- A keyframe is one point within the timeline of a track's scene, which denotes a change in property for the floating box (such as a directional change or stacking order).

To add an animated sequence to your page, it's easiest to go back to the floating box in the Layout Editor and drag to the desired points on the page. First, select the floating box, which isn't as easy as you think. The grabber hand is turned sideways to denote that you're selecting the floating box. Next, click the Record button in the Floating Box Inspector. Go back to the Layout Editor, grab the floating box, and drag it to a new location. To add another movement on the page, return to the Floating Box Inspector and repeat the previous steps, clicking Record before each movement.

The points at which you stopped along the path are marked by squares; these correspond to the keyframes that have been added to the track for that floating box in the Timeline Editor (see Figure 3-52).

Figure 3-52
Relationship between Layout and Timeline editors

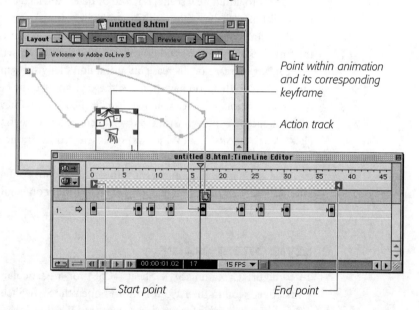

Point within animation and its corresponding keyframe

Action track

Start point

End point

At the bottom of the Timeline Editor, you can click the Play button to display your animation. You can also view it one frame at a time by clicking the Backward and Forward buttons. Your position in the timeline, viewed at the top of the editor, is displayed in two ways to the right of these buttons: in time format broken down by hours, minutes, seconds, and frames; and in total number of frames. To change the number of frames played each second, select from the range in the Frame Speed popup menu.

To keep your animation playing as long as a page is being viewed, click the Loop button; click the Palindrome button if you want the animation to reverse itself once it reaches the end of its cycle. (For Palindrome to work, you must first click Loop.)

Clicking the Autoplay button, which is on by default, begins the animation as soon as the page is loaded into a browser. However, if this is turned off, the animation can't begin unless an Action is assigned to start it.

To add an Action, Command-click (Mac) or Control-click (Windows) in the Action Track—the gray track line directly above the editor's first track—to position an Action placeholder at that point (a question mark icon appears as you position your mouse). Use the menu in the Action Inspector to select an appropriate Action and configure its attributes. You can also place Actions to trigger at any point within an animation.

Clicking the Options button below Autoplay displays a popup menu that allows you to add a new scene, rename or delete a selected scene, and select from a list of available scenes within a track.

The total length of animation is displayed in the area immediately below the timeline by a yellow band bounded by two red boxes with inset arrows. You cannot increase or decrease an animation's length by moving either of these points. Rather, you have to move the keyframes at the beginning or end of an animation, or create a new keyframe. Command-click (Mac) or Control-click (Windows) within a track to create a new keyframe, or Option-click (Mac) or Alt-click (Windows) on a selected keyframe and release the mouse at a new point to copy the original item.

See Chapter 27, *Animation*, for information about configuring DHTML animations. See Chapter 14, *Floating Boxes*, for more on configuring individual floating boxes.

Style Sheet Editor

To configure Cascading Style Sheets (CSS) for a particular page, click the stairstepped icon in the Layout Editor to open the Style Sheet Editor. This is only a collection point for the classes, tags, and IDs that you add to your page. The real work is performed through the Style Sheet toolbar, covered earlier in this chapter, which allows you to add items to the Style Sheet Editor; and the CSS Selector Inspector, which allows you to configure individual styles (see Figure 3-53).

Figure 3-53
Style Sheet
Editor

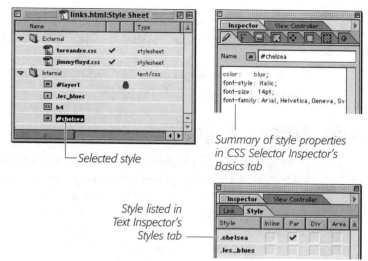

Selected style

Summary of style properties
in CSS Selector Inspector's
Basics tab

Style listed in
Text Inspector's
Styles tab

After determining the type of style you want to configure for your page, click the New Tag, New Class, or New ID button in the Style Sheet toolbar. A new item is placed under a folder named "Internal" and the CSS Selector Inspector appears. You can give your style a name in the Name field of the Basics tab, then configure your style using the other tabs.

You can reference style definitions that you've created and collected in a standalone style sheet file. Click the New Style Sheet File button; a folder named "External" is created and holds a placeholder file icon that references the external style sheet. Select the file icon, then navigate to your desired file using the External Style Sheet Inspector.

The file's location is listed under the Info column in the Style Sheet Editor's External folder, while its status—good links indicated by a checkmark, broken links by a stop sign—is listed in the column to the immediate right of the Name column. If you have a page that references several external style sheets, you can change the order in which they take precedence by selecting a file and moving it up or down the list by clicking one of the two Priority arrow buttons on the External Style Sheet Inspector (see Figure 3-54).

Figure 3-54
Selecting
external
style sheet

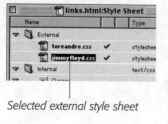

Selected external style sheet

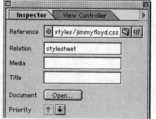

Move style
sheets up
or down in
the list using
the Move
buttons.

To edit these styles, open this external file by either double-clicking the file icon or selecting a file and clicking the Open button in the External Style Sheet Inspector.

For more information, see Chapter 29, *Cascading Style Sheets*. Also see the CSS section of Chapter 2, *The Inspector*.

Putting Pieces Together

GoLive's drag-and-drop approach makes it easy to construct sites from individual parts stored in palettes. This organization, combined with the WYSIWYG nature of the program, allows you to quickly create an enormous amount of sophisticated content—or just place text and images on a page and rapidly format them.

In the next chapter, we tell you how to take all that you've learned up to now and set it to your liking: tweak all the preferences that GoLive provides in order to really maximize your use of the program and get a display that meets your needs.

CHAPTER 4

Preferences and Customizing

So you're humming along—building pages, developing your site, and publishing to the Web—and you're getting the hang of working with your new friend, GoLive. You could continue along this way quite nicely, but perhaps it's time to make a larger commitment to this relationship and deepen the communication and understanding between the two of you—using preferences.

Perhaps this is stretching the relationship metaphor a bit far, but the configurations you set in GoLive's preferences help you work more effectively with GoLive and, in turn, make GoLive that much more efficient in meeting your needs. Within the Preferences dialog, GoLive provides you a range of customizing options, from basic interface to usage of GoLive modules to designating network proxy servers.

This chapter covers each section within the Preferences dialog, as well as the Site settings, and global HTML formatting options found in Web Settings (which duplicates GoLive 4.0's Web Database in just about everything but its name). Additionally, we introduce two items new to GoLive 5.0: specifying your own keyboard shortcuts and linking up with Adobe's Web site to download GoLive updates.

Preferences Basics

To get to Preferences, press Command-Y (Mac) or Control-Y (Windows), or select Preferences from the Edit menu. Preferences displays a list of panes for each major setting area on the left side of the window. Those with a toggle triangle (Mac) or plus sign (Windows) to their left have additional preference sections. To reveal and hide those items, simply click the triangle or plus/minus signs.

TIP:
Panes and
Arrows

You can use the up and down arrow keys to navigate through the menu on the left side. To open or close an item that has other items below it (such as General), press Command-right/left arrow on the Mac, or just the right/left arrow on Windows. You can press a letter key (such as B) to go to an item starting with that letter, but in our experience it can be a little persnickety about highlighting the correct entry.

On the Mac, your preference settings are written to a file named "Adobe GoLive 5.0 Prefs" and placed in the System Folder's Preferences folder. In Windows, the preferences file (PrefFile.prf) is placed in the GoLive application folder (which in turn is buried in the Windows folder).

NEW IN 5:
Automatic
Preferences
Update

When updating to version 5 from version 4, GoLive reads the previous version's preference file: "Cyberstudio Preferences" on the Mac, and "PrefFile.prf" on Windows. GoLive writes a new version 5 preferences file based on these old values.

TIP:
Keeping
Preferences
When
Quitting

Although GoLive 4 didn't save preferences changes until you quit out of the program, GoLive 5 updates the preferences file as soon as you click OK in Preferences as well as when you quit. So if, for some "unlikely" reason, GoLive up and quits on you (i.e., crashes) or you perform a forced quit (Command-Option-Escape on the Mac or Control-Alt-Delete under Windows), your preferences should be safe.

TIP:
Swapping
Prefs

If you're sharing GoLive with someone who requires different settings (such as for networking) or you just have distinct ways of working, you can easily swap in and out each other's customized preference files. Set up a workflow system with your GoLive partner where, after quitting the application, you drag the preference file out of its system-designated home to a special user folder. Whoever opens GoLive next either gets the default settings or can drag in his or her own customized preference file before opening the program.

TIP:
Delete
Preferences
for Clean Start

If you are having problems with GoLive crashing, or if you just want to start from scratch, quit GoLive and delete the preferences file. When you start GoLive again, your preferences are restored to the program's default settings.

General Preferences

When you open Preferences for the first time, GoLive deposits you at the top in the General pane, which sets a variety of standard program behaviors.

When you launch the program, GoLive defaults to opening a blank, new document. If you want to change this, from the At Launch popup menu select either Show Open Dialog (allowing you to navigate to a file automatically) or Do Nothing (opening no document windows, but displaying your previous set of open palettes).

If you want the Document window to open in a mode other than the Layout Editor (such as the Outline Editor), select the desired item in the Default Mode popup menu (see Figure 4-1).

Figure 4-1
General
Settings

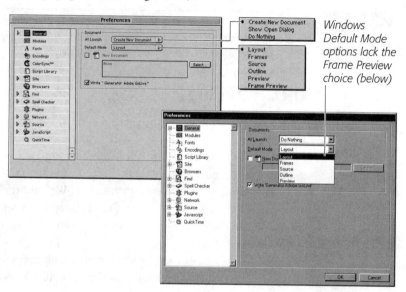

Windows Default Mode options lack the Frame Preview choice (below)

To open a specific file each time you create a new HTML document in GoLive (by selecting New from the File menu), check the New Document box, then click the Select button and navigate to the desired file. If you uncheck this option later, then decide that wasn't such a good idea, GoLive retains the location of the file as an inactive entry in the file field.

TIP:
Use
Stationery

If you work with a specific design structure for new pages in your site, designate a Stationery file as your default new file. See Chapter 21, *Files, Folders, and Links*, for more on Stationery files.

GoLive also defaults to inserting a Meta tag into a page's Head section that tells the world GoLive 5 created the page; here's the code:

```
<meta name="generator" content="Adobe GoLive 5">
```

If you don't want to add this to your page, simply uncheck Write "Generator Adobe GoLive".

There's no particular reason to tell the world or not tell the world that you're using GoLive 5 to edit your pages. It's a marketing message for Adobe, in particular; or, a point of pride for you if you think it's neat to share the editor you use.

Reveal the other General preference items by clicking the triangle (Mac) or the plus sign (Windows) to the left of the General pane.

The order and inclusion of General preference items have changed with GoLive 5: file mapping preferences have been moved to Web Settings while the Mac-only Cache settings have been dropped altogether.

URL Handling

Click URL Handling under the General pane to configure a couple of basic URLisms.

Select the Check URLs Case Sensitive option to allow GoLive to treat internal URLs as if capitalization counts. On Unix and under Windows, two files named identically with different capitalization (like "ags.html" and "Ags.html") are treated the same; however, on the Mac, capitalization is retained, but the Macintosh can't distinguish between two identically named files with different case.

If you want GoLive to add "mailto" automatically in front of email addresses typed in a URL field, check Auto Add "mailto:" to Addresses.

Be sure to select this option, as it's best to always have mailto in front of an address; there's no reason we can think of not to, and this option saves a step in typing.

To change all links to absolute URLs (in reference to the base URL of the site) rather than relative (which uses the current site's root location as the reference point), check Make New Links Absolute. (See Chapter 21, *Files, Folders, and Links*, for how to find, change, or use the root location of a site.)

Checking Cut URLs After This [sic] Characters (a grammatical whoops still not corrected from GoLive 4) allows you to trim the way that URLs with arguments attached to them are displayed. A URL can include information that gets passed to a server, generally after a question mark to mark the start of the data part of the URL; GoLive distinguishes URLs from one another by the entire URL unless you check this box.

The URL Filter area allows you to set patterns, like file extensions or directory paths, that GoLive treats as special files; these are ignored when the program creates a list of missing linked files and other errors. The filter allows you to keep GoLive from wanting to find CGI scripts, for instance, that aren't stored on your local hard drive; we typically add /cgi-bin/ to the list.

To change which files GoLive considers to be missing, click the New button and type a file extension or directory pattern (like .pdf or /pdfs/) in the URL Filter text field. Any file or folder that matches this pattern has its own icon replaced with a gear icon to indicate that it's a special file (see Figure 4-2).

Figure 4-2
URL Handling
settings

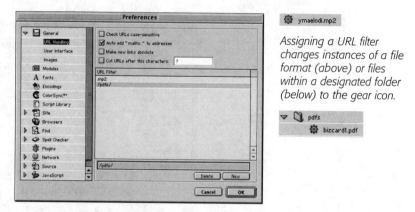

Assigning a URL filter changes instances of a file format (above) or files within a designated folder (below) to the gear icon.

After you make changes to some of these items and click OK, GoLive brings up a dialog which asks whether you want to update your site to reflect the changes you've made. Clicking OK to that prompt causes GoLive to revise your currently open site to reflect the new settings (see Figure 4-3).

Figure 4-3
Updating site
to reflect
changes to
URL Handling

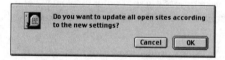

User Interface

Click the User Interface settings under the General pane to configure how link warnings and resize buttons on images are shown. (Most of this information was formerly collected in the GoLive 4 Display settings.)

At the top of the options list, Mac users encounter two items that don't exist on the PC, which only support Mac OS 8.5 and later. Checking Appearance Theme Savvy enables Golive's support for the Appearance Manager, while checking Use Navigation Services enables Navigation Services in Open and Save dialog boxes (see Figure 4-4).

Figure 4-4
User Interface
settings

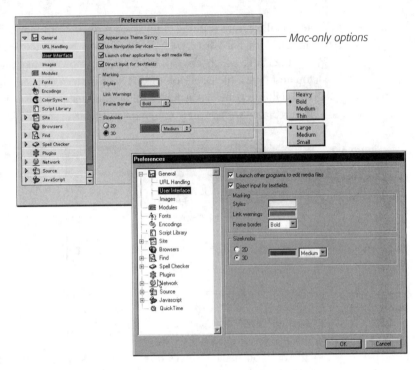

Mac-only options

TIP:
Turn Off
Navigation
Services

We have to applaud Apple for updating its old Open and Save dialog boxes by re-placing them with Navigation Services (which offers more options and control over files). However, in our experience, Navigation Services is glacially slow. In this case, we're happy to forsake new features in order to avoid waiting a few seconds each time we need to open or save a file. We recommend keeping this box unchecked.

Check Launch Other Applications/Programs to Edit Media Files to auto-matically open the parent media application when double-clicking the item in a GoLive page or site document (such as opening RealPlayer to access a RealAudio file).

Checking Direct Input for Text Fields causes GoLive to apply a value to an Inspector text field as soon as you move away from it, such as simply clicking outside of it.

NEW IN 5:
Direct Field
Input

For you GoLive 4 veterans, Direct Input for Text Fields is quite a welcome change from having to press the Tab or Return/Enter key, or to click the carriage return icon. If you really do miss having to accept every modification, uncheck this op-tion to bring back the carriage return icon...most of the time. GoLive still isn't fully consistent, and you still find some text fields (such as on the Text Inspector) that don't heed this preference and allow a deselected field to accept edits.

Under Marking, click the color field to the right of either Styles or Link Warnings to bring up the Color Picker (Mac) or the Color dialog box (Windows) to choose a new color. The Link Warnings color is displayed when Show Link Warnings is checked in the Layout View Controller and broken links are discovered in a page. The Styles color is displayed when you select an item from either the Mark Style or Mark Tag popup menu in the same Controller. In the Frame Border popup menu, select a weight for the line that surrounds the style, tag, or broken link (see Figure 4-5).

Figure 4-5
Marking examples

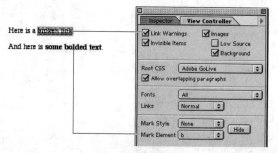

Under Sizeknobs, you can choose how resize handles are displayed; they appear at the bottom, corner, and right side of HTML objects. Select a size from the popup menu, a color using the Color Picker or Color dialog box, and choose between 2D and 3D buttons.

See Appendix A, *Macintosh Issues and Extras,* for details on GoLive's support for Appearance Themes and Navigation Services.

Images

Click Images to set GoLive's image drag and drop support and low-source image creation preferences (see Figure 4-6).

Figure 4-6
Image settings

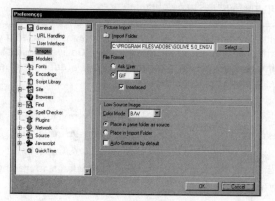

Dragging images. A great way to quickly create design comps is to drag an image from an open file (such as in Photoshop) or from a page in a Web browser and drop it into an open GoLive page. GoLive displays the Save for Web dialog, giving you the ability to control the image's compression settings of saving it as a GIF, JPEG, or PNG formatted file (see Figure 4-7). For more on the Save for Web options, see Chapter 9, *Images*.

Figure 4-7
Save for Web
dialog

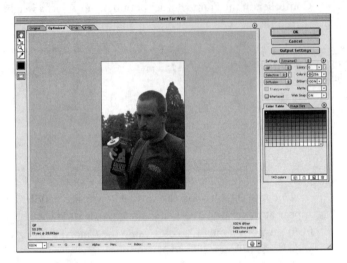

<table>
<tr><td>

TIP:
Disabling
Save for
Web

</td><td>

So, if GoLive uses Save for Web to handle incoming images, why are the Picture Import settings still in GoLive 5's preferences at all? Although Save for Web is now the default method of handling incoming image files, the Picture Import functionality is still built in to the program. And it can be useful too: if you're building lots of comps on the fly, Save for Web can be a speed bump to your productivity. Letting GoLive create temporary files of images you're not going to keep anyway is much faster. To disable Save for Web, turn off the Smart Links option in the Modules pane of Preferences.

</td></tr>
<tr><td>

TIP:
Temp Images
with Save for
Web Active

</td><td>

Even with Save for Web active, temporary images are used if you're adding an image that's less than 8-bit. Unfortunately, GoLive doesn't let you drag in a CMYK image (you get an error message) or a duotone (the dragged image becomes a plug-in placeholder).

</td></tr>
</table>

If the Save for Web option is disabled, the image preview GoLive creates is saved as a temporary browser-compatible image file (with a generic numerical name, such as image7106732.jpg). Under Picture Import, you can select a folder where these collected images reside. GoLive defaults to placing these images in the Import Images folder.

TIP:
Temporary
Image
Storage
(Windows)

Dragging images from Internet Explorer into a GoLive document does not place a temporary image file into the Import Images folder. Rather, GoLive references the image found in the Windows folder's Temporary Internet Files folder. To import an image into GoLive's Import Images folder successfully, right-click on the browser image and select Copy from the contextual menu. Then return to the GoLive document, right-click at your desired insertion point, and select Paste.

Also, you can't just drag a linked image from IE, and it seems rather impossible to drag any image from Navigator. For both of these instances, you must use the copy and paste method.

Under File Format, select the browser-compatible file format to use when saving dragged and dropped images—GIF, JPEG, or PNG.

TIP:
Disabling
PNG

If you don't use PNG image files, you can turn support for them off in the Modules section, discussed later.

With GIF and PNG, you can check Interlaced, which creates the image file in a manner that allows rendering to start immediately when the browser receives the first data representing the image, and gradually improves its resolution as the entire file is delivered. This option increases the file's size slightly. With JPEG, you can check Progressive (which acts like Interlaced), as well as your desired compression level from the popup menu. On the Mac, you can also check Use QuickTime, which uses QuickTime's JPEG encoding algorithm instead of Adobe's (see Figure 4-8).

Figure 4-8
JPEG and PNG
file format
options

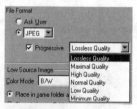

JPEG options

PNG options

If you check the Ask User option, you are met with an Import Image dialog box, which allows you to navigate to a desired directory folder and choose the format of the file. This is handy, as it allows you to give the file a coherent name (instead of something like "image-1276465113.jpg"); however it does take away a bit of control over the formatting of the file. For instance, if you choose JPEG, GoLive automatically saves the file as a progressive JPEG, and you don't know which level of compression is selected. In addition, this import/save dialog doesn't contain the nifty GoLive Save button that lets you choose to go directly to either the site's Root, Stationeries, or Components folders (see Figure 4-9).

Figure 4-9
Image file
saving options

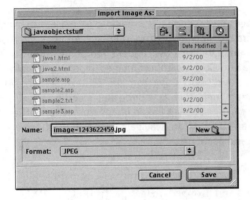

Low-resolution images. If you want to generate low-source versions of images placed into GoLive pages, you can choose to store those either in the same folder as the original image or into the folder designated as the Picture Import location. Choose B/W (black and white) or Color from the popup menu. If you want GoLive to generate these low-resolution images automatically, check that option. Remember you can also create low-source images via the Image Inspector Basic tab (See Figure 4-10).

Figure 4-10
Generating
low-source
images

GoLive Modules

You can control several aspects of GoLive's functionality via the Modules pane. You can turn modules on and off to increase responsiveness and memory requirements for GoLive. If you make a change to the Modules list in Preferences, you must quit and then restart GoLive to make the changes take effect.

Say, for instance, you decide you can do without the Document window's Outline Editor, as you really only use the Layout and HTML Source Editors to build your pages. Click the Modules pane, scroll down the list, and select the Outline Mode module. To learn more about it, click the Show Item Information toggle triangle below the list. This reveals the size of the module, as well as its version number and when it was last modified. You can also read a brief description of what the module does in the text box to the right.

If, after digesting this information, you decide you really want to do away with the HTML Outline Editor, uncheck Outline Mode in the list; GoLive then reminds you that you must quit the program and restart it for this action to take effect (see Figure 4-11).

Figure 4-11
Module
settings

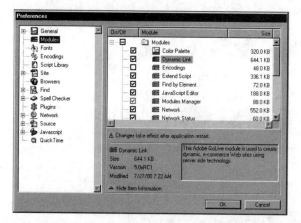

Color Palette. Displays GoLive's integrated Color Palette and allows for dragging and dropping color swatches. If unchecked, the Color Palette isn't available and you have to rely on the Color Picker (Mac) or the Colors dialog box (Windows) for choosing colors.

Download Page (Mac). Allows you to download the entire contents of a Web page, including embedded images and style sheets. If unchecked, the Web Download option is removed from the Mac's File menu. For details on this feature, see Chapter 18, *Page Specials*.

Dynamic Link. Checking this item allows you to use server-side actions to create dynamic pages on the fly; it also adds a set of Dynamic Link preferences.

Encodings. Accesses a plethora of international text encodings, from Japanese to Chinese (Traditional and Simplified) to Greek to Devanagari. This option is off by default.

Extend Script. Enables the customization of GoLive via JavaScript using a Software Developer's Kit (SDK). You can actually add dialog boxes, tabs in the Objects palette, and other controls.

Find by Content (Mac). Activates Apple Information Access Toolkit (AIAT), which gives you the ability to simulate Internet search engine queries. This module is turned off by default. Checking this option adds the Content tab to the Find dialog and allows you to find all instances of a word or phrase within a site's pages for index-based search capability of an entire Web site (see Figure 4-12). See Appendix A, *Macintosh Issues and Extras* for more details.

Figure 4-12
Find by
Content
searching

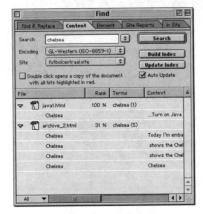

Find by Element. Adds the Element tab to the Find dialog, which enables you to search for specific tags and attributes.

JavaScript Editor (Windows). Allows Windows users to work with JavaScript and access the JavaScript Editor. If this is unchecked, the JavaScript Editor coffee bean icon doesn't appear in the Layout Editor.

Modules Manager. In theory this would allow you to enable or disable GoLive's collection of modules. However, since it is checked by default and appears in the module list as inactive, you can't turn it off. But you can still admire it, nonetheless.

Network. Used to support a File Transfer Protocol (FTP) connection. If unchecked, the FTP tab in the Site window's Extras tab isn't available, and all FTP fields in the Site Settings dialog (accessed via the Site toolbar) are inactive.

Network Status. Helps you troubleshoot network problems through the display of FTP and WebDAV log information.

Open Recent Files (Mac). Provides access to documents (pages, site documents, and media files) most recently opened. If unchecked, the Open Recent menu item doesn't appear in the Mac's File menu.

Outline Mode. Allows you to view and edit HTML source code in the HTML Outline Editor's graphical format. If unchecked, the HTML Outline Editor tab isn't available.

PNG Image Format. Allows you to use images saved in the Portable Network Graphics (PNG) format. If this is unchecked and you try to bring a PNG image into a page, you receive either a broken image icon under Windows or an unsupported image icon on the Mac. In addition, you aren't given the choice to save imported images in PNG format.

Preview Mode. Allows you to preview the layout of pages and frame sets. If unchecked, the Document window's Layout Preview tab is not available (nor is the Frame Preview tab on the Mac).

QuickTime Module (Mac) or QuickTime (Windows). Activates GoLive's QuickTime editing features (such as the Movie Viewer and Timeline Editor).

Site Design. Activates GoLive 5's Design tab in the Site document, which enables you to prototype new pages or structures in a site or map existing pages by navigation hierarchy or links.

Site Module (Mac) or Site (Windows). Manages Web sites via the GoLive site file, including all links, images, external URLs, colors, font sets, etc. If unchecked, GoLive doesn't allow you to create or open site documents.

Smart Links. Enables you to synchronize original Photoshop, Illustrator, and LiveMotion image files (TIFF, EPS, PSD, etc.) with their Web-friendly cousins (GIF, PNG, JPEG). Adds the Smart Photoshop item to the Objects palette's Smart tab, and activates the Save for Web feature for images that are dragged into GoLive.

Smart Objects. Activates the DHTML/Javascript items in the Objects palette's Smart tab (such as Rollover and URL Popup).

Spell Checker. Allows you to check spelling within an individual document or an entire site. If unchecked, the Check Spelling option is removed from the Edit menu.

SWF Module (Mac), SWF (Windows). Manages links embedded within Shockwave/Flash files.

WebDAV. Allows you to connect to and exchange files with WebDAV servers.

WebObjects. Used for designing components based on Apple's WebObjects technology. If checked, a WebObjects Declaration tab is added to the Document window, as is a WebObjects tab in the Palette (see Figure 4-13). This is turned off by default.

Figure 4-13
WebObjects

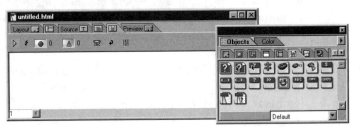

WebObjects tab in Document window   WebObjects tab in Objects palette

Languages and Fonts

If you're working with non-English Web page content, you can set default display fonts and preferences for different language character sets in the Encodings pane.

Fonts

In the Fonts pane, you can set the default font that GoLive uses to display text within your documents. Remember that these are not font set preferences, which determine how your audience views your published Web pages; these are interior GoLive-specific font designations.

Click a toggle triangle (Mac) or plus sign (Windows) to the left of a language group to reveal the types of fonts you can set (Proportional, Monospaced, Serif, Sans Serif, Cursive, and Fantasy). Click a font selection to activate the Font popup menu at the bottom of the window, then choose from the list of available system fonts and point sizes using the Font and Size popup menus. On the Mac, GoLive also provides a preview pane when you click the Font Sample toggle triangle (see Figure 4-14).

Figure 4-14
Font settings

Click OK to return to a Document window. Content that is typed as GoLive's Default Font is then displayed using the font you chose.

Encodings

If you leave the Encodings module turned off, you only see the GL-Western encodings (for ISO-8859-1 and X-MAC-ROMAN). However, with the Encodings module turned on, you see the full range of non-Roman-alphabet character from outside this Western European group, and are able to add those characters to your GoLive pages.

In the Encodings pane, go through the list and select all language encodings you want to make available to GoLive (see Figure 4-15).

You can select all encoding subsets for a group (revealed by clicking the group's toggle triangle or plus sign) by checking the group.

TIP:
**Showing
Encoding
Subsets**

If you uncheck certain subsets within a group, GoLive on the Mac denotes that not all subsets are checked by displaying a dash in the group checkbox. Windows, however, doesn't display this dash, so you could be tricked into thinking the entire list of subsets are unchecked.

Figure 4-15
Encoding
settings

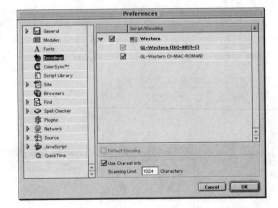

The Use Charset Info option is checked by default, which tells GoLive to place character set information in the Head section's Meta content tag. If this is unchecked, the Scanning Limit # Characters field becomes inactive; the value in this field tells GoLive how many bytes to search to find encoding and character set information when it opens. To make an encoding subset your default, select it from the list and check Default Encoding; it is then displayed in the list in bold. The selected default encoding used when a file was created appears in the File Inspector's page tab (see Figure 4-16).

Figure 4-16
Viewing
encoding via
File Inspector

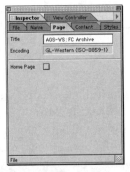

ColorSync (Mac Only)

On the Mac, you can use Apple's ColorSync color management system (CMS) to display colors within images consistently. This can be done either globally (for all images within GoLive via Preferences), regionally (for all images on a single page via the Page Inspector), or locally (for an individual image via the Image Inspector).

Under ColorSync in Preferences, GoLive defaults to selecting ColorSync as your global CMS. With Display Images Using ColorSync checked, you can also check Use Default RGB Profile If Not Specified, which then uses a color profile built into GoLive when ColorSync is activated but no RGB profile is specified. If Display Images Using ColorSync is unchecked, the Use Default RGB Profile becomes inactive (see Figure 4-17).

For more information, see Chapter 9, *Images*.

Figure 4-17
ColorSync
settings

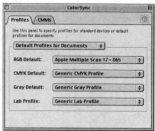

ColorSync control panel

Global ColorSync settings in Preferences

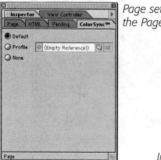

Page settings in
the Page Inspector

Single image
settings in the
Image Inspector

Script Library

When you bring DHTML or JavaScript objects into a page from the Objects palette's Smart tab, GoLive writes the JavaScript for the object in the page's source code by default. If you want to handle code in this way, keep the Write Code in Page option selected in the LiveObjects pane. But if you use components in your pages, you need to choose Import GoLive Script Library to write the code for all Actions and other JavaScript features into a script library named CSScriptLib.js; it places a reference to this common file in the Head section of each new page.

If you have a site document open, GoLive creates this library file in a new folder at the root level of the site in a folder called GeneratedItems. You can modify both the folder and file names in the Folder for Script Library and Name of Script Library respectively.

Selecting Import GoLive Script Library only shifts this code to the library file for new pages. To move code from existing pages with dynamic components to the library file, you must go into an individual page, open the Page Inspector to the HTML tab, check the Import CSS Library radio button, then save the page (see Figure 4-18). Clicking the Rebuild button doesn't perform this task, as you might expect. Instead, Rebuild is used whenever you change the Actions you have loaded into GoLive; clicking the button rebuilds the library file to reflect the new set of Actions.

For more information, see Chapter 26, *JavaScript* and Chapter 28, *Actions*.

Figure 4-18
Script Library
settings

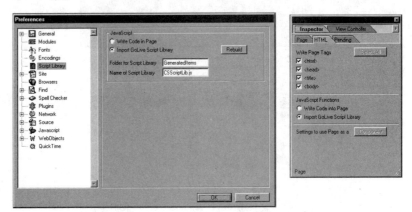

Making the change for new pages in Preferences (left) and for existing pages in the Page Inspector (right)

Site

The Site pane allows you to configure how GoLive's site management features work, from folder names and the way files are deleted to defining page status and export parameters.

Selecting Site itself allows you to configure the following (see Figure 4-19):

• Reparse Only Modified Files works in conjunction with site documents. If this is checked when you open a Site window or when you select Reparse from the Site menu, GoLive verifies only those references that were modified since the last check.

Figure 4-19
Site settings

- Reparse Files on Harddisk Rescan forces GoLive to perform a full reparse (opening and checking all HTML in all files in a site) whenever Rescan is selected from the Site menu.

- Create URL Mapping for Shortcut to Folder allows you to build a one-to-one relationship between any aliases or shortcuts in the site folder and other sites. This allows you to create manageable links between several sites, each of which has its own site file and folder, but all of which exist on local hard drives or volumes.

- Ask Before Deleting Objects forces GoLive to prompt you before you delete objects off a page using Clear from the Edit or contextual menu, or the Delete key.

- Spring-Loaded Folders allows you to open a closed site folder and display its contents when dragging a Point & Shoot lasso, links, or files on top of the desired folder for a few seconds. If this is unchecked, you can hold the Point & Shoot lasso over a folder, but it only expands the contents below the folder.

- Display Full Path shows the full directory path of an opened folder at the top of the Site window's left- and right-hand panes (such as in the Files and FTP), as well as a popup menu showing the path. Click the popup menu and select a directory with the site's root folder to open that directory (see Figure 4-20).

Figure 4-20
Display
Full Path

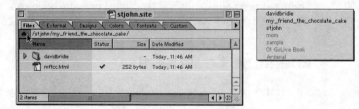

- Automatic Backup of Site File automatically creates a copy of your site file when you first open it up (adding the word "Backup" to the file name). This file reflects the state of the site document at your last save; if you manually save your site file (or close the site file, which automatically saves it), the backup file is updated with the information from the previous save. You probably won't notice this file if you don't crash; the file disappears when a site file is successfully closed, but is there waiting for you should something go kerflooey.

The Names for New Items area brings in options found in GoLive 4's Folder Names preference section, allowing you to specify basic file and directory information for your site. Here you can enter a custom HTML suffix in the File Extension field (for instance, choosing .htm instead of .html) and type a name for your default home page (welcome.htm instead of index.html) in the Home Page Name field.

The option for Folder for Generated Items allows you to name a default folder in the root level of your site into which empty pages are placed when not otherwise directed. For instance, if you add pages to a design in the Design tab and don't use an anchor to link them into the existing site, selecting Submit Design copies the files into your default generated items folder. GoLive offers no automatic default, but if nothing is selected a folder titled "NewItems" is added. If you return to Preferences, you notice that the name "NewFiles" is added to the Folder for Generated Items field, yet subsequent new folders that get created ignore "NewFiles" and continue to be named "NewItems".

Under the When Removing Files section, you can choose to move files to GoLive's site trash (which saves the files within the site data folder) or move deleted files directly to Trash (Mac) or the Recycle Bin (Windows). If Show Warning is checked, you receive a gentle reminder about the action you're about to perform.

For more information, see Chapter 19, *Site Management*, and Chapter 21, *Files, Folders, and Links*.

TIP:
Deleting Files

To delete files, select a file or range of files (by shift-clicking), then click the Delete button on the Site toolbar. You can also use the contextual menu by Control-clicking and choosing Clear (Mac) or right-clicking and choosing Delete (Windows). On the Mac, you can also select a file and press Command-Delete.

Filename Constraints

This section sets preferences for your site's file naming convention based on what type of Web server your files are living on (see Figure 4-21). Choose your desired convention from the Selected Constraints popup menu; the fields below change to reflect the constraint's specifics: name, a brief description, maximum character length, required length for extensions (if any), and character parameters in the Regular Expression field.

Figure 4-21
Filename
Constraints
settings

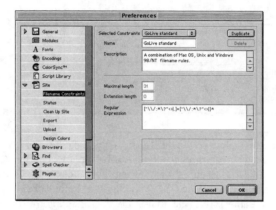

GoLive defaults to its standard set, which is a mix of Mac, Windows, and Unix rules that combine for maximum flexibility. You can also choose GoLive Strict (which allows a mix of small and capital letters, numerals, period, dash, and underscore) or GoLive lower case, which disallows upper case letters.

You can choose a specific server constraint from among Mac OS, Unix, Windows 98/NT, and DOS/Windows 3.1. Additionally, you can create your own file naming convention. Select a constraint from the list, then click the Duplicate button; this allows the fields to become editable so you can specifiy your server's parameters.

Status

You can add another layer of identification to the files collected in your site by creating a set of color-coded page status entries in the Status settings (see Figure 4-22). If you're a Windows user, the ability to assign a Status color might be new to you, but Mac users are familiar with the concept, thanks to the Finder's Labels feature. To add a new status item, click the New button. In the highlighted text field, type a name for this status item, then click the color field to the left and choose a color from the Color Picker (Mac) or Color dialog box (Windows). To do away with a status, select it from the list and click the Delete button.

Figure 4-22
Status settings

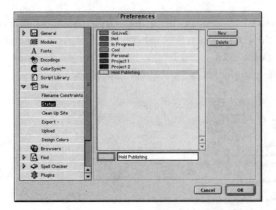

TIP:
Deleting
Status
Entries

GoLive doesn't allow you to delete any of the default set of seven status settings. In Windows, you can modify a default Label's name. On the Mac, however, you can only edit the default set by setting the Labels in the Finder's Preferences under the Edit menu (Mac OS 8.0 and later) or in the Labels Control Panel (Mac OS 7.5 and earlier). This is all to assist with cross-platform conversion of the site file, by the way, which was also added in GoLive 5.

TIP:
Adding
Status

If you add a new status item, it doesn't become active in site documents that have already been created—it's only added to new site documents.

To assign a status to a file, go to an open Site window and select any file (page, image, media, text, etc.). In the File Inspector, select the Page tab and choose an item from the Status menu. You may assign No Status (default) or one of the status items you set up (see Figure 4-23). You can view objects with their status label in the Site map in the Display tab of the Site View Controller.

For more information, see Chapter 21, *Files, Folders, and Links*, and Appendix A, *Macintosh Issues and Extras*.

Figure 4-23
Changing
Finder labels

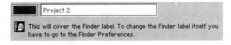

Clean Up Site, Export, Upload, and Design Colors

When you select Clean Up Site from the Site menu, GoLive updates your site with files linked from outside your root folder; adds referenced items that aren't yet in the External, Colors, or Font Sets tabs; and deletes unused files or items in any of the Site window tabs.

We cover cleaning up sites and how the preferences in the Clean Up Site pane affect the command, in greater detail in Chapter 21, *Files, Folders, and Links.*

Similarly, the Export and Upload options are found in Chapter 21, while the Design Colors pane is discussed in Chapter 20, *Prototyping and Mapping.*

Previewing in Web Browsers

GoLive's Layout Preview feature gives you a decent, quick 'n' dirty look at how your page looks when actually viewed in a browser. However, to get a more precise look at how your page elements are represented, click the Show in Browser button from the Toolbar. GoLive then opens the page (or a page highlighted in the Site window) in a browser or set of browsers designated in the Browsers pane.

If you click the Show in Browser button without first designating a browser, you receive an error dialog box reminding you of this fact. Simply click the Specify button to open up the Browser preferences.

To gather a list of all browsers found on your system, click the Find All button. After GoLive searches your hard drive, a list appears in the pane above. To remove a browser from the list, select it and click the Remove button. To add a new browser, click the Add button and navigate to that browser application.

Check the box next to a browser that you want to set as your default. After exiting Preferences by clicking OK, clicking the Show in Browser button opens the browser (if it's not already open) and previews your selected page. If you want to preview a page in another browser in the list not designated as default, click and hold the Show in Browser button to reveal the entire list of browsers found on your hard drive, then choose your desired browser. Additionally, if you didn't check a default browser and you click the Show in Browser button, GoLive reminds you that you didn't set this option with the previous error dialog (see Figure 4-24).

Figure 4-24
Browsers
settings

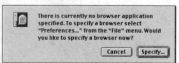

If you click the Show in Browser button and haven't specified a browser or set of browsers as your default, GoLive reminds you with this dialog (above).

TIP:
**Checking
Different
Browsers**

To get a feel for how a page behaves in different browsers (i.e., Navigator 4 versus Internet Explorer 5.5), check a version of each different browser flavor in Preferences. Then, when you click the Show in Browser button, your page automatically opens in each application. Be careful, though, not to check multiple versions of the same browser (such as Navigator 4 and 4.5), as you typically can open only one version at a time.

Document Editing

GoLive provides two text-based tools to help you make changes to documents inside and throughout your site. The Find feature allows you to perform searches as well as make replacements both in an individual file and across all the files within a site; the Spell Checker feature checks spelling on individual pages and across a site, and can keep a list of custom spellings.

Find

To set general Find preferences, go to the Find pane (see Figure 4-25). The When Match Is Found popup sets how the Find dialog behaves. Activate Document brings the document window to the front when a search term is located, while Keep Find Window in Front keeps the Find dialog active. Choosing Close Find Window closes the Find dialog as soon as your search item is located, though if nothing is returned the Find dialog remains open.

Figure 4-25
Find settings

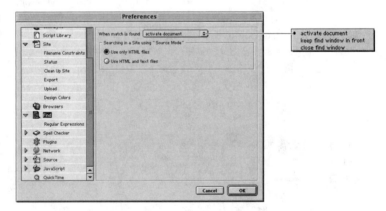

You can search across a site for items in a file's HTML source code by selecting Source Editor from the Treat Files In popup menu. When an item is found, GoLive opens the page to the highlighted item in the HTML Source Editor. In Preferences, you can choose to search only Web pages (Use Only

HTML Files) or all Web pages and associated style sheets (Use HTML and Text Files).

Under the Find pane's Regular Expressions settings, you can set up a list of wildcard search options for GoLive to use as prefabricated searches when using regular-expression pattern matching (see Figure 4-26). Wildcard searching uses special characters to represent one or more characters in a search string. For example, "David B[a-z]+" finds all instances of "David B" that are then followed by any combination of lower case letters (from "David Batty" to "David Beckham"). The "[a-z]" designates the range of lower-case letters you want to find, while the plus sign tells GoLive to find one or more occurrences of the characters contained within the two brackets.

Figure 4-26
Find Regular
Expression
settings

GoLive comes with several built-in patterns. To create a new pattern, click the New button and type a descriptive name for this item in the highlighted Name field. In the Expression field, type what you want to search for, such as any number that follows the word "GoLive" or a common change you make across your site. If you plan on using the Replace feature as well, enter the word or string that replaces the found text in the Replacement field. After exiting Preferences, open up the Find dialog, click the popup menu button to the right of the Find field, and select the item you just created from the list.

To learn more about GoLive's Find feature, see Chapter 16, *Source Editing* (basic Find on page and the Find by Element feature), and Chapter 25, *Advanced Features* (site-wide searches and regular expressions).

Spell Checker

When checking spelling on GoLive pages, you can store unrecognized words in a personal dictionary by pressing the Learn button. To edit this customized collection, go to the Spell Checker pane of the Preferences, select a word from the list, and make your edit in the text field below the list pane (see Figure 4-27). Choose All Languages from the Personal Dictionary For popup menu above the list pane to have words in the list appear across the spectrum of languages, or create a customized list for an individual language.

Figure 4-27
Spell Checker
settings

As with the Find feature, GoLive also provides a Regular Expressions section for spelling where you can create a list of wildcard spelling strings for GoLive to ignore (see Figure 4-28). GoLive's built-in list includes a pattern for normal URLs (like ftp and http) to keep them from popping up left and right while you attempt to check spelling.

To learn more about using GoLive's Spell Checking feature, see Chapter 18, *Page Specials*.

Figure 4-28
Spell Checker
Regular
Expression
settings

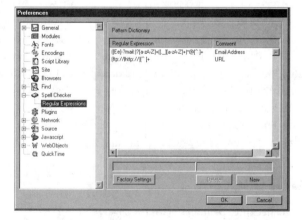

Plug-ins

GoLive works with media files (like QuickTime, Flash, etc.) in much the same way that Web browsers do, with plug-ins that handle the media's playback stored in the Plug-ins folder within the GoLive application folder. If you place a media file onto a page without including the plug-in, you can't preview the file directly in GoLive.

TIP:
Adding
Plug-ins

Remember that if you make any additions to the GoLive Plug-ins folder, they don't show up in the Plug-ins pane (nor can they be used by media files inserted into GoLive pages) until you quit and open the application again.

Under the Plug-ins pane, you find a collection of media players placed into the Plug-ins folder listed with the MIME type, the player that handles this type, and the file name extension that triggers GoLive to use this plug-in player. Below the list pane, you can make modifications to these fields, as well as choose another plug-in player that can handle that file type (if one is available). You can also designate whether GoLive should or should not play the file when previewed.

To add a new item, click the New button and enter a valid MIME type. If an appropriate plug-in player already resides within the Plug-ins folder, GoLive assigns that in the popup menu. Type the file suffix in the Extensions field, then any comments in the Info field (see Figure 4-29).

For more information, see Chapter 17, *Media*.

Figure 4-29
Plug-ins
settings

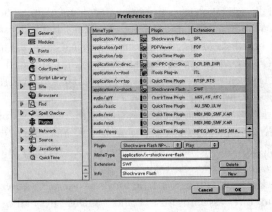

Network

In the Network pane, you can set up basic connectivity (see Figure 4-30). If your ISP or network requires that you connect via a proxy server (for filtering or security reasons), check either the Use FTP Proxy or Use HTTP Proxy options and fill in the server address and Port number below. Check Keep Connections Alive to continue to ping the Web via your Internet connection so it doesn't close down due to lack of activity. Keep the Use ISO 8859-1 Translation option checked to use the Latin1 character encoding set, which covers the majority of Western European languages.

Figure 4-30
Network
settings

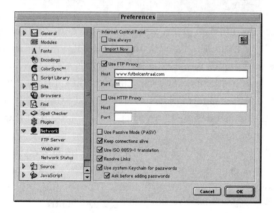

Checking Resolve Links compares your local files with those on your Web server; if this resolution takes an inordinate amount of time, uncheck the option.

On Windows, you can check Resolve Links, but it doesn't have a documented function. (This reminds us of when National Public Radio's *All Things Considered* program called humor columnist Dave Berry and got his answering machine. The message was, "If you'd like to press 1, press 1. If you'd like to press 2, press 2…" And so on.)

On the Mac, you can alternately choose to use the network settings from the Internet control panel; see Appendix A, *Macintosh Issues and Extras,* for details on the Internet control panel (which replaces Internet Config for System 9.0 and above).

Checking Use System Keychain for Passwords allows users of Mac OS 9.0 or later to store passwords for FTP and WebDAV sites in the system Keychain feature, which encrypts passwords using a passphrase.

FTP and WebDAV Servers

You can collect a list of frequently used FTP addresses under the Network pane's FTP Server settings (see Figure 4-31). Click the New button, then type the address in the highlighted Server text field (where GoLive places a generic "ftp.company.com" placeholder). If your FTP location goes deeper than the main server address, type its directory after the forward slash in the Directory text field. Leave the Username field blank if the FTP server accepts anonymous users ("Anonymous" appears listed in the Username column in the FTP list pane); otherwise type in your required name. Type your required password in the Password field; if this is left blank, you are prompted to type your password when accessing this FTP address. In the unlikely event your system administrator advises it, click the Advanced button to add a port number (GoLive defaults to 21) or to use passive mode when connecting.

Figure 4-31
FTP Server
settings

GoLive adds FTP Server settings to a popup menu in the FTP Browser under the File menu and in Site Settings (see Figure 4-32). From both locations, select any server setup listed in the popup menu to fill in the FTP server fields automatically.

In both the FTP Browser and Site Settings, you can add new FTP information to the FTP Server preferences (selecting Add Current Server from the popup menu) or edit an existing FTP Server entry (selecting Edit from the popup menu).

The WebDAV preferences section is where you can set up a workgroup server that uses the Web Distributed Authoring and Versioning protocol. GoLive uses this feature to work with a server that locks files that are being edited, preventing others from changing them until the current owner checks those files back in.

Figure 4-32
FTP Browser
and Site
Settings
dialogs

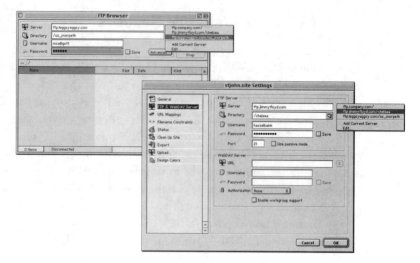

The WebDAV preferences section is similar to the FTP Server section, allowing you to collect a list of frequently used servers (see Figure 4-33). Click the New button to add a server. Add its URL in the Address field (GoLive places "server.golive.com" by default) and your name or the name of the administrator in the Username field (GoLive places the name used to register the application by default). If a password is required, type it in the Password field, and make sure to press Return or Enter to accept the change. Also, select Basic from the Authorization popup menu (if no password is required, leave None selected).

Figure 4-33
WebDAV
preferences
and Site
Settings

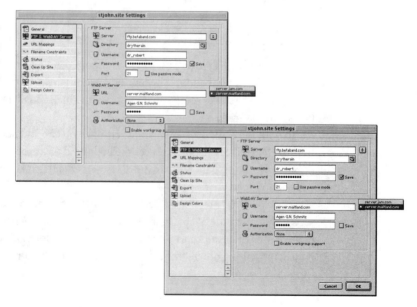

As with FTP Server, the global WebDAV settings that you create in Preferences are also found in the Site Settings. However, if you add a new WebDAV server in Site Settings, you don't have the option of adding those settings to Preferences like you do with FTP Server.

Network Status

Network Status works in conjunction with FTP and WebDAV, showing any errors or just plain system messages, depending on the options you've chosen (see Figure 4-34). Checking Warnings and Status Messages increases the amount of feedback that GoLive offers, which can help debug problems with connections or file transfers—if not for you, then for the person from whom you ask for help. Use the popup menu to choose the maximum number of items in the list, which ranges from five to unlimited.

To learn more about the features referenced in the Network pane, see Chapter 23, *Synchronizing Sites*.

Figure 4-34
Network
settings

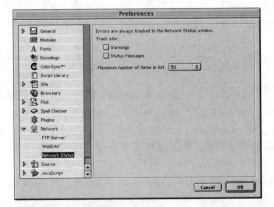

Code Appearance

The Source and JavaScript panes let you control how your code appears in the Document window and JavaScript Editor, respectively, from colors for specific pieces of code to font appearance. Additionally, you can turn on and off drag-and-drop support and configure how the code appears when printed. In Source, you can also configure browser sets to act as a base for syntax checking of HTML.

Source

Click Source to set the general source code preferences, the top three of which control certain behavior within GoLive (see Figure 4-35). To turn off drag and drop support, uncheck Enable Dragging of Marked Text. Uncheck Relaxed Checking of &xxx; Characters if you plan to use special characters (such as é, which is é in HTML). If Do Not Mark Unknown Attributes as Errors is unchecked, GoLive's HTML Source Editor syntax checker marks non-HTML tags and unknown attributes as errors.

Figure 4-35
Source settings

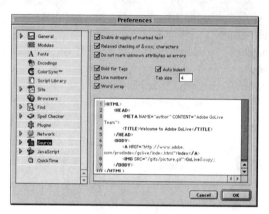

The next section controls how code is displayed in the Source Editor, and includes a preview window to show you an example of what you've just modified. GoLive defaults to checking Bold for Tags and Auto Indent. To play around with the size of this indent, type a value in the Tab Size field. If you want to add line numbers or make your code soft wrap (so that long lines don't run off the right side of the window), check those options.

Browser Sets

The Source pane's Browser Sets settings control code specifications that the HTML Source Editor's syntax checker uses to find errors and warnings (see Figure 4-36). For instance, the default choice of Netscape & IE 3, 4, 5 (denoted by a bullet) checks your code against the combined specifications for those three versions of Netscape Navigator and Microsoft Internet Explorer. However, if you're designing pages for an audience that still uses older browsers (such as Navigator 2.0), you want to check for errors against those specifications. These sets are found in the HTML Source Editor's Browser Compatibility popup menu, which enables you to check your code against any of the sets you've created in this Preferences section.

Figure 4-36
Browser Set
settings

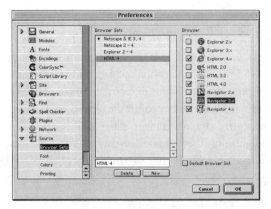

To modify an existing set, select it in the list, then check the browsers or HTML standard you want to include in that set. To create a new set, click the New button, type a name in the text field, then check the browsers or HTML standards you want to include in the set.

For more information, see Chapter 6, *Layout*, and Chapter 31, *Web Settings*.

Font

In the Source pane's Font settings, choose a font found on your system to display code in the HTML Source Editor (see Figure 4-37). Click the Name popup menu to select from your list of available fonts (Mac), or choose from the Font, Style, and Size lists (Windows), and then select a point size from the Size popup menu. If you want all code to appear bold, check that option. Checking Condense shortens the space between letters, while Extend adds space.

Figure 4-37
Source Font
settings

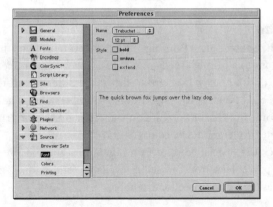

Colors

The top section of the Source pane's Colors settings allow you to choose your default view option when you open the Source Editor (see Figure 4-38). Choosing No Syntax Highlighting displays all text in your default font color, while choosing Detailed assigns different colors to each of a plethora of code syntax, from HTML attributes to special characters. Choosing Media & Links only colors entire tags for images, plug-in files, and links, while choosing URLs highlights only the link reference in hypertext and image tags. Choosing Server Side Code highlights code such as that generated via the Dynamic Link feature (such as ASP).

Figure 4-38
Source Colors
settings

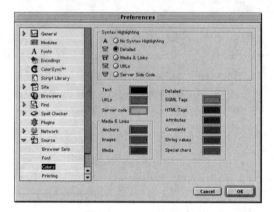

You can set the colors for the various items in the color fields below. The color you choose in the Text color field is displayed for all page content; or, it's the color used if no syntax highlighting is selected.

Printing

Under the Source pane's Printing settings, you can configure how your source gets output to a printer (see Figure 4-39). Check Printer Specific Settings to have the options below take effect, such as the different colored syntax highlighting, bold typeface for tags, and line numbers along the left side of the page. (Some of these options are only effective on a color printer, but black-and-white printers simulate colors as grays.)

Check Use Special Font for Printing to use a specific font style with your printed pages. Here you can set an available font, its size, and whether it's printed as bold, condensed, or extended.

Figure 4-39
Source Printing
settings

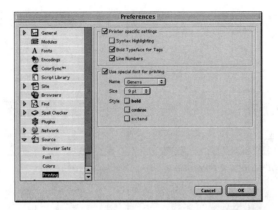

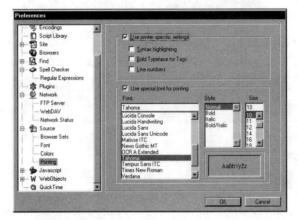

JavaScript

The preferences for how the JavaScript Editor displays and prints code are nearly identical to the HTML Source Editor preferences; however, no section appears for determining which JavaScript version the syntax checker uses (see Figure 4-40). (The browser-specific version of JavaScript is determined in the JavaScript Inspector's Language menu.)

For more information, see Chapter 26, *JavaScript.*

TIP:
Where's
JavaScript?

If you open Preferences and don't see the JavaScript section at the bottom of the right pane, don't panic. You probably just turned off the Scripting Module (Mac) or JavaScript Editor (Windows) in Modules. To return those preferences to the list, check the option in Modules, then quit and run GoLive to bring them back.

Figure 4-40
JavaScript
settings

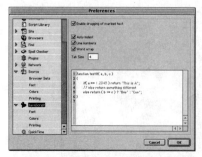

JavaScript general preferences

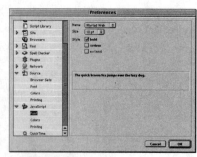

Font preferences

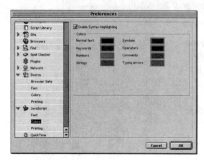

Color preferences

Printing preferences

Dynamic Link

Selecting Dynamic Link in the Modules section of Preferences turns on GoLive 5's ability to add dynamic content to pages using Active Server Pages (ASPs). Enter a value in the HTTP Timeout field that GoLive observes before reporting an error when it can't access a content source from an open page. Keep the Cache Responses from Server option checked to keep responses in memory, or click the Clear Cache Now button to delete them.

You can also configure the colors used to highlight valid and invalid bindings; the Frame Border popup controls the width of the binding indicators.

For much, much more on adding dynamic content in GoLive, see Chapter 30, *Dynamic Link*.

QuickTime

The QuickTime section of Preferences allows you to set a scratch disk, where GoLive saves temporary movie files (much like Photoshop and Premiere).

Additionally, you can configure the color, style, frequency, and subdivision of layout grids when you're editing QuickTime movies in the Layout tab of GoLive's built-in QuickTime editor (see Figure 4-41).

Figure 4-41
QuickTime
settings

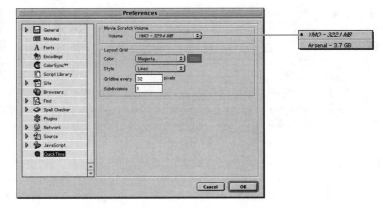

Keyboard Shortcuts

GoLive 5.0 provides a new feature where you can specify keyboard shortcuts (instead of using a third-party utility to personalize your keyboarding environment). You can access Keyboard Shortcuts under the Edit menu (or by pressing Command-Option-Shift-K on the Mac, or Shift-Alt-Control-K under Windows).

You can create different sets and assign different keyboard shortcuts for different users or different functions (see Figure 4-42).

Figure 4-42
Keyboard
Shortcut
settings

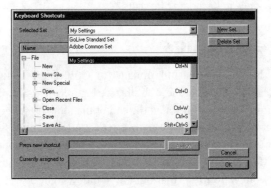

Keyboard Shortcuts comes with three settings—GoLive Standard Set, Adobe Common Set, and My Settings, which is the active set by default. When first accessing GoLive, GoLive Standard Set and My Settings are the same. The GoLive Standard Set cannot be modified, so you edit shortcuts in My Settings or in a new set. If you try to edit GoLive Standard Set anyway, you're prompted to create a new set (see Figure 4-43).

Figure 4-43
Unmodifiable
shortcut set

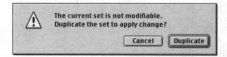 

To create a new set, click the New Set button, which opens up the New Set dialog. A copy of the name of the currently viewed set is placed into the Set Name field, preceded by "Copy of". Keep this designation or type your desired name, then click OK.

To add a shortcut to a menu item that has no existing shortcut, or edit a menu item's existing shortcut, select the item from the list. For example, expand the Edit section and select Group. In the Press New Shortcut field, type a new keyboard combination. If you choose a command that's already in use, such as Command-G, the Currently Assigned field notes that the shortcut is already paired with the Edit menu's Find Next item.

You could simply choose another keyboard combination, or you could be stubborn and click the Assign button to switch shortcut assignments from the original menu item to the newly selected item.

TIP:
Print Your
Shortcuts

On the Mac, you can print a list of a set's keyboard shortcuts; simply press Command P or select Print from the File menu. The trick is to expand all items that you want to be printed; items that aren't expanded don't have their underlying items printed. Unfortunately, Windows doesn't allow you to access print functions while in Keyboard Shortcuts.

Adobe Online Settings

Get the latest tutorials and updates to GoLive direct from the horse's mouth... er, from the Adobe Web site (see Figure 4-44). Simply click the ever-present Adobe Online button at the end of the toolbar (see Figure 4-45).

To set up your connection settings, select Adobe Online Settings from the Edit menu, or click the Preferences button on the main Adobe Online screen. On the Mac, check Use Internet Config Settings to use your already stored Internet connection information. On Windows, check Use System Default Internet Settings. Otherwise, configure the network settings as needed (see Figure 4-46).

Figure 4-44
Adobe Online

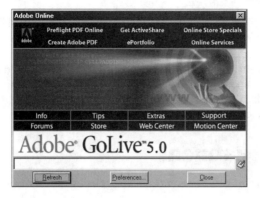

Figure 4-45
Adobe Online
Toolbar button

 — *Adobe Online*

Figure 4-46
Setting Adobe
Online
preferences

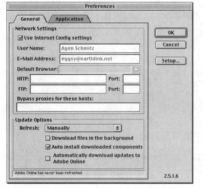 

Under Update Options, select how you'd like your machine to connect with Adobe Online, either manually or automatically (from once a day to once a month). Check Download Files in the Background to continue working in GoLive (or other programs) while a file downloads to your hard drive. Check Auto Install Downloaded Components (Mac) or Automatically Install Downloaded Files (Windows) to automatically open an installer file and begin installing it on your hard drive. If you want to automatically receive updates to Adobe Online, check the last option.

On the Application tab, configure how Adobe Online notifies you of its actions, either when new files are found or once they're completely downloaded. We like to check the Notify Me Before Starting Any Connection option on the Mac to make sure we know when some application is making an outside connection. Finally, if you're not getting quite enough email from Adobe, you can always ask for more in the Subscription Options section.

TIP:
Step-by-Step
Setup

As John Cougar (pre-Mellencamp) once sang, everyone needs a hand to hold on to—and if you're that someone, click the Setup button to have GoLive lead you by the hand through a step-by-step dialog that configures these same preferences.

Preferential Treatment

Tuning up GoLive's preferences before starting to work can save you endless hours and frustration. Discovering hidden preferences you've forgotten or never known about that can help color-code your text or produce better output can be a great surprise and pleasure. Many folks leave configuring their settings to the very end, but we've discovered that setting up the program right—detailing it to *your* needs—is like tuning a piano before you sit down to play: the results are always better.

Pages
PART 2

CHAPTER 5

Page Overview

GoLive's primary function is to create and edit the basic unit of the Web: the *page*, a set of text, images, and other items that comprise the contents of a browser window. You add these elements by typing or dragging them to GoLive's Layout Editor, much as you would edit a page in a desktop publishing program like InDesign or QuarkXPress. However, when you take a closer look at it, the Web page is quite different from its bound-for-paper cousins. The structure of HTML presents several advantages and limitations for designers; understanding them will help you avoid unexpected problems and unneccessary work.

Page Structure

The whole point of using a graphical program like GoLive is to avoid hand-coding HTML. It's easier to drag an image file from the Desktop onto a GoLive page, for example, than it is to write the HTML that describes the file's location and dimensions. (Even if you've been hand-coding Web pages for years, it's usually faster to drag and drop elements—and it's better for your hands and fingers in the long run.) But unlike pages in InDesign or QuarkXPress, which allow you to place elements anywhere within the workspace, Web pages are more dependent upon how browsers read and display the underlying HTML.

Top-Down Design

Although GoLive offers plenty of control over precise positioning of elements, building pages is more akin to working in a word processor than a desktop-publishing program. Everything on a page is *inline*, treated like just another text character. When you place an image, GoLive doesn't calculate its position based on the number of pixels between the image's border and the edge of the page. Instead, GoLive recognizes that the image appears as the first character of the second paragraph (see Figure 5-1).

Figure 5-1
Inline vs. DTP
placement

GoLive

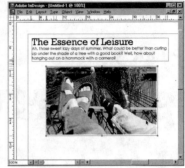

InDesign

TIP:
Pushing
Pixel
Positioning

If you're familiar with Cascading Style Sheets, you're probably thinking that we've gone out of our heads (and so early in the book, too). In fact, CSS *does* allow you to position elements with pixel-level control (one of its coolest features). But as you'll see, even the code required to accomplish this still appears inline within the HTML. See Chapter 29, *Cascading Style Sheets*, and Chapter 14, *Floating Boxes*, for more on precise positioning.

Designers employ many techniques to give the illusion that objects aren't tied to this structure, such as wrapping text around images, or using tables or layout grids to position elements. But underneath, every element exists as an inline object within the page's text—even in cases where there's no text to be seen.

When a Web browser builds a page, it reads the HTML from the first character to the last, placing elements based on the order they appear in the code.

For a practical example, let's look again at positioning an image. We want a photograph to appear against the right side of the page, with text wrapping around its left side. In a typical desktop-publishing program, you'd position the image on the page, then drop a text block alongside it. (You could also put the text behind the image and enable the program's text-wrapping features, but in this case we'll keep things simple.) However, in standard HTML, the image is treated as just another character: placing it at the beginning or end of the paragraph produces different results (see Figure 5-2). For now, put the image at the beginning of the paragraph.

To wrap the text, set the image's alignment to Right in the Image Inspector. The image shifts to the right edge of the screen, with its top edge aligned with the height of the first line of text. Now, drag and drop the image so it follows the last character in the paragraph. Although the photograph is still aligned against the right edge of the screen, the text of the next paragraph is wrapped (see Figure 5-3).

Quirks like this can sometimes drive traditional designers crazy, and illustrates the importance of understanding the limitations of one's medium.

Figure 5-2
Image placement within text

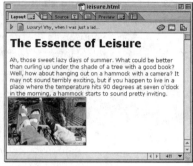

Image at start of paragraph   *Image at end of paragraph*

Figure 5-3
Right alignment

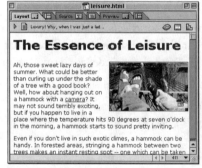
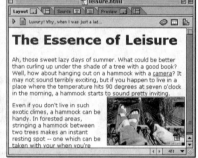

Start of paragraph   *End of paragraph*

Netscape's Nerdiness

Of course, in this example, there's still a fly in the ointment. Depending on the version of Netscape a user might employ, this might cause text to run right over the image. It's a bug in Netscape, and one they fixed quite late in their history.

Anatomy of a Web Page

No matter the length or complexity, a Web page is divided into two parts: the Head section and the Body section. Chapter 6, *Layout*, covers how to access the various elements invovled in a Web page. The other chapters in this part of the book are devoted to what you can do in these two sections.

Head Section

Like the rounded (and attractive, we might add) protuberance supported by your shoulders, a Web page's Head is vital to the operation of the whole organism. At its simplest, the Head section defines the title of the page (which appears in the browser window's title bar).

However, over the years, the Head section has become home to a big junk pile of things, most of which are rarely seen by people viewing the page in a browser. Chapter 7, *Head Section*, explains how to use the following elements.

- **Base tag.** You can identify a URL to act as the basis of all links on the page.

- **Meta tags.** Search engines and other archival systems read Meta tags to gain overview information about your page, including a brief description and relevant keywords.

- **Link tags.** You can define special relationships between the Web page and other pages on the Web.

- **Scripts.** Code that's used for effects, like image rollovers or advanced functionality, is stored in the Head section and referenced from commands in the rest of the page. Examples include JavaScript, Jscript, and VBScript.

- **Cascading Style Sheets (CSS).** You can gain advanced typographic control and precise positioning using CSS. The code either appears directly in the Head section, or exists in an external file that is specified in the Head.

Body Section

The Body section contains everything else in a Web page, most of which comprises what a Web browser displays. Separate chapters cover each aspect of the following elements and tools.

- **Layout:** the basics of building pages

- **Head Section:** the information, like meta tags and style definitions

- **Text and Fonts:** everything about specifying typographic characteristics, using typefaces, and structuring paragraphs

- **Images:** inserting and manipulating images, creating image maps, using the new Tracing Image feature, using ColorSync (Mac only); sharing pixels and code with Photoshop, ImageReady, LiveMotion, and other tools

- **Color:** managing all the options in the voluminous Color palette

- **Tables:** the ins and outs of creating tables

- **Layout Grids:** GoLive's near-exact positioning tools

- **Frames:** how to use GoLive's Frame icons, Frame Editor, and Layout Preview or Frame Preview to create frames that work
- **Floating Boxes:** break out of inline constraints by building boxes that use CSS for positioning and manipulation
- **Forms:** an explanation of form elements, structuring forms, and integrating with a server
- **Source Editing:** editing the underlying HTML code
- **Media:** QuickTime, plug-ins, and other media
- **Page Specials:** spellchecking, Web downloading, file mapping, and other primarily page-based features

Structure Isn't Restrictive

HTML may seem like a restrictive environment in which to bring up a healthy Web page, but it's not necessarily so. Like all artistic mediums, once you understand what's going on beneath the surface—whether you're building four-color brochures or mixing photographic chemicals—the more adept you are at achieving consistently better Web designs.

CHAPTER 6

Layout

We all have our favorite places, the spots where we tend to gravitate. You could own a house with a hundred rooms, but we bet you would spent most of your time in only one or two. The same idea applies to GoLive. Although the program has a wide variety of editing and preview screens, the bulk of your time is spent in its main rooms: the Document window, and more specifically, the Layout Editor.

The Document window brings together all the different elements necessary to create a page. You drag icons from the Objects palette into it; add keywords and other items to the Head section; and, of course, you place images, text, tables, and other items to create your final Web page.

Document Window Basics

At the top of each Document window are tabs for GoLive's different modes of editing and previewing, each of which allows you to view your page in a different manner: Layout Editor, Frame Editor, HTML Source Editor, HTML Outline Editor, Layout Preview, and the Mac-only Frame Preview (see Figure 6-1). When you first launch GoLive, the Document window displays the Layout Editor by default.

If you collapse the Document window on the Mac to a width of 301 pixels or fewer, the Layout, Source, and Preview tabs are represented only by icons (the Frame Editor and Frame Preview tabs are normally represented only by icons). In Windows, the tabs do not collapse when minimizing the Document window.

Like most windows, the Document window's size can be adjusted by dragging the lower-right corner on the Mac, or dragging any outer edge under Windows. The value at the bottom of the screen is the window's current width. GoLive also includes six preset widths, from 50 to 780 pixels (you can't type in another value, unfortunately). GoLive defaults to a 580-pixel window size, (620-pixel width under Windows) which is its suggested setting for displaying Web pages on a 14-inch monitor.

Figure 6-1
Page views

Layout Editor   HTML Source Editor   Layout Preview
        Frames Editor   HTML Outline Editor   Frame Preview (Mac)

TIP:
Change Your
First View

If you'd rather have another editing mode—such as Frame Editor—as your default when creating a new document, you can set your preference through the General pane's Document settings in the Preferences dialog box. Select a view from the Default Mode menu (see Figure 6-2).

Figure 6-2
Setting Default
Mode

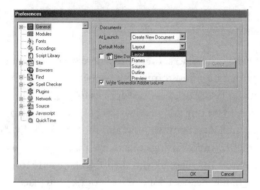

What if your Web pages need to be targeted to a different size? You can set up a new default window size by resizing it to your desired width and height, then selecting Window Settings (Mac) or just Settings (Windows) from the popup menu. Make sure HTML Windows is checked in the Window Settings dialog box. Then click OK. From here on, every document opened—new and old—appears at both this pixel width and height. To return to GoLive's default width, return to the Window Settings dialog box and click the Use Default Settings button. Note that the Window Size popup menu is not available in source or outline editors, nor is it available in the Preview tab in Windows.

If you have a tracing image specified (see Chapter 9, *Images*), select Tracing Image from the Change Window Size menu to collapse the window's size to the image's dimensions.

TIP:
Maximum
Width

If you're designing for both Mac and Windows, which most designers must, consider using 520 pixels as your default window rather than 580. For reasons we've never determined, a Macintosh and a Windows box both displaying a resolution of 800 by 600 pixels don't have the same horizontal screen territory available. On a Mac, a site designed for 580 pixels wide and displayed at 800 by 600 forces a user to scroll left and right, which—unless a specific effect is intended—we find just annoying.

TIP:
Collapsing Mac Document Windows

On the Macintosh, Control-clicking the title bar of any document window collapses it to a tab at the bottom of the screen (similar to the Finder's popup folders). You can also drag the window to the screen bottom.

Layout Editor

The Layout Editor is where you will likely spend the most time when developing content for individual pages. (Of course, if you're an old-school hand-coder who can't "see" a page without a panoply of tags and attributes, there's the HTML Source Editor, which is detailed in Chapter 7, *Head Section*.) The Layout Editor has a number of icons on the bar below the Document window's tabs (see Figure 6-3).

Figure 6-3
Layout Editor

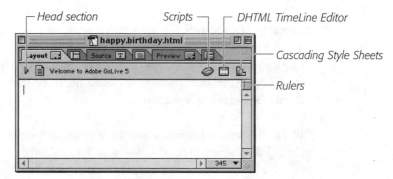

Head section. If you click the arrow at the far left of the bar, the Head section opens up below, which is where you can configure items that contain information about the page, such as keywords and a page refresh rate. You find icons for these tags under the Head tab of the Objects palette (the fourth tab in).

TIP:
Opening the Head Section

If you don't have the Head section already open, you can drag an icon from the Palette's Head tab and place it over the toggle arrow for a second. The Head section then opens for you to place the tag.

Moving to the right, clicking the Page icon calls up the Page Inspector, which allows you to configure a page's basic attributes, including page title, background and link colors, and a designated ColorSync profile. (Learn more about the Page Inspector in the "Document Layout Inspectors" section of Chapter 2, *The Inspector*.) You could also click the default "Welcome to Adobe GoLive 5" text to the right of the Page icon to rename your page's title, bypassing the Page Inspector. When finished typing, press Return, Enter, or Tab, or click elsewhere, to accept the change.

Scripts. Clicking the coffee-bean icon opens the Scripts Editor and displays the JavaScript Script Inspector. To begin writing a script from scratch, click the New Script Item button (labelled Create Script under Windows) and start typing the script in the main window area. Scripts can be stored in either the Head section or the body of your HTML document. (See Chapter 26, *JavaScript*, for more information on using JavaScript in GoLive.)

DHTML Timeline Editor. Clicking the filmstrip icon brings up the DHTML Timeline Editor, where you can configure DHTML-based animations. (QuickTime movies are edited with a similar-looking, but not identical, interface; see Chapter 17, *Media*.) The DHTML Timeline Editor allows you to arrange objects in sequences over periods of time using Dynamic HTML (see Chapter 27, *Animation*).

Cascading Style Sheets. Clicking the stairstepped icon opens up the Style Sheet Editor, from which you can add text and paragraph styles to a page using the Cascading Style Sheets (CSS) specification. The Toolbar changes to the CSS toolbar, which contains the controls for defining new styles (see Chapter 29, *Cascading Style Sheets*).

Rulers. To view and measure your layout against vertical and horizontal rulers, click the Ruler button located at the top of the right-hand scroll bar. If you are editing a table cell, the ruler recalculates its horizontal and vertical zero settings to match the cell. To get rid of the rulers, simply click the Ruler button again (see Figure 6-4).

Figure 6-4
Layout rulers

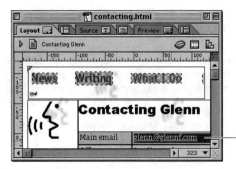

Rulers reset to the borders of a table cell that's being edited.

TIP:

**Quieting
Noisy Rulers
(and Vice
Versa)**

Who says rulers can't be fun? On the Macintosh, clicking the Ruler button doesn't just display the rulers, it animates them quickly emerging from the upper-left corner of the window, accompanied by a "swoosh" sound. If you think the Web already has enough animation and sound, Option-click the Ruler button to make them appear and disappear immediately and without noise.

Under Windows, the options are reversed (perhaps the average Windows user is too business-minded to enjoy the show? We doubt it!). Control-click the Ruler button to animate the ruler (which remains silent, unfortunately).

View Controller. If you're spending most of your time in the Document window anyway, shouldn't you be able to control what gets displayed? Using the controls in the View Controller, you can configure how GoLive looks and acts as you work in the Layout Editor, HTML Outline Editor, and Preview (see Figure 6-5). These controls also let you preview how links appear (either active or visited) and which fonts are displayed; or highlight elements, such as low-source images and elements with Cascading Style Sheet definitions applied. The View Controller is also covered in "Document Layout Inspectors" in Chapter 2, *The Inspector*, but the options here apply directly to the Layout View Controller (which applies to the Preview window as well) and the Outline View Controller.

Figure 6-5
View
Controller

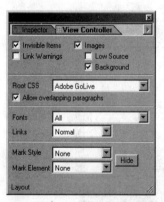

Invisible Items. Unchecking the Invisible Items box causes GoLive to hide line breaks and tag icons on the page. You can also press Command-I (Mac) or Control-I (Windows) to hide and show invisible items, or select the corresponding option under the Edit menu.

Link Warnings. If you check the Link Warnings box, GoLive displays a colored border surrounding all links and images that have an empty or invalid reference. Pressing Command-Shift-L (Mac) or Control-Shift-L (Windows), or selecting Show/Hide Link Warnings from the Edit menu, also turns link warnings on and off. Additionally, you can click the Link Warnings button in the Toolbar (represented by a green bug) to turn the warnings on and off. (Invoking the Link Warnings option makes the toolbar button appear pressed.)

Images. If you uncheck the Images box, images disappear from your page, with only the border, a generic image icon, and any Alt text remaining. The Background box hides or displays a page's background image. If you've specified low-source previews of your images, checking the Low Source box displays them instead of the original ones.

Root CSS. Web browsers have supported a mixed bag of Cascading Style Sheets definitions over the years, making it a challenge to know which effects work with which programs. If you're using CSS in your document, select a browser version from the Root CSS popup menu to see how the page will display in that browser (see Figure 6-6). The Allow Overlapping Paragraphs box controls the display of text with negative margin values. (See Chapter 29, *Cascading Style Sheets*, for more on CSS.)

Figure 6-6
Root CSS

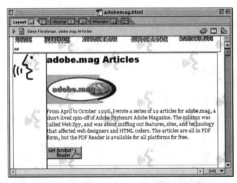

GoLive preview

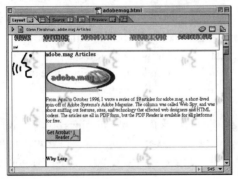

Netscape Navigator 3

Fonts. GoLive can display text in any font you choose, but that doesn't guarantee that people viewing your page will have those fonts installed on their computers. The Fonts popup menu lets you view text only in Times, or using any font except for Web fonts such as Georgia or Verdana. (See Chapter 8, *Text and Fonts*, for more on applying different type styles.)

Links. As we talked about in Chapter 2, *The Inspector*, you can define colors for linked text, including colors for active links (when you click on them) and visited links. To easily see how your links will look in your selected colors, choose Normal, Active, or Visited from the Links popup menu.

Mark Style, Mark Element, and Set Mark. It's easy to see which CSS definitions are applied to the objects on your page using the Mark Style and Mark Element popup menus. When a style or object is selected, text with that definition is set off by a yellow outline (see Figure 6-7). (You can change the color in GoLive's preferences.) Choosing None from the menus removes the highlighting; clicking the Hide button sets both menus to None.

Figure 6-7
Mark Style and
Mark Element

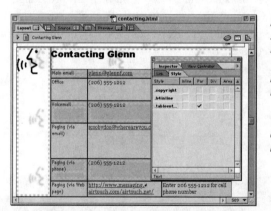

Mark Style is set to .tableentries, used for row names.

Mark Element is set to TD, marking all table cells.

The CSS selector has an outline to show it's the marked style.

TIP:
Highlight in Style Tab
When you select a CSS style via Mark Style, the name of the style is also highlighted in the Style tab of the Text or Image Inspector (see Figure 6-7, above).

Set Mark, which appears in the Outline View Controller, operates the same as Mark Style. Choose to display text, comments, or generic elements (see Figure 6-8). The Unfold Marked button expands marked outlines if they're retracted.

Figure 6-8
Marks in the
Outline View
Controller

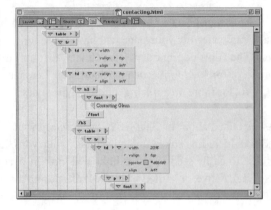

Frame Editor

At the top of the Document window, click the Frame Editor tab. GoLive displays a window chock full of nothing but a reminder in the middle that there are "No Frames." To add a frame configuration to your page, click the Object palette's Frames tab and select one of the many pre-designed frame sets. (The icons give you an idea of the basic layout of the frame set.) Drag the icon of your desired set into the Document window; double-clicking the icon doesn't work (see Figure 6-9).

Figure 6-9
Frame Editor

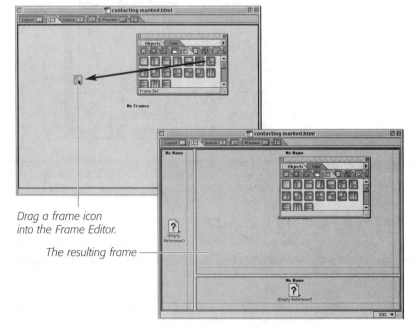

*Drag a frame icon
into the Frame Editor.*

The resulting frame

The Document window is then filled with the layout of the frame set, with an Empty Reference icon in each frame indicating that it needs to be linked to an HTML page. The Frame Set Inspector also pops up and allows you to configure orientation (either horizontal or vertical) and borders (size, color, and framing).

Click within one of the individual frames, and the Frame Set Inspector changes to the Frame Inspector (see Figure 6-10). (If you want to return to the Frame Set Inspector, click a frame border.) Here you can specify the frame's size—choosing either Pixel or Percent from the popup menu to the right of the Size field—as well as its name.

Figure 6-10
Frame
Inspector

To specify a content file for the frame, type the name and directory location of the file or click the Browse button and navigate to the file. If you are adding a content file from a site file, you can use the URL Getter controls or drag and drop a file from the Site window.

On the Mac, you can preview the frame's content within the editor. (We're not sure why this ability isn't available in the Windows version. Our best guess is that since Windows GoLive uses Internet Explorer's engine to display previews in the Layout Preview window, it would have been too difficult to implement it on a frame-by-frame basis in the Frame Editor. But we're not programmers, so consider this as just our own theorizing.) Click the Preview Frame button on the Frame Inspector; toggle it back off to turn off the preview. On the Frame Set Inspector, you can also preview all frames by clicking its Preview button. Or, you can preview by selecting the Frame Preview tab at the top of the Document window.

To edit a frame's content, double-click the frame to open the referenced file. To change the size of a frame, click and drag a border. To change a frame's location on the page, click a frame and drag it over another frame, which turns gray.

If you want to add another frame to the mix, choose an icon from the Frames tab of the Objects palette and drag it into the Document window. The layout is modified according to the frame that was added.

TIP:
Layout Editor Reflects Frame Changes

If you return to the Layout Editor after placing your frame set, notice that the Page icon has changed to indicate that frames have indeed been added (see Figure 6-11). Clicking the icon still calls up the Page Inspector for you to configure link colors, etc. You can type text and add material into the Layout Editor, but if you have content files selected for the frames, whatever you add is placed into a Noframes tag and is not visible in the browser.

Figure 6-11
Page icon and frameset icon

More information. For a whole bunch of frame examples and how they relate to their icons, see Chapter 3, *Palettes and Parts*. For the skinny on frames and frame sets, see Chapter 13, *Frames*. Also see "Creating a New Site" in Chapter 1, *Getting Started*, for details on configuring a site.

Layout Preview and Frame Preview

To see how your work previews in a browser and test your links, click the Layout Preview tab (which is the only preview tab in Windows). GoLive's previewing capabilities give you a close approximation of how your page's layout behaves when viewed by your audience.

GoLive doesn't preview JavaScript effects coded into a page. However, if you've placed plug-in players into the Plug-ins folder found in the GoLive application folder, you can preview a page's plug-in files. If not, preview the page in an external browser that includes the plug-in.

TIP:
I Can Preview Clearly Now

If you aren't seeing the Layout Preview tab, it's probably because the module isn't loaded. Go to the Modules pane in Preferences and make sure that the Preview Mode Module is checked. Then quit and relaunch the program.

Moving the mouse over a link turns your cursor into a pointing hand, denoting that the link is indeed hot. Click a link to an internal page (one that is stored on your hard drive) to open that page. However, if you click a link to an external URL, GoLive opens the link in your default browser or browsers (defined in the Preferences dialog box's Browsers pane).

Since GoLive's previewing feature is limited, it's best to use the actual external browsers your audience might use to preview your pages. After setting up a list of available browsers found on your hard drive in Preferences, click and hold the arrow just to the right of the Toolbar's Show in Browser button (available in just about every contextual toolbar) to reveal the list. If you just click the button, your page opens in the default browser(s). You can also preview a page in your default browser(s) by pressing Command-T on the Mac or Control-T under Windows (or accessing this item, as well as your browser list, from the Special menu).

As in the Layout Editor, use the popup menu at the bottom right corner to adjust the size of the window and to set the default size for opened documents.

Frame Preview. If you're designing a page with frames and using a Mac, click the Frame Preview tab to preview the page. If you haven't built frames and click the Frame Preview tab, GoLive reminds you that you have no frames. Windows users need not worry about this, as the Preview tab handles both non-framed and framed pages. (Unlike in Layout Preview mode, the View Controller does not appear.)

More information. For a reminder of how to configure settings for viewing pages in external browsers, see the "Browser Sets" section of Chapter 4, *Preferences and Customizing*. See Chapter 31, *Web Settings* for more on setting up style sheets.

Turn the Page

No doubt at some point you've woken up in the middle of the night and made your way through your house without turning on the lights. How is it you can make it all the way to the kitchen in the dark? Your familiarity with the locations of walls and doors, and your memory of where furniture is placed, keeps you from stumbling around blind.

After you've used GoLive a dozen or so times, you gain the same sense of familiarity. Moving through its layout editors and around the document quickly becomes second nature, so you can focus on the task of creating great Web pages.

CHAPTER 7

Head Section

Okay class, don your lab coats and grab your scalpels, because it's time to delve into one of the most important—and most overlooked—portions of a Web page's anatomy: the Head section. Like the control centers of the human brain, which regulate your breathing and heart rate, the Head section provides fundamental information required to display a Web page. Without it, your hard-won designs appear as nothing more than plain text.

When used successfully, the Head section directs JavaScript scripts and CSS styles, and also describes the meta information—information about the rest of the information, like a précis or summary—for search-engine placement and easier archiving.

A browser reads and interprets the Head section of a page before it moves on down to the body, so things that affect the rest of the page—like scripts—need to be stored in the Head section unless there's a highly specific reason not to. Don't worry; although this section is important, it's not overly oblongata. In fact, you may come to lobe it.

TIP:
What's in Your Head?

The Head section, as GoLive calls it, is really just the part of the page that starts with <HEAD> and ends with </HEAD>. The rest of an HTML page is the body part, which is—you guessed it—surrounded by Body tags.

Several kinds of objects wind up in the Head section in HTML and in GoLive.

- **Title.** The name that appears in the browser window's titlebar.

- **Base.** The Base tag identifies a static URL that gets used as the root of any relative link on the page. This overrides the current location of the page within its site, which typically gets used to determine relative links.

- **Meta tags.** Meta tags contain information about the contents of the document, including a description of the content, keywords derived from the page, and so on.

- **Link tags.** Links are a special kind of tag that create a relationship between the page they appear on and other pages or objects. For instance, you can embed fonts in a Web page using Netscape's TrueDoc system via a Link tag to connect to the font file elsewhere on your site or on the Internet. (Note how these differ from hypertext links which don't contain information about the kind of link they are, but simply point to another location.)

- **Scripts.** JavaScript, Jscript, VBScript, and other scripting languages generally—though not exclusively—put all their scripts in the Head section. (See Chapter 26, *JavaScript*, for more on where to locate JavaScript code and when to use the Head Script icon versus the Body Script icon.)

- **Cascading Style Sheets (CSS).** CSS enables advanced typographic control and the ability to position elements precisely on a page (see Chapter 29, *Cascading Style Sheets*).

TIP:
Other Head Tab Tags

The Head tab of the Objects palette also holds the Isindex, Tag, and Comment tag, which are fully described in Chapter 2, *The Inspector*, and Chapter 3, *Palettes and Parts*.

Base

The Base tag lets you change the local context in which relative links get interpreted (see sidebar, "It's All Relative"). Drag the Base tag into the Head section, and the Base Inspector lets you set the reference (see Figure 7-1). Check the Base box and choose a location to which relative links are appended.

Checking Write Base Always Absolute ensures that all references are written back to the root of the site, or the starting slash after the server name for your site.

Using the Target field, you can direct all your page's links to a specific window; for example, a target of "_blank" causes every link destination to open in a new browser window.

Figure 7-1
Setting Base
URL via the
Base Inspector

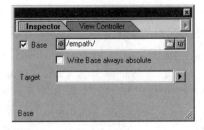

Meta

Meta tags allow you to specify information about the page on which the tag appears, such as a description of its content or keywords that describe the content. You can code numerous Meta tags by hand, and GoLive provides the framework for that. However, GoLive also prefabricates three kinds of commonly used Meta tags.

Plain Meta Tag

Drag the Meta icon from the Head tab into the Head section, and GoLive brings up the Meta Inspector. You can set the Meta tag through the popup menu to either Name or HTTP-Equivalent. Names are used for information about the page; HTTP-Equivalent is used for simulating header information that accompanies a Web page when it's sent by a server to a browser.

In the field beneath the popup menu, enter the Meta tag's title, such as "description". In the Content text area below that, enter the contents of the tag, such as a description of the page.

A great explanation of a variety of available Meta tags and their specifications can be found at http://www.webdeveloper.com/html/html_metatags.html (see Figure 7-2).

Figure 7-2
Meta tags in
Layout Editor
and HTML
Source Editor

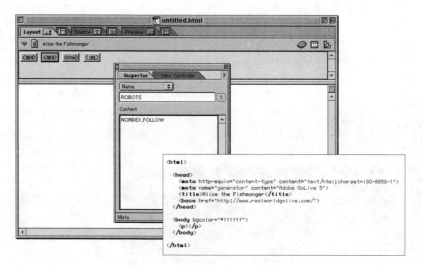

It's All Relative

HTML pages use two different ways of linking to other resources: fully qualified "absolute" links and relative links. We explain this distinction in great depth in the "Absolute versus Relative" sidebar in Chapter 21, *Files, Folders, and Links*, but here's a sneak preview.

Fully qualified absolute links (as opposed to GoLive's Absolute Link) require a resource type, a server name, and a file location. For instance, a file link might look like:

```
http://www.necoffee.com/flavor/
syrup/doubletall.html
```

The "http" is the resource type (Web protocol), the server is www.necoffee.com, and the file location includes the whole path after the server: /flavor/syrup/doubletall.html.

A relative link uses the location of the page on which it appears to navigate to the resource, which has to be stored locally. So if you're viewing a page that's located at

```
http://www.necoffee.com/flavor/
syrup/doubletall.html
```

and you put a relative reference to the page of

```
snickerdoodle.html
```

a Web browser constructs a full reference of

```
http://www.necoffee.com/flavor/
syrup/snickerdoodle.html
```

If you need to navigate to a higher folder, use two dots plus a slash to signify "up one folder level." So a relative link up two levels from doubletall.html of

```
../../decaf/notenough/whybother.html
```

causes a browser to construct a link of

```
http://www.necoffee.com/decaf/not
enough.html
```

Refresh

The Refresh tag lets you set the time before which the browser loads another page in place of the one on which the Refresh tag appears. It can even be the same page if you're providing updated information that changes every few seconds or minutes, and the user can just leave the page open, like a traffic status page.

Figure 7-3
Refresh
Inspector

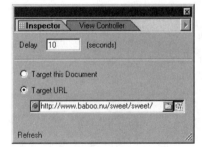

The Refresh Inspector sports only a few settings (see Figure 7-3). You can set the delay before the page reloads; it can be set to zero for an instant redirection to another page. You can either choose Target this Document or select Target URL to specify another page to load through the URL Getter.

Keywords

A well-produced page includes keywords in a Meta tag. Internet search engines consult Meta tags, in part, to construct their indexes and place those pages in order of precedence on their results pages.

There are two ways to add keywords in GoLive: by selecting words on a page and using the contextual menu's or the Special menu's Add to Keywords item; or, by typing them in via the Keywords Inspector.

Using the Add to Keywords item automatically creates a Keywords icon in the Head section. You can also drag the icon from the Head tab of the Objects palette. Selecting it brings up the Keywords Inspector where you can type in words and hit Return or Enter to add them to the keywords list (see Figure 7-4).

Figure 7-4
Keywords
Inspector

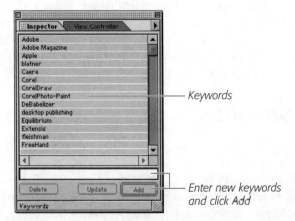

Keywords

Enter new keywords
and click Add

If you want to re-order keywords, select a word or group of words and click the move up/move down buttons in the lower-left corner of the inspector. The order of keywords may effect the ranking in some Internet search engines, though results vary among different engines.

TIP:
Search
Secrets

We recommend consulting Danny Sullivan's Search Engine Watch (http://www.searchenginewatch.com) for the best information on the subject.

Link

The Link tag lets you create relationships between the current document and other documents on a site or on the Internet. Typically, you use this tag for two purposes:

- To connect the contents of external CSS style sheets, as described in Chapter 29, *Cascading Style Sheets*. There's no reason to code this kind of Link tag by hand, as GoLive has a built-in linking feature that automatically creates the right Link tag code. (In fact, if you create one of these by hand, GoLive "takes it over"—that is, removes it from the Head section's graphical display and shows the file in the Style Sheet Editor's External folder.)

- To reference fonts that get retrieved by a 4.0 or later Netscape browser or Internet Explorer running an ActiveX object rendered to display type in a browser window. (Internet Explorer uses a different method to link in fonts as part of the CSS specification; see Chapter 29 for more on that, as well.)

The Link Inspector lets you enter the appropriate attributes depending on the kind of link. However, few common uses for this tag currently exist.

If you'd like more information on what values you can use with the Link tag, see http://www.w3.org/TR/html401/struct/links.html#edef-LINK. It's a little dense, but it's the best resource available.

Head and Shoulders

On the Web, having a good Head section not only can affect how your page displays in a Web browser, but also how your page is displayed by search engines and other tools that use Meta tag information. In the real world, we compliment people's intelligence by saying they have "a good head on their shoulders." Employing a good Head section in your Web pages complements the wisdom of the head on your shoulders.

CHAPTER **8**

Text and Fonts

Despite the flash and glitter of images on the Web, and despite the maxim of a picture equaling a thousand words, text forms the majority of what you peruse on a page. But text has received the least amount of hype and attention. While advances in sound, animation, and image compression have transformed the look and experience of the online world, most of the Web's words are still viewed in browsers' default fonts. Like the flashing "12:00" display on millions of VCRs, 12-point Times is the modern user option that never gets changed. (Most people don't even know they can change it.)

Granted, things could be much worse. Anyone raised on the green- or amber-on-black block letters of early computers may think that just having fonts with serifs and letterspacing is a quantum leap towards greater legibility. In HTML, we can specify a fairly broad range of type styles: bold, italic, underline, strikethrough, paragraph alignment, bulleted lists, and more. But only recently have we been able to apply attributes such as different fonts, variable type sizes, and colors—and even then it was a chore to code the necessary tags in HTML.

In GoLive, you can set specific visual formatting like bold or italic, as well as structural definitions like Code, Pre, and heading styles. How these appear is defined by the defaults in each browser, some of which can be modified by users. GoLive also offers tools for managing fontsets—or designer-specified sets of fonts for a browser to display type in—to broaden compatibility among browsers.

TIP:

More on Text in GoLive

This chapter explains how to manipulate and style text. Chapter 12, *Layout Grids*, and Chapter 14, *Floating Boxes*, cover GoLive's positioning controls for text and objects on a page. Cascading Style Sheets, which represent a huge leap in text control for the ever-increasing majority user-share of current browser users, are covered in Chapter 29, *Cascading Style Sheets*.

Entering Text

After installing GoLive for the first time on our systems, one of the first things we did to test the program was type a few lines of gibberish into the Layout Editor, then preview the file in a Web browser. You can type directly into the Layout Editor as if it were a dedicated word processor, copy and paste text from another program, or drag text from an open application directly into GoLive.

Paragraphs and Line Breaks

As you type or edit text, two types of line breaks—methods of starting text on the next line at the margin—are available. Following word-processing convention, GoLive formats text in paragraphs by default. Pressing Return (Mac) or Enter (Windows) inserts a paragraph break, which on the Web signals that extra vertical space is added following the end of the paragraph.

If you'd rather not let Web browsers determine how much space belongs after each paragraph, you can insert line breaks by pressing Shift-Return (Mac) or Shift-Enter (Windows). If you're feeling particularly mouse-happy, you can also double-click the Line Break icon in the Basic tab of the Objects palette, or drag it to the desired location in your document. Some designers use multiple line breaks to separate paragraphs in order to maintain more control over how much space appears before and after their paragraphs (see Figure 8-1).

Figure 8-1
Paragraph and
line breaks

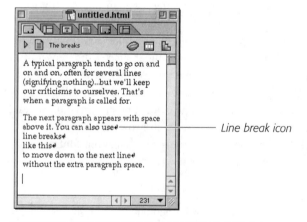

Line break icon

TIP:
Oh, Bad
Break!

The BR tag is a hack, or a trick designed to solve a specific problem that's not easy to generalize. Each browser, platform, and release tends to handle BR differently. If you must control the space between paragraphs more precisely, you may want to opt for CSS (see Chapter 29, *Cascading Style Sheets*), or preview your choices extensively.

TIP:
Pasting Text
Corrects
HTML
Entities

If you copy and paste text from an outside source into the Layout Editor, GoLive automatically converts some nonstandard text elements into their HTML entities. For example, an ampersand (&) becomes "&", the copyright symbol (©) turns into "©", and an accented letter like the "e" in "café" is transformed into "é". This helps ensure that readers don't see strange characters when their browsers hit those elements in the HTML source code. (See "Characters Tab" in Chapter 31, *Web Settings,* for a discussion of HTML entities.)

Navigating Text

With so many words on the Web, you need effective ways of navigating them all, whether you're traversing a couple paragraphs or several screens' worth of text. This may seem like a basic point, but, like designing a Web page, you'd be surprised at the difference good navigation makes.

Navigating with the Mouse

The easiest method to move around is to use your mouse to place the text-insertion point where you want to type or edit. Double-clicking selects a single word; triple-clicking selects a line, and quadruple-clicking selects an entire paragraph. If you right-click in Windows, or Control-click on a Macintosh, the contextual menu offers the option to Select All. (Typing Command-A on a Mac or Control-A under Windows also selects all text and objects on a page.)

GoLive supports drag-and-drop editing, so you can select a block of text, then drag the selection to a new location—even onto another open page window. To make a quick copy of a text range, hold down Option (Mac) or Control (Windows) while you move it (see Figure 8-2).

Figure 8-2
Drag-copying
text selections

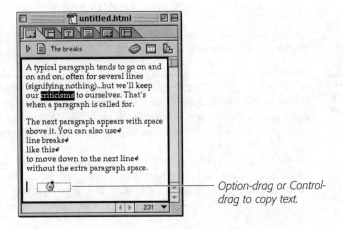

Option-drag or Control-
drag to copy text.

Not only can you drag text blocks to other documents within GoLive or other open applications, you can also create a text clipping on the Macintosh by dragging text to the Desktop. This can be handy if you need to use a block of text frequently, but don't want to set up a GoLive Component. Dragging text from the HTML Source Editor works the same way.

Navigating with the Keyboard

You may not always want to reach for the mouse when you're typing, so it's important to know how to get around via the keyboard using the arrow keys and modifiers. Table 8-1 lists the results of the possible key combinations. Holding down Shift when performing any of the following actions selects the text range from the cursor's starting position.

Table 8-1
Modify your
keys to
success

Arrow Key	Macintosh	Windows	Result
Up/ Down			moves cursor up/down one line
Left/Right			moves cursor one character to the left/right
Left	Option	Control	moves cursor one word* to the left
Left	Command	Alt	moves cursor to beginning of line
Right	Option	Control	moves cursor one word* to the right
Right	Command	Alt	moves cursor to end of line**

* The cursor jumps between the beginnings and ends of words when using Option, rather than just the beginnings.

** The exception is when a line ends with a line break, rather than a full paragraph character, in which case the cursor is placed at the beginning of the next line.

Pressing the Home, End, Page Up, and Page Down keys changes what's displayed in the Layout Editor, but doesn't move your cursor to those locations. If you want your cursor to appear at the end of the document, for instance, you must either move it with the arrow keys, or scroll to the end and click where the cursor should appear.

On the other hand, this method of navigation makes it easier to locate your cursor if you've scrolled elsewhere on the page: just press one of the arrow keys to force GoLive to display the cursor. If the page structure makes it difficult to see the cursor by itself, press Shift plus an arrow key to spot the newly-highlighted text.

Formatting Text

Before launching into the specifics of styling text on a Web page, we need to take a step back and explain the difference between structural formatting and styled-text formatting. Although GoLive, for the most part, treats the variations as general text formatting, the underlying distinction between the two helps you understand why some formats, like bold and strong, seem to produce the same visual results, and to give you a taste of what's to come as Web formatting matures.

A Brief History of Formatted HTML Text

The Web wasn't necessarily intended to be a designer's playground. HTML provided a convenient framework for displaying information in a more readable format, featuring text styles and inline images (and, of course, connecting pages using hyperlinks), that could be read on any computer with a Web browser.

Since there was no guarantee that someone reading your document had the same typefaces or support for styled text, such as offered in a word processor, HTML was devised as a set of tags defining a document's structure rather than the specifics of its appearance. (This is the theory behind Extended Markup Language, or XML, which provides an even more generic structure.) Structuring tags also circumvented the need to support several proprietary file formats; HTML files are plain text, readable by nearly every computer system from Palm handheld to Unix workstation to IBM mainframe.

So, for example, instead of creating a headline in 36-point Franklin Gothic type, the relevant text was simply tagged as a headline, letting the browser format it to the program's settings for what a headline should be—in most cases, this meant bold type set two to three times larger than the body text. This structural approach provides more flexibility when sharing information because it identifies sections of a document—such as headlines, quotations, and code examples—as objects, not as text with local formatting applied.

Unfortunately, structure tended to drive designers nuts in early implementations of HTML, because designers are accustomed to specifying exactly how something will look. That's why HTML also allows styled-text formatting, letting you display text in italics, or underlined, or in a monospaced font without assigning a structural classification to it.

As HTML has evolved over the years, this type of local formatting has lost favor with the architects of the HTML spec at the World Wide Web Consortium (W3C). The HTML 4.0 specification, while calling for backwards compatibility with the formatting introduced in earlier versions of the specification, recommends styling text using Cascading Style Sheets (CSS). Although in the long run this may prove to be the better implementation, especially in terms of ease in updating a site's appearance, sometimes we just want to make a word italic and move on.

Text Styles

GoLive currently supports text styling in a number of ways, available either from the Toolbar or the Type menu and applied to any highlighted text in the Layout Editor. Styles can also be combined with one another. Table 8-2 displays the basic styled text options.

Table 8-2
Text styles

Text Style	Example
Plain Text	Typefaces by Josef Stylin'
Bold	**Typefaces by Josef Stylin'**
Italic	*Typefaces by Josef Stylin'*
Underline	Typefaces by Josef Stylin'
Strikeout	~~Typefaces by Josef Stylin'~~
Superscript	Typefaces by Josef Stylin'
Subscript	Typefaces by Josef Stylin'
Teletype*	Typefaces by Josef Stylin'
Blink	(see next tip)
Nobreak**	

* Teletype is a method of applying local formatting to display text in a monospaced font.

** Nobreak lets you specify that the highlighted text not wrap to the next line if it's being displayed in a narrow browser window, a table cell, or beside an aligned image.

TIP:
Don't Blink

The Blink tag was introduced by Netscape and quickly became one of the most derided tags ever, since not everyone wants to be repeatedly flashed by text. GoLive does not display the blink effect in either the Layout Editor or the Layout Preview; you have to open the page in a Netscape browser to see it in action. Although we have seen an occasional clever use of Blink (it convincingly reproduces a word processor's flashing cursor), we don't recommend its continued use.

NEW IN 5:
Contextual
Text
Formatting

Tired of reaching for the menus whenever you want to apply text formatting? GoLive 5 introduces extensive contextual menu support for applying all of the formatting found under the Type menu. With text selected, simply Control-click (Mac) or right-click (Windows) to access the contextual menu (see Figure 8-3).

Figure 8-3
Contextual
choices

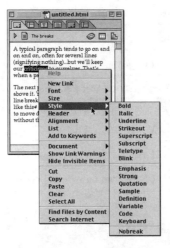

TIP:
Mix and
Match Styles

You don't have to pick just one text style or text structure tag; feel free to mix and match them as you wish. If your style soup gets to be too murky, simply go to the Type menu and select Plain Text from the Style submenu, or Plain Structure from the Structure submenu, or both.

Text Structure

The Structure submenu of GoLive's Type menu lists the structural formatting options, which are also applied to any highlighted text. Unlike the text styles above, the appearance of text formatted with these tags depends on how a browser is configured to display them. Structural definitions tend to identify the kind of content rather than the formatting that should be applied to them; for instance, "quotation" instead of "italic."

Structural definitions are helpful when using Cascading Style Sheets as well; for example, you could specify that text marked as Emphasis appear not only in italics, but colored red and slightly larger than the rest of the text (see Chapter 29, *Cascading Style Sheets*). The descriptions in Table 8-3 note GoLive's display as well as the common appearance in Web browsers (though they may differ among products, platforms, and versions).

Table 8-3
Structural
styles

Structure	Appearance
Plain Structure	The default style offers no frills
Emphasis	Text appears in italics
Strong	Text appears in bold
Quotation	Text appears in italics
Sample	Text appears in a monospaced font
Definition	A truly structural tag, the text doesn't change its appearance in GoLive
Variable	Text appears in italics
Code	Text appears in a monospaced font
Keyboard	Text appears in a monospaced font

Paragraph Formatting

In addition to formatting snippets of highlighted text, HTML includes the ability to choose a format that gets applied to an entire paragraph. Unlike text styles, you cannot mix and match paragraph formats.

Headings. Web browsers include built-in definitions for six heading levels. Structurally, headings act as classifications whose appearances easily can be manipulated with Cascading Style Sheets; stylistically, headings often pack an obvious "this is clearly a headline" punch to your text. You can apply headings from the Type menu's Header submenu or the Paragraph Format popup menu on the Toolbar (see Figure 8-4).

Figure 8-4
Heading
formats

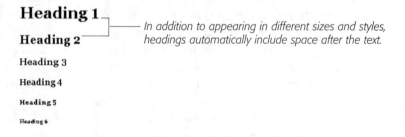

In addition to appearing in different sizes and styles, headings automatically include space after the text.

Preformatted. Preformatted text disobeys a few laws of HTML for the sake of making things easier for Web authors. Normally, Web browsers ignore line breaks and multiple spaces in an HTML file, relying on paragraph and other vertical markers—like the end of a list—to identify paragraphs and other blocks of text that should be separated vertically. Preformatted text instead reproduces the text exactly as it appears in the HTML, in a monospaced font including any hard returns, even without paragraph or line break tags (see Figure 8-5). Preformatted text works well when showing longer code samples or content, like bracketed text, that would normally require HTML entities to display properly.

Figure 8-5
Preformatted
text

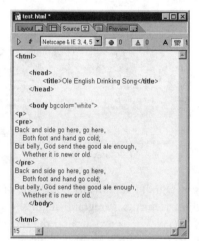 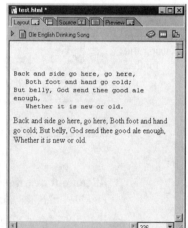

The line breaks of the preformatted section (within the Pre tags in the HTML Source Editor) are applied, where the line breaks in the bottom paragraph are ignored by GoLive and Web browsers.

TIP:
Exporting and Uploading with Pre

In Part 3, *Sites,* we discuss using features like Export and Upload to Server to strip unwanted white space and other useless HTML from Web pages. If you use Preformatted text, which uses the Pre tag in HTML, some of this superfluous spacing may be useful for page formatting. We recommend not stripping HTML on pages that use the Pre tag.

Address. This format is used for addresses or other contact information that Internet search-engine indexers look for when scanning your Web site. GoLive and most browsers display the text in italics.

Text Alignment

Most of the text we read in Western European languages is aligned to the left edge of a page or column, but that doesn't mean there isn't room for a little nonconformity here and there since GoLive handles all kinds of text encodings, multiple alignment styles can be handy for that purpose.

In addition to left-side alignment, GoLive can center or right-align paragraphs: click the desired alignment button on the Toolbar or choose from the Alignment submenu of the Type menu. To return to the paragraph's default alignment, either select Default Alignment from the Alignment submenu or click a highlighted alignment button to deactivate it (see Figure 8-6).

Figure 8-6
Text alignment using the Toolbar

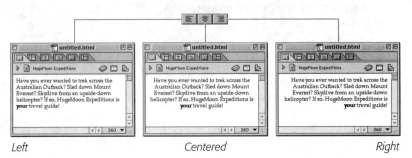

Left   Centered   Right

Alignment overrides. Paragraph alignment is only one of several methods GoLive offers for aligning elements. Paragraph alignment is much different than image alignment, which wraps text around the image (see Chapter 9, *Images*). You can also align text within a table cell by setting the cell's alignment attribute (see Chapter 11, *Tables*). And, as you might expect, the various alignments can be combined depending on the layout you're aiming for. In this case, it's good to know how the alignments interact with each other, and which ones override the others.

In general, paragraph alignment dominates. If you enter text within a table cell and set its paragraph alignment to Right, the text remains aligned right even if the table cell's horizontal alignment is set to Left or Center. When setting image or table alignment for purposes of wrapping text, however, you can get both effects simultaneously. An image with its Alignment set to Left, but placed at the front of a paragraph that's been aligned right, sticks to the left of the screen while the wrapped text appears beside it aligned right (see Figure 8-7).

Block indent. Although not technically an alignment attribute, GoLive supports block indentation of paragraphs, which simply indents the paragraph using HTML's Blockquote tag. From the Alignment submenu of the Type menu, choose Increase Block Indent or Decrease Block Indent, depending on how far you want to indent the text. Unlike using an unnumbered list to indent a paragraph (see "Unnumbered List" later in this chapter), Block Indent brings the paragraph's margins in from both the left and right sides (see Figure 8-8).

Figure 8-7
Alignment
overrides

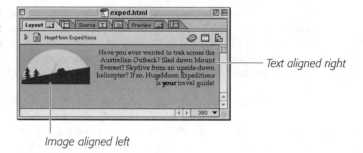

Text aligned right

Image aligned left

Figure 8-8
Block indent

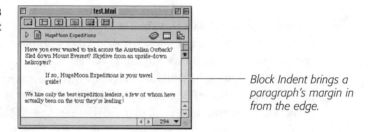

Block Indent brings a
paragraph's margin in
from the edge.

Text Size

Text size in HTML isn't expressed in points, as it is most everywhere else on your computer, because HTML doesn't understand descriptions like 10-point Times. In order to make the Web more accessible, text size is expressed structurally, not stylistically, based on the text-size settings in most Web browsers. This way, it doesn't matter how large your monitor is, or whether you're viewing it at its maximum resolution—the text on a Web page is almost guaranteed to be readable. To further complicate the issue, text sizes in HTML are relational, so trying to emulate 10-point Times, for example, might mean setting the type size at 3, -1, +1, or others depending on the user's browser settings. Don't be daunted, however: you still have plenty of control over the appearance of your text.

Choose from 22 size options by using the Font Size popup menu on the Toolbar, or the Size submenu under the Type menu; the default text size is None (see Figure 8-9).

Figure 8-9
Text sizes

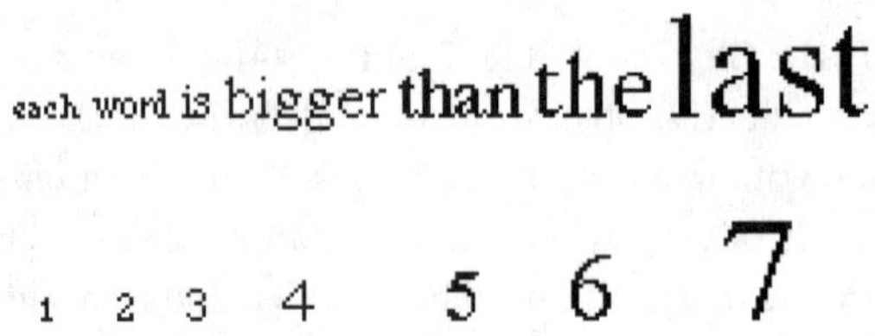

each word is bigger than the last

1 2 3 4 5 6 7

NEW IN 5:
How Big
Is None?

How nitpicky do you want to get? Earlier versions of GoLive tracked text size solely on a scale of 1 to 7, with 3 being the default size. With the addition of relative text sizes, it's harder to convince Web designers that 3 is the default, so the None option has been introduced in GoLive 5.

One could argue that "none" represents nothing, or zero, which would mean that the text wouldn't even exist, and therefore theoretically all of your hard work would be obliterated when you chose the None option. But we're sure you have much better uses for your time than theorizing about nonexistent numbers.

Absolute versus relative text sizes in HTML. There are two ways to express font size within HTML. Absolute sizing specifies a number on a 1 to 7 scale; relative sizing tells the browser to use a size that's equal to a number more or less than the browser's default font size, ranging from -7 to +7.

In reality, each method is somewhat relative, since there's no way outside of using CSS to define a specific point size (however, see the sidebar "Covering the Bases with the Basefont Tag," later, for an exception). So, if you've set your browser to display a larger font size by default (like the "Text Zoom" option in Internet Explorer, or a larger point size in Netscape Navigator's preferences), the browser is always computing the correct size based on those settings. In the code, however, the difference is plain: absolute sizes are referenced by their number, while relative sizes look like this:

```
<FONT SIZE="+2">
```

Glancing at the results in most browsers, there seems to be no difference. Assuming that a browser is using "3" as the default, specifying a size of "+2" or "5" achieves the same results. The difference comes when the user selects a new browser default font size. In this case, assuming the new default is "4," the absolute size of "5" still renders text at what the browser knows to be a size of "5." The relative size comes out at "6" instead, being two more than the default size (see Figure 8-10).

If you prefer to use relative sizes, choose the positive or negative values from the Font Size popup menu, or from the Type menu's Size submenu.

Figure 8-10
Absolute and relative text sizes

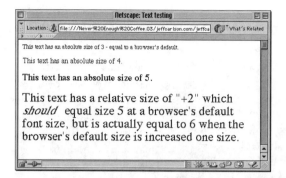

Covering the Bases with the Basefont Tag

You can gain a small measure of control over a page's default font size by employing the Basefont tag in your HTML. This tag, which must be entered directly into the page's source code, specifies a base text size from which a browser can calculate the results of relative font sizing. It appears after the Body tag, and is expressed like this:

`<BASEFONT size="2">`

For example, if using smaller type is part of a page's design, specifying a Basefont size value of 2 means you won't have to manually adjust the page's text using GoLive's text size settings (you also drastically reduce the amount of code in the HTML file in place of Font tags). When you use a relative text size, such as +2, the text is measured from a size of 2, rather than the browser default of 3 (see Figure 8-11).

The downside to the Basefont tag is that the W3C has deprecated it in favor of Cascading Style Sheets, which provides much more control over text size. Also, even though most people probably don't change the default size values of their Web browsers, you still can't know for sure what size your words will appear across the board. (See sidebar, "Why Windows Web Pages Have Tiny Text," for more information on how text size differs among browsers and platforms.)

Figure 8-11
Basefont's effect on font sizes

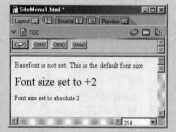

With no Basefont tag, font sizes work as expected (left). Setting the Basefont increases relative sizes (below).

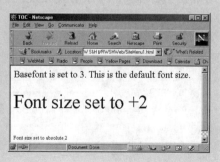

Why Windows Web Pages Have Tiny Text

by Geoff Duncan, Technical Editor,
TidBITS *(http://www.tidbits.com/)*

Most Macintosh users have encountered Web pages with unbearably tiny text. If you haven't, spend a few minutes browsing Microsoft's Web site (http://www.microsoft.com/windows/)—especially pages devoted to Windows itself—where it's not uncommon for Mac users to see text one to four pixels in height.

This phenomenon isn't limited to the Web. Do all Windows users have some sort of telescopic vision that makes text appear larger to them?

Why, yes. They do.

Making points. The confusion begins with a unit almost everyone uses: the point. People use points every day, choosing a 12-point font for a letter, or a 36-point font for a headline. But do you know what a point is?

Many people tell you that a point is ½-inch. That's correct, but only for the imaging systems used in most computers (including Apple's QuickDraw and Adobe's PostScript). Outside of a computer, the definition of a point varies between different measurement systems, none of which put a point precisely equal to ½-inch.

For the purposes of understanding why text on Windows Web pages often looks too small on a Macintosh, you can do the same thing your computer does: assume there are 72 points to an inch.

Not your type. When you refer to text of a particular point size, you're describing the height of the text, rather than its width or the dimensions of a particular character (or glyph) in a typeface. So, if there are 72 points to an inch, you might think 72-point characters would be one inch in height—but you'd almost always be wrong. The maximum height of text is measured from the top of a typeface's highest ascender (generally a lowercase d or l, or a capital letter) to the bottom of the face's lowest descender (usually a lowercase j or y). Most glyphs in a typeface use only a portion of this total height and thus are less than one inch in height at 72 points. With that in mind, how does a computer use this information to display text on a monitor?

Let's say you're writing a novel, and you set your chapter titles in 18-point text. First, the computer needs to know how tall 18 points is. Since the computer believes there are 72 points in an inch, this is easy: 18 points is $^{18}\!/_{72}$-inch, or exactly one-quarter inch. The computer then proceeds to draw text on your screen that's one-quarter-inch high.

This is where the universe gets strange. Your computer thinks of your monitor as a Cartesian grid made up of pixels or "dots." To a computer, your display is so many pixels wide by so many pixels tall, and everything on your screen is drawn using pixels. Thus, the physical resolution of your display can be expressed in pixels per inch (ppi) or, more commonly, dots per inch (dpi).

To draw 18-point text that's one-quarter inch in height, your computer needs to know how many pixels fit into a quarter inch. To find out, you'd think your computer would talk to your display about its physical resolution—but you'd be wrong. Instead, your computer makes a patent, nearly pathological assumption about how many pixels fit into an inch, regardless of your monitor size, resolution, or anything else.

If you use a Mac, your computer always assumes your monitor displays 72 pixels per inch, or 72 dpi. The exception is Microsoft Internet Explorer 5 and later, which uses a base of 96 dpi. If you use Windows, your computer most often assumes your monitor displays 96 dpi, but if you're using "large fonts" Windows assumes it can display 120 pixels per inch (120 dpi). These assumptions mean a Macintosh uses 18 pixels to render 18-point text, a Windows system typically uses 24 pixels, a Unix system typically uses between 19 and 25 pixels, and a Windows system using a large fonts setting uses 30 pixels.

Size does matter. This leads to the answer to our $20 question: why text on Web pages designed for Windows users often looks tiny on a Mac. Say your computer's display—or Web browser's window—measures 640 by 480 pixels. Leaving aside menu bars, title bars, and other screen clutter, the Mac can display 40 lines of 12-point text in that area (with solid leading, meaning there's no extra space between the lines).

Under the same conditions, Windows displays a mere 32 lines of text; since Windows uses more pixels to draw its text, less text fits in the same area (see Figure 8-12). Thus, Windows-based Web designers often specify small font sizes to jam more text into a fixed area, and Macintosh users get a double whammy: text that was already displaying using fewer pixels on a Macintosh screen is further reduced in size, even to the point where the text is illegible to even those with the best eyesight.

The fundamental issue is that the computer is trying to map a physical measurement—the point—to a display device with unknown physical characteristics. A standard computer monitor is basically an analog projection system: although its geometry can be adjusted to varying degrees, the monitor itself has no idea how many pixels it's showing over a particular physical distance.

Thus, in terms of raw pixels, most Windows users see text that's 33 percent larger than text on a Macintosh—from a Macintosh point of view, Windows users do, in fact, see text with telescopic vision. When you view the results on a single display where all pixels are the same size, the differences range from noticeable to dramatic. The Windows text is huge, or the Mac text is tiny—take your pick.

[This sidebar was adapted from a longer article first published in TidBITS #467/15-Feb-97, copyright 1998 TidBITS Electronic Publishing. To read the entire article, go to http://db.tidbits.com/getbits.acgi?tbart=05284]

Figure 8-12
Text size differences between Mac and Windows

Both screens viewed in Internet Explorer with the text size set to Medium.

Lists and Indents

Without the margin and indent features of a word processor, formatting list material would be a frustrating endeavor. Fortunately, GoLive supports and previews HTML's list features, not only making it easy to create typical lists of items, but also lists for presentation purposes.

Numbered List. To create a list that includes numbers before each paragraph, highlight the text and click the Numbered List button on the Toolbar, or select Default Numbered List from the List submenu of the Type menu. You can choose which style of numbering you want displayed by choosing the other options from the same menu (see Figure 8-13).

Figure 8-13
List types

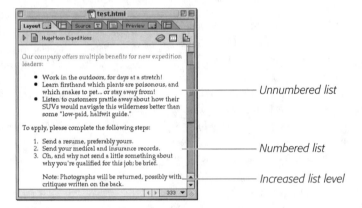

Unnumbered list

Numbered list

Increased list level

TIP:
No Need to Select All Text

Since lists are a paragraph (or block) setting, you don't need to select every character in a paragraph before applying the list-level commands. As long as a portion of the paragraph is selected, the entire block between returns is formatted in the list style.

Unnumbered List. If your list isn't dependent on numbering, create an unnumbered list by clicking the Unnumbered List button on the Toolbar or selecting Default Unnumbered List from the List submenu of the Type menu. The menu also includes the option to use bullets, circles, or squares at the beginning of list items.

TIP:
CSS Bullets

With CSS, you can specify a wider variety of bullets for unnumbered lists, including images you specify yourself. However, so far only Microsoft Internet Explorer 4.0 and later supports this very cool design feature.

Increasing and decreasing list levels. One advantage to using lists is that you don't have to precede each item with a number or bullet; a list can just as easily serve as an indented margin for the selected range of text. Click the Increase List Level button on the Toolbar or select it from the Type menu's List submenu to push the text horizontally to the right. The Decrease List Level button and menu item move the text back toward the left margin.

TIP:
Removing Bullets or Numbers

You'd think that turning a list back into regular text would be a matter of clicking the Numbered List or Unnumbered List buttons to toggle the setting, but that's not the case. To rid your text of bullets or numbering, use Decrease List Level instead.

Term and Definition. Harking back to its academic origins, HTML includes the capability to define terms and definitions (structural formatting). Select part of a paragraph and choose Term from the List submenu of the Type menu to tag it as a term; the appearance doesn't change in the Layout Editor. To create a definition for the term, select the text and choose Definition from the same submenu. This action formats the text indented from the left margin without the vertical space imposed by normal paragraphs (see Figure 8-14).

Figure 8-14
Terms and definitions

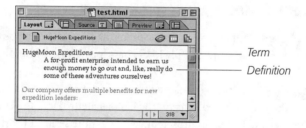

Term
Definition

Indenting using horizontal spacers. Another method of indenting text is the use of HTML-defined spacers called Horizontal Spacers in GoLive. Despite their name, these spacers are not limited to being just horizontal.

TIP:
Spacers are Netscape Only

The downside to spacers is that they're only recognized by Netscape browsers (and not likely to be adopted by the other major browser developers), limiting their usefulness across a broad range of viewers.

Double-click the Horizontal Spacer icon from the Objects palette's Basic tab, or drag it to the Layout Editor to add a spacer. You can specify its width in the Spacer Inspector to create a single line indent by changing the value in the Width field or stretching the spacer element by its object handle. A spacer also can be set to Vertical, which fills the length of the text and offers a variable height value; or Block, which creates a rectangular space that can be aligned like an image (see Figure 8-15). The Block style can be aligned similar to an image (where text wraps around it) by choosing an option from the Alignment popup menu.

Figure 8-15
Horizontal
Spacer tag

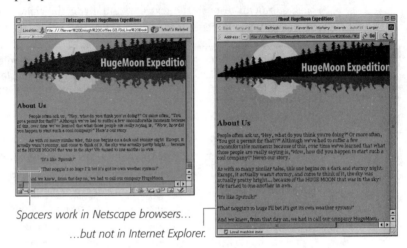

Spacers work in Netscape browsers…

…but not in Internet Explorer.

Text Color

A page's default text color can be set in the Page Inspector, but there are times when you may want to apply local color formatting within the body text.

Applying text color. To color a range of text, first select it in the Layout Editor, and then choose a color from the Color palette. Drag the color swatch from the Preview Pane and drop it anywhere on the selected text to apply the new color (see Figure 8-16).

Figure 8-16
Coloring text

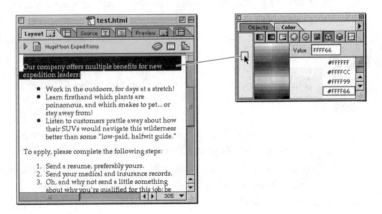

You can also take advantage of GoLive 5.0's new Text Color field, located on the Toolbar. Drag a color swatch from the Color palette to the Text Color field to define a color. If a range of text is selected, the color is applied to the text; if no text is selected, however, any text you type beginning at the insertion point's location assumes that color.

TIP:

Many Unhappy Returns

GoLive likes to keep its text formatting orderly within the underlying HTML, which means that the style you're typing with in one paragraph won't carry over to the next when you hit Return or Enter. To test, specify a color in the Text Color field and apply bold formatting; type a few words, then hit Return to make a new paragraph. The text now shows up in the default formatting. The only attributes that get carried into the next paragraph are structural ones: header, alignment, and list items. Applying other text formatting after you've entered the text will likely save you time and frustration.

If that's too much dragging and dropping for you, select a text range and then click once on the Text Color field to use it in active mode. The highlighted text dynamically changes colors as you click on colors in the Color palette.

TIP:

Popup Text Color

To quickly choose a Web-safe color, Control-click (Mac) or right-click (Windows) the Text Color field to display a popup grid of the Web Color List. Hold down Option (Mac) or Control (Windows) to view a grid of the Web Name List.

If you're editing text in the HTML Source Editor and don't know the hex value of a specific color, dropping a color swatch in your text inserts the following code, which you can use in a FONT tag:

```
COLOR="#000000"
```

Removing text color. If you decide that colors just aren't working visually within your text, highlight the colored area and select Remove Color from the Type menu to return to the page's default text color.

Using Fonts

A welcome change in modern Web browsers is the ability to specify typefaces other than the limited selection used in a browser's preferences. Just as color and text formatting can affect the tone and presentation of your text, using different fonts adds to the character of Web pages. Font support also allows you to employ faces such as Verdana or Georgia that were created specifically for onscreen reading.

Unfortunately, there's no guarantee that all the viewers of your page have your specified fonts installed on their systems. However, this doesn't turn out to be too much of a downside (maybe it's more of a slightly-vertically-declined plane?) because of the flexible way HTML handles font selection.

Specifying Fonts

Before leaping into how GoLive handles font selection, we quickly need to explain how Web browsers treat fonts. As with text size, typefaces are defined using the Font tag, which tells the browser which font to use for the text that follows it. But if the viewer's computer doesn't have that face installed, the viewer sees only the default text—still acceptable, but it misses the mark on communicating the designer's vision. That's why designers typically define several fonts in the Font tag, separated by commas.

A Web browser looks at the first font listed, and uses it if it's installed. If it's not available, the browser moves on to the next font, then the next, and the next, until either a match is found or the list ends, at which point the default font comes back into play. For greater compatibility, designers choose fonts that are more likely to be installed on users' machines, such as the faces used by the operating system. In HTML, the code looks something like this:

```
<FONT face="Helvetica,Arial,sans serif">
```

In this example, most browsers and platforms are accounted for: Helvetica ships with the Mac OS, Arial is a default Windows font, and "sans serif" is a general descriptor that tells the browser to use whichever font has been set up for sans-serif use in its preferences.

GoLive recognizes the fonts in these types of groupings, called "fontsets," in order to present the most compatible front to its Web pages.

Applying fontsets. That said, styling text in a particular font is an easy task: select a font by going to the Type menu, then navigate to the Font submenu. The fontsets are noted only by the name of the first font in the set, but the backup font options get applied as well (see Figure 8-17).

Figure 8-17
Applying
a fontset

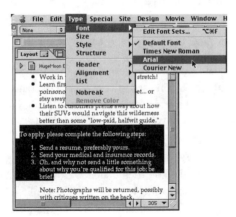

Seen Onscreen

Most of the fonts installed on your computer herald from a long history of printed typography. Being able to view on your computer screen close approximations of what a typeface would look like when printed was one of the strengths behind early desktop publishing. The problem is, those fonts were designed with print in mind, and aren't necessarily designed to be read onscreen.

With the popularity of the Web and CD-ROM-based multimedia, typographers are devoting more efforts to making fonts that read better onscreen—some of which may never see the printed page. After a bit of trial and error, we've become partial to a handful of faces that we use when designing for (and browsing) the Web, reading email every day, and using word processors. Favorite faces include Microsoft's free fonts Verdana and Georgia; Adobe's Minion Web and Myriad Web; and Apple's venerable New York and occasionally even Geneva.

Each of these fonts features, on average, a taller x-height (the vertical measurement of a lower-case letters), roomier letterspacing, and a pixel-level attention to detail that avoids mis-shapen or overly jagged letters. If you've been suffering with Times all this time, try a font that's been designed expressly for onscreen reading; the difference is an eye-opener (and an eye-saver).

Editing Fontsets

GoLive is preconfigured with three common fontsets that all but ensure that any viewer sees the fonts displayed. Although they work well, we have enough typographical sense behind our eyeballs to want to customize the fontsets and use other typefaces (see the sidebar, "Seen Onscreen").

TIP:
Local, Global, and Sitewide Fontsets

GoLive tracks three kinds of fontsets: local to the page, global to the program (any page opened in the program), and specific to a site. We discuss working with global fontsets in Chapter 2, *The Inspector;* site fontsets are covered in Chapter 22, *Sitewide Sets.*

Font Set Editor. To edit or create fontsets, choose Edit Font Sets from the Font submenu of the Type menu. Specify either default fontsets (or global fontsets), which appear on the Font list in every GoLive document, or page fontsets, which are used only for the frontmost open document. Click a set in the Font Sets pane at left to view its contents in the Font Names pane to the right (see Figure 8-18).

To create a new, empty fontset, click the New button at left. A new font set (appropriately named "New Font") appears at right. Type the name of the font you want to use, then press Enter; since that's the first font in the new set, the set takes its name. If you want to add more fonts, simply click the New button beneath the Font Names pane and type their names in the field below. You can also click the popup menu near the field and select fonts that are currently installed on your system.

When you're finished, click OK. As far as we can tell, you can enter as many fonts as you like, or stick with only one. With your fontsets created, apply them from the Font menu as normal.

Figure 8-18
Editing
fontsets

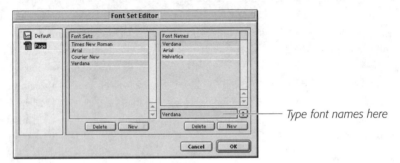

Type font names here

TIP:
**Careful
Typing
Produces
Better
Typography**

When you type the names in the Font Names field, it doesn't matter whether you have these fonts installed on your system, or whether the fonts exist at all. GoLive assumes that you know what you're typing, and accepts it. If you make a spelling mistake or typo, such as "New Yurk" instead of "New York," a Web browser looks for New Yurk, then moves on to the next font in the list.

TIP:
**Default and
Page Sets
Don't
Mingle**

If you want to create a set that appears in both the current page and GoLive's fontset defaults, you have to create the set twice. There's no way to create one and then duplicate it to the other except by hand. Also, creating a new default set doesn't make it appear in the page set, even though by definition the page becomes subordinate to the default; you must quit and relaunch GoLive for it to show up.

TIP:
**Make Your
Fonts
Available**

If you're worried someone may not possess the font you have in mind for your page, consider using one that is freely accessible. Microsoft has made several fonts, such as Verdana, Georgia, and Trebuchet, available as free downloads from its Web site at http://www.microsoft.com/typography/; they're also now added when you install a recent version of Internet Explorer or Outlook Express. The downloads are fairly small, so your viewers can install them easily and return to your site later to get the full effect of what you've designed.

You Look Simply... Fontastic

Text on the Web used to be about as exciting as the endless columns of copy on old-time newspapers: it seemed to go on and on and on, without offering any pizzazz. What most people don't realize is that a lot of hard work went into making those newspaper columns as readable as possible—legibility wasn't sacrificed, just a bit of excitement. The Web, finally, is reaching the point where legibility and control can co-exist, and the presentation of type can be just as interesting as the snazziest graphics.

CHAPTER 9
Images

The Web existed before it could handle images, but it wasn't as exciting. To make it more useful, the early browser engineers threw in support for poor-resolution, limited-color-range images that displayed at excruciatingly slow speeds and—presto—the commercial Web was suddenly a hot property. Folks began banging down the doors to be let in, no matter how pokey it was.

Combining images with text on a page also marked the beginning of wide-scale online publishing and opened the field for graphic designers to make an impact. You can simulate graphics with text for just so long.

Before visual page editors existed, adding images to a page by hand coding HTML tags was a laborious process. GoLive, in contrast, lets you add images by dragging them into a document window from the Desktop or Site window, or by browsing local drives and other networked resources.

Once an image is on a page, you can assign attributes, like alignment and spacing, via the Image Inspector, which let you immediately preview how the settings look on a page.

Image Formats

Before the Web, bigger seemed better: larger images had more resolution, and image formats that were *lossless*—that is, preserved all the data and color variation in an image—were the ideal choice. But the Web shook things up. The relatively small amount of bandwidth available to most Web users gets overwhelmed by the size of most uncompressed, full-resolution, high-fidelity color images. Obviously, some kind of accommodation had to be made.

To that end, two image formats, GIF and JPEG, rose to the top. GIF was the first format that the earliest graphical Web browser supported—that's Mosaic, for you history buffs. And, for better or for worse, we're stuck with it. JPEG, on the other hand, offers some superior tradeoffs in image quality versus image size. As most users' systems can now handle displaying thousands or millions of colors on their monitors at once, its use has really taken off.

PNG, a third format designed from the ground up to meet the needs of Web users, offers a variety of tradeoffs among compression, color palette, and image quality. Although PNG has found some takers, many browsers can't display PNG images properly.

GoLive doesn't have the ability to edit images directly—otherwise, why would we all have so many megabytes of applications like Adobe Photoshop or Equilibrium DeBabelizer sitting on our systems?—but it's helpful to know the advantages and limitations of each format to get the best performance out of your pages.

GIF. Images saved as GIF (Graphics Interchange Format, pronounced "jiff") files are the universal language of the Web, with all browsers in all versions displaying almost all kinds of GIFs. The GIF format compresses data in two ways: first, by reducing the number of colors in the image to a palette of no more than 256 different colors, meaning that color takes less space to store; and second, by analyzing patterns of repeated color and replacing them with tokens that take up much less space (see Figure 9-1). Line art, like logos or simple drawings, work best when saved as GIF files.

What's New in 5

GoLive's image-editing features are significantly beefed up in version 5. Using GoLive Smart Objects, you can directly add Photoshop, Illustrator, and LiveMotion files to your pages. Any changes made to the original are automatically applied to the version on your page. Also, resizing a Smart Object in the Layout Editor prompts GoLive to re-render the image in its host application, removing undesirable artifacts that appear when you make a Web browser resize a GIF or JPEG image.

This is all made possible via Adobe's Save for Web software, which has been integrated into GoLive, and which now underlies nearly all image processing in the application. The Save for Web dialog box offers a surprisingly thorough level of control over optimizing Web graphics, from changing color palettes to the way sliced images are split up and named. Save for Web now handles converting all graphics that aren't Web formatted, such as TIFF, PICT, BMP, and others.

Another new feature in GoLive is Tracing Image, a handy way to bring in rough templates created in an image-editing program for use as a background guide to building pages. You can extract portions of a tracing image for use on the page, which appear in floating boxes.

Figure 9-1
GIF image

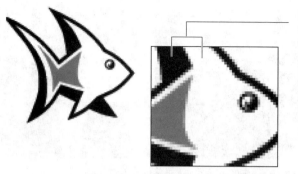

Large areas of solid color, combined with a low number of colors in the image, make logos and line-art excellent candidates for the GIF format.

GIFs also support two extra features, both of which are useful for Web page design. You can set a transparent color in a GIF so that the background shows through, allowing you to simulate the layering of images over other images or a background. And, you can include multiple frames in a single GIF to provide simple animation; many Web ad banners use GIFs to cycle through a message.

JPEG. For images that are more "photographic" in nature, turn to JPEG (Joint Photographic Experts Group, the body that came up with the specification). JPEG is a *lossy* compression format, meaning that the algorithm that creates the JPEG throws away information when creating the compressed image file. The JPEG algorithm can provide more or less faithful color and image quality on a sliding scale from most faithful (in which the most accurate representation of the image is created at about a 2 to 1 ratio), to least faithful—in which visible artifacts in the image show, including pixelization, but the ratio can be as high as 100 to 1. JPEG uses a perceptual system so that the least important color distinctions are removed first; it also has built-in compression to further reduce the amount of space the final data takes up.

Although it sounds like the end result would resemble a patchwork of pixels, JPEGs can be surprisingly accurate to the original image while being drastically reduced in file size (see Figure 9-2). JPEG images don't support transparency or animation, however.

PNG. The newcomer to the graphics world is PNG (Portable Network Graphics), pronounced "ping." PNG images compress slightly better than GIF images (anywhere from five to 25 percent improvement), and feature alpha-channel transparency like Photoshop's (providing more options than GIF's one-bit transparency), gamma correction, and improved interlacing for faster perceived downloading. PNG offers completely faithful image reproduction

Figure 9-2
JPEG image

JPEG compression actually degrades the quality of your image (compare the original at left to the JPEG version at right), but does so in a way that is barely detectable to most viewers depending on the level of compression. (We've degraded the JPEG to its lowest setting in this example to prove the point.)

in which no color or quality is lost; or, you can use a GIF-like palette to reduce the number of colors to 256 or fewer.

The problem, so far, is that PNG has yet to be fully adopted by the major Web browsers. Netscape Communicator, for example, can view inline PNG graphics, but doesn't support alpha-channel transparency as of this writing; the closest full implementation so far is Microsoft Internet Explorer 5.0 on the Macintosh (see Figure 9-3). At least 25 percent of browsers still in general use can't display PNG images in any form. There's little doubt that PNG will be the wave of the future; it offers too many features that designers would love to take advantage of. Adoption of the format will take some time, however. For a more detailed look at the PNG specification, see http://www.libpng.org/pub/png/.

TIP:
Patent
Medicine

The PNG format arose for a reason in addition to building a format specifically for the Web: patent payments. Both GIF and JPEG are encumbered with patent licensing and payment issues that make it virtually impossible to release entirely free, non-problematic versions of source code for programs that create and/or read GIF and JPEG images. PNG is purposely designed to use only public-domain algorithms and requires no licensing fees for any part of its system.

Inserting Images

Like most page elements in GoLive, inserting an image is a simple drag-and-drop operation. Drag the Image icon from the Basic tab of the Objects palette to a location on the Layout Editor; you can also double-click the Image icon to insert an image placeholder.

Figure 9-3
PNG
transparency

If you're in the HTML Source Editor, you can drag or double-click the Image icon to insert the appropriate HTML code into the document. Similarly, dragging the icon to the HTML Outline Editor inserts an image object (though double-clicking does nothing). Each of these actions inserts a blank image placeholder sized to match the icon's dimensions (32 pixels square).

Enter the pathname of the image you want to use in the Source field of the Image Inspector's Basic tab, click the Browse button to locate the file, or use the Point & Shoot tool to specify a source image (see Figure 9-4).

Figure 9-4
Inserting
images

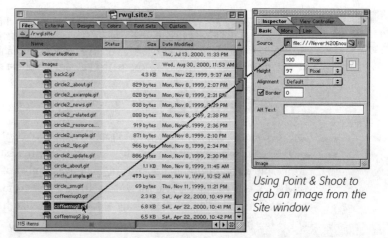

Using Point & Shoot to grab an image from the Site window

NEW IN 5:
Choosing a New Image

You can use these steps to specify a different image for the placeholder, but GoLive 5 introduces two contextual menu items that may be quicker. Bring up the contextual menu on the image and choose either Browse Link, which is the same as clicking the Inspector's Browse button, or Edit Link, which brings up the Edit URL dialog. Don't confuse this with the New Link item, a few items down the list, which creates a new hyperlink (see Figure 9-5).

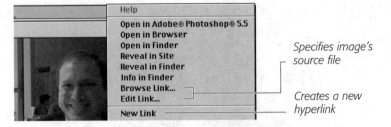

Figure 9-5
Changing
images
via the
contextual
menu

*Specifies image's
source file*

*Creates a new
hyperlink*

If you already know which graphic file you want to use, drag it from the Desktop or the Site window to the Layout Editor. You can also drag images between open files. Unlike inserting an image placeholder, however, dragging an image file directly to the HTML Source Editor creates a link to the file, not the code required to display the image.

Working with Images

An image isn't just a picture on the screen. Although a Web browser can figure out how to display an image based solely on the name of the graphic file, HTML provides several attributes for defining images and how they relate to surrounding material.

**TIP:
What about
Rollovers?**

Even though designers constantly use image rollovers (moving the mouse over an image changes the image to something else), GoLive supports them via a special Smart Object that works like a GoLive Action. We cover Actions and related Action-like Smart Objects in Chapter 28, *Actions*; flip forward to get the skinny.

Image Attributes

Control over the display of images has rapidly become one of the factors that sets the newer browsers apart from the older ones. The newest HTML specifications and extra features in browsers offer a huge number of settings that let you better control the appearance of an image. Some options have been around since practically the beginning of the visual Web; others are more recent. A few features are dedicated to improving how quickly or crisply browsers display images.

Width and height. It's our shared opinion that every Web page should include the height and width tags for every image; fortunately, GoLive offers this feature by default when an image is placed or imported. Providing width and height measurements to browsers helps speed up page loading because the browser doesn't have to retrieve images to know their size.

TIP:
**Dimensions
in Files**

GIF, JPEG, and PNG image file formats all list their dimensions in the first few characters of the data that comprises the file. But the browser still has to retrieve part or all of the file before it grabs that information if you don't specify width and height.

GoLive automatically pulls the height and width values from each image when placed on the page and displays the information in the Basic tab of the Image Inspector. If you really don't want the values to appear in the HTML, select Image from the Height and Width popup menus, and GoLive leaves the fields blank.

TIP:
**Other
Dimensions**

If you edit the height and width that GoLive fills in for the image, a browser resizes the image to fit the dimensions you specified—though with degraded results. See "Resizing Images," later in this chapter.

Border. HTML provides a method for drawing borders around images, but we guess that 90 percent of border usage is to apply a setting of "0" to help suppress the ugly blue line that shows up around linked graphics by default when no border is specified (see "Linking Images" later in this chapter). If you want a border of greater than zero to appear, enter a number in the Border field to specify the border's width in pixels (see Figure 9-6). If the image is linked, the border displays as the page's link color; otherwise, it shows up as the page's text color. (See Chapter 2, *The Inspector*, for how to set a page's link and text colors.)

**Figure 9-6
Image
Inspector
Basic settings**

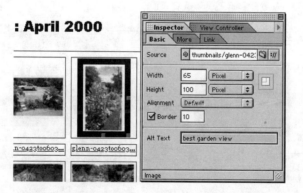

If you turn the Border setting off, GoLive's Layout Editor and Preview mode show a standard browser default border of two pixels for linked images (though it doesn't appear for unlinked images).

NEW IN 5:
Zero Default

Recognizing that most designers set their image borders to zero (or realizing that most bordered images are ugly, especially when linked), GoLive's developers rightly changed the default border width to zero.

Alt Text. The Alt Text attribute holds text that gets displayed before images load on a page or when the user doesn't want to or can't load images. In GoLive, type the text in the Alt Text field, located on the Basic tab of the Image Inspector.

The Alt Text is usually a description of the image that should load in its place, giving the viewer a quick preview of what's to appear while waiting for the rest of the graphics and text to load. Adding Alt tags to your images also makes your pages more accessible for those text-only Web warriors who surf with images turned off or in the pure text Lynx browser for Unix (we know several people who prefer to surf the Web this way, especially on slower modem connections). It's also a great aid to the visually impaired who require non-graphical elements to navigate a page.

Hspace and Vspace. These attributes define the space, in pixels, that pads the image from surrounding text or other items; Hspace adds space both to the left and right of an image, while Vspace adds it to the top and bottom (see Figure 9-7). The two corresponding fields are found in the Spec. tab. Padding an image comes in handy when wrapping text around an image, so the text and the picture aren't crammed against each other.

Figure 9-7
Hspace and
Vspace

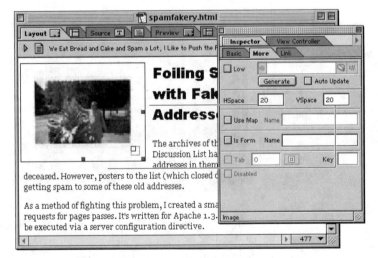

TIP:
Padding
with Pixels

Because the Hspace and Vspace options add space to both directions of an image, not just either side, we prefer using a transparent GIF to the right of a flush-left image, or to the left of a flush-right one. This allows us to space just in one direction and leave the other flush with the margin.

Resizing Images

As you should expect from a visual editor, GoLive supports resizing any images you place on a page. You can stretch, squash, or proportionally resize them to your heart's content.

However, we suggest thinking twice before publishing a page with images that have been resized in GoLive (or any visual editor, for that matter). The problem with resizing is that Web browsers generally don't display resized images very well because they're trying to compensate for the graphic's new size based on the limited amount of information available in the original. Also, a browser is not Photoshop; it doesn't have the algorithms and tools to provide the kind of resampling and smoothing that a photo-editing program can.

TIP:
Resizing
Smart
Objects

The information here refers to just changing an image's dimensions in the HTML for a standard Web graphic format (GIF, JPEG, PNG). If you're using Smart Objects, such as native Photoshop files, you're actually causing GoLive to resample or recreate the image itself, retaining a higher degree of quality. See "Smart Objects," later in this chapter.

Resized images, though not horrible, do tend to appear blocky or have misplaced pixels—a trained Web designer can usually spot immediately if the height and width values in the HTML don't match the intrinsic dimensions of the graphic. Plus, you're asking the browser to do extra work, which can slow its rendering time, making viewers wait a bit longer to see a full page. For finished pages, it's always better to resize the original in a true image editor, then save it as a new file (like "doggy_sm.gif").

TIP:
Resize While
Designing

We don't want to make a blanket statement that resizing in GoLive is a bad tool. Resizing images is good for mocking up pages during development; it allows you to experiment with different image sizes and placement on the page without having to create multiple resized versions. Just remember to create a final image that matches the final specifications you choose.

Resizing in the Image Inspector. To change the dimensions of an image, enter new values in the Width and Height fields in the Basics tab. When the values don't match the graphic's actual measurements, a resize warning icon appears in a corner of the image (see Figure 9-8). Clicking the resize button to the right of the Width and Height fields returns the image to its original dimensions and proportion.

Figure 9-8
Resizing
Images

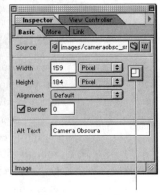

Resize warning icon appears in image...

...and resize warning button becomes active in Image Inspector

You can also choose to express the dimensions in percentages by selecting Percent from the popup menus to the right of the Height and Width fields. Be aware, however, that you're not specifying a percentage of the original image size, but a percentage of the page. So, an image with a width set to 100 percent would fill the width of the entire window when viewed in a Web browser (see Figure 9-9).

If you'd rather not include the size values at all, select Image from the popup menus to remove the values and restore the image's actual dimensions.

Figure 9-9
Choosing
percent for
width and
height

Percentage resize in relation to size of the browser window

Resizing using object handles. Dragging an image's object handles also re-sizes the image, allowing you to change the size manually without using the Image Inspector's numeric values. To resize the image proportionally, press the Shift key while dragging. Pressing the Control key lets you preview the image dynamically as it resizes, rather than displaying a bounding box to indi-cate the dimensions (see Figure 9-10).

If you've opted to resize the image using percentage values, you can't use object handles to manipulate the graphic.

Figure 9-10
Dynamically
resizing
images

Dragging the resize handle displays only a bounding box.

Control-dragging dynamically resizes the image as you drag.

Aligning Images

As with text, you can specify how an image is aligned on the page. However, image alignment offers more than just the ability to push a picture to one side of the screen or the other; text can wrap around aligned images.

Unlike placing images in a page-layout program, images on the Web are treated as if they were just another character or element. (They were original-ly called "inline images," which fell out of fashion some time ago.) In fact, be-fore browsers featured object alignment, pictures would display at the beginning, end, or sometimes in the middle of a line of text—resulting in un-even line spacing to compensate for the height of the graphics. So when you're specifying an image's alignment, you're telling a Web browser how the image should display in relation to the line of text in which it's contained.

TIP:
Place
Images at
the Front
of the Line

You can put an image anywhere you like, but we prefer to position them at the beginning of a line or paragraph of text. If you're using left or right alignment (see below), text wrapping is much more consistent than if the image appears at the end of a paragraph. Keep in mind that a Web browser reads the page the same as you read text—left to right, top to bottom—and formats it accordingly.

With an image selected, choose one of the following options from the Basic tab's Alignment menu.

Left, Right. These are the most commonly used alignment settings, and it's plain to see why: text and other elements wrap around an image, making the best use of space and generally presenting a more professional look to the page (see Figure 9-11). Unlike the rest of the alignment options, left and right alignment can change the location of the image itself. Depending on the size of your image, the wrapping can be unflattering, so watch out for odd results. If several pictures are left-aligned without much text between them, an awkward stairstepping effect happens (see Figure 9-12).

Top, Middle, Bottom. Not surprisingly, these settings place text at the top, in the middle, or at the bottom of the image. That's fine for single lines of text, but if your graphic appears at the beginning of a paragraph, only the first line is affected; the rest of the paragraph in that case falls below the image (see Figure 9-13).

Figure 9-11
Aligning
images

Alignment Left

Alignment Right

Figure 9-12
Stairstepping
effect

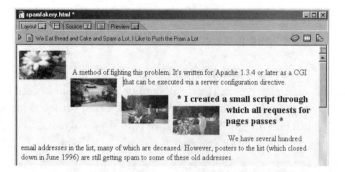

Depending on the height of the line, however, these settings can position an image above or below the text surrounding it. For example, if the line of text includes a large image that increases the line height, placing a smaller image on the same line and setting its alignment to Top would align the tops of both images, lifting the second image high above the text (see Figure 9-13).

TIP:

**Easy Margin
Control
Using
Alignment**

If you don't like the various ways HTML indents text (such as block indent or unnumbered lists as described in Chapter 8, *Text and Fonts*), you can control the size of a text margin by placing an aligned image to the left of it. Insert a transparent GIF at the beginning of the text section, and specify its height to be large enough to span the depth of the text; make its width the distance you want from the edge of the page's true margin. Then, set the image's alignment to Left or Right and watch the text snap into place. This won't work in all circumstances, since text sizes can vary widely among browsers and platforms, but it's often a simpler method than building tables or using other means.

Figure 9-13
Top, Middle,
and Bottom
alignment

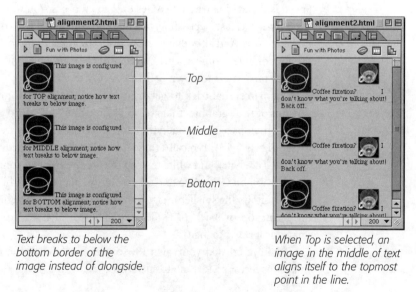

Text breaks to below the bottom border of the image instead of alongside.

When Top is selected, an image in the middle of text aligns itself to the topmost point in the line.

Text Top, Baseline. Images aligned to Text Top or Baseline stick to the height of the text, regardless of the text's line height (see Figure 9-14).

Abs Middle, Abs Bottom. This pair of alignment settings positions text and other elements at the absolute middle or bottom in relation to the aligned image, which may not necessarily be based on the midpoint of the text's height. This is often useful when centering images used as bullets to text lines (see Figure 9-14).

Figure 9-14
Text Top,
Baseline, Abs
Middle and
Bottom

Lowsource Images

Speed is everything when it comes to Web graphics. You want your viewer to see the page as fast as possible, but not everyone has a fast connection to the Internet—yet. And although you can optimize most graphics down to a small number of bytes, some images end up just large enough that it's going to take time for most users to download and display them.

One perceptual trick to get around this dilemma is to offer sneak-peek versions of your graphics that are small enough to download quickly, but take up the same space and contain the same image as the higher resolution graphic (see Figure 9-15). Typically, these "lowsource" images (defined in HTML as "lowsrc") are black and white to keep the file size smaller; sometimes the lowsource is a 1-bit GIF, while the full-resolution image is a 24-bit color JPG. The browser shows the smaller image first, and then displays the higher-resolution image on top of it when it's done loading (or, if it's a progressively saved image, as it starts to load).

If you've created your own lowsource image, click the Low box in the Image Inspector's More tab to specify the file.

Figure 9-15
Generating
lowsource
images

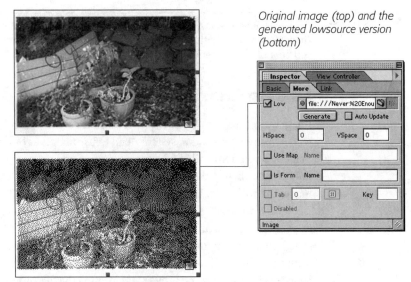

Original image (top) and the generated lowsource version (bottom)

TIP:
**Use Any
Image as
Lowsource**

Although the purpose of using lowsource images is to load a preview version of a graphic quickly, you can actually specify any graphic as a lowsource image. Some designers have used this to create some surprising effects.

Generating lowsource images. GoLive can generate a lowsource image for you when you click the Generate button.

By default, the lowsource image GoLive creates is a black-and-white GIF that exists in the same directory as the original image. Check the Auto Update box to make GoLive update the the lowsource version whenever the referenced image changes.

In GoLive's preferences, you can choose to save lowsource files in the Import Images folder—but see the tip "Import Images Files Aren't Uploaded," later in this chapter, before you do. You can also set whether the preview image is rendered in black and white or color. If you check the Auto-Generate by Default box, GoLive creates lowsource images for every graphic you place on your pages.

TIP:
**Clever Color
Previews**

GoLive features a clever way to create color lowsource images. Since GIFs compress best when they have a limited number of colors, black-and-white images are great because they feature only two. What GoLive does for color images is reduce the color palette; it also shrinks the image down to half the size of the original, thereby reducing the number of pixels in the file. When displayed at the same size as the original, you get a rough preview that's still in color, but also loads quickly.

TIP:
Animated
GIF
Lowsource

GoLive generates a lowsource GIF of any image you throw at it, even animated GIFs. However, only the first frame of the animation is rendered as the low-source, not the full series of frames.

Linking Images

Images can stand out from their surroundings in more effective ways than text. Also, most navigation systems tend to use images as buttons or other elements. So you frequently find yourself turning an image into a hypertext button, which, when clicked, works just like a text link. Any image can be turned into a link with a minimum of fuss.

With an image selected, choose one of the following: select New Link from the Special menu; click the New Link button on the Toolbar; click the New Link button in the Link tab of the Image Inspector; or select New Link from the contextual menu. Then specify the link's destination using Point & Shoot navigation, clicking Browse and locating the file, or by entering the file's pathname in the URL field. If you want, enter the link's title text and a target for the link.

Smart Objects

It's a rare day when GoLive is the only application running on our computers. Typically, we switch between GoLive and a host of graphics programs in order to create the hundreds of prototype pages and images required to test our ideas and their iterations. Before GoLive 5, testing and development meant lots of time in Photoshop converting all our graphics—even the scrap ones we knew weren't going to be final production images—to GIF or JPEG format just to view them in a Web browser.

GoLive's Smart Objects promise to significantly change our Web workflow. Using what Adobe calls Smart Links technology, you can drag and drop native Photoshop, Illustrator, and LiveMotion files onto your Web pages. Adding these files activates the Save for Web feature, which creates an optimized GIF, JPEG, or PNG version of the original. Editing the original file automatically updates the Web version. Making changes to the Web version (such as resizing the image) prompts GoLive to re-render it using data from the original.

In short, you can add an image to your page once, then edit it innumerable times without pointing to new versions of the file. Even better, the source application can remain closed.

To add a Smart Object, select the Smart tab of the Objects palette and drag a Smart Photoshop, Smart Illustrator, or Smart LiveMotion icon to your page. You can also drag and drop a native file from the Site window or the Desktop (see Figure 9-16).

Figure 9-16
Smart Objects
icons and
placeholders

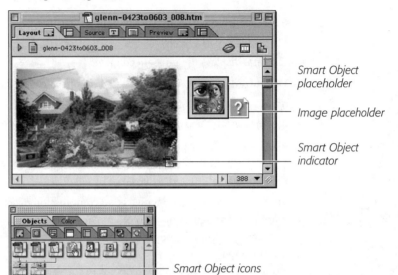

Smart Object
placeholder

Image placeholder

Smart Object
indicator

Smart Object icons

TIP: **Smart Sign**	Smart Objects include an icon in the lower-right corner of the image to indicate they're not regular images.
TIP: **Missing a Smart Object Icon?**	If you don't see an icon for the smart module you want, be sure you have the appropriate application installed. If you own Photoshop and Illustrator, but still don't see the icons, you may have to upgrade to a more recent version of those applications. Photoshop 5.5. and Illustrator 9 are the minimum requirements for Smart Objects. (LiveMotion is at 1.0 at this writing, so any version including or following 1.0 works.)

Save for Web

Adding a Smart Photoshop or Smart Illustrator object to your page activates the Save for Web feature, a surprisingly sophisticated dialog box that optimizes your images for the Web. LiveMotion files contain vector-based data, and are converted directly to the Shockwave Flash (SWF) format; therefore, the Save for Web dialog doesn't appear (see "Smart LiveMotion Objects" later in this chapter).

NEW IN 5:
**Familiar
Face?**

If Save for Web looks familiar, that's because the programming code for this addition to GoLive 5 was lifted from Photoshop, which itself borrowed it from
ImageReady. Integrating this standard feature across programs makes it easier
to switch back and forth.

Save for Web offers four views of your source image, accessible by clicking
the tabs at the top of the dialog box:

- **Original** displays the unchanged image.

- **Optimized** previews the image based on the values in the Settings area.

- **2-Up** shows the original image and its optimized preview. You can view
  any preview in the panes by clicking one and selecting new settings values.

- **4-Up** shows the original, its optimized preview, and two alternate opti-
  mizations. Like the 2-Up view, you can use the four panes to preview any
  settings, not just the ones displayed by default.

Suppose you've come up with a good combination of settings, but want to
compare your configuration with others. In the 4-Up view, select Repopulate
Views from the Optimize popout menu to use the selected pane as the baseline for the other panes.

Additionally, you can zoom in on any of the versions using the Zoom tool
or by changing the value in the Zoom Level popup menu (see Figure 9-17).

As you're working, if you don't like what you've done to the poor image,
holding down Option (Mac) or Alt (Windows) changes the Cancel button
into a Reset button, which reverts to the initial Save for Web settings. Holding
the modifier key also changes the OK button to Remember, which defines the
reset state. The next time you use Reset, the settings revert to the state at
which you clicked the Remember button.

After you've added the Smart Object to your page, you can return to the
Save for Web dialog by clicking the Settings button in the Live Image
Inspector's Basic tab.

Image Settings

With Save for Web, you almost don't need Photoshop or other image editors.
Use the controls in the Settings area of the dialog box to compress and optimize images for the Web (see Figure 9-18). The Settings popup menu provides a number of saved sets that load the most common settings
combinations, but you can also save your own custom settings by selecting
Save Settings from the Optimize popout menu.

Figure 9-17
Save for Web
view controls

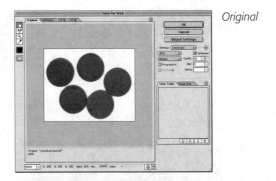

Original

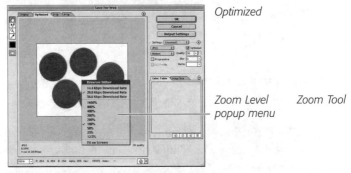

Optimized

*Zoom Level
popup menu*

Zoom Tool

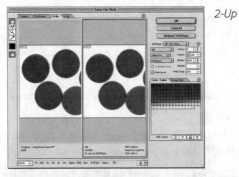

2-Up

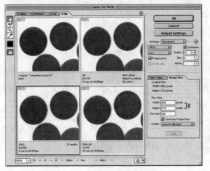

4-Up

Figure 9-18
Settings
overview

Optimized File Format ——
Color Reduction
Algorithm ——
Diffusion Algorithm ——

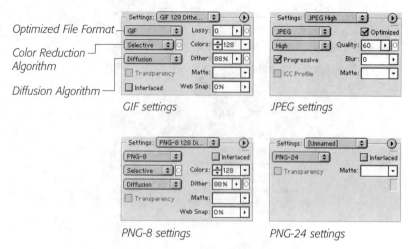

GIF settings   *JPEG settings*

PNG-8 settings   *PNG-24 settings*

Optimized File Format. Choose which type of file you're creating: GIF, JPEG, PNG-8 (8-bit), or PNG-24 (24-bit).

Color Reduction Algorithm (GIF and PNG-8). Save for Web can compress the image data using a handful of different methods of determining the image's color table.

- Perceptual uses an algorithm based on colors that are commonly perceived by the human eye.

- Selective is similar to perceptual, but with an eye (ahem) toward favoring Web-safe colors.

- Adaptive builds a color table based on the colors most frequently appearing in the image.

- Web uses the strict Web-safe color table, which comprises 216 colors shared by the Mac OS and Windows color palettes.

- Custom effectively freezes the current color table, so that any further changes to the image retain the same set of colors.

- Mac OS and Windows use the 8-bit color palette used by the two operating systems. It can be helpful to target an OS palette if you know your audience will be using just one or the other; otherwise, the differences between the two mean the image quality will suffer when viewed under the system not chosen.

- Other color tables are listed if you load them into the Color Table panel (see "Color Table," later in this chapter).

Compression Quality (JPEG). The default compression qualities—Low, Medium, High, and Maximum—are general shortcuts for assigning Quality values (see next).

Quality (JPEG). The Quality value determines how much JPEG compression is applied to the image. Since JPEG is a lossy algorithm, a lower Quality setting means more image data is being thrown away. Type a new number or use the slider activated by the popup menu button to change the value.

Blur (JPEG). One strength of JPEG compression is that it can remove redundant image data based on how the eye perceives color. When an image is more blurry, more data can be extracted, diminishing the file size. The Blur setting applies a Photoshop-style Gaussian Blur effect on the image, smoothing compression artifacts. Of course, unless you're trying to convince users that they need to buy a new computer display, a lower Blur setting is recommended.

Optimized (JPEG). Checking the Optimized checkbox can produce smaller JPEG files, but some older Web browsers can't display optimized JPEGs. However, in this day and age when more people are using modern browsers, we recommend checking this option to squeeze every last pixel out of your files.

Dithering Algorithm (GIF and PNG-8). Dithering is a method of simulating colors by positioning similar colors near one another. For example, you could create a green image without using any green pixels by making a pattern of alternating blue and yellow pixels. Fortunately, you don't have to go to that much trouble to employ dithering in your Web images. From the Dithering popup menu, select No Dithering, Diffusion, Pattern, or Noise. Each one combines pixels in its own way (except for No Dithering, of course), so try each one to arrive at the best result.

Dither (GIF and PNG-8). Choosing the Diffusion dithering algorithm gives you an additional control: the amount of dithering applied. Higher percentages produce images that are more grainy, while low percentages create larger areas of flat color.

Transparency (GIF, PNG-8, and PNG-24). If image formats didn't have a method for specifying transparent colors, the Web would be an ugly stack of rectangular image blocks. Fortunately, each format except for JPEG allows you to set one color (or more, in the case of PNG) as transparent. Save for

Web gets its cue from the source application to designate a transparent color. Empty pixels in Photoshop (indicated by the presence of the workspace's white and gray grid pattern) become transparent when you click the Transparent box (see Figure 9-19).

Figure 9-19
Transparency

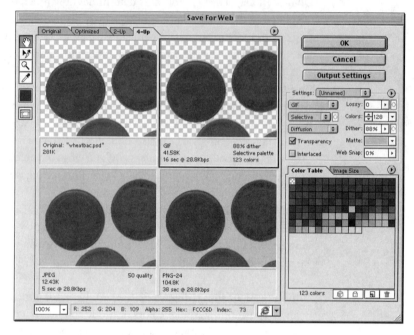

Matte. Instead of transparency, you can choose to matte unused portions of an image, filling them with a solid color. In most cases, the matte color is the same as the page's background color, but you have some control over this setting. The Matte popup menu lets you select None, the Eyedropper Color, White, or Black. Choosing Other opens the operating system's color picker in order to select any color; you can also just click the Matte color field.

TIP:
**Transparency
Only Works
on Unused
Pixels**

Unfortunately, there's no easy way in the Save for Web dialog to choose a different color to be marked as transparent. If all pixels are active, the Transparency option is inactive, and Matte settings have no effect. In that case, it's time for a quick trip back to the source program to delete or hide the necessary pixels.

Interlaced (GIF, PNG-8, and PNG-24). Check the Interlaced box if you want your images to incrementally display as they load, creating a perceptual increase in the time it takes to draw the page in a browser.

Progressive (JPEG). Like the Interlaced option, checking the Progressive box casuses JPEG files can be partially viewed as they load.

ICC Profile (JPEG). Check this box if you want to use Photoshop images that contain embedded ICC Profiles, which some browsers can use to color-correct images.

Lossy (GIF). Save for Web attempts to create an optimized image that's as true to the original as possible. However, this can result in larger-than-ideal file sizes (and, therefore, longer download times). The Lossy field gives you a scale of 1 to 100 that determines how much information can be thrown out of the image ("lost") in order to achieve better compression (see Figure 9-20). The more lossy an image is, the better it compresses, but the lower its quality.

TIP:
Lost Lace

Checking the Interlaced option disables the Lossy setting for GIF images. Depending on how high the Lossy setting, this can significantly increase the size of your file.

Colors (GIF and PNG-8). Another way of controlling image compression is to limit the maximum number of colors used by the image. To change that number, click the up or down arrow buttons in the Colors field, type a new value into the field directly, or select a number from the popup menu to the right of the field. Save for Web calculates which colors to use by analyzing the

Figure 9-20
Lossy setting

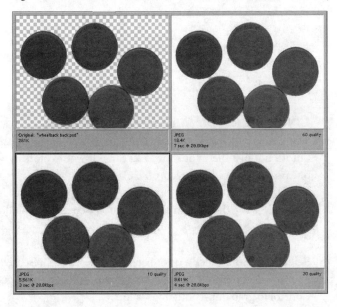

ones used most in the image. The file size is smaller with less colors, but also of lower quality.

Web Snap (GIF and PNG-8). Unless you've set the Color Reduction algorithm to Web, the colors in your image aren't likely to be Web safe. The Web Snap setting determines a percentage of tolerance for automatically switching colors to the Web-safe palette. A higher Web Snap setting means more colors are Web-safe, which improves compatibility but can often degrade quality.

Optimize to File Size. Kilobytes are the reigning currencies in some production environments, where strict quotas are established to ensure that Web page sizes don't expand to infinity (and beyond!). If you know that an image needs to be a certain size, Save for Web can apply the settings required to hit that goal.

From the Settings popout menu, select Optimize to File Size and enter a number in the KB field (see Figure 9-21). The Start With option can build on settings you've already applied, or use its built-in guesses for GIF and JPEG settings. If slices have been defined in the original image, you can apply the optimization to each one separately, all of them together, or just the current slice (see "Working with Sliced Images," later in this chapter).

Figure 9-21
Optimize to
File Size

Color Table (GIF and PNG-8 Only)

The Color Table tab is a handy guide to which colors appear in your image, but it's not just there for show. You can edit your colors as well as see which ones are being used (see Figure 9-22).

Color values corresponding to the cursor's position are also displayed numerically along the bottom of the Save for Web dialog; you don't have to click a color to see its numbers.

Selecting colors. Click a color square to select it, represented by a white outline. To select multiple squares, hold down Shift for a contiguous selection or Control to grab non-contiguous colors.

Figure 9-22
Save for Web
Color Table

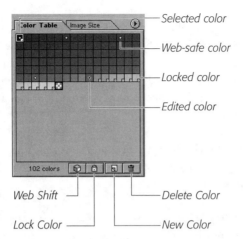

Selected color

Web-safe color

Locked color

Edited color

Web Shift

Lock Color

Delete Color

New Color

The Color Palette popout menu (not to be confused with the Color palette) to the right of the table lets you select all colors, all Web-safe colors, and all non-Web-safe colors; you can also deselect all colors.

Changing colors. Double-click a color square to bring up your operating system's default color dialog and choose a new color.

Sorting colors. The Color Palette popout menu also includes commands for sorting the table's colors. Choose from Unsorted, Sort by Hue, Sort by Luminance, and Sort by Popularity. This type of control is helpful when you want to isolate or change a single color or a small range of colors.

For example, to easily change the background color of an image (without using the Matte feature), select Sort by Popularity from the popout menu, then click the first image square. In many cases, the background color appears the most, so it becomes the first square. You can then change the color value by double-clicking the square and choosing a replacement color.

Locking colors. Select a color square, or a range of squares, and click the Lock Color button or choose Lock/Unlock Selected Colors from the Color Palette popout menu. Locking a color ensures the color doesn't change as you apply more settings to the image.

Snapping to Web colors. Although you could easily set the Color Algorithm popup menu to Web in order to work with just Web colors, the colors chosen by Save for Web occasionally aren't the ones you want to use. An orange might get switched to a Web color that's more yellow than red, for example.

To gain some control over the decision, select a color square and then click the Web Shift button, or choose Web Shift/Unshift Selected Colors from the Color Palette popout menu. If the Web-safe color chosen by Save for Web isn't what you had in mind, click the button or choose the popout menu item again to unshift the color, then choose a different color closer to what you expect and try again.

Deleting colors. To selectively remove colors from the image, highlight them and click the Delete Color button or choose Delete Color from the Color Palette popout menu.

Saving and loading color palettes. Of course, you don't have to rely on what Save for Web throws at you. Some Web sites use a strict color palette to maintain consistency throughout all pages. To bring in an outside color palette, choose Load Color Table from the popout menu. Similarly, you can save a color palette by selecting Save Color Table.

Image Size Tab

Even if your image is an actual-size photo of a Cray supercomputer, you can add it to your Web page at any size you like. The Image Size tab allows you to numerically change the dimensions of your image and control the way Save for Web recalculates how the image is resized.

In the New Size area, enter new measurements for width and height fields. If the Constrain Proportions box is checked, you only need to change one of the fields. Alternately, you can specify a percentage of change in the Percent field.

The Quality popup menu determines the type of calculation that's performed: Smooth (Bicubic) results in better, but sometimes blurry, images; Jagged (Nearest Neighbor) doesn't try to compensate for quality and stays closer to the image's pattern of pixels (see Figure 9-23).

Figure 9-23
Quality settings for resized images

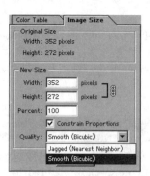

Original

Smooth (Bicubic)

Jagged (Nearest Neighbor)

Browser Preview

Lest you think that Save for Web doesn't offer enough options for previewing your final image, you can click the Browser button at the bottom of the dialog box. Not only will you see the optimized version of the image, but Save for Web also writes a summary box containing the image's optimization settings and HTML required to view the image.

The Browser button works the same as the Show in Browser button located on the Toolbar, and is based on the browser settings in GoLive's Preferences. Use the popup menu to choose among multiple installed browsers, or select Other to locate a browser not listed.

Smart LiveMotion Objects

In our discussion of Smart Objects so far we've largely avoided talking about files created in LiveMotion. While Photoshop and Illustrator images are processed through the Save for Web feature, LiveMotion files are simply added to the page. Their data is vector-based, which means that the browser draws (and animates) images based on mathematical commands instead of noting colors for each individual pixel. The advantage of this approach is that LiveMotion files tend to be smaller in size, and therefore load faster. They can also be scaled to any size without a loss of resolution; smooth curves stay smooth and type stays crisp.

As with other Smart Objects, add LiveMotion files to your page by dragging them from the Desktop or Site window; or, drag the Smart LiveMotion icon from the Smart tab of the Objects palette and specify a file in the Source field of the Live Plugin Inspector. GoLive asks you to specify a conversion setting, even though your only option is Shockwave Flash (see Figure 9-24).

With the exception of providing a Smart Link to the original LiveMotion file, GoLive treats Smart LiveMotion objects no differently than Flash plug-in objects. (See Chapter 17, *Media*, for more on working with plug-ins and their Inspector settings).

Figure 9-24
Adding Smart
LiveMotion
object

Working with Smart Objects

Using the Save for Web feature to process your images on their way into GoLive is powerful stuff, but the real utility of Smart Objects happens within the Layout Editor.

From an HTML point of view, the only thing that distinguishes a Smart Object from a regular image is the Smart Link that points to the original source file, implemented using the Livesrc attribute.

```
<img src="images/coffeegood.gif" livesrc="graphics/coffee-
good.psd" width="201" height="70">
```

To strip out the Livesrc attribute in your page or site, use GoLive's Find by Element feature. Select Find from the Edit menu and click the Element tab. Enter "img" in the Name Is field, and choose Keep Element from the first popup menu in the Action area. Click the New Action button, select Delete from the Action popup menu, and type "livesrc" into the Attribute field. Finally, specify the files you wish to process, and hit the Start button.

This operation can't be undone; make sure you have backups handy.

Did you place your images already, but now want to link them to their Photoshop or Illustrator originals? Simply go into the HTML Source Editor, locate the Img tag, and add the following to the tag's attributes.

```
livesrc="fluctuating/self/images/weird.liv"
```

When you switch back to the Layout Editor, your formerly dumb image has become a smart object.

In addition to the standard Web formats, Smart Illustrator objects also give you the opportunity to convert Illustrator 9 files into SVG (Scalable Vector Graphics), SVG Compressed, and Shockwave Flash formats. In each case, the appropriate plug-in is used to display and handle the file.

Resizing Smart Objects. So you've optimized your image and placed it on a page, only to realize that its width should be 275 pixels instead of 300. Previously, you'd have to go back into Photoshop or Illustrator, resize the image, then resave it in its optimized form.

Now, simply resize the image on your page by either dragging the image's control handles or entering new values in the Width and Height fields of the Live Image Inspector. GoLive temporarily displays a resize warning icon, then recreates the optimized image using data from the source application (see Figure 9-25).

Figure 9-25
Smart versus
normal
resizing

Original Smart Object

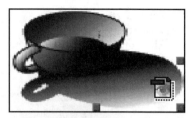

*For a normal
image, this
would be the
end result
after resizing.*

*Image is
smoother
after being
automatically
processed in
Photoshop.*

TIP:
**Resizing
Multiple
Copies of
Same Image**

If you have two or more instances of the same Smart Object on your page, re-sizing one doesn't resize them all. Although the Web image file gets optimized for the new dimensions, only the active object has its Width and Height values changed; the others display the resize warning icon. You can manually select each one and click the Resize button on the Inspector, or better yet, use the Find feature's Element tab to quickly update the dimensions in one pass (see Chapter 16, *Source Editing*, for more on GoLive's search-and-replace features).

TIP:
**Resize
Button
Shifts to
Original**

Clicking the Resize button on the Live Image Inspector resets the dimensions of the image to those of the original source file, not the size of the first generated Web version.

In the case of Smart LiveMotion objects, changing their dimensions in the Layout Editor doesn't prompt GoLive to get new data from LiveMotion. There is no resizing calculation because vector art has to be rendered from scratch to display on screen. The Flash plug-in installed in a user's browser renders the LiveMotion content.

Instead of displaying a resize warning icon, Smart LiveMotion objects retain a dotted outline of the original file's dimension (see Figure 9-26). To get back to the original size, drag the resize handles to make the object borders match the outline.

TIP:
**Use Active
Resizing**

Hold down the Control key when dragging Smart LiveMotion object handles to see a live preview of how the image is being resized. Otherwise, it takes several attempts to nail the target when working with GoLive's standard dotted-line re-sizing indicators.

Figure 9-26
Resized Smart
LiveMotion
object

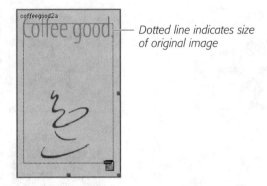

— Dotted line indicates size
of original image

TIP:
**Dispropor-
tionate
LiveMotion
Resizing**

When you resize a Smart LiveMotion object proportionally (hold down Shift when dragging the lower-right corner's handle), the image is similarly resized in a browser. However, if you resize in one direction, or disproportionally, the image doesn't appear stretched as you would expect (despite the fact that GoLive shows a stretched preview in the Layout Editor). Instead, the image resizes proportionally, but based on the narrowest dimension, height or width. Any extra defined area just fills with blank space (see Figure 9-27).

Import Photoshop as HTML

It's not uncommon to find designers who "think Photoshop." For them, illustrations aren't made up of different graphics; instead, they're different Photoshop layers, and anything can be fixed with a few Curves and Levels tweaks. Using GoLive's Import Photoshop as HTML feature, you can bring in any Photoshop file containing multiple layers, each of which is converted to a floating box. This allows you to do much of the prep work for animations or other special effects in Photoshop, and then get right to work by moving items around in GoLive.

Select Photoshop as HTML from the File menu's Import submenu and then choose the Photoshop file to add. After selecting the file, specify a folder as the root for the images that are created. GoLive uses Save for Web to process each layer, giving you the chance to save each image in its own format.

When Save for Web is finished, your page includes a series of floating boxes, each of which contains the image corresponding to one of the Photoshop layers. (See Chapter 14. *Floating Boxes*, for more information.) GoLive also assigns a depth setting to each box in order to replicate the layer order (see Figure 9-28).

Import Photoshop as HTML doesn't function like a Smart Photoshop object. Changes made to the original file do not update the referenced file on the

Figure 9-27
Dispropor-
tionate
LiveMotion
resizing

*Stretching a Smart
LiveMotion object
disproportionately
in GoLive…*

*… does not
display as you
would expect in
a browser.*

Figure 9-28
Import
Photoshop as
HTML

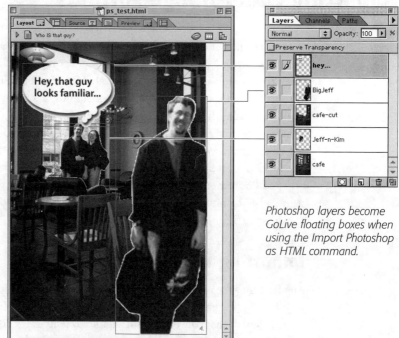

*Photoshop layers become
GoLive floating boxes when
using the Import Photoshop
as HTML command.*

GoLive page. On the other hand, if changes are warranted, it's easy enough to re-import the changed file in place of the older version.

TIP:
Bypassing Save for Web

You can bypass the Save for Web dialog for each layer by Control-clicking the OK button. This takes the image settings of the first layer and applies it to the remaining ones.

TIP:
Name Your Photoshop Layers

If you're not already in the habit of naming layers in Photoshop, we encourage you to do so. GoLive automatically uses the layer name as the name of its corresponding floating box. However, because of how some browsers interpret the code needed to work with floating box information, be sure that none of your layer names begin with a number.

TIP:
First Layer and Background Image

The GoLive manual states that the first layer of an imported Photoshop layer becomes the background layer for your Web page, but in our testing this doesn't appear to be true. The first layer becomes a floating box like the others, with a Depth setting of 0 (zero).

Importing Other Image Formats

It would be nice if every image file that came across our desks was ready for the Web, but that just isn't the case. Designers regularly have to deal with client files or high-resolution images created for print publishing. Fortunately, you can bring these into GoLive without running them through Photoshop or other image editors. GoLive lets you import any PICT, TIFF, or BMP (a Windows bitmap format) image file directly into the Layout Editor: simply insert the image as if it were any Web-ready format using drag and drop, or via the URL Getter in the Image Inspector. You can also drag an image from an open Photoshop document (or even an open browser window) without using a key combination. GoLive's Save for Web dialog box takes over and converts the file into the format of your choice.

Importing Without Save for Web

The Save for Web approach can be time consuming if you just want to throw together a quick page draft. Instead, you can use GoLive's Image preferences to set a default that converts imported files to temporary GIF, JPEG, or PNG files. The images aren't production-quality—don't upload them to your site for use—but they're certainly good enough for roughing out your ideas.

To use this feature, open Preferences, select the Modules pane, and then uncheck the Smart Links module. Quit GoLive. When you restart GoLive, the Save for Web feature is disabled, as well as the ability to work with Smart Objects. When you're finished with your roughs, simply re-enable the Smart Links module and quit and restart the program.

TIP:
Merge Layers in Photoshop

You don't need the full-blown features of Smart Objects to transfer images between Photoshop and GoLive. But when you drag an image from Photoshop, only the active layer of a multi-layered image is imported into GoLive (see Figure 9-29).

If you need the composite image, be sure to merge the layers before dragging; you can always select Undo in Photoshop to get your layers back, or, since you were no doubt smart enough to save your file before merging, select Revert to go to the last saved version. Any transparent pixels in Photoshop are changed to white during import, and only the size of the active image (not the entire canvas) is copied into the GoLive document.

Figure 9-29
Dragging active Photoshop layer

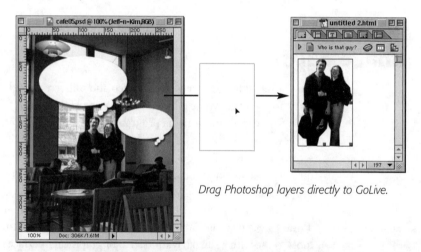

Drag Photoshop layers directly to GoLive.

The converted files are stored in the Import Images folder, which is located in the same folder as your GoLive application; they're given names like "image-1275542589.gif". You can choose to control whether they are imported as GIF, JPEG, or PNG files by opening GoLive's Preferences window and choosing a format from the Picture Import options in the General pane's Image settings. Or, you can click the Ask User button to be prompted each time you import a file. (See Chapter 4, *Preferences and Customizing*.)

Converted files aren't high-quality versions of the originals, but there's another reason you don't want to rely on them as final images on your page: Files in the Import Images folder aren't recognized if you're uploading your site using GoLive's FTP or WebDAV synchronization features(Chapter 23, *Synchronizing Sites*). You should create final versions by the time the site goes live, but if you're staging draft pages on a Web server for a client, you need to manually move the temporary files to another location where GoLive recognizes them as valid files the next time you upload the site.

For this reason, we use the Ask User setting in GoLive's image preferences to specify a folder in our site's directory. (We usually name that location something like "tempgifs" to keep them separate from the final files.) Alternately, you can change the location of the import folder in the preferences, but that can get hairy if you're working on multiple sites concurrently.

If you have image preferences set to Ask User, and if you cancel a drag-and-drop import, GoLive leaves an orphaned image placeholder on your page. Be sure to delete this.

Imagemaps

One of the differences between the Web and full-screen multimedia development tools is that you can't define any area on the screen as a link with the Web, where most multimedia programs use the whole screen as an interface. However, the Web does let you turn images (which could take up an entire screen) into an analogue of multimedia by letting you define one, several, or dozens of areas on an image that each have separate links and other image properties.

These images with definable areas are called imagemaps; they've been around since near the dawn of the Web, and they're one of the most common tools to use with a site navigation strip or graphical interface on the Web.

You can define the regions in an imagemap using a variety of shapes, including rectangles, circles, and polygons. Each region's exact pixel coordinates at each point on the shape (or the oval's center point and width and height) are stored in the HTML file. When a Web browser is told that an image is acting as an imagemap, the browser examines the pixel location where a user clicks, and loads the corresponding URL for that region.

In the olden days, imagemaps required a server to process the user's clicks—the imagemap's region file resided on a server, and a special program there, often called htimage, handled the translation. These were called server-side imagemaps, as opposed to in-the-HTML client-side imagemaps. If you find old HTML files that still reference a server script, consult Chapter 24, *Importing a Site*, which offers a section on refurbishing old sites.

Before GoLive and other visual editors, building imagemaps required a third-party mapping program—or a great deal of patience and graph paper—to calculate each region's coordinates by hand. Now, creating an imagemap is a matter of switching tabs in the Image Inspector. With an image selected, click the More tab and check the Use Map box. GoLive creates a name for the map based on the filename, but you may want to change the name to something that doesn't look like the name of a future android's serial number.

To link a portion of an imagemap, use the region tools located in the Toolbar to highlight an area for the link, and enter the destination address using the URL Getter in the Map Area Inspector. The other fields for that region (Title, Target, Alt, etc.) act the same as if you were defining a single image link (see Figure 9-30).

Unlike GoLive 4, the imagemap tools are no longer located in the Inspector. Instead, they've been relocated to the Toolbar. Although it makes some sense (storing tools in the Toolbar), it's a jarring change if you've gotten used to the old Map tab of the Image Inspector. Progress marches ever onward…

Figure 9-30
Imagemap region tools

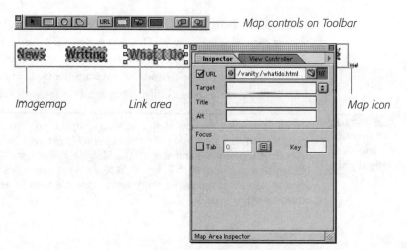

Map controls on Toolbar

Imagemap   *Link area*   *Map icon*

NEW IN 5:
Map Icon

Creating an imagemap adds something more to your page besides clickable regions: a small M icon, similar to the one used for floating boxes. The icon represents the block of text used to define the map coordinates, and appears after the imagemap image. If you want, you can move it anywhere on your layout without adverse affects; some designers prefer to store all their imagemap code at the beginning or end of the page. The only problem you may run into with the M icon is when you disable an imagemap; unchecking the Use Map box on the Image Inspector turns the imagemap off, but leaves the icon, which you have to delete manually.

TIP:
Grab Imagemaps by Their Edges

If the Is Map box is checked, GoLive won't let you grab or move the image as you normally would. The internal area is reserved for the imagemap tools, which take over when your cursor is in that region. So, to select the image, click on its edge (the cursor changes into an object-select cursor), then move or resize the image as usual.

TIP:
Imagemaps and Smart Objects

You can build imagemaps out of Smart Photoshop and Smart Illustrator objects as well as normal images. If you resize the image, GoLive even adjusts the map sizes accordingly.

Region Tools

The region tools are used to define and select areas in your image that lead to other URLs.

Selection tool. An all-purpose pointer, the Selection tool is used to select, move, and resize imagemap regions.

Rectangle and circle tools. Use these tools to create simple rectangular or circular regions (see Figure 9-31). Don't worry if the shapes you create aren't pixel-perfect; since imagemap areas aren't visible on the Web, they only need to cover the approximate area where you want the viewer to click to follow a link. The Circle tool creates only proportional circles, not ovals.

TIP:
Imagemap Browser Highlights

Actually, the only time you might see imagemaps appear on the Web is when you tab through a page using Windows Internet Explorer or Netscape Navigator, or Internet Explorer 5.0 and later on the Macintosh. Because Windows uses the Tab key to move from each link or field to the next, even the shapes on an imagemap can show up. We've seen some scary maps on occasion, but it's not quite like letting your slip show.

Figure 9-31
Rectangle,
Circle, and
Polygon
map tools

Rectangle   *Polygon*   *Circle*

Polygon tool. For regions that don't fit nicely into the rectangular or circular molds, the polygon tool provides a highly flexible way to build custom-shaped link fields. With the Polygon tool selected, click to create a series of points connected by straight line segments around the area; GoLive automatically closes the selection, so you won't have any open-ended polygon fields (see Figure 9-31).

When you're finished defining the region, select one of the other region tools to deselect the polygon. If you then click the polygon with the Selection tool, the object is selected as a grouped object, which you can resize. If you resize the image, the regions scale in proportion.

If you want to edit the shape's individual points, double-click the region with the selection tool to activate the polygon's defining points. After modifying them, click outside the shape or select another region tool to deselect it again. Once you've created a polygon, you cannot add new points or remove existing points.

TIP:
**Adding
Points in
HTML**

If you're really desperate not to start from scratch, you can insert extra point coordinates in the HTML. A point in a polygon requires two values: the x and y coordinates, which are listed in the code that defines the shape, as in this example:

```
<area href="poly_gone.html"
coords="102,189,64,160,115,103,150,179" shape="polygon">
```

Each pair of numbers represents one point, which means there are four points to this polygon. To add another, get the location values of the new point (open the image in Photoshop and use the Info palette to indicate where your cursor is), then add them to the list, x before y.

If you're fanatical about keeping your HTML files as small as possible so they load quickly, try not to use too many complex polygons in an imagemap. Unlike rectangles and circles, which require only a few pixel coordinates, each point of a polygon must be defined in the HTML (see Figure 9-32). Granted, we're talking about text, which loads much faster compared to almost everything else on the Web; but the less work the browser has to do, the faster the page loads and responds.

Figure 9-32
Polygone code

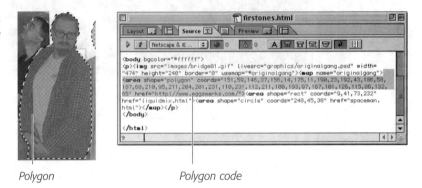

Polygon   *Polygon code*

Region Display Tools

GoLive makes it easy to identify and control the appearance of imagemap regions while you're working in the Layout Editor (see Figure 9-33).

Display URLs. For a quick reference of where the region's link takes viewers, the Display URLs button writes the HTML link on top of the appropriate area of the mapped image.

Frame regions. Clicking this button displays a dotted line around region edges.

Color regions. With this button selected, regions are filled with a color to make them even easier to find. Colored regions are semi-transparent so you can still see the images beneath them.

Select color. Everyone has their own color favorites. If a hot pink region color clashes too much with your page's ochre-colored background, feel free to select a new color for the region highlight. The color you select applies to all regions; you can't color-code different regions with different colors (though that would be a neat feature in a future version of GoLive).

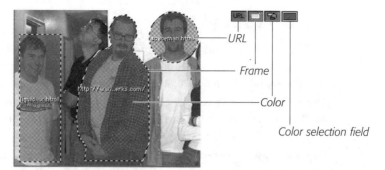

Figure 9-33
Region
display tools

URL

Frame

Color

Color selection field

Organizing Regions

GoLive also includes two buttons for changing the layer order of imagemap regions. If you wind up with overlapping regions and you don't want to re-draw boundaries, you can use the Bring Region to Front or Send Region to Back buttons to bring the right one to the top.

TIP:	Although layered regions aren't really a function of HTML imagemaps, Web
Reordering Directives	browsers do read the imagemap directives (the lists of shapes and coordinates) in the order they appear in the file. So a directive coming earlier than another is the equivalent of being a higher layer. When you use Bring Region to Front or Send Region to Back, GoLive shuffles the HTML; very neat.

TIP:	Another use of imagemap layers in GoLive would be as a quick method of ro-
Storing Other Links	tating links for the same image that change often. You could set them up all at once, then bring an inactive link region to the front when the need arises. It does bulk up your HTML and it does slow down an imagemap's processing time in a browser when a user clicks, so don't go hog wild.

Working with Sliced Images

A common technique when designing images for the Web is to take a larger composition and slice it into several smaller images. Perhaps you want to ani-mate just a portion of an illustration with an animated GIF, or you've created a navigation bar with elements that change on a regular basis. Designers were forced to create the image in Photoshop, then manually split up the pieces and place them onto a Web page. ImageReady and other applications put an end to that in the last few years. These programs have included methods of automatically slicing images into regular pieces, and building an HTML structure (typically using tables) which holds the pieces together.

Smart Sliced Images

Using options found in the Save for Web feature, GoLive 5 handles sliced images with ease. In Photoshop, or ImageReady, set up the slices for your image. Then, bring the native file into GoLive using the Smart Photoshop icon (which also works with ImageReady 2.0 files) or the Smart Illustrator icon. Or, you can drag the file into the Layout Editor. GoLive prompts you to specify the location of the data folder it creates to store the image slices, then brings up the Save for Web dialog (see Figure 9-34).

Figure 9-34
Slices in
Save for Web

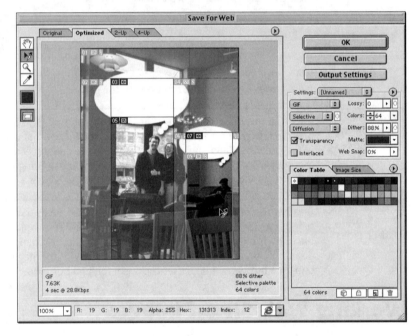

After you define your settings, the sliced image appears in the Layout Editor like any other image, but you can click directly on the slices. How does GoLive accomplish this magic? Underneath that image is a bit of GoLive trickery called a live grid—yep, it's just a layout grid, which in turn is just a table (see Chapters 11 and 12 for more information). To return to the Save for Web optimization features, select the entire object (click at the edge of the sliced image when the cursor turns into an object select cursor). In the Live Grid Inspector, click the Settings button.

Using Save for Web with Slices

At this point, most of the typical Save for Web settings are inactive, because your image has become a set of multiple images. Use the Slice Select Tool and choose a slice to work with. Shift-click multiple slices to select them, or click and drag with the Slice Select Tool; any slices within the selection marquee are highlighted.

TIP:
Optimizing Individual Slices Glitch

It would appear that you can apply different settings to each slice, but in fact this only works once. To see an extreme example, bring in a sliced JPEG image, then set one slice as a 1-bit (2 color) GIF. When you click OK, the image looks correct in GoLive, with one slice showing up as black and white. However, if you try to apply settings to more than one slice, the entire image assumes the settings. As a workaround, create separate versions of the sliced image in the formats you prefer, then sort them manually.

To preview the image without the overlay indicating where slices occur, click the Toggle Slices Visibility button; clicking a sliced area with the Slice Select Tool automatically displays the overlay again.

Applying properties to slices. While in the Save for Web dialog, double-click a slice to bring up the Slice Options dialog box. Although the settings here can also be applied in the Layout Editor, doing it in Save for Web means they are retained in the event that the original image changes. Slices show up with dark blue outlines if they have attributes applied.

You can modify a slice in several ways: change its name, add a link to it, set a target for it, specify its Alt text, and compose a message that can be shown when a user rolls their cursor over the slice in some browsers (see Figure 9-35). If transparency is applied, you can also set a background color for a slice.

Figure 9-35
Slice options

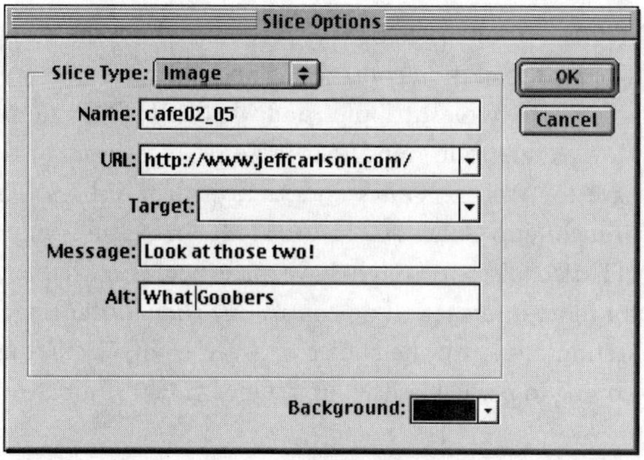

Slice Options

Slice Type:	Image ⬍
Name:	cafe02_05
URL:	http://www.jeffcarlson.com/ ▾
Target:	▾
Message:	Look at those two!
Alt:	What Goobers

OK
Cancel

Background: ▾

In addition to Image, the popup menu at the top of the dialog offers a No Image option. Frequently, designers use sliced images in order to create areas within the image to swap text or other images into. Type some text into the Text Displayed in Cell field, or leave it blank for none. In the Layout Editor, GoLive uses a Layout Text Box to hold the text.

TIP:
Edited Text
Not Updated

In the Layout Editor, you can freely edit the text placed into a blank cell, but if you go back into Save for Web and double-click that slice, your new text does not appear, only what was entered in the dialog the last time.

TIP:
Space
Makes Color

If you choose No Image and leave the text field blank, any color you specify in the Background popup menu won't appear. Add a space to the Text Displayed in Cell field to see the background color.

TIP:
Text Styling,
No Image

The Text Displayed in Cell field only lets you type in straight text...or does it? Although you can't access any of GoLive's text formatting features, feel free to type HTML tags to customize the display of the text.

TIP:
Return
Slices after
No Image

Images with slices set to No Image aren't permanently stricken. Switching the popup menu back to Image restores the image data from the original file.

Save for Web Output Settings. Taking an original image and creating slices involves managing not only several files, but also the HTML code used to display them. As you would expect, GoLive includes settings for controlling every last tag and filename involved. (We swear, Save for Web is the most Swiss-Army-knife-like software feature we've seen in a long time.)

With the Save for Web dialog open, click the Output Settings button. The popup menu at the top takes you to the four categories of options, or you can use the Prev and Next buttons (see Figure 9-36).

- **HTML.** Do you like to be very particular about the output of your HTML? The HTML section controls tag and attribute case, style of line endings, whether to quote attributes, and whether HTML comments are included. However, keep in mind that these settings apply to the HTML file that Save for Web generates and saves with the slices. This HTML is then brought into GoLive. GoLive's HTML formatting options prevail over any HTML choices you might have made here (see Chapter 16, *Source Editing*, for more information on controlling code formatting). The Slice Output section gives you the choice between using Cascading Style Sheet positioning to place the slices, or a standard table framework.

Figure 9-36
Output
Settings

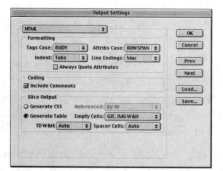

HTML Output Settings

*Background
Output Settings*

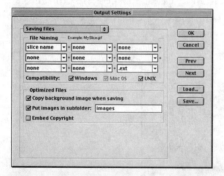

*Saving Files
Output Settings*

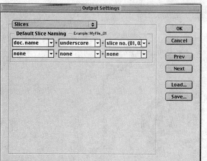

*Slices
Output Settings*

- **Background.** The Background setting lets you specify an image or color for the HTML file generated by Save for Web.

- **Saving Files.** Use the popup menus in the File Naming section to specify file names when working with rollover images. The Optimized Files options lets you define a folder for the generated images, copy the background image you specified in the Background section, and embed an optional copyright notice.

- **Slices.** The Default Slice Naming option in this section determines how slices are named when the image is converted. As with the previous section, use the popup menus to set which information (including date-stamps) is incorporated into the title.

Importing Other Sliced Images

Although not as convenient as working with smart sliced images, it's easy to take a sliced composition created in an application like Fireworks and add it to your GoLive page.

In GoLive, open the HTML file created by the other program containing the composition. In most cases, the slices are built into a table structure, so simply select the table and drag it to your Web page or copy and paste it (see Figure 9-37).

Figure 9-37
Importing other sliced images

Sliced image built in Fireworks.

Sliced Fireworks image brought into GoLive as a table.

Tracing Image

It would be nice if Web pages could leap in final form from our brains to the computer screen. There are even some late nights when it feels like we've stared at a monitor long enough to accomplish that feat. But unlike Mozart, who had the annoying tendency to compose his symphonies in completed first drafts, we find ourselves creating Web pages in several stages.

Many designers work up dummy pages in Photoshop or Illustrator as sketches, and then use those roughs as the basis for building pages with more refinement. To support this common tactic, Adobe added the Tracing Image feature to GoLive. Simply put, it lets you display an image in the Layout Editor as a point of reference. Unlike other images, a tracing image can't be selected directly, which means you can build objects on top of it.

But a tracing image can be more than just a background template or guide. You can cut out portions of the image to be used on your page, rather than grab them from their original source file (or rebuild them).

TIP:
There Can
Be Only One

Only one tracing image can be active at a time. However, any portions that have been cut out remain on the page, so once you're done with one tracing image, feel free to load another and work on another section of the design.

Before you can begin tracing, you need to specify your source image. If it's not already visible, select Tracing Image from the Window menu to bring up the Tracing Image palette (see Figure 9-38).

Figure 9-38
Tracing Image
palette

Click the Source box and choose the source image. GoLive can use the following formats: 8-bit RGB Photoshop, JPEG, GIF, PNG, BMP, TARGA, PCX, PICT, PIXAR, TIFF, and Amiga IFF. The image appears aligned to the upper-left corner of the Layout Editor, and has a 50-percent opacity. The Opacity slider controls how see-through the image is (see Figure 9-39).

Figure 9-39
Tracing image
on a page

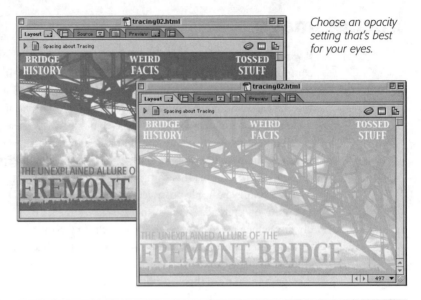

*Choose an opacity
setting that's best
for your eyes.*

**TIP:
Resize to
Tracing
Image**

To collapse the Document window to the size of your tracing image, select Tracing Image from the Change Window Size popup menu at the lower-right corner of the window.

To remove a tracing image, just deselect the Source box. GoLive remembers your last tracing image if you haven't closed the file, so if you enable the image again later, you won't have to go in search of the image file.

Positioning a Tracing Image

A tracing image can appear anywhere within the Layout Editor. Four controls let you easily position the image (see Figure 9-40).

- **Position fields.** Enter values into the two Position fields on the Tracing Image palette. The left field controls horizontal position, while the right field controls the vertical, both measured from the upper-left corner of the image. Entering negative numbers moves the image off the window.

- **Move Image Tool.** As its icon suggests, the Move Image Tool lets you grab the image and reposition it freely. It's possible to place the image beyond the visible area of the page; use the Position fields to bring it back.

- **Reset Position command.** To quickly restore the image's position to the upper-left corner of the window, select Reset Position from the Tracing Image palette's popout menu.

Figure 9-40
Positioning a
tracing image

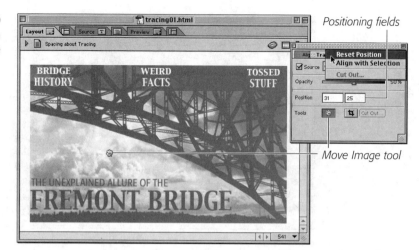

Positioning fields

Move Image tool

- **Align with Selection command.** Also available on the palette's popout menu, the Align with Selection command sets the tracing image's top-left corner to match the position of an object selected on the page. Any object works, including text selections.

Cutting Out Sections of a Tracing Image

Click the Cut Out Tool and drag a selection on the tracing image corresponding to the area to be cut out. You can use the resize handles on the selection box to resize it, or move it by clicking and dragging within the box.

When you've determined the area to be extracted, either click the Cut Out button on the Tracing Image palette, or select Cut Out from the popout menu. In the Save for Web dialog, set the optimization settings for the image, then click OK.

Cut out portions appear as floating boxes in the Layout Editor, and can be placed anywhere on the page (see Figure 9-41). (Also see Chapter 14, *Floating Boxes*.)

TIP:
**Cut Out
Section
Retain
Dimensions**

When you cut out subsequent areas of the same tracing image, the last selection is activated when you choose the Cut Out Tool. This is helpful when breaking out a navigation bar or similar element where each button or link needs to be the same size and shape as the last.

Figure 9-41
Cut out
sections of a
tracing image

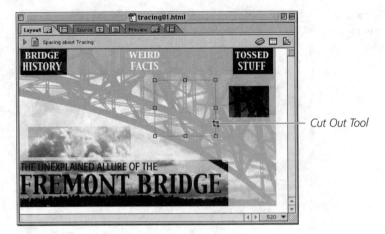

Cut Out Tool

ColorSync (Macintosh Only)

If you work with more than one computer system, you can see that what you view on one screen may not be exactly the same as what you view on another. Monitor brands and hardware differ, and software treats images differently depending on the company and the platform. Apple's answer to this is ColorSync, a system that attempts to make images appear as the designer intended no matter which combination of hardware and software is being used.

For ColorSync to work in GoLive, make sure the Display Images Using ColorSync box is checked in the ColorSync section of GoLive's preferences.

TIP:
ColorSync
Installation
in Mac OS

You need to have ColorSync installed on your Macintosh; some versions of Mac OS didn't install it by default (or you might have chosen not to install it). You can install it typically off the latest CD-ROM you have with your system, but we recommend getting the most up-to-date version. Go to Apple's ColorSync Web site at http://www.apple.com/colorsync/, to find the latest version.

TIP:
Great Idea,
Minimal
Support

We like the possibilities that ColorSync offers, but currently there's very little support for it on the Web; at this writing, only Internet Explorer 4.5 and higher for Macintosh can display an image with a ColorSync profile applied. Apple promises to release a Windows version of ColorSync, but Microsoft allegedly isn't very happy about this—though no global CMS solution for Windows is currently available.

ColorSync Profiles. This feat of color management magic is accomplished through the use of ColorSync Profiles, sets of data that describe how your monitor, scanner, digital camera, or other device "sees" color. These characterizations generally rely on feeding color into them and using a colorimeter to measure their output values so that their subjective notion of color can be compared to an absolute, physical property of color.

TIP:
Roll Your
Own
Profiles

If you don't have a profile set up for your monitor, you can use either the Monitors or Adobe Gamma control panel to use your eyeballs to create a rough profile. Click the Colors button in Monitors, then the Calibrate button, and follow the instructions. With Adobe Gamma, select the control panel, and it walks you through a calibration process. Remember to name your custom profile something intelligible, like "Glenn's 420GS monitor" (see Figure 9-42). This process can take you a surprisingly high degree closer to what images should objectively look like on your screen.

Figure 9-42
Creating a
ColorSync
profile

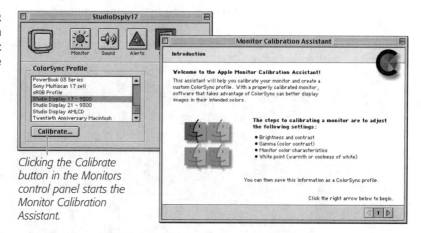

Clicking the Calibrate button in the Monitors control panel starts the Monitor Calibration Assistant.

In GoLive, you can apply a ColorSync profile to an image by switching to the Link tab of the Image Inspector, and clicking the Profile button in the ColorSync section. Use the URL Getter to locate the profile that represents your hardware configuration.

From here you can also choose to use GoLive's built-in profile or not use it at all by selecting Default or None, respectively.

TIP:
Embedded
ColorSync
Profiles

Photoshop 5.0 and later support the ability to embed a ColorSync profile into an image when saving it. If a profile already exists within the image file, its name appears in the Embedded field.

Page-wide implementation. You can specify profiles for every image on your page, but since it's more likely you'll set the same profile each time, GoLive has a way to apply a single profile to an entire page. Click the Page icon in the Layout Editor, then switch to the ColorSync tab of the Page Inspector to link to a profile.

To make an externally-referenced profile work, you need to upload it to your Web site along with the HTML and image files that use it. So although you can link to a profile located in the ColorSync Profiles folder within the System Folder, it doesn't get automatically uploaded to the site, and therefore isn't referenced.

Imagine Great Images

It's not an understatement to say that inline images turned the Web from an interesting way to share information into a new designers' medium. GoLive makes it easy to add images to your Web pages, freeing you to spend your time making great images.

CHAPTER 10
Color

We've each taken our fair share of art and design courses throughout school and beyond. Littered amid that history of paper, canvas, brushes, and charcoal lie dozens, even hundreds, of mostly-squeezed paint tubes covering the full visible-color spectrum (and maybe even some ultraviolet and infrared colors too). Although we were taught that color is actually the perception of light interacting with a surface, our stained-hands-on experience told us that color was usually a combination of pigments that eventually swirled into a brownish muck at the center of our palettes.

Today, most of our color usage has returned to the realm of light, with trillions of photons projected daily to ignite pixels with specific hues on our screens. Coming up with a certain color on the Web is a matter of combining numerical values, not watercolors or oils. But that doesn't mean you have to suppress your inner fingerpainter. GoLive's color capabilities let you easily choose the tone you want, or experiment with several different ones.

In fact, the robustness of GoLive's color features continues to surprise us: not only does it offer a palette of the 216 "Web safe" colors for use on the Web, it includes resources for defining colors in RGB, CMYK, and HLS color spaces, long the bastions of print publishing. And as you'd expect, GoLive makes working with color incredibly easy, with most operations requiring a simple drag and drop of a color swatch.

TIP:
The Slightly Misleading ColorSync Name

GoLive supports Apple's ColorSync technology on the Macintosh, which is an effort to make the colors viewed on one computer appear the same on other, dissimilar machines. However, ColorSync deals with synchronizing the color of images, not HTML-based color found in objects like table cells or text. See Chapter 9, *Images*, for more information about this unique approach to providing a consistent viewing experience.

Color on the Web

Color is a subjective thing; for example, the paint in Jeff's living room is perceived as cream by some people and slightly pink by others (cream is the intended perception). Depending on the lighting, the time of day, the colors of objects in the same field of vision, and dozens of other factors, one color can take on multiple appearances. The same is true on the Web, where we must deal with hundreds of different monitor types and calibration settings, plus the default color values of different browsers and operating systems.

We also have to deal with color in a historical context. Although these days you can buy a fully-loaded PC system for less than $500, it was only a few

A Bit About Bits

Everything in computing is represented, at its foundation, in bits. You're probably more familiar with massive amounts of bits counted as bytes (each of which contains eight bits), kilobytes, megabytes, gigabytes, and upward. A bit is the smallest increment of binary data, and can have a value of 1 (on) or 0 (off). When we talk about monitors and screen resolution, we sometimes express it in bits, like 8-bit color, which represents 256 colors (see Table-10-1). This may sound overly geeky, when all you want is to make a table cell purple, but understanding this fundamental unit of measurement makes it easier to mix and match color values in the Color palette.

Table 10-1 Deep bits	Bit Depth	Math	Total Colors	Also Known As...
	1	$1+1$ or 2^1	2	
	2	2^2	4	
	3	2^3	8	
	4	2^4	16	
	5	2^5	32	
	6	2^6	64	
	7	2^7	128	
	8	2^8	256	
	15	2^{15}	32,768	Thousands of colors (older Macs)
	16	2^{16}	65,536	Thousands of colors (newer Macs)
	24	2^{24}	16,777,200	High color, millions of colors

years ago when even moderate-quality hardware was expensive. We didn't have 17-inch monitors that displayed millions of colors, because the horse-power and memory requirements to drive them were affordable only to very wealthy corporations. As a result, many of today's Web standards are based on the state of computing when those standards were first created.

The field of color management has slowly evolved with the technology in order to work toward color's holy grail: everyone seeing the same color. We're not there yet, but we are getting closer.

Color Between Platforms

One of the frustrations of Web designers is that Macintosh and Windows operating systems use different bases for displaying color. This is especially evident in images, but carries over to background and text colors as well because the two systems feature different gamma defaults. Gamma is a representation of how the same input value, like a specific percentage of black defined in software, gets displayed as the output in a given physical system, like a monitor or printer. Due to the ways in which the two operating systems translate color values for display at the software level, colors tend to be lighter on a Macintosh, or darker under Windows, depending on your point of view.

TIP:
Adjusting and Simulating Gamma

You can tweak gamma settings on both platforms to varying degrees by using the Adobe Gamma control panel that ships with Photoshop 5 and later for both platforms (see Figure 10-1). This control panel allows you to simulate Windows gamma on a Mac more effectively than the reverse. Also, Adobe ImageReady (Mac and Windows), which ships with Photoshop 5.5 and later, features a gamma simulator for the opposite platform when previewing images (see Figure 10-2).

Figure 10-1
Adobe Gamma

The Adobe Gamma control panel is used to aid hardware calibration, but you can also use it to simulate Windows or Mac gamma levels.

Figure 10-2
Simulated
gamma using
ImageReady

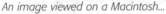

An image viewed on a Macintosh...   *... appears darker under Windows*

The Web-safe color palette. Color also differs among platforms because the engineers who built color into each system's operating system chose slightly different color values to use for each default color palette. Of the 256 colors available in an 8-bit color system, 216 of them match up across all platforms, including Mac, Windows, and typical Unix interfaces. This is what's commonly called the Web-safe, or sometimes browser-safe, color palette (see Figure 10-3). Using colors from this palette makes it more likely that what you see on your

Figure 10-3
Web-safe
color palette

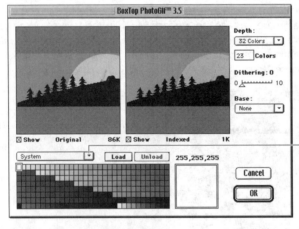

The Web-safe color palette, unlike your computer's system palette, is usually associated with Web images, as shown here. But the colors apply just as well to page backgrounds, table cells, etc. (which is admittedly difficult to show here in grayscale).

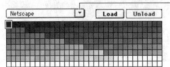

Choosing the Web-safe color palette (in this case referred to as the Netscape color palette) offers fewer total colors to work with, but increases the chance that colors display the same on all platforms.

screen looks the same on another computer system, even if that system has old equipment or is set to a low bit depth.

Keeping this information in mind can help prevent problems later on, and underscores the point that you should be sure to test your pages on as many platforms as possible.

TIP: **Quick** **Web-Safe** **Color** **Palette**	Be careful: after reading this tip you may not want to read the rest of this chapter! No matter which color space you have selected in the Color palette, you can always access the Web-safe palette by Control-clicking the Preview Pane or any color field. This brings up a table of the 216 "safe" colors, plus their hexadecimal equivalents. Release the mouse button over the color you want to load into the Color palette's color well. If you Control-click a color field in the Inspector, the new color is applied immediately to your selected object. You may never need the Color palette again—but stick around, there's more valuable information in the rest of this chapter.

Applying Colors

Normally, we would make a point of explaining all the options available before telling you how to implement a feature. But in this case, applying colors is so easy we wanted to give away the how-to first. The section following this one, "Selecting Colors," offers the skinny on how best to find the color you're looking for.

To bring up the Color palette—if it's not visible—select Color from the Window menu. You can also click any color field in an inspector or the Text Color field on the Toolbar.

Drag & Drop Color

GoLive lets you apply colors to text, tables, layout text boxes, floating boxes, frame borders, and just about anything else that contains a color field in its inspector. From one of the color tabs, select a color to load into the Preview pane, then drag a color swatch from that pane to an object's color field (see Figure 10-4). If you're using the Web Color List, Web Name List, or Site Color List, you can drag the swatch directly from the color list in each tab.

Some items allow color to be applied directly, rather than through the Inspector palette. You can drop a color swatch on a highlighted selection of text, for example, or drop directly onto a floating box or layout text box. If you try to drop a color onto an area of text that isn't highlighted, the text you type from that point will be that color.

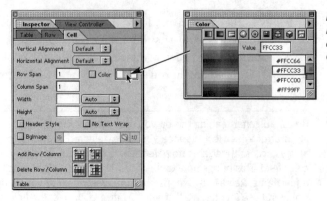

Figure 10-4
Applying color

Drag from the Preview pane to an inspector's Color field.

TIP:
Color Field Dragging

Typically, when you click a Color field, its color appears in the Color palette's Preview Pane. If you want to apply that color to an object from the Color field (instead of making a trip to the Color palette), hold down Command (Mac) or Control (Windows) and click to grab the color swatch and drag it out.

TIP:
Drag to Select a Background Color

To change the background color of a page, you normally must drag a color swatch onto the appropriate field in the Page Inspector. However, a shortcut is to drag a color swatch directly onto the Page icon in the Document window's Layout Editor.

TIP:
Applying Text Color Without the Text

Ever the inquisitive types, we tried dropping color swatches on everything to see what would happen, including images and table borders. Unfortunately, we weren't able to apply table background colors without using the color field in the Table Inspector, nor turn photos of pets and family members hot pink. We did discover that dropping a swatch onto an object that doesn't directly react to the color actually adds a font color to that area. So, any text typed immediately following an image appears in that color. "You never know until you try" is our motto (for today, anyway).

Active Color

Sometimes, especially if you're experimenting with a number of color combinations, you don't want to drag and drop swatches like they've been ripped out of some torn-up Pantone guide. GoLive 5's active color mode enables you to apply colors to an object as you highlight it.

First, select an object whose color can change, such as a table cell. To switch modes, click once on the Color field in the Inspector; a colored border surrounds it to indicate the mode shift (see Figure 10-5). As you click on different colors in the Color palette, the object's color changes too.

Figure 10-5
Active color
mode

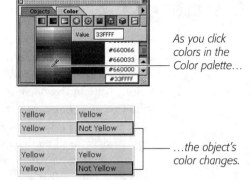

*As you click
colors in the
Color palette…*

*…the object's
color changes.*

*Click once on the Color field
to enter active color mode.*

TIP:
**The Pop-Up
Color
Palettes**

Control-click (Mac) or right-click (Windows) any color field to display a grid of the 216 Web-safe colors and their hexadecimal values. If you also hold down the Option (Mac) or Alt (Windows) key, the grid displays the Web Name List colors, including the color names, instead.

Applying Colors in Other Editors

Although setting colors in the Layout Editor is the easiest and most visual approach, GoLive offers a couple of interesting color uses in the HTML Source Editor and the HTML Outline Editor.

HTML Source Editor. You can't apply a color to objects while editing their HTML code, but you can use the Color palette to help you grab the right hexadecimal values that define colors. If you drag a color swatch anywhere in the HTML Source Editor or the Source Code window, GoLive inserts

```
color="[color value]"
```

at the point where you dropped the swatch. This way, you can set up a tag (like a font definition or table cell), then insert the color you want without having to look up the hex value.

HTML Outline Editor. Drop a color swatch onto the color attribute of a tag to change it. This can be especially useful for setting attributes that aren't directly supported in the Layout Editor, such as a table's border color (see Chapter 11, *Tables*, for information on editing tables and cells).

Selecting Colors

It's great to select color by eye in a visual editor rather than imagining color while looking up, and then typing in, hexadecimal values; it's another reason we like working in a WYSIWYG editor. Now all we have to do is click on the Color palette and we don't even have to worry about what the color's numeric values are. (Of course, you could simulate the Color palette by buying a Web-safe color poster listing hex, RGB, and named values, and hang it near your desk…which we admit to having done before GoLive appeared.)

But which color palette to click? GoLive includes nine different tabs on the Color palette that each offer a different way of selecting colors. (See Chapter 3, *Palettes and Parts*, for a visual overview of each.)

TIP:
The Color Palette's Color Palette?

Before you begin to think we're repeating ourselves, we just wanted to point out the difference between Color palette (capitalized) and color palette (not capitalized). The Color palette is the floating window where GoLive's color controls are located. A color palette is the portion of a tab on the Color palette where the actual colors are located. This is a good example of how real-world metaphors can get confusing in the computer world. A physical palette is what we use to hold and mix colors on, but the notion of a digital palette that can hold other things (like commands, text fields, etc.) works well when describing the floating windows. Now, before you begin to think we're repeating ourselves, we just wanted to point out….

The Value of Color Values

If the Web were a box of crayons, there would be a lot of confused kids. Although we would look at a color and call it "red," computers need a numeric definition of what constitutes red. With the exception of the Web Name List tab, the values in the Color palette tabs are expressed either as digits, percentages, or in hexadecimal notation.

Digits. Colors are defined using an 8-bit scale, which gets its roots from the amount of information required to draw a colored pixel onscreen (see the sidebar "A Bit about Bits," earlier in this chapter). Values range from 0 (none of the color) to 255 (all of the color), for a total of 256; mixing different colors this way gives you a full spectrum of color (see Figure 10-6).

Percentages. Choosing Percent Values from the Color palette's popout menu switches the value display to percentages in the RGB, CMYK, Grayscale, and Indexed Color tabs. Offset printers mix percentage amounts of inks to arrive at a desired color, and the technique has migrated to the digital realm as well.

(We won't even begin to address additive versus subtractive color here; if you're interested, a book like *Real World Photoshop 5* can tell you more than enough about the topic.)

Figure 10-6
Color notation

The same color expressed in digits, percentages, and hexadecimal notation.

Hexadecimal notation. When it comes down to adding color to HTML code, the values end up in hexadecimal, or base 16, notation, which is just a more compact and neat way to specify the color value. GoLive's great color strength is that you don't need to mess with hexadecimal; choose a color visually, and GoLive supplies the correct hex value. Then again, if you know the hex value but not its color, type the code into the Value field to see its match.

GoLive's Color Palette Tabs

With the Color palette displayed, clicking the color palette buttons brings up the following palettes; you can also select them from the popout menu's list. To display or hide the buttons, choose Show Buttons from the popout menu.

Gray Slider. Classic like old movies and early television, the grayscale palette displays up to 256 levels of gray.

RGB Sliders. The RGB palette selects colors using mixtures of red, green, and blue, which is the combination that monitors use to display color. Technically, everything you're looking at onscreen is being represented in RGB.

CMYK Sliders. If you're trying to match a color from a printed color swatch, enter its values in the CMYK tab. Cyan, magenta, yellow, and black (represented by K, since B already stands for blue) are the four ink colors used in process-color printing.

HSB Wheel (indexed color). The HSB Wheel palette displays the full range of colors compatible with your existing monitor and screen depth; choose your color, then use the Brightness slider to achieve just the right shade. (HSB is short for Hue (or sometimes Hue Angle), Saturation, and Brightness. Hue is calculated based on a 360-degree scale—hence the circular representation—and saturation is measured from the middle of the wheel to the edge.) For example, if your screen is set to display 256 colors, or 8-bit color, you see more dithering (where the computer pairs different-colored pixels in an attempt to approximate the original color if it's not available) than if you were viewing at a resolution of thousands of colors, or 16-bit color (see Figure 10-7).

Figure 10-7
Dithering

 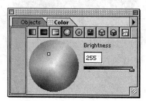

Fewer colors are displayed on 8-bit screens.   *16-bit and higher screens display more colors.*

TIP:
Slider Slickness

The Grayscale, RGB, CMYK, and Indexed Color palettes feature sliders as well as numeric fields for defining a color. Click and hold the slider knob while dragging to change the color amounts. If you click along a slider's path, the knob jumps to the mouse arrow's location.

Apple and Windows palettes. These palettes, available on their respective platforms, present the built-in 256-color system palettes. (The popout menu in the Color palette refers to these simply as Palettes.) From the popup menu on these tabs, you can also choose to display a reduced palette of 16 colors or 16 grays, desktop colors (the ones the system reserves for its own use), or a custom palette of colors you can drag from the Preview pane (see Chapter 3, *Palettes and Parts*).

TIP:
Access System Colors

To access the full range of colors on your system, Command-Option-click (Mac) or Ctrl-Shift-click (Windows) the Preview Pane; use Option-Click (Mac) or Shift-click (Windows) within a Color field. The operating system's color options window appears, enabling you to choose colors, for example, from Apple's Crayon Picker (see Figure 10-8).

HSV Picker. The HSV tab displays colors based on their hue, saturation, and value. Hue is represented as a number between 0 and 360 (creating the circle);

saturation and value are expressed in percentages. Some people find this to be a quicker and more visual way to nab the color they're looking for. Note that the RGB values are also shown here.

Figure 10-8
Apple's Crayon
Picker

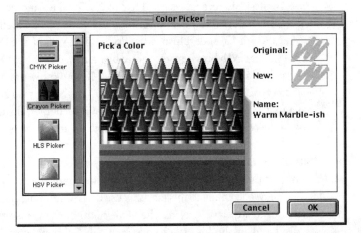

Web Color List. Honestly, this is the tab we keep open 90 percent of the time we use GoLive. It offers an overview of the colors available as well as a scrolling list (with hex labels) showing larger swatches of the colors. But the main reason is that the Web Color List displays only the Web-safe color palette. Sticking to this ensures that our colors are viewable on any system;

Why So Much Color?

As we mentioned at the beginning of this chapter, there are only 216 Web-safe colors. In most cases, you want your site to be available to the most possible viewers, which is why most designers stick to the Web-safe color palette. So why does GoLive include support for color spaces that don't necessarily show up on the Web, like CMYK?

We can think of a few reasons. Hopefully, there will come a day when we're not limited by the number of colors that can be displayed safely, so GoLive has the functionality required to scale up when needed. Virtually all the tens of millions of machines shipping in the last few years have video display cards that show thousands or millions (16- or 24-bit) of colors on a monitor, but there are many millions of older machines that are still being phased out and upgraded. So that day isn't decades off—it's a year or two away.

Second, if you're working with a group that you can identify as having more modern equipment or if you're designing for a corporate intranet in which you know that everyone's machine is capable of more than the Internet mean, you can use the full breadth of color.

there's nothing worse than spending a lot of effort choosing the perfect color, only to realize it looks like garbage on other computers.

Web Name List. Some days, we'd like to give it all up and become the people who name colors—did they hire these folks away from mail-order catalogs (PapayaWhip? Lavenderblush? Mistyrose?). The Web Name List displays a list of colors that Web browsers recognize by name (so in the HTML, "#FFDAB9" is actually substituted with "PeachPuff"). If you know the name of a color, you can type it, or even part of its name, into the Name field and hit Return to get a match. Despite the often-creative naming schemes, the downside is that not all the colors in this tab display the same on all browsers.

Site Color List. The Site Color List simply reflects the contents of whatever colors are present in the Colors tab of the Site window when a site file is open. You cannot add colors to this tab, only use it as a quick reference to select colors that you already have in a site. The name of the current site reflected in the tab is displayed in the lower-left corner of the Color palette. See Chapter 22, *Sitewide Sets*, for information on how to create and store site colors.

TIP:
Select a Color from Anywhere on the Screen

Frequently, we have an image or other element that contains the exact color we want to use on our page. Instead of trying to match it to a value in one of the Color palette tabs, you can grab the value directly. Switch to the Apple/Windows palette (depending on your machine), or Web Color List, then click within the color proxy to the left of the tab, but keep the mouse button pressed. Now, feel free to roam the eyedropper cursor over any part of your screen, even the menu bar or applications that are visible behind GoLive. When you release the mouse button, the color beneath the eyedropper is loaded into the Preview pane.

TIP:
The Quicker Color Picker-Upper

GoLive's active color mode can be especially handy if you want to quickly pick up a color that appears elsewhere on the page. For example, if you want a table cell to match the color of another cell, but don't know the latter's color, simply select the first cell, click the Color field to enter active mode, then use the eyedropper tool mentioned in the tip above to point at the second cell's background color.

The Art of Color

In some respects, GoLive has made color a more complex issue than in other Web design applications. With nine color palettes available, selecting the right hue or background shade can be almost overwhelming. *Almost.* In reality, the simplicity of applying colors to Web objects overcomes the number of methods for selecting those colors. It's almost enough to make us hang up our paints and brushes for good. Almost.

CHAPTER 11

Tables

The Web hasn't always been a designer's medium. As we mentioned in Chapter 8, *Text and Fonts*, HTML is a *structural* formatting language, which shows anyone with a browser the same information regardless of his or her choice of font, type style, or screen size. However, this flexibility became a problem when representing tabular information, like spreadsheet results. Netscape soon introduced HTML tables, which became the tool of choice to display this kind of data in structurally defined rows and columns.

We've spent enough time around graphic designers (and each other) to know that designers not only appreciate useful tools, they also like to discover new uses for those tools that the tool makers never dreamed about. Needless to say, it wasn't long before the Web's first designers turned the tables on tables. Now the unassuming HTML table has become one of the most reliable and flexible tools used by Web designers. With tables, you can build a framework that controls where elements appear, paint in colors without using images, and add variety to your pages.

The "traditional" cost of wielding this tool has been complexity. Even veteran HTML coders can be found glued to their computer screens deciphering which tags belong to which table cell (and trying to find the one errant tag that's preventing the table from being drawn at all in some browsers). Fortunately, GoLive's table tools make it easy to create, edit, and bend tables to your will in ways that barely resemble a standard table—and with a minimum amount of direct code wrangling.

Creating a Table

If you've ever used a spreadsheet application like Microsoft Excel, tables are a familiar sight. No matter how you stretch, shift, or align them, tables always remain rectangular blocks of *cells* (see Figure 11-1). Because of this structure, cells naturally fall into rows (horizontal, left-to-right) and columns (vertical, top-to-bottom). As you'll see, tables are highly configurable. They can contain column headings and captions, nest within other tables, and be manipulated in a variety of ways. You can specify the size and number of cells, the amount of space between their internal edges and contents, the width of their border, their alignment, and, as they say, much, much more.

Figure 11-1
Elements in a
table

Building a New Table

To take advantage of these features, you first need to create a table, a quick and painless process. From the Basic tab of the Objects palette, drag and drop the Table icon on your page; you can also double-click the icon to insert a table at your current text insertion point on the page. A perfectly useful three-column by three-row table appears (see Figure 11-2).

To start entering information, click inside a cell—not on its border—and begin typing. Or, drag page elements from the Objects palette, such as images or forms, or items from any of the tabs in the Site window; consider each cell to be a microcosmic Web page. You've just accomplished in a few seconds what formerly took hand coders several minutes to set up.

With a basic table in place, you can now begin to modify most of its

What's New in 5

Tables are still tables after all these years, so Adobe didn't so much change GoLive's approach as refine and extend its reach.

GoLive 5's Table palette provides three powerful new options: a schematic outline of the currently active table (if any) that you can use as a proxy or stand-in for selecting cells, rows, and columns; a tool to sort information by rows and columns; and a styles feature with which you can apply and capture color and font schemes for a table.

The Hidden tab of the Table Inspector disappeared, as the Table palette's proxy replaces it and adds the selection functionality.

attributes from within GoLive's Table Inspector tabs. Virtually all of these attributes display correctly in all current Web browsers.

Figure 11-2
Default table

Three rows

Three columns

Working around the Table Default

Having tables spring full-formed into the world is a wonderful thing, especially if you've ever spent time writing them by hand. (We explain how the underlying code works later in this chapter.) But sometimes you don't want to apply GoLive's default table attributes, which have these specifications every time: three columns, three rows, a width of 180 pixels, border set to 1, cell padding set to zero, and cell spacing set to 2.

Why would you want to change GoLive's table defaults? Perhaps you know that every table throughout your site will have five columns, or you need a white background color every time. Whatever the reason, you'll be happy to know that you have choices beyond a 3-by-3 default table.

The secret is in GoLive's Web Settings. Open the Web Settings window, then click the HTML tab. Expand the Table option, then expand the "table" item within. From here, click the at-

tribute you wish to change. For example, you can give new tables a width of 500 by selecting the "width" attribute and entering the number in the Value field of the Web Settings Attribute Inspector. For more on how to use this powerful portion of GoLive, see Chapter 31, *Web Settings*.

If you'd rather just keep a template of the table handy, you can also use the Custom tab in the Objects palette, which can hold any object you create on an HTML page except for simple text selections (see Chapter 3, *Palettes and Parts*). Create a new table and apply your settings. Highlight it by positioning your cursor to the right or left of the table and selecting it as you would select any other character or image. Grab the selection and drag it to the Custom tab of the Objects palette (see Figure 11-3). Double-click your new icon to give it a descriptive name. You can then drag and drop the icon onto any page, instead of dropping the standard Table icon.

Figure 11-3
Adding a table as a Custom palette item

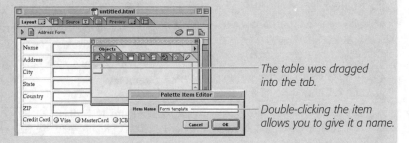

The table was dragged into the tab.

Double-clicking the item allows you to give it a name.

TIP:
HTML 4.0
and Tables

The HTML 4.0 specification offers additional table attributes, but GoLive doesn't support all of them visually. See Elizabeth Castro's book, *HTML 4 for the World Wide Web*, for descriptions of the available attributes.

Border. You can specify a table's border thickness in pixels by changing the value in the Border field of the Table Inspector's Table tab; GoLive's default border setting is one pixel. The higher the border setting, the larger the "picture frame" appears (see Figure 11-4).

If you don't want borders to appear at all, set the border value to zero. GoLive displays invisible borders using gray lines. (If you don't see them, make sure you have Show Invisible Items active in the Edit menu.) Note that

Figure 11-4
Table borders

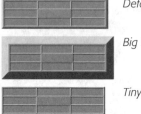

Default border of 3 pixels

Big border of 15 pixels

Tiny border of 1 pixel

Where's the Column Tab?

It's like one of those "What's missing from this scene?" tests. The Table Inspector contains tabs for Table, Row, and Cell. Why not a tab for Column?

The reason hearkens back to ye olde days of code: HTML allows you to specify the settings for a row because cells are defined as elements that exist within rows. Tables are built sequentially left-to-right, then top-to-bottom.

As a browser reads HTML that constructs a table, it's working much like an old-fashioned typewriter. It reads an enclosing Table tag followed by a row tag, followed by individual cell tags. It puts each new cell to the right of the previous cell until it reaches an end-of-row tag. It then moves down to the next row starting at the same left margin, and builds cell-by-cell

across. (See Figure 11-5, built from the following HTML.)

```
<TABLE>
<TR>
   <TD>Left Cell, Row 1</TD>
   <TD>Right Cell, Row 1</TD>
</TR>
<TR>
   <TD>Left Cell, Row 2</TD>
   <TD>Right Cell, Row 2</TD>
</TR>
</TABLE>
```

Since all the settings for formatting the cells are contained either in the row (TR) or cell (TD) tags, there's no need for a separate column tag.

Figure 11-5
Left to Right

| Left Cell, Row 1 | Right Cell, Row 1 |
| Left Cell, Row 2 | Right Cell, Row 2 |

the value you assign in the Border field applies only to the border surrounding the table, not to the borders of the cells inside, unless the value is set to zero.

Width and Height. The Width and Height fields control the size of tables, rows, and cells in their respective tabs in the Table Inspector. Rows, however, can only have their height set, not their width.

There are three ways of controlling width and height, all of which are found in the popup menus that accompany the fields.

- **Auto.** The default setting tells the Web browser to take the current window's width and height, add in the contents of the cells, and figure out how wide and tall to make each cell and the entire table. Auto is often good for tables that don't require specific dimensions, as the browser tries to ensure that everything fits.

Provide the Numbers — the *Correct* Numbers

When a Web browser encounters table code that's missing width values, it has to read and examine the HTML code for the entire table to determine its dimensions before drawing it. For large tables, that can take a long time.

(Every time we upgrade to new computers, we are pleasantly surprised that many Web pages display much quicker—a result of the faster processors parsing table-heavy pages, even on the same slow modem connections. It's odd that we continue to be surprised, but that's progress for you.)

To help make your pages load faster, be sure to include table and cell widths when you specify your table settings.

But even those specifications can introduce problems if your math happens to be more art than science. Although GoLive does its best to make sure your numbers add up correctly, it relies on you to get your figures straight. For example, create a new table that's 400 pixels wide. Now select the top cells in each row and specify widths for each so that the numbers don't add up to 400 (let's say 75, 10, and 35). The table retains its width, but also retains the values you assigned, which only add up to 120 pixels (see Figure 11-6).

Most browsers are forgiving enough to approximate the widths. But we've seen unexpected results when the numbers don't add up.

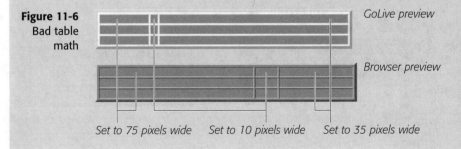

Figure 11-6
Bad table math

GoLive preview

Browser preview

Set to 75 pixels wide   Set to 10 pixels wide   Set to 35 pixels wide

- **Pixel.** Enter a number to specify the number of pixels wide or tall a table or cell should be. If your table is part of a page's structure, you most likely want to use pixels (see "Tables as Structure," later in the chapter).

- **Percent.** Because not all Web browser windows share the same dimensions, you can set a table to take up a percentage of the space in a browser window, or set a cell to use a certain percentage of the table's dimensions. You can choose numbers higher than 100 to force a table off the edge of the screen, if you want, but why?

It's a good idea to include table and cell widths to help speed up the display of your Web pages, but you don't have to get carried away. A table column always stretches to fit the width of the widest cell, pulling the other cells in the column with it. So don't feel obliged to set the width for every cell in your table. Specifying the width of just one cell in a column saves you a little time, and streamlines your code. When you click another cell in that column, GoLive displays the correct value in the Width field.

Cell spacing and cell padding. The Cell Space field in the Table tab (called cell spacing in HTML) controls the thickness in pixels of a table's internal cell borders. The Cell Pad field (called cell padding in HTML) controls the indent on all four sides of a cell from the cell and table borders (see Figure 11-7).

Figure 11-7
Cell Pad and
Cell Space

Configuring cell padding and cell spacing in the Table Inspector

Cell spacing and cell padding accomplish similar tasks: they both add breathing room to the cells' contents. However, in the case of colored backgrounds in table cells, the difference can be drastic (see "Adding Color to Tables," later in this chapter). Suppose you're using different colors for different cells, and have applied a separate color to the entire table. If you set the Cell Pad amount to zero, your text gets crammed right against the cell's edges; by contrast, a larger value adds space around the cell's contents to better offset the text (see Figure 11-8).

Figure 11-8
Offsetting text
with cell
padding

Teams	Top Scorer	Top Assists
Chelsea	Vialli	Lebeouf
Tottenham	Anderton	Ginola

Teams	Top Scorer	Top Assists
Chelsea	Vialli	Lebeouf
Tottenham	Anderton	Ginola

Cell padding set to 0 (left) and 4 (right)

Using a higher Cell Space value increases space between cells, but has its own pitfalls. In the example table above, the background color of the table shows through the wider cell borders in Internet Explorer (see Figure 11-9). Under Netscape's browsers, however, the larger cell borders become transparent, leaving you with multiple cell islands separated by the Web page's background color or image (see Figure 11-10).

Figure 11-9
Cell spacing
border colors
in Explorer

Figure 11-10
Cell spacing
border colors
in Navigator

Since cell spacing and cell padding are table-wide values—you can't set them for individual cells—it's easy to experiment with different combinations and view the results immediately.

Header style. With a cell selected, check Header Style in the Cell tab to center the cell's contents and apply bold formatting to its text (see Figure 11-11). Although you could just as easily apply bold to the text and specify the cell's alignment to get the same effect (see below), the table header style is treated as a unique element in HTML—another example of structural formatting versus visual formatting.

Figure 11-11
Applying
Header Style
to a table cell

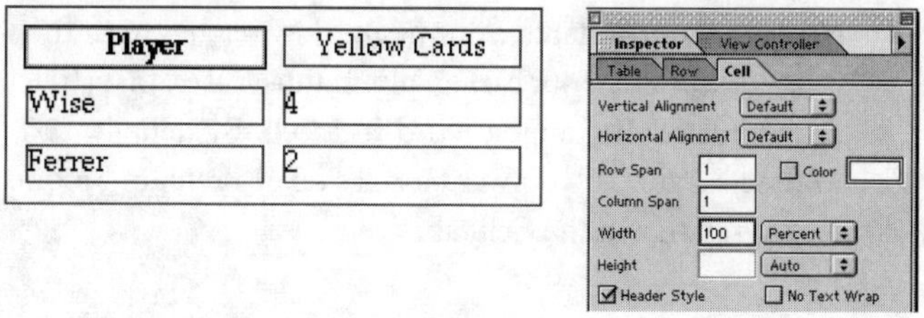

You generally use table headers for column or row headings at the top or left of a table, but you can apply the style to any cell. You can also apply local formatting on top of the table header style.

Cell spacing and cell padding have a tendency to confuse a table's Width value. When you increase cell spacing or cell padding, you're adding pixels that increase the overall width and height of the table (see Figure 11-12). However, the table Width field remains the same, and doesn't reflect the increased width.

Unless you want other elements on your page crowded out by swelling tables, factor the cell padding and cell spacing amounts into the table width value. For example, if your 200-pixel table with a border set to 0 (zero) contains two columns that are both 100 pixels wide, but you want a cell spacing of 10 pixels, you would need to add a total of 30 pixels to the table width: 10 each for the left and right edges, plus 10 for the border separating the two cells (see Figure 11-13).

Figure 11-12
No added width with cell padding and cell spacing

Note that only the interior spacing changes, not the overall width of a table, when configuring these two attributes.

Cell padding   Cell spacing

Figure 11-13
Adding width to compensate for cell spacing

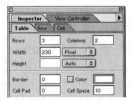

Add to the table's width the amount of Cell Space (10 pixels here) for the left and right edges and for each border separating the table's columns (in this case, adding up to 30 extra pixels).

No Text Wrap. A table column always stretches to fit the width of the widest cell, as we pointed out earlier. But in most cases, that stretching applies only to the width of the longest word in a cell. By default, text within cells wraps to the next line. If you want a cell's text to remain on one line, check the No Text Wrap box in the Cell tab.

Background color. Applying colored backgrounds within tables adds color to a page without having to download images, speeding up a page's load time. You can apply color to entire tables, rows in a table, individual cells, or all three, by checking the Color box located on the Table, Row, or Cell tabs in the Table Inspector.

Clicking the color field beside the checkbox displays the Color palette (if it's not already visible). Select a color from the Color palette—which is covered in greater detail in "Adding Color to Tables," later in this chapter—and drag it to the color field in the Table Inspector to apply the color.

A table color is applied to the entire table. In the Layout Editor, cell colors stop at the edges of their cells, so in a table with wide border sizes, the page's background color shows through the borders. (See "Cell Spacing and Cell Padding," earlier in this chapter.)

Cell colors override row colors which override table colors, so you can specify all three and use that hierarchy to determine which color a cell will ultimately be. For instance, you might want to use an overall table background to contrast with the page's background color, and alternate colors in every other row to make the contents easier to read. Specific cells might be in yet another color to highlight certain facts or figures (see Figure 11-14).

Figure 11-14
Coloring parts
of a table

Setting the color for entire table

Specifying colors for different rows

Specifying color for specific cell

TIP:
**Fill Cells to
Show Their
Colors**

Even if you've applied a color to a table cell, you don't see the color unless the cell has something in it. In otherwise empty cells, insert a non-breaking space to solve the problem: Option-spacebar on the Macintosh, or Shift-spacebar under Windows.

You can also insert non-breaking spaces into multiple cells at once. Select the cells, then choose Insert   from the contextual menu.

BgImage. Alternately, you can apply a background image to the table, which is tiled like a page's background image. Check the BgImage box and choose an image file via the URL Getter. Be aware that background images display differently in various Web browsers.

In Internet Explorer, the image appears behind the entire table, even the borders; set a higher Cell Space value to see this at work. If you have a cell color selected, the color supercedes the background image (see Figure 11-15).

Figure 11-15
Table
background
image in
Internet
Explorer

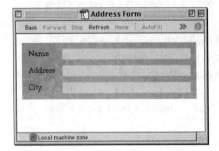

Netscape's browsers take a different approach (see Figure 11-16). Only the cells themselves include the background image, not the borders, and the cell color shows up behind the image (if the image contains transparency; otherwise, you don't see the cell color at all). If the cell is empty, the background doesn't appear at all.

Figure 11-16
Table
background
image in
Netscape

Alignment. Tables support two types of alignment: the alignment of the table itself, which forces other elements to wrap around it, and alignment of the contents of table cells.

With the table selected, select either Left or Right from the Alignment popup menu in the Table tab. Just as with images, the text that follows wraps around the table. Unlike images, however, you can't control how much space appears between the edge of the table and its surrounding items.

Controlling the alignment within cells offers much more flexibility (see Figure 11-17). When you select a cell, you can access both Vertical and Horizontal alignment menus on the Cell tab. Contents can be set vertically to

Top, Middle, or Bottom, while the horizontal options include the expected Left, Right, and Center.

Figure 11-17
Vertical and horizontal alignment

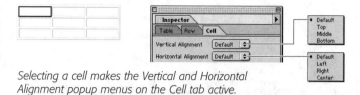

Selecting a cell makes the Vertical and Horizontal Alignment popup menus on the Cell tab active.

TIP:
Fast Cell Application

You can select many cells at once and apply horizontal and vertical alignment options to them via the Cell tab.

You can also apply the same settings to the contents of a row by switching to the Row tab and making your choices. This is a quicker method of applying the settings across multiple cells. If the Row and Cell alignment settings contradict each other, Cell settings override Row settings.

All the alignment popup menus also include Default as an option, which applies the settings found in Table 11-1.

Table 11-1
Default table alignment settings

Attribute	Setting
Table	Left*
Row, vertical	Middle
Row, horizontal	Left
Cell, vertical	Middle
Cell, horizontal	Left

* Naturally, alignment can vary depending on your Web browser's settings, providing yet another reason why testing on a variety of platforms and browsers is essential.

TIP:
Check Paragraph Alignment

Paragraph formatting surrounding a table also affects the table's alignment on the page. If the paragraph is set to be right-aligned, for example, the table hugs the right side of the page, even though you haven't specified any table alignment within the Table tab.

This applies even if your table isn't embedded in a paragraph. If you had set text alignment, then delete the text and replace it with the table, it's likely that the alignment settings could still exist.

Select the table by highlighting it as you would a character, and check the alignment buttons on GoLive's Toolbar. The table alignment settings are as much about controlling how elements wrap around the table as they are about pushing elements to the left or right sides of the pages.

Caption. A table can also optionally contain a caption. With the table selected, check the Caption box on the Table tab, then choose whether the caption appears above or below the table (see Figure 11-18). A space appears where you can place your cursor and begin typing. Just as with regular text, you can apply local formatting (font face, size, color, etc.), but it always appears centered in GoLive.

Figure 11-18
Table caption

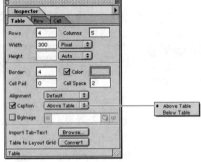

Checking Caption places a text field above or below the table.

TIP:
Aligning Captions

Here's yet another example of how different browsers choose to interpret HTML. When you choose Below from the Caption popup menu, GoLive places an Align="bottom" attribute in the Caption tag. (It adds nothing if Above is chosen, since that's the default.) If you don't want your caption to be aligned in the center of your table, and you're using Internet Explorer, you can change the HTML source to substitute Left or Right in the Align attribute. However, this only applies to the caption's default positioning, which is above the table; if you choose to put the caption below the table, it is automatically centered. If you're using Netscape, the point is moot, since the browser only supports top and bottom alignment.

When you select the table, the caption is selected as well. This symbiosis is great if you need to reposition the table, but it can be dangerous if you decide to detach the caption. Be sure to copy and paste the text in the body of your page, because the text gets deleted if you uncheck the Caption box.

The Fine Art of Table Selection

Despite the painstaking care taken to develop any software program, there are always bits—even in a 5.0 software release—that make you feel more like a Swiss watchmaker instead of a designer: some task that requires intense concentration and focus to get just right. A little slip and that there watch don't tell time too well no more. In GoLive, selecting tables takes a good eye and a steady hand too, especially in a complicated or nested table.

Every good lesson has a fundamental key idea, and here's the one that transforms table selection from random guesswork to precision selecting: it's not how you use your mouse, but where you use it. Being a visual Web editor, GoLive takes a spatial approach to table selection, so the position of your cursor on the table determines what's going to happen when you click the mouse button. The cursor also changes shape depending on the table region it's pointing at.

Selecting the Contents of a Cell

It's likely that you want to start entering information into your table first thing, so click in the middle of a cell to place your text cursor within it. The cursor becomes an I-beam or text insertion cursor (see Figure 11-19), which you can use to type text or provide a target for placing other elements such as graphics.

Figure 11-19
Selection and insertion cursors

The text insertion cursor   The cell selection arrow   The table selection arrow

---

TIP:
Can't Get a Cursor to Appear

You may find yourself unable to get a text-insertion tool to appear when you click at the top of a large cell (see Figure 11-20). That's because the default setting for a newly created cell is to center text top to bottom within the cell. When you click at the top, GoLive doesn't associate that action with text because there's no text at the top.

You can solve this dilemma of two ways: set the table cell's vertical alignment to Top (see later in this chapter); or, if clicking in the top of the field doesn't bring up an I-beam, click in the middle of the field.

Figure 11-20
Accessing text tool in large cells

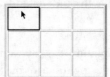

If at first you don't succeed, click within the middle area of a larger cell to acquire the text-insertion tool, or select a Top vertical alignment for the cell.

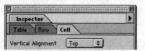

Typically, choosing Select All would seem to select everything on your page. But the engineers at Adobe get extra credit for making GoLive smart about selecting items within a cell. With your text cursor active within a cell, choose Select All from the Edit menu, or type Command-A (Mac) or Control-A (Windows), to highlight objects and text within that cell only.

We use Select All within cells constantly, especially when we want to copy the contents of one cell (including font, color, and size attributes) and paste them into another.

Tables can be particularly mouse-intensive items in GoLive. Give your wrists a break by using the Tab key to move among cells, left to right, then down to the next row. Pressing Shift-Tab reverses the direction.

Selecting an Entire Table

Move the cursor to either the top or left side of a table and you notice that the arrow becomes an object selection cursor. Clicking the table in this state selects the table and displays the Table tab in the Table Inspector. If you continue to hold on, you can drag and drop the entire table to another location on the page, in another open window, or into the Custom tab of the Objects palette.

You can also place the cursor at the right edge of the table to select it. However, if the table's width is set in pixels, the cursor becomes a dark blue icon with arrows pointing left and right. This is technically the tool for manually adjusting the table's width, but as long as you just click and don't drag, the cursor still just selects the table. The cursor remains an arrow if the Table's width is set to Auto or Percent.

It's not immediately obvious, but you can select the whole table using the table's proxy in the Select tab of the Table palette. Position your cursor either at the top-left or bottom-left edges of the table, making sure the cursor is outside the table's edges, and click. Clicking anywhere outside the right or bottom borders also selects the whole table. This trick unfortunately doesn't work under Windows.

You can also select a table by highlighting it as you would a block of text, or by placing the text cursor at the left or right side of the table and pressing Shift with either the left arrow or right arrow key. Unfortunately, this only selects the table as an object on the page, like text or an image. You need to click the top or left edges of a table to be able to bring up the Table Inspector and access GoLive's table-editing features.

Selecting a Cell

You'll probably spend more time selecting individual cells than other table elements, because cells are where most of a table's formatting happens. Position your cursor over a cell's bottom border or its right border (making sure the pointer is not an I-beam), and click. The cursor in this case doesn't change.

If the table's width is set in pixels and the cursor turns into the dark blue resizing cursor when you're attempting to select the rightmost cell, you've moved too far to the right, and clicking here selects the entire table instead.

Another option is to click a cell's corresponding proxy in the Select tab of the Table palette (see Figure 11-21).

Figure 11-21
Selecting a cell
in the Table
palette

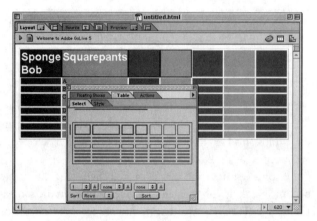

With a cell selected, you can return to editing its contents by pressing the Return or Enter key. This can come in handy if a cell is so small that you can't get the mouse's I-beam cursor to appear; simply select the cell and hit Return or Enter.

TIP: **Increase Cell Spacing for Easier Cell Selection**	If you're having trouble positioning your cursor to select cells, it's okay to cheat a little. Increase the Cell Space value in the Table tab while you're editing, which gives you larger borders between cells; anything higher than 10 works nicely. GoLive considers the border between cells part of the cell, so your pointer doesn't even have to be touching the edge of the cell to select it. When you're finished editing, just restore the previous Cell Space value. (Since it's a table-wide setting, you only have to change it once.)
TIP: **Table Editing Through Cell Selection**	When you select a cell, the Cell tab automatically comes up in the Table Inspector. But it can be helpful to remember that although the cell is the primary item selected, you can also make changes to values that affect the whole table. If you switch to the Table tab or the Row tab, you don't need to deselect the cell and reselect the table or row to edit those attributes.

Selecting Multiple Cells

The ability to select more than one cell and apply settings to them all is one of the great benefits of using GoLive instead of hand-coding HTML table tags. Hold down the Shift key when selecting cells to select multiple, non-contiguous cells. This also applies to clicking areas of the table's proxy in the Table palette.

To choose a contiguous range of cells, hold down Shift, click a cell, then drag without releasing the mouse button. Or, simply click and drag on the Table palette's proxy. If any cells in that range were previously selected, they become deselected. Blue horizontal and vertical indicator lines make it easier to see the range selection.

TIP:
Resize Proxy

The Table palette can be made much larger to increase the size of the proxy when you're trying to select proportionately tiny cells.

With one or more cells selected, you can also choose Select All to choose all the cells.

With multiple cells selected, you can't add or delete rows or columns (see "Editing Tables," later in this chapter). However, you can change the values for the Width and Height fields, and change whether selected cells' dimensions are specified as Pixel, Percent, or Auto.

If some settings conflict, such as cell alignment, the affected popup menus become blank. If you then choose an option from the same affected menu, it resets all cells selected to that popup choice. Leaving it alone preserves the original settings.

Selecting a Row or Column

Holding down the Shift key while the cursor is at the top or left edge of a table changes the cursor to an arrow pointing right. Clicking the left edge selects all the cells in the nearest row; clicking the top edge selects all the cells in the nearest column.

To select an entire row using the Table palette, click to the left of the table proxy; click at the top of the table proxy to select a column. Holding down the Shift key allows you to select multiple, non-contiguous rows or columns.

This technique also works for inverting a cell selection. If one or more cells are already selected in a row or column, Shift-clicking the top or left edge deselects those cells and selects the others. However, by selecting a row or column in the Table palette, you choose all cells in that row or column; it's not a toggle for selection.

Nesting Tables

You can place whole tables within the cells of a surrounding table, commonly referred to as nesting. This is often done when a page's overall structure is defined by a table, and a standard table needs to be displayed on the page (see "Tables as Structure," later in this chapter). The problem sometimes is that selecting individual cells from within nested tables can be difficult if the tables' borders run against each other.

Fortunately, GoLive has implemented a nice keyboard shortcut to get around the problem. Select a cell and then press Control-Return (Mac) or Control-Enter (Windows) to select the cell's parent table. If that table is nested within another table cell, then that (grandparent?) cell is selected (see Figure 11-22). You can repeat this process for as many levels as it takes to get to the top of the table hierarchy.

Figure 11-22
Nested tables

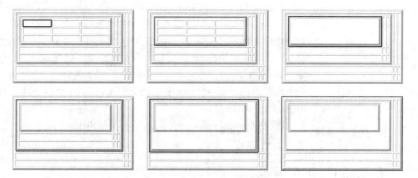

Starting with a single selected cell, press Control-Return to select the cell's table, again to select the cell where that table is nested, again to select that cell's entire table, and so on, and so on....

TIP:
Quick Cell Selection Without Leaving the Keyboard

If your text cursor is within a cell, you can use Control-Return/Enter to select the cell and bring up the Table Inspector. If we're typing with both hands on the keyboard, it can be a pain to grab the mouse, locate the cursor's position, maneuver the pointer to an edge of the cell, and finally click to select it. This way, one Control-Return/Enter keyboard action saves us four steps, some unnecessary hand-flailing, and a bit of brainpower too!

Editing Tables

It's highly unlikely that every table you create needs to look like the default you get when creating a new table. Using the flexible table editing tools in GoLive, you can resize a table's dimensions, add and remove cells, and "span" cells over others to customize the table's appearance.

Resizing Cells and Tables

There are two methods of resizing table elements. With the table or a cell highlighted, you can input pixel or percentage values into the Width or Height fields in the Table, Row, or Cell tabs. If you already know the table's dimensions, this is the best way to set specific values.

Sometimes, though, you don't have the math worked out, or you just want to begin with a boring old table and see how you can mold and stretch it into a close approximation of the masterpiece in your head. This is where the second method comes in: manipulating table dimensions by dragging the table's borders. In some cases, you can resize elements by simply clicking and dragging; other capabilities require the use of a modifier key, like Command or Control, as you click and drag.

As we mentioned earlier, in "Selecting a Cell," the results from manually resizing tables and cells depend on whether the Width and Height values are set to Pixel, Percent, or Auto. If the cells' width attributes are set to Auto, you can squish and stretch as much as you want; if you've previously specified pixel widths for the cells, the table's dimensions are constrained to accommodate those settings. Also, remember that cells never shrink narrower than their contents, so the longest word or object in a cell defines that cell's (and column's) minimum width.

The following rules apply when manually resizing (see Figure 11-23).

Figure 11-23
Dragging to
resize tables
and cells

Dragging a table wider using dark blue resizing cursor

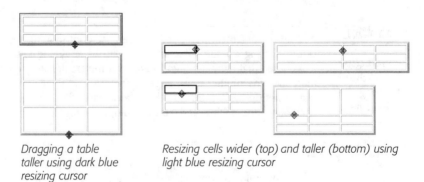

*Dragging a table
taller using dark blue
resizing cursor*

*Resizing cells wider (top) and taller (bottom) using
light blue resizing cursor*

Table width. Position your cursor at the table's far right edge until it becomes a dark blue resize cursor (a left-and-right arrow icon) to change the width of an entire table. Clicking and dragging lets you expand or compress the width; GoLive automatically adjusts the internal cell widths to maintain their individual settings.

If your table and cells are set to Auto widths, however, the dark blue resize cursor doesn't appear. Hold down the Option (Mac) or Alt (Windows) key when the pointer is in the right edge region to invoke the resizing control. When you click and drag, your table's Width setting automatically switches to Pixel.

Table height. Similar to setting table width, position the cursor at the lowest edge of the table until it becomes a dark blue resize cursor (in this case an up-down arrow), then click and drag to adjust the height. Also, like table width, you may need to hold down the Option or Alt key to invoke the resize control if the table's height is set to Auto, which changes the setting to Pixel.

TIP:
Cell Width Restricts Table Width

If the rightmost column's cells are set to a pixel width, GoLive doesn't allow you to resize the table any narrower.

Cell width. Follow the same basic procedure when resizing table cells. If a cell is set up to be measured in pixels, you see a light blue resize cursor appear; if not, press Option or Alt when you drag. You can only adjust cell widths from the right border.

Cell height. Position your cursor at the bottom of a cell. If you don't see the light blue resize cursor, press Option or Alt and then drag to change the height.

TIP:
"Live" Resizing Display

Normally, GoLive displays only a dotted outline to indicate the table's or cell's dimensions as you drag them to a new width or height. However, GoLive can also actively redraw the table with all its attributes (such as cell spacing, background colors, etc.). Hold down the Control key as you drag.

Adding and Deleting Cell Rows and Columns

You can attack the problem of adding and deleting cells in four ways: using the Table Inspector, dragging table borders with command keys held down (adding cells only), using keyboard shortcuts, or using the contextual menu. However, these methods don't all produce the same results. Knowing what to expect saves you time and hopefully prevents you from unintentionally deleting table data, as GoLive happily dispenses with the contents of deleted rows or columns without warning you.

TIP:
Add and Delete Apply to Rows and Columns

It's important to mention here that these add and delete functions only apply to rows and columns. If you're trying to remove a single cell within a table so that another cell expands to take its place, what you really want to do is hide that cell using the spanning techniques mentioned later in "Cell Spanning."

Adding and deleting using the Table Inspector. If you've just created a new table and know the number of rows and columns it needs, enter those numbers in the Rows and Columns fields of the Table tab. New columns are added to the right of existing columns, while new rows are appended to the bottom of the table. Enter a number smaller than the current number of rows or columns to remove cells from the right side or bottom of the table. You can change these figures at any time.

At the bottom of the Cell tab in the Table Inspector are four buttons for adding and deleting rows. They are only active when a single cell is selected, even if you're removing a column and have only cells in that column selected. Clicking the Delete Row or Delete Column button deletes whichever row or column contains the selected cell.

Clicking the Add Row/Column buttons adds a row or column, but with one essential twist: new rows appear *above* the row containing the selected cell, while new columns appear to the *left* of the selection—the opposite of adding rows and columns using the fields in the Table tab (see Figure 11-24). This subtle difference makes it possible to control how existing cells shift within the table, bypassing the need for a lot of cutting and pasting of cell contents.

Figure 11-24
Adding rows and columns

Original table with selected cell

After clicking Add Row and Add Column button in Cell tab of Table Inspector

After increasing row and column count to 5 in the Table tab of Table Inspector

Adding by dragging table borders. As a rule, we like to avoid making frequent trips to the Table Inspector, which is why we like the capability of adding rows and columns by dragging their borders. This only works on the table as a whole (you can't drag a cell border in the middle of the table and expect a new column to appear there), but it's a great way to expand a table quickly and easily. (Unfortunately, you can't delete rows or columns using this method, though it's a feature we'd like to see.)

Position your cursor on the table's right edge (for adding columns) or the bottom edge (for adding rows), just as if you're going to resize the table. With the Command key (Macintosh) or the Control-Shift keys (Windows) held down, drag the table's border. A plus sign (+) appears on the arrow cursor, and dotted outlines representing new cells appear. Continue to drag until you've added as many columns or rows as you'd like, then release the mouse button.

Adding and deleting using keyboard shortcuts. As you've no doubt guessed, we love keyboard shortcuts. Select a single cell and quickly add or delete rows and columns using the keys described in Table 11-2.

Table 11-2
Keyboard shortcuts for adding and deleting

Action	Numeric Keypad or Standalone Key	Standard Keyboard
Add a row	* (asterisk)	* (asterisk)
Add a column	+ (plus sign)	+ (plus sign)
Delete a row	Shift-Del	Shift-Delete (Mac) or Control-Shift-Delete (Windows)
Delete a column	Del	Delete (Mac) or Control-Delete (Windows)

NEW IN 5:
Copying and Pasting Cells

To copy the contents and attributes of a cell, simply select the cell and use the Edit menu's Copy command, then paste it into another cell. If you select a contiguous range of cells, like a two-by-two square, you can paste it into a similar range of cells. Using the Cut command works the same, but clears the contents of the original cell or cells.

Adding and deleting using the contextual menu. With a cell, row, or column selected, bring up the contextual menu by Control-clicking on the Mac, or right-clicking under Windows. In addition to the standard insert or delete options for rows and columns available in the Table Inspector, the contextual menu adds the capability to add a column to the right of the selection, or add a row below it (see Figure 11-25).

The contextual menu also offers another way to delete rows or columns, with an interesting twist. Select an entire row or column, then choose Clear Selected Cells from the contextual menu to delete the selected cells. If you have multiple cells selected that don't belong to the same row or column, applying Clear Selected Cells clears the contents of the cells (including text formatting), not the cells themselves.

Figure 11-25
Adding and
deleting using
the contextual
menu

TIP:
Clearing Cells

Selecting Clear from the Edit or contextual menu works the same as choosing Clear Selected Cells.

Cell Spanning

Even if you're really using a table to display tabular information instead of as a formatting element, it's rare that you want to maintain an even grid of cells. There are times when a cell's contents need to fit across the two cells below it, for example, or you want an image to run down the length of the table. Cell spanning enables you to instruct one cell to extend or span, like a bridge, across other cells (see Figure 11-26).

Figure 11-26
Cell spanning

Cell spanning follows the same directional principle as table cells, operating from left to right, top to bottom. So, select a cell that is either to the left or the top of the cell that's going to be overtaken by the span. With the cell highlighted, go to the Table Inspector and enter the number of cells it covers in the Row Span or Column Span field of the Cell tab. Alternately, you can hold down the Shift key and press the right arrow or down arrow key to apply the span; pressing Shift and the left or up arrow removes the span.

When dealing with cells that are part of a column or row span, think of that area as a single cell—the upper left one in the spanned section—that has simply grown to hide the other spanned cells. The cells that are "hidden" behind the spanned cell aren't affected by changes applied to them, such as when you select a column by Shift-clicking at the top of the column. There is no way to select a cell that is "hidden" by a span.

The contextual menu offers an extra cell-spanning goodie. With contiguous cells selected, bring up the menu and choose Merge Cells. If you have cells that occupy columns and rows in the selection, the Merge Cells command takes care of both span adjustments and turns it into one large cell.

TIP:
**Inserting
Oversized
Contents into
Spanned Cells**

A cell resizes to fit its contents; a graphic or set of text too large to fit into a cell's existing dimensions causes it to grow. If you plan to use cell spanning to accommodate a large graphic or text, it might be easier to apply the dimensions before inserting the element to avoid throwing off any preset values in the surrounding cells.

Adding Color to Tables

Originally, the only method for adding color to a Web page was by specifying its background color or image, or by adding other images to the layout. When you start adding colorful images, as we're all too aware, your download times begin to crawl under the weight of all those pixels. The emergence of colored table cells offered a refreshing change: visual variety without loading a single image! Even better, applying colors to tables in GoLive is a simple matter of dragging and dropping swatches from the Color palette—with only a few oddities to watch out for.

The Table, Row, and Cell tabs in the Table Inspector each contain a Color field, plus a checkbox for activating or deactivating the color. If the Color palette is not visible, clicking the Color field displays it, and, if there's a color in the field, drops that color into the preview pane. Clicking the field once also switches to active color mode, where you can apply colors by clicking swatches in the Color palette. (See Chapter 10, *Color*, for more about color in GoLive.)

Applying a cell or row color. With a cell or group of cells selected, choose a color from the Color palette and drag it to the Color field in the Row or Cell tab. Dropping the color in the field automatically checks the Color box if it wasn't already selected, and applies the color. Once a color has been loaded into the Color field, you can check or uncheck the Color box to apply or remove the color without erasing it.

Cell colors override row colors, so if you apply a different color to a cell within that row, the cell's color is displayed (see Figure 11-27). Unchecking the Color box in the Cell tab reverts the cell's color to the row color.

Figure 11-27
Cell color
overrides row
color which
overrides table
background

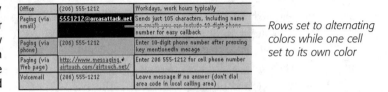

— *Rows set to alternating colors while one cell set to its own color*

TIP:
Adding Non-Breaking Spaces

In order for cells to display a background color, they need to be populated. If they're completely empty, then the Web page's background color or image shows through. The traditional solution to color empty cells has been to insert a non-breaking space by typing Option-spacebar on the Mac or Shift-spacebar under Windows. However, doing that in a complex table can be a time-consuming, and annoying, process. Instead, select the cells or the entire table and choose Insert   from the contextual menu to automatically insert the non-breaking space tag. GoLive is even smart enough to ignore cells that already contain content.

Applying a table color. Like setting a background color for your page, you can specify a background color for an entire table. Follow the same procedure for applying a color as above, but drop it onto the Color field in the Table tab.

As we mentioned in "Cell Spacing and Cell Padding," earlier in the chapter, Web browsers don't display table colors consistently. GoLive's Layout Editor displays only the table's cells filled with the background color, not the space occupied by its borders (increase the Cell Pad and Cell Space values to see a vivid example of this). When you view the table in Netscape Navigator, the borders are transparent and reveal bits of a page's background color or image; but if you look at it in Internet Explorer, the table color is applied to the entire table, borders included (see Figure 11-28). Also remember that the color doesn't show up at all in cells which are completely empty. See the tip "Fill Cells to Show Their Colors," earlier in the chapter. Also, individual cell colors, as well as row colors, override the table color.

Figure 11-28
Background
show-through

In a table with exaggerated cell spacing, it's clear how Internet Explorer (left) shows the table's background color, while Netscape Navigator (right) shows the background image through the interstices.

TIP:
Nest Tables to Create Colored Borders

Build a table containing only one cell, set the Border value to zero, and apply your desired border color to the entire table. Then, create a new table within the cell, sized smaller than the first depending on how thick you want the colored border to be. Set this table's background color so that the back table doesn't show through. Not only do you have more control over the border effect, the result is more consistent than current HTML implementations in 4.0 and later browsers (especially in terms of border size and line weight).

TIP:
Don't Drag Colors to the Cell Itself

You can only apply a cell color using the Color field in one of the Table Inspector's tabs. If you drag a swatch from the Color palette to the table itself, GoLive thinks you're specifying a text color.

A Bad Idea Gone Even Badder

We mentioned at the outset of this chapter that you can use tables to paint without images—clearly a catchy overstatement used to grab your interest, right? Well, you'd be surprised. Most table and cell coloring is used as a backdrop to text or other elements on a page. But an April Fool's joke proved that you can also use tables to reproduce images, pixel-for-pixel.

Every Web image is made up of rows and columns of colored pixels, aligned in a rectangular grid. Sound familiar? For the April 1, 1998 issue of the electronic journal *TidBITS*, Jeff wondered if it would be possible to reproduce an image by substituting colored pixels with colored table cells, thereby eliminating the need to load an image at all.

Travis Anton of BoxTop Software (http://www.boxtopsoft.com/) took the idea one step further and created PhotoHTML, a fully-func-

tional Photoshop plug-in that converts images into HTML tables (see Figure 11-29).The only graphic used is an invisible spacer GIF to make sure that each cell is populated to make the background color display in all browsers.

As with too many brilliant ideas, alas, PhotoHTML has one major flaw: the code required to reproduce even a small image in table format winds up being larger than the graphic it replaced! And if the pseudo-image is large, most browsers either tend to take a long time to parse and render the code, or choke on it entirely. Designers, please don't try this at home! (Unless you really want to, in which case it can be downloaded from www.realworldgolive.com.)

Warning: a really good way to crash GoLive is to open a PhotoHTML file larger than about 50K; GoLive really tries to open it, but it *kinna handle it, cap'n!*

Figure 11-29
A handsome lad blown to smithereens

The original (left) turned into a table with PhotoHTML and opened in GoLive (middle); cell spacing added for cool, new age effect (right).

Table Styles

Tables are complicated elements, especially now that designers often rely on them for adding visual punch to otherwise basic pages. In many cases, such as coloring table cells, making changes throughout a site can be a time-consuming process. GoLive's table styles feature lets you set up formatting options such as cell color, padding, and spacing to automate (but not centralize) repetitive table making.

Applying a table style. GoLive ships with several prefabricated styles to get you started. With a table selected in the Layout Editor, click the Style tab in the Table palette and choose a style from the popup menu. Click the Apply button to activate that style (see Figure 11-30).

Figure 11-30
Applying a
table style

Before styling

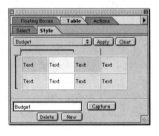

After styling

You don't have to select the whole table to apply a style. As long as a cell is selected or the text cursor is placed within a cell, the style affects the entire table.

Creating and editing new styles. Of course, you're not limited to using just GoLive's built-in styles; one big advantage of table styles is the ability to create your own.

Start by building a table in the Layout Editor. The following elements can be stored in a style definition.

- Cell padding
- Cell spacing
- Border size
- Cell and row color (but not table color)
- Font face
- Font size
- Type style (bold, italic, etc.)

- Text structure (strong, quotation, etc.)

- Text color

Once your table appears the way you like, go to the Style tab of the Table palette and click the New button, which creates a copy of the style selected in the popup menu. Rename the style (if you want), and click the Capture button to grab the settings from your table (see Figure 11-31). To change the style's settings, simply edit the table in the Layout Editor, then recapture them again.

Figure 11-31
Capturing a
table style

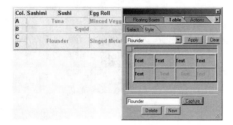

**Restore
Default
Table Styles**

We anticipate that nearly everyone will make this mistake at first: you bring up the Table palette's Style tab, then click the Capture button to create a new style from your table. Unfortunately, this changes the currently selected style (Grey, in most cases) instead of making a new style. Don't worry, there's an easy fix.

Navigate to the folder where the GoLive application resides, open the Modules folder, then open the TableStyles folder. Delete the file styles.xml, the restart GoLive. The default tables will return when GoLive rebuilds the file.

The blue bars appearing above and to the left of the style preview on the Table palette control how cell styles repeat throughout the table. Cells falling in the range of the bars repeat horizontally or vertically, depending on the bar (see Figure 11-32). To change the definitions, click and drag the edge of a bar: the portions appearing within the thicker blue bars are the repeated portions.

Figure 11-32
Repeated style
patterns

Simple table

Captured style

Simple table expanded

TIP:
Define Styles with Small Tables

When you're creating a new style, GoLive uses the entire table as reference; the thin blue lines along the top and left-side edges of the table proxy indicate the original size of the table. (If you can't see the thin blue lines, resize the Table palette as large as you can.) If you base your style on a large table, the style you expect may only be repeated for a few rows or columns, after which the original style goes into effect (see Figure 11-33). Creating a new style based on a smaller table ensures a consistent pattern.

Figure 11-33
Define styles with small tables

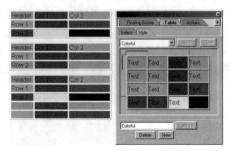

Small table used for capture

Table made from capture set to three rows and columns

Table made from capture set to one row and column

TIP:
Style Power

Are you switching to a different table style, but a few cells refuse to change? Check the cell styles in your style definition. When you apply styles, cell attributes overpower row attributes. If the new style specifies a row color of green, for example, but the existing style calls for a cell color of white, that lone cell remains white unless you change it by hand.

TIP:
Export Table Styles

We thought it would be a good idea to export table styles so other members in your group can have access to them. But before we thought to ask Adobe for the feature, we realized we could do it ourselves! Simply create the table style you want, and save the table in its own HTML file. Send that page to your coworkers, who can then open the page, click the table, and capture a new style based on yours.

Sorting Table Cells

Web tables have always been just for show: they can approximate the type of tables found in spreadsheets, databases, and some word processors, but once the table has been created, you might think you'd tediously have to copy and paste an enormous amount to get the order just right.

Fortunately, GoLive 5 has a sort feature like the one in Excel and Word that makes it a snap to reorder rows by the contents of columns.

NEW IN 5:
All Sorts

The table sorting feature is new in GoLive 5, bringing it up to speed with some other Web page development tools. It's incredibly useful, so we're glad that Adobe had "feature envy" in this case.

The table sorting controls sit at the bottom of the Table palette's Select tab. The three numbered popup menus correspond to the number of qualifiers used to define the sort; the numbers represent the column or row number. For example, a table of college donors can be sorted to group all donors by their state of residence, then listed by the amount donated (see Figure 11-34).

The popup menu at the lower left specifies whether to sort according to column or row, while the pyramid buttons to the right of each numbered menu specify ascending order (1, 2, 3…x) or descending order (x…3, 2, 1). Click the Sort button to rearrange your data. To sort only a few rows or columns, first select them before hitting the Sort button.

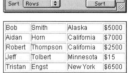

Figure 11-34
Sorting rows
by multiple
criteria

Bob	Smith	Alaska	$5000
Tristan	Engst	New York	$6500
Aidan	Horn	California	$7000
Jeff	Tolbert	Minnesota	$15
Robert	Thompson	California	$2500

Unsorted table

Jeff	Tolbert	Minnesota	$15
Robert	Thompson	California	$2500
Bob	Smith	Alaska	$5000
Tristan	Engst	New York	$6500
Aidan	Horn	California	$7000

Sorted table

Bob	Smith	Alaska	$5000
Aidan	Horn	California	$7000
Robert	Thompson	California	$2500
Jeff	Tolbert	Minnesota	$15
Tristan	Engst	New York	$6500

Sorted table

TIP:
GoLive Doesn't Understand Values

GoLive is good about sorting, performing numerical and alphabetical sorts depending on the cells' contents. However, it doesn't know the difference between a dollar ($) and a euro (€) if you've used those symbols in front of numbers. Further, if you've used characters like this in front of numbers, GoLive no longer recognizes them as numbers; so, this means "$70" will appear *after* "$500" because "$5" is alphabetically higher than "$7". If you need to do more complicated sorts, you're better off doing them in a spreadsheet program before bringing them into GoLive (see next section).

Importing Table Content

So far, we've been concentrating on building and editing tables from the ground up. Often, however, we need to build a table from preexisting data, such as a spreadsheet. Although it's possible to create a table and then type the values into the cells, GoLive's Import Tab-Text feature is much more efficient.

GoLive reads and parses delimited text files, which simply means that each cell of spreadsheet information is separated by a specific character. You can import files delimited by tabs, spaces, semicolons, or commas into GoLive. If you haven't done so already, open your spreadsheet and save it as a text-only delimited file.

Tabular data almost always comes from a spreadsheet program, but that doesn't mean you have to buy Microsoft Excel for this purpose. The delimited format can be created in any word processor or text editor, and can be easily exported from most database programs, like Microsoft Access and FileMaker Pro. What's important is that the data lives in a text-only file.

TIP:
Choosing the Right Delimiter

The point of a delimiter is to pick a character that doesn't get used for any other purpose in the file in question unless it's enclosed with two sets of quotation marks. The quotation marks denote that everything between them is data.

So if you use tabs, spaces, semicolons, and commas throughout your data, make sure to set up your output so quotation marks surround all cell data. (Some programs do this by default, like FileMaker Pro.)

We often use tabs as delimiters because most spreadsheet and database programs don't let you enter the tab character as data; we can be sure it's unique.

Now, switch to GoLive and create a new table. Don't worry about specifying the number of rows or columns; GoLive automatically generates the cells it needs. Select the table and click the Import Tab-Text button labeled Browse in the Table tab, or choose Import TabText from the contextual menu. When prompted for the file, be sure to specify the type of delimiter from the Col. Separator popup menu before clicking OK or Open.

TIP:
Importing with a Cell Selected

It's quicker to select the table as a whole, which displays the Table tab in the Table Inspector, then click the Import Tab-Text button. However, the process also works if you have one or more cells in the table selected. Switch from the Cell tab to the Table tab and click the Browse button; the incoming data automatically begins at the upper-left cell of your table, no matter which cell was selected when you began.

TIP:
Don't Span Cells Before Importing

GoLive's table import feature lets you start with a default 3-by-3 table and changes its dimensions to accommodate the imported information. However, if you've applied cell spanning to the table before importing, those cells remain spanned, possibly throwing off the cell order of your incoming data.

TIP:
Importing into a Populated Table

If you want to merge two sets of tabular data into one table, you're better off using your spreadsheet or a word-processing program to paste the text of the second table after the first. You can import delimited data into a table that already contains data, but the results are less than desirable. GoLive starts filling the table from the upper-left cell, even if it's occupied. You don't actually lose your original data, but it is forced to coexist with the new information, resulting in cells containing both.

Importing into nested tables. Earlier in the chapter we mentioned that you could nest tables within tables, and you can do the same with nested tables based on imported data. After you build a table, simply create a new table within one of the parent table's cells and click the Browse button on the Table tab.

Applying Text Formatting to Multiple Cells

Since we can select multiple cells, it makes sense that we should be able to set formatting on those selected cells. Unfortunately, some attributes work across multiple selections while others don't. Table 11-3 lists how much control you have with more than one cell selected.

Table 11-3
Multiple
Formatting
Hits and
Misses

Can Change	Cannot Change
Font color	List formatting
Cell color	Text alignment
Font set	
Cell alignment	
No text wrap	
Font style (bold, italic, etc.)	
Header style	
Remove font color	
Nobreak style	

TIP:
Apply
Formatting
to Cells

Most formatting is applied at the cell level, so if you want to change the text font throughout your table, you need to select all the cells and make the change, instead of selecting the table as a whole.

Tables as Structure

Web browsers were created to suit the user, who could specify his or her own fonts and sizes and expect that the text would wrap to fit any browser window size. Unfortunately, this had the side effect of driving some graphic designers completely insane, because they had such limited control over the visual presentation. From a graphic design standpoint, the original approach was akin to making every printed brochure a letter-size sheet of white paper with Courier text.

But when HTML tables appeared, designers realized they didn't have to be restricted to traditional tabular data. Instead, tables can provide the framework necessary to invite all sorts of design flexibility. We know designers who start every page by creating a table enclosing its contents. With a table as the structure of your page, you can specify columns or sidebars or special areas for navigation graphics.

Fixed Versus Percentage Measurements

If you know the dimensions of your design, you can specify fixed pixel widths to establish—and retain—the design's measurements, regardless of the size of the browser window. This enables you to control where images and other elements are placed. Instead of working on a sliding, unpredictable layout, you've created a framework which has predictable results.

Using tables doesn't mean you lose the ability to create a page that adapts to the viewer's screen. A fixed-width table that occupies the first 500 pixels of a window may look fine in most browsers, but can get lost amid the expanse of a window opened to its fullest on a large monitor. (Similarly, the right edge of your layout gets cut out of smaller windows.) In times like this, consider tailoring your design to use percentage widths instead; you still maintain control over where objects load, but the cells expand or contract to make the best use of the available space (see "Width and Height" earlier in the chapter).

TIP:
Create Structural Templates

If you've created a design that relies on the same underlying table structure, or frequently-used structures like navigation bars, speed up your work by using the Custom tab of the Objects palette. Create a blank table with the dimensions you need (including any static elements such as logos, etc.), then drag it to the Custom tab. When you create a new GoLive document, simply drag that table template to your page to start building its contents.

TIP:
Stitching Together Split Images

If you're using a larger image that's been split into smaller ones, placing these smaller sections into a table ensures that they don't drift apart in some layouts. Create a table cell for each section, setting each cell's alignment so that the images get pushed together; for example, in a 2-by-2 table, the upper-left corner's horizontal alignment would be set to Right while its vertical alignment would be set to Bottom. Make sure that the cell padding, cell spacing, and border values are set to zero to remove spaces introduced by those attributes. (Programs that slice-and-dice for you, like Adobe ImageReady, Photoshop 5.5, or Macromedia Fireworks automatically create a table structure like this.)

Building Forms Using Tables

Forms are notoriously tricky to lay out on a page, since the size of text fields and other form elements vary widely among browsers and platforms. Building your form with table cells, however, imposes a structure that helps keep your forms visually consistent (see Figure 11-35).

Figure 11-35
Form
embedded in
a table

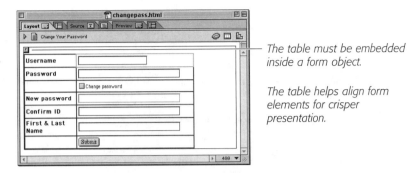

The table must be embedded inside a form object.

The table helps align form elements for crisper presentation.

Place item labels in the first cell in a row, and then put form elements like text fields or checkboxes into their own cells to the right on the same row. This lines up the left edges of all your fields, making the form easier to follow and enter data into.

TIP:

Nest Table in Form Object

Forms in GoLive comprise a form object as a container holding the form elements. To properly let GoLive work with a form and to create the right underlying HTML, first drag a form object onto the page, and then put the table entirely inside it (see Figure 11-35, above). Any elements you place in the table are nested correctly inside the form.

You can use cell-alignment settings to balance descriptive text naming a field or set of fields and the form-entry fields themselves. We often set vertical alignment to Middle to offset font size and automatic leading discrepancies, especially when placing checkboxes or radio buttons alongside text.

Converting Tables to Layout Grids

Perhaps you're using GoLive to edit an existing site with a table-based structure, or maybe you've decided that the extra elements your client wants added to a site would be better off created with one of GoLive's layout grids. Whatever the reason, you don't have to throw away your previous tables and start over.

Select a table, then click the Table to Layout Grid button (labeled Convert); or, select Convert to Grid from the contextual menu. The dimensions of the table change to a layout grid. Images and other objects in the table remain in the same places; cells containing text become layout textboxes (see Figure 11-36). Unfortunately, GoLive offers no easy method of converting a grid back into a table. It's unfortunate because in the underlying HTML, grids are tables—just highly complicated ones. (For more on working with layout grids, see Chapter 14, *Floating Boxes*.)

Figure 11-36
Table turned
into layout grid

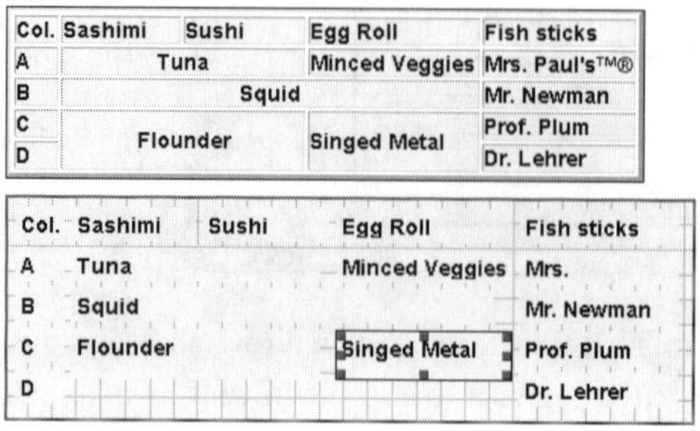

This simple form was
turned into a layout
grid, transforming each
cell into a layout text
box, each of which can
hold any kind of HTML
content, not just text.

Ubiquitous Tables

Whether they're displaying complex tabular data or providing the skeletal structure of an entire page, tables have evolved into a tool that very few designers can live without. It might take you a little time to learn the subtleties of creating and modifying tables in GoLive, especially to get the hang of selecting individual cells. But the time you save later is well worth suffering that initial burst of feature-shock.

Turning Layout Grids Into Tables

Although there's no built-in support for converting layout grids into tables, that doesn't mean it's impossible. Grids don't exist in HTML, which means GoLive is performing a clever hack to create a complex table at the source code level that responds according to its grid features.

Click a layout grid to select it, then uncheck the Show checkboxes. Switch to the HTML Source Editor and locate the beginning of the grid, which looks something like this:

```
<table cool width="394"
height="305" border="0"
cellpadding="0" cellspacing="0"
gridx="16" gridy="16"
bgcolor="#ffffcc">
```

Looks familiar, doesn't it? To turn the grid into a genuine table, remove the attribute "cool". When you switch back to the Layout Editor, you see a standard table, which you can edit and clean up using GoLive's table tools. It's not exactly beautiful, but it could mean a lot less work required to manipulate the information.

Once you've performed this change, it's unlikely you can switch the table back to a grid without performing major surgery. Make sure and save the page (or back it up) before trying.

CHAPTER 12

Layout Grids

From the dawn of time—1994—designers have had one ambition: to have the ability to place an object precisely where they want it on a Web page. GoLive supports two major solutions to this goal, layout grids and floating boxes. However, each has its own set of drawbacks and considerations.

GoLive's layout grids are actually complex arrays of table cells carefully spaced and controlled so that they force objects to appear in specific positions based on the table formatting. Floating boxes, which are covered in more detail in Chapter 14, employ Cascading Style Sheets (CSS) to specify the absolute position of a block of HTML on a page (see Table 12-1).

TIP:
Design Grids

As noted in Chapter 20, *Prototyping and Mapping*, the Design tab of a design window uses many of the same conventions and tools as layout grids. We note those similarities in tips throughout this chapter.

Creating Layout Grids

Layout grids use a graph-paper metaphor for locating items on a page (see Figure 12-1). You can set a grid to rigidly lock all items dragged onto it to the defined grid lines, or you can disable that control for horizontal and/or vertical directions to freely drag objects around.

Getting started couldn't be simpler. From the Basic tab of the Objects palette, drag the Layout Grid icon onto an HTML page (see Figure 12-2). GoLive inserts a 201-by-201 pixel grid with 16-pixels-square grid spacing. This also brings up the Layout Grid Inspector and adds layout controls to the Toolbar when the grid is clicked.

Table 12-1	Feature	Grids	Floating Boxes
Grids versus floating boxes	HTML basis	Table cells and special tags	Standard CSS
	Browser support	Table complexity requires 3.0 or higher major browser	Only 4.0 and higher major browsers that are CSS1 compliant for positioning tags
	Positioning units	In units as small as one pixel, which is the only available measurement unit	In any increment of any absolute units, such as whole pixels, fractions of an inch, etc.
	Arbitrary positioning anywhere on page	No, grids are inserted into normal HTML flow; objects on grids can be placed	Yes, floating boxes can be positioned precisely anywhere on a page
	Animation	No	Yes, used with JavaScript as the basis of DHTML animation
	HTML beauty	Pretty dense, impossible to hand edit, proprietary GoLive tags	Compact and straightforward, but all coordinate-based, so still quite difficult to hand edit
	Overlapping objects	No, each grid is its own object on the page in the HTML flow	Yes, each floating box has its own layer setting which allows transparency and overlap between any number of boxes
	Contain the other	Grids can't contain floating boxes except inside Layout Text Boxes	Floating boxes can contain grids (as well as any HTML)
	What can be put on or in them	Every kind of HTML object except text, which requires a special Layout Text Box; the Layout Text Box, however, can hold floating boxes and all other kinds of HTML, including other grids	No limitations; like a mini-HTML page

Figure 12-1
Text and
objects on a
layout grid

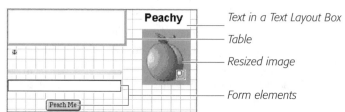

Text in a Text Layout Box

Table

Resized image

Form elements

Figure 12-2
Dragging in a
layout grid

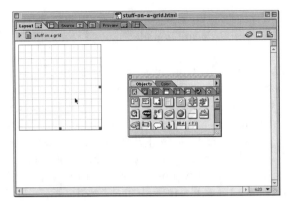

Editing the Grid

Grids have a set of properties including dimensions, color, and alignment that can be set or edited through dragging or through the Layout Grid Inspector.

Location. Like nearly everything else in HTML, layout grids are inline objects. You can move a grid to a new location within the text on a page by dragging or copying and pasting it, but you can't give it an arbitrary location.

TIP:
**Put the Grid
Where You
Want It**

We hate to contradict ourselves like this, but in reality you *can* specify an arbitrary location for a layout grid. However, it's not always a pretty sight. Create a floating box (which uses CSS to achieve absolute positioning), then place a layout grid inside the box. Chapter 14, *Floating Boxes*, explains more about using floating boxes.

Grid units. Grid units are preset at 16 pixels in both directions, but you can modify these through the Horizontal and Vertical fields in the Layout Grid Inspector. If you uncheck Snap for either or both directions, objects can be dragged to any spot on a grid regardless of the grid lines. Unchecking Visible for either or both directions removes the grid lines display. Note that if the

Browser Compatibility

Grids use table tags and elements, and therefore require browsers newer than Netscape 2.0. But because of the intensity and quantity of table elements GoLive uses to make a grid, 3.0 browsers and higher are really required.

Floating boxes only work with 4.0 browsers and higher because they rely on CSS properties.

Both features may work differently on different platforms and releases of the same browser because of the juryrigging that make this work.

Snap box is checked for a direction, but the Visible box is not checked, objects will still snap to the invisible guides.

Resizing. The Layout Grid Inspector includes fields for changing the height and width of the grid, but often it's easier to drag the grid into shape using its resizing handles. To make them appear, click the edge of the grid (your mouse pointer will include a small gray box to indicate you've hit the spot). The grid always grows or shrinks on the right and bottom edges.

Holding down the Shift key while dragging keeps the grid proportionate. Pressing the Control key provides an interactive display (the grid is entirely visible, rather than showing just the dotted outlines of its borders). You can't resize a grid smaller than the width of the largest object's right or bottom edge.

Optimizing. When the grid is populated by other objects, clicking the Optimize button in the Layout Grid Inspector resizes the box to the farthest right and bottom edges of the objects (see Figure 12-3).

Figure 12-3
Optimizing the
layout grid

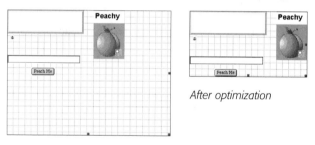

After optimization

Before optimization

Alignment. Like an image, a grid can be aligned by default (to the uppermost and leftmost location available), or to the left or right. Text and other objects wrap around the grid when the Align setting is set to Left or Right.

Background color. Drag a color swatch onto the Color field to set the background of the entire grid. Or, click the field once to enable its active color mode, so you can apply colors by clicking values in the Color palette's tabs.

Layout Grids: Web Design Revolution, or the Work of the Devil?

We believe it's important to make it clear up front that we've never really liked layout grids. Although the idea is good—make a Web design program more flexible, like a desktop publishing application—the implementations over the years have left us scratching our heads.

Our main problem with grids is the code required to make them work. Perhaps it's because we both come from backgrounds in hand-coding our HTML. When we started designing for the Web, no graphical Web design packages existed; Yahoo was just a screen full of hyperlinks, and it would be years before we'd see a URL in a public place. Any Web page change involved poring over the HTML to find the appropriate tags. Then layout grids appeared, adding control by building an overly complicated table, and we squawked whenever we had to dive into that mess.

And it wasn't just the complexity of the code. To achieve pixel-level positioning without turning to CSS (by way of floating boxes) requires a complex framework of table cells to hold everything in place. The result was substantially more HTML for a Web browser to handle, slowing down the times required to download the page and then render it correctly. We know people whose dedication to performance makes them go out of their way to shave a few hundred *bytes* from images; so why waste that savings with dozens of *kilo*bytes of table text?

Our secondary problem, up through GoLive 4, is the simple fact that grids often don't work well in a browser. Objects don't line up the way they did in GoLive, spacing is shot, and text becomes sized incorrectly.

We were forced to conclude that layout grids, while a novel idea, just didn't cut it in the real world. If you're building a quick design mockup, layout grids can't be beat; but even then you're likely to find yourself spending more time cleaning up the table code in order to start building the real design.

And yet…

To our surprise, layout grids in GoLive 5 weren't the beasties that we had remembered. The code is leaner and cleaner; in some cases, we've seen a 35 percent decrease in code! And our testing on various platforms and browsers indicates that the more efficient code is making the grids more compatible too.

We reserve the right to be curmudgeonly, of course. We're not completely sold on grids, preferring to create a simple table and build from there when we need underlying structure in our pages. And we bristle whenever we hear someone begin a GoLive tutorial by starting with a layout grid, regardless of the page's requirements.

But we also applaud GoLive's developers for taking an idea whose time we thought had come and gone, and turning it into a more effective tool for real world Web work.

Grid Objects

Nearly any HTML object from the Objects palette can be dragged directly onto a layout grid. GoLive displays a bounding box of the item as you drag it around the grid, so you can see its size and to which grid lines it adheres if Snap is set for either direction. You can also drag image files from the desktop, though the bounding box does not appear.

TIP:
Stacking Multiple Objects

You can select and drag multiple objects from the desktop at once and drop them onto a layout grid. They arrive overlapped, and colored red to indicate a warning (see Figure 12-4). When you drag them to new locations, GoLive removes the warning. This only applies when dropping files from the desktop; GoLive won't allow you to stack objects once they're on the grid.

Figure 12-4
Stacking multiple objects

Colored object indicates overlap

Layout Text Box

The exception to the rule is adding text, which requires a Layout Text Box, which can contain any kind of HTML object itself, including layout grids and floating boxes.

TIP:
Indecent Nesting

You can nest a floating box with a layout grid inside a Layout Text Box inside a layout grid (see Figure 12-5). Only a higher power knows exactly how any given browser would react to this abomination, however.

Figure 12-5
Nesting layout grids inside floating boxes ad infinitum

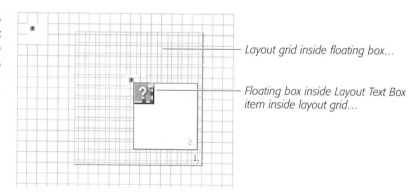

Layout grid inside floating box...

Floating box inside Layout Text Box item inside layout grid...

Drag the Layout Text Box icon from the Basic tab of the Objects Palette to create a new 32-by-32 pixel box. Then, simply click to insert your cursor and begin typing. As you add more text, the box's height automatically increases (see Figure 12-6).

Figure 12-6
Typing in a
Layout Text Box

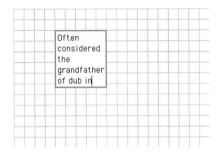

Use the handles along the Layout Text Box's border to resize the box. As with the grid, holding down Shift resizes proportionally, while holding down Control gives you an interactive preview. (If you don't see the resizing handles, click the box's border.)

GoLive is smart about text boxes: by default you can't resize the box to be smaller than its contents. To get around this limitation, check the Allow Content Overflow option in the Layout Text Box inspector to change the box's dimensions (see Figure 12-7).

Figure 12-7
Allow Content
Overflow

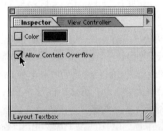

TIP:
Unintended
Overflow
Indicator

If Allow Content Overflow is turned off, and you inadvertently change the text box's height attribute (Csheight) within the HTML so that the box is smaller than the text, a small plus-sign icon appears in the lower-right corner indicating there's more content (see Figure 12-8).

Also in the Layout Text Box inspector, choose a background color for the box using the Color field. (Applying color to the text itself is the same as in the rest of the Layout Editor; see Chapter 8, *Text and Fonts*.)

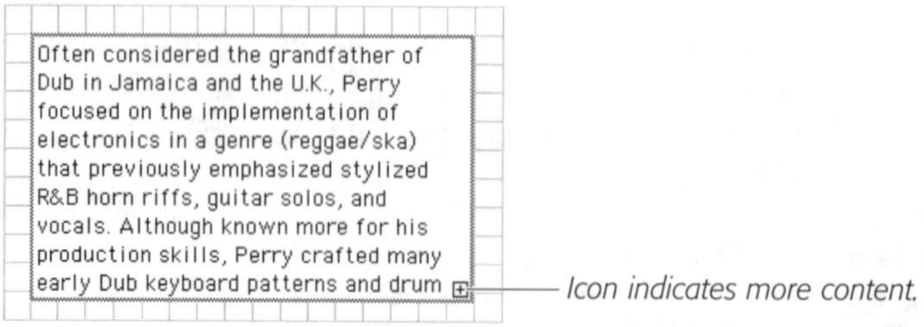

Figure 12-8
But wait,
there's more

```
Often considered the grandfather of
Dub in Jamaica and the U.K., Perry
focused on the implementation of
electronics in a genre (reggae/ska)
that previously emphasized stylized
R&B horn riffs, guitar solos, and
vocals. Although known more for his
production skills, Perry crafted many
early Dub keyboard patterns and drum
```
—— *Icon indicates more content.*

TIP:
Visual Text
Buffers

Being able to fill a Layout Text Box with color makes it easy to display text as a separate entity from the grid or page background. Unfortunately, a Layout Text Box offers no way to add a margin to keep the text from butting up against the box's edge. Instead, create an empty Layout Text Box, sized to approximately the grid width, and run it alongside the main text box.

Working with Grid Objects

The whole point of layout grids is to put objects where *you* want them to appear, not where HTML tells you they belong. The grid gives you a canvas to do just that.

Moving. After an object is placed, it can be dragged around and positioned almost anywhere on a layout grid, provided that the object doesn't overlap other objects or won't fit on the grid. If you drag it near the edge, the bounding box for the item stops previewing if its left or top edge goes too far to the right or down (see Figure 12-9).

You can also move an object from the keyboard by selecting it and using the arrow keys; it will move in grid increments if Snap is checked in the Layout Grid Inspector, or one-pixel increments if Snap is turned off. Pressing Control-Alt (Windows) or Option (Mac) plus an arrow key moves using the opposite method to the one that's selected.

To reposition an object numerically, use the Horizontal Position and Vertical Position fields on the Toolbar or on the Transform palette (see Figure 12-10).

Resizing. Objects on a layout grid can be resized by grabbing their control handles and dragging (see Figure 12-11). You can also enter values into the Width and Height fields in the Toolbar and the Transform palette.

Objects can be resized using the keyboard starting in GoLive 5. Hold down the Shift key and press an arrow key to resize by a grid increment; add Control-Alt (Windows) or Option (Mac) to modify in pixel increments. If Snap is disabled, the key combinations are reversed.

Figure 12-9
Dragging an
object off the
layout grid

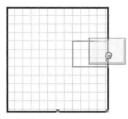

The bounding box displays only while the object is on the grid (left); the layout grid's highlight and the object's bounding box disappear when it leaves the grid (right).

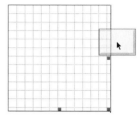

Figure 12-10
An object's
coordinates in
the Toolbar

Behind the Grid

Layout grids are just tables at heart, which is why they can be displayed in any Web browser. However, to take advantage of their special editing features in GoLive, grids make use of non-standard HTML, which is ignored by browsers when displaying the page. Here's what the code used to define a grid looks like:

```
<TABLE cool width="201"
height="201" usegridx usegridy
showgridx showgridy border="0"
cellpadding="0" cellspacing="0">
```

By removing these tags, you can end up with a normal—though more confusing—table. The following custom HTML tags control aspects of the grid.

- **Cool** identifies the table as a layout grid. We can only guess that the early GoLive engineers thought the feature was so great as to give it the moniker "cool."

- **Usegridx** makes objects on the grid snap to the horizontal grid lines.

- **Usegridy** enables objects to snap to vertical grid lines.

- **Showgridx** displays the horizontal grid lines.

- **Showgridy** displays the vertical grid lines.

Other grid-specific tags appear throughout the rest of the table:

- **Xpos** indicates a Layout Text Box's origin from the left side of the grid.

- **Csheight** tells GoLive how tall the Layout Text Box appears, even if its text occupies part of that space. (Also see the tip, "Unintended Overflow Indicator," earlier in this chapter.)

- **Cntrlrow** appears at the end of the table's code, and indicates a row that's used as a guide for sizing the table's columns. A control column is also added to the right-most edge of the table, though it isn't identified as such.

The last non-standard HTML element that appears frequently throughout a grid is the Spacer tag, which GoLive uses to make sure empty table cells display properly in Netscape. See Chapter 8, *Text and Fonts*, for more on the Spacer tag.

Figure 12-11
Resizing an
object in a
layout grid

*Dimensions change as you
drag the resize handles.*

Resize cursor

Figure 12-12
Alignment
options

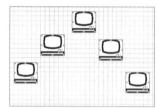

Random

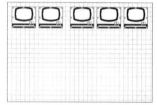

Align top edges

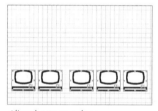

Align bottom edges

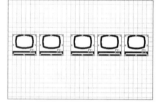

Align middles

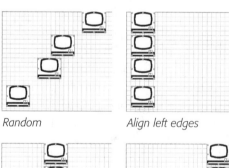

Random

Align left edges

Align centers

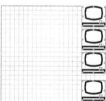

Align right edges

Aligning. With two or more objects selected, you can use the alignment features in the Toolbar or in the Align palette (see Figure 12-12).

All the features described here work identically with objects in the Design tab of a design window.

The horizontal and vertical alignment buttons in the toolbar use the layout grid as a base, so clicking the Align Top button, for example, shifts the selected objects as a group and aligns the highest object with the top of the layout grid. These are the same buttons labeled Align to Parent on the Align palette. To align objects with each other, use that palette's Align Objects buttons (see Figure 12-13).

Figure 12-13
Align to Parent
versus Align
Objects

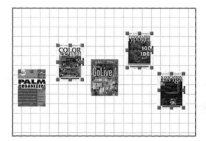

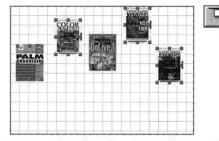

Align to Parent

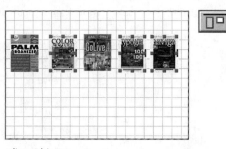

Align Objects

Distributing. With three or more objects selected, the Distribute Objects and Distribute Spacing portions of the Align palette provide options for scattering or reshuffling the objects in relation to each other (see Figure 12-14).

Figure 12-14
Distribute

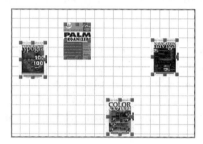

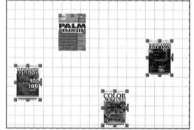

Distribute Objects

Like a chess champion, GoLive tries to stay a few moves ahead of you to anticipate your actions. Depending on the positions of the objects you've selected, only the alignment and distribution buttons that would work successfully are active. If you think you're in the clear but GoLive won't let you perform an alignment or distribution, double-check that a piece of an object isn't jutting into another item's horizontal or vertical space.

Grouping. To work with multiple objects as a united whole, click the Group button in the Toolbar or on the Transform palette to turn them into a single larger object (see Figure 12-15). The Group Inspector includes a Protection

Figure 12-15
Grouped
objects

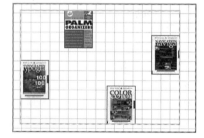

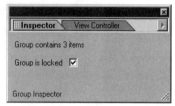

button marked with a lock icon. When the lock is active, clicking an object within a group selects the entire group. When the lock is off, you can select individual items—though you can't move or resize them while they're part of the group.

Select the group and click Ungroup to turn them back into individual objects.

You Control the Vertical, You Control the Horizontal

Designers want more control over their Web designs, and layout grids seem to promise that control. Although they're not a perfect implementation, they can be great for mocking up quick design ideas or simple layouts which contain frequently changed elements.

CHAPTER 13

Frames

In the physical world, windows serve a specific purpose: the clear glass allows us to enjoy the sunshine and look outside without actually having to go outside (an important distinction if you've ever lived in a sunny, but cold, climate). The window's frame usually acts as a border for the stuff that's happening outside—the window's "content." You can change the size and shape of the window, but the content remains the same.

Now picture a church or cathedral—preferably something older, gothic, European. There are lots of windows, all made of glass, but the multicolored panes stretching to the ceiling take on a completely different purpose. Each window is something to look at, not through, and its different panes tell their own stories—content existing for the ages.

In the digital world, we usually employ one window through which to view a section of the Internet. That Web browser window frequently changes shape and position on our screens, and occasionally joins other similar browser windows when we're "multitasking." But essentially, the window is a single pane of clear glass looking outside at the Web.

At least it was until Netscape introduced the concept of *frames*. Like the stained-glass cathedral window, frames allow you to split a browser window into multiple sections. They can simultaneously display different parts of the Web, different parts of your site, or even act as graphical interface elements.

Frames Versus Framesets

Looking at a framed page in a Web browser, it's easy to see what's happening on the surface: within your browser's window, the separate panes are set to display different pieces of information, even including other Web sites that weren't necessarily built with frames in mind (see Figure 13-1). The structure beneath the surface, though, can be a bit confusing at first, especially if you're accustomed to building non-framed Web pages (see Figure 13-2).

Frameset. To create a framed collection of pages, first create an HTML document that contains one or more *framesets*: HTML code that contains the geometry of the frames in the browser window, including their absolute locations and dimensions of each frame. Each frameset references individual HTML files that make up the contents of the framed page. Framesets also contain any properties specific to each frame, such as its border width and border color.

Keep Your Framesets and Frames Separate

Indulge us if we repeat an important point: the contents of a Web page can be displayed within a frame, but the Web page must be a separate entity from the frameset. Fortunately (or unfortunately, if you don't like crashing programs), a self-reference problem in GoLive illustrates this point beautifully.

Suppose you've been working on a page in GoLive's Layout Editor, and realize midway into editing it that the page would work better in frames.

The *right* thing to do would be to save and close the existing file, create a new GoLive document, and start over by building your frameset. The current file would then be referenced by this new frameset .

However, the logical, intuitive action—if you hadn't worked much with frames in GoLive—would be to click on the Frame Editor, drag over a frame icon, and start creating a frameset.

The next logical act would be to reference the page you were just working on in the Layout Editor by using Point & Shoot to select it from the Site window's Files tab, as the source of one of the frames.

If you now were to switch to Frame Preview, you'd instigate a self-referencing loop that can't be broken without forcibly quitting GoLive (press Command-Option-Esc on the Macintosh and click Force Quit); in Windows, it's sometimes possible to click on another view to break out of the loop, though you may have to resort to hitting Control-Alt-Delete to end the task…ouch!

GoLive is helpful in one important respect in this situation: the content you added in the Layout Editor is still there, surrounded by Noframe tags which separate it from the frameset-specific code. This way, people using browsers that can't (or won't) display frames can still see the material you've created in the Layout Editor. See "Using the Noframe Version of a Frameset," later in this chapter.

Remember: create framed pages from scratch, not by starting in the Layout Editor and switching to the Frame Editor.

Figure 13-1
Framed page
in browser

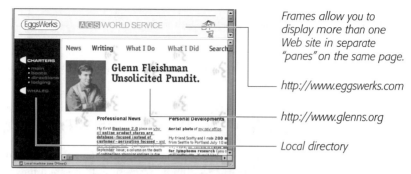

Frames allow you to display more than one Web site in separate "panes" on the same page.

http://www.eggswerks.com

http://www.glenns.org

Local directory

Figure 13-2
GoLive's Frame
Editor

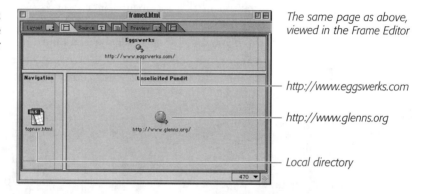

The same page as above, viewed in the Frame Editor

http://www.eggswerks.com

http://www.glenns.org

Local directory

In GoLive, the document you create and save in the Frame Editor contains one or more framesets. In fact, when GoLive creates a frameset that contains both horizontal and vertical frames, it's actually placing a pair of nested framesets (see "Creating Nested Framesets" later in this chapter for more information).

Frame. The window panes created by the frameset are the frames themselves, and contain the external HTML files referenced by the frameset. In GoLive, you can specify each frame's size and name, whether or not its scrollbars are visible, and if the user can resize the frame borders manually by dragging them. These attributes are all defined within the frameset file, not the HTML files that make up the frames' contents (see "Creating Frames," below, to configure these settings). With Web frames, you're pointing at separate HTML files that comprise the frame's content. At first, this may seem like an awkward solution, what with having to pull together several files to create one Web page, but it's clean and it works. (Also see the sidebar, "Keep Your Framesets and Frames Separate.")

Creating Frames

GoLive's frame-creation tools are some of the best we've seen, and make setting up frames no more difficult than the steps we've covered so far to build basic pages.

Building and Populating a Frameset

GoLive includes 16 preset frameset layouts, plus one Frame icon for adding individual frames to existing framesets. To create a new frameset, click the Frame Editor tab in the document window, choose a layout icon from the Frames tab of the Objects palette, then drag it to the Frame Editor (see Figure 13-3). If you drag the single Frame icon onto a blank document, the file automatically turns into a frameset. Don't worry if the layout doesn't initially reflect the structure you're trying to build; you can easily manipulate the frames later.

Figure 13-3
Dragging
frame layout
icons

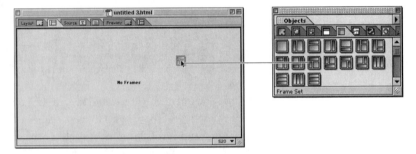

Do You Really Need Frames?

Before you start going frame-happy, determine if you really need to use frames on your site. Most of the frame examples we've seen while cruising the Web really don't require frames; a much simpler Web page can do just as well. Frames in current browser versions are more stable than their earlier incarnations, so they tend to be more reliable (some browsers had a tendency to crash if you even mentioned the word "frames" within earshot of the computer). But frames also introduce a layer of complexity to a site that, in many cases, is completely unnecessary. This isn't to say that frames should be avoided; we just don't like seeing people struggling through unnecessary amounts of work when a simpler solution is at hand.

Use the site's content and your own design sense to determine if frames are appropriate.

TIP:
**Single
Frame Icon
Versus Other
Frameset
Icons**

It could be argued that GoLive's Frames tab really only contains one tool, despite the presence of 17 icons. The single Frame icon, in the upper-left corner, is used to create individual frames in the Frame Editor; wherever you drop it on a page, GoLive automatically builds or edits framesets to accommodate the new frame. The other 16 icons are really just templates whose structure could easily be rebuilt by repeatedly dragging the single Frame icon to the page. This is another example of why we love using GoLive: dragging one or two icons saves a huge amount of time compared with writing the frameset code by hand.

Clicking anywhere within a frame selects it and displays the Frame Inspector, which controls settings for individual frames. To select a frameset instead, click a border separating the frames; this displays the Frame Set Inspector, which handles global frame options and values.

TIP:
**Frameset or
Empty
GoLive
Document?**

If you view an existing HTML file in GoLive through the Layout Editor and discover no content on the page, don't be alarmed. It could be just a frameset. To make a quick determination, look at the document's Page icon (see Figure 13-4). A frameset file displays a frame icon; regular HTML files feature a regular page icon design with horizontal lines.

Figure 13-4
Two flavors of
the Page icon

Page icon as seen in the Layout Editor   Page icon indicating a framed page

TIP:
**Identifying
the
Frameset
Icons**

The Frameset icons have been designed to easily tell the relative size and place-ments of frame borders you're likely to end up with when you drag them into the Frame Editor. However, the last four icons seem redundant; the only differ-ences among the two vertical frames and the two horizontal frames are their color schemes. Or are they? Figure 13-5 illustrates what you should expect when you drag them to your document.

Adding and deleting frames. If you want to create a framed page that has a different look or a different number of frames than the prefabricated icons in the Frame tab of the Palette, drag the single Frame icon from the Objects palette to the location you want to insert a new frame.

Dragging this icon onto an existing horizontal frame generally splits it into two vertical frames. Likewise, dragging it onto a vertical frame usually splits it into two horizontal ones (see Figure 13-6).

Figure 13-5
Identifying
the four
"redundant"
frame icons

Vertical, wide center

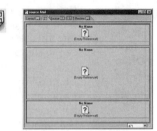

Horizontal, wide center

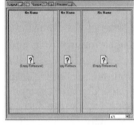

Vertical, narrow center

Horizontal, narrow center

Figure 13-6
Adding frames
with the single
Frame icon

*Original frameset layout
dragged in from the Palette...*

*...and after adding single
frame icon to top frame*

TIP:
**Controlling
How New
Frames Are
Inserted**

Dragging the single Frame icon from the Frames tab of the Objects palette creates a new frame in your layout, but which orientation? In our semi-scientific testing—meaning we repeatedly created new frames until we were sick of it—dropping the icon most anywhere in a single-frame frameset created a new vertical frame to the right of the existing frame. However, dropping the icon directly on top of the existing frame's icon, or near the bottom of that frame, caused a new horizontal frame to appear below it. When more than a few frames existed on the page, new frames usually appeared vertically. Fortunately, moving frames into new positions is a simple matter of dragging the frame.

If you make too many new frames, delete them one by one by clicking within each frame's borders to select it, and then pressing the Delete key. You can't select multiple frames and delete them at once.

Creating Nested Framesets

Like tables, you can nest framesets within frames. As mentioned earlier, when GoLive creates a frameset that contains both horizontal and vertical frames, it's actually creating a pair of nested framesets (see Figure 13-7). Simply drag a new Frameset icon from the Objects palette into an existing frame. The existing frame doesn't act as a container, the way a table cell holds a nested table; instead, the frame resizes to accommodate the new incoming frameset. For example, suppose you have a frameset containing two horizontal frames. If you drag one of the two-framed frameset icons from the palette, you end up with four separate frames, not three. You can select a nested frameset by clicking one of its frame borders; a dark outline indicates the current selection.

Figure 13-7
Nested
framesets

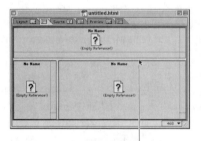 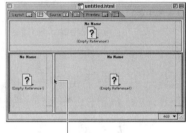

Clicking the horizontal divider highlights the page's master frameset, indicated by a bold box surrounding the frameset.

However, clicking the vertical divider reveals that the bottom two panes belong to their own frameset, which is therefore nested within the master frameset.

Using the Noframe Version of a Frameset

Frames aren't for everyone nor everyone's browsers. Some browsers have the option to not view frames, while other, mostly older, browsers don't recognize frame coding at all. Users in these situations typically would see a blank page when encountering a frameset.

Fortunately, GoLive automatically adds the simple Noframe tag to every framed document. With Noframe in the HTML, the browsers mentioned above ignore the frameset code and display the content included within the Body tags.

Use the Layout Editor to build the Noframe page, just as you would a normal document, without worrying about it interfering with your frames (see Figure 13-8). To preview the page in GoLive for Macintosh, switch to the Layout Preview.

Figure 13-8
Noframe page

People who can't view frames see the Noframe page, which you build in GoLive's Layout Editor.

In most cases you can add a line or two of text explaining that the viewer has happened upon a framed page. But you can also build a full page that echoes the contents of the frames and leads the user either to the pages that load within the frames (see below), or to alternate pages set up specifically for folks who can't or won't view frames. This way, your pages' content is available to everyone in one form or another.

TIP:
Frames and Search Engines

Frames can often confuse search engines, because the content of your frameset file doesn't actually include the content of the framed page. If you've put a lot of time and effort into including descriptive Meta tags in your files, your work may be ignored by search engine robots which look only at the frameset information. So, be sure to put your Meta tag information in the frameset file as well.

If you're running the Windows version, you can't preview the Noframe page because Windows uses an embedded version of Microsoft Internet Explorer to preview pages. Internet Explorer supports frames, which is why Adobe doesn't provide a non-framed preview tab. You just have to rely on the Layout Editor's view as the preview of your Noframe content.

TIP:
Previewing Noframe Pages on Windows

Depending on the browser, you may be able to turn off frames. Or you could install an old version of Netscape Navigator or Internet Explorer that doesn't support frames and preview your Noframe content in that browser. However, older browsers have their own sets of problems when used with newer operating systems, especially when you're running, say, IE 3 and IE 5 on the same machine.

TIP:
Provide a Link to Unframed Pages

It's good Web etiquette to give the viewer a choice between framed or unframed pages by providing a link in one of your frames that leads to an unframed version of the site. Perhaps visitors won't see the full brilliance of your design, but at least they won't click away in search of someone else's brilliance.

Specifying the Contents of a Frame

With a basic frameset built, it's time to populate the frames within it. There are three methods for linking frames in a framed page to HTML files (see Figure 13-9).

Drag and drop existing files. From either the Desktop or an open Site window, drag an HTML file's icon to the desired frame. You can also grab the Page icon from an open document and drop it onto a frame.

Point & Shoot. Here's another area where GoLive's Point & Shoot tool comes in handy. With your cursor placed anywhere within a frame, hold down the Command key (Mac) or Alt key (Windows) and drag from the frame to the file you want to use in the Files tab of the Site window. You can also "shoot" at the Page icon of an open file. The Frame Inspector's Point & Shoot button works too.

Figure 13-9
Methods of
populating
frames

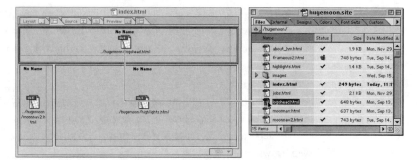

Point & Shoot from a frame to the Site window...

...drag and drop a file from the Site window...

...or type the filename in the Frame Inspector's URL field.

TIP:
**Point &
Shoot for
Anchored
Links**
You can display a specific section of an HTML file, other than its beginning, within a frame. With the destination page open, use Point & Shoot from your frame and aim for an anchor within that page. Similarly, you can direct your cursor to an anchored link within a file being displayed in the Site window (indicated by a gray anchor icon beside the link). If an anchor doesn't currently exist in the destination page, using Point & Shoot will create a new anchor in an open file at the point where you release the mouse button.

Direct entry. When a frame is selected, type the path name of the frame's source file into the Frame Inspector's URL Getter, or click the Browse button to search for the file. Option-clicking (Mac) or Alt-clicking (Windows) the Browse button brings up an Edit dialog box where you can see more text as you type. This path can be a pointer to a file on your hard disk, or a page that exists elsewhere on the Web, in which case a globe icon appears within the frame.

Previewing Framed Content

The Frame Editor makes it easy to see which files appear in each frame, but displaying just the file icons is contrary to the whole idea of creating Web pages visually. Two options are available for seeing what your frameset looks like in a real browser.

Frame Preview and Preview windows. If you're running the Macintosh version of GoLive, click the Frame Preview icon in the document window to get a fairly accurate representation of what the framed page will look like in a Web browser.

The Mystery of the Macintosh GoLive Preview Set

The Frame and Frame Set inspectors contain a bit of mystery; they're both full of buttons that appear to duplicate other features. But the choice to use VCR-style buttons stumps us.

In the Frame Inspector, clicking the Preview Frame button causes it to appear "pressed" while previewing is active. In the Frame Set Inspector, however, the same functionality requires two buttons: Preview Set, which resem-
bles a "play" button, and Stop Preview, which looks like a "stop" button. Neither button appears pressed when active. Hopefully, consistency and simplicity will improve in a future version. (We first noted this in the previous edition of the book, and remain perplexed as to why it lives on in version 5. If it kinda sorta works, don't fix it, we assume.)

The Windows version uses only one Preview window. If the document contains framesets, the frames are previewed there. On both platforms, only local files are displayed, so any external URLs referenced in the Frame Inspector's URL field remain blank, even if you have an active Internet connection. You cannot edit the frames in the Frame Preview window (see Figure 13-10).

Figure 13-10
Previewing a framed page

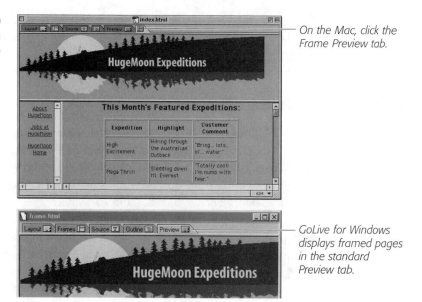

On the Mac, click the Frame Preview tab.

GoLive for Windows displays framed pages in the standard Preview tab.

Frameset and frame previews in the Frame Editor (Macintosh only). As you're working in the Frame Editor, you can opt to display the contents of the entire frameset, or just individual frames, to get an idea of how the frames interact with one another. You can't edit the referenced HTML files directly, but previewing them helps to establish the overall look of the frameset.

Click a frame border to bring up the Frame Set Inspector, then click the Preview Set button. Each frame containing a local file displays the page's contents. Clicking the Stop Preview button reverts back to the default file icon view (see Figure 13-11).

To view only the contents of selected frames, select one and click the Preview Frame button on the Frame Inspector. Click the button again to stop previewing.

Figure 13-11
Previewing
individual
frames

*Click here to preview
the contents of the
selected frame.*

Editing Frames

Real-world objects only go so far when used as computer-interface metaphors, and this is where the idea of the stained-glass window begins to break down. Unlike solid windows made of glass and lead, framesets feature the ability to move panes around easily, allow users to stretch their dimensions, load information in specific frames, and more.

Editing the contents of a frame. Rare is the occasion when all the HTML files you place into frames are in perfect shape. Invariably, something must change; when it does, simply double-click the frame to open its associated HTML file in a new window. GoLive adds a nice touch to this action: the new window appears the same size as your frame, in roughly the same location. You can open all your frame content files this way and work on them as if they were in a virtual frameset (see Figure 13-12).

Figure 13-12
Editing frame
contents

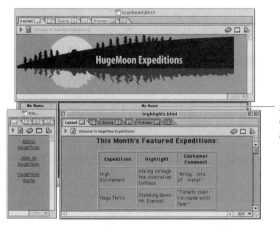

*Double clicking a frame
opens the HTML file that
it contains.*

Moving and Resizing Frames

Moving frames and framesets is fairly intuitive; click within a frame to select it, then drag the selection to where you would like the frame to appear. However, you can only move individual frames within their parent framesets. If you want a frame to appear in a separate nested frameset, use the Frame icon to add a new frame where you'd like to move an existing one, make sure it's pointing to the same HTML source file, then delete the old frame (see Figure 13-13). To move an entire frameset, Control-click and drag the frameset's border.

Resizing a frame is also easy, provided you're aware of how GoLive handles the settings that regulate frame size. When you add to an existing frameset by dragging the single Frame icon from the Frames palette, the Size attribute in the Frame Inspector is set to Scale, which simply balances the size automatically with other frames in its row or column. In this case, although you can grab the divider and drag a ghosted version of it, the size won't actually change.

Figure 13-13
"Moving" a frame into another frameset

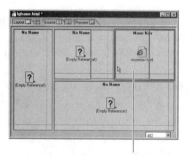

We want to move the Moon Nav frame into the left column frameset, but Moon Nav will only move within its own frameset.

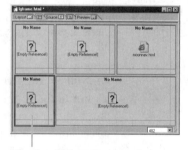

Use the single Frame icon from the Palette to create a new frame within the left column frameset.

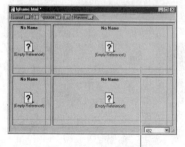

Delete the old Moon Nav frame.

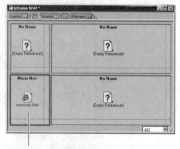

Rename the new frame to Moon Nav and set its source as the original HTML file.

To make the size change permanent, you must first set the Size option either to Pixels or Percent, depending on whether you want to set the size in absolute or relative terms. You can either drag the frame border to set the size, or you can enter values directly into the Size field. Switching back to Scale re-balances the frames.

If you build your frameset by dragging a prefab Frameset icon from the Frames menu, you can just drag the borders to resize the frames, because at least one frame's Size attribute is set to either Pixels or Percent.

TIP:
Awkward Inspector Display When Resizing

To resize a frame, you need to click the frame's border. To select a frameset, you need to click the frame's border. Spot any similarities? Unlike resizing table cells, you can't resize a frame and view its exact pixel or percentage dimensions as you drag its border, because the Frame Set Inspector appears in place of the Frame Inspector as soon as you release the mouse button. So, if you're shooting for a specific height or width for your frame, it's better to enter that value in the Frame Inspector's Size field.

TIP:
Balancing the Scales

Web browsers like balance, because it means they don't have to work as hard to interpret the dimensions of a page. If you specify a frame's height or width in pixels or percentages, make sure at least one more frame in that row or column has its size set to Scale to avoid any potential browser problems.

Controlling users' resizing options. Not all the frame settings are intended to control the page from the designer's side. A unique feature of frames is the ability for users to resize their frames within Web browsers. Checking the Resize Frame box in the Frame Inspector gives users this option, and puts a small indented circle in the middle of the frame's border (see Figure 13-14).

Figure 13-14
Resizable frame indicator

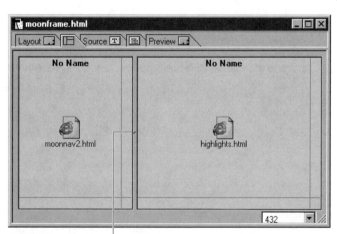

This indicates that users can resize the frame within a Web browser.

Since GoLive assumes that you want absolute control over your frame sizes, this option is turned off by default.

You may have to turn on the Resize Frame option on both frames that share the resizable border in order to make it work. If one frame has Resize Frame turned on, but the other frame has it off, your users won't be able to move the border.

You can also control whether or not a frame's scrollbars are displayed in the browser. If the contents of the frame exceed the size of the window, browsers automatically show horizontal or vertical scrollbars. But you can force them to remain hidden by setting Scrolling to No. Similarly, choosing Yes draws scrollbars (even if they're inactive) every time. Since scrollbars in most browsers tend to take up a lot of space, especially in smaller frames, this feature can be useful for controlling a frame's appearance as well as its functionality. The Auto setting leaves the decision to draw the bars to the browser (see Figure 13-15).

Figure 13-15
Controlling
scroll bar
appearance

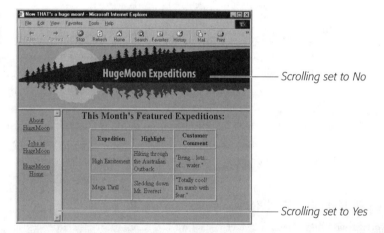

Scrolling set to No

Scrolling set to Yes

Frame Borders

Frame borders can be part of how you navigate or interpret a page, and they can be modified in a few ways to control their effect and display. Click a border to bring up the Frame Set Inspector, where you can change the following options.

BorderSize. GoLive assigns borders with a default thickness of six pixels—big enough to grab and manipulate, but not so large they become obnoxious. Checking the BorderSize box lets you enter a pixel size to change the border's thickness. Often, designers set frame borders to zero so that the page doesn't blatantly look like it's been split into frames (see Figure 13-16). One downside is that zero-pixel borders can't be dragged to resize frames in most browsers, even if the Resize Frame box is checked.

Figure 13-16
Invisible frame
borders

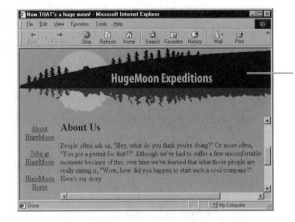

With borders set to zero, the page has a more uniform look. Frames with content exceeding the frame size display scrollbars— the only indication on this page that frames are being used.

BorderColor. If a border's size is set larger than zero, you can apply a color to it. Check the BorderColor box, then drag a swatch from the Color palette to its color field. Unlike table colors, where dropping a swatch onto a color field automatically checks the Color box, you must first check BorderColor, then select a color.

BorderFrame. The BorderFrame setting is a bit confusing on the surface, and requires a brief dip into the HTML being used in the page. Some settings, like table border sizes, are only set numerically; telling a browser to render a table

Border Skirmishes

If you play around with frame borders in GoLive, you'll discover that you can apply different attributes to separate borders within nested framesets. For example, a vertical border at left could be dark green, while a horizontal border at right could be bright yellow, and sized at 20 pixels.

What you see in your browser is a different matter; some programs we tested favored one setting over another. But which settings override others? Logically, it would make sense that the parent frameset would win out, but experience proves otherwise. In the example above, the bright yellow border wins out in Netscape Communicator 4.7, despite being the child frameset. The two border colors draw correctly under Internet Explorer 5.0, though.

As with too many aspects of HTML, the final results vary depending on which browser and platform you're using. Until the mythical day comes when all browsers treat HTML the same, you're better off testing your pages' effects with as many variations as you can get your hands on.

with a border of zero effectively produces a borderless table. In the case of frame borders, two triggers come into play: the numeric size, and also an on/off toggle for displaying the border. In HTML, the Frameborder tag can have a value of "1" or "Yes" to indicate that a border is visible, or "0" or "No" to hide the border.

Therefore, if you really want your borders hidden, you need to set GoLive's BorderSize to 0 and specify that the BorderFrame is set to No. This also applies to border colors; if you specify a border color but BorderFrame is set to No, the color doesn't display (though in some browsers, a larger-sized BorderSize setting causes that much space to be filled with the browser's default background color).

FrameSpacing. Although it doesn't appear in the Frame Set Inspector, you can adjust the FrameSpacing value from the HTML Outline Editor. Select the frameset block and click the gray triangle to select frameSpacing from its attribute popup menu. FrameSpacing increases the size of the frame borders in Internet Explorer (Netscape ignores the attribute). In fact, if you haven't applied any frame border settings, then enter a FrameSpacing value, GoLive assumes that you really meant to change the BorderSize value when you return to the Frame Editor (though the source code remains unchanged). Why use FrameSpacing instead of the border commands? Honestly, we have no idea. But the capability is there if you want to experiment.

TIP:
Using Frames as Layout Elements

A good way to avoid some of the unpredictability of how browsers display frame borders is to circumvent the border settings altogether. If you want a thick black border separating two vertical frames, for example, you could set the border's size to 10, its color to black, and make sure that BorderFrame is set to Yes.

Or, you could create a frameset containing three frames, with the borders hidden. The left and right frames hold the page's contents, as you would have done with a two-frame frameset. Then specify that the middle frame's width is 10, and use a source HTML file that contains nothing but a background color of black. You've cut down the number of variables at work, and you can also reuse that black-background page in other framesets.

Naming and Targeting Frames

We've covered the structure of frames and framesets, and how to manipulate their appearance. Moving still further away from our stained-glass metaphor, frames are designed to interact with one another so that all of them in combination work together as a whole on the page. To use a common example, if you're using a vertical frame to the left as a navigation bar, clicking a link should change the contents of a main content frame to the right. To accomplish this, you have to identify each frame with a unique name; otherwise, the link's destination page is likely to override your frameset and fill the entire window.

When you create a new frameset, each frame is titled "No Name" in the Frame Inspector's Name field. Whenever we build framed pages, one of the first things we do is name the frames to prevent confusion later in the process: simply type in a new name.

Creating frame links. Linking to a frame is essentially the same as linking to a file (see Chapter 1, *Getting Started*), only in this case, you must specify a name to go along with the link's source. This is why naming frames is so important.

To start, open a frame's HTML file by double-clicking the frame. For purposes of explanation, let's assume that you want to create a link in the left-most frame, titled "left-nav," that displays a new page as the contents of the bottom right frame, titled "right-main" (see Figure 13-17). Perform the following steps to create the link.

Figure 13-17
Targeting
frames

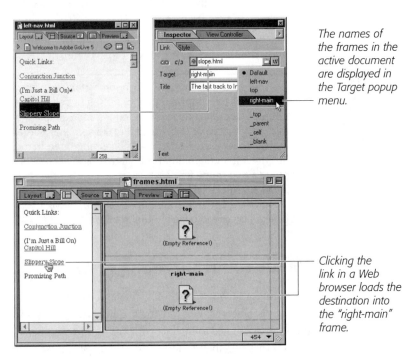

The names of
the frames in the
active document
are displayed in
the Target popup
menu.

Clicking the
link in a Web
browser loads the
destination into
the "right-main"
frame.

1. Select the text or image to be linked, and choose New Link from the Special menu.

2. On the Link tab of the Text or Image Inspector, enter the link's destination in the URL Getter by typing the filename or using the Point & Shoot tool.

3. Specify the intended frame by entering its name in the Target field. If your frameset file is still open, the popup menu at right includes the names of all frames at the top of the list. In our example, use "right-main" as the target.

4. Be sure to save the content file.

Now, when you click the link, your browser first looks for a frame with that name before loading the page. If one is found, the contents are loaded into that frame.

TIP:
Multiple Open Frameset Files

When you have more than one frameset file open, the Target popup menu lists all the names available. If your frames share the same names across several files, close the frameset files that you're not using to make sure the link is pointing to the correct frame.

TIP:
Renaming Frames

If you rename a frame, you run the risk of breaking the links to it. GoLive's ability to manage links automatically throughout a site is great, but unfortunately the feature doesn't extend to target names. The good news is that you can easily use the Element tab or Find & Replace tab of the Find feature to find the old frame name and replace it with the new name across all the files within your site (see Chapter 21, *Files, Folders, and Links*).

Special built-In targets. The Target popup menu also features four targets that let you direct the contents of a link without using a specific frame name.

- **_top** directs your browser to load the targeted page into the existing window, overriding the frameset.

- **_self** replaces the contents of the frame containing the link with the targeted page.

- **_blank** loads the targeted page into a new browser window.

- **_parent** acts like _top, but is applied when you have nested framesets, loading the contents into the parent frameset.

Are You Game for Frames?

Over the last few years, we've grown accustomed to looking at the Web on our computers, though it's more accurate to say that we look through our computers to glimpse the Web. With frames, you can multiply that view dramatically, using the same screen space to display and interact with more of the Web at the same time.

CHAPTER 14
Floating Boxes

In Chapter 12, *Layout Grids*, we covered one way of achieving precise positioning using complicated tables known as layout grids. Although grids can do a good job of gaining control over where objects are placed on a page, they remain, at best, a sophisticated hack: imagine building a road not by laying asphalt in a continuous path, but by constructing a maze of guardrails that prevents your car from going anywhere other than the designated route. For the most part, layout grids work, but there's also a more advanced way of controlling your page: floating boxes.

You can put objects or text into a floating box, then position the box anywhere on a page. Floating boxes use Cascading Style Sheets (CSS) to specify pixel coordinates, so you're not limited to inserting them into a position forced by the word processor-style sequence of HTML. And the amount of code to make a floating box appear is simpler and more standardized than grids, meaning less strain on the browser, which creates a greater chance of it looking like you expected.

The only real disadvantage is that you and your site's visitors must use version 4.0 or later of Netscape Navigator and Microsoft Internet Explorer to view floating boxes. People without 4.0 or later browsers (or the Opera browser's 5.0 or later release) see lumps of material scattered around the screen. Although most U.S. Web users are running these modern browsers, take heed of your audience—especially a worldwide one—before committing to floating boxes.

Creating Floating Boxes

Creating a new floating box is just as easy as adding nearly every object in GoLive: drag the Floating Box icon from the Basic tab of the Objects palette into the Layout Editor (see Figure 14-1). GoLive inserts a small yellow placeholder labeled SB, which indicates the spot in the HTML code where the contents of the floating box are inserted. However, the placeholder's location doesn't affect the positioning of the box on the page.

Figure 14-1
Dragging
in a Floating
Box icon

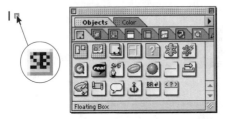

**German
Lesson**

Why SB for a floating box? In the first edition of this book, we speculated that SB was German for floating box: Schwebende Büchse, which literally means floating boxes, as in floating in the air. Many of GoLive's developers are based in Hamburg, Germany, so the explanation made a bit of sense. However, subsequent correspondence reveals the truth to be less clever: SB stands for Style Box, but the engineers thought our explanation was pretty funny. Eine Schade. At least we were able to provide amusement to developers on a deadline (always a good skill to have).

You can type or drag any kind of object into the floating box. If you drag in objects larger than the box, the box's size increases to fit them (see Figure 14-2).

Figure 14-2
Resizing the
floating box

*Default
floating box*

*Floating box
automatically resized*

Floating Boxes Palette

The Floating Boxes palette serves two purposes: it's the hiding place for some handy floating box preferences, and it provides a single location from which to help manage multiple boxes that may overlap or be spread throughout your page (see Figure 14-3).

Figure 14-3
Floating Boxes
palette

Each floating box on a page shows up in the Floating Boxes palette with the name assigned to it in the Floating Box Inspector; you can change these names at any time through the Inspector (we discuss names a bit later in the chapter).

Floating Box Grid Settings. With the Floating Boxes palette visible, select Floating Box Grid Settings from its popout menu at the upper right. Although you can move a floating box anywhere on the page, it can be helpful to use a grid for positioning. As with layout grids, you can set the grid size, the horizontal and vertical visibility, and whether objects snap to the grid. To make sure objects don't bleed into each other, check the Prevent Overlapping box. With these options enabled, a grid appears when you drag a floating box (see Figure 14-4). These settings apply only to the active document.

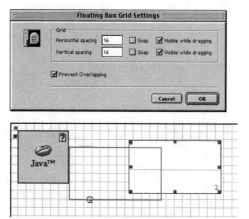

Figure 14-4
Floating
box grid

Convert to Layout Grid. In addition to using a grid for reference, you can also opt to abandon floating boxes altogether and convert the page to a layout grid. Select Convert to Layout Grid from the Floating Boxes palette's popout menu. Fortunately, when you invoke this command, GoLive creates a new untitled document containing the grid, leaving the original and its floating boxes intact.

TIP:
Collision
Alert

If you have overlapping floating boxes, GoLive doesn't let you convert the page to a layout grid. Move the boxes away from each other manually, or by using the options on the Align palette.

Visibility and editing control. Clicking the eye icon next to a layer's name hides both the box and its contents. Clicking the pencil icon renders the box immobile and its contents uneditable.

The Visible checkbox in the Floating Box Inspector and the eye and pencil controls in the Floating Boxes palette interact in a complex enough fashion that they need a table to explain them all (see Table 14-1). Generally, you use the Visible checkbox to control the object's display in a browser and in the Layout Editor and Layout Preview, while the eye icon controls a floating box's display only in GoLive.

Table 14-1
Checking or unchecking Visible with Floating Box Controller options

State	Action	New State	What's Visible
Visible checked Eye black	Uncheck Visible	Eye and pencil dim	Box remains but its contents are hidden
Visible unchecked Pencil either black or dimmed Eye dimmed	Click eye	Eye turns red	Box and contents both visible
Visible unchecked Eye red	Click eye	Eye changes back to black, dims	Box and contents both hidden
Visible checked Eye black	Click eye	Eye turns red, dims, and pencil dims	Box and contents both hidden
Visible checked Eye black Pencil black	Uncheck and recheck Visible	Eye and pencil both dim, then both turn black	Box and contents both visible

Locking. Tucked below the popout menu is a lock icon. Changing the icon to its "locked" state preserves any settings in the Floating Boxes palette that you've made while editing; if you switch to another editing view then return to the Layout Editor, the settings are unchanged.

Editing Floating Boxes

Like so many actions in GoLive, multiple methods of doing things are available. You can position and resize floating boxes using the mouse, the keyboard, or by entering values in the Floating Box Inspector or the Toolbar.

Positioning

If you mouse over any of the four borders of a floating box, the cursor changes to a left-pointing gloved hand (see Figure 14-5). This indicates you can drag the box anywhere on the page.

Figure 14-5
Floating box
movement
cursor

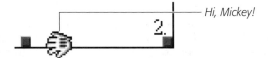

TIP:
**Boxes
Overboard!**

You can also drag a floating box partially off a page, provided that enough of the box remains sufficiently visible to grab with the mouse pointer. This technique is frequently used in animations, where an object appears from one edge of the screen; see Chapter 27, *Animation*.

The Floating Box Inspector, of course, allows you to set the left and top origin position of the box in pixels. But you can also change the box's dimensions in pixels, as a percentage of the browser window, or as an automatic resize to fill the necessary space (see Figure 14-6).

Figure 14-6
Setting floating
box size

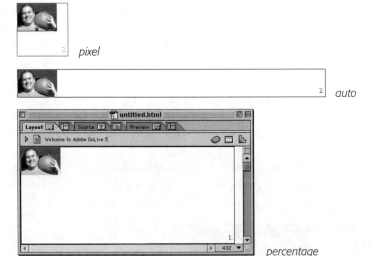

Press the arrow keys to move boxes in one-pixel increments; holding down Option (Mac) or Alt (Windows) shifts the box according to the grid values found in the Floating Box Grid Settings dialog box. If the Snap option is enabled for horizontal or vertical spacing, holding down the modifier key achieves the opposite effect.

TIP:
**Multiple Box
Keyboard
Manipulation**

The keyboard modifiers for positioning (and resize, as discussed later) also apply when you have more than one floating box selected.

You can also use the positioning tools located on the Transform and Align palettes, as well as the Toolbar. We cover these operations in more detail in Chapter 12, *Layout Grids*.

TIP:
**Centering a
Floating Box**

Being able to put an object anywhere on the page by using a floating box is an impressive advantage—but also a serious liability if you're trying to dynamically center the object on a page that's designed to accommodate varying browser window widths. In many cases, you can't center the object on the page, because the floating box is positioned at specific pixel coordinates. However, it *is* possible, depending on your design.

Create the floating box and set the Left value to 0 in the Floating Box Inspector. Then, set the Width value to Auto, which pushes the right edge of the box against the far side of the window. Add an object to the box, making sure that the objects inside are centered within. When you preview the page in a Web browser, the object remains centered even if you change the size of the window.

Resizing

For precise control, change the width and height values in the Floating Box Inspector, and specify whether the dimensions should be expressed in pixels, by percentage, or automatically.

As with layout grids, floating boxes can be resized by using the mouse. When you mouse over any of the control handles on the box, the cursor changes into an arrowhead (see Figure 14-7). Dragging resizes the box. Adding the Shift key constrains the resizing to the proportions of the existing box. Pressing the Control key (both Mac and Windows) provides a live preview as you drag.

To resize using the keyboard, hold down the Shift key and press the arrow keys. As with positioning, the resizing increments are based on the settings in the Floating Box Grid Settings dialog box.

Figure 14-7
Resizing the
floating box

If you change the Width or Height fields to Auto or Percent, the appropriate control handles disappear, so you can't drag that dimension any more but must set it through the Floating Box Inspector.

TIP:
Auto Width, Height

Selecting Auto for Width appears to resize a floating box from its current coordinates to the full width of the browser window. However, setting Height to Auto resizes the box to only the depth necessary to fit the objects it contains.

Naming

You can (and should) name each floating box to better identify it in the Floating Boxes palette. But it's also useful and pretty necessary to name them when creating animations; see Chapter 27, *Animation.* When you create a new box, GoLive automatically increments the name (such as layer, layer2, layer3, etc.).

TIP:
Duplicate Boxes

If you've created a floating box and need another one just like it, simply copy the SB icon, move your cursor, then paste the new box. Not only does it share the same dimensions and content as the first one, the name is automatically incremented based on the original name. This makes it easy to set up a series of similar floating boxes that are named sensibly, such as Navigation1, Navigation2, etc. Even if you begin with a box named Navigation42, GoLive correctly assumes that the next pasted one should be Navigation43.

Layer Depth

Floating boxes may overlap one another, and you control their stacking order by entering a value into the Depth field, which is also known as the Z-Index field in CSS (Z being the top-to-bottom dimension in a coordinate system).

The higher the number, the closer to the top the floating box, um, floats (see Figure 14-8). Numbers do not have to be sequential; you can assign numbers 7, 21, and 50 to three boxes, and that still places them in order from bottom to top (or most occluded to least).

Figure 14-8
Layering floating boxes

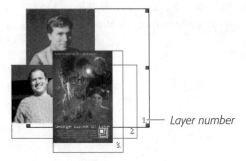

Layer number

Visibility

You can hide the contents of the floating box both in the Layout Editor and in a browser window by unchecking the Visible box. (This setting interacts in interesting ways with the Floating Boxes palette, described earlier.)

Color

A floating box's background color may be set by dragging a swatch into the Color field. Click the field once to enable its active color mode, where you can dynamically apply colors to the box's background by clicking previews in the Color palette.

Background Image

Floating boxes are like mini-HTML pages, and can have their own tiled background images (see Figure 14-9). Set the background image for a floating box exactly as you would for an HTML page: browse or Point & Shoot from the URL Getter to specify an image.

Figure 14-9
Background in
a floating box

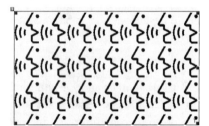

Animation Settings

A whole chunk of the Floating Box Inspector is labeled Animation and includes features that relate to using floating boxes in Dynamic HTML (DHTML) animation. We address this advanced feature at length in Chapter 27, *Animation*. None of these options affects using floating boxes for absolute positioning on a page.

Behind the Box

Floating boxes use a somewhat more elegant and simple approach for inserting a precisely positioned item on screen. (This explanation requires some knowledge of CSS, which you can acquire from Chapter 29, *Cascading Style Sheets.*)

First, all the material that appears in the floating box is inserted in the HTML using a Div (division) container. The Div tag is used just for CSS to help divvy up areas of a site into self-contained blocks. Each floating box is assigned a unique identifier in the Div tag.

Next, the positioning and other characteristics of the box are written to the page's style sheet as an individual style that has the corresponding unique identifier.

For instance, if we named a box "bingle," in the Head section of the page in the style declaration, you might see this in the HTML code:

```
#bingle { position: absolute; top:
17px; left: 24px; width: 100px;
height: 100px; visibility: visible }
```

The box itself would be represented in the HTML as

```
<div id="bingle">Whole lotta shakin'
goin' on</div>
```

Dragging or reshaping the floating box or changing specifications in the Floating Box Inspector cause the style #bingle to be rewritten. Editing the contents of bingle changes the material in the Div container labeled bingle.

It's surprisingly straightforward, but again, not something you generally want to manage by hand.

TIP:
Boxes from Styles

We've noticed that if you create a CSS unique identifier that has block properties—like position, margin, or border—GoLive turns it into a floating box. You can demonstrate this by switching to the HTML Source Editor and back to Layout Editor, or closing and opening the document. Back in Layout Editor, the paragraph or range of text now appears as a floating box. Nothing to be done about this; it's almost a feature!

A Floating Box Doesn't Drift

It's ironic that in order to achieve precise positioning, we turn to a tool that offers the most flexibility for locating objects on a Web page. As advanced Web browsers continue to proliferate, the day may come when all of our pages are built out of floating boxes. In the meantime, though, we continue bobbing in this sea of code and grabbing onto floating boxes whenever we need a handle on more page control.

CHAPTER 15

Forms

Most interaction on the Web involves users clicking links. Pressing buttons is fine when you're in an elevator moving from floor to floor, or after putting your money in a soda machine (unless the dreaded "selection unavailable" sign lights up). But most Web sites eventually need to gather more than clicks from their users; they need names, addresses, credit card numbers, shirt sizes, movie preferences, and credit card numbers—for some, *especially* credit card numbers.

Users can enter text and make choices via HTML forms, which consist of an opening and closing tag (making a form object) and any of a number of structured elements that allow users to enter information or select items from a list. A form also contains a button for submitting the form, and may have buttons to clear all values in the form or trigger programmed actions.

GoLive offers a clean and straightforward method of graphically constructing forms. You can drag and drop elements from the Forms tab of the Objects palette onto a page and customize their values via individual Inspectors. You do have to tweak almost every element you drag into place—by adding settings, resizing fields, or typing in precise sequences of data or directory paths—but GoLive's management of the process lets you create complex forms without much fuss.

If you open a page with existing forms, GoLive will display all its parts using its own symbols, and all elements will be just as editable as if you'd created the page using GoLive's tools. (Some exceptions having to do with the new Form object are discussed later in this chapter.)

GoLive's Preview window gives a reasonable indication of the appearance of form elements, but if you try to type or select items, the preview is less exact. It's much better to test forms in actual browsers, especially since different browsers offer different support and display of the various form elements.

In addition to constructing the forms themselves, you can set up JavaScript code that can validate whether a user has entered information into a given field, and, if so, whether what's entered conforms with what you expect. For instance, if you ask for an email address and get back something that contains spaces and no at-sign symbol (@), a JavaScript script could pop up a dialog box that asks the user to re-enter the address in that field.

Parts of a Form

GoLive supports all standard form elements and attributes, using the Forms tab of the Objects palette and various form element Inspectors to insert and set up a form. GoLive also lets you use form features from HTML 4.0 that are not supported by all browsers.

A form comprises two parts: an enclosing container (made visible as a box in GoLive 5.0) and a set of fields. The container is made by inserting a Form object (see Figure 15-1). Many forms can co-exist on a single page, each in its own Form container. (Nesting forms in HTML is a no-no, but GoLive allows you to do so. A browser won't like it, resulting in failed form submission.)

The fields may be any of a dozen or so types of input elements, including text fields and buttons, discussed in "Input Elements," later in this chapter.

Figure 15-1
Form object in
GoLive 4 and 5

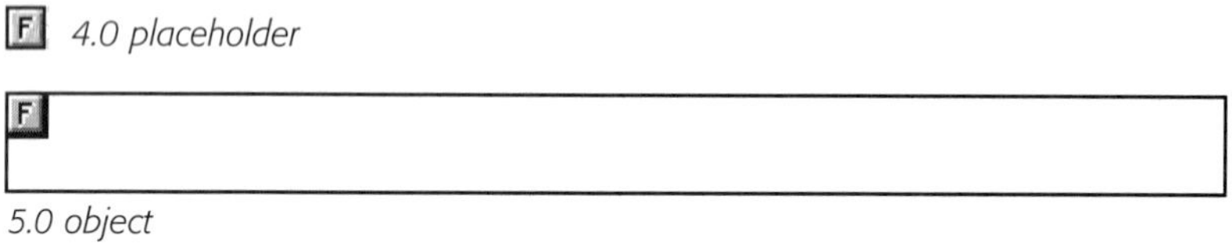

4.0 placeholder

5.0 object

Form Submissions and Servers

When a user clicks a form's Submit button, the Web browser sends the contents of the form to a specified server script or program. The server processes and acts on this information in some fashion; it might store the form's contents in a database, send email with its details, or deliver a custom page that depends on values selected in the form. The server, after processing the form, typically returns a Web page, though it could also provide a file to download, a RealAudio file to play, or something more complex.

GoLive allows you to create forms graphically, but it lacks support for integrating forms with Web servers. You can use Dynamic Link to connect a database to a form (see Chapter 30, *Dynamic Link*), but most people want to pass information from a form to a CGI (Common Gateway Interface) script that runs on a Web server. It's important to be clear at the outset that GoLive offers no features to help with this task.

You must work with a programmer or system administrator (or learn scripting yourself) to connect the data that comes out of a form submission with a script that performs some action, such as emailing you the results or adding the results to a text file.

Mixed Reaction to GoLive 5 Form Objects

The Form object found in the Forms tab of the Objects palette is the only significant change between 4.0 and 5.0. You may also notice that the close form tag is now missing (see Figure 15-1 for the 4.0 and 5.0 icons).

We have mixed feelings about this new element. In 4.0, you dragged a Form icon in to "open" the form, and then a Form Close icon to close it. This corresponds directly to the HTML: <FORM> and </FORM> enclose a form. It can be hard to conceptualize what is contained in a given form, because you have to look for the tiny Form icons.

In GoLive 5, you drag a Form object, which is a container for all form elements, into the Layout Editor. The Form object includes both the opening and closing tags for a form in its underlying HTML. The Form object creates a rectangle that automatically sizes in the Layout Editor to the full width of your window. This seems like a logical way to organize a form, no?

But HTML forms are odd beasts. Most HTML elements require nesting: table cells are inside table rows which are inside tables. Or, they stand as separate, complete objects, like a heading (<H3>Headline Here</H3>). Forms, on the other hand, can be inside, around, or across any other part of HTML, but cannot nest inside each other.

The GoLive engineers may have squeezed the round peg into the square hole of forms in order to make it easier to see the entire form as a shape and to enforce the use of a close form tag. The Form object skews the display of forms in the Layout Editor, especially if you're putting a form in a line of text with non-form items before and/or after it. It also allows you to nest forms, which you'd think the Form object was designed in part to prevent.

The Form object also interacts poorly with tables. You can put a Form object into a single table cell, but you can also span table columns or rows. Many designers do what we do and use tables to provide a better visual layout for form elements. You can still go into the HTML Source Editor and move the close form tag to wherever you want, but that defeats the benefits of visual editing.

If you open a form created in another application or in GoLive 4.0 that spans table cells or rows, GoLive 5 displays the Form object in the first cell. The closing form tag shows up in the last cell as a "misplaced closing tag" which cannot be moved in the Layout Editor (see Figure 15-2).

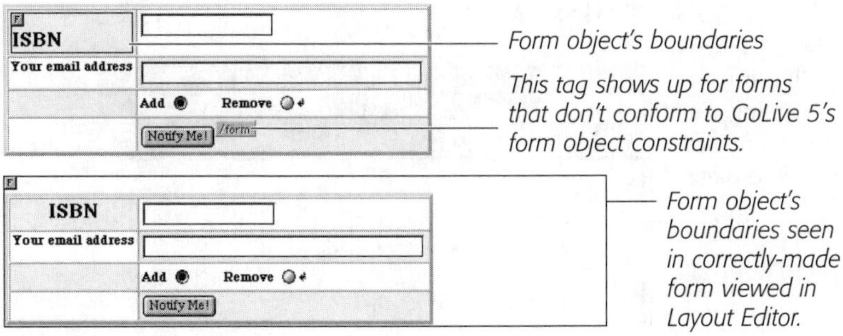

Figure 15-2
Misplaced closing tag when opening existing page

Form object's boundaries

This tag shows up for forms that don't conform to GoLive 5's form object constraints.

Form object's boundaries seen in correctly-made form viewed in Layout Editor.

TIP:
Form Elements and JavaScript

GoLive offers support for adding JavaScript "handlers" to form elements; these provide actions based on selecting items in a list, checking a box, or submitting a form. These handlers have to be entered through the JavaScript Inspector's Event tab, explained in Chapter 26, *JavaScript*.

TIP:
Where to Find Form Pieces

All the pieces to create forms are found in the Forms tab of the Objects palette (see Figure 15-3). Any item referenced in this section as something you can drag into place must be dragged from this palette; or, you can double-click the item to have it inserted wherever your cursor is in the text. See Chapter 3, *Palettes and Parts,* for a visual reference to the items in this palette.

Figure 15-3
Forms tab of Objects palette

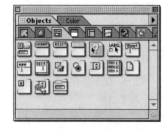

TIP:
Using Tables for Forms

The GoLive manual wisely suggests dropping your form elements into a table; otherwise you can't line up text and fields. You can see some examples of setting up form elements in a table in "Building Forms Using Tables" in Chapter 11, *Tables.* The new Form object complicates this task, but it's still possible using some raw HTML editing. See the sidebar, "Mixed Reaction to GoLive 5 Form Objects," earlier in this chapter.

Form Object

To set up a form, first drag a Form object to your page (see Figure 15-4). The Form object contains the HTML for opening and closing the form on the page. All your input tags, described below, get inserted into the Form object's container.

Figure 15-4
Dragging the Form object into page

New Endings

GoLive has gone through a few iterations of how to set up forms. In GoLive CyberStudio 3, dragging a Form icon on the page automatically inserted a </FORM> tag at the end. This got confusing as the end wasn't explicitly shown.

GoLive 4 added a Form End icon that looked like a little slash-F. But you had to manage that Form End icon and put it in the correct place.

GoLive 5 uses the Form object to contain visually all the elements of a form. Older forms still open fine in 5.0, but your close form tag might float as a grayed-out element if your form doesn't conform to GoLive 5's notions (see Figure 15-5).

Figure 15-5
Lack of Form object compliance

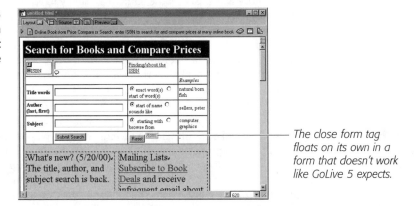

The close form tag floats on its own in a form that doesn't work like GoLive 5 expects.

With the Inspector palette displayed, selecting the Form object brings up the Form Inspector (see Figure 15-6), which includes five items you can set.

Figure 15-6
The Form Inspector

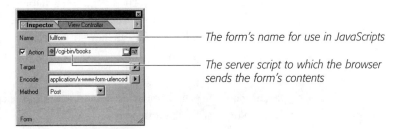

The form's name for use in JavaScripts

The server script to which the browser sends the form's contents

Name. Naming a form isn't required; in fact, all your forms could have the same name. But if you want to use JavaScript to modify or interact with a form, it's a good idea to name each form differently and, probably, descriptively (see Chapter 26, *JavaScript*).

Action. When you click a submit button, your browser bundles up the data you've entered and sends it as part of a regular request to the Web server. But the browser needs to know what script to request to pass the information to, which is what the Action field provides.

TIP:
Actions and Action

The Action field has nothing to do with GoLive Actions. GoLive Actions are pre-fabricated JavaScript tools; the Action field tells a browser where to send the contents of a form when submitted.

The Action field typically specifies the location of a processor: a script or program that's accessed on the same Web server on which the form is located—but not always.

If the processor exists on the same machine, you would generally enter a full path from the root of the server, such as /cgi-bin/form-process, and then depress the Absolute Link button in the Form Inspector. (See Chapter 21, *Files, Folders, and Links,* for an explanation of absolute and relative links.) You can also browse to find a script to link to, or use the Point & Shoot tool, but typically you directly enter a path provided by your system administrator or Webmaster.

If the program is located on another machine, you need to enter a full Web address starting with http://.

TIP:
Avoiding mailto: as an Action

It's possible to make a form's action be a mailto: link, but we warn against that. Unless the user's browser is correctly configured to send mail, it won't work; the user gets an error. Even if it will work, most browsers pop up a security dialog box warning that the form is being sent via email. It's much more reliable to use a script, even one that just emails you the form contents, as that will work 99.99 percent of the time.

Target. With framesets, you can use this popup menu, located to the right of the Target field, to target the returned page (see Chapter 13, *Frames*). This menu includes four standard target destinations; you can also type in a destination or select it if you have frames already created.

- **_top** loads the page within the current window, but independent of the current frameset

- **_parent** loads the page within the frame containing the current frameset when you're using nested framesets

- **_self** loads the return page within the same frame as the form

- **_blank** works independently of frames, opening a new browser window to load the return page

Encode. A Web browser has to turn any "illegal" characters in a form—certain text and non-text characters that can't be sent through standard Web protocols—into representations that can be sent. It encodes these characters in one of two ways, available from a popup menu next to the field.

NEW IN 5:
Encode not Encrypt

This field was incorrectly named Encrypt in version 4.0; you could thank Glenn for prodding the developers to change this, except that they had already planned to revise the name before he prodded them.

The default encoding is the same as the "application/x-www-form-urlencoded" option in the popup menu. If you've seen text like "%2E" in a URL, then you were looking at part of that encoding; the % sign means that the two characters that follow are the hexadecimal (base 16) number for the ASCII character code. In this case, 2E is the code for the equals sign (=).

The other method of encoding, "multipart/form-data," gets used to transmit files to a Web server correctly by identifying where they start and end. (We cover this a bit later in the chapter).

GoLive provides a field here to enter another value in case a new method is developed, but we haven't seen any yet.

Method. You can have a Web browser send data to a server by one of two methods: Get or Post. The Get method sends form data as part of a standard file request to a server. The browser appends all the data to the end of the file request for the script you specified in the Action field.

Encoding and Decoding in Perl

We don't want to scare anyone, but it's often tricky to track down how to encode or decode URLs. Here's the perl code if you're scripting using that language for a CGI:

```
sub URLencode {
    my ($urle) = $[0];
    $urle =~ s/ /\+/g;
    my ($qm) = quotemeta ";.,/?\|=-_)(*&^%$#@!~`:";
    $urle =~ s/([$qm\"\']{1,1})/"%" . sprintf("%2.2x", unpack("c",$1))/eg;
    s/ /\+/g;
    return $urle;
}
sub URLdecode {
    my ($urle) = $_[0];
    $urle =~ s/%(..)/pack("c",hex($1))/ge;
    $urle =~ s/\+/ /g;
    return $urle;
}
```

The problem with Get is twofold. First, you expose all your information in the URL, which can look ugly and might display passwords or other private information on screen or in a browser's cache or history file. Second, Get requests are limited to less than 256 characters on some browsers, so form data could be truncated.

The solution is to use Post, which is the better choice in almost every case. With a Post request, the browser still asks the server to process the data with a specific script, but it sends the form data as a separate stream of text, hidden from the user, and with no apparent limit with newer browsers. (We did have problems with Netscape 1.0, but none since.)

Input Elements

Once your form is all set up and ready to submit, you need to add elements that a user can type data into or select values from. If you've ever worked with FileMaker Pro or Microsoft Access, many of these terms, types, and concepts will be familiar to you.

Input elements may contain preset data, like months of a year in a popup menu, or they may require a user to enter data from scratch, like a last name. HTML provides several kinds of input elements tailored to each of these needs. We've divided them into similar categories.

To access settings for each type of element, drag them into an HTML page, make sure the Inspector palette is displayed, and select the item to bring up the appropriate Inspector. There are Inspectors, of course, for every kind of element.

Text Fields

Text fields allow users to enter any arbitrary set of characters, like someone's name, email address, or credit card number. If you want the field to appear with a value already filled in or selected, enter it in the Content field of the Inspector.

The number of characters shown onscreen is set via Visible. You can also drag the handle on the field's right side to resize interactively; the number of characters changes in the Inspector as you drag the handle. Unfortunately, each browser interprets width slightly differently, so there's absolutely no guarantee that setting Visible to "10" allows for only or as many as 10 characters to be visible onscreen. Setting the field size with Visible doesn't constrain the user from exceeding that length. You can limit the number of characters a browse accepts in a field by entering a maximum number in the Max field.

HTML lets you hide the contents of a field as they are being entered by using a password field. GoLive supports this feature with the Is Password Field checkbox, which replaces the letters typed with characters (usually bullets or dots). GoLive offers both a Text field icon and a Password field icon in the Forms tab, but you can change the state of either one later using the checkbox.

If you use the Password field, be aware that it's not as secure as it may sound. All a password field does is prevent someone from reading a password as someone types it. The value in a password field is not encrypted when it's sent to a server; it's sent in plain text, so it could be intercepted or logged in some fashion, though that's unlikely. Many sites use a password field combined with a secure server as the right mix of caution and protection.

Text Area

For longer text entry, like user comments on a feedback form, use the Text Area field. You can roughly control the dimensions of a Text Area field by specifying its width in characters in the inspector's Columns field, and its height in lines of text in the Rows field, or by dragging its control handles. However, as with text fields, every browser interprets these dimensions differently.

You can set text to wrap automatically to the next line as a user types or pastes it in by setting Wrap to Virtual or Physical. Setting Wrap to Off turns off automatic line wrapping, so text just keeps scrolling off the left margin as a user types (see Figure 15-7 for the differences).

If you leave Wrap set to Default, Netscape Navigator interprets this as Off, while Internet Explorer automatically wraps.

The Content field lets you prefill a value to be displayed whenever the user retrieves the page, which the user can type over.

Figure 15-7
The Wrap
attribute in
different
browsers and
platforms

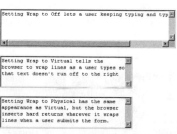

Mac Internet Explorer 4.5 and later, Windows Internet Explorer 5.0 and later, and Windows Netscape Navigator 4.6 and later all interpret Wrap settings the same, correct way.

Mac Netscape Navigator 4.6 wraps text with Wrap set to Off, which is incorrect.

TIP:
W3C Rap on
Wrap

"Users should be able to enter longer lines than this, so user agents should provide some means to scroll through the contents of the control when the contents extend beyond the visible area. User agents may wrap visible text lines to keep long lines visible without the need for scrolling." —W3C on Wrap.

Translated, this means, "that the browser is responsible, but we're not going to provide you an attribute to allow a designer to define this behavior." See http://www.w3.org/TR/REC-html40/interact/forms.html#h-17.7 for more information.

Lists

Forms can have preset lists of items to choose from in two formats: a popup menu or a scrolling list (called a "list box" by GoLive). The main difference between the two styles is that you can only make a single selection from a popup menu, while a scrolling list allows multiple selections; the HTML is the same for both objects.

You can drag either a Popup or List Box icon from the Forms tab into a form and use the Inspector palette to change one into the other (see Figure 15-8). Browsers typically display a popup menu when the Rows value is set to 1 and Multiple Selection is unchecked. If either attribute is different (more than one row or multiple selections allowed), browsers tend to display a scrolling list. GoLive honors this behavior in its previews. With Multiple Selection checked, a user can choose more than one item from the list by holding down the Command key on a Mac or the Control key under Windows and clicking on different items.

GoLive automatically inserts three placeholder items in the list of items when you create a Popup or List Box element. You can create an indefinably large number of items for a list. The text in Label shows up on the Web page; the text for Value represents what's sent to the server if that option is chosen.

Naming Elements

All input elements share one attribute: Name. When a form is submitted to a server, the name identifies which field a value came from. Because of this, you should name elements carefully. Sometimes scripts require highly specific names for different fields, and a Webmaster may need to tell you exactly what to name each item.

If you're using JavaScript for form verification (discussed in Chapter 26, *JavaScript*), your script will most likely address each element by the name you provide. Radio buttons are the one exception to this rule, as they share a group name that identifies members. But you still have to choose that group name. See "Checkboxes and Radio Buttons," later in this chapter.

Figure 15-8
Popup menus
and scrolling
lists

Mac Internet Explorer 5

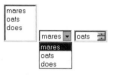

Windows Internet Explorer 5

Popup menus and scrolling lists display differently in each browser depending on how many rows are displayed and whether Multiple Selection is checked.

The settings are, from left to right in both illustrations: Multiple Selection, show four rows; no Multiple selection, show one row; and Multiple selection, show one row. (One row is empty in each example.)

Click New to create a new list item and edit it. To edit an existing item, select it in the list and type over the current values. You can also select an item and duplicate or delete it by clicking the appropriate button.

To preselect an item so that it's highlighted in a list or displayed in a popup menu, select it and click the checkbox to the left of the entry fields. If you preselect more than one item without having Multiple Selection checked, GoLive allows it, though it's "illegal" HTML, and browsers don't know quite what to make of it.

Bad Wrap

Wrap is a funny attribute. Neither the HTML 3.2 nor 4.0 specifications support it as a facet of the Textarea tag, so it's not an official part of HTML. Netscape introduced it in Navigator 2.0 using the terms Off, Soft, and Hard, according to WebReference.com (http://www.webreference.com/).

A Soft wrap automatically breaks text at the end of a line onscreen, but the line breaks aren't sent as part of the form submission to the server. A Hard wrap inserts line break characters wherever the text wraps onscreen when submitting the form.

Internet Explorer formerly used the terms Virtual and Physical to mean Soft and Hard, but according to Microsoft's developer resource site, the browser now uses Soft and Hard.

The developers of GoLive went with the new Internet Explorer terminology. But if you examine the settings in the Web Settings for Textarea you see that GoLive shows this tag as having Netscape 2, 3, and 4 compatibility only (see Chapter 31, *Web Settings*). This is correct in that Netscape supported wrapping back as early as 2.0, but incorrect in terms of terminology and current support.

Windows Navigator and Internet Explorer as well as the Mac version of Internet Explorer correctly use GoLive's Wrap settings; Netscape Navigator for Macintosh ignores the Off setting.

For consistency with the newest terms and settings, you could also edit the HTML directly, and change Wrap to be set to Soft or Hard. Or, if you're overly ambitious, you can edit your Web Settings to use Hard and Soft.

TIP:
**Editing
Sources in
List**

Sometimes we find it easier to edit list elements in Source view because GoLive's editor doesn't have the ability to rearrange items. If you first select the list, and then click the Source tab in your page window, the HTML for the list is highlighted. You can then drag and drop items to rearrange their order, or copy and paste to insert new items (see Figure 15-9). When you click the Layout tab, all your work is reflected in the inspector .

Figure 15-9
Rearranging popup menu values by cutting and pasting HTML

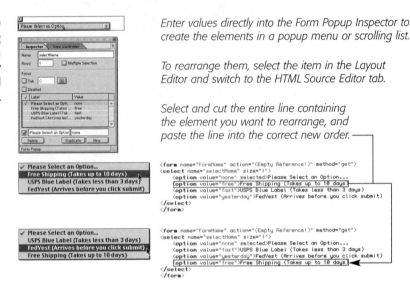

Enter values directly into the Form Popup Inspector to create the elements in a popup menu or scrolling list.

To rearrange them, select the item in the Layout Editor and switch to the HTML Source Editor tab.

Select and cut the entire line containing the element you want to rearrange, and paste the line into the correct new order.

TIP:
**Label in
GoLive Isn't
Label in
HTML**

What GoLive calls the Label in the List Item Editor is actually the Value attribute in HTML. This is confusing, as HTML 4.0 has a new attribute for the items in a list (called Label) which allows you to specify a label to appear instead of text if you're using the new hierarchical menu feature described in "HTML 4.0 Features," later in the chapter. This is only an issue if you want to hand-code this new feature—which GoLive still doesn't support in version 5—and get confused about what attributes are named.

Checkboxes and Radio Buttons

When designing a form, you often want to present information that the user can simply check or click to choose. HTML provides checkboxes, which offer a binary checked/unchecked choice, and radio buttons, which work like a single selection popup menu in that only one item from the set may be selected.

Both objects have a Value attribute, which is what the browser sends to a server when the form is submitted. You can precheck or preselect these elements by checking the Selected box in the inspector.

Checkboxes are all standalone elements, but radio buttons are created in sets with at least two members. (A single radio button makes no sense, as one member of a group must always be selected, and a single-member group can't have its button turned off.)

You can create a radio button set by dragging a Radio Button icon from the Forms tab onto a page and bringing up the Form Radio Button Inspector. Entering any text in the Group field creates a new group which is automatically added to the popup menu next to the Group field. For the next button you create, you can select the group from the popup menu to the right of the field.

TIP:
Mass Button Production

If you know you're going to have several radio buttons belonging to a set, start by creating one and giving it a group name and value. Highlight the button, copy it, then paste however many you need. All of them will already be set to the correct group, avoiding multiple trips to the Group popup menu.

Laying out checkboxes and radio buttons requires some extra work in spacing. You want to prevent the label for the button or box from being confused with one on the right or left. We often insert non-breaking spaces (Option-space or Alt-space, or " " in HTML) to better distance one button from the next (see Figure 15-10). It's also easier if you use a table and cells to control placement.

Figure 15-10
Non-breaking spaces for button legibility

If you use the Label element, described under "HTML 4.0 Features," later in the chapter, you can associate a bit of text which, when clicked, also selects a radio button or checks a box.

Standard Buttons

Two buttons have traditionally been used in HTML forms to perform actions: a submit button sends a form to the server; a reset button causes the browser to empty all the fields and change the form back to its default state. Submit Button and Reset Button icons can be dragged directly from the Forms tab onto an HTML page. Selecting either button with the inspector open brings up the Form Button Inspector.

428 Real World Adobe GoLive 5

You can convert a Submit Button into a Reset Button by clicking the appropriate radio button in the Form Button Inspector. The Normal option invokes an HTML 4.0 kind of button which has no built-in behavior, but which can be coded for behavior via JavaScript; we explain how to use it under "HTML 4.0 Features."

If you check the Label box, you can change the text that appears inside the button from Submit and Reset to anything you wish. We often change Submit to "Send the Form" and Reset to "Erase All Entries" to reduce visitors' confusion.

You can also use a custom image as a submit button by dragging the Form Input Image icon onto an HTML page. This item can only be used to submit, not reset. GoLive presents you with a full array of image options in the Form Input Image Inspector, but most browsers don't support special attributes for this kind of image. The Use Map checkbox on the More tab is dimmed when Is Form is checked because of this as well.

**TIP:
Spittin'
Image**

GoLive offers two image icons in the Objects palette, depending on the context, but they're exactly the same. The only functional difference between the Image icon on the Basic tab and the Input Image icon on the Forms tab is that the latter automatically checks the Is Form box on the More tab in the Inspector. So if you already have an image on your page that you want to use as a submit button, simply check the Is Form box, which is quicker than deleting the existing image, dragging the Input Image icon from the Forms tab, and linking to the image again.

Hidden

Some server programs require a bit of extra identifying data to be sent along with a form, that the user shouldn't be able to see or modify. To include this information, use a Hidden input tag. GoLive represents hidden items with a small H, which, when selected, activates the Form Hidden Inspector.

Set the Name and Value as instructed by your system administrator. Often, a hidden field is inserted as a placeholder in a template that a server program uses to insert identifying data.

Upload Files

You can let users upload files via a Web page using the File Browser element. When a user clicks the Browse button, the browser displays a file dialog in which the user can choose a file. The file chosen is inserted into the field portion of the element; you can use the Visible field or drag on the control handle to display more or fewer characters of the file name.

When the user clicks a submit button, the browser transmits the file as part of the form data. You must set Encode to "multipart/form-data" in the Form Inspector, as described earlier, for file upload to work. The server also must be configured to interpret the file data.

Key Generator

GoLive includes the Key Generator icon to be thorough, but it appears that support for this feature is limited to Netscape 3.0, and documentation is scarce—sort of an evolutionary dead-end. For more info, read the dense explanation provided by Netscape at http://home.netscape.com/eng/security/ca-interface.html.

HTML 4.0 Features

Forms haven't changed much since the early years of HTML, but the HTML 4.0 specification, a guideline to implementing standardized advanced HTML features, includes some nice refinements and new tags that help create forms which are easier to use and more visually appealing. Only some of these features are currently supported in either Internet Explorer or Navigator in their 4.0 releases. Because of this, if you use any of these elements or elaborations, you're potentially limiting your audience.

We discuss all the 4.0 elements as if they actually work for the purposes of describing how to use them and their intended function. We're relying heavily on a combination of how GoLive encodes the specification, how existing browsers display it, and what the actual 4.0 specification states. But we suggest that you:

- Carefully read WebReference.com's explanation of HTML 4.0 features in Netscape Navigator and Internet Explorer (http://www.webreference.com/dev/html4nsie/forms.html) to figure out whether the specific set of features you want to use are supported by the browsers you want to apply them to.

- Test your forms in your anticipated users' most typical browsers to ensure that, at best, they look the way you want, and, at worst, new things don't display but also don't disrupt the page.

Most of the HTML 4.0 features that relate to existing elements are grouped in the Focus section of various Form inspectors. Some features are new elements that provide new capabilities.

According to W3C documents in preparation for the third version of the Cascading Style Sheet (CSS) specification, some HTML 4 tags might be rendered obsolete by fundamental changes in form elements. Because many of these features are currently unsupported, it's possible that CSS3 might eliminate them. It's all in flux at this writing. See http://www.w3.org/Style/CSS/ for the latest information.

Focus and Field Modifiers

Focus refers to which field or element is currently being edited or selected. On the Macintosh, focus is less clear (so to speak) because the Macintosh interface doesn't highlight checkboxes, buttons, and other similar elements, only fields that you can type into. (The exception is Internet Explorer 5, which introduced a default setting that adds focus to all links and items; see Figure 15-11.)

Figure 15-11
Macintosh
Internet
Explorer focus

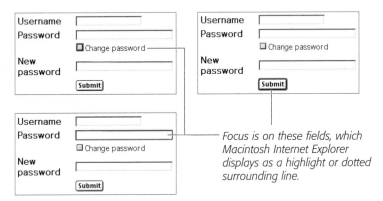

Focus is on these fields, which Macintosh Internet Explorer displays as a highlight or dotted surrounding line.

But under Windows and Unix, any item that's being manipulated—like a checkbox being selected—gets highlighted in some manner and has the focus put on it (see Figure 15-12). GoLive lets you apply focus settings to most fields

Figure 15-12
Focus on fields

```
Bill Buxlety
1930 W. Hoodoo Ave. #4
Flibbity, WI
10345
(954) 212-5867
```

On the Mac, except for Internet Explorer 5.0 and later, focus only appears on text fields; clicking a checkbox does move focus there without a visual cue to indicate it.

☐ Overnight ☑ Saturday Delivery ☐ Insured ☐ Unbroken

Windows puts focus on any form element, including radio buttons and checkboxes.

☐ Overnight ☑ Saturday Delivery ☐ Insured

Windows Internet Explorer focuses on the box. Windows Netscape Navigator focuses on the text following it.

that allow input; Focus is located in the lower section of each form element Inspector. The kinds of focus are broken into discrete settings.

Tabbing Chains

You can help a user logically fill out a form by letting them press the Tab key to jump through fields in a specified order. This is especially handy when using tables and forms together, as the default tab order might run from left to right across columns, while the items occur in more logical order (like name, address, city, state, zip) from top to bottom.

GoLive offers two ways to set the tab order. You can select an item, check the Tab box in its inspector, and number the item in the order you want it to appear (see Figure 15-13). The tab numbers have to follow one another in increasing order, but don't have to be the next higher number. So whether you number tabs 10, 15, 20, 25 or 1, 2, 3, 4, both work the same way. This can be helpful if you plan to insert fields later and want to leave a gap in numbers so you don't have to renumber the entire form.

Figure 15-13
Tab order

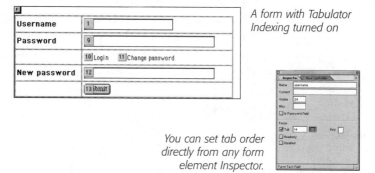

A form with Tabulator Indexing turned on

You can set tab order directly from any form element Inspector.

You can also use a more point-and-click method of ordering tabs, either by selecting Start Tabulator Indexing from the Special menu, or by clicking the icon to the right of the Tab field in a form inspector. If an item has already been assigned a number, that number appears adjacent to the item in a yellow box; otherwise, a question mark is displayed. As you click from item to item, the current number is assigned to that element, and the counter increases.

Clicking the icon in the Inspector again or selecting Stop Tabulator Indexing from the Special menu turns off the tab-order display and brings everything back to normal.

TIP:
Tab Numbering Bug

Whenever you have tabulator indexing turned on, every click increments the tab order counter, whether you click on an item that already has a number or just click anywhere on a page. However, the gap between numbers doesn't affect tab order. So each time a user presses Tab, the browser determines the next highest numbered field, and moves the focus there.

Read-only

Checking Readonly in fields that support this attribute causes compatible browsers to display the field and any content you pre-filled, but does not allow modification. This might be useful for showing the user information in the same manner as the rest of a form and implying that it's being submitted as part of the form data.

Disabled

Checking Disabled makes a field act just like a read-only element. Since JavaScript can turn the disabled status of a field on or off, programmers might want to use the Disabled checkbox to keep certain fields inaccessible, and then activate them based on a user's actions.

For instance, if you provide a user login where a radio button allows users to choose between logging in and changing their password, you might want the new password field to be disabled unless the user clicks the correct radio button (see Figure 15-14).

Figure 15-14
Setting up a way to toggle a disabled field

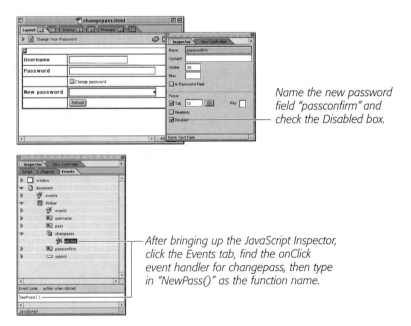

Name the new password field "passconfirm" and check the Disabled box.

After bringing up the JavaScript Inspector, click the Events tab, find the onClick event handler for changepass, then type in "NewPass()" as the function name.

1. On your HTML page, name the Change Password checkbox "changepass" and click Disabled in its inspector.

2. Click the JavaScript coffee bean button, bring up the JavaScript Inspector (if it's not already visible), then click on the Events tab.

3. Expand the view under document, your form name (FormName by default), and the checkbox that you've named changepass.

4. Select OnClick and enter "NewPass()" in the Event Code field.

5. Click the new Head Script button in the JavaScript Editor and enter this as its contents:

```
function NewPass () {
    if (document.forms[0].changepass.value == "yes") {
        document.forms[0].passconfirm.disabled = false;
    } else {
        document.forms[0].passconfirm.disabled = true;
    }
}
```

Keystrokes

Users can move to a specific field or element by pressing a keystroke combination if you assign a letter in the Key field. On the Mac, a user types Command plus that key; under Windows, Alt plus that key. If you use this shortcut, you need to mention it alongside the element, as there's no other indication.

Keep in mind that on a Mac, most alphabetic Command key combinations are already assigned, so this feature doesn't provide much utility.

HTML 4.0 Resources

Of the myriad books about HTML that burden bookstore shelves, we have consistently recommended one title as the best HTML reference you can buy. *HTML 4 for the World Wide Web: Visual QuickStart Guide, 4th Edition*, by Elizabeth Castro (Peachpit Press, ISBN 0201354934) offers easy-to-understand information about the current specification. (We have a link to buying this book online at http://realworldgolive.com/.)

You can also read the W3C's technical final draft section on forms online (http://www.w3.org/TR/REC-html40/interact/forms.html).

If you want to see what's technically different between HTML 3.2 and 4.0, see the W3C's list of changes (http://www.w3.org/TR/REC-html40/appendix/changes.html#h-A.1.9).

WebReference.com provides an excellent guide that outlines which form features are supported in which browsers (http://www.webreference.com/dev/html4nsie/forms.html).

New Buttons

Standard HTML forms can have buttons that submit and/or reset a form, or an image that serves as a submit button. HTML 4.0 extends the standard button and adds a new, rich media button.

If you drag a Submit or Reset icon to your page and click Normal in the Form Button Inspector, you're actually turning the button into an HTML 4.0 button—the underlying HTML changes the button to a, well, "button" type of button. This kind of button has no action associated with it, like submit or reset; it can be used with JavaScript to trigger actions to better simulate an interactive user interface.

The rich media button is simply called Button in the Forms tab. This kind of button supports content inside its frame, which includes anything you can express in HTML, like images or even QuickTime movies. This button can be set via the Form Button Inspector to work as a submit or reset button, or like the Normal button described just above.

Better Labeling and Grouping

HTML 4.0 provides a couple of nice interface subtleties that make an HTML form look more like a program's dialog box—more familiar and easier to use at the same time.

List Hierarchies

In a popup menu, items are all displayed at the same depth—flat. HTML 4.0 adds tags and attributes to lists so you can code submenus without losing legible display in previous browsers. GoLive lacks support for these two features, resulting in the need for hand coding (see Figure 15-15).

The Optgroup tag allows you to group a list of elements into submenus. Label becomes the submenu name. <OPTGROUP> can have a number of elements, and is then closed with its mate, </OPTGROUP>.

The Label attribute of the Option tag gets displayed as the submenu item, while the Name's value is sent as form data if that item is selected. In older browsers, the text following the Option tag gets displayed, and the Label attribute and Optgroup tags are ignored.

Label

A label is a piece of text that may be associated with a given field, such as a checkbox or radio button. Clicking the text has the same effect as clicking the field, bringing the focus to that field, or, in the case of a button, selecting or checking it.

Figure 15-15
Optgroup tag

```
<SELECT name="Shipping">
<OPTGROUP label="UPS">
<OPTION label="UPS Ground"
value="UPS Ground">UPS Ground
Shipping (3-10 days)
<OPTION label="UPS 2-day"
value="UPS 2-day">UPS Blue Label (2
days)
<OPTION label="UPS overnight"
value="UPS overnight">UPS Red Label
(overnight)
</OPTGROUP>
<OPTGROUP label="US Postal
Service">
<OPTION label="USPS First Class"
value="USPS First Class">USPS First
Class (3 to 7 days)
<OPTION label="USPS Priority Mail"
value="USPS Priority Mail">USPS
```

```
Priority Mail (2 to 3 days)
<OPTION label="USPS Express Mail"
value="USPS Express Mail">USPS
Express Mail (1 to 2 days)
</OPTGROUP>
<OPTGROUP label="FedEx">
<OPTION label="FedEx Two-Day"
value="FedEx Two-Day">FedEx Two-Day
(afternoon following next day)
<OPTION label="FedEx Standard"
value="FedEx Standard">FedEx
Standard (next business day after-
noon)
<OPTION label="FedEx Priority"
value="FedEx Priority">FedEx
Priority (next business day morn-
ing)
</OPTGROUP>
</SELECT>
```

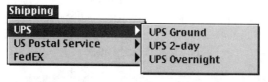

The HTML above would produce something like the menu at left in a fully HTML 4.0-compliant browser, which is yet to appear.

GoLive uses Point & Shoot to create the association between a label and its object. If you bring up the Form Label Inspector, you can point-and-shoot onto the element you want. Later, pressing the Show button draws a line to the associated object.

The value that GoLive automatically creates for the Reference field is best left alone, as it requires hand tweaking the associated field's HTML in Source view if you want to change the reference name.

TIP:
Pointing Out the Wrong Place

GoLive has a problem with pointing the label to the right place if you associate it with an identically named field on the page. GoLive points to the first instance of the field's name, rather than to the one you've chosen. Even renaming the correct field doesn't seem to help; it just keeps pointing to the wrong field.

Fieldset and Legend

You can group elements together into nifty boxed sets, just like GoLive does in its Inspector palettes, by using the Fieldset icon. Dragging this icon over creates two different HTML tags: the Fieldset tag groups the set of items; the Legend tag provides the label for the set.

Unchecking Use Legend removes the text and deletes the tag. You can also position the legend by selecting from the Alignment popup menu. GoLive doesn't preview Bottom alignment.

A Script to Test Forms

This isn't a programming book, so we're not going to reveal the secrets of creating the server scripts necessary to process forms via CGI. These scripts vary greatly by platform and server setup. You may not even have access to write or install programs on your site's Web server.

However, we want to give you a little help, as testing forms can be mystifying. If you are using a Web server on which you can run scripts and the perl scripting language is installed, you can enter and run the following script. (This script is also found at http://realworldgolive.com/simplecgi.txt.)

Enter everything exactly as seen here, remembering to use straight quotation marks, not curly, typographer's quotes. The first line requires the

path to your system's copy of perl; under Unix, you can enter "whereis perl" and replace "/usr/local/bin/perl" (the first line) with the results.

This script, when called via the Action attribute in a form that a Web browser submits, simply produces an alphabetical list of all the field names and values submitted by the form. This gives you a chance to run a test and make sure the values are being transmitted properly.

We also have a copy of this script running at the Real World GoLive Web site (http://realworldgolive.com/cgi-bin/simplecgi), which you are welcome to use as well. Just enter the URL above in the Form Inspector for your Form placeholder.

```perl
#!/usr/local/bin/perl
if ($ENV{'REQUEST_METHOD'} eq "GET") {
    $in = $ENV{'QUERY_STRING'};
} elsif ($ENV{'REQUEST_METHOD'} eq "POST") {
    read(STDIN, $in, $ENV{'CONTENT_LENGTH'});
}
@in = split(/&/,$in);
foreach (@in) {
    s/\+/ /g;
    local($key, $val) = split(/=/,2);
    $key =~ s/%(..)/pack("c",hex($1))/ge;
    $val =~ s/%(..)/pack("c",hex($1))/ge;
    $in{$key} .= " and " if (defined($in{$key}));
    $in{$key} .= $val;
}
print "Content-type: text/html\n\n";
print "<HEAD>\n<TITLE>Results of form</TITLE></HEAD>\n<BODY
BGCOLOR=\"#FFFFFF\">\n<TABLE BORDER=\"1\" CELLSPACING=\"2\"><TR>
<TH VALIGN=\"TOP\" ALIGN=\"LEFT\">Field name</TH>\n<TH VALIGN=\"TOP\"
ALIGN=\"LEFT\">Value</TH></TR>\n";

foreach (sort { $a cmp $b } keys %in) {
    print "<TR><TD VALIGN=\"TOP\" ALIGN=\"LEFT\">$_</TD>";
    print "<TD VALIGN=\"TOP\" ALIGN=\"LEFT\">$in{$_} </TD></TR>";
}
print "</TABLE></BODY>\n";
exit 1;
```

CGI and Forms

Forms get processed by a Web server through the Common Gateway Interface (CGI), a method by which a browser sends data requiring a script to process it, and then the server hands off this data to a separate program. That program performs whatever manipulations it requires and hands off a Web page to the server; finally, the server feeds the Web page out to the browser.

Form a Line

Since forms make up a significant portion of the Web's interactivity, the importance of getting them right is paramount. GoLive's approach to forms makes them easy to construct, maintain, and modify, and in the process you'll find that it helps you make them good-looking as well.

Source Editing

Updating software is a matter of addition: new buttons, new menus, new look, new features, even new spins on old features. So imagine our surprise when we learned that one of GoLive 5's new features does absolutely *nothing*—which is exactly what it should do. Adobe calls it 360Code, a slick way of saying that GoLive doesn't modify the underlying HTML code unless you ask it to.

Why is this important? HTML is the language of the Web, the set of directions that browsers interpret as Web pages. In some ways it's like PostScript, the page-description language used in desktop publishing to describe to a printer or imagesetter what a printed page looks like; the output device builds a picture of that page from the PostScript "recipe" and outputs it.

Unlike PostScript, however, HTML is accessible to Web designers and even average mortals. Only a few years ago, the only way to create Web pages was to hand-code HTML, and as a result, it's often necessary for designers to fine-tune the HTML, or include functionality offered by JavaScript, XML, ASP, ColdFusion, or other varieties of Web content. But few things are more frustrating than formatting your HTML and having GoLive reformat it when you switch to the Layout Editor. In GoLive 5, the code that goes in is the code that goes out.

But don't start to think GoLive's source editing tools are featureless. Although GoLive is primarily a visual editor, it's easy to jump between the layout and the HTML, and manipulate the code with more finesse than a simple text editor.

GoLive offers three main approaches for interacting with the HTML underlying a page: the HTML Source Editor, the HTML Outline Editor, and the Source Code palette. From these areas you can write and edit the code directly, add attributes to tags, and check the HTML's syntax for errors. Other helpful methods of accessing code include the Markup Tree palette and GoLive's powerful search and replace functions.

HTML Source Editor

Click the Source tab at the top of the Document Window to view the HTML source code for your page. Here you can type and edit your HTML as you would in any other text editor. You get no help from the Inspector, but you can insert element placeholders by adding icons from each of the Object palette's tabs except Site, Site Extras, and QuickTime.

Syntax Highlighting

To make the code display more legibly, GoLive offers options to highlight different parts of HTML syntax, or the parts of "speech" in that language. These options appear on the row of buttons just below the Source tab (see Figure 16-1).

Detailed Syntax Highlighting   *Highlight URLs*

Figure 16-1
Highlight
buttons

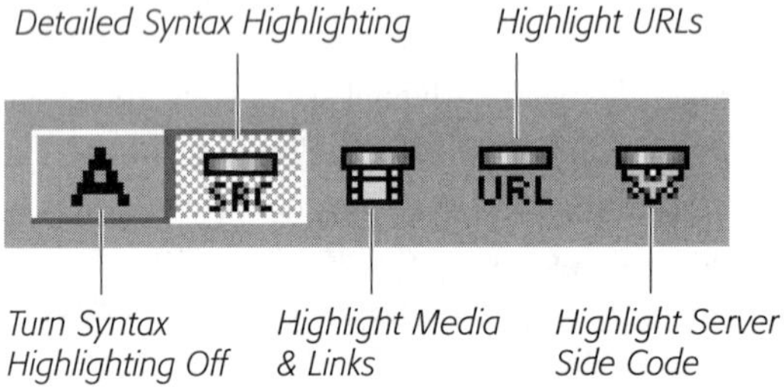

*Turn Syntax
Highlighting Off*   *Highlight Media
& Links*   *Highlight Server
Side Code*

By default, the Detailed Syntax Highlighting option is chosen, which makes GoLive color HTML by category: black for text, blue for HTML tags, green for special characters (like), and so on. There are four other options; only one form of highlighting may be active.

- Set your code to black text by clicking the Turn Syntax Highlighting Off button.

- Highlight just links and pieces of media (images, QuickTime files, etc.) by clicking the Highlight Media & Links button.

- Highlight links only by clicking the Highlight URLs button.

- Highlight code that activates instructions from the Web server by clicking the Highlight Server Side Code button.

To keep your code from running off the side of the page, click the Word Wrap button. This option only affects the display in the editing window; it doesn't create a "hard" wrap by inserting carriage-return characters after each line.

Click the Display Line Numbers button, and the line numbers that show up in syntax checking also appear along the left edge of the window. If you have Word Wrap turned on, the line numbers don't apply to long lines which wrap around (see Figure 16-2).

Figure 16-2
Word Wrap
and line
numbering

Word Wrap turned off

With Word Wrap activated, line numbers appear only on actual lines, not wrapped lines.

Syntax Checking

To check for errors in the HTML, first select the browser range from the browser compatibility menu, which shows you how a given browser reacts to tags that you're using. GoLive defaults to three browser sets: Netscape and Internet Explorer 3, 4, 5; IE 2-5; and Netscape 2-4.

Next, click the Check Syntax button which opens the HTML error log directly below the option buttons. (You can also press Command-Option-K on the Mac, press Control-Alt-K under Windows, or select Check Syntax from the Special menu.)

With Display Errors and Display Warnings turned on, you see a list of what makes browsers in the selected set go haywire. The total numbers of errors and warnings appear in the counters to the right of their buttons.

TIP:
Errors
Without
Warning

If these buttons are toggled off when the Check Syntax button is clicked, you don't see a list of errors and warnings. But they are still detected and enumerated by the counters to the right of the buttons.

Select an error or warning to highlight and then jump to the offending code.

When you check a page's syntax, GoLive examines the browser compatibility information stored for each HTML tag in Web Settings. It uses this information to determine whether any given bit of HTML should be marked as an error or with a warning for a particular range of browsers. So, if you have a custom tag that's not in Web Settings (or if a tag is misspelled in your code), you will receive a warning that GoLive doesn't recognize the tag.

GoLive also warns you when the contents of attributes don't work with the browser set you selected. A few examples:

- When Netscape & IE 3, 4, 5 is selected, the program incorrectly warns you that the Size attribute for the HR tag in Figure 16-3 is not supported. Although the HR tag is marked as supported by all browser and HTML versions in Web Settings, GoLive itself only marks it as valid for Explorer 4.x and HTML 4.0.

Figure 16-3
HR warning

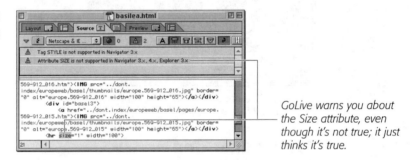

GoLive warns you about the Size attribute, even though it's not true; it just thinks it's true.

TIP:
Viewing HR Attribute Settings

To see this attribute's browser setting, bring up Web Settings, switch to the HTML tab, and find the HR tag. Expand the tag, and select the Size attribute. Finally, click the Version tab of the Web Settings Attribute Inspector (see Figure 16-4).

Figure 16-4
Size attribute setting

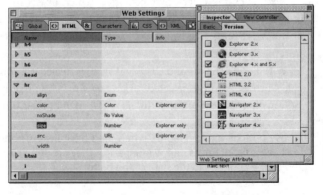

The attribute's browser compatibility in Web Settings

- Also in Figure 16-3, note that the attribute's value is marked as an error. The Web Settings value for this attribute is set to Number, which means GoLive marks any other kind of information as an error.

- What's the difference between an error and a warning? That's a good question, and one that GoLive doesn't really help to define. With the <TITLE> tag misspelled as <TTLE>, you might expect to get an error (see Figure 16-5). Instead, the misspelled tag provokes just a warning. However, an error appears for its closing tag, </TITLE>, because GoLive can't detect a matching start tag.

Figure 16-5
Misspelling alert and warning

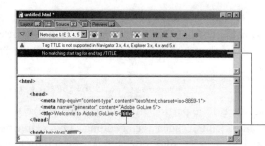

GoLive doesn't catch that the tag's misspelled, just that it doesn't know the first one (ttle), and the second one isn't paired with a start tag.

To check syntax for other browser versions, select another set from the Browser Compatibility menu, then click the Check Syntax button to display those warnings. New browser sets can be created and configured in Preferences, discussed later in this chapter.

TIP:
Syntax Error, or HTML Spec?

In some cases, what may appear to be a syntax problem is actually valid HTML, causing GoLive to not flag what appears to be a problem. For example, the HTML 3.2 and 4.0 specifications for a table requires that it begin with <TABLE> and end with </TABLE>. However, the rows and cells within the table, expressed as <TR> and <TD>, don't require closing tags—although most coders consider it good form to include them. To make these (and other) tags required, go to Web Settings, locate the tag, and select Required from the End Tag popup menu in the Web Settings Element Inspector.

Editing HTML Source

Those familiar with HTML are likely to edit the code by typing tags and text directly into the HTML Source Editor. But you don't need an encyclopedic memory of the language to edit the source.

TIP:
Quicker Keyboard Navigation (Mac)

You can move around using the arrow keys, of course, but by themselves you won't get very far. Adding Option to a left or right arrow key moves the cursor from word to word. Command-left arrow or -right arrow takes you to the beginning or end of a line. When moving up and down the page, Option-up arrow or -down arrow moves a screen's distance (like the Page Up and Page Down keys); using Command instead jumps to the top and bottom of the document (like the Home and End keys).

TIP:
Quicker Keyboard Navigation (Windows)

GoLive for Windows offers fewer navigational keystrokes. Control plus the left or right arrow key moves the cursor from word to word.

Drag icons from the Objects palette.   Nearly any icon from the Objects palette can be dragged onto the HTML Source Editor to insert its code. For example, dragging the Image icon produces the following HTML at the point where the icon is dropped:

```
<img src="(Empty Reference!)" width="32" height="32">
```

This feature can be particularly handy when you're not sure of an element's tags and attributes, such as embedding a QuickTime movie (see Figure 16-6). True, you can accomplish this in the Layout Editor as well, but if you're already editing the source, you may as well stay in the HTML Source Editor.

Figure 16-6
Adding code from the Objects palette

QuickTime object dragged onto Source window...

...with resulting code

Apply styles to highlighted text. You can also edit the appearance of text on your page using the text formatting controls covered in Chapter 8, *Text and Fonts*. Select some text, then choose formatting from the Toolbar or the Type menu. However, you can't toggle formatting on and off as you can in the Layout Editor. Clicking the Italic button in the Toolbar will add <I> and </I>

around your selected text, but clicking it again doesn't remove it—in fact, it adds those tags again.

Drag and drop links. When you're creating links, GoLive offers another helpful tool: you can drag and drop a file from the desktop or a site window to create a link to that object. In this case, GoLive uses the file's name as placeholder-linked text; to make the link apply to an existing object or text, simply move the <A HREF> code in front of your desired link (see Figure 16-7). Don't forget to place the </A> closing tag after the link.

Figure 16-7
Drag and drop files to create links

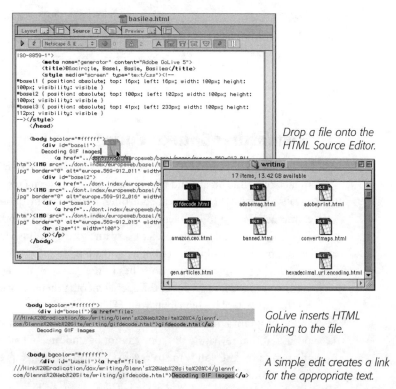

Drop a file onto the HTML Source Editor.

GoLive inserts HTML linking to the file.

A simple edit creates a link for the appropriate text.

The Noedit tag. Although GoLive is good about leaving a page's source code alone, there may be times when you want to be absolutely sure the program doesn't change a range of text, especially when using the Pre tag to format text with hard returns. At times like that, use the Noedit tag. Either type <NOED-IT> and </NOEDIT> around the text, or drag the Tag icon from the Basic tab of the Objects palette onto your page (see Figure 16-8). The text enclosed within the Noedit tag doesn't appear in the Layout Editor, but you can feel secure that it's protected in its virtual source wrapper.

Figure 16-8
The Noedit tag

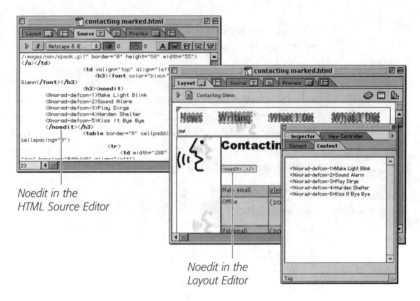

Noedit in the
HTML Source Editor

Noedit in the
Layout Editor

Formatting Source Code

Although Web browsers don't care about the appearance of HTML—you can, in fact, omit line breaks and other empty space between tags and get the same result—people who hand-edit code often prefer to control how it's displayed. Some people like to see elements like tables and forms indented for easier identification, while others prefer every line to appear flush left but with generous amounts of white space before and after.

The key to reformatting code lies in the scary-sounding Rewrite Source Code command located under the Special menu. Whenever you invoke Rewrite Source Code, GoLive reformats your HTML code based on the settings found in the program's preferences and in Web Settings. GoLive displays an alert to point out that rewriting the code cannot be undone, so have a backup of the file handy in case you want to reverse the formatting you've applied. Don't worry, though: unless you've completely trashed your Web Settings information, your HTML appears clean and orderly on the other side.

Web Settings. GoLive's preferences let you specify how code shows up in the HTML Source Editor, including colors for syntax highlighting, typefaces, and whether tags appear styled bold or not (see Chapter 4, *Preferences and Customizing*). To control how new code is written, as well as how it's optionally rewritten, take a trip to GoLive's Web Settings. Although we cover these options to some degree in Chapter 31, *Web Settings*, their usefulness applies most when editing source code.

Playing with Power

Messing around with Web Settings can cause ugly results if you don't know what you're doing. Although the bulk of the features mentioned in this section are located in the general Global tab of the Web Settings window, a few interact with the HTML definitions that GoLive relies on to write its code. We don't mean to put up a sign reading, "Beware Ye Who Enter Here," but you may want to take a quick look at Chapter 31, *Web Settings*. Better yet, make sure you have a backup of the Web Settings folder located in the Modules folder (which in turn lives where the GoLive application is stored on your hard disk).

The Global tab of the Web Settings window is devoted to source formatting (see Figure 16-9). Here, you can specify options such as the case for tags and attributes (UPPER, lower, or Capital), and the method of indenting text.

The HTML tab contains the definitions for the tags themselves, and this is where you can fine-tune the way your code displays on a tag-by-tag basis.

Figure 16-9
Global tab of
Web Settings

Basic tab. Clicking a tag name brings up the Web Settings Element Inspector. For the most part, you should probably leave the settings here alone since they derive from the HTML specification. Pay attention to a few items, however.

Although tag capitalization is controlled by the Tag Case popup menu found in the Global tab of Web Settings, it's possible to selectively capitalize tags by renaming them in the HTML tab's Web Settings Element Inspector's Basic tab. Simply retype the name in the Tag Name field the way you'd like it to appear. If it's easier for you to identify Table in upper case, but want the other tags in lowercase, you can do that. You can even write "tAbLE" if you want. Don't change the spelling, though, unless you want GoLive (and Web browsers) to ignore it. When you've changed the name, be sure that the Tag Case popup menu is set to Database Driven.

Mind Your Ps

The <P> tag gets special treatment, since it lets the body section of the page accept text. If you open a blank, default GoLive page, a <P> and </P> tag set is already inserted. This allows you to begin typing or adding elements right away when you're in the Layout Editor.

In the Basic tab of the Web Settings Element Inspector, <P> adds two options: Avoid every first <P>, and Avoid every last </P>. This protects the original tags from being reformatted to the other specifications found in the Basic tab. Otherwise, you run the risk of deleting the tags that are holding the body together.

As we just said, every blank page's body section includes a paired set of P tags by default. Although you can still enter text, the first line doesn't include the paragraph tags, causing formatting problems. But some people don't need the ubiquitous tag pair, especially designers creating documents containing DHTML or other code variants.

To get around them, create a new blank file, delete the <P></P> pair, then save the file. In the General section of GoLive's preferences, check the New Document box and specify the file as your default. From now on, every new page will be created without the tags. (You can do this for any object on any page—if each page of a site needs your company logo in the upper-left corner, you can add the HTML that defines the logo and set that file as the default.)

Output tab. A more dramatic method of controlling the code formatting is found on the Output tab of the Web Settings Element Inspector. The Separation options dictate how much white space (line breaks) appears before and after each instance of a tag (see Figure 16-10).

Figure 16-10
Separation
options

- **None.** With None selected, text surrounding a tag runs right against the tag's brackets.

- **Small, Medium, Large, X Large.** The size differences refer to the number of line breaks separating the tag and its surrounding text. Small adds one line break, Medium adds two breaks, etc.

- **Before Start, Behind End, Behind Start, Before End.** These options determine whether the tag shares the same line with its preceding text and following text.

- **Indent.** With Indent checked, the contents between open and close tags is indented to increase its readability and relationship to the tag.

Multiple Text Indent Controls

Indenting source code is one of those personal preferences that seem to polarize HTML coders. Is a page more readable when sections are indented to indicate their structure, or does the added horizontal space cause your eyes to zigzag down the screen? GoLive offers no fewer than three methods of controlling how source code is indented.

In GoLive's preferences, the Source section includes an Auto Indent checkbox where you can specify how many characters make up a Tab character.

In the Global tab of Web Settings, the Indent With value determines the base number of Tab characters or spaces used when applying indents for each tag set (see next item). To make your source run flush left against the window, set this value to 0 (zero).

The Output tab of the Web Settings Element Inspector lets you choose to indent the text between open and closed tag sets.

Macros

If you spend a lot of time working in one of the three text-editing views—HTML Source Editor, JavaScript Editor, or the WebObjects Editor—you can set up shortcuts or "macros" to insert longer bits of commonly typed text. This is handy if you have a logo image or boilerplate text that appears frequently.

Macros have a short name, which you type, followed by a key combination to transform what you typed into the text it stands for. For instance, in the HTML Source Editor, you can type the letter A plus Command-M (Mac) or Control-M (Windows) to insert

```
<A HREF="http://where"></A>
```

with the word "where" highlighted (see Figure 16-11). You can also type "A" and then select Use Macro from the Special menu.

Figure 16-11
Using text macros

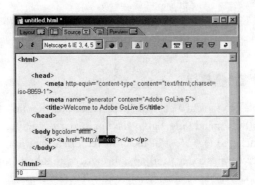

Entering an "a" and pressing Control-M (Windows) or Command-M (Mac) inserts an anchored href with the word "where" highlighted.

Creating macros. You can define your own macros by editing the appropriate file in the Text Macros folder in the Modules folder found in the GoLive application's root folder. GoLive has four files in this folder:

- **Default.macro** holds macros that work in all three editors
- **HTML Source.macro** for the HTML Source Editor
- **JavaScript Source.macro** for the JavaScript Editor
- **WebObject Source.macro** for the WebObjects declaration editor

Macros consist of the macro name and the macro's content surrounded by a unique character or delimiter that defines the start and end of the macro. You can insert marks in the macro that cause text to be highlighted or the cursor to be positioned in a location after GoLive inserts the macro.

TIP:
Multiple-Line Macros

Although the macros found in GoLive's definition files are all on one line, you can add however much text you want. Just make sure that the whole section is enclosed within the single quote marks.

If you want to write a macro that inserts a specific font set in a Font tag whenever you type f1 but requires you to enter a size, you enter it into either the HTML Source.macro file or the Default.macro file:

```
f1 '<font face="Geneva,Helvetica,Arial,Swiss,
SunSans-Regular" size="%size%">'
```

The single quote marks indicate the beginning and end of the macro. The percentage signs mark the area to highlight after insertion. You can also just position the cursor in the right place without providing helpful text by inserting a vertical bar:

```
f1 '<font face="Geneva,Helvetica,Arial,Swiss,
SunSans-Regular" size="|">'
```

The GoLive online help offers extensive insight into the nomenclature, syntax, and special conditions affecting macros.

Source Code Palette

Some people can look at a page of HTML code and mentally see the page that it creates; others spend long, happy days in the Layout Editor without viewing a single bracketed tag. Most of us, however, open the door between the two rooms several times a day (and, we admit, occasionally slamming the door), twiddling code, then previewing the results. The Source Code palette provides a convenient window to your HTML.

With the Source Code palette visible, you can see the code and the layout at the same time. As you type or select objects in the Layout Editor, they are highlighted in the palette (see Figure 16-12). The palette also works with the Frame Editor, though you only see the code that defines the frame set (see Chapter 13, *Frames* for more on creating framed pages).

Figure 16-12
Source Code
palette

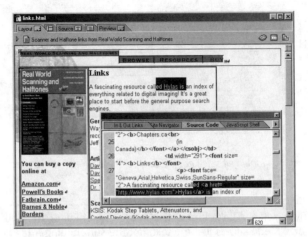

Using the Source Code palette is simple: click the palette's title bar or anywhere in its window to make it active, then edit the HTML by hand. To apply the change, return to the main document window.

TIP:
**Edit in
Layout
Preview
(Mac)**

Normally, the Layout Preview is only good for viewing your page as it would appear in a browser. However, you can make changes to the HTML in the Source Code palette and view the change in the Layout Preview.

Viewing Options

It's simple, straightforward, and it works. What more could you want? Using the palette's popout menu, you can change how the HTML is displayed.

Local Mode. By default, the Source Code palette shows as much HTML surrounding the position of your cursor as the window size allows. Depending on the amount of code, however, it can be difficult to immediately see where you're typing. Selecting Local Mode from the popout menu on the right displays only the code selected in the Layout Editor. GoLive is pretty strict about how this works: if nothing is selected, the palette is empty; selecting a word displays only that word. But when you select an object (such as an image or table), or even a range of formatted text, the applicable HTML tags appear (see Figure 16-13).

Figure 16-13
Local Mode

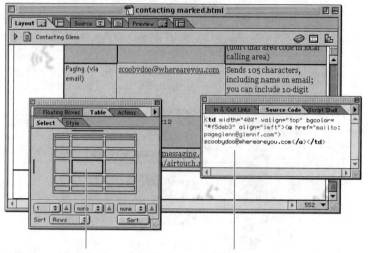

With the Table cell selected, the Source Code palette set to Local Mode shows just the code for that cell and its contents.

TIP:
The Missing
Link

If you select a linked bit of text in the Layout Editor, the Source palette set to Local Mode shows just the text, not the surrounding A tag and Href attribute. Include the characters just before and after the link in your selection to display the A tag.

Word Wrap. Unless GoLive stretches across multiple 21-inch monitors, there are some lines of HTML that won't fit the width of the Source Code palette. Selecting Word Wrap from the popout menu wraps the text to the current window size (see Figure 16-12, above). We typically leave this turned on since there's no reason to worry about line ending unless you're formatting pages with the Pre tags.

Display Line Numbers. Some people prefer to use line numbers to help track down problems in their code. With Display Line Numbers activated, a column of numbers appears at the left side of the palette. If you have Word Wrap turned on, the line numbers correspond only to lines ending in line breaks (see Figure 16-12, above).

Dim When Inactive. A nice but subtle preference is the Dim When Inactive option, which shows the HTML text at about half the intensity of normal text when the palette isn't active. Not only does this make it easy to tell when you're editing the source code, it also minimizes the distraction of all that code when you're not working with it directly (see Figure 16-14).

Figure 16-14
Dim When
Inactive

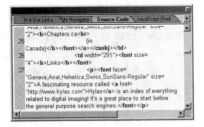
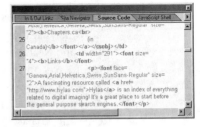

Active   *Inactive*

Markup Tree Palette

"Do you know what we really need?" we can imagine a GoLive engineer asking at an early meeting. "Another palette!"

Such was our first impression (albeit less enthusiastic) when we first set eyes on the Markup Tree palette. What appears to be another nefarious plot to steal our desktops actually has a few surprises hanging from the branches.

The purpose of the Markup Tree palette is to give you a quick overview of the HTML hierarchy above the placement of your cursor in the Layout Editor. On a standard page, you're likely to see only the HTML, Body, and P tags listed. The palette really comes into its own when you're in the midst of a complex nested table or similarly more advanced formatting (see Figure 16-15). Clicking a tag automatically selects that area or object on the page in the Layout Editor.

Using the popout menu to the right of the palette, choose whether the tags are indented or not, and displayed with bevels (so they look like tiles) or not.

Figure 16-15
Markup Tree
palette

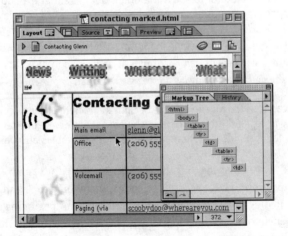

Previous and Next items. The surprises come in the form of the rounded arrow keys at the lower-left corner of the palette, indicating Select Previous Item and Next Item (these two commands are also available from the popout menu). Not only does the Markup Tree palette show you the structure of your HTML, it remembers which items you've clicked, and in what order. So, if you select an object at the top of your document, then jump around the page, you can easily go back to that first element by stepping through the list of previously selected items.

Don't confuse this with the Undo feature, though. If you make an edit to your page, the internal list of selections in the palette is reset.

HTML Outline Editor

Click the tab to the right of the HTML Source Editor tab and you open the HTML Outline Editor. At first, you might wonder what alternate dimension you just stepped into. You're met with a collection of hierarchical "container tags" that can be collapsed by clicking the toggle triangle to the right of the beveled tag handle. For instance, if you click the toggle triangle of the Head container tag, you close up all the code associated with the Head tag appearing indented below it, plus the closing Head tag. Meanwhile, the Body tag is still visible. To close up the containers for the entire page, click the toggle triangle on the HTML container (see Figure 16-16).

TIP:
Expand or Contract All

Hold down the Option (Mac) or Shift (Windows) key when switching to the HTML Outline Editor to show the entire outline either expanded or contracted (it applies the opposite setting of how it was previously displayed).

The objective of working in Outline mode is to configure code in containers. Each tag may have its own attributes; it may also contain other tags and text. All the values attached to any tag are accessed through popup menus on the containers.

TIP:
Expand Attributes

You can hold down the Option or Shift key when clicking an element's toggle arrow to expand the entire hierarchy of that element. For example, clicking the Body tag expands everything within it, including tables and paragraphs.

It's a bit daunting, but the HTML Outline Editor can be very helpful for moving around large sections of code (by grabbing the handle of a container tag and dragging it to a desired spot), as well as for beginning coders who gain the benefit of using the popup menus of a container to see what attributes can be used with that particular tag. Some programmers also favor an object model where they know exactly what they're getting into so they're not just typing, but actually manipulating elements.

Figure 16-16
Viewing code
in the HTML
Outline Editor

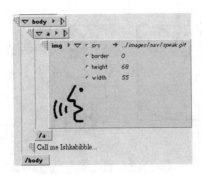

*An image and
accompanying
text added in
Layout Editor...*

...then viewed in HTML Source Editor...

```
<body bgcolor="white" background="../images/nav/speak.bk.blur.gif">
<a href="../welcome.html"><img src="../images/nav/speak.gif" border="0" height=
"68" width="55"></a>Call me Ishkabibble...

</body>
```

...then viewed in HTML Outline Editor...

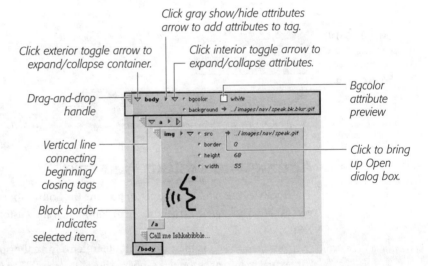

Say you want to add an alignment attribute to the Img tag shown in Figure 16-16, above. Click and hold the show/hide attributes triangle. This is the smaller, gray triangle to the right of the HTML tag—not to be confused with the larger, outlined toggle triangle at the front of the container. Holding this triangle brings up a popup menu of available attributes. Select Align from that menu (see Figure 16-17).

The Align attribute is then added to the container's list of attributes, from which you can click the gray triangle to its right and call up another popup list, this time showing the available values for the attribute.

Figure 16-17
Modifying
code in the
HTML Outline
Editor

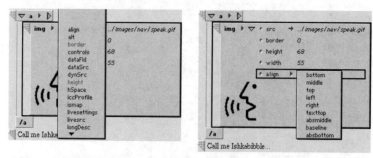

Adding an attribute to the Img tag (left), and then adding the attribute's value (right).

You could also click the space to the right of the gray triangle and type the attribute's value. If you've entered the value name incorrectly, the HTML Outline Editor doesn't warn you that you've made a syntax error. The only way to check errors is to return to the HTML Source Editor and run the Syntax Checker (see Figure 16-18).

Figure 16-18
Checking code
in the HTML
Source Editor

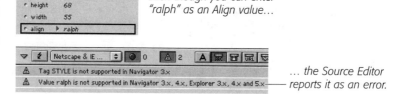

Even though you can enter "ralph" as an Align value...

... the Source Editor reports it as an error.

Adding and Editing Elements

The Toolbar contextually changes to become the Source toolbar, from which you can insert elements, attributes, text, comments, and custom elements (for XML, ASP, etc.).

You can also access these Source toolbar items from the Special menu, the contextual menu, or through keyboard shortcuts (see Table 16-1).

Most HTML tags are binary, meaning they operate in a matched opening and closing pair. In the opening tag, attributes appear (if any are needed) that modify the tag, such as width and background color for a Table tag. Inside the pair, the information in question appears, such as the text for a link or elements in a table cell. The pair of tags forms a container—sound familiar?

Some elements (such as Img) are called unary because they stand on their own without requiring a closing tag. (There are also a few tags, such as P, that can operate either way due to early confusion over the direction of HTML.)

Clicking the Toggle Binary button adds a closing tag to an HTML element that doesn't necessarily require a closing tag. For example, click a P tag to select it (a black boundary surrounds the entire element), then click the Toggle Binary button from the Toolbar to add a closing tag directly below the selected tag.

Table 16-1
Outline
keyboard
shortcuts

Command	Mac	Windows
New Element	Command-Option-Shift-E	Control-Shift-E
New Attribute	Command-Option-Shift-A	Control-Shift-A
New Text	Command-Option-Shift-T	Control-Shift-T
New Comment	Command-Option-Shift-C	Control-Shift-C
New Generic Element	Command-Option-Shift-G	Control-Shift-G
Toggle Binary	Command-Option-Shift-B	Control-Shift-B

Find and Replace

In case you hadn't noticed, most Web pages tend to require a lot of code to operate, which means it can be harder to find the sections you're looking for when editing the HTML. GoLive offers several methods of searching for text and elements—so many, in fact, that we've had to scatter them throughout the book where they're most applicable, even though they all come up in the general Find dialog box.

In this chapter, we talk about the Find dialog's Find & Replace and Element tabs. For information on generating site reports and performing searches throughout sites, see Chapter 21, *Files, Folders, and Links.* Lastly, we cover regular-expression pattern matching, an option for finding complicated strings of characters in several places in GoLive, including the Find feature, in Chapter 25, *Advanced Features.*

TIP:
Multiple
Tabs

You can invoke the Find feature by selecting it from the Edit menu, or by pressing Command-F on the Mac or Control-F under Windows. The Find feature has several tabs, including the Find & Replace and Element tabs.

Find & Replace Tab

For longer pages or pages on which you need to change the same element multiple times, consider using the Find & Replace tab. It offers some simple and powerful controls for locating items on a page.

Figure 16-19
Find & Replace
tab

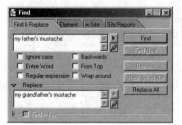

Find field. Enter the text you want to find here. The Find field keeps track of your most recent searches, so you can "replay" them by selecting from the popup menu next to the field. To edit a longer string of text, click the Edit Field button (indicated by the image of a pencil) to bring up an Edit dialog.

Ignore Case. Checking this box ignores the capitalization both in what you've entered and what's on the page. So searching for "EaRtH" matches earth, EARTH, Earth, and eArTh.

Entire Word. This option limits the find to whole words, which are defined as characters between white space (returns, spaces, and tabs).

Regular Expr. (Mac), Regular Expression (Windows). GoLive offers the powerful option of using regular-expression pattern matching to specify wildcard patterns to find (and replace) items in text. As we noted above, we devote a section to its power and complexity in Chapter 25, *Advanced Features*.

Backwards, From Top, Wrap Around. If you check Backwards, GoLive searches from the current point in the text to the start of the document. Checking From Top searches from the start of the document to the bottom. To search the entire document in either direction, regardless of where your cursor is located, check Wrap Around.

Find button. Click Find to find the first instance of the text in the Find field. When a match is made, the document window moves to the foreground by default. You can change this behavior in the Find section of GoLive's Preferences using the When Match Is Found popup menu.

Find Next button. This button finds the next instance of your search text. A more practical incarnation of this command is to use Command-G (Mac) or Control-G (Windows) with the document window frontmost to find the next occurrence without switching back to the Find dialog.

Replace field. Finding isn't enough: the Find & Replace tab can handle the useful task of replacing items wherever they occur on a page or in selected instances. Click the expand triangle next to the word Replace at the bottom of the Find dialog box to open the Replace field if it's not already expanded. As with the Find field, recently used Replace entries appear in the popup menu to the right of the field.

Replace button. Click this button to replace the current instance, and leave the cursor at that point on the page.

Replace & Find button (Mac), Repl. & Fnd Nxt button (Windows). This button performs the replace operation, and then performs Find Next.

Replace All. It's dangerous, tempting, and generally useful: clicking Replace All changes all instances in the document that it finds. Just in case, make sure you have a backup copy of the file before replacing all. (This is especially critical when using Find & Replace on multiple pages, as discussed in Chapter 21, *Files, Folders, and Links.*)

Element Tab

It's one thing to perform a search for a word like "mocha" and replace it with "espresso" throughout a page or site. But what if you want to change all table borders sized 4 points down to 2 points? You could jump into the HTML Source Editor and search for the following code and change its value from 4 to 2.

```
border="4"
```

But that would also change the size of image borders, leaving you to construct more elaborate searches or make the adjustments by hand.

A better method is to use the controls found in the Find dialog's Element tab. Unlike the straightforward Find command, the Element feature's controls understand HTML and tag structure.

Defining search elements. Choose either Name Is or Name Matches from the Element Name popup menu, and type the name of the tag in the field.

Alternately, you can choose a tag name from the popup menu to the right of the field.

You can also enter regular expressions in the name field; this is covered in Chapter 24, *Importing a Site*, to great advantage, as well as in Chapter 25, *Advanced Features*. For instance, entering ".*" allows you to search for an attribute that might occur in any tag, as ".*" matches any tag's name.

If you're searching for a particular attribute of that element, select its name from the Attribute popup menu, or type its value into the Attribute field (see Figure 16-20). This menu changes depending on which tag name is selected. The Operator popup menu defines the relationship you're applying to the search. You can set up more than one attribute at a time using the operators "and," "or," "not," or "()" between each attribute definition.

Figure 16-20
Setting up
search
elements

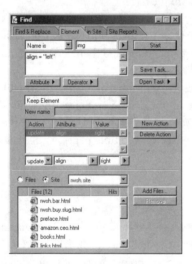

For instance, if you want to find a Font tab that contains both a Color and Size attribute, you enter Font in the Name field and the following in the Attribute field:

```
color <> "" and size <> ""
```

You can also find all instances of the tag without any attributes or their values by leaving the Attribute field blank.

Defining actions. With the search defined, it's time to take action. In the Action section of the dialog (the middle), select one of the following actions from the popup menu.

- **Keep Element** does nothing to the tag name itself, but makes it possible to change the attributes. This is the most typical setting; most tasks involve changing attribute values.

- **Rename Element** retains the tag's attributes, but changes the name of the tag itself. Enter a replacement name in the New Name field.

- **Delete Element** removes the entire element, including start and end tags.

- **Replace Element by Its Content** removes the start and end tags, but keeps the information appearing between them. This is a great way to remove A tags around anchors or links while leaving the text intact.

- **Delete Content Only** keeps the start and end tags, but deletes the information they enclose.

Click the New Action button to define how the element changes. The Action popup menu gives you the option to set, update, or delete an attribute's value. The Attribute popup menu is similar to its namesake in the Search section above. If you wanted to add a Color attribute to all Font tags, for instance, whether or not the Font tag had a Color attribute already, you would leave the Attribute field blank and use the Set choice for the action.

Finally, type the text to be changed in the Value field; the popup menu to its right lists predefined options when applicable. To add more actions, click the New Action button.

| **TIP:** |
| Changing |
| Color Values |
| (Mac only) |

If you're specifying a new color, such as for a font or background color, drag and drop a color swatch from the Color palette onto the Value field to insert its hexadecimal value. However, be sure to clear the field first, or else the value is added to the existing contents.

Performing the search. When your search criteria is all set up, the last step is to choose the files on which the search will run. Click the Add Files button to select the files from your hard disk. On the Mac, you can also click and hold the Page icon in an open document window, and then drag that into the files list area.

If you have a site file open, choose the site's name from the site popup menu, which automatically selects the Site radio button and adds the site's files to the list. You can also drag files from the Site window into the file list.

Unfortunately, even if you have only one file open, you must still add it to the list—it doesn't assume that you want to use the file like the Find & Replace tab.

To remove a file, select it and click the Remove button.

When your element and attributes are all set up, click the Start button. Be sure you have a backup of your files, as the search action offers no undo once you've applied it. (If the file you're editing is open when the change occurs, you can select Revert to Saved from the File menu, but we would caution you not to count on that as your first line of defense.)

Using and saving tasks. The Element search and replace feature is especially useful if you find yourself regularly modifying or cleaning up Web pages created by others. To store the definitions for later, click the Save Task button. When prompted to name the task, save it to the Find by Element Tasks folder located in the GoLive's Module's folder.

To retrieve a saved task (including a handful that Adobe included with GoLive), select one from the Open Task popup menu. If you don't see the one you're looking for, select Browse from the menu and locate the task file on your hard disk.

TIP:
Saved Task
Locations

Tasks can be saved anywhere, but they'll only appear in the Open Task menu if they're located in the Find by Element Tasks folder.

TIP:
Clear
Element
Fields

If you've performed a complex Element search and want to start fresh, you need to manually delete the data in the fields. Or do you? We've created a task called ClearFind that resets the Element dialog. Download it at http://www.realworldgolive.com/example.html.

Getting Back to the Source

You can scream, "Pay no attention to the geek behind the curtain!" all you want, but designing for the Web means you must face HTML source code at some point. GoLive's source-editing features become more robust with every new generation of the program—whether it's manipulating the text or keeping its paws off—which means you can move between the two worlds with ease.

CHAPTER 17

Media

When you're building a multimedia Web site, you can wind up with all sorts of content: Acrobat PDFs, Flash files (SWFs), RealAudio and RealVideo files, and lots of other bits and pieces. GoLive offers support for previewing, inserting, and editing a whole range of rich media and rich formatting languages. In addition, GoLive also offers you the ability to create and edit QuickTime movies directly via the Timeline Window.

But first, a word of warning: If you thought you'd escaped the wrath of the Inspector, think again. Like configuring images in GoLive, most of the editing and modifications to embedded media and QuickTime tracks are done almost exclusively through the various and sundry Inspectors (hence the decision to focus on them here rather than back in Chapter 2, *The Inspector*).

Netscape-Style Plug-ins

At this point in the history of the Web, using browser plug-ins—modules added to a browser to handle specific file formats—is no big deal. Let's say you come across a page or link that utilizes a plug-in. If the file is one that your browser can handle natively, or via a plug-in that's already installed, it simply handles it. The file then plays within the browser window (for Flash files, for instance), or an appropriate application is launched that can handle the file (for streaming media like RealAudio, for instance).

GoLive supports any multimedia file that Netscape's browsers or Microsoft Internet Explorer can handle, from QuickTime to Flash to Beatnik. GoLive works in much the same way as a browser. If you've inserted the plug-in file into the Plug-ins folder within the GoLive application folder (see Figure 17-1), you can view your media files using GoLive's Layout Preview. If these plug-in files aren't placed there, you see only a generic plug-in icon.

Figure 17-1
Plug-ins folder

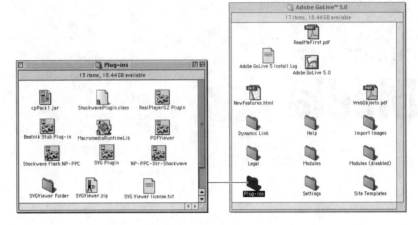

Adding plug-ins to GoLive is just as easy as adding them to your browser. Either place them directly into the GoLive Plug-ins folder via the plug-in's installer, or duplicate the files and move them into the folder. Plug-ins placed here while GoLive is open don't become active until you quit and relaunch the program.

Adding Plug-in Objects

Yes, Flash, Real, and QuickTime plug-in media files are very different breeds of animals, and GoLive acknowledges that fact by adding specific plug-in items in the Objects palette, in addition to a generic plug-in item. That said, you really only get one Inspector to deal with these different media types, but one that adapts to the different plug-in types.

Plug-in Inspector

Drag the Plug-in icon from the Objects palette's Basic tab to the Layout Editor. The placeholder icon that appears includes a question mark in the top right corner until you attach a file using the Plug-in Inspector or contextual menu (see Figure 17-2). Alternatively, you can drag a media file from the Site window or a directory location on your hard drive.

Figure 17-2
Plug-in icons

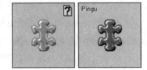

TIP:
Organizing
Plug-in
Files, Part 1

If you drag a file onto a page and it only appears as a text link, you do not have the proper plug-in stored in the GoLive Plug-Ins folder. To rectify this, either add the plug-in to the folder (then quit and restart GoLive), or use the Plug-in tag icon from the Objects palette, then navigate to the plug-in.

After finding the source file, the question mark icon disappears and the file's name is placed in the upper-left corner of the placeholder. In addition, the generic puzzle icon becomes active instead of dimmed. Depending on what kind of file you reference, GoLive switches the plug-in icon to something more specific (yet still rather generic) for plug-in media that match items from a list of icons for recognized MIME types (see Figure 17-3).

Figure 17-3
Plug-in icons

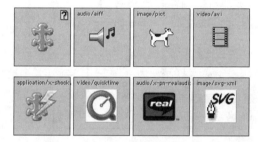

TIP:
A MIME You
Look
Forward to
Seeing

MIME started its life as Multipurpose Internet Mail Extensions, a standard promulgated by a few prominent email gurus (including one of Glenn's idols, Nathaniel Borenstein). MIME was an attempt to bring order to mail attachments, allowing any mail user to encapsulate all kinds of content as parts of an email message and have any MIME-compliant mail reader understand enough about the attachment to, at worst, turn it into a separate file, and at best, decode, play, or display its content.

This standard was useful enough on its own, but the emergence of the Web with lots of operating systems and lots of rich media brought MIME to the forefront as a standard that enables all kinds of software—email clients, browsers, FTP software, etc.—to correctly mix, match, and exchange files without losing their essential nature.

The file's URL is entered in the Plug-in Inspector's File field. If you add a plug-in file that is recognized by GoLive, the inactive Player and Medium fields are pre-filled with the plug-in that should play the file, and the type of multimedia file you're linking to, respectively. GoLive gathers this information via the Plugins pane in Preferences, where you can assign a plug-in to play media based on the file extension (like .wav or .mov). If you link to a file without an extension, the field remains blank.

The MIME type should also be filled, but you need to check the box to make it active and add it to the source code. If the MIME type doesn't appear automatically, check it to make it active, then either enter the MIME type in the field or select one from the popup menu (see Figure 17-4). (Checking MIME also changes the placeholder's generic plug-in icon from grayed-out to more active.)

Figure 17-4
Plug-in
Inspector's
Basic tab

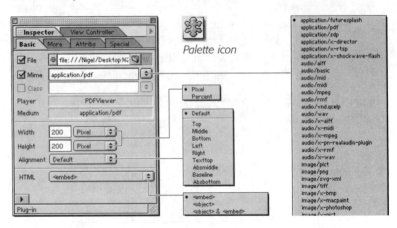

Palette icon

| | TIP: |

Recognizing
Plug-in
Files, Part 2

As mentioned before, the question mark icon in the top-right corner of the placeholder also disappears once linked to a known file (i.e., one found within your site). However, if you're linking to a URL outside the site, the question mark remains. It only goes away once you check MIME and select the correct file type.

| | TIP: |

More Media
Info

For more information on configuring which plug-ins play what media, see the Plug-ins section of Chapter 4, *Preferences and Customizing*. To learn more about modifying current and creating new MIME types, see the File Mappings section of Chapter 2, *The Inspector*.

GoLive enters a multimedia file's dimensions into the Width and Height fields. To change dimensions, enter values into either or both of these fields, or drag the placeholder icon by one of the blue handles. Select either Pixel for fixed dimensions, or Percent to resize the plug-in file relative to the size of the viewed page. Note that selecting Percent eliminates the placeholder icon's blue handles. To align the object on the page, select an option from the Align popup menu.

To preview the object in the Layout Editor, click the Play button at the bottom-left corner of the Plug-in Inspector, which is accessible on all the Inspector's tabs. Turn off previewing by clicking the depressed Play button, which brings back the placeholder icon. Preview is also turned off if you click away from the Layout Editor to one of the other modes, then return to the Layout Editor.

The HTML popup menu at the bottom should automatically be filled with the required tag according to the plug-in file's MIME type. Embed is used as the default tag to bring in multimedia files to a page. If Object is selected (or a choice between Embed and Object, such as for Flash files), the Class field becomes active, allowing you to specify the class ID or select an ID from the popup menu (see Figure 17-5).

Figure 17-5
Selecting a
class ID

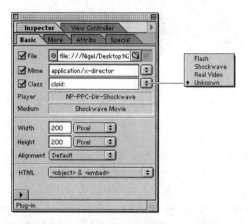

TIP:
**Objectifying
Plug-ins**

If you drag in a generic plug-in placeholder, change its HTML tag from Embed to Object, click on another tab in the Document window, then return to the Layout Editor, the plug-in placeholder changes to become an object.

More Tab

Click the Plug-in Inspector's More tab to add a name to the object (see Figure 17-6). You can assign a destination link for a page that includes installation instructions by checking Page and entering the URL or navigating to it. If you need to assign a link to a plug-in's code base (such as the location of the Flash player ActiveX control that the browser can download if not installed), check Code and enter or navigate to that URL. The Palette menu configures whether the plug-in appears in the Foreground or Background palette. If left as Default, the palette appears in the background.

To add blank space surrounding the plug-in file, type values in the HSpace and VSpace fields. If you want a multimedia object to play in the background (such as a sound file), check Is Hidden. Checking Is Hidden for a visual object defeats the purpose of including it on the page, as it is invisible—but we thought you'd want to know it was possible, anyway.

Figure 17-6
Plug-in
Inspector's
More tab

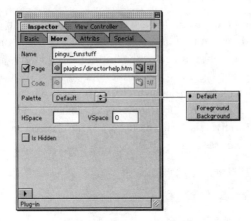

Attribs and Special Tabs

The Attribs tab allows you to configure a plug-in's attributes manually if you're working with a multimedia plug-in not recognized by GoLive. You can also find a blank Special tab for unrecognized plug-ins—though this becomes active for the specialized plug-in items from the Objects palette, as well as for audio files.

Click the New button, type the attribute name in the left Attribute field, then type its value in the right Value field. A common attribute is Autoplay, which starts the plug-in file once the page is loaded; enter either true or false as its value. To modify an attribute, select it from the list and edit either of the two fields. To delete an attribute, select an item from the list and click the Delete button (see Figure 17-7).

Figure 17-7
Plug-in
Inspector's
Attribs tab

Audio Tab

If you add an audio plug-in file (such as AIFF, WAV, or MP3), (representing the various sound file varieties, such as AIFF, WAV, etc.), you're still working within the Plug-in Inspector. However, the Special tab morphs into the Audio tab, from which you can configure the following attributes (see Figure 17-8).

Figure 17-8
Plug-in
Inspector's
Audio tab

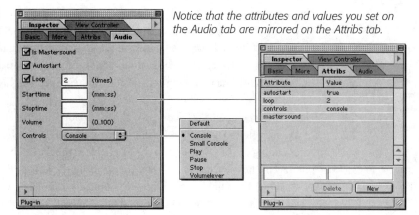

Notice that the attributes and values you set on the Audio tab are mirrored on the Attribs tab.

- Is Mastersound groups sounds together using the Name attribute. In addition, checking this option allows you to spread the controls for a single sound around a page (such as placing the play, stop, and pause buttons in different table cells). If you use this attribute, remember that all sounds in a group must use the Name attribute, and only one sound within the group can have Is Mastersound checked. (This only works with Netscape browsers.)

- Autostart plays the audio as soon as the page begins to load.

- Loop repeats the audio over and over, unless you specify a number of loops in the text field.

- Starttime and Stoptime values specify when to begin a sound clip at a certain point within the file and when to stop it at another point. Disregard GoLive's example to the right of each field. The values should be typed in a minute:second: $\frac{1}{100}$-seconds format (i.e., 01:30:05 to start or stop at one minute and thirty-$\frac{5}{100}$ seconds).

- Leave the Volume field blank to default to 100-percent volume; or, specify a desired percentage (0 to 100).

- The Controls popup menu allows you to specify a player interface. Console displays the default player interface with stop, play, and pause buttons and a volume lever, while Small Console displays a thinner version with only stop, play, and volume controls. Choosing one of Play, Pause, Stop, or Volume Level displays only that interface item. Note that this is a Netscape-only attribute.

Specialized Plug-in Inspectors

The specialized plug-in items added to your Objects palette arsenal don't change much of the Basic, More, and Attribs tabs found in the Plug-in Inspector; in fact, the Inspector retains the Plug-in name. However, each of the four (QuickTime, Real, Flash, and SVG) adds its own tab, overwriting the Special tab, as well as making some slight modifications to attributes in the first three tabs. The following sections detail these specific plug-in items.

Flash files. Drag an SWF icon (no, it's not a code from the personals section of a weekly newspaper, but a Flash file) from the Objects palette to your page. After adding the file's location to the File field on the Basic tab, you should see a preview of the file with its default dimensions in the Layout Editor (see Figure 17-9). The Mime field is filled in with "application/x-shockwave-flash", while "clsid:D27CDB6E-AE6D-11cf-96B8-444553540000" is added to the Class. The HTML menu defaults to choose both Embed and Object; the latter is required for referencing the Macromedia Flash player ActiveX control that is needed by Internet Explorer and America Online browsers on Windows 95 (and above) and Windows NT.

Figure 17-9
Previewing
SWF file

Before   *After*

On the More tab, the Page field is prefilled with a link to download instructions, while the Code field includes a link to the Flash ActiveX control (Windows browsers only) that can be downloaded if not already on the viewer's system (see Figure 17-10).

Figure 17-10
SWF-specific
Plug-in
Inspector's
Basic and
More tabs

Click the SWF tab to modify Autoplay/Autostart (corresponding to Play on Attribs), to start the file playing automatically (see Figure 17-11). Check Loop to have the file play over and over. The Quality field controls the appearance and playback speed of a file. Leave it at Default to use the player's settings, or choose from the following:

Figure 17-11
SWF-specific
Plug-in
Inspector's
SWF and
Attribs tabs

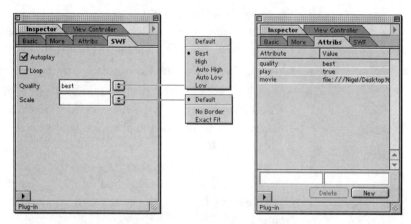

- High emphasizes appearance over playback speed.

- Auto High emphasizes appearance, but improves speed when the frame rate drops below a specified frame rate.

- Auto Low emphasizes speed but improves appearance when Flash player determines a viewer's system can handle it.

- Low emphasizes speed over appearance.

The Scale field controls how the Flash file appears if its original dimensions are different from those specified in the Basic tab's Width and Height fields.

- Default displays the file in the specified area and maintains the original aspect ratio; a border may appear on two sides of the file.

- No Border scales the file to the specified area and maintains the original aspect ratio, though some portions of the file may be cropped.

- With Exact Fit, the file displays exactly in the specified area, though no attempt is made to preserve the original aspect ratio and distortion may occur.

TIP:
Shocking
Previews

To get the best representation of how a Flash file scales, be sure to preview your page in an external browser. The Document window's Preview tab doesn't seem to make a true distinction between No Border and Exact Fit. However, if you've previewed an Exact Fit Flash file, the preview icon does scrunch down when you return to the Layout Editor.

QuickTime files. When a QuickTime icon is added to a page from the Objects palette, the Basic tab checks the Mime field and adds "video/quicktime" and selects Embed from the HTML menu; the More tab remains unchanged. The QuickTime tab checks Autoplay, but leaves Show Controller off (see Figure 17-12). Here's the skinny on configuring the QuickTime tab's attributes:

- Checking Show Controller (GoLive defaults to leaving this unchecked) reveals the QuickTime playback controls when the plug-in is viewed in a browser. The playback controls add 16 pixels to the height of your object.

- Checking Cache allows the file to be cached by the browser while playing.

- Autoplay (checked by default) allows the file to start playing immediately. Unchecking this option lets the viewer decide when to start playing a file. (Make sure if you uncheck Autoplay to also check Show Controller, or else the file just sits there.)

- If you check Loop, the file repeats itself endlessly. In addition, if you check Palindrome, the file repeats back and forth (i.e., reversing itself when it hits the end; perfect for discovering backward messages in your favorite Beatles songs).

- If Play Every Frame is checked, the browser doesn't take any shortcuts by omitting any frames from your file (a trick used to improve playback).

- Check Link to add a destination URL to the file (by adding the location into the Link field, or navigating to the page via Point & Shoot or browsing your hard drive), as well as set a Target (typing the information in the text field or choosing an item from the popup menu).

- Click the Open Movie button to preview the file in a GoLive window. For more information on Inspectors you meet when editing QuickTime files, see "Movie Inspector," later in this chapter.

Figure 17-12
QuickTime-specific Plug-in Inspector tabs

- Set a background color by checking BGcolor and dragging a swatch from the Color palette into the preview field.

- Type a value into the Volume field at which you want the sound to be played back. A value of 100 places the volume slider at the top, while 50 places it in the middle and 0 (zero) places it at the bottom, thus playing no sound. Leaving the Volume field blank produces a default 100-percent QuickTime volume. If you're looking for some Neil Young feedback, you don't get it here; a value greater than 100 just places the volume control at 100 percent.

- Type a value in the Scale field to increase the size of the QuickTime pixels. A value of 1 is the default, while 2 doubles the size, and so on.

After configuring the attributes for a file, click back to the Attribs tab and notice all attributes that were marked are mirrored in the attributes list.

Real files. Adding the Real item from the Objects palette adds "audio/x-pn-realaudio-plugin" to the Basic tab's Mime field and sets the HTML menu to Embed. On the Real tab, check Autostart to begin playing the file immediately. Checking No Labels stops display of such information as title, author, and copyright (see Figure 17-13).

Figure 17-13
Real-specific
Plug-in
Inspector tabs

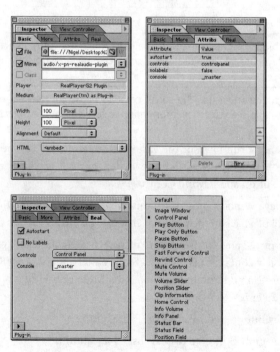

Select a type of control button you want to include with the file from the Controls menu. Only one control is allowed per Real placeholder icon added to the page; to add more controls, you must add more Real plug-in items. For instance, to set up the basic playback interface for a streaming audio file, you'd add two Real items from the Objects palette. Add the first and link to the Real file in the Basic tab's File field. On the Real tab, choose Control Panel from the Controls menu and give this Real object a unique name in the Console field (or choose either _master or _unique from the popup menu). After adding the second Real item, choose Status Bar from the Controls menu and make sure to give this item the same name in the Console field (see Figure 17-14).

Figure 17-14
Adding Real
controls

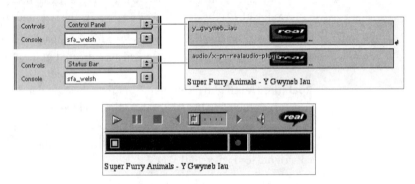

TIP:
Real
Formatting

Real objects can be formatted on a page much like form objects—add spaces or paragraph breaks between items, or place individual objects into a table layout.

TIP:
Real Names

Though you must use the same console name for all Real objects, you only need to add file reference information to just one of the objects.

Here's a rundown of the various Real items that can be selected via the Controls menu (we've intentionally left out self-explanatory items such as Pause Button and Rewind Control):

- Image Window provides a contextual menu that allows the viewer to control playback in the playback area using controls such as Play and Stop.

- Control Panel (or Default) to display the default RealPlayer control panel, which contains Play, Pause, Stop, Fast Forward, and Rewind buttons, Position and Volume sliders, and a Mute button that appears when the speaker is selected.

- Play Button to display a Play/Pause button.

- Play Only Button to display just a Play button.

- Mute Control to display a Mute button.

- Mute Volume to display a mute button and volume slider.

- Position Slider to display a slider indicating the location in the file of the current data being played.

- Clip Information to display an information field for information on the Real media clip.

- Home Control to display the Real logo.

- Info Volume to display presentation information as well as a volume slider and a mute button.

- Info Panel to display the presentation information panel.

- Status Bar to display informational messages, the network congestion LED, and the position field, which indicates the current place in the presentation timeline along with total clip length.

- Status Field to display the message text area of the status bar. If no status field or status bar is embedded, error messages display in the browser's status bar.

- Position Field to display the clip's current place in the presentation time line and the total clip length.

From the Console popup menu, choose _master to group the control with other controls on the page, or _unique to keep it separate. Choosing default assigns no Console attribute.

SVG files. Scalable Vector Graphic (SVG) files use an open-standard vector graphics language (based on XML) that allow you to include rich and sophisticated graphic elements, from animation to filter effects to dynamic charting—using just plain text commands.

There's not a whole lot going on with SVG-specific options. The Basic tab displays "image/svg-xml" in the Mime field. In the SVG tab, check Use Compressed SVG if you are linking to a compressed SVGZ file (see Figure 17-15).

Figure 17-15
SVG-specific
Plug-in
Inspector tabs

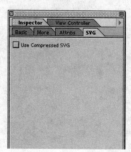

QuickTime Editing

If you're working on a high-end movie file, you'll probably still want to use Adobe Premiere or a comparable video editing program; but it's nice to know you can add some final touches to your files within GoLive.

NEW IN 5:
More Track Controls

GoLive's support for QuickTime editing has improved in version 5, with several more track options added to the QuickTime tab of the Objects palette.

Movie Viewer

QuickTime movie and sound files can be opened directly within GoLive from the Site window or by double-clicking the plug-in placeholder in the Document window while in the Layout Editor. When a new or existing movie is opened, GoLive displays it in the Movie Viewer (see Figure 17-16). Meanwhile, the Toolbar changes to the QuickTime Toolbar which works in conjunction with the Timeline Window and the Layout tab of the Movie Viewer.

Figure 17-16
Viewing
QuickTime files
in GoLive

*Viewing QuickTime
movie in Layout Editor*

*Viewing QuickTime
movie in Movie Viewer*

To create a new movie from scratch, choose QuickTime Movie from the New Special submenu of the File menu (see Figure 17-17). Add a title to the Name field, then choose the movie's dimensions from the Size menu (or enter custom values in the Width and Height fields). Choose a background of white, black, or a color of your choice, then click OK. If you select Custom, clicking the color box opens your system's color picker and not GoLive's Color palette.

Figure 17-17
Creating New
QuickTime
movie

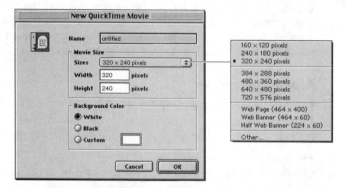

The Movie Viewer in GoLive 5 includes two tabs. The Preview tab is where you find the basic QuickTime control bar, such as Play, Volume, and frame-by-frame stepping. The Layout tab displays a set of rulers and allows you to select individual tracks and edit their properties via the various Inspectors (see Figure 17-18). The Timeline Window lets you edit individual tracks using the Inspectors as well, but the Layout tab provides a more visual environment for editing as well as better precision when selecting tracks. Additionally, the QuickTime Toolbar's Position, Skew, and Rotate buttons become active when a movie is viewed in the Layout tab.

Figure 17-18
Movie Viewer's
Preview and
Layout tabs

TIP:
Playing
Tricks

On Windows, you can start playing a QuickTime file in the Movie Viewer by pressing Enter. To pause, press the 0 (zero) key on your keyboard's keypad. To start back up again, press Enter, or press 0 again to return to the beginning of the file. On both Windows and the Mac, double-click within the movie's image once to begin playing, then double-click a second time to pause.

TIP:
Speedy
Slider

With a movie previewed in the Movie Viewer, Control-click (Mac) or Alt-click (Windows) on the single frame buttons in the control bar (the two buttons at the right) to bring up a slider. Keeping the slider in the middle pauses the movie, while sliding to the right goes forward and sliding to the left goes backward. Depending on how far you place the slider determines the speed at which the movie plays (i.e., the farther right, the faster forward it plays).

Movie Inspector

Opening a QuickTime file in the GoLive Movie Viewer brings up the Movie Inspector. The Inspector's Basic tab provides information about the file, including file size, window size, data rate, and duration (see Figure 17-19). These values are inactive, and can only be modified using the QuickTime application. If you modify the size of a movie manually by dragging the border of the Movie Viewer, the Current Size field updates the dimensions, but the Normal Size field continues to display the movie's original dimensions.

Figure 17-19
Movie
Inspector

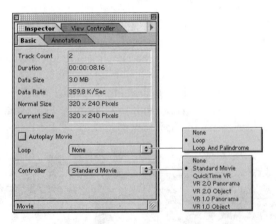

Check Autoplay to start the movie automatically when viewed in either the GoLive Movie Viewer or in the QuickTime Player. This does not affect how a movie is played when viewed within a browser; that functionality is handled by the Plug-in Inspector's QuickTime tab.

In the Loop popup menu, choose Loop to have the movie play over and over or Loop and Palindrome to have it play endlessly forward then backward. To play it only once, choose None.

TIP:
Loopy
Looping

To make these options active within the movie, you must close and save the file and reopen it. If you change Loop to None, you can return to the Layout Editor, then revisit the Preview tab to stop the looping (however, this doesn't work the other way around).

TIP:
Save at the
Beginning

If you view a movie at a point other than the beginning, then save and close it, it subsequently opens in the Movie Viewer or QuickTime Player at that point.

The Controller popup menu enables you to choose the type of controller for your movie file. Choosing one of the VR options for a file without any VR content has no effect; the selected controller must be compatible with the movie's content.

On the Annotation tab, enter copyright information, creation date, director (yes: you, too, can be an auteur!), and a brief note about the movie. A file's annotations can be viewed when opened in QuickTime by choosing Get Info from the Movie menu (see Figure 17-20).

Figure 17-20
QuickTime file
annotations

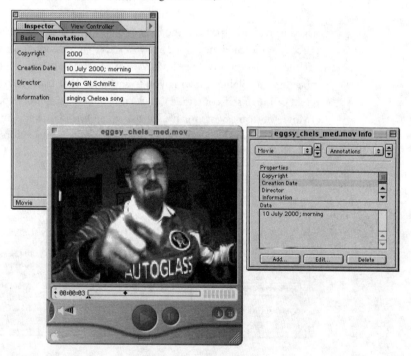

TIP:
Other
Annotation
Fields

Not all of the Annotation fields that GoLive 4 included (and that are read by the QuickTime Player) are included in this Inspector; these include Author and Description. The Writer annotation (which indicates the application that created the file) is written automatically.

QuickTime Toolbar

Click the Show Timeline Window button from the QuickTime toolbar (see Figure 17-21). When working within the Timeline Window, you can toggle back to an open movie by clicking the Show Movie Window button (or by simply clicking the Movie Viewer window).

Figure 17-21
QuickTime
Toolbar

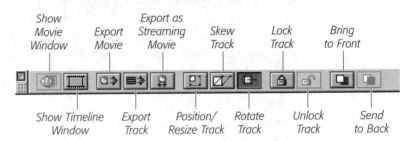

To save a QuickTime movie into a different file or compression type (from WAV to AIFF to AVI and more), click the Export Movie button. Choose a compression type from the Export menu, and then choose settings from the Use menu (see Figure 17-22). If you select an individual track (either via the Timeline Window or the Movie Viewer's Layout tab), the Export Track button becomes available, allowing you to save only that track into another file format or into a self-contained QuickTime file. Clicking the Export as Streaming Movie button saves your file for use on a QuickTime streaming server; click the OK button in the Save dialog to bring up the Hint Explorer Settings dialog (see Figure 17-23).

Figure 17-22
Exporting a
QuickTime
movie

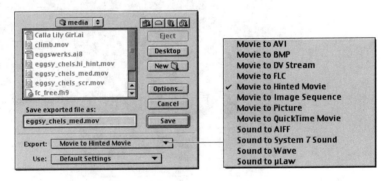

Figure 17-23
Exporting into
a Streaming
QuickTime
movie

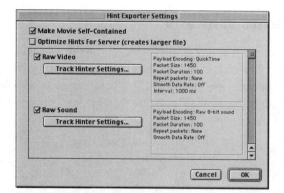

With the Layout tab open in the Movie Viewer, the next three buttons become active. First, select a track viewed in the Layout tab or one of the tracks from the Timeline Window's Tracks column. Click the Position/Resize Track button to drag the track to another point within the movie. Clicking the Skew Track button stretches the track, while the Rotate Track button lives up to its label. To stretch or rotate the track, click and drag one of a track's blue handles (see Figure 17-24).

Figure 17-24
Skewing and
rotating tracks

Clicking the Lock Track button for a selected track prevents any modifications being made to it; the word "Locked" appears in the Timeline Window's blue track bar. To allow editing for a locked track, simply select it and click the Unlock Track button.

To change positions of a track within a movie, select it and click either the Bring to Front or Send to Back button.

Timeline Window

The Timeline Window is where you can modify and add individual tracks (video, sound, text, Flash, etc.) by dragging them from the Objects palette's QuickTime tab (see Figure 17-25). These items can also be added to the Layout tab of the Movie Viewer, but the Timeline Editor provides more editing controls.

Figure 17-25
Timeline
Window

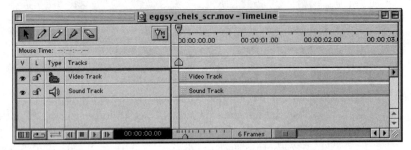

NEW IN 5:
Better, Faster,
Stronger Than
Before

The Timeline Window is much more robust in GoLive 5 than in the previous version, adding more controls for editing and manipulating elements of a QuickTime movie.

To access the Timeline Editor, open a QuickTime file in the Movie Viewer, then click the Show Timeline Window button in the QuickTime Toolbar.

TIP:
Don't Confuse
Timeline
Windows

Remember, clicking the filmstrip icon in the Document window opens the DHTML Timeline Editor, not the QuickTime Timeline Window as you would guess it might from the icon's metaphor.

The Timeline Window is divided into two sections: track controls (left) and a display of tracks (right). The track controls oversee playback and sampling, and display track information, such as locked status. The track view offers a graphical display of tracks measured against the Time Ruler, which is displayed across the top of that side of the window.

Track View

To view your movie at a certain point within the file, click the Time Cursor above the Time Ruler and drag it to the desired point. Alternatively, click the Time Ruler to place the movie at that point. As you move your mouse over the Time Ruler, the Mouse Time field in the Track Controls pane displays the point in time. Selecting a point in the Time Ruler displays that time in the inactive time field at the bottom of the window (and to the left of the Time Scale Slider).

Click the popup menu on the right border of the Timeline Window to configure a movie to loop from start to end, or to loop back and forth (palindrome); these controls are also found at the bottom of the Track Controls area (see Figure 17-26).

To change the measurement amount displayed in the Time Ruler—which can range from one frame to one minute)—click and move the Time Scale Slider at the bottom of the editor; the frame amount appears in the text box to its right. By default, the Time Scale Slider is set to displaying six-frame increments.

Figure 17-26
Timeline
Window's
track view

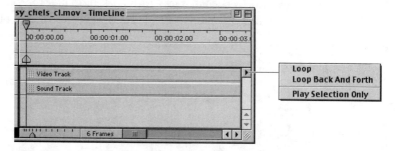

TIP:
One-Minute
Timing

Clicking the text box to the right of the Time Scale Slider changes the scale to one-minute increments.

Click one of the blue tracks and drag with the grabber hand to adjust its starting point; as you drag, you see a ghosted display of the track, showing you its original position.

TIP:
Set a
Starting
Time

If you need to start a track at a specific time point, click the track handle (the dotted area at the far left of a track) and start dragging, keeping an eye on the Mouse Time field. When you reach your desired point in time, release your mouse to place the track.

TIP:
Stretching
Tracks

To stretch a track's length (or make it more compact), position your cursor at the end of a track; the cursor changes from a pointing hand to an icon with bi-directional arrows. Click the track and drag to your desired point. Note that stretching a track makes it play back slower, while scrunching it up plays it faster (and, if it's a Sound track, gives it a Chipmunks effect).

If you want to view a specific segment while editing in the Timeline Window, position the left and right Locator Sliders (below the Time Ruler) to your desired points, and then choose Play Selection Only from the popup menu. The configured segment shows up as highlighted in the Movie Viewer's slider bar, and clicking Play in either the Movie Viewer or Timeline Window plays only this segment. It's important to remember that this segment is not saved and is not displayed in the QuickTime application.

Track Controls

The Track Controls area features a listing of the types of tracks included in a movie, as well as their names, visibility, and editability (see Figure 17-27). Click a track's name to select and bring up its associated Inspector. Click a track's eye icon to turn the track invisible, or click the lock icon to prevent it from being edited; by default, tracks are unlocked. To hide the Visibility, Lock, and Type columns, click the Show/Hide Track Info button in the bottom left corner.

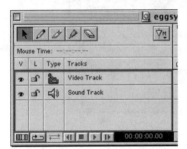

Figure 17-27
Timeline
Window's track
controls

You can configure a movie to play repeatedly from start to finish by clicking the Loop button; if this is clicked, you can also click the Palindrome button, which plays the movie first forwards and then backwards repeatedly. Use the playback buttons to preview the file in the Movie Viewer. Clicking the Forward or Backward button once moves the movie one Time Ruler increment at a time, based on the increments set by the Time Scale Slider. Clicking and holding either the Forward or Backward buttons speeds through a file.

Selecting the Inspect/Move/Copy Sample button (which, for our sanity, we prefer to call the Pointer button) enables basic selecting of tracks in the Timeline Window. Using the pointer, you can copy and paste a selected track as well as click and drag a track to another position in the track list.

TIP:
Track Names

You can select a track name after clicking the Pointer button or any of the Sample buttons just to the Pointer button's right. Then copy, paste, or modify the track's properties using its Inspector.

The other Sample buttons enable you to create keyframes or samples within certain tracks, including the HREF, Text, Chapter, Sprite, and three Filter tracks. Tracks that can accept samples display an expanding/collapsing arrow to the left of a track name, which toggles open to a second track line where the samples are added. The Sample buttons include:

- **Create Sample.** Expand a track and click this button to create a Sample track bar or sprite keyframe; your cursor changes from a pointer to a pencil. Click at your desired starting point within the track, drag to an end point, then release the mouse; this also brings up the Sample Inspector (see Figure 17-28). If you click one point in the track then another, you can drag backwards from the second sample point (back to the first sample point, using the bi-directional cursor) to create a sample track.

Figure 17-28
Creating a
sample track

- **Divide Sample.** Click the Divide Sample button, then click at various points within the Sample track to separate it into pieces. With the Pointer button selected, you can then move the different pieces to different points in the track.

- **Glue Sample.** With this button selected, clicking a sample piece sets its end time to be flush with the start time of the next sample piece in the track.

- **Delete Sample.** To delete a Sample track or keyframe, click this button then click a desired item to be rid of it.

You can create special points within your movie that you can quickly jump to using the Marker popup button. To set a marker, move your cursor over the Status row (located between the Time Ruler and the Left/Right Locator); the cursor becomes a downward pointing triangle. Click within the Status row to set a marker, and a text field appears to its right; enter a name for this marker. When you want to return to this marker, simply click the Marker popup button and choose its name from the menu. To move a marker, click and hold its triangle icon, then drag with the grabber hand. To delete a marker, click, hold, and drag its icon out of the Status row; you cannot select a marker's icon and then Delete or Clear it.

Track Inspectors

Within the Timeline Window, you can add and edit individual track attributes using a gaggle of Inspectors. To add a track to a movie, drag an icon from the QuickTime tab of the Objects palette into the Timeline Window (see Figure 17-29). To edit a track within a movie, select it by clicking its name or clicking the blue track bar (with the Pointer button clicked, just to be safe).

Figure 17-29
Objects
palette's
QuickTime tab

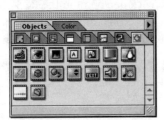

TIP:
Clearing
Your Tracks

To delete a track, select it by clicking its name (this fails if you select a blue track bar), then choose Clear (Mac) or Delete (Windows) from the Edit menu. Alternatively, press the Delete (Mac)/Backspace (Windows) key.

TIP:
Double-click
to Edit

Double-click a track's name to edit it, bypassing the need to make the edit in the associated Inspector.

Track Inspector Basics

There are a number of elements that are shared by many (and, in some cases, all) QuickTime track Inspectors (see Figure 17-30).

Figure 17-30
Track Inspector
basic elements

Title field

This track is set to begin at 1 second into the movie, and last for 8.11 seconds.

Tracks are positioned by default at 0,0 on the x,y axis in the movie file.

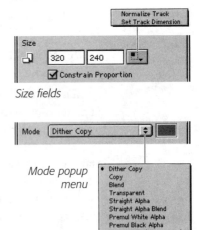

Size fields

Mode popup menu

Title. Enter a name for the track in this field; by default, the type of track is entered. If subsequent types of a track are added to a movie, the default track name is followed by a number (2, 3, etc.).

Start Time and Duration. In the Start Time and Duration fields, enter a specific beginning time or the length of time the track will run, respectively. Clicking the buttons to the right of either field begins or ends a track at the point selected in the Time Ruler by the Time Cursor.

TIP:
Scaling
Samples

The Scale Sample Time option is inactive with the Video Track Inspector, and is only active for those tracks that can accept samples or keyframes (i.e., HREF, Text, Chapter, Sprite, and Filter tracks). With Scale Sample Time checked, the duration of a Sample track changes proportionally if the end point of a track is changed.

Position. Enter a pixel value in the first field to position a track horizontally, and a value in the second field to position it vertically.

Size. The dimensions of a track are automatically entered into the size fields. If you modify a value in either field with Constrain Properties checked, the second field changes in proportion.

   If you enter size changes and want to return to the original setting for the movie (such as 320 by 240), choose Normalize Track from the popup menu. If you want to set a newly entered size as the normal dimensions of the movie, choose Set Track Dimension.

Mode. In the Mode popup menu, select how you want a video track to overlay other tracks in the movie. Your options include:

- **Dither Copy.** (GoLive's default.) Lays the video track over the track directly beneath it and applies dithering to improve how it looks to the viewer. (Dithering creates additional colors and shades by varying the proportions of colors from an existing palette.)

- **Copy.** Essentially performs the same job as Dither Copy. However, because it does not dither, this isn't optimal for display using 256 colors (though it might be a good solution for viewers with low system memory).

- **Blend.** Makes the track translucent, allowing you to see the track lying beneath the current track; in the Track Editor, a track at the top of the list is overlaid by tracks added to the list below it. To change the degree and color of the transparency, choose a color from the Color palette and drag its swatch into the Mode color field.

- **Transparent.** Allows you to define a transparent color as you did for Blend.

- **Alpha channel options.** With 32-bit graphics, you have three 8-bit color channels (red, green, and blue) and one 8-bit alpha channel. The alpha acts as a mask and specifies how the pixel's colors should be merged with another pixel when the two are overlaid. Thus, you are specifying what part of a visible image should be left out. With Straight Alpha, the color components of each pixel are combined with the background pixel. Straight Alpha Blend combines straight alpha with the properties of Blend, causing the masked areas to be transparent and the non-transparent areas to be translucent. Premul White Alpha works with images created on a white background with a premultiplied alpha channel, while Premul Black Alpha does the same with images created on a black background.

- **Composition (Dither Copy).** Similar to Dither Copy's properties, but works best when adding animated GIFs as video tracks.

Video Track Inspector

Select a video track in the Timeline Window, or drag in the Video Track icon from the QuickTime tab of the Objects palette, to bring up the Video Track Inspector (see Figure 17-31). If you drag in a new Video Track icon, an Open dialog appears with which you can navigate to another movie (or QuickTime-compatible video file) to place as your video track. Follow instructions from "Track Inspector Basics," earlier in this chapter, for the fields in the Video Track Inspector.

Figure 17-31
Video Track
Inspector

Sound and Music Track Inspectors

Select either a music or sound track to bring up its respective Inspector. When you drag either the Sound or MIDI (Music) Track icons in from the QuickTime tab, GoLive asks you to navigate to the file you want to bring into the movie; sound tracks accept a wide variety of sound files (from .aiff to .wav), while music tracks only accept MIDI files. Both Inspectors only include Title, Start Time, and Duration fields (see Figure 17-32).

Figure 17-32
Sound and
MIDI Track
Inspectors

Picture Track Inspector

To insert still images into your movie (or create a slide show), drag a Picture Track icon into the Timeline Window. On the Image tab, select whether you are importing images or replacing an image that has already been imported, then click the Import button (see Figure 17-33).

Figure 17-33
Picture Track
Inspector

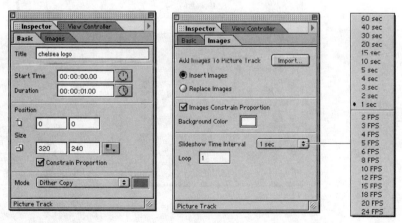

GoLive supports images in BMP, GIF, JPEG/JFIF, MacPaint (Mac only), Photoshop, PICT, PNG, QuickDraw GX (Mac only), QuickTime Image Format, SGI, Targa, and TIFF. This is true for all QuickTime tracks that can import images.

Using the Import dialog box, navigate to your directory location (see Figure 17-34). Select an image file and click the Add button; you can add multiple images to create a slide show. When you've selected all necessary files, click the Done button, which brings up a Compression Settings dialog. Choose an image format compressor from the top popup menu. Choose a color depth in the lower menu, which offers choices based upon the compression method selected; most format compressors offer just grayscale and color (256 colors), while some offer more choices (such as Cinepak, offering 256 grays, 256 colors, and millions of colors). To modify the quality of compression, drag the slider to one of the preassigned settings. If you click the slider and hold it while dragging, you can view the numerical scale.

Figure 17-34
Importing
image files

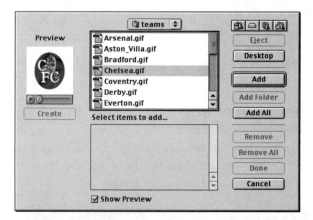

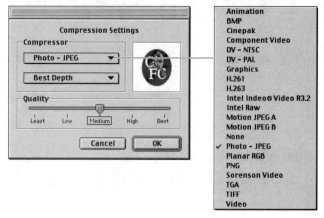

Check Images Constrain Proportion to scale down an image larger than the current movie's dimensions, preserving the original aspect ratio of the image. If you choose a Background Color, it appears if the chosen image is smaller than the movie's dimensions.

If you are creating a slide show with multiple images, choose the duration that each image is visible from the Slideshow Time Interval popup menu. If you wish to loop this slide show, enter a value for the number of times it should repeat.

Generic Filter Track and Sample Inspectors

Drag the Generic Filter Track icon into a movie's Timeline Window to apply one of three basic effects: ripple, fire, and clouds. In the Generic Filter Track Inspector, fill in the basic info (see Figure 17-35).

Figure 17-35
Generic Filter
Track and Filter
Sample
Inspectors

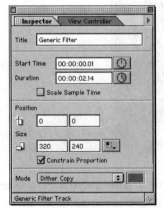
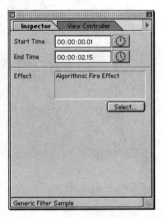

To add a filter, click the toggle arrow to the left of the track name, click the Create Sample button, and add a Sample track. Click the Sample track to bring up the Generic Filter Sample Inspector. Click the Select button to open the Select Effect dialog, from which you can configure one of the three basic effects (see Figure 17-36). If you choose None, you can import your own effect by clicking the Load button and navigating to the filter file. You can also load in filter effects when ripple, fire, or clouds are selected; additionally, you can save the settings from these effects by clicking the Save button (which creates a .qfx file).

Play around with the Mode popup menu on the Generic Track Inspector to display the effect into your movie. For instance, the effect in Figure 17-37 uses the Straight Alpha mode to blend the movie's video track with the effect.

Figure 17-36
Select Effect
dialog

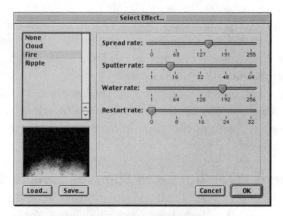

Figure 17-37
Fire effect

*As Bruce Springsteen
once sang: "Ohhh, ohhhh,
ohhhh, I'm on fire."*

One Source Filter Track and Sample Inspectors

Adding a One Source Filter track enables you to add a filter to a single track, and it requires one video source track. Using the One Source Filter, you can create such effects as emboss, blur, film noise, color tint, sharpen, and lens flare.

After adding the filter track, click the Source popup menu to choose a video track to attach this effect to. To add an effect, create a Sample track as specified for the General Filter Track (see Figure 17-38). Select the Sample track to open the One Source Filter Sample Inspector, from which you can add a name and configure start and end times. Click the Select button to choose an effect and configure its settings; remember, you can also save settings and load previously saved .qfx files.

Select the One Source Filter track, and play around with the Mode settings to blend the effect with the video track; the emboss effect in Figure 17-39 uses the Copy mode.

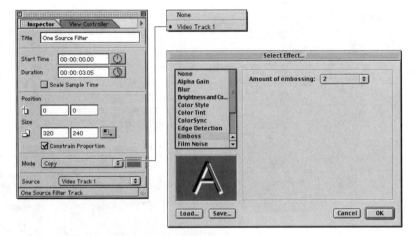

Figure 17-38
One Source
Filter Track and
Filter Sample
Inspectors

Figure 17-39
Emboss effect

To quote Black Sabbath:
"I am Iron Man..."

Two Source Filter Track and Sample Inspectors

The Two Source Filter track enables you to transition between tracks, fading from one track to another. This effect requires two video source tracks, and includes such transitions as implode, slide, wipe, and zoom.

After adding the filter track, choose your video source tracks in the Source A and Source B popup menus. To add an effect, create a Sample track as specified for the General Filter Track. Select the Sample track to open the Two Source Filter Sample Inspector, from which you can add a name and configure start and end times (see Figure 17-40). Choose how you want the transition to work, either from Source A to Source B or vice versa. Click the Select button to choose an effect and configure its settings.

TIP:
**Transitional
Reading**

The GoLive online manual does a pretty thorough job in describing each of the transition effects available with the Two Source Filter track.

Figure 17-40
Two Source
Filter Track and
Filter Sample
Inspectors

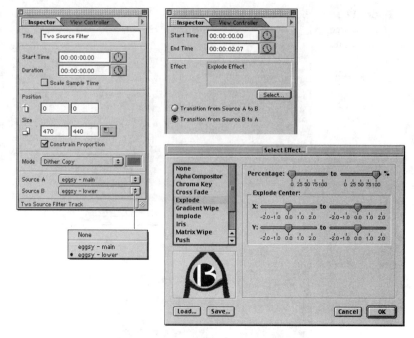

Select the Two Source Filter track, and play around with the Mode settings to blend the effect with the video track; the explode effect in Figure 17-41 uses the Dither Copy mode.

Figure 17-41
Explode effect

As the Soundgarden song goes: "Black hole sun, won't you come..."

MPEG Track Inspector

Dragging an MPEG Track icon into a movie brings up an Open dialog, from which you can navigate to an MPEG audio or video file; the MPEG Track Inspector features just the basic fields (see Figure 17-42).

Figure 17-42
MPEG Track
Inspector

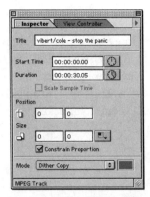

**No MPEG in
Windows**

QuickTime for Windows does not support MPEG video, so no MPEG icon appears in the QuickTime tab of the Objects palette.

Sprite Track Inspectors

Sprite tracks are handy tools for adding low-impact animation to your movies. Unlike adding an animated sequence as a video track, which streams a continuous set of pixel images, sprite tracks mark individual references to pixel- and vector-oriented and 3D objects placed into a common gallery, which helps to keep the file size down. You can also apply Actions to sprite tracks (which are called wired sprites) that can make the user's experience even more interactive.

Drag the Sprite Track icon from the Objects palette to the Track Editor and set up your baseline attributes (such as start point, duration, and positioning) on the Inspector's Basic tab (see Figure 17-43).

Figure 17-43
Sprite Track
Inspector

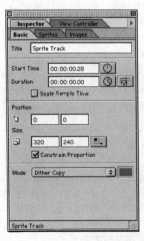

On the Sprites tab, check Visible to display the sprite track in the Movie Viewer; if this is unchecked, the sprite track can be temporarily hidden to display any tracks below it (see Figure 17-44). Check Scale Sprites When Track Is Resized if the images you include are vector graphics; if left unchecked, vector graphics could look jaggy after a movie is resized. To add a background color, drag a color swatch into the Background Color field.

Figure 17-44
Sprite Track
Inspector's
Sprites tab

The Add New Sprites field is inactive until you import images into the Sprite track. (The GoLive manual's instructions say otherwise, but the import action must take place before this field becomes editable.) You have two options to add images: using the Import button on the Sprites tab (which only works with Photoshop .psd files), or using the import function on the Image tab (which allows you to choose other image formats, from JPEGs to TIFFs).

The more typical route to employ is via the Images tab. Click the Import button, and you're met with the Import dialog box. Navigate and select your image, and choose the file format and compression level. The image file's name appears in the list area field; click it to see a preview of the image and information about the original file. To manage imported images, select an item from this list to rename (in the Name field), delete, or replace it with another image.

TIP:
Sprite-ly
Strength

An image cannot be deleted after it is added to a sprite keyframe (explained in conjunction with the Sprite Sample Inspector); you must remove it first from the sprite before you can delete it. You can, however, replace an image added to a sprite, but this action cannot be undone.

If you check Import Photoshop Layers (Mac) or Import Multiple Layers (Windows), each layer within an image file is imported and is displayed in the list area; select separate layers to see a preview and view information (see Figure 17-45).

Figure 17-45
Sprite Track
Inspector's
Images tab

You can also import a Photoshop image file's layers using the Import button back on the Sprites tab. However, importing via this method requires a bit of setup work first: you can only import three layers and they must follow a strict naming convention of Layer_main, Layer_over, and Layer_click. You can, however, modify the main, over, and click portions. To view the imported layers, click the Images tab, then select layers from the list area.

TIP:
Import
Fourth Layer

Actually, you can import four layers using the above method. If your image has a background layer (named as such), check Import Background Layer to bring it into your Sprite Track.

So what's the difference between these two import methods? While you can create Actions (or wired sprites) via both methods, the Create Sprites from an Adobe Photoshop File (on the Sprites tab) allows you to create a rollover effect with an image file's layers (or with other images stored in the Sprite Track).

Sprite Sample and Sprite Object Inspectors. Now that you've added an image (or several layers of an image), you need to add a sprite to make the image visible. Back on the Sprites tab, enter a number into the now active Add New Sprites field; click the Sprite Track toggle arrow to expand the view to see an empty Action track and the number of sprite objects that were entered into the field. Each sprite object appears as a keyframe (a diamond icon) set to 0:00:00.00.

Click the sprite object name (under the Tracks column) to open the Sprite Object Inspector and give it a unique name (see Figure 17-46). (Alternatively, you could double-click the sprite name and enter a new name in the active field that appears.)

Figure 17-46
Sprite Object
Inspector

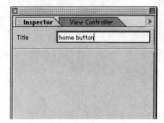

Click the keyframe icon to bring up the Sprite Sample Inspector (see Figure 17-47). Place your sprite image in the movie by adding pixel measurements in the horizontal and vertical positioning fields; keep Visible checked in order to see the image. Determine how the sprite overlays other sprites in the movie by choosing a method from the Mode popup.

Figure 17-47
Sprite Sample
Inspector

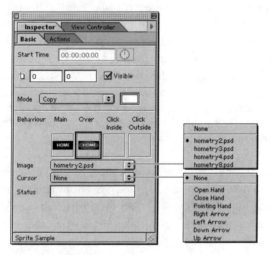

The first image in the import list is added to the Main box. If you've imported multiple images (or Photoshop layers), you can choose another image from the Image popup menu. Select the other Behaviour [sic] boxes to set the following actions:

- **Over** creates a basic rollover effect, revealing the second image when the cursor passes over the Main image.

- **Click Inside** reveals the selected image when a user clicks within the Main image.

- **Click Outside** doesn't work exactly as it sounds like it might. Instead of simply clicking outside of the Main item to reveal this second image, you must first click within the Main image then hold and drag your cursor outside of its boundary. If your image fills up the entire movie window, your viewer has to click and drag to outside of the movie viewer.

Choose the type of cursor you want to display to your user when their cursor passes over the sprite. In the Status field, add a message you want to appear in the Web browser status bar (at the bottom of a browser window). The movie must be viewed in a browser using the QuickTime plug-in for this message to appear.

To create a simple sprite-based animation, add more keyframes to a sprite object row. Click the Create Sample button (pencil icon) and click within the track to add keyframes. Additionally you can copy a keyframe by selecting and Option/Alt-dragging. Once a keyframe has been added, you can click and drag it to another point along the timeline; note, however, that the beginning keyframe (set at 0:00:00.00) cannot be moved.

TIP:
Deleting Keyframes

To delete a keyframe, click the Delete Sample button (eraser icon) and click desired keyframes.

TIP:
Adjust Sprite Start

You can't adjust the time of the beginning sprite: its Start Time field is inactive and it can't be dragged. But you can create a second keyframe in the sprite object track. A blue bar appears in the Sprite Track row, covering the range from beginning to ending keyframes; click and drag the bar along the timeline to adjust its beginning point.

TIP:
Adjust Ending Keyframe

If you move the ending keyframe to a later point along the timeline, the blue bar expands to that point. However, if you move the ending keyframe to an earlier point, the blue bar doesn't adjust. To make this adjustment, return to the Sprite Track Inspector's Basic tab and click the Snap Duration to Last Keyframe button, then click anywhere within the Timeline Window to make the change occur.

On the Actions tab you can configure wired sprites, which respond to actions performed by your viewer (see Figure 17-48). Select the type of input (Mouse Down, Up, Click, Enter, and Exit), click the new action button, choose your desired action from the popup menu, then click Apply.

Figure 17-48
Sprite Sample
Inspector's
Actions tab

Action Sample Inspector. You can also add Actions to a sprite track by adding keyframes to the action row; the Action associated with these keyframes occurs when the frame is loaded and not dependent upon user activity. To add a keyframe, click the Create Sample button and click in the Action row at the desired point in the timeline. Select the keyframe to bring up the Action Sample Inspector, which only includes Frame Loaded in the Events pane (see Figure 17-49). Select it, click the New Action button, then select your Action from the popup menu.

Figure 17-49
Action Sample
Inspector

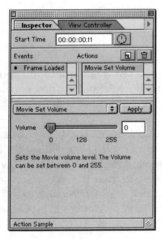

TIP:
Supplemental
Sprite Source

See the "About Sprite Actions" section in the GoLive manual for a pretty thorough description of the different actions available in the Sprite Actions popup menu.

SWF Track Inspector

To add a Flash (SWF) file to your QuickTime movie, drag the SWF Track icon into the Timeline Window (see Figure 17-50). If your movie's dimensions are smaller than the Flash file's dimensions, the Movie Viewer adjusts its size accordingly and the new dimensions become the normalized size.

3D Track Inspector

Drag a 3D Track icon into the Timeline Window to add QuickDraw 3D files to your movie (see Figure 17-51). Use the Open dialog to navigate to a 3D Meta file (with a 3DMF extension), then set the basic information for the track.

Figure 17-50
SWF Track
Inspector

Figure 17-51
3D Track
Inspector

HREF Track and URL Sample Inspectors

Drag the HREF Track icon into the Timeline Window to add a destination URL to your movie. This URL can be one that either automatically causes the browser to jump to the new page or allows the viewer to click a link. Again, configure the usual suspects, however, the Title field is inactive with the default HREFTrack (sic) name (see Figure 17-52).

Figure 17-52
HREF Track
and URL
Sample
Inspectors

To add a link, click the toggle arrow to the left of the track name, click the Create Sample button, and add a Sample track. Click the Sample track to bring up the URL Sample Inspector. Modify the Start Time and End Time fields if necessary. In the Link field, enter a URL or navigate to it using Point & Shoot or Browse. In the Target field, type a frame name or select an item from the Target popup menu.

Checking Autoload URL automatically opens the specified link; if left unchecked, the QuickTime movie must be clicked to open the link.

The URL added to this track is displayed in the Movie Viewer; if Autoload URL is checked, an "A" appears before the link, and if a Target is selected, "T" follows the URL with the specified target (see Figure 17-53).

Figure 17-53
Viewing the
HREF track

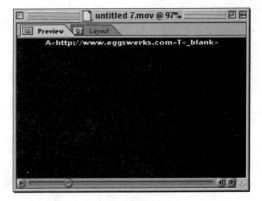

Chapter Track and Sample Inspectors

You can divide a QuickTime file into sections by dragging the Chapter Track icon into the Timeline Window, which brings up the Chapter Track Inspector. These chapters appear in the status line of the QuickTime Player; in version 4.0, the chapters are accessed by clicking the up and down arrows (see Figure 17-54).

Figure 17-54
Viewing a
chapter in
QuickTime
movie

Add a Title to the Chapter Track Inspector, and Start Time and Duration if necessary. In the Act As Chapter Track For popup menu, select the track you want these chapters to be associated with.

To add a chapter, click the toggle arrow to the left of the track name, click the Create Sample button, and add a Sample track. Click the Sample track to bring up the Chapter Sample Inspector (see Figure 17-55). Provide a Chapter Title, and modify the Start Time and End Time fields if necessary.

To add more chapters to this track, add more Sample tracks using the Sample tools (i.e., adding samples using the Create Sample tool, or dividing a longer Sample Track using the Divide Sample tool). Note that if you leave any gaps in time between samples, no chapter title is displayed in the QuickTime application during that section of the movie.

Figure 17-55
Chapter Track
Inspector

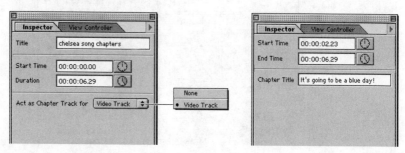

Text Track and Sample Inspectors

To add a text message to your movie, drag the Text Track icon into the Timeline Window and add any necessary information into the Text Track Inspector's fields (see Figure 17-56).

Figure 17-56
Text Track
Inspector

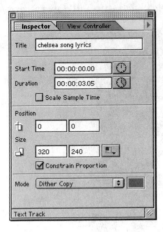

To add text, click the toggle arrow to the left of the track name, click the Create Sample button, and add a Sample track. Click the Sample track to bring up the Text Sample Inspector.

In the Text tab, provide a Start Time and End Time if necessary (see Figure 17-57). Enter your message into the text field, making sure to click the Apply button. If Apply is not pressed, you lose whatever you typed. Choose an

Figure 17-57
Text Sample
Inspector

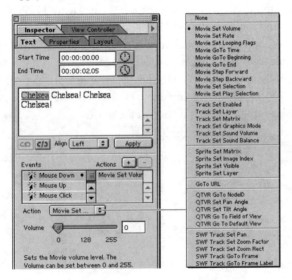

alignment from the Align popup menu. You can create a link that triggers an action, such as setting a movie's volume, jumping to the end or beginning of a movie, or simply going to another URL.

On the Layout tab, entering a value in the Margin Width field positions the text by that amount of pixels from the left and right borders, while the Margin Height field controls the spacing between the top and bottom borders (see Figure 17-58). Format the text by checking Drop Shadow and/or Anti Alias. To make the text invisible, check Transparent. To provide a background color, click the color field to open the Color palette.

Figure 17-58
Text Sample
Inspector's
Layout tab

Click the Properties tab to set the following options (see Figure 17-59):

• Check Don't Display to suppress text from displaying in the movie.

• Check Don't Auto Scale to keep text from scaling automatically.

• Check Use Movie BG Color to use the same background color as defined for the movie.

• Checking Shrink Text Box uses the Margin Width and Margin Height values from the Layout tab to shrink the display area of the text, which

Figure 17-59
Text Sample
Inspector's
Properties tab

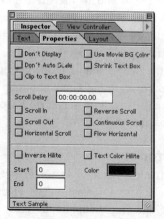

gets rewrapped. Checking Clip to Text Box also uses these Layout tab values, but does not rewrap text and displays the text within a box.

If you have negative values entered into Margin Width or Margin Height, text may not appear in your movie file, depending on how far the negative offset is.

- Enter a time value in Scroll Delay. This only works when scrolling is enabled (i.e., Scroll In or Scroll Out) and the delay time is shorter than the sample duration.

- Scroll In sets the start time of the scrolling text, while Scroll Out sets the end time.

- Horizontal Scroll sets the text to scroll horizontally.

- Check Flow Horizontal to allow horizontally scrolled text flow within the text box. Leaving this unchecked (the default) causes the text to flow as if the text box has no right edge.

- Check Reverse Scroll to reverse the original direction of scrolling text.

- Continuous Scroll causes two text samples to scroll in and out. Scroll In and Scroll Out need to be set along with Continuous Scroll for this to work correctly.

- Checking Inverse Hilite reverses the highlighted text color and the text color, while Text Color Hilite sets the highlighted text color.

- Set the start and end times of scrolling text by entering values in the Start and End fields.

Streaming Track Inspector

Adding a Streaming Track allows you to prepare a movie for use on a QuickTime streaming server using RTSP (Real Time Streaming Protocol). Add your basic information in the Streaming Track Inspector's Basic tab (see Figure 17-60). In the RTSP tab, specify the location of the streaming content file in the Link field. Click the Get Streaming Properties button to open the connection to this RTSP reference. In the Timeout popup menu, set a time when attempts to connect to the streaming server from GoLive should stop; this doesn't affect a live Web connection.

Folder Track Inspector

Dragging a Folder Track icon into a movie allows you to group tracks together. It features just the basic of the basic information (see Figure 17-61). To add tracks to a folder, click, drag, and drop them into the folder track.

Figure 17-60
Streaming
Track Inspector

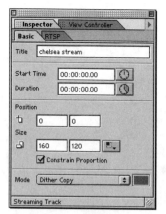

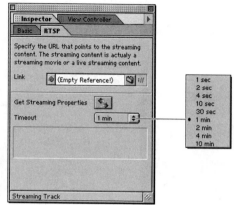

Figure 17-61
Folder Track
Inspector

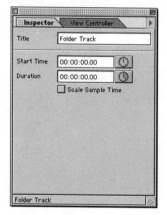

Plug In, Log Out, and GoLive!

GoLive offers a powerful set of previewing and editing options for working with rich media. Mastering these features can help you take material that has to appear on your Web site and make it work in the best and most reliable fashion with any browser that dares to cross your threshold.

Page Specials

Although you'd think we would have covered every possible page feature in this part of the book, a few items that already help create and manage pages still defy categorization. These include spellchecking, previewing a page's download time, and a couple of tweakier issues that affect how GoLive opens and downloads files.

Spellchecking

Spellchecking is the best thing ever to hit computres. Computres. Computers. But it requires human intelligence to operate successfully. GoLive's spellchecking offers most of the standard features found in Microsoft Word and other applications.

You can spellcheck an entire site or a single page; the controls are almost identical. If you want to spellcheck a site, you need to have the Site window as the frontmost window when you select Check Spelling from the Edit menu; otherwise, bring the page you want checked to the fore (see Figure 18-1).

Figure 18-1
Spellchecking

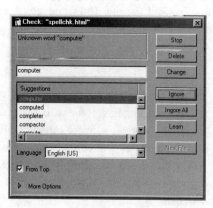

Language. Select a language from your installed dictionaries if the default doesn't match the language of the page.

Because GoLive was designed for an international audience, you can spellcheck for any of the languages you have installed. GoLive includes dictionaries for almost all Western European languages and all their "Americas" versions (French Canadian, US English, and Brazilian Portuguese).

From Top. Check this option to examine the entire page; otherwise, the spellchecking starts at the text-insertion point.

More Options. Sometimes a spellchecker will flag words that you know aren't in its dictionary, but are correct anyway. The More Options section (click the triangle at the bottom of the screen to display) provides the following features, which can be activated by clicking their check boxes:

- Find Uncapitalized Begin of Sentences
- Find Repeated Words
- Ignore Single Characters
- Ignore Words with Only Uppercase
- Ignore Words with Numbers
- Ignore Numbers
- Ignore Roman Numerals

Spellchecking can also ignore patterns of text using regular expressions. If you reveal the Regular Expressions settings under the Spell Checker pane in Preferences, you can add patterns that GoLive excludes when it spellchecks. It has two built-in patterns to avoid flagging URLs and email addresses. See Chapter 25, *Advanced Features,* for details on using this feature.

Checking

Click the Start button to begin spellchecking. GoLive displays each word it finds misspelled at the top of the dialog box, along with a brief description of the problem (such as "Unknown word" or "Space missing"). If it suggests a replacement, it places it in the field below the misspelling. This field can be edited, or you can enter a word when GoLive offers no suggestions. Other choices appear in the Suggestions list; select a word to have it automatically inserted in the replacement field.

The other options are controlled via the buttons along the right edge of the window.

Stop. During a spellchecking operation, the Start button becomes the Stop button, which predictably stops the process. Closing the Check Spelling dialog box also ends the operation.

Delete. GoLive deletes the word from the page where the misspelling was found.

Change. Click Change to apply the word suggested by GoLive's dictionary, or your own replacement if you typed it in.

Ignore. This skips just the current instance of the word.

Ignore All. GoLive remembers this word during the spellchecking "session" and skips all subsequent instances of it.

Learn. GoLive adds the word to its exception dictionary, which you can edit via the Preferences dialog box's Spell Checker pane.

Next File. This option is only available when you're spellchecking a site, and it allows you to force GoLive to move to the next file, even if the current file hasn't been completely checked.

TIP:
Switching to Document

You can click the Layout Editor to make changes at any time while spellchecking. If you position your text-insertion point elsewhere in the document, though, the Spellchecker continues its search where it left off, not the new cursor position.

Document Statistics

You usually have to wait until a page is fully designed and created to test how long it might take for an average user to download, images and all. Fortunately, GoLive offers the Document Statistics feature, which can provide a total size for all the content on the page, a word and character count, and an estimate for download time at different speeds (see Figure 18-2). With a document open, choose Document Statistics from the Special menu.

Figure 18-2
Document
Statistics
feature

GoLive doesn't take into account real-world issues in its estimates, however, like latency. Latency is the amount of time it takes to get data from point A to point B, not how fast it's moving. An analogy would be a stream of cars that gets stopped on a slow stretch of road between two exits on a highway: they might travel 60 mph before and after the slow stretch, but it still takes each car a while to get through the bottleneck.

Go Live also doesn't account for Internet slowdowns and platform and browser overhead (how long they take to deal with content once it's arrived). For instance, a page with eight images that's only 20K total would take 21 seconds to download at 9,600 bits per second (bps), according to GoLive. However, most browsers are configured to download only four to eight items at a time (four is typically the default). Plus, a 9,600-bps modem has high latency, meaning that it takes a while to get data gushing through the pipe. The slower the connection, generally the higher the latency, slowing down the whole process.

So for up to 28,800 bps, we'd multiply GoLive's estimate by three for real-world purposes; up to ISDN, we'd multiply by two. For T1 (about 1.5 megabits per second or Mbps) and T3 (about 45 Mbps), the estimates are useful for pages with lots of multimedia, but the mechanisms by which data gets sent across the Net seems to limit all Web transfers to an effective throttle of about 400 kilobits per second (kbps) maximum, or one-fourth of a T1 line. (FTP can be much faster, but the Web seems to max out lower.)

TIP:
Missing
Bandwidth
Options

Oddly, this feature doesn't note any DSL or cable modem speeds, despite at least a million people (including office workers) using that technology. DSL and cable modem speeds fall between ISDN and T1.

Download Page

Download Page is a special, standalone, Mac-only feature that lets you type in any Web page location starting with http://, and have GoLive download the page, as well as any images or other objects that appear on the page (see Figure 18-3). (The exception is anything referenced in JavaScript or other scripting languages; it only downloads media mentioned in HTML tags.) Select Download Page from the File menu, type the Web page's address, then click the Save As button to specify a destination for the files.

Figure 18-3
Download
Page

GoLive opens a page with the same title, but all of the images are stored in the same folder as the HTML page; so, you cannot retain the original page's file structure (such as having images in a separate folder). You can edit and save this page with its new image references, and then upload it back to the server. However, doing so usually breaks all of the links on the page, as they have been rewritten to reflect the local storage location of the downloaded images.

If you use the FTP or WebDAV Browser features described in Chapter 23, *Synchronizing Sites*, double-clicking a page in those windows brings up a page in the exact manner as using Download Page. The difference is that with the Browsers, you must have access to a server; with Web Download, you need merely enter a URL.

File Mappings

Most kinds of documents can be viewed or edited by more than one application. GoLive maintains a list of document types and the programs that can handle working with them in its File Mappings settings, so you can open files directly by double clicking them inside GoLive just as you could from the Windows or Macintosh Desktop.

The File Mappings tab is found in the Web Settings dialog box on both Macintosh and Windows (see Figure 18-4). File Mappings reveals the defaults that Adobe built into the program, including the notion that GoLive itself can open a whole variety of files for editing. For instance, if you have the QuickTime Module installed, GoLive "knows" it can open and edit AIFF sound files, QuickTime ".mov" (movie) files, and other video and sound formats.

Figure 18-4
File Mappings
settings

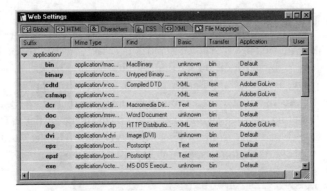

GoLive relies on the bit at the end of a file following a dot—the extension—the same way Windows does. For instance, a PDF file is named "folderol.pdf" while an HTML file could be named "snooker.html" or "scrabble.htm" (either .html or .htm).

The structure of File Mappings is pretty straightforward, and it's identical for Mac and Windows. To make it a bit easier, the mappings are broken into groups like application, audio, and video. Click the triangle to the left of a heading to view its mappings settings.

Click a column's title to sort the list according to that heading. To hide or show a column, bring up the contextual menu while your cursor is on a column title, then select a column name from the list (see Figure 18-5). You can also opt to show or hide all columns.

Figure 18-5
Displaying File
Mappings
columns

TIP:
Using File Mappings in Files Tab

We discuss how File Mappings affects opening files in the Site window's Files tab in Chapter 21, *Files, Folders, and Links,* where it's more contextually appropriate. For now, we want to concentrate on how to edit and manage the settings.

TIP:
Internet Control Panel (Mac)

The Internet control panel is a program that, among other things, maintains a list of file types and programs associated with them for use in programs like GoLive. If you check Use Internet Control Panel, any preferences you've changed in GoLive are overwritten. For more on using the Internet control panel, see Appendix A, *Macintosh Issues and Extras.*

Suffix. The Suffix column lists the file type's extension.

MIME. MIME defines the kind of data a given file type contains. This is necessary for feeding out content over the Internet.

Kind. Kind is a text description created by Adobe; it identifies the variety of content.

Basic. Basic describes the type of file, to give GoLive an idea of how it's structured: Binary file, Text, HTML, XML, SGML, or XHTML.

Transfer. Transfer specifies how the data should be carried across the Internet: as bin (binary) or as text.

Application. Application lists the application that should open the file if double-clicked. The Default setting means that GoLive relies on its mappings or information stored in the file, but you can change Default to a specific program to override this.

Type and Creator (Mac). If you're using a Macintosh, these two columns specify the Type and Creator codes, which the Mac OS uses to identify which applications can open the file.

User. When you add a new file mapping to the list, a bullet appears in the User column to indicate that the file isn't part of GoLive's built-in library of mappings.

Modifying Settings

File Mappings allows all of its settings to be changed by clicking the line containing the settings and entering new values in the File Info Extension Inspector. For instance, if you want to map PDF files to be opened in Adobe Acrobat, you'd click the line starting pdf, and find Adobe Acrobat using the Application field's Browse button in the Inspector.

New Items

You might find it necessary to add extensions for files you regularly work with that GoLive doesn't currently list or that aren't available. Adding extensions is extremely simple. Click the New Extension button on the Toolbar, or select Add Suffix from the contextual menu. Enter the extension, choose an application to open the file, enter the MIME type (if you know it), choose an option from the Basic popup menu, select a Transfer type, and then type a description in the Kind field. Deselect the item to apply the changes.

Open Files

Trying to open or launch an item has a different effect depending on what characteristics we or the program's developers assigned to the file.

No extension or an extension that's not listed. If the file lacks an extension or has one that GoLive doesn't list in File Mappings, GoLive for Windows brings up the Open With dialog box that presents likely suspects for being able to open the program—if no extension exists, it's possible that Windows would list a very large number of applications (see Figure 18-6).

Figure 18-6
Windows
Open With
dialog box

On the Macintosh, GoLive's behavior depends on whether you have a file translator installed; this translator exists in many incarnations over many system versions; you can buy commercial versions that support more file types than the built-in one Apple provides. If you have anything in your Control Panels folder called EasyOpen or File Exchange and it's set to ask you about files it doesn't know how to open, double clicking an unmapped file in GoLive brings up a dialog box which prompts you to choose an appropriate application (see Figure 18-7). As on Windows, the Mac might present a list of dozens or even hundreds of applications.

Figure 18-7
Macintosh File
Exchange
dialog box

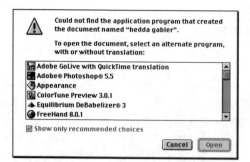

> ⚠ Could not find the application program that created the document named "hedda gabler".
>
> To open the document, select an alternate program, with or without translation:
>
> - 🖼 Adobe GoLive with QuickTime translation
> - 🔷 Adobe® Photoshop® 5.5
> - 🔶 Appearance
> - 🔷 ColorTune Preview 3.0.1
> - 🔸 Equilibrium DeBabelizer® 3
> - ⚫ FreeHand 8.0.1
>
> ☑ Show only recommended choices
>
> [Cancel] [Open]

Listed extension. For file types that list an extension, the information for that type affects the options GoLive presents. If you use the contextual menu to select an option, GoLive shows Open in Adobe GoLive if the extension is mapped to Adobe GoLive or if GoLive knows that it can open that file type even if it's mapped to another program. The menu also shows Open in "Program Name" if anything but GoLive has been mapped to the extension (see Figure 18-8). If the application that's been mapped to the extension doesn't exist, despite the fact that it's listed, GoLive shows an error stating that the document can't be opened with the specified program. In that case, your best solution is to change the listed program to another application you do have available.

Now That We're on the Same Page...

At this point, you've probably learned more about Web page creation in a short amount of time than most of us absorbed in the same amount of time hand coding HTML. That's the magic of using GoLive—plenty of the Web workings behind the scenes remain behind the scenes, allowing you to focus more energy on design than on code.

But you haven't reached the end (if you have, go get a new copy of this book, because there should be several hundred more pages following this one!). If you want to put your pages together into a *collection* of pages, GoLive can offer you an entirely new set of options: its site-management features. The next part of this book, Sites, is devoted to just that.

Methods of Opening

There are several methods of opening a file (see Figure 18-8).

- Right-click (Windows) or Control-click (Mac) a file in the Site window, and select Open in "Program Name" from the menu.

- Double click the item on a page or in the Site window's Files tab.
- Select the item in the Site window's Files tab and select Launch File from the Site window's Finder (Mac) or Explorer (Windows) menu.

Figure 18-8
Different ways of opening a file

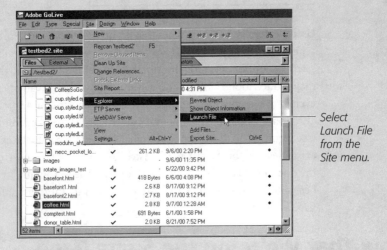

Select Launch File from the Site menu.

Open the file using the contextual menu.

CHAPTER 19

Site Management

The basic units of the Web are pages and sites. A page is a discrete file containing HTML which forms something that is clearly its own object. Sites are collections of pages, images, media, and other files (CSS style sheets, JavaScript libraries, etc.) that collectively form a navigational whole in which all (or most) elements can be reached in some manner by starting at the home page or root of the site.

Sites can exist as a few pages on one server in someone's basement in Twin Falls, Idaho, or comprise hundreds of thousands of pages on servers around the world. But what differentiates a site from a random list of files is that pages link to each other in an organized fashion.

GoLive uses this notion of linked pages in its approach to site management. In GoLive, you create a site file that stores all the information about the objects and links found in a site's HTML, media, and code files; a site folder that contains the actual site documents; and a GoLive data folder where all special templates and reusable items for a particular site reside.

You can always see precisely which files are in your site and the relationships between them and other linked files and objects. Behind the scenes in the site file, GoLive maintains a database of this information, which allows it to manage aspects of a site that are embedded in individual HTML and media files. Change the name of a file and GoLive can update references to it everywhere, including within PDFs, Flash (SWF) files, and QuickTime movies. Update a recurring element, like a navigation bar, and GoLive can update it on all pages on which it appears.

This aspect of site management is highly satisfying. Using GoLive, you no longer have to keep track of practically anything. Creating new objects is a snap, as is updating thousands of links on thousands of pages and prototyping multiple designs while working out a new Web site.

This chapter covers how GoLive deals with a site: where all the parts live, what commands are available, the specifics of working with the site management tools, and how the program divides different aspects of site management into sections.

What's New in 5

Most site-management features work the same way in GoLive 5 as they did in 4. The main exception is the new Design tab, replacing the Site tab. In GoLive 4, the Site tab created and modified simple site maps that reflected a site's navigational structure. The Design tab in GoLive 5, however, allows you to prototype sites, see an accurate representation of the link hierarchy, and create multiple maps of a site. This is covered in Chapter 20, *Prototyping and Mapping.*

GoLive 5 includes site templates that have graphics and text placeholders, as well as CSS style sheets, that can act as the basis of a new site. You can use the built-in templates or create your own (covered in this chapter).

WebDAV file transfer supplements existing FTP support. WebDAV is a tool for checking files in and out of a Web server while marking their status as in use or updated. With WebDAV, several people can work on a Web site simultaneously with the firm knowledge that only one person is editing a given file at a given time. It also allows two-way synchronization, so you can refresh the Web site with your updates, and download changes others have made—all in a single action. WebDAV is covered in Chapter 23, *Synchronizing Sites.*

Each major platform—Mac OS, Windows , and Unix (including Linux)—has different requirements for what files can be named. GoLive 5 offers Filename Constraints, which alerts you when you have files that don't conform to what a given platform can handle. (See Chapter 21, *Files, Folders, and Links*).

Most tabs in the Site window, whether on the left side (Files, External, Designs, Colors, Font Sets, and Custom) or the right (Extras, Errors, FTP, and WebDAV) can be "torn off" and made into freestanding windows for greater utility (discussed later in this chapter).

A 40-inch monitor would help you use version 5's site-management features alongside its page tools. Or two 19-inch screens—one for the palettes, one for the windows (see Figure 19-1).

The Split-pane view is now available in every left-hand tab view; the left- and right-hand tabs are essentially independent. Also, Windows GoLive is now in sync with the Mac: the pane showing Extras, Errors, etc., is on the right, not the bottom. And the Windows version of the Files tab is now almost identical to the Mac's.

Trivia question: How long did it take you to figure out how to open that split-pane view with GoLive 5? *Answer:* Longer than you want to admit. The two-triangles button at the bottom right corner of the Site window opens the split-pane view (see Figure 19-2); you can also reach it by choosing some of the options on the Site menu's View submenu.

The View Controller palette customizes the display of columns and other aspects of Site window tabs. Formerly, the Inspector handled this. The Inspector and View Controller are dockable; you can customize a site view while still seeing your Inspector palette options.

You can finally see a file's modification date in the Files tab itself, rather than having to rely on the File Inspector. The Files tab shows a number of file characteristics, such as date, kind, and size; you can sort files by any of them.

A new Find feature, Element, allows you to make changes based on specific HTML characteristics in individual files or sitewide (covered in Chapter 16, *Source Editing*).

Figure 19-1
Spanning
many monitors

*You might want
to mortgage
your house…*

Figure 19-2
Splitting the
panes

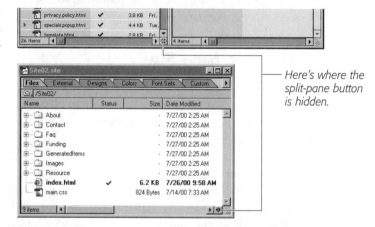

*Here's where the
split-pane button
is hidden.*

The rest of this part of the book covers the individual aspects of site management:

• Prototyping and mapping a site using the Design tab (Chapter 20)

• Working with files, folders, and links, including templates and troubleshooting using the Files, External, Extras, and Errors tabs (Chapter 21)

• Managing colors and font sets using the Colors and Font Sets tabs (Chapter 22)

• Synchronizing your local copy of a site with a remote Web server using the FTP and WebDAV tabs (Chapter 23)

• Importing existing sites into GoLive (Chapter 24)

TIP:
**Reviewing
the Basics**

If you find yourself needing a review, or you want to get a visual breakout of every element, flip back to Part 1, *GoLive Basics,* in which the interfaces, elements, palettes, toolbars, and menus are fully annotated.

Site Setup

GoLive offers a few different methods to set up a site, depending on whether you're starting from scratch or working from an existing site. You can create a blank site with no contents, or use one of the new templates provided in GoLive 5. Existing sites can be imported from a folder on a local hard drive or network volume, or from a directory via FTP.

No matter how you get started, your site will end up with a site file, which contains the underlying information about a site (the link database, site designs, and preferences) and two folders (one containing your actual site files, the other containing special objects, like Components and Stationery).

Creating a New Site

When you're starting from scratch, you have two choices: you can create an entirely blank site that contains just a placeholder home page and no contents, or you can use one of GoLive's templates to create a fleshed-out structure into which you can pour content.

Blank. If you select the Blank item from the New Site submenu in the File menu, or type Command-Option-N (Mac) or Control-Alt-N (Windows), GoLive prompts you for a site name and creates a site file, a site folder, and a site data folder. The default name is "New Site" which creates a "New Site.site" file, a "New Site" folder and a "New Site.data" folder. If you choose your own name, GoLive adds ".site" to name the site file and ".data" to name the site folder.

We recommend you check the Create Folder box when naming the site to create an enclosing folder for those three items; the folder is named whatever you call the site plus a space and "folder".

NEW IN 5:
Same Names on Mac and Windows

Macintosh and Windows versions of GoLive formerly named the site file and folders somewhat differently, and each had different default values. This has been nicely synchronized in version 5.

Copy from Template. Selecting Copy from Template from the New Site submenu of the File menu allows you to choose a template, view a preview of its structure and layout, and then create a copy for your use.

Creating a Site Template

Creating a site template is extremely simple, you'll be happy to hear. First build a site with pages, links, objects, Stationery, and Components in as generic a fashion as you want. Then copy that site's enclosing folder—the one that contains the site file, site folder, and site data folder—into the Site Templates folder in the GoLive application folder (see Figure 19-3). The site is now available as a template.

To customize the preview display, make two screen captures of 72 pixels square of the site's structure and navigation, or anything you want, really. Save these somewhere handy; they can be located anywhere, but inside the Site Template folder probably makes sense. Open the site template's site file, and then hold down the Shift key and click the Site Settings button on the Site Toolbar. This enables an additional setting that allows you to enter a description and link to the screen captures (see Figure 19-4).

Figure 19-3
Site Templates folder

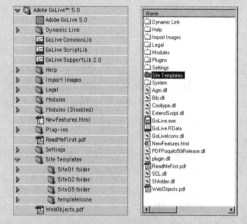

Figure 19-4
Accessing site template settings

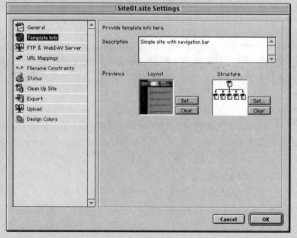

Importing a Site

If you already have a site created, or in progress, that you want to bring under GoLive's management, you can import your current working site into a fresh GoLive site file. The site can be stored locally (on your hard drive or on the local network) or somewhere on the Net (in a place you can access via FTP).

TIP:
Make New Sites from Old

Making imported sites sing can be a more or less difficult task depending on the size and age of the site. This process includes rooting out dead files, bad links, old imagemaps, and many other examples of rot. We devote an entire chapter to handy strategies for this routine task: Chapter 24, *Importing a Site*.

GoLive offers two import commands corresponding to bringing in local and remote sites.

Import from Folder. Select the Import from Folder option from the New Site submenu to bring up a dialog box which prompts you to specify your existing site's folder location and a home page file inside that location.

Click the Browse button under the top field, and use the standard file selection dialog box to find your existing folder. GoLive creates its own site files and folders at the same level as your existing site folder, so you may want to create a new folder that contains just the existing site before importing into GoLive; this prevents new items from mingling with older files and folders.

The home page should be the first page users retrieve when they type in your URL without a page selected, such as http://realworldgolive.com. GoLive considers the home page as the root of all navigation and links. Choose this page by clicking Browse under the bottom field.

TIP:
Automatic Home Page Selection

If the home page in the folder you're importing is named the same as GoLive's default home page (index.html), GoLive automatically chooses it and displays it in the home page field of the Import Site Folder dialog. (This only works for index.html at this writing, even if you've chosen a different default home page value in Preferences or Site Settings.)

If you don't have something you consider a default home page or want to defer that decision, check the Create Generic Home Page box. We discuss making the decision about what your home page is in Chapter 21, *Files, Folders, and Links*.

Import from FTP Server. After choosing Import from FTP Server from the New Site submenu, GoLive prompts you with its typical FTP connection dialog, described at length in Chapter 23, *Synchronizing Sites*.

When you click the Browse button, GoLive connects to the FTP server using the settings you provided. You can browse the remote directories and files to find the home page.

After clicking Import, GoLive prompts you for a location to save the downloaded site.

TIP:
No Import via WebDAV

Although you can manage a site via WebDAV, you cannot use it to import a site. You can create a blank site and then use the Synchronize feature to make a local copy of the content. See Chapter 23, *Synchronizing Sites,* for more details on WebDAV.

TIP:
Local FTP or WebDAV

If you want to synchronize a copy of your site over your Local Area Network (LAN), see Chapter 23, *Synchronizing Sites,* for a discussion on how to set up a local FTP or WebDAV server to let GoLive carry out this task.

Site File and Folders

As we mentioned earlier in the chapter, GoLive creates three items on your local hard drive when you create a new site or import an existing site: the site file, the site folder, and the site data folder (see Figure 19-5).

Figure 19-5
Site folders

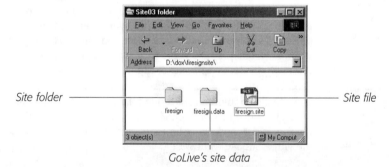

Site folder ——————   —————— Site file

GoLive's site data

TIP:
Changing Site Names

The names of the site file, site folder, and site data folder are coordinated to start with the same text. Although you can change these outside of GoLive, we don't recommend it. If you change the name of the site folder, GoLive asks you to locate it the next time you open the site file; if you change the name of the site data folder, a new, blank one is created. If you really need to change the root name of your site, be sure to make the change on all three elements. GoLive will ask you to specify the site folder once the next time you open the site file, but from then on the change will stick.

Site file. The site file contains the database of items found on the site: a list of HTML files, images, and other documents, and their internal references; the database of external links; a list of colors and font sets; the structure of any site maps or designs you're working on in the Design tab; and all your local preferences. (The files that comprise a prototype are stored in the Extras tab's Designs folder in the site data folder.)

The site file can be saved after changes are made to any of the attributes that are part of it. Its save-to-disk behavior is a little too transparent for us cautious types, though. If you quit without saving changes to the site, GoLive saves changes to the site file anyway, but doesn't warn or ask you about saving changes. However, you can manually Save the file at any point after changes are made.

TIP:
Save Often

Your site file isn't automatically saved until you exit the program, and you could easily spend hours working in GoLive without a save—which we don't recommend. Since the site file contains all the above-mentioned items, you lose any information not contained in the Web site itself that you may have manipulated.

For instance, if you create folders to organize your links in the External tab and unceremoniously crash, those folders will not appear when you reboot; the links will still be intact if they're present in the site's individual HTML files, but not if you created them from scratch in order to add them to pages.

TIP:
Automatic Backups

The site file is automatically backed up when you close it or quit GoLive. It's also backed up when you open the file, which can add tens of seconds to either process. It's only a small time loss, so we recommend leaving this option on unless you have a really great backup procedure in place. You can disable backups by unchecking Automatic Backup of Site File in the Site pane of the Preferences dialog.

TIP:
Where the Site File Belongs

The site file should be stored one folder level above the site folder (see Figure 19-6). We once received email from a poor soul who had stored his site file in his site folder, and every time he uploaded his site to his FTP server, the 1+ megabyte site file went with it.

Figure 19-6
Positioning site folders

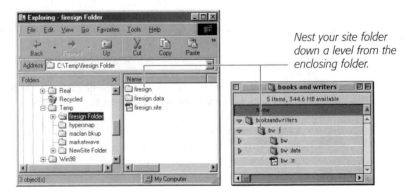

Nest your site folder down a level from the enclosing folder.

The site file, when opened in GoLive, is represented by the Site window. The site itself, comprising real documents and folders, is stored entirely in the site folder.

Site folder. This folder contains all the files that comprise your Web site. It is essentially a local, identical representation of your remote Web site, with all files and folders intact.

If you reference files that live outside the site folder by browsing via the URL Getter, GoLive offers a few tools to copy or move them into the site folder before you upload your site or synchronize it. See discussion of the Clean Up Site feature in Chapter 21, *Files, Folders, and Links*. Ultimately, anything you reference locally has to be copied into the site folder so that it can be uploaded to your Web server.

You can, conversely, keep files in the site folder that you don't upload to the Web site. We discuss how to prevent files from being uploaded in Chapter 21, *Files, Folders, and Links*, and Chapter 23, *Synchronizing Sites*. (You can run into trouble here with references to files, like aliases, symbolic links, and shortcuts; we also discuss solutions for maintaining references in Chapter 23.)

Site data folder. The site data folder holds the GoLive miscellany: Stationeries, Components, in-progress design prototypes, even trash, as a temporary holding bin before you empty it.

You can view the contents of the site data folder by opening the split-pane view of the Site window: click the two-way arrow at the lower-right corner of the window (see Figure 19-7). The Extras tab shows the four folders contained in the site data folder, even if those folders are empty: Components, Designs, Site Trash, and Stationeries.

Figure 19-7
Split-pane
view

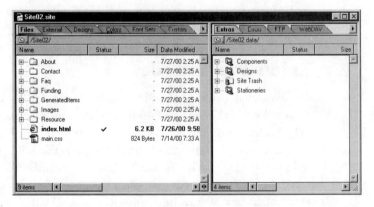

Site Window

GoLive organizes a site into five categories inside a Site window (see Figure 19-8). The Site window contains five tabs which handle specific aspects of site management. (The sixth tab, Custom, allows you to store text and HTML "snippets" you might want to use later.)

Figure 19-8
Site window
tabs

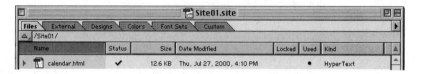

The five tabs starting at the left of the Site window—Files, External, Designs, Colors, and Font Sets—divide into three categories.

- References and files: the Files and External tabs help you manage HTML files, and folders containing items, media and other files, email addresses users can click on, and any external URLs.

- Prototyping and mapping: the Designs tab offers a graphical and outline view of the navigational structure and linking relationships among all the elements in a site. It also offers powerful tools for prototyping and extending sites with the ability to test and stage changes.

- HTML attributes: the Colors and Font Sets tabs provide a central location to view the Font tag's Face attribute and the general Color attribute applied to text, tables, and other items anywhere in a site.

By centralizing all this management into one window, it's a simple task to view all the elements by category in a site. For instance, you can find out which colors have been used for a site that may have been created elsewhere and imported into GoLive; or, you can change a reference to another location on the Internet with a single Point & Shoot action.

References and Files

The Files tab in GoLive shows all the files that make up the site and are stored on your local hard drive. The Files tab also manages all references made inside HTML files that point to other objects on your site, such as other HTML pages, GIF and JPEG images, Flash SWF files, and PDFs. We get into more detail about the Files tab in Chapter 21 *Files, Folders, and Links*.

If you click the split-pane button in the Site window, you can also examine errors, Stationery, Designs, items thrown in the GoLive trash, and Components;

you can also access an FTP file list displaying the contents of remote FTP servers, and interact with a WebDAV workgroup file server (see Figure 19-9). The FTP and WebDAV tabs let you manage uploads and downloads to your Web site.

Figure 19-9
FTP and
WebDAV
windows

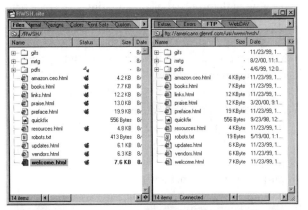

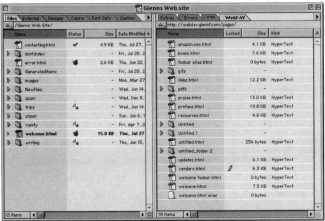

The External tab shows all references to URLs that reference external Web pages or other objects like public FTP servers and downloadable PDFs. Any item inside an HTML hyperlink that starts with a resource identifier link, like http://, ftp://, or mailto:, gets extracted and turned into an object you can manage in the External tab. We examine the External tab in Chapter 21, *Files, Folders, and Links*.

GoLive can handle links embedded in several kinds of media files: QuickTime, Acrobat PDF, and Flash SWF files. This media file management means you can update URLs and internal references to files on the site without having to go back to the source program and data to recreate a new media file.

Designs

The Designs tab serves two separate functions: site prototyping and site mapping. The prototype feature lets you drag in blank pages or templates and create links between them, essentially populating a Web site before you have all the content to put into place. It also allows you to directly modify those pages in a prototype "stage" so you can test them locally before adding them to your Web site. You can add them to your live site and then remove them, too, if you need to make more revisions.

The other feature of the Designs tab shows a graphic relationship between pages and objects in a site through either a navigational view (top-down from the home page showing the main links) or through a links view which shows all inbound and outbound links from every page and object.

Both views offer significant opportunities for visualizing what's going on without resorting to paper and pencil.

For more detail, see Chapter 20, *Prototyping and Mapping*.

HTML Attributes

The Colors and Font Sets tabs land in the same bucket because both let you view a summary of a single HTML attribute. The Color attribute is found in many different HTML tags, including those for table cells, page backgrounds, and individual text ranges.

The Font Sets tab shows a summary of the contents of the Font tag's Face attribute. Font sets are lists of font names that dictate a Web browser's display of text (see Chapter 8, *Text and Fonts*, for a deeper explanation.)

The Colors and Font Sets tabs both offer tools to create and name specific uses of colors or font sets, and extract a list of all those items used in a site. However, the tabs don't offer a quick method for changing colors or font sets throughout your Web site. In Chapter 22, *Sitewide Sets*, we explain more about each tab and discuss multiple methods of simulating site management for these two attributes using the Find feature's Element tab.

Custom

The Custom tab is an odd bird. You can drag text or HTML objects into this tab and edit them directly in the Custom Object Inspector. The functionality is identical to the Custom tab of the Objects palette.

For instance, you could create a table with complex formatting and drag it into the Custom tab. When you want to use this table again, you simply drag

it from the Custom tab into a document window, and GoLive faithfully duplicates it for you (see Figure 19-10). It's unclear why you need the ability to
store custom HTML and text in two locations; our best guess is that it may be
more convenient to manage and organize chunks of site-related data without
having to switch to the Objects palette's Custom tab.

Figure 19-10
Custom HTML
objects

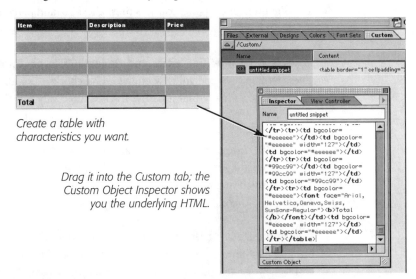

*Create a table with
characteristics you want.*

*Drag it into the Custom tab; the
Custom Object Inspector shows
you the underlying HTML.*

Site Preferences

GoLive offers a number of application-wide site preferences that affect your
current site and new sites created later. These are found in the Edit menu,
under Preferences, by clicking the Site icon and the triangle (Mac) or plus sign
(Windows) next to it (see Figure 19-11).

Figure 19-11
Site preferences

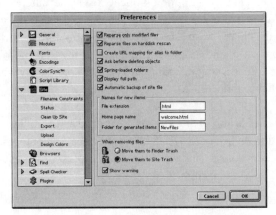

Most of these preferences are described in detail in other chapters, which we'll indicate below.

Site

The Site preferences panel controls most checking and parsing behavior; that is, how and when GoLive checks files and URLs.

Reparse Only Modified Files, and Reparse Files on Hard Disk Rescan. These two options control how often GoLive checks the source HTML to see if changes were made that it hadn't tracked internally. See Chapter 21, *Files, Folders, and Links.*

Create URL Mapping for Alias/Shortcut to Folder. URL mappings are a highly powerful, yet confusing feature for splitting content over multiple Web sites, for which we provide some step-by-step clarification in Chapter 21, *Files, Folders, and Links.*

Ask Before Deleting Objects. If this isn't checked, you can delete items with impunity without any warnings. Danger, danger, Will Robinson! Starting with GoLive 5, you can undo many operations several steps back—but this doesn't include restoring deleted files!

Spring-Loaded Folders. If this option is checked, folders automatically open when you drag files over them or use the Point & Shoot tool and hover over them.

Display Full Path. This option is unchecked by default, placing the Path icon at the lower left of each pane in the Site window. Checking it moves the Path icon to the upper left, and shows a path display to its right, including the protocol (ftp or http) and fully qualified URLs for the FTP and WebDAV tabs. We recommend checking it, because it's easier to see exactly where in a site you are with this option on.

Automatic Backup of Site File. As mentioned earlier in this chapter, checking this option (which is on by default) creates a backup of the site file every time you open or close it. This adds time to both operations, but it ensures that you always have a recent copy.

Names for New Items. These three fields control how new, blank pages are created when dragged from the Objects palette's Site tab, added from the Site menu, or otherwise plopped into a site. File Extension controls the part of the file that defines its content after a period; this is almost always .html, even on Windows boxes, but DOS demands just .htm.

The Home Page Name defines what a new, default site uses as its home page file name. The Folder for Generated Items field lets you chose a name where new, unlinked pages appear in the Files tab's folder hierarchy.

When Removing Files. These radio buttons allow you to select a Trash folder for your deleted files: either the internal one in the site data folder handled by GoLive (Move Them to Site Trash); or your system's own waste elimination device (the Desktop Trash can on Macintosh, the Recycling Bin on Windows). For the latter option, select Move Them to Finder Trash on the Macintosh or Move Them to System Trash under Windows. Unchecking Show Warning removes files without displaying a warning when you delete them. These options are covered in depth in Chapter 21, *Files, Folders, and Links*.

Other site preference tabs. The Filename Constraints, Status, Clean Up Site, Export, and Upload preferences are covered in Chapter 21, *Files, Folders, and Links*; Design Colors is covered in Chapter 20, *Prototyping and Mapping*. All of these settings can be set globally in Preferences, as well as overriden for each site in Site Settings.

Site Features and Objects

The same site feature or object can be found in several different places in GoLive, sometimes under a different name in each place. Some commands are available only from the Site menu, while others might be activated from the Site menu, the Site toolbar, and the contextual menu. Objects can be inserted by dragging from, or double-clicking in, the Site tab of the Objects palette, and sometimes by selecting an option from the contextual menu.

The Site menu, the contextual menu (Control-click on Mac and right-click on Windows), and the Site toolbar display choices in gray that aren't available for the tab you have selected; the menu items may change their contents as well. The Site tab of the Objects palette lets you drag objects that aren't applicable, but when you release them, they snap back to the Objects palette; if they're appropriate, the whole tab highlights on its edges, just like dragging files into a folder on the Desktop.

TIP:
Design Menu

The Design menu contains all features and objects needed for the Designs tab of the Site window. The Site tab of the Objects palette features only four objects needed in the Designs tab: Generic Page, Design Section, Design Group, and Design Annotation.

Because we run down all the toolbar's options in Chapter 3, *Palettes and Parts*, we won't recapitulate them. Here are all the site-specific commands found on the Site menu, Site toolbar, contextual menu, and Site tab of the Objects palette.

New Generic Page, URL, Address, Color, Font Set, and folders for each. The Site menu's New submenu creates all the objects you need in each tab except Designs. The submenu only shows appropriate objects for the tab you're viewing (see Table 19-1). You can also insert them from the contextual menu.

Table 19-1
Tabs and objects

Tab	New object
Files	Generic Page
External	URL or Address
Color	Color
Font Sets	Font Set

If you want to group any items in any of the tabs except Designs, insert a folder by selecting Folder from the Site menu's New submenu, clicking the New Folder button in the Site toolbar, or selecting New Folder from the contextual menu. In the Files tab, this step creates a new folder into which you can drag files. In the External tab, inserting a folder creates a URL Group; the Colors and Font Sets tabs each has its own folder type as well.

The Site tab in the Objects palette contains 13 icons: the first five are Generic Page, URL, Address, Color, and Font Set; the next five are the respective folders for each kind of object, including an Address Group which can only be created by using its group icon. The Custom tab's icon and folder icons aren't available in the Objects palette.

Rescan..., Reparse All, Create Thumbnails (Files and Extras tab). With the Files or Extras tab selected, the Rescan menu item appears, followed by the current location in quotation marks. Selecting Rescan checks the site folder or site data folder on the local hard drive, depending on whether you've clicked on one top or another, and depending on what level of folders you've clicked down into. Rescan updates the Files or Extras tab to reflect its current state following any changes to files, organization on the Desktop, or in another program.

Holding down the Option or Alt key changes Rescan to Reparse All, and causes GoLive to rebuild its database of links from the source HTML of your pages. This option is necessary when hand-editing HTML files or using the Find feature to change HTML. (We give you more information on this subject in Chapter 21, *Files, Folders, and Links,* and Chapter 24, *Importing a Site.*)

Press Command-Option (Mac) or Control-Alt (Windows) to change the Rescan menu item to Create Thumbnails. This option opens every single bloody HTML file in your site and creates previews of them for display in the Content tab of the File Inspector. Worth it? Mebbe. But it can take a long, long time on larger sites. (More on this in Chapter 20, *Prototyping and Mapping.*)

Removed Unused…, Get…Used (External, Colors, and Font Sets tabs). If you delete URLs, addresses, colors, or font sets from pages in your site, they persist in the appropriate tab; or, if you create new objects and don't apply them to pages, they also remain. Selecting Remove Unused… deletes any item that isn't used somewhere in the site.

Get…Used and Remove Unused… for the External tab are covered in Chapter 21, *Files, Folders, and Links*; and for the Colors and Font Sets tabs in Chapter 22, *Sitewide Sets.*

Clean Up Site. Clean Up Site offers the same kind of functionality as Remove Unused…, but it allows you to remove all kinds of unused objects simultaneously, including files that aren't linked into the navigation hierarchy. This is covered in Chapter 21, *Files, Folders, and Links.*

Change References. Selecting this option from the menu or clicking the Change References button in the Site toolbar brings up a Change References dialog box that allows you to change all instances of an internal or external link. We cover this in Chapter 21, *Files, Folders, and Links.*

Finder/Explorer. Mac users see a Finder item, while Windows users see Explorer in the Site menu. The items in this submenu let you interact with files locally. Sounds a bit vague, but they've lumped a number of features into one menu, so let's cover them each on its own, shall we?

The Reveal Object, Show Object Information, and Launch File options affect any files you have selected in the Files tab. The corresponding items in the Site toolbar are out of order and named differently: Reveal in Finder/Explorer, Show Information in Finder/Explorer, and Open (see Figure 19-12).

Figure 19-12
Object
manipulation

Reveal, Show Information, and Launch

Reveal Object switches you to the Desktop (or to the Windows Explorer), opens the folder containing the file, and selects it. Show Object Information repeats that action, but brings up the information window in the Desktop (Info on the Mac or Properties in Windows).

Launch File (or Open on the Site toolbar) opens the file with the application it was created in. You can change the application through various means, including changing the creator code on the Mac, editing the Registry in Windows, or updating File Mapping in GoLive on either platform. Because File Mapping is more of a page-based feature, we provided some guidelines to modifying its settings in Chapter 18, *Page Specials*; there's a few Mac-specific tips in Appendix A, *Macintosh Issues and Extras*, and for Windows in Appendix B, *Windows Issues and Extras*.

The Add Files item lets you choose files that fall outside the current site folder. Select the items you want to add and GoLive copies them into the default new items folder in your site folder. You can then move them to whatever location you want in the site.

Export Site creates an exact duplicate of your site folder while allowing you to remove GoLive-specific tags, remove extra white space, and/or reorganize the site's hierarchy. See Chapter 21, *Files, Folders, and Links*, for all the options.

FTP Server and WebDAV Server. The FTP and WebDAV features get full coverage in Chapter 23, *Synchronizing Sites*.

Settings. The Settings item brings up Site Settings, which contains any preferences customized for your site. This always includes the General setting, which has the name of the home page of the site. Clicking Show reveals that page in the Files tab. You can use Point & Shoot navigation to link to another page.

TIP:
Easier Home Page Switch

You can also change the home page by clicking on any page in the Files tab, bringing up the File Inspector's Page tab, and checking Home Page.

The other settings available for customization allow you to override any global preferences you've set via Preferences in the Edit menu. The Preferences dialog box contains settings that control any currently open site or any site opened after you change to the settings. Site Settings allows you to customize a given set of options on a per-site basis.

FTP & WebDAV Server corresponds to FTP and WebDAV settings in the Network pane of the Preferences dialog box. Their intricacies are covered in Chapter 23, *Synchronizing Sites*. The Filename Constraints, Status, Clean Up Site, Export, Upload, and Design Colors settings have identical entries in the Site pane of the Preferences dialog box. Everything but Design Colors is covered in Chapter 21, *Files, Folders, and Links*; Design Colors gets what's coming to it in Chapter 20, *Prototyping and Mapping*.

URL Mappings controls a very complex set of behaviors that allows you to split your Web site among multiple remote locations. We cover this topic with some examples in Chapter 21, *Files, Folders, and Links*.

Set Your Sights

With the big picture in mind, let's set our sights on setting up sites, and walk through the details of each aspect of creating, maintaining, and updating sites using GoLive.

CHAPTER 20

Prototyping and Mapping

You can build a site two ways: as accretions of links and pages that you add and name chaotically as the need arises, and not according to any system or schedule; or, as a carefully thought-out set of sections and pages which are consistently structured, named, and linked, and which correspond to an overall navigational theme that users can handle.

Can you tell our bias?

Actually, like most Web designers, we work in a state that is often a combination of anal-retentive and free-love hippie-child tendencies. Depending on the site's size and our available time, we can either cobble together pages and graphics to produce something; or, spend months with programmers, editors, and information architects trying to figure out how to build a site that can expand sensibly for months or years.

We all yearn for a tool that would answer both needs: a kind of electronic paper and pencil that would let us draw in a site with quick strokes, making multiple illustrations, each serving their own purpose, and erasing and redrawing lines and boxes as the design progresses.

The electronic design sketches would eliminate the tedium of drawing each individual box or line, and as we move pages around, the lines would redraw themselves. Sounds like an unreachable ideal, but GoLive's new design features aren't too far from utopia.

GoLive vastly improved its prototyping and mapping features in version 5, allowing a designer to map the outlines of a site, including links between pages and hierarchical relationships, with a minimum of effort. After a few keystrokes and mouse movements, your prototyped site is completely reorganized on screen. (They also renamed the feature from the Site tab to the Designs tab.)

The approach GoLive takes to prototyping is to let you use templates and blank pages to sketch in the structure of a site. You can edit those pages directly in a staging area, in which nothing is committed to the existing live site until you're ready. That way, you can test and work on the structure and content without disturbing the rest of the site.

GoLive lets you develop any number of sets of these prototypes at the same time without interfering with one another. When you're ready, you can stage these prototypes into the live site, while still being able to revoke a prototype after it's become live.

These prototypes can be used as roughs for clients or for yourself to preview how new features and sections of a site might look and work. In a collaborative environment, different people could open the same site file (over a file server, for example) and create and annotate different designs.

TIP:
Old-
Fashioned
Linking

You can, of course, still add pages and links to the live site without using these design features; we discuss how to do that in the next chapter, *Files, Folders, and Links*.

The Design menu includes two site mapping views, navigation and link, which are similar to those views in GoLive 4. However, the link view of a Web site now works correctly, unlike in version 4, so that you can see the full in-

What's New in 5

Adobe completely revamped the prototyping and mapping features. The Designs tab and Design menu are entirely new, and the whole idea of prototyping offline (i.e., not inside your existing site) and being able to have several prototypes in progress at the same time is a huge addition. Some of the features that help you create designs come over from GoLive 4's Site tab, but most of them are new.

And GoLive even has improved mapping features. The Navigation View and Links View in GoLive 4 seemed hard to distinguish; they were just never entirely fleshed out. But in GoLive 5, the Links View truly shows you all links. Any page you bring up can show all outgoing and incoming links, including links to pages that are that page's parent. You can create quite a cyclical view. This feature alone will cause you print thousands of pages you otherwise wouldn't to better visualize and troubleshoot your current site designs.

The Navigation View is only slightly changed. You can still insert pending links via its interface, but it also offers a high degree of assistance in visualizing relationships, including a very cool Spotlight feature that puts big colored shapes behind all files that meet a set of constraints. For instance, you can choose to highlight all members of a "family," meaning parents, siblings, and children (see Figure 20-1).

Figure 20-1
Highlighting
family
relationships

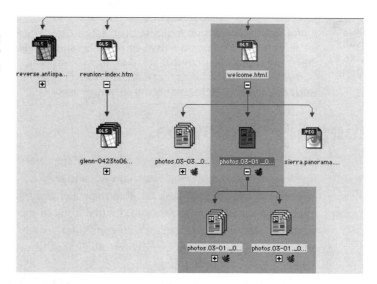

bound and outbound links for every page. The Navigation view lets you add pages and pending links to the live site.

NEW IN 5:
Site, Site, Site

The Designs tab was called the Site tab in GoLive 4, which was pretty confusing. You had the Site tab, the Site window, the Site menu, and so forth. GoLive 5 cleans up the nomenclature by renaming the tab to Designs, and adding a Design menu full of all the specific features used in the Designs tab.

TIP:
Family
Relationships

GoLive follows the standard Web design practice of naming pages "parents" that are above other pages in a hierarchy; the pages below parents are their "children." "Siblings" are pages down a level in the hierarchy from a parent that are all linked from the same parent, and may be linked to each other (see Figure 20-2).

Figure 20-2
Family
relationships

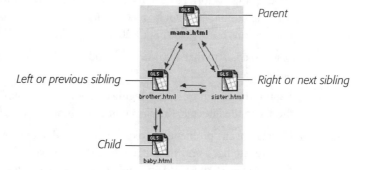

TIP:
**Existing
Sites Stand
Alone**

Unfortunately, there is no facility to build a new design based on existing sites or sections. For instance, a parent could be the home page, with the children being the section divisions that are all siblings to each other. GoLive sometimes allows left and right siblings that indicate previous or next items in a sequence, such as a tutorial that has an organized flow of pages.

Creating Site Prototypes

The design features in GoLive are built around the idea that you start with a site map on paper or in your head, and you add sections (pages with special properties) and pages to flesh out that map, including the relationship between pages as siblings, parents, and children. You can also add pending links between pages that get stored for later application to items on the page. And you can leave notes like stickies all over a design, either attached to a page or just floating out there in space.

The basic order of prototyping a site works like this. The first three steps can happen concurrently (see Figure 20-3).

1a. Add sections and pages that correspond to all the pages you need in the new site or area you're creating.

1b. Create pending links between pages that correspond to connections you need to make in the actual content of a page.

1c. Nail down the overall structure and prettify the appearance using tools to clean up alignment, distribution, and display, and add visual groups to lump content together. Customize with the View Controller.

2. Fill pages with content and add the pending links to the items on pages that need to be linked in.

3. Send in digital form to clients and/or others for comments. (If you're working alone, just look at it yourself.) Make remarks using the Annotations feature (see Figure 20-4).

4. Test and confirm that all content is good, and that all comments in annotations are answered.

5a. Submit the design from the staging area into the current local version of the site in the Files tab. Confirm that everything works as you expect.

5b. If there are any problems, revoke the design (which moves the files out of the live site back into the staging area), and make notes and/or corrections. Repeat steps 5a and 5b as necessary (see Figure 20-5).

6. Upload the new files to your live site via FTP or WebDAV.

Figure 20-3
Prototyping
a site

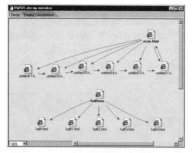

Step 1a: Add pages & sections

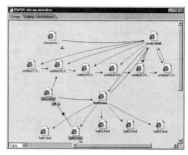

Step 1b: Create pending links

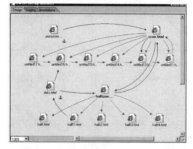

Step 1c: Nail down structure

Figure 20-4
Annotating a
design

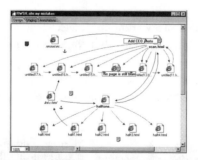

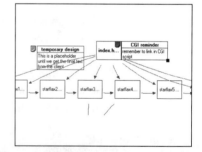

Step 3: Use Annotations to mark up design for review and feedback.

Figure 20-5
Submitting a
design

Step 5: Submit design

Step 6: Upload new files

Most of the actions you can perform in the Designs tab are fully undoable (i.e., you can revert after committing to the action), from dragging objects around the tab, adding and removing pages, and changing links. Consult the History palette to go backward and forward. (See Chapter 3, *Palettes and Parts*, for more about the History palette.)

Managing Designs

Like many features in GoLive, the Designs tab appears to have no functionality when you first open it. It's a tabula rasa (empty slate), which can be daunting. But it's easy to start adding to the tab and to get up and running with prototyping.

Once again, GoLive defeats simplicity by naming two similar things the same. The Designs tab of the Site window is where all the designs from a site are stored. The Design (note singular) tab of a specific site design is where the pages and relationships are stored. A single site can have many site designs, so you could have several design windows (each containing a Design tab) on screen at once.

We call an individual layout a "design" and the view into it a "design window." The Design, Staging, and Annotations tabs appear in a design window.

Adding a design. With a Site window open, select New Site Design from the Design menu, or in the Designs tab select New Design from the contextual menu (see Figure 20-6). A new design is untitled and empty, and represented by a icon in the Designs tab's design list. The Designs tab can hold multiple designs which are alphabetized by name, although you can sort by modification date as well.

Figure 20-6
Adding a new site design

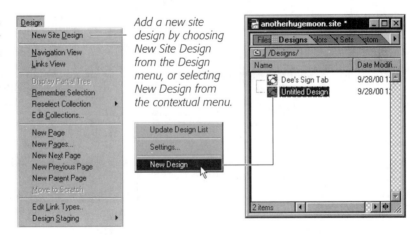

Add a new site design by choosing New Site Design from the Design menu, or selecting New Design from the contextual menu.

Opening a design. Double-click the design to open a design window in which you create your prototypes and relationships between parts, as well as stage and annotate designs. There are three tabs corresponding to these tasks in every design window: Design, Staging, and Annotations.

Deleting a design. Select one or more designs and choose Clear or Delete from the Edit menu or contextual menu, or simply press Command-Delete (Mac) or Delete (Windows). GoLive prompts you about whether you want to delete the designs; this action cannot be reverted with Undo.

Changing a design's name. The design's name is highlighted after creation so you can directly edit it. You can also select the name later and modify it, or use the Site Design Inspector.

Building Site Designs

The Design tab of a design window provides you with a drawing pad in which you can sketch out the structure and content of your new site, new section, or new pages. The Design tab of a design window is empty when first opened, just like the Site window's Designs tab.

Designs are created by dragging the Generic Page icon or the Design Section icon from the Site tab of the Objects palette. A section is a special kind of page to which you can assign properties that apply to new pages created inside that section. You can also drag in Stationery items and pages you've already created that are listed in the Files tab of the Site window. Links can be created automatically when you insert new pages, or by using Point & Shoot to connect pages.

You can drag pages all over the place and GoLive preserves the relationships between them, redrawing any link lines as needed. Once you've achieved optimal results, you can clean up the Design tab through alignment and distribution features. It's a visual tool, so don't be afraid to act visually.

Viewing Designs

The Design works like a big canvas, similar to the canvas or pasteboard found in desktop publishing programs. You generally see only a fraction of the canvas at any given time (depending on the size of your window and the complexity of your prototype). GoLive provides several tools you can use to pan and zoom around.

Drag. Holding down the spacebar turns the cursor into a grabber hand just like in other Adobe applications (see Figure 20-7). You can then click and slide the view around.

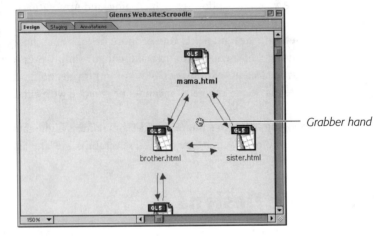

Grabber hand

Zoom menu. The Zoom menu, located at the lower-left corner of the Design tab, allows you to select a magnification amount; the default is 100 percent, where thumbnail previews are displayed at 72 dpi.

The Zoom menu offers preset enlargement and reduction factors: 10, 20, 50, 80, 100, and 150 (see Figure 20-8). You can also select Fit Site in Window or Fit in Window, and GoLive reduces the site map to very tiny proportions to accommodate the window size. The Zoom menu displays the currently selected percentage.

The Zoom menu also appears in the Display tab of the Design View Controller. You can enter values directly into the a field as well as select default values from the popup menu.

Figure 20-8
Zoom menu
presets

TIP:
Thumbnail
Scaling

The page thumbnails GoLive creates are sized for 72 dpi at 100 percent view in the Design tab, and are pixilated at larger sizes.

Magnifying glass. Holding down Option (Mac) or Shift (Windows) turns the cursor into a zoom-in magnifying glass to enlarge the site map. Clicking once zooms to 200 percent and changes the icon to a zoom-out magnifying glass which, if you click, zooms back to 100 percent.

You can also zoom to higher magnifications (up to 500 percent) by dragging to create a marquee, which fills the window with the selected area. Dragging works with both a zoom-in and zoom-out magnifying glass.

Site Navigator palette. For true ease in panning around the site map, invoke the Site Navigator palette from the Window menu (see Figure 20-9). The Site Navigator gives you a thumbnail of the entire design canvas, with a marquee which you drag to control the section that appears in the main window.

Figure 20-9
Site Navigator
palette

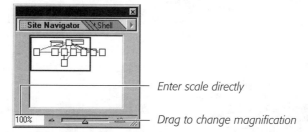

Enter scale directly

Drag to change magnification

When you drag the marquee, the window scrolls as you drag; or just click points on the site thumbnail, and the Design tab instantly changes its focus to display that section.

Zoom options are available at the bottom of the palette. Clicking the larger and smaller "mountain" buttons increases or decreases the design window's zoom factor by standard increments. Or, you can use the slider to dynamically change the zoom value. Just to round things out, you can enter a value into the Zoom field at lower left. The palette is resizable within small bounds (see Figure 20-10). If you need a bigger preview, try the Panorama pane.

Figure 20-10
Resizing the
Site Navigator
palette

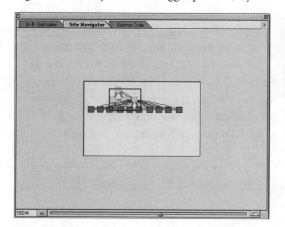

You can only resize the palette within certain bounds.

Panorama pane. The Panorama pane works remarkably like the Site Navigator palette, but it's an integrated part of a design window and shows a larger area (see Figure 20-11). It's also a proxy for selection, just like the Table palette is for tables: you can select items in the Panorama exactly like you would in the main design window. Display the Panorama pane by checking its box in the Display tab of the Design View Controller. (See "Design View Controller," later in this chapter.)

Figure 20-11
Panorama
pane

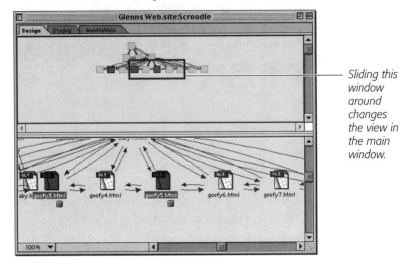

Sliding this window around changes the view in the main window.

Pages

The simplest way to start a design is to add pages—whether empty or derived from Stationery—to the blank design canvas. Once placed in a design, pages can be opened and edited just like a page in the Files tab.

Adding by dragging. Drag a Generic Page icon from the Site tab of the Objects palette, or drag Stationery from the Site Extras tab (see Figure 20-12). If you simply drag the page into the window, a new page icon is created which is either blank (Generic Page) or a copy of the Stationery.

New generic pages are named "untitled" plus a number and extension (like "untitled5.html"). Stationery pages are named "New from " plus the name of the Stationery and a number and extension (like "New from template2.htm").

If you drag near an existing page, a new relationship is added via links, depending on the point on the compass you drag to and indicated by a solid bar near the existing page's icon. Dragging to the top creates a parent relationship; to the left, a previous sibling; to the right, a next sibling; and below, a child (see Figure 20-13).

If the page you drag near is derived from Stationery, the new page is also copied from the same Stationery. If the page is a section, the section rules for naming and folders apply.

Figure 20-12
Adding pages

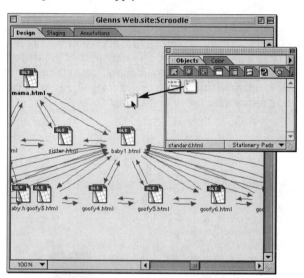

Figure 20-13
Dragging
relationships

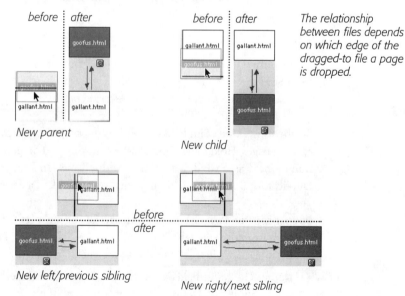

The relationship between files depends on which edge of the dragged-to file a page is dropped.

Adding by menu. You can also add pages by choosing one of the new page items from the Design menu or the contextual menu with an existing page selected. You can't add more pages unless one is already there.

The options in the Design menu are New Page (which creates a new child), New Next Page, New Previous Page, and New Parent. In the contextual menu, these options appear as items in the New submenu. (The New Pages item is explained in "Sections," below.)

TIP:
Smart
Directions

The GoLive engineers threw in a neat feature for helping you create site sketches. Create a page and then add a parent or child to that page. Drag that parent or child left or right, up or down. Now, create the next relationship from it— GoLive remembers the direction you dragged, and adds the latest item in that same direction (see Figure 20-14). Pretty nifty!

Figure 20-14
Predicting
positions

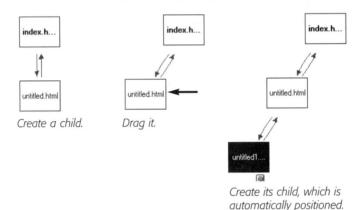

Create a child.   Drag it.

Create its child, which is
automatically positioned.

Just like with dragging in a new page, if the page you selected is derived from Stationery, the new page uses the same Stationery; if it's a section, the new page uses the section's rules, as described below.

Duplicating (Mac). Similar to using Stationery, you can create duplicates of existing pages. Hold down Option when clicking and dragging a page or section in the design window to create the duplicate. (In a surprising glitch, the Duplicate option under the Edit menu doesn't work in a design.)

Page Inspector. Pages have their own special Page Inspector, which is entirely different from the Files tab's Page Inspector (see Chapter 21, *Files, Folders, and Links*). It has a single tab, Object, with four fields (see Figure 20-15).

• **Name.** The Name field has nothing to do with any underlying HTML; it's used only in the Design tab when you view the name of files by their

Figure 20-15
Page Inspector

"design name." (See "Design View Controller," later in this section, for details on customizing the display using the Design View Controller.)

- **Target Dir.** A new page is placed in your default directory for new pages, which is set in the Site pane of Preferences in the field marked Folder for Generated Items. If you enter a name in Target Dir, however, GoLive puts this page into the directory you specify. You can use slashes to create subdirectories; each slash creates a new directory and GoLive creates any folders that don't exist.

> **TIP:**
> **Revoking Directories**
>
> Under "Staging," later in the chapter, we discuss how you move a prototype into the live site. If you've specified new directories, GoLive creates them, but it doesn't delete them if you revoke the design.

- **Filename.** The filename is the actual name of the file. Changing it here modifies the name of the file on the local hard drive.

> **TIP:**
> **Filename Constraints**
>
> The Design tab doesn't honor Filename Constraints; it allows you to name a file anything. Read about Filename Constraints in Chapter 21, *Files, Folders, and Links*.

- **Page Title.** The page title is the text placed between Title tags in the Head section of an HTML page. (This is one of about nine ways to change the title of a page in GoLive.)

Sections

Pages are fine, but you have to add them one at a time and name them individually. What if you create a template for an entire set of pages—a new section of the site—and want to add five or even 50 pages for that section? The Design tab's section feature helps with that task.

Sections look and act like pages, but they have additional properties assigned to them in the Section tab of the Section Inspector that allow you to automate adding new pages as children. Adding pages then becomes a cookie cutter operation in which the section is the template for the naming, location, and contents.

TIP:
Object Tab of Section Inspector

The Object tab of the Section Inspector is identical in appearance and function to the Object tab of the Page Inspector described earlier.

Adding sections. You add a section to a design through one method only—surprising for GoLive—which is to drag the Design Section icon from the Site tab of the Objects palette into the Design tab (see Figure 20-16). You can also convert pages into sections; see below.

The section symbol on a page looks like a regular page except that its name displays in bold type and is named by default with the home page name specified in the Site pane of Preferences. This is a small problem, as you have to either pay close attention to the file or select it and check out which Inspector palette appears.

Section Inspector's Section tab. All the properties of a section are defined through the Section tab of the Section Inspector (see Figure 20-17).

- **New Filename.** The name you enter here becomes the stub prefix for any pages created through this section. If you enter "scooby", pages are created

Figure 20-16
Adding a
section

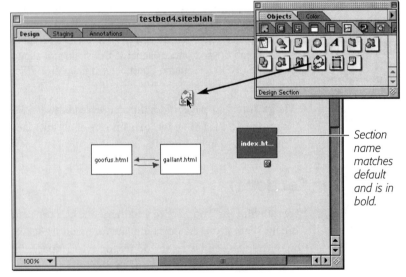

Section name matches default and is in bold.

Figure 20-17
Section tab

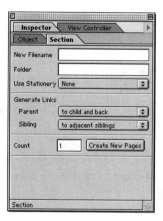

named "scooby1.html", "scooby2.html", and so forth. (The number following the file name varies based on whether you're using Windows or Mac.)

- **Folder.** You can specify an enclosing folder or path with slashes for where
  pages created in this section should be stored.

- **Use Stationery.** Any Stationery in the site is available through this
  popup menu. Choosing a Stationery template creates new pages using
  that template.

- **Generate Links.** The section page is the parent, in this case, so selecting
  items from the Parent popup menu controls which visual links are drawn
  between the section and the pages you're creating. The None option is
  self-explanatory; for the rest, see Figure 20-18. The Sibling popup menu
  affects all the pages created in the section: The To Next Sibling option
  links just from one page to each subsequently created page; To Adjacent
  Siblings links bidirectionally (see Figure 20-19).

Figure 20-18
Link types

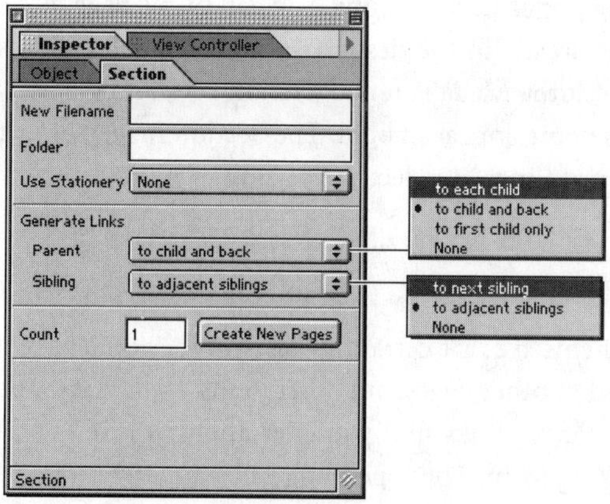

Figure 20-19
Sibling
relationships

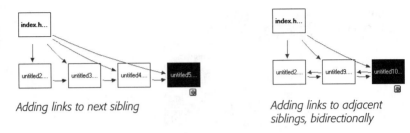

Adding links to next sibling

Adding links to adjacent siblings, bidirectionally

- **Create New Pages.** The section menu gives you a shortcut to creating new pages, as discussed just below. Enter the number of pages to create and click Create New Pages.

Adding pages to sections. You add pages to a section by selecting the section and choosing one of the new page options from the Design menu or contextual menu, or by dragging a Generic Page icon or Stationery template onto the section. With a section selected, the rules of that section apply to any new page created when it's selected or dragged onto. These methods create just a single page.

But if you bring up the Section tab of the Section Inspector, you can use the Create New Pages button to make multiple pages: enter a number in the Count field following the rules in that tab.

The New Pages item in the Design or contextual menu offers similar choices, but you don't need to have a section defined to use section-like rules: you can select any page in the site from which to spring new pages. (The one missing feature in the New Pages dialog is the Folder field, so you must create a section page first in order to nest new pages in a folder.)

Converting pages into sections. You can turn a page into a section by selecting a page already in the design and choosing New Pages from the Design menu. Check the Make Parent a Section box, and GoLive converts the page, making its name appear in bold. The Section Inspector, with its two tabs, appears the next time you select the page.

Links

Pages by themselves are certainly nice, but they only have worth once they've been linked to other pages and other items. In the Design tab, you're creating pending links, or links that you later apply to text and images on the page you're linking from. These pending links appear in two places: in the visual preview you edit in the Design tab of a design window, and in the Pending tab of the Page Inspector, discussed below in "Adding Pending Links."

GoLive offers three kinds of links in the Design tab: hyperlink, navigation, and tour. Navigation links include parent, previous, next, and child which GoLive breaks out as separately defined items. You can also define your own link styles to color-code certain links differently than others; or, you can redefine the colors so that parent and child links are more distinct.

Currently, only the hyperlink and navigation link options work as pending links; the tour link and any links you define on your own are for visual impact only. We expect this will change in a future release.

Link Inspector. Selecting one or more links brings up the Link Inspector, which has blessedly few settings. The Link Type defines the kind of link out of six defaults or any user-defined link types. You can change a link from one type to another through the popup menu.

You can also define new link types or change the color or name of an existing type through the Edit Link Types button. You can't delete or rename the six defaults, although you can change the color assigned to them.

TIP:
Editing Links through Menu

The Design menu also sports the Edit Link Types item for editing links without requiring that a link be selected.

Deflection describes the angle of arc assigned to a link. You can use the prefabricated values in the popup menu or simply drag the handle in the middle of a link to arc it out or in with a much higher degree of control.

Adding navigation links. Navigation links are added when you drag a page onto another page, by using any of the new page items with a page selected, or by using the Create New Pages button in the Section Inspector. These links appear green by default.

Navigation links appear in the Pending tab of the Page Inspector, but they do not have their orientation (parent, child, next, or previous) in the Nav column of that tab because they are not active links; they're still in a staging area.

TIP:
Navigation View Links

If you use the Navigation view of a site map, any links added there show up in the Pending tab with green arrows to indicate their navigational direction. See "Mapping Sites," later in this chapter.

Adding hyperlinks. Use Point & Shoot to add hyperlinks. These appear blue by default. Hyperlinks appear in the Pending tab.

You can't Point & Shoot anywhere except in the Design tab, because you can only link to other files in the same design sandbox. Once you drag anchors in, which are proxies for real pages on your active site, you can link to and from them (see Figure 20-20). See "Anchors," next page.

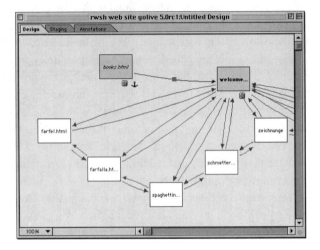

Adding tour and custom links. The only way to add custom links is to convert a link you've made through the methods described for hyperlinks and navigational links. Select the link or links, bring up the Link Inspector, and choose your new link from the popup menu, such as Tour.

Adding any type of link by selection. Another way to create links is to select two or more pages and choose Add Design Line(s) from the contextual menu; it's not available from any other menu. You can choose any type of link from the submenu to add. The order of selecting pages determines the direction of the arrows of the links you add (see Figure 20-21).

Figure 20-21
Page selection
order

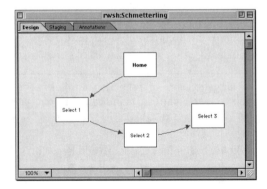

Anchors

If you're creating an annex or new section for an existing site, you need to link in the new pages to at least one point on an existing page—otherwise, how does a user navigate to your new section? You create these links through anchors.

An anchor is an alias or shortcut to a file in the existing site. Drag a file from the Files tab or the Navigation or Links views into the Design tab, and GoLive creates an anchor (see Figure 20-22). You can then use Point & Shoot to link the anchor to an existing page. This adds a pending link on the anchor page. You can have as many anchors as you like. Anchors are identified by their names appearing in italic type.

Figure 20-22
Creating an anchor

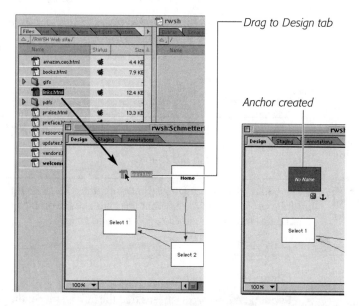

Once the anchor is created, you can treat it just like any other page in the Design tab. You can Point & Shoot links to it from other pages, or use any of the options to create new navigational relationships. You can even use the New Pages menu item to convert the anchor into a section.

Adding Pending Links

After you construct a set of linked pages, you need to fill them with at least *some* content. The links you've added visually are recorded by GoLive as pending links, accessed through the Page Inspector's Pending tab. Open any page in the Design tab and click the Page icon at the top of the page to bring up the Page Inspector. Click the Pending tab.

The Pending tab shows every link to other HTML pages and media files already present on the page, but, more importantly, it also displays any pending links to other objects on the site (see Figure 20-23).

Figure 20-23
Pending tab

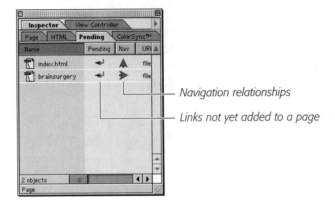

Navigation relationships

Links not yet added to a page

TIP:
Navigation and Pending

Because you can add links to the existing site via the Navigation View, the Pending tab is applicable for those relationships you create as well. See "Mapping Sites," later in this chapter.

TIP:
In & Out Links Palette

While you're editing a page in the Design tab, the In & Out Links palette is a useful tool to help figure out what links are already on a page. It's discussed in great detail in Chapter 21, *Files, Folders, and Links.*

The Pending tab has four columns:

- **Name:** The link's name.

- **Pending:** A blue arrow means that the link is still pending and hasn't been added on the page itself to text or an object.

- **Nav:** This column only applies to pending links added via the Navigation View; see "Mapping Sites," later in this chapter.

- **URL:** Displays the full local path to internal links or media files.

You add objects from the Pending tab onto a page in one of the following three methods. After applying any of them, the pending icon disappears from that object in the Pending tab (see Figure 20-24).

Dragging. Drag the link from the Pending tab onto the page. GoLive creates a hyperlink using the link's file name.

Figure 20-24
Adding
pending links
and objects

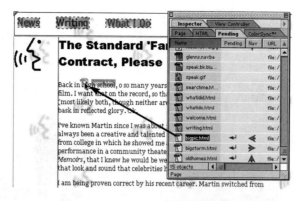

Pending link gets dragged onto a page.

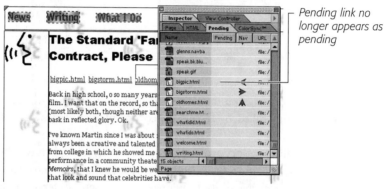

Pending link no longer appears as pending

Selection. First, select text to be linked on the page. With the Page Inspector visible, drag a pending link from the Pending tab onto the selected text.

Other tabs. You can drag pages from the Files tab, Navigation View, or Links View onto an HTML page (whether you have something selected on that page or not). This isn't the most efficient method, nor does it directly use the Pending tab, but it does remove the pending status from the Pending tab once you've dragged the object into the page.

Selection

The selection options center around selecting one or more files and identifying them as a collection you can reselect later. You can make, edit, and retrieve selections in the Design tab as well as the Navigation View and Links View.

TIP:
**You're a
Star!**

Selections are especially useful in conjunction with the Spotlight display option in the Navigation View. Spotlight can highlight a variety of relationships, including selections (see Figure 20-25).

Figure 20-25
Remembering
a selection

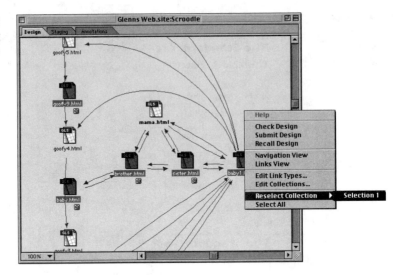

Making a selection. Choose one or more pages and select Remember Selection from the Design or contextual menu. This creates a new selection group called, by default, "Selection " plus a number, such as "Selection 4".

Editing selection. You can't edit the actual files chosen by a given selection through the Edit Selections menu item in the Design or contextual menu, but you can change its default name and assign a different color to the selection.

Toggling selection. The Toggle Collection submenu, available only in the contextual menu, allows you to change the contents of a selection. Confusingly, toggle doesn't toggle the members: this would mean it would add files in your selection that weren't members, and subtract those that were. Instead, if merely adds any files in your selection to the current set (see Figure 20-26).

Retrieving selection. Choose a selection from the Reselect Collection submenu in the Design or contextual menu. The pages in the selection are highlighted so that they can be acted upon as a set.

Grouping

The grouping features allow you to create a colored container into which you place pages; or, you can select pages and have a visual container drawn around them. Groups don't affect any underlying HTML. They're all about appearance and organization.

Figure 20-26
Toggling
selections

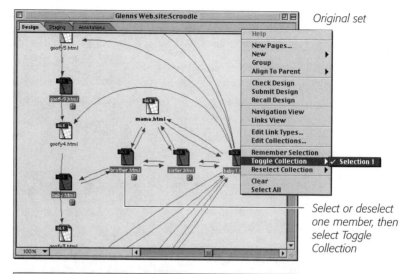

Original set

*Select or deselect
one member, then
select Toggle
Collection*

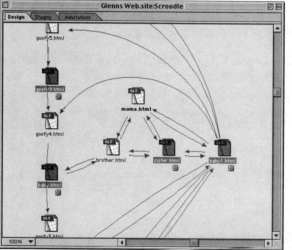

*The next time you
use Reselect
Collection, the
newly-defined
collection is used.*

Creating a group. There are three ways to create groups (see Figure 20-27):

- Drag a Design Group icon from the Site tab of the Objects palette. You can drag files into the newly created group.

- Select one or more pages and select Group from the Edit or contextual menu.

- Select one or more pages and click the Group icon under the Grouping area in the Transform palette.

Figure 20-27
Creating
groups

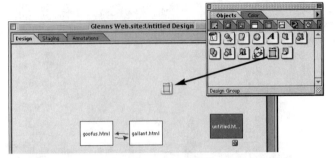

*Drag from
Objects
palette*

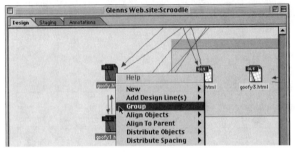

*Use
contextual
menu*

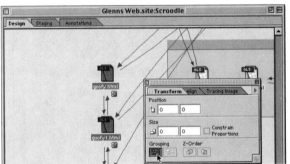

*Group items
in Transform
palette*

Modifying a group. You can drag items in and out of a group at will. The group's borders highlight if the item or items is inside the group. If you slide items around a little, the group's borders enlarge or shrink.

You can also drag groups around the Design tab, in and out of other groups, or near other groups to bump them out of the way.

Group Inspector. You can name and set a color for a group through the Group Inspector. You can also set two preferences. Unchecking Display Title Bar removes the name of a group from the group's top as well as the titlebar. Auto Resize controls whether the group changes shape as you drag items in and out of it.

Ungrouping. Select a group by its edge or titlebar and choose Ungroup from the Edit or contextual menu. You can also click the Ungroup button in the Transform palette under the Grouping area.

Deleting a group. Select any edge of the group or the group's titlebar and press Delete or select Clear from the Edit menu or the contextual menu. This removes the group and all of its enclosed items.

Alignment and Distribution

Like any good page-layout program, GoLive offers tools to better shuffle icons around on screen to clean them up. The alignment and distribution tools, available from menus and palettes, are exactly the same as those available for objects in layout grids. Would we be so crass as to waste your time and several pages by repeating that information here? No way! (See Figure 20-28; also see "Working with Grid Objects" in Chapter 12, *Layout Grids*.)

TIP:
Consistent
Interface

We'd certainly like to thank the engineers for being consistent. It's nice that one set of skills transfers to another part of the program.

Also, you should know that GoLive likes to let the pages rock and roll in the Design tab. Every time you move any file or add one, it seems like GoLive is compelled to rearrange all the links and icons near whatever you changed. The way to avoid this behavior is to turn off Collision Avoidance (unchecking both Horiz. and Vert.) in the Display tab of the Design View Controller, and to uncheck Auto Resize in every group you create; you can't set that as a default behavior. There is no simple way to lock a file or link's position in the design window.

Design View Controller

So far, we've discussed only how to manipulate objects, but GoLive also offers a large list of display options to customize how you view pages and their relationships in the main design window. Click the View Controller and you see two tabs: Design and Display.

TIP:
Panorama
Pane

The Design View Controller also affects the Panorama pane, described below.

Figure 20-28
Aligning and
distributing

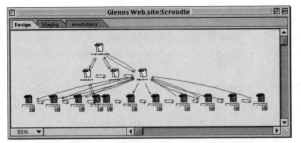

Out of alignment

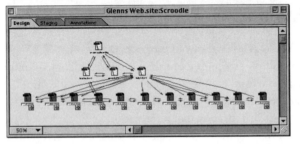

Horizontally aligned

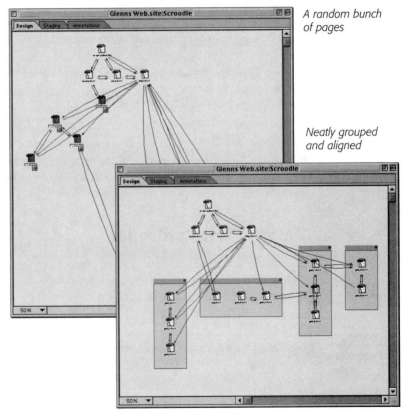

*A random bunch
of pages*

*Neatly grouped
and aligned*

Design Colors

The Design View Controller doesn't set the colors for everything in the design window. The Design Colors settings let you set the background color for all the panes and windows in the Design tab, as well as the colors for links and items (see Figure 20-29).

You can set global defaults for Design Colors through the Preferences dialog box. Open the Site pane and select Design Colors. Design Colors are set on a site-specific basis by clicking the Site Settings button on the Toolbar with a Site window open. Check Site-Specific Settings.

The colors under the Background Colors column set the background for the panes or windows noted. (The Files View doesn't appear to exist; this may be an artifact of some development effort that didn't get implemented.)

The Item Color swatch sets the default color for pages added to a prototype. The Link Colors swatches affect the Navigation View and Links View colors: the Navigation field colors all links in Navigation View; Links covers all links in Links View; and Pending covers pending links when displayed via the View Controller in the Navigation View.

Default Design Link Colors control the links in a design window's Design tab.

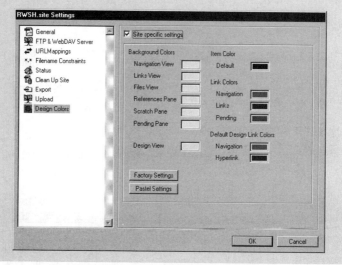

Figure 20-29
Design Colors settings

Design Tab

The Design tab controls the main window's orientation and which panes are displayed.

Orientation. The Tall or Wide settings for orientation affect how the panes arrange themselves, but have no impact on whether links get made from left

to right or top to bottom (see Figure 20-30). (In the Navigation View and
Links View, Orientation affects the display of pages.)

Show Panes. GoLive uses four panes in conjunction with the Design tab of a
design window. In the Design tab, three are available: Panorama, Reference,
and Pending.

TIP:
Site View
Controller

The Site View Controller, described later in this chapter, controls the appearance
of the Pending and Reference panes.

- Panorama is also discussed earlier in the chapter in the sidebar, "Viewing."
  It's a proxy for selection, meaning that you can select items in it just as if
  you were selecting them in the main window. You can drag items around,
  delete them, group them, and edit links. The one thing you can't do is use
  Point & Shoot.

- Reference shows any media items included on a page, such as images and
  QuickTime movies.

Figure 20-30
Orientation

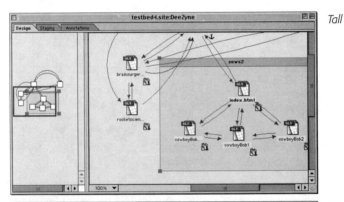

Tall

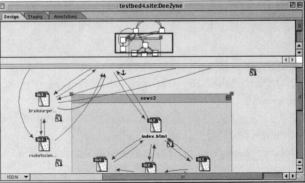

Wide

- Pending displays all pending links. It's identical to the items tagged with a blue arrow in the Page Inspector's Pending tab. GoLive displays a status icon next to pages in the Pending pane to show their status, such as a yield sign for new, empty pages.

Display Tab

The Display tab formats the individual items in the design window's panes.

Show Items As. The Show Items As heading offers four options (see Figure 20-31):

- **Icons:** the icons for objects as seen in the Desktop. The name appears below the page.

- **Thumbnails:** a small rectangle containing HTML page thumbnails, if available, with the item's name below the box. (See the sidebar, "Thumbnails.")

- **Frames:** a box with the page's name inside of it.

- **Ovals:** big, ol' ovals with the page's name nestled in the middle.

Figure 20-31
Show Items As

Icons   Thumbnails   Frames   Ovals

Item Label. The Item Label can be set to Page Title (the name in the Title tags), the File Name (the actual name of the file), or the Design Name (the name set in the Name field of the Object tab of either the Page or Section Inspector). If you set Item Label to Page Title and the page has no title, GoLive wisely displays "No Title." Ditto for Design Name, which displays "No Name."

Grid. The grid settings work here just as in layout grids: they control the minimum increments to which items get snapped. You can turn off both Horizontal and Vertical grid settings to move items around willy-nilly.

Collision Avoidance. This feature allows you to drag pages wherever you want in the design window without two pages overlapping. However, if you want this to happen (to group related pages together in a small space), disable this feature by unchecking both boxes. If you're trying to create a neat, perma-

Thumbnails

Thumbnails are tiny previews of HTML pages which GoLive can generate from the pages' contents. We discuss this feature thoroughly in Chapter 21, *Files, Folders, and Links*. However, thumbnails get used in the Design tab, too, if you set Show Items As to Thumbnails in the Design View Controller or Site View Controller. You can create thumbnails for pages in the Design tab by selecting Update Thumbnails from the Design menu. This can take quite a while to carry out, as GoLive has to open each page, then render and store each thumbnail.

A simpler way to create a thumbnail for a particular page is to open it, make a small change, and save it. GoLive then automatically creates a thumbnail.

nent display of your prototype, you really should disable Collision Avoidance. Otherwise, every new link or page can cause other pages to jump about.

Frame Size. The Frame Size controls the height and width of the page icons in the design window. We don't find much reason to change these unless we want to see more of a thumbnail's preview.

Item Color. You can choose a custom color for each page in a design window. This option is disabled if you are viewing items as icons.

Zoom. This controls the current zoom percentage. See the "Viewing" sidebar, earlier in this chapter.

Site View Controller

The Pending and Reference panes use their own View Controller to handle the objects they show. This is due, in part, to a broader array of files that might show up in these two panes. The main design window and Panorama show only Web pages. The Pending and Reference panes can show any media file or external reference that is already linked to a Web page, that is pending, or is to be linked.

TIP:
Navigation View and Links View

The Site View Controller is virtually identical for these two views. When we discuss them later, we'll reference you back to this section.

Pending Tab and References Tab

The Pending and References tab work exactly like the Display tab of the Design View Controller, described earlier. Orientation modifies how the various panes are displayed in the design window.

Display Tab

The Display tab is mostly the same as that in the Design View Controller. There are a few differences, though.

Graphical or Outline. Graphical view is the default for all panes. Selecting Outline shows the items in the Reference or Pending tab as a list with all their properties, just like in the Files tab (see Figure 20-32). See Chapter 21, *Files, Folders, and Links*, for more information about these properties.

Item Labels. Because the items referenced in the Reference and Pending tabs aren't prospective pages, the Design Name option is excluded here. You can show either the Page Name or File Name.

Cell Size. The Cell Size settings define the maximum width and height for the space for each item's preview or icon. GoLive won't let you reduce it too low, and changing the Height's value doesn't seem to affect the display.

Filter Tab. The Filter tab is common to both the Reference and Pending tabs as well as the Navigation View and Links View. This tab allows you to select which files and link types appear in the panes or views.

Each of the checkboxes is a toggle, controlling whether the file type listed is displayed in the current pane or view (see Figure 20-33). The Toggle Media and Toggle Links buttons don't work exactly as expected. They don't actually toggle the settings (turning inactive ones on and active ones off), but rather turn them all on or all off.

Figure 20-32
Outline view

Figure 20-33
Toggling
selections

The media types are pretty straightforward: GIF, JPEG, and PNG are image types. Link types include the two references found in the External tab—URLs and email addresses—and missing files. The two grayed out items, Links to Self and Cyclic Links, are explained under "Links View," later in this chapter.

Staging

If you made it this far, the rest is a lot easier. Most of the work you do on a prototype site is in the Design tab of a design window. But when you've tweaked the design as much as it needs and you're ready to link it into your existing site, switch to the Staging tab for some straightforward action, Jackson!

TIP:
Anchors

Remember that you can't stage your site until you have created at least one pending link between an anchor and a page in your prototype design. See "Anchors," earlier in the chapter.

Staging a site causes GoLive to copy all or selected files in your prototype to either the default folder for new files (as defined in the Site pane of the Preferences dialog box) or to folders you specified for each file or section when creating them. GoLive keeps track of which files it copies so that it can move them back to the staging area on request.

The Staging tab has three folders: Anchor Pages, Live Pages, and Design Pages. Anchor Pages contain any anchors you've dragged into the Design tab; these pages appear as aliases or shortcuts, just like they do in the Design tab. Live Pages show the pages that you've staged, even though they are actually now located in the site folder itself. The Design Pages folder shows the hierarchy of pages before they are staged into the live site. You can sort files and folders in this tab by any of the column headers.

Check Design

This option—found in the Design Toolbar, the Design Staging submenu of the Design menu, and in the contextual menu—confirms that the contents of the files in your site are up to snuff. The Status column shows typical file problems; for an explanation of these codes, see "Status Icons" in Chapter 21, *Files, Folders, and Links.*

Any problems with staging are reported in the Check column:

- **File in use.** Close the file; GoLive needs all files to be closed in order to stage a page.

- **Target folder.** GoLive can't create the folder you specified for that page in the Target Dir field of the Object tab of either the Page or Section Inspector. Check that you're not asking it to create something impossible.

- **Section name.** The section name you've chosen is already in use in the location you want to locate a section. Rename the section or opt for a different directory through the Section Inspector's Object tab.

- **Stage in scratch.** If the file isn't linked to a navigation hierarchy starting with an anchor page, this error shows up. What it means is that when you stage that page, it doesn't have a connection to the site.

- **File rename.** GoLive needs to rename the file when the design is staged.

Submitting a Design

You can copy files from your design to the live site in one of three ways:

- **Submit Design.** Choose this option from the Design Toolbar, the Design Staging submenu of the Design menu, or the contextual menu to copy all files to the default New Files folder or any folders you specified in the live site.

- **Make Items Live in Site.** This option, available only from the Design Staging submenu of the Design menu, copies any selected items to the live, local copy of the site, allowing a selective staging operation. However, you can only copy items that are children of an anchor page (see Figure 20-34).

- **Make Items Live in Scratch.** The Scratch pane of the Navigation View replaces the old missing files display, showing all files in a site that aren't linked to the main navigation tree. By selecting files and choosing Make Items Live in Scratch from the Design Staging submenu of the Design menu, GoLive copies the selected files in the Design Pages folder to the live site whether or not those files selected are linked to an anchor. You can

Figure 20-34
Make Items
Live in Site

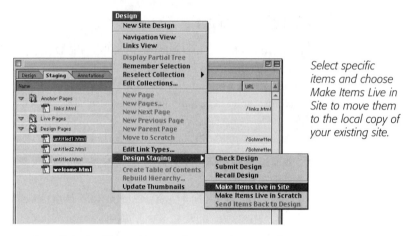

Select specific
items and choose
Make Items Live in
Site to move them
to the local copy of
your existing site.

then link the file or files via the Scratch pane of the Navigation View or
any other linking method.

Recalling a Design

As with submitting, you have a few options for recalling a design. When you
recall a design or files in a design, GoLive moves these files back to the staging
area, removing them from the live site.

*   **Recall Design.** Choose this option from the Design Toolbar, the Design
    Staging submenu of the Design menu, or the contextual menu to copy all
    files back to the staging area.

*   **Send Items Back to Design.** This option, available only from the Design
    Staging submenu of the Design menu, retrieves any selected items in the
    Live Pages folder and moves them out of the live site back to the staging
    folders.

Annotations

Like any good piece of electronic paper, you can put electronic sticky notes on
it (and they don't even leave adhesive on the screen!). Annotations let you
apply notes that can be displayed in a variety of configurations attached to
pages or areas of the drawing board.

TIP:
Ote-nay
Ost-it-pay

We can't call them what you think they should be called or a certain Minnesota-
based firm's lawyers would be after us. Besides, if we revealed the name here
in this book, we'd have to also go on the Web and post it.

Add an annotation by dragging a Design Annotation icon from the Site tab of the Objects palette. If you drop it anywhere in the design window, it stays put. If you drag it near a page, you see an annunciation-style focus (cue angel choir) appear around the page indicating that the note will be stuck to that page when you release the mouse button (see Figure 20-35).

Annotations can be grouped, selected, aligned, and distributed along with page icons (see Figure 20-36).

Annotation Inspector

The Annotation Inspector lets you set the parameters associated with an annotation, such as the text and positioning.

Subject. The subject is the header for the annotation and is displayed separately from the text. It should be relatively short, as it's the item by which the annotation is listed in the Annotations tab.

Figure 20-35
Annunciation
of the
annotation

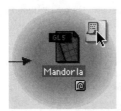

Figure 20-36
Moving
annotations
with pages

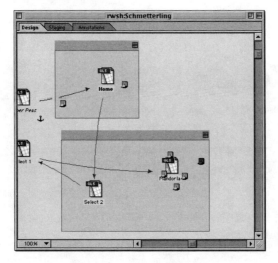

Text. The text is the body of the annotation and can be arbitrarily long.

Display Subject and Display Text. Checking neither, either, or both of these boxes controls whether the respective item displays in the Design tab (see Figure 20-37). These two options are available as Expand Subject and Expand Text in the Annotation submenu of the contextual menu.

Position. You can set the position of the text attached to the annotation to be to the left or right of, below, or centered over the icon (see Figure 20-38).

Annotations Tab

The Annotations tab is the control center for annotations, making it easy to review them all in one place. You can see that there aren't a whole lot of options, but we can suggest a few things.

When you or other designers in your workgroup add annotations, start the subject with your initials or a number (with leading zeroes). This helps organize annotations when it's time to review them. Otherwise, annotations are alphabetized entirely by text or subject (depending on which column you choose; subject is the default).

Figure 20-37
Annotations
with subject
and text

*Subject and text
displayed*

*Subject hidden and
text displayed*

*Subject displayed
and text hidden*

*Subject and text
hidden*

Figure 20-38
Positioning
annotations

Left

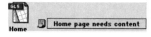

Right

Above

Below

We imagine that in future release of GoLive, you'll be able to set a status to an annotation and/or color code them and/or display only active annotations that haven't been dealt with.

Mapping Sites

Although GoLive offers a powerful prototyping tool, it can't show or modify pages in your existing site. To visualize and add pending links and new pages to your current site, you need to use one of GoLive's two mapping views: Navigation and Links. Both views are available from the Design menu or from the contextual menu in any Design tab.

TIP:
Accessing Views

The two mapping views don't show up as an item in the Window menu, so if the window displaying the view is obscured, you must go to the Design menu and select Navigation View or Links view.

The two views represent two distinct approaches. Navigation View shows the top-down organization of a site, where the home page is the root, and pages are shown linked by their relationship to one another. Navigation also allows you to add new pages and pending links in a similar manner to a design window. Links View works much like the In & Out Links palette, showing all the inbound and outbound links from every page. This makes it easy to see the relationship of any page or file in a site to every other file.

Views Interface

The Navigation View and Links View share many features in common for viewing and handling files.

Opening. Double-clicking a file in either view opens it. If it's an HTML file, it opens in GoLive. For other files, the preferences you set take precedence for controlling which applications open which files (see Chapter 21, *Files, Folders, and Links.*)

Revealing files. Simply selecting a file reveals it in the Files tab of the Site window (see Figure 20-39). This saves a vast amount of time by allowing you to use either view as a navigation map for your site. No more clicking through endless folders and scrolling. You can select one or more files at the same time.

Figure 20-39
Revealing files
via View

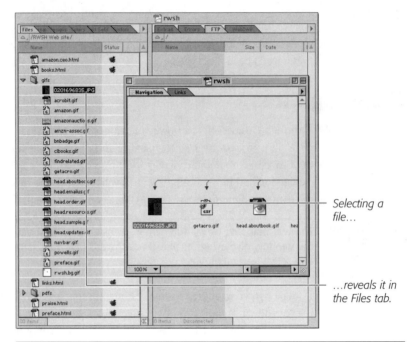

Selecting a
file...

...reveals it in
the Files tab.

**Closing Up
Shop**

After we've messed around in the Navigation View or Links View, we find our Files tab to be really out of sorts—practically every folder is opened. On a big site, it's a mess! But there a simple solution. 1. Click anywhere in the Files tab. 2. Select All from the Edit or contextual menu. 3. Command-Option-left arrow (Mac) or Control-Alt-left arrow (Windows). This collapses all the folders back down again, closing each one as GoLive carries out the task. When you reopen any folder, the ones beneath it are also closed.

**Status and
Color**

If you assign any Status labels to page or files, the Navigation View and Links View display those items using the color associated with that label. It's a handy way to see what's going on all at once, especially when scanning via the Panorama pane.

Graphical view. The Graphical option in the Site View Controller's Display tab displays pages as icons, thumbnails, frames, or ovals. You can control spacing and the size of the preview, just like in the Pending and Reference panes as discussed earlier in this chapter.

You can open and close files above and below a given page by clicking a plus sign or minus sign. If the plus sign is showing, that means that files exist as children below or parents that page in the Navigation View, or that page has additional links inbound or outbound in the Links view (see Figure 20-40).

Figure 20-40
Collapsing and
expanding
links

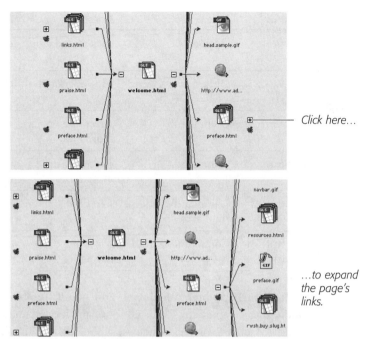

Click here...

*...to expand
the page's
links.*

Selecting any page and clicking the Unfold All button in the Design Toolbar completely expands all links below the current one in the Navigation View, or just a single level in the Links View.

Although the Graphical view doesn't offer a method to collapse or expand all from a given point, there a simple way out. Switch to Outline, collapse or expand as needed (all or some), and then switch back to Graphical.

Outline view. The Display tab's other option is Outline, which turns the view of relationships (link or navigation) into a file list with status and other information, just like in the Files tab. Opening a file by clicking its triangle (Mac) or plus-sign (Windows) shows the children (Navigation View) or outbound links (Links View). You can also use a variety of keyboard shortcuts to expand and collapse single and multiple levels (see Table 20-1).

Remembering selections. You can use the Remember Selection and Reselect Collection features just as you can in the Design tab.

Page and other Inspectors. Selecting an item brings up the appropriate Inspector with the same range of offerings as if you were in the Files tab and had selected one or more files.

Table 20-1
Keyboard
shortcuts for
expanding and
collapsing in
Outline view
(any pane)

Windows	Mac	Action	Result
Alt	Option	click closed icon	expand all from that point
Alt	Option	click open icon	collapse all from that point
Right arrow	Command	select one or more files	expand selections one level
Left arrow	Command	select one or more files	collapse selections one level
Control-Alt- right arrow	Command-Option- right arrow	select one or more files	expand all selections
Control-Alt- left arrow	Command-Option- left arrow	select one or more files	collapse all selections

Finder (Mac)/Explorer (Windows), Edit menu, Toolbar, and contextual menu. You can apply any file-based command located under the Site menu's Finder (Mac) or Explorer (Windows) submenus, the Edit menu, the Toolbar, and the contextual menu. You can also use the Change References command, or the Point & Shoot icon in the In & Out Links palette, to redirect files and links, including pointing at files in the site map itself (see Figure 20-41).

Deleting files. If you press the Delete key or choose Clear from the Edit or contextual menu, the selected file or files are thrown into whichever trash you specified (see "Trash," Chapter 21, *Files, Folders, and Links*).

GoLive warns you about deleting files, but if you have multiple items selected, all of them are thrown into the trash, and you have sort the trash to restore their locations. The History palette and Undo don't help out here.

If you choose to use GoLive's Site Trash in the Extras tab, which is the program's default, you can drag any item you trash back to where it belongs in the Files tab.

Navigation View

The Navigation View organizes the contents of a site hierarchically starting with the home page. Each link from the home page is listed as a child; each page in the site is listed just once, as the child of the first page that links it (see Figure 20-42).

Figure 20-41
File-based
commands

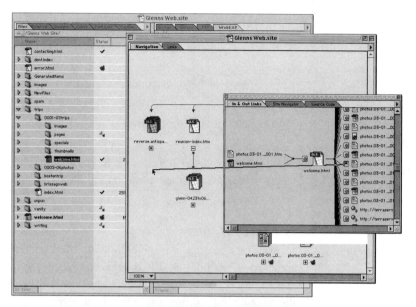

Figure 20-42
Navigation
View

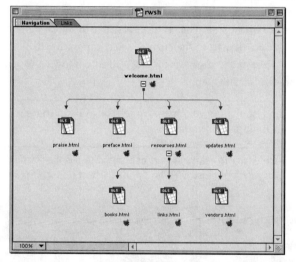

This is not always how a site is organized. For instance, if you use a common navigation bar on every page, those items are referenced just from the first page on which they appear. The Links View (described in more detail later) helps sort through that particular set of issues, however, by showing every link.

Fortunately, virtually every aspect of the interface for Navigation View is identical to the Design tab of a design window. You can zoom, use the Site

Navigator palette, add panes through the Site View Controller, use the grabber hand to move pages around, etc. However, there are a few key differences:

- Navigation View shows only pages that exist in the live site; the Design tab shows prototype pages that are in the staging area.

- You can't rearrange pages in Navigation View; they are locked to the grid. You can change spacing, however.

- The Scratch pane can be enabled in Navigation View, showing files in the site folder that aren't linked into the navigational hierarchy. These can then be dragged into the Navigation View to be added as pending links to existing pages.

Customizing View

The Site View Controller for the Navigation View matches the Design tab's Design View Controller closely, so we won't repeat the identical items (see Figure 20-43). (Consult "Design View Controller" and "Site View Controller" in the "Prototyping" section earlier in this chapter.)

Display Partial Tree. This feature, available in the Design menu, truncates the Navigation view from the current selection on down. This allows you to see just a piece of the site at once. The option is a toggle, so selecting it again restores the full site map.

TIP:
Narrow Esc

You can also narrow your focus by selecting one or more pages and hitting the Esc key to display only those files.

TIP:
Printing Partial

It's much easier to print out part of a site with Display Partial Tree selected. That way, you can show just what you think is most important.

Figure 20-43
Navigation View's Site View Controller

TIP:
Table of Contents

The Navigation View offers a table of contents builder that's based on the files you're showing in that view when you select Create Table of Contents from the Design menu. The TOC GoLive generates is always a plain text file; hopefully, a future release will add TOC placeholders, so you can update a template with new pages without having to regenerate and rebuild a file.

Navigation tab. The Navigation tab offers a great and unique feature that you'll find yourself using all the time: Spotlight. By selecting one of the five options for Spotlight you can view relationships between multiple pages in an extremely clear highlighted fashion (see Figure 20-44). GoLive puts a spotlight or highlight around the items in question; in the case of Pending, it actually adds more link arrows. The five types of Spotlight work as follows:

- **Family.** Choosing Family and selecting a single page highlights the parent, siblings, and children of that page, if any or all of those exist.

- **Incoming.** Selecting any file highlights all files or items that point to that file; this works for media and HTML pages.

- **Outgoing.** Ditto as Incoming, but selecting any file highlights anything the file links to.

- **Pending.** Pending puts a spin on Spotlight by introducing a link between all files that have pending links to one another. This is a great aid for figuring out what's left to link in. Unfortunately, you can't drag files from the Navigation view onto pages to create links.

- **Selection.** Remember our friend Remember Selection? Well, not only can you select multiple files and create new collections of selections in the two maps of your site, but you can also Spotlight any collection you've already made. Note that the selection doesn't reselect the files; it just highlights them.

You can also show all four panes listed in the Navigation tab: Panorama, Reference, and Pending, which work just like they do in the Design tab, as well as Scratch.

- **Panorama.** Panorama is even more useful in Navigation View, as the number of files shown at once can be staggering. We like to select items in Panorama or hover over them to see their names. It's a great way to select multiple items with a marquee, too (see Figure 20-46).

- **Scratch.** Scratch shows all pages in the site that aren't linked into your main navigation hierarchy (see Figure 20-46). You can drag pages out of any of these into the main navigation window to add new pending links (see "Adding Links and Pages," below).

Figure 20-44
Spotlighting
options

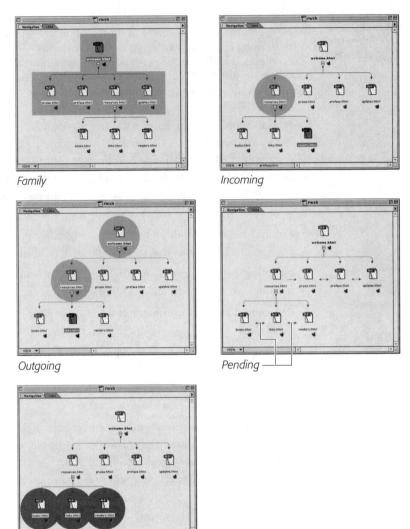

Family

Incoming

Outgoing

Pending

Selection

- **Reference.** Reference works just the same as in the Design tab, showing any items referenced on the selected page or pages.

- **Pending.** This shows you all the items pending for any selected file or files. As you add real links to pages that have pending links, these items disappear from the Pending tab.

Display tab. This tab is discussed under "Site View Controller," earlier in this chapter, and "Views Interface," earlier in the chapter. The only unique aspect is

Figure 20-45
Panorama
selection

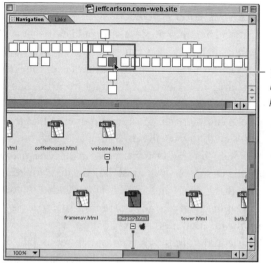

You can select items using Panorama as a proxy for the actual files.

Figure 20-46
Scratch pane

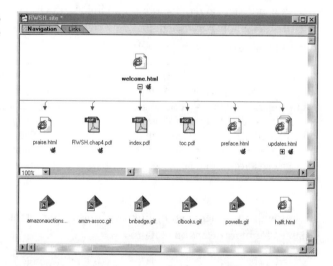

that with Outline selected, you can't display the Panorama pane through the Navigation tab of the Site View Controller.

Filter tab. This is identical to the Reference and Pending tabs Filter tab described under "Site View Controller," earlier in this chapter. The HTML Pages checkbox is disabled because you really have to show HTML pages to show the Navigation View!

Adding Links and Pages

The Navigation Hierarchy mode lets you add entirely new pages to a site just as you would in the Design tab of a design window. (You have to set Navigation View to Graphical in the Display tab of the Site View Controller.)

You can drag in a Generic Page icon from the Site tab of the Objects palette or a Stationery file from the Site Extras tab of the Objects palette or the Reference or Pending pane. You can also drag in files from elsewhere in the Navigation View. Or, you can select a file and click one of the New buttons (Next, Previous, Child, and Parent Pages) in the Design Toolbar.

Unlike the Design tab, you must drag the item you're adding on top of an existing file. Blank pages and Stationery are added to your default new files folder, while other items already exist in the site; so, a pending link is simply added, but the file itself is otherwise unaffected.

With Orientation in the Navigation tab set to Tall, dragging left adds a pending parent link, top and bottom add pending next and previous links, and dragging right adds a pending child link. With Orientation set to Wide, the traditional top: parent, left: previous, right: next, and bottom: child relationships apply.

TIP:
Dragging around Media

If you drag a file on top of a media file, you can only drag it to the parent, next, or previous compass points. Media can't have children—a sad, but true fact. The same behavior happens if you drag in a media file on top of other files, HTML or otherwise, in the Navigation View.

Granted, you can have links that come out of a PDF, SWF, or QuickTime file, but you cannot create these as pending links in the Navigation View because GoLive can't access pending links for anything but HTML files.

The pending links you add via this method still have to be put on a page just as with any other pending link. See "Add Pending Links," earlier in this chapter, for more details on that process.

Links View

The Links View is a hall of mirrors: links linking to links linking to links (you're back on the chain gang). The Links View lets you see the full panoply of media and HTML references to and from any item or page in a site. Many of the features work like those in Navigation, so we've highlighted just the unique parts here in the main display window and the Site View Controller's Links and Filter tabs.

Links display. The main display shows files with link lines between them. It also shows the status icons next to each file; these are discussed in Chapter 21, *Files, Folders, and Links.*

You can select any file and choose Move to Center from the Design menu to make the world rotate around it: GoLive shows just the inbound and outbound links for that file (see Figure 20-47). (It's the equivalent of Show Partial Tree in the Navigation view.)

Figure 20-47
Using Move
to Center

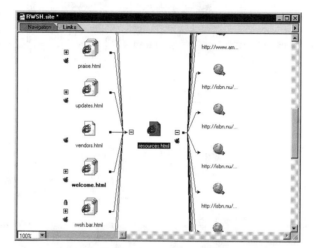

The selected file becomes the center of the axis around which links are shown.

TIP:
Escape to
the Center

Similar to the Navigation View, selecting a file and pressing the Escape key is the equivalent of selecting Move to Center from the Design menu.

Selecting a file can appear odd: because each file can show up many times in the Links View, selecting a single file actually selects all instances of that file in the current display. Any changes you make to the file obviously affect all views of it because it's really the same file (see Figure 20-48).

Links tab. The Links tab lets you turn Incoming Links and Outgoing Links on or off. Turning both off is senseless, as you would be left with a single page in the middle; however, these are checkboxes, because you need to be able to have both or either turned on.

The Explore choices are split between Multiple and Single Link Paths. If you have Multiple Link Paths selected, each time you click a plus sign to open a node, it simply opens it without affecting any other items displayed. With Single Link Paths selected, all other open nodes at that level are closed when the new node is opened (see Figure 20-49).

Figure 20-48
Selecting a file

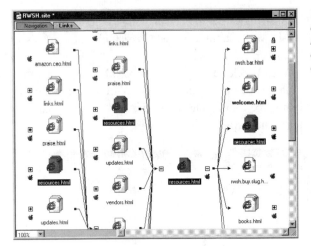

*The same file
can appear
many times, so
all instances
are selected.*

Figure 20-49
Choosing Link
Paths

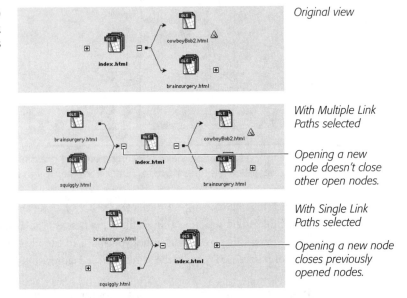

Original view

*With Multiple Link
Paths selected*

*Opening a new
node doesn't close
other open nodes.*

*With Single Link
Paths selected*

*Opening a new node
closes previously
opened nodes.*

Filter tab. Two options in the Filter tab are only available for the Links View: Links to Self and Cyclic Links. If you enable Links to Self, GoLive shows incoming and outgoing links that point to the file from which those links emerge (see Figure 20-50). Turning this off can simplify the display, although it reduces the amount of information you're seeing, too.

If you turn on Cyclic Links, GoLive displays self-referencing links. For example, suppose you have a navigation bar with three links that appears on every

Figure 20-50
Filtering links

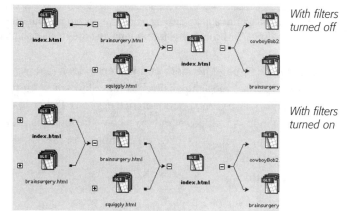

With filters turned off

With filters turned on

page. If you've selected one of those three pages, the Cyclic Links option displays that page as if it were a separate page, because the link to itself is present.

Printing

It seems that printing a site map was not a top priority for GoLive's developers, as there are no options, and the printed output is not great. When you print from any part of the Design tab, GoLive essentially prints out a screen grab, tiling the onscreen map onto several pages. (These features are unchanged from GoLive 4.)

You cannot control tiling, nor preview the results. Lines around objects scale to be hairline thin or monstrously large. Whichever colors you choose in the Design Colors settings for backgrounds and items get used in the printing process, whether you're creating Acrobat PDFs or printing to a color output device.

**TIP:
Collapsing Views**

When you want to print just selected portions of the site map, collapse the hierarchies that don't need to appear on the printout.

**TIP:
Print at 100 Percent**

The best output we get is at 100-percent view. The type looks reasonable, and the thumbnails or other graphics display without too much pixelization.

**TIP:
Print PDF; Edit in Illustrator**

You can print your site map to a PDF file and then open it in Adobe Illustrator to tweak the previews and type for better visual allure.

You can also print a links display using the popup popout menu of the In & Out Links palette. This can useful for printing just the relationships to one file.

Customizing page headers and footers (Mac). GoLive for Macintosh has settings in the Page Setup dialog box that allow you to customize the text that appears on the top and bottom of each page (see Figure 20-51). (GoLive 4 and 5 for Windows lack these options, although Windows previews output in a sort of funky manner.) GoLive offers choices for the left, middle, and right of the header and footer:

- **Date:** the current date
- **Title:** the site file's name
- **Username:** Whatever name is entered in File Sharing (Macintosh)
- **Page Number**

You can also set whether a line appears below the header and above the footer.

Figure 20-51
Print options

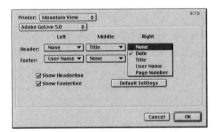

Macintosh print options

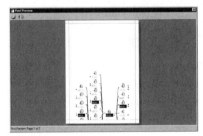

Windows print preview

The Big Picture

By combining prototyping in your design stage and mapping your completed site, you can achieve a real big picture—graphical, even—of how your site is built and continues to be expanded. Using these features, you not only get to work out ideas, but put them into action with a minimum of fuss, and then see how they work out.

CHAPTER 21

Files, Folders, and Links

Managing links forms the heart of GoLive's superlative site-management system. Not only can GoLive show the file organization of all pages, media, and special code libraries graphically, but it can also show the relationships between all of them. It accomplishes this task by keeping a lot of information behind the scenes where you don't even have to know about it. The graphical approach to site management allows you to make powerful, sitewide changes with single clicks and by dragging and dropping files.

When you create any site, you're really creating a set of relationships between resources. Some of these resources may be files stored at the Web site, like HTML pages and GIF images; others may be documents stored elsewhere on the Web or on an intranet, like a PDF file containing a form that a user can print out, or a simple Web page with more information on a subject.

Whenever a Web browser retrieves a page or file, it undergoes the same fundamental process, regardless of whether that file is linked from another page on the same Web site, or if it's linked from a site in Turkey. The user's Web browser still has to go out on the Internet, make a connection to the site, negotiate the file's transfer, and download it.

GoLive cleverly recognizes these similarities by providing management tools for local files that reflect the contents of your Web site as well as a view into all of the "external" resources your site links to elsewhere on the Web.

This chapter covers working directly with files and folders (or directories), managing and updating links, creating and working with templates, troubleshooting errors, and cleaning up sites by stripping out the dead brush.

Files Inside GoLive

Ordinary documents on the Macintosh or Windows Desktops don't have much intelligence. On its own, a file might have an icon and a file extension or file type that identifies it to the operating system. But unless a file is opened by an application which can act on the data in that file, the Desktop can't peer inside those files and tell you what's what. However, when those same files are viewed through the Files tab in GoLive, they exhibit lots of smarts, revealing links and other object relationships.

The Files tab mimics the display of files and folders in the Mac OS Desktop or in My Computer under Windows 98 and later. Files can be moved up and down folder levels, renamed, and deleted.

GoLive maintains a hidden database in the site file, stored on your local hard drive, that contains every link and image reference in all HTML files. If you have the right GoLive Modules loaded, any external URLs used in QuickTime movies, SVG (Scalable Vector Graphics) files, Flash SWF files, and Acrobat PDFs (Portable Document Format) are also put into this database (see Chapter 4, *Preferences and Customizing*, and Chapter 25, *Advanced Features*, for more on modules).

Because every link and image is managed by this database, whenever you act on a file, GoLive prompts you to update all references to that file. If you agree—which you should—GoLive rewrites every link within HTML or supported media files to reflect your changes, and also updates its internal list.

For instance, let's say while building a site you put all images at a single folder level, the main level of your site. This is pretty typical for a small site that unexpectedly gets bigger. You may suddenly find yourself with hundreds of files at the main level and want to reorganize them to make the site's files display for easier browsing.

What's New in 5

The Files tab changed only slightly in GoLive 5; it still anchors the site window. You can now view file modification date and time in that main window and sort by any field.

Filename Constraints, a new feature, allows you to see if any filenames you've chosen fail to conform to the name length and legal characters (like only alphabetic, or no spaces) of the platform you're going to load the files onto.

CSS external styles can now be applied to multiple files by selecting them in the Files tab and using the File Inspector's Styles tab.

The Copy Files feature, which appears in many forms for different tasks in GoLive, can show files by folder or without any folder hierarchy.

Checking link validity in the External tab now works the way it should; in GoLive 4, it could crash or fail to start without explanation.

Due to the way GoLive tracks references, you can just drag and drop to your heart's content in the Site window. In this case, you could create a folder named "images" in the Files tab, and drag all your image files into it (see Figure 21-1). GoLive would then prompt you to change all of the HTML and media files that contained links pointing to those images. Clicking OK would allow GoLive to rewrite the links, move the files, and everything on the site would remain working and correctly linked into place.

Figure 21-1
Reorganizing files in the Files tab via drag and drop

Select and drag images in a flat layout into the images folder, and GoLive prompts you to rewrite all of the HTML and media files that link to these images.

Images in their new location

Working with Files in a Site

Opening the site window displays the Files tab, which shows the list of files already in the site; if you started from scratch, the Files tab is empty except for a blank home page (see Figure 21-2).

Root Location

A site exists as a collection of files and nested folders in a given directory. That directory is the root; all files are referenced from that location, either at the

Figure 21-2
An empty Site
window

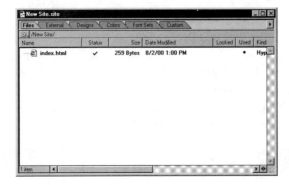

same level or in nested folders. Folders might be nested several layers deep, but they're referenced from that main, root folder that marks the headwaters of the site (see Figure 21-3).

When you create a new link within a page and click the Absolute Link button in the URL Getter, the URL is displayed with the full path based on the site folder—even if the link is in the same directory as the file itself. For example, suppose you're working in a file called "hobbes.html" located in the "comics" folder. Linking to a file called "calvin.html" in the same folder would normally display just the file name in the URL field of the Inspector. However, with Absolute Link enabled, the URL would show: "/comics/calvin.html" (see Figure 21-4).

In traditional computer parlance, "root" refers to the base level of your hard drive, like "C:" in Windows or "Macintosh HD" (or whatever you may

Figure 21-3
Root of a site

Mac root

Windows root

The list of folders and directories from the hard drive's root level to your site folder's location

Figure 21-4
Absolute links

Relative link (Absolute Link disabled)

Absolute link (Absolute Link enabled)

have renamed it) on the Mac; GoLive is smart enough to treat your site file's directory as the root for its Web site. See the sidebar, "Absolute versus Relative," for a more detailed explanation.

TIP:
Absolute
Testing

If you link to an image or media file using Absolute Link, you cannot preview it locally in a browser. Unlike GoLive, browsers assume the root of an Absolute Link is the top of the hard drive; GoLive automatically "deflects" that in order to preview. To test Absolute Links, you must upload the files to a server.

In the upper left of the Files tab, GoLive displays a Path icon, to the right of which is the name of the current root folder (see Figure 21-5). Holding down the mouse button on the Path icon for almost two seconds displays the local hard path (grayed out) in which your site folders are nested (see Figure 21-6).

Figure 21-5
Files tab's full
path display

Path icon

Figure 21-6
Path from root

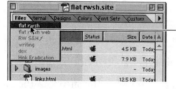

Hold down the mouse button to get the path popup.

If you're down a level or two in either the site data folder or site folder, you can click the Path icon to move up a level, or navigate up by selecting the higher-level folder from the popup list.

TIP:
Full Path

The default for GoLive is to not show a file's full path. Check Display Full Path in the Site pane of the Preferences dialog box, and the Path icon moves to the top of the Site window and shows the fully qualified URL or path for each file. For FTP and WebDAV, it shows the protocol (ftp or http) as well (see Figure 21-7).

Home Page

The home page of a site is typically in the root, and it forms the basis of the navigational hierarchy of the site. GoLive creates a default home page if you create a site from scratch, but you can choose any page to be the home page.

Figure 21-7
Display Full
Path options

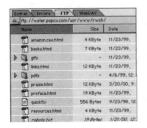

Display Full Path unchecked

Display Full Path checked

Select the HTML file in the Files tab and bring up the File Inspector. From the Page tab, check the Home Page box. You can also use the contextual menu's Set as Home Page option.

File Information

Each file and folder is shown in the Files tab with several characteristics in columns (see Figure 21-8):

- **Name:** editable by selecting the file or folder name
- **Status:** links are all working, filename is legal for uploading, empty page
- **Size in bytes**
- **Date modified**
- **Locked:** whether the file is editable or not
- **Used:** whether a file is referenced in the site from the navigational root
- **Kind:** document, folder, HTML file, etc.
- **URL:** the path from the root
- **Filename Status:** whether the file or folder's name meets the filename constraints set for this site or globally; this column is off by default (see "Filename Constraints," later in this chapter)

The View Controller allows you to toggle off any and all of these columns. Clicking the column's name sorts the items alphabetically, by size, or by date depending on the contents of the column. Click the pyramid button to re-

Figure 21-8
Files tab

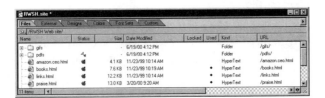

verse the sort order. Hover over the division between columns to resize their horizontal width. Hold down the Command key (Mac) or Control key (Windows) and a grabber hand appears; use it to rearrange the order of the columns from left to right.

TIP:
Tabbing Through Files

Pressing Tab moves you forward through files, just like the down arrow key, and Shift-Tab works like the up arrow key. If you have a folder expanded, tabbing still hits files alphabetically, so don't be surprised if you tab from "about.html" to "arden.gif" in the "images" folder. If you sort files by anything other than alphabetically, tabbing still works alphabetically, while the up and down arrows move through the items in the order they appear.

TIP:
Switching Sides (Mac)

Pressing Option-Tab or Command-Tab toggles between the left and right panes of the Site window if the right pane is open.

Absolute Versus Relative

All references in GoLive, whether they're hypertext links or media links, fall into one of two categories (see Table 21-1):

- **Absolute:** the entire URL is specified, including what's called a "scheme": http, ftp, file, etc., like http://www.bootyc.com/foo/bar/path.html or ftp://ftp.windbagx.com/mish/e/gas/nonsense.pdf
- **Relative:** just the part containing a filename or a path to a filename is included, like "bar/path.html" where "bar" is a folder

A relative reference uses the context of where you are within a site to generate the rest of the link. If you're at http://www.bootyc.com/foo/welcome.html, the relative URL above treats "bar" as a folder without having to know about the enclosing "foo" folder, and path.html as a file in that folder.

GoLive mixes up the issue by calling a certain kind of relative URL "Absolute," counter to the HTML specification that defined these terms. Every URL Getter has an Absolute Link button which, when enabled, doesn't turn the file reference into a true, absolute URL (sometimes known as a fully qualified URL); rather, Absolute Link provides the entire path from the root of the Web site down to the file.

So in the above example, if we made path.html into a GoLive Absolute Link, the URL would turn into:

`/foo/bar/path.html`

This kind of reference always works on a given server, no matter where in the directory the linking file is located. Using GoLive's Absolute Link makes your files somewhat more portable without adding too much of a management burden, as GoLive can cope with its own form of Absolute as well as any kind of relative link to a file on the site. You can also easily rewrite Absolute Links into relative ones by using Change Reference, described later in this chapter.

You can force GoLive to make all new links Absolute ones by checking Make New Links Absolute in the URL Handling settings of the General pane in the Preferences dialog box.

Table 21-1	Type of link	User is at...
Absolute and relative references	Relative	http://www.etaoin.com/shrdlu/welcome.html
	Relative folder	http://www.etaoin.com/shrdlu/welcome.html
	GoLive Absolute Link	http://www.etaoin.com/pdevil/welcome.html
	Relative with ".."	http://www.etaoin.com/pdevil/welcome.html
	Real absolute	http://www.etaoin.com/pdevil/dvorak.html

TIP:
Item Count

We're not sure how useful this is, but the lower-left corner of the Files tab displays the item count, or the number of items currently displayed in the Files tab.

TIP:
Magic Fingers

Typing the first few letters of a file name selects the file in the list. The letters you type show up briefly in the item count box in the lower-left corner of the Site window.

Viewing Folder Contents

Double-clicking a folder in the Files tab expands it to fill the Files tab and updates the file path shown next to the Path icon if you have the Display Full Path option enabled (see Figure 21-9). You can click the expand triangle (Mac) or plus sign (Windows) to show nested items inside folders in the same view (see Figure 21-10).

TIP:
Files Tab Display

Although the Files tab looks almost identical in Mac and Windows versions, they both pick up "local" conventions. Mac users are accustomed to seeing right-pointing triangles which indicate that the user can click and expand the display to see nested contents underneath, as in a folder. Windows users are accustomed to a plus sign in a box for the same effect. The two icons work identically (see Figure 21-11).

Revealing and Opening Files and Folders

With a file or folder selected, you can manipulate a file in various ways, from revealing its enclosing folder on the Desktop, to duplicating it, to opening it in the application that created it.

TIP:
Many Places to Select

Most of these options can be accessed through both the Edit menu and Site menu's Finder (Mac) or Explorer (Windows) submenu, and under slightly different names in the contextual menu by right-clicking under Windows or Control-clicking on the Mac (see Figure 21-12). They are also paralleled in the Site toolbar; here, they appear on the left-hand side with different names and in a different order than in the Site menu and contextual menu.

Link in HREF is...	User winds up at...
letterpress.html	http://www.etaoin.com/shrdlu/letterpress.html
oldstyle/numerals.html	http://www.etaoin.com/shrdlu/oldstyle/numerals.html
/shrdlu/welcome.html	http://www.etaoin.com/shrdlu/welcome.html
../shrdlu/welcome.html	http://www.etaoin.com/shrdlu/welcome.html
http://www.qwerty.com/index.html	http://www.qwerty.com/index.html

Figure 21-9
Opening a
folder

 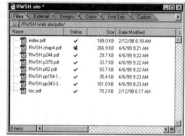

Windows display of closed and opened folder

Mac display of closed and opened folder

Figure 21-10
Expanding
folders

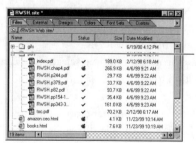

Clicking the plus sign (a triangle on the Mac) expands the folder's contents.

Figure 21-11
Triangle and
plus sign

Macintosh expand triangle

Windows plus sign in a box

Figure 21-12
The many
ways of
opening

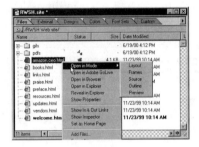

Windows contextual and Site menus

Mac contextual and Site menus

The Finder (Mac) or Explorer (Windows) submenu in the Site menu offers three options when you select one or more items in the Files tab: Reveal Object, Show Object Information, and Launch File. Although Reveal Object and Show Object Information are pluralized to Objects if you have more than one item selected, you cannot open multiple items at once. (These items were discussed briefly in Chapter 19, *Site Management*; here's the fuller explanation of all three.)

The Edit menu makes available Clear, Duplicate, and Select All for files and folders. The Site toolbar offers a final option, Update, available only in the Toolbar and in the contextual menu, which corresponds to the Rescan option in the Site menu (detailed in Chapter 19).

Clear and Duplicate work on multiple selections; Select All and Update don't require any selection to work.

Reveal Object(s). Selecting this command opens the item's enclosing folder in the Desktop with the item selected in it (see Figure 21-13). The contextual menu reads Reveal in Finder (Mac) or Reveal in Explorer (Windows).

Figure 21-13
Revealing
objects on
Desktop

 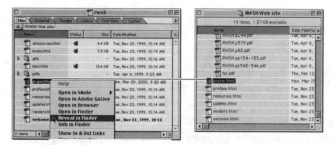

*Select a file and choose Reveal in Finder from the contextual menu
to open the appropriate folder with the item selected.*

Show Object(s) Information. This option brings up the Information window
on the Macintosh or the Properties window under Windows, showing the file
system characteristics and values, such as modification date, file size, and so
forth. GoLive has Inspectors that do much the same; see "File Inspector," later
in this chapter. This option is called Info in Finder (Mac) or Show Properties
(Windows) in the contextual menu.

Launch File. The most complex option is Launch File, as it relies on quite a
bit of underlying detail to work correctly.

Selecting Launch File or double-clicking a file opens the file in the application specified in the File Mappings tab in Web Settings (accessed from the
Edit menu). This is a sufficiently complex subject, so we devote a whole section to it in Chapter 18, *Page Specials*. In brief, you can set GoLive to open certain kinds of files and choose applications (or use defaults) to open others. If
there's no program set, different options control what program or dialog box
appears when you double-click the file.

Using the contextual menu shows two to five options (see Figure 21-16):
Open in Mode (one of the document window modes for HTML files only),
Open in Adobe GoLive (if it's a file type GoLive has built-in support for), Open
in "Program Name" (if another program is listed in File Mappings), Open in
Browser (GoLive opens the file in the default browser), and Open in Finder or
Open in Explorer (GoLive launches the file from the Desktop). For file types
GoLive doesn't support and for which it has no program associated, the Open
in Adobe GoLive and Open in "Program Name" options are both omitted.

TIP:
File Icons
(Mac)

The Site window's Files tab displays the files as the Macintosh Finder sees them,
which means you may see different icons for the same type of file, like a GIF or
HTML document. The most common example on our systems is a mixture of
HTML files that show icons for GoLive and the text editor BBEdit. (The icons are

Status Icons

The Files tabs share with the External and Designs tabs a set of status icons which indicate the state of a file's links (see Figure 21-14). Even though only one icon appears at a time, each of the icons represents a distinct condition for a file.

Folders can also have status icons, which look like smaller versions of file status icons with an expand arrow. They show whether the folder contains files with links that are broken, has empty files, or has files that should be in the folder but are missing (also see Figure 21-15).

Checkmark. All of the item's links are up to date and GoLive has confirmed that the item is where it thinks it is on the local hard drive.

Green bug. A page's links to some items are missing. In the Layout Editor, clicking the green bug or Link Warnings icon in the Toolbar highlights all the broken links on the page with a colored outline (see Chapter 6, *Layout*). In the Site window, clicking the green bug in the Toolbar displays the Errors tab in the right pane. In the External tab, the URL has been tested and failed.

Yield sign. The page is empty; typically, it was created from a template or through the Designs tab. It could also have been created by dragging a Generic Page icon from the Site tab of the Objects palette into the Files tab.

Stop sign. When this icon appears in the Files or Designs tab, the file is missing; the icon also shows up in the Missing Files folder in the Errors tab (see "Errors," later in this chapter).

Question mark. This icon gets attached to a file when GoLive can't find the actual item on the local hard drive. It shows up in the Errors tab and in the In & Out Links palette.

Crossed-out folder. This icon, which symbolizes orphaned files—ones that aren't stored in the site folder but are referenced by the site from somewhere else on the local hard drive—helps you troubleshoot before uploading a site to a server.

Filename Warnings. The Filename Warnings icon appears only in the Errors tab of the Site window to indicate which files in your site don't conform to the filename settings you set up globally or for this particular site. (See "Filename Constraints," later in this chapter.)

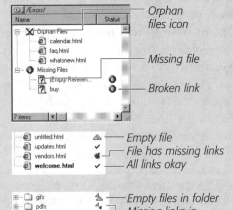

Figure 21-14
File status icons

Orphan files icon

Missing file

Broken link

Empty file
File has missing links
All links okay

Figure 21-15
Folder status icons

Empty files in folder
Missing links in contained files

Figure 21-16
Contextual
menu for
opening

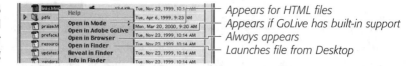

— Appears for HTML files
— Appears if GoLive has built-in support
— Always appears
— Launches file from Desktop

just a reflection of what program that file has been associated with in the file's internal Creator flag; see Appendix A, *Macintosh Issues and Extras*, for an explanation of this subject.)

If you were to double-click them in the Finder, the program associated with the icon opens the file. But within GoLive's Site window, the File Mappings setting overrides the file's Finder flag every time. This way, you don't have to worry about accidentally launching a different program for the same type of file.

TIP:
Alternate
HTML
Editors
(Mac)

File Mappings and contextual selection are especially useful for setting an alternate HTML editor on the Mac. If you set up a program for the .htm and .html extensions in File Mappings settings, GoLive still "knows" it can open the files; so double-clicking them opens the files with those extensions in GoLive. However, Control-clicking on the Mac reveals the Open in (Other HTML Editor) option, which allows you to more easily access that editor.

Clear. Selecting Clear prompts GoLive to ask if you want to delete the selected file or files. The files are moved to the trash location specified in the Site pane's setting in the Preferences dialog box.

Duplicate. The selected item or items are duplicated.

Select All. All items in the Files tab are selected. Pressing Command-A (Mac) or Control-A (Windows) accomplishes the same thing.

Update. This feature is identical to Rescan in the Site menu, but is contextual to the location currently selected. See Chapter 19, *Site Management*, for the complete explanation.

Inspectors

The Files tab features two inspectors that help you examine and modify the properties of files and folders: the File Inspector and the Folder Inspector. For HTML files, there are four tabs in the File Inspector: File, Page, Content, and Styles; for media files, just the File and Content pages appear. If you have Filename Constraints enabled, the Name tab also shows up for any kind of file. (This is different for certain special kinds of rich media; see Chapter 17, *Media*.)

Aliases and Shortcuts

Most platforms let you create pointers to files that serve as proxies for them: the Macintosh uses aliases and Windows uses shortcuts (see Figure 21-17). However, GoLive treats both kinds of pointers as plain files, showing the File Inspector's Basic and Content tabs when an alias or shortcut is selected.

GoLive lets you map folder aliases to other sites if you've split your content among multiple Web servers; and it supports, to some extent, links that are used on Web servers to point to content elsewhere on your Web site.

But support remains a bit tricky to sort out, and we'd recommend not using aliases at all, and only folder aliases for URL Mapping, described later in this chapter. We also provide a much fuller explanation of how links and pointers work in uploading and downloading sites in "Aliases, Shortcuts, and Symbolic Links" in Chapter 23, *Synchronizing Sites*.

Figure 21-17
Shortcuts and aliases

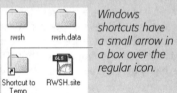 *Windows shortcuts have a small arrow in a box over the regular icon.*

Mac aliases have an arrow as well; the name is also in italics.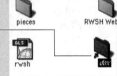

TIP:
Multiple Selections

Selecting multiple files or multiple folders disables most of the options in the File and Folder Inspectors except for Status, Publish, and the Mac-only options. The Styles tab also remains active in the File Inspector as described below.

Basics. The File tab of the File Inspector is almost identical to the Folder Inspector's only display: the Folder tab (see Figure 21-18). The Name field allows you to change the file's or folder's name.

TIP:
Renaming

You can also change the name of an item by clicking on the name portion in the file list and waiting for it to highlight, then editing or typing over it. GoLive prompts you to rewrite any links pointing to that item after you press Return or Enter.

Figure 21-18
Basic items in File tab of File Inspector

NEW IN 5:
Renaming
Main Name

When you highlight a file in the Site window to change its name, only the main part of the name is highlighted, not the extension. Although it takes a little getting used to, especially for those of us who find ourselves typing ".html" all the time, this feature makes it faster and easier to change filenames without accidentally messing up their extensions.

The URL field, which can't be edited, shows the location of the file or folder relative to the site's root. This is the same information as in the URL column of the Files tab.

You can set a color and name via the Status menu; formerly, this was available only on the Macintosh. The color and name allow you to sort items by Status and identify, for instance, the stage of a project's files (such as, "completed" or "first draft"). The colors also show up in the site mapping display; see Chapter 20, *Prototyping and Mapping*.

NEW IN 5:
Improved
Status

Status is a built-in feature of the Macintosh Finder that allows you to set a color and name label to any file or folder. GoLive picked up this feature, but also used its own internal Status indicator so that Windows users could get similar functionality.

Unfortunately, this was confusing for users, as there were two statuses vying for attention. GoLive 5 combines the two, offering the options from the Macintosh's built-in labels, but carrying this over through the same interface and preferences to Windows. You can't delete these basic labels in Windows. On the Mac, you can't edit them via GoLive; see Appendix A, *Macintosh Issues & Extras*.

The Publish menu allows you to choose under what circumstances a file or folder gets uploaded to a Web server when you use the built-in FTP features of GoLive. (See Chapter 23, *Synchronizing Sites*, for an in-depth discussion of this option and how it interacts with other GoLive preferences.) The Used column of the Files Inspector identifies whether a file is referenced.

The Created and Modified fields, which can't be edited, show the date and time of the file's creation and last changes.

The Size field appears only in the File Inspector, not the Folder Inspector, and simply shows the size of the file in bytes.

The Stationery Pad checkbox and the Type and Creator fields only appear in the File Inspector on the Macintosh; for a discussion of them, see Appendix A, *Macintosh Issues and Extras*, as they don't affect how you work with files or folders.

Page tab. The Title field shows the page's title, which you can edit here without opening the file.

We joked with the GoLive engineers that there were seven ways to change the title of a page. They disagreed: more like eight or nine! Among the many methods, you can open the file, click the Page icon, and rename it via the Page Inspector; or just click the title text next to the Page icon and edit it directly. There's also the Title tag in the Head section, which you can edit via the Title Inspector, and many, many, perhaps too many, more.

The file's encoding is listed in a non-editable box. You can change encoding by opening the file and selecting another option from the File menu's Encoding submenu. See Chapter 1, *Getting Started*, for more on encoding.

The Home Page checkbox lets you change the root page for your site—the page from which all the hierarchical links are mapped for uploading referenced files or creating a site map. However, you can't simply uncheck the box with the home page selected. Instead, select the page you want to become your new home page, and check the box there; that filename turns bold in the Files tab, and the other page's Home Page box becomes unchecked. (You can also reset your home page via the Site Settings, discussed in Chapter 19, *Site Management*.)

Content tab. A preview of the content of the file appears here if GoLive knows how to preview it (see Figure 21-19). For HTML files, GoLive must already have opened, modified, and saved the file for a thumbnail to show up. For other media, the appropriate module must be loaded. For instance, without the QuickTime Module loaded, QuickTime movies and sound files don't preview in this tab (see "Modules" in Chapter 25, *Advanced Features*.)

Styles tab. The Styles tab allows you to set an external style sheet for multiple files at once. This subject is fully addressed in Chapter 29, *Cascading Style Sheets*.

GoLive 5 added the Styles tab so that you could avoid the tedium of opening files one at a time to apply external style sheets. Bravo!

Adding Files to the Site

GoLive lets you add content to the Files tab in several ways, making it convenient to use whatever method you prefer. The methods include:

- Using the Add Files menu item under the Site menu's Finder submenu (Mac) or Explorer submenu (Windows)
- Dragging and dropping from the Desktop into the Files tab

Figure 21-19
Content
previews

*QuickTime
preview*

HTML preview   *GIF preview*

- Creating new, blank files to fill with content
- Using Stationery to create new pages
- Copying files from the Desktop into the Web site folder, bypassing GoLive

Using either the Add Files command or dragging items into the Files tab copies the files in question rather than moving them.

TIP:
Hooking
Content

When files are added via the first two methods, GoLive scans them for links and adds those relationships to the site file. If you add files to the Web site folder on the Desktop, you have to go through a few more steps, described below, to hook in the content of the files.

Add Files. The only method to add files to your site from within GoLive is to select Add Files from the Site menu's Finder submenu (Mac) or Explorer submenu (Windows). The dialog box allows you to navigate to any location reachable through the file dialog box and add files to the list by selecting them and clicking Add (see Figure 21-20).

TIP:
Contextual
Add Files

It's quicker to right-click (Windows) or Control-click (Mac) to bring up the contextual menu and select Add Files directly from it.

Figure 21-20
Adding files

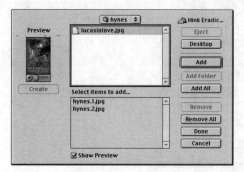

Clicking Add Folder adds the folder's contents to the list, including nested subfolders; clicking Add All adds the entire current contents of the file browser's display, including all nested subfolders. You can individually remove items by selecting them and clicking Remove, or delete your entire selection of files by clicking Remove All.

Clicking Done copies all the items, wherever they are, to the site folder; the files appear immediately in the Files tab and are located in the site folder unless you're viewing the contents of a subfolder, in which case they're copied into that folder. Clicking Cancel is the equivalent of clicking Remove All and Done: the end result is no action taken.

Dragging into Files tab. Sometimes, it's just easier to find what you need on the Desktop, select it, and drag it into the Files tab. GoLive is perfectly content to let you act this way; in fact, it's just as good as using the Add Files option. (We applaud the developers for not straitjacketing users by giving them just one method!)

Before dragging items into the Files tab, it's a good idea to arrange the window so that you can see the area you're dragging into when you're on the Desktop. If you want to nest the items inside a folder—that is, not put them at the root level of the site—open that folder (Mac) or select it from the Explorer (Windows) so it's the only thing in the Files tab (see Figure 21-21).

Items you drag are immediately copied to the site folder and appear in the Files tab. If any of the files are HTML or media files that have embedded links in them, GoLive brings up the Copy Files dialog box and notifies you that the links need to be updated (see Figure 21-22). Generally, you click OK. Clicking Cancel halts the copy, so if you want to copy the files without updating links, uncheck the boxes for those files (or the box at the top for all files), and then click OK.

Figure 21-21
Dragging files
into an open
folder

Figure 21-22
Updating links
in added files

Dragging into the Desktop folder. Although we think it a bit uncouth, you can bypass GoLive altogether and copy or move files directly into the site folder on the Desktop. The problem with the direct route is that when you return to GoLive, the program doesn't know the files have been added. Don't worry! There's a solution: see "Tuning Up," later in this chapter, on how to get GoLive to add these files and folders.

Adding empty files. When you're prototyping a site to build out content, it can be useful to add empty files that will eventually have real content. Using the Designs tab, you can add templates or absolutely blank pages with link placeholders (pending links) to other items in the site. (See Chapter 20, *Prototyping and Mapping*, for the details on prototyping.)

You can also drag a Generic Page icon directly from the Object palette's Site tab; GoLive creates an untitled page with a yield icon in the status column indicating that it has no links. If you double-click the Generic Page icon, the program creates a "NewFiles" folder (if it doesn't already exist) and places the untitled files inside it.

TIP:
New Items
Name

You can change the name of the default folder into which new items are added by editing the Folder for Generated Items field in the Site pane of Preferences.

Adding Stationery. GoLive lets you create templates in the form of Stationery, which are stored in a special folder in the split-pane view of the Files tab. You can drag Stationery from that folder into the Files tab, or double-click it to create a new copy that you can save in the site. See "Stationery," later in this chapter.

Moving Files

Because GoLive tracks every link in every file, moving and reorganizing items in a site is a cinch. Select any file, folder, or set of items, and drag it to a new location; GoLive prompts you with a dialog asking which files should have their links rewritten to reflect these new locations. This list includes files you're moving as well as any files that have links to the items you're moving.

Unless you have a specific reason not to, you should click OK, so that GoLive updates the links; otherwise, links get broken, and GoLive reports missing and orphaned files (see "Errors," later in this chapter).

Creating Links

It's also a snap to add links in GoLive through the URL Getter, which is the bar containing all the methods of linking files. You can use Point & Shoot visual linking; direct entry, where you type in a path; and Browse, through which you find a file on a local or remote hard drive (see Figure 21-23).

GoLive also offers a method of creating placeholder links in the Designs tab when you're prototyping sites, briefly discussed here.

Figure 21-23
URL Getter

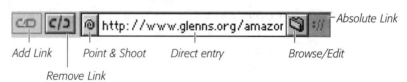

Add Link   Point & Shoot   Direct entry   Browse/Edit
                                                          Absolute Link

          Remove Link

Point & Shoot

GoLive's Point & Shoot navigation lets you simply drag from any link field or from certain selected items directly onto the object you want to link. It's as simple as that. Although you can use Point & Shoot on individual open pages to make anchors—specific locations on a page to jump to—it's most powerfully employed in creating hypertext links and links to media files.

TIP:
The Basics

We devote a section in Chapter 1, *Getting Started*, to the Point & Shoot tool with all its ins and outs. If you're having any trouble using it, consult that chapter for more information.

TIP:
External Links

Everything described in this section that works for local links in your site functions just as well for external URLs found in the External tab. See "External Links," later in this chapter.

Point & Shoot button. The most common use of Point & Shoot is via the URL Getter in the Image Inspector's Link tab and Text Inspector's Basic tab, although the field and tool are found in the Map Area Inspector for individual mapped areas, and numerous other places in the program (see Figure 21-24).

To use Point & Shoot, drag the icon onto the Site window, bringing that window to the front after a few seconds delay. If you drag on top of the Files, Designs, or External tabs, GoLive switches to that tab, and then you can drag to items in those locations. If you drag on top of a folder, after a slight pause, GoLive opens the folder to reveal its contents. Dragging over the Path icon lets you move up folder levels as well. You can even drag your cursor onto the Select Window icon in the Toolbar, and GoLive swaps the Site window in front.

Figure 21-24
Some of the many appearances of Point & Shoot navigation

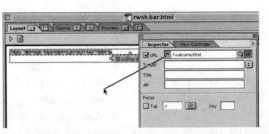

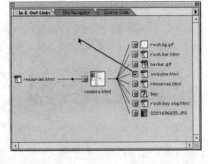

Point & Shoot navigation is available, for example, in the Map Area Inspector, the Link tab of the Text Inspector, and for each of the links in the In & Out Links palette.

TIP:
Disabling Spring-Loaded Folders

You can disable the ability to drag onto folders and tabs to open them by unchecking Spring Loaded Folders in the Site pane of the Preferences dialog box. We prefer keeping this feature active as it allows us to move items around easily without perfectly positioning everything first.

When you hover over a linkable object, like an HTML file or an external link, the item highlights (see Figure 21-25). If you release the Point & Shoot tool's link line on top of that item, the link is added into the URL Getter's direct entry field.

Figure 21-25
Adding a link
via Point &
Shoot

Adding the link (left);

the new link (top)

If you release the mouse button on top of the wrong kind of item—for instance, a font set in the Font Sets tab—or if you release it without having anything selected, the line snaps back like a broken rubber band. Hey, no one can accuse us of not liking good eye-candy! (We'd like to show this effect in a figure, but it's an animation, so try it on your own.)

Point & Shoot shortcut. With any text selected on a HTML page, holding down the Command key (Mac) or Alt key (Windows) turns the cursor into a Point & Shoot tool (see Figure 21-26). You can drag from that text onto any kind of object or tab as described above to complete the link.

If you drag to a location on the same HTML page or on another open HTML page, GoLive creates an anchor link pointing to that exact location on the page. Clicking that link takes the user directly to that spot.

Figure 21-26
Point & Shoot
shortcut

Holding down Command (Mac) or Alt (Windows) changes the cursor to a Point & Shoot tool.

Dragging Links

Although it's not quite as elegant, you can drag a file or folder from the Files tab directly into an HTML page. Wherever you release the mouse, the item's name is inserted in the direct-entry field, and it's automatically linked back to the source. You can then rename the link.

Browsing

Clicking the Browse button (the icon that looks like a folder) brings up a dialog box from which you can select a file. The file doesn't have to be in the site folder to select it. However, if you choose an item that's not in the site folder, it shows up in the Orphan Files folder in the Errors tab, and you must eventually copy it over (using Clean Up Site, for instance) to keep the site working when you upload it.

Direct Entry

You'd hardly believe it in a WYSIWYG program like GoLive, but you really can just type in links in the URL Getter's direct entry field instead of using Point & Shoot or drag and drop. Of course, that's about as déclassé as paying with green paper at the supermarket these days (you should see the looks we get). It's almost always better to use Point & Shoot because it constructs the links perfectly. But you can certainly type in a filename in the same folder, an Absolute-style path, or a URL for a file location elsewhere.

Editing

Holding down the Alt key (Windows) or Option key (Mac) changes the Browse button to the Edit button, which, when clicked, brings up the Edit URL dialog box displaying the full text in a larger, modal dialog box (see Figure 21-27).

Figure 21-27
Edit URL
dialog box

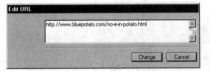

TIP:
Up a Level

GoLive follows the Web convention for relative links, so if you want to refer to a file located in a folder level up from where the linking file is located, insert two dots and a slash (../); this means "go up a folder level." For instance, if you want to link to wonderbro.html which is located two levels higher in the "jerry" folder, you'd use a link like

```
../../jerry/wonderbro.html
```

We received email on our moderated discussion list about GoLive from a user whose Web hosting company told him that the ".." was some weirdo Mac thing. It's not. It's a) Unix in origin and b) completely standard on virtually every Web server.

Pending Links

In the Designs tab, you can add pending links, or placeholders where links should be added, as you prototype a site's structure. By creating these in-process links, you can later go back and turn the pending links into actual ones by inserting items on the page and adding the links to them.

For instance, when you're prototyping a site, you might know that page A needs links to pages B, C, and D, but the elements that will link to B, C, and D aren't yet created. After you create those elements, you can go to the Pending tab of the Page Inspector and connect the items with the pages they point to. Chapter 20, *Prototyping and Mapping*, covers this subject in great detail.

Modifying and Examining Links

The features for looking at existing links and modifying them are equally as strong as the tools for creating links. For examining links, GoLive offers the powerful In & Out Links palette; for modifying existing links, you can use either the In & Out Links palette or the Change References feature.

In & Out Links Palette

The In & Out Links palette is your best friend in managing a site. It can show all the inbound connections to a given file. For HTML and media files with embedded URLs, it also shows all the items the file links to (see Figure 21-28).

Figure 21-28
In & Out Links
palette

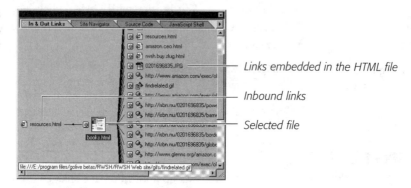

— Links embedded in the HTML file

— Inbound links

— Selected file

TIP:
**What You
See Is What
You Get**

To set the options for which files are shown in the In & Out Links palette, click the popout menu in the upper right to bring up the Palette Options dialog box. The specific options are covered in greater depth in Chapter 3, *Palettes and Parts*.

Invoke the In & Out Links palette by selecting it from the Windows menu. Select any file in the Files tab or any design in the Designs tab to create a display in the In & Out Links palette of all the inbound and outbound links relating to that file. Use Palette Options from the popout menu to specify whether the palette should show inbound or outbound links at all, and, if so, which kinds of outbound links to display. Filter the external links and other types to help clarify the outbound links.

Selecting the file at the center brings up the File Inspector. Selecting one of the linked-to or linked-from objects makes that object the star, putting it in the central position of the In & Out Links palette.

Any item that is linked to, including the selected item if it has any inbound links, has a Point & Shoot icon next to it. By using Point & Shoot, you can redirect the link that points at that object to any other object. This allows you, for instance, to update an old external link on a page by viewing it in the In & Out Links palette, and just dragging the Point & Shoot link line onto the External tab and on top of the correct new external link. (You can also click the Change References button or select that from the Site menu; this action enters the current item in the center of the palette into Change All References To.)

This feature is especially useful for troubleshooting errors. Select the file with an error from the Errors tab in the split-pane view of the Files tab, and the In & Out Links palette displays all the files that point to the missing or broken item. Use the Point & Shoot icon to reconnect the error icon to the correct item, and GoLive rebuilds the links. Voilà!

TIP:
Printing
Links

The popout menu of the In & Out Links palette has a Print option that prints precisely what's displayed in the window. This can be useful as a mini-site map, although you can customize it more completely in the Links View via the Design menu. Selecting this option brings up the Print dialog box.

Change References

The Change References feature allows you to change a reference throughout a site to another reference. It even works within the In & Out Links palette. Bring up the Change References dialog box by selecting it from the Site menu or clicking its button in the Site toolbar.

With an item selected in the Files, Site, or External tab, or with an item showing at the center of the In & Out Links palette, choose Change References to display the dialog box with the Change All References To field prefilled with the selected item (see Figure 21-30). That field is non-editable if an item was selected when you chose Change References. GoLive generates an error if you have an item selected with no inbound links, as there's nothing to transform references to.

With nothing selected and nothing in the In & Out Links palette, bringing up the dialog box allows you to type, browse, or Point & Shoot a value for the Change All References To field. In either case, you can navigate the replacement value for the Into References To field.

Figure 21-29
Change
References
dialog box

Existing link

Replacement link

TIP:
Not "To"
Clear

Let's be clear: Although both fields of the Change References dialog box use the preposition "to," the top field (Change All References To) means "from the current setting" and the bottom field (Into References To) means "to this new setting."

Change References, like most site features, is immune to the History palette and Undo features, so be sure to make a backup first—the changes you make are permanent.

If you want to ensure that everything's normal after using Change References, use Reparse All as described under "Tuning Up," next.

Filename Constraints

Filename Constraints allows you to make sure that any file or folder name you choose can be uploaded correctly to the specific server hardware configuration you're working with, whether Mac, Unix, DOS, Windows, or something more unusual.

The "constraints" refer to which characters (whether letters, numbers, or symbols) a given platform and operating system can handle correctly, and the length and format of the name. For instance, Unix filenames can be up to 256 characters long and contain any character except a forward slash (/). But DOS names must not include all sorts of characters, and must be eight characters at most, followed by a period, then followed by a maximum of three characters.

TIP:
Files Versus
Folders

Most of these constraints are true for both files and folders, except in DOS where folders can be a maximum of eight characters total.

Hunt the Wumpus

One of the best ways to use Change References is to clean up older HTML pages that might have a variety of references to the same file. We recommend one method in Chapter 24, *Importing a Site*, that our friends at Adobe thought involved too many steps. They suggested a simpler alternative for some cases: use Change References and type in all the old references one at a time in the top field, while leaving the bottom field set to your new value. For instance, if we want a whole variety of files to point to /foobar/sniggle.html, we might search for these three URLs:

```
http://www.snark.com/foobar/
sniggle.html
/home/users/wumpus/foobar/
sniggle.html
~wumpus/foobar/sniggle.html
```

Then we could replace those, one at a time, with the new location. This works sitewide and cleans up the management task of having lots of different URLs that point to the same file.

GoLive comes with several prefabricated sets of constraints for the major platforms and some good combinations of the major platforms. The explanations that Adobe provides for each set is top notch, noting all the peculiarities of the required naming scheme.

Filename Constraints manifests itself in several places in the program, so let's cover each in turn.

TIP:
Fixing Bad Names

Because Filename Constraints is an integral part of GoLive, you can fix a "bad" filename by simply editing the name in the Files tab. You can't have bad filenames for Windows or Mac on those platforms, as GoLive won't allow you to rename files to names that can't work on those two platforms; and, you can't even create files or download them with "illegal" names.

Preferences. Filename Constraints preferences are found in both the Preferences dialog box's Site pane under Filename Constraints, as well as in each site's Site Settings (see Figure 21-30).

Figure 21-30
Filename Constraints

TIP:
Site Versus Global Settings

As with other site settings, you can make global changes that affect all open sites or sites opened subsequently; or you can make changes just to the currently opened site.

From the Selected Constraints popup menu, you can select the most appropriate setting for the Web server you're uploading or transferring your files to. If you don't know, ask your Webmaster, ISP, or system administrator. The default choice, File System Default, sets the Constraints to Mac or Windows 98/NT, depending on the machine you're running GoLive on.

The best choice is GoLive Standard, which only allows file names that work on Unix, Mac OS, and Windows 98/NT machines. Since the vast majority of Web servers are running on one of these operating systems, you should never have problems.

If you want to create your own sets, you have to click the Duplicate button; there is no new set button. The Maximal Length and Extension Length fields control the number of characters in each part of the name; the Regular Expression field uses a regular expression as discussed in Chapter 25, *Advanced Features*, to identify legal patterns in file names.

Filename Warnings. One of the easiest ways to find any items in your site that don't meet the constraints is to look at the Errors tab in the Site window. If any non-conforming files or folders exist, the Errors tab shows a Filename Warnings folder containing all the bad files. Selecting a file allows you to edit the faulty filename in the File Inspector.

File Inspector's Name tab. When you select a non-conforming file or folder in the Errors tab or the Files tab, the File Inspector's Name tab explains that the filename or folder violates the site or global constraints.

Filename Status column. By default, the Filename Status column is not displayed in the Files tab. In the View Controller, select it from the Show Columns popup menu to display it. It shows the standard red *.* icon for any file or folder not up to snuff.

Tuning Up

After you've done quite a bit of work in the Files tab, it could seem, well, a bit out of sorts. Generally, GoLive tracks all the elements in a site, but if you've clicked Cancel here and unchecked a box there, and edited your HTML in a text editor way over there, some of your links and files might need a bit of tidying.

GoLive offers a few tools for helping in that department. Here are three tips for cleaning up missing files or deleted files, updating problems, and missing thumbnails. (We offer more tips under "Errors," later in this chapter.)

Rescanning Site
If you've added content by dragging it into the Web site folder on the Desktop or otherwise manipulated files without using GoLive, you need to rescan the site. Rescanning forces GoLive to re-examine all of the items in the folders that comprise the site.

Select Rescan from the Site menu; the current site name is inserted after Rescan in the menu. Rescan is context-sensitive: if you've selected a folder's contents so that it fills the file list, the Rescan menu item appends that folder's name (see Figure 21-31). Rescan also works to update items in the Extras tab if the highlight is on that tab (by clicking anywhere in that tab), or if a nested folder is displayed or selected (see Figure 21-32).

Figure 21-31
Rescan in
Files tab

Figure 21-32
Rescan in
Extras tab

Reparse All

If you've been a little naughty and worked on raw HTML in an editor other than GoLive's HTML Source Editor, GoLive isn't up to speed on the contents of that file. You have two choices:

- You can open any files you've edited elsewhere, make a small change (like typing and erasing a space character), and then save it.

- Hold down the Option key (Mac) or Alt key (Windows) and select Reparse All from the Site menu.

Reparse All walks through all of the HTML on the site and recreates the invisible GoLive database of links and other information.

TIP:
Reparse Only Modified Files

If you check Reparse Only Modified Files in the Site pane of the Preferences dialog box, GoLive checks the modification date of the file against its record of the last time it dealt with the file. If the modification date is more recent, only then does it reparse the file. We're not sure why you'd want to turn this off.

TIP:
Reparse on
Rescan

If you check Reparse on Hard Disk Rescan in the Preferences dialog box's Site pane, then Rescan and Reparse All have the same functionality.

Creating Thumbnails

GoLive automatically makes thumbnails—tiny previews—of HTML pages after you've modified them at least once in the program and saved those changes. These thumbnails are used in the Content tab of the File Inspector as well as in one of many possible views in the Site tab.

However, if you've brought in HTML from other sources, GoLive hasn't had the opportunity to create a preview for the file. Press Command-Option (Mac) or Control-Alt (Windows) and then select Create Thumbnails from the Site menu; it only appears when these keys are depressed.

For larger sites, creating thumbnails can take some time, as GoLive has to open every page, internally render a preview, save the preview, and move on. GoLive puts up a progress bar to show you how far it's gotten on larger sites. You can cancel the operation midstream.

TIP:
Image
Previews

Create Thumbnails has no effect on images. If you want previews of images in the Content tab, make sure the appropriate file format modules are turned on in the Modules pane of the Preferences dialog box (see Chapter 25, *Advanced Features*).

To get thumbnail previews in the Site tab when viewing items as icons on the Mac, you need to enable the thumbnail feature in Photoshop or a similar program so that it makes thumbnails when you save files (see Figure 21-33). You can use a batch process in Photoshop or Equilibrium DeBabelizer to open and resave all of your images with thumbnails if it helps you create a better site map (see Figure 21-34).

External Links

So far, we've been talking mostly about links from resources that are all located on your hard drive and in your Site window. But many sites contain extensive links to other Web resources; others may simply have a few scattered URLs throughout the site. Managing these resources can be eased with a couple of GoLive features while using the same controls for adding and modifying external links as those you use for internal links.

Two of the biggest problems in keeping a site fresh and functional are tracking when those links go bad, and changing them throughout the site when the original reference changes. GoLive automates both features in the External tab.

Let's walk through managing link objects, editing the values stored in them, and then discuss link validation.

Figure 21-33
Creating
previews in
Photoshop

Preview settings

Figure 21-34
Batch
processing in
DeBabelizer

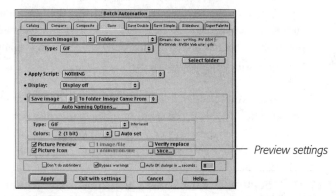

Preview settings

Link Objects

When you import a site, GoLive automatically generates a list of external references (see Figure 21-35). It also adds external references as you enter new items in files in your site. The External tab shows both "external" URLs—links to other sites referenced from your site—as well as any email addresses that you can click on as links (ones you specified using "mailto:").

The External tab also has a column indicating whether a given address or URL has been referenced or "used" somewhere in the site. The Status field indicates whether or not the link has been confirmed as good using GoLive's link validator tool, discussed later in this section.

Figure 21-35
External tab

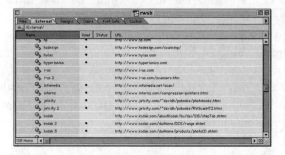

Grouping. If you have a large number of external references, you might want to group them by category for easier viewing. With the External tab active, click the New Folder button in the Toolbar, name the folder, and then drag and drop your external URLs and email links into them.

You can also drag in a URL Group or Address Group folder from the Site tab of the Objects palette. If you select a group, the Group Inspector appears, allowing you to change the icon for the group; the functionality is identical whether you choose URLs, Addresses, New URLs, or New Addresses. Really, none of these names matter; it just makes it easier to visually inspect which links are in which categories.

Updating. If you've added or removed external URLs or email addresses from your site after importing or creating it, you can select either Get References Used from the Site menu to update the External tab, or Remove Unused References to delete entries you are no longer using anywhere in the site.

TIP:
Clean Up
References
The Clean Up Site feature allows you to group features like removing unused references, getting used references, and other cleaning operations for font sets, colors, and files into one dialog box. See "Clean Up Site," later in this chapter.

GoLive adds new addresses and URLs to the first group it finds tagged as New for that category; if no such group exists, GoLive creates it.

If you use Remove Unused References and you've created items in the External tab that haven't been added to pages in the site, those items are removed from the tab and can't be restored.

Creating. It's easy enough to create links from scratch. Drag an Address (for email) or URL icon into the External tab, or double-click either icon to insert one. Use the Reference Inspector to edit the value or the shortcut name that appears in the External tab. Addresses must start with "mailto:", which GoLive prefills when you add an empty Address icon.

Renaming. You can name the link objects anything you want via the Reference Inspector. References are named, by default, with part of the hostname after "www.", or for names like "store.apple.com", with the start of the name. For multiple URLs with similar names, the program adds a number following the name (see Figure 21-36).

Figure 21-36
Links for same
domain

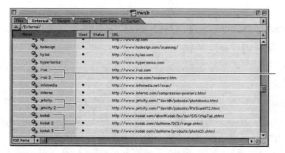

*When there's more than
one link to the same
domain or host name,
GoLive adds a number
to the object's name.*

Managing Links

Each URL or email address in the External tab consists of two parts: the name
that GoLive or you assign to it (which appears in the Name column of the
tab), and the actual URL or address (which appears in the URL column).

GoLive tracks the URL or address so that each one is unique in the site, regardless of the name assigned to it. The URL or address is centrally managed
so that changing it in the External tab changes it wherever it appears throughout the site.

You can modify the values for URLs that aren't referenced in the site (ones
you've created from scratch to insert later), as well as ones that have links to
them using a few methods.

TIP:
Viewing References to Links

The In & Out Links palette works just as well on URLs as it does on files. Select an
item from the External tab and bring up the In & Out Links palette to see all the
files that reference that URL (see Figure 21-37). Using Point & Shoot, you can redirect links to an external reference just as you can to an internal page or object.

Reference Inspector. The Reference Inspector appears when you select either
a URL or an email address in the External tab. It allows you to change the
name of the object, or the URL or address the object represents. The Edit button allows you to bring up a dialog box for easily editing longer Web locations.

Figure 21-37
Showing
external links
in the In & Out
Links palette

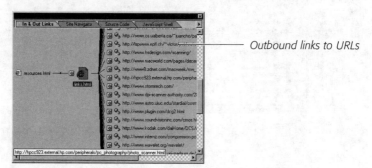

Outbound links to URLs

Importing Bookmarks from Browsers

For those of you who have accumulated a massive number of links in your Web browser, GoLive offers a quick way to turn those links into entries in the External tab. Choose the Favorites as Site Externals command from the Import item in the File menu. Adobe has set up GoLive with the link format styles for Netscape Navigator's bookmarks file and Internet Explorer's favorites file—as well as Netscape's mail client address book format for email addresses—so that all you need to do is select Favorites as Site Externals and navigate to your bookmarks or favorites file. GoLive can even preserve the folder structure, if you've applied one (see Figure 21-38).

On the Mac, both browsers store their bookmarks in the System Folder's Preferences folder. Internet Explorer has its items in the Explorer folder in a file called "Favorites.html". Netscape Navigator keeps its links in the Netscape Users folder, generally under a user's name in that folder; the file is called "Bookmarks.html".

Under Windows, Netscape and Microsoft store their information in very different places. Netscape stores its "Bookmarks.html" file in Program Files\Netscape\Users\ and then under the individual user's name (which might be just you). Internet Explorer places its favorites as individual files in the Favorites folder of the root Windows directory, which can be named Win32, Win98, and other names depending on the flavor of Windows. Windows 2000 may store favorites in the root "documents" folder, as well as in individual user folders in the "settings" directory.

Some browsers let you select subdirectories in your favorites or bookmarks area and export just those as a separate HTML file. For instance, in Macintosh Internet Explorer, select Organize Favorites from the Favorites menu, open a subfolder, and then select Export Favorites from the File menu. That exported file can be directly imported into GoLive.

Figure 21-38
Imported
bookmarks

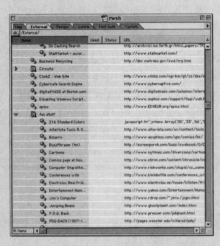

*External tab preserves same
folder structure as in browser's
bookmarks*

If you edit the URL field and that URL is used anywhere in the site, GoLive brings up the Change Reference dialog box letting you know and approve which files need to be rewritten to reflect the new URL. If you only change the URL on certain pages, instead of accepting all of the ones that GoLive proposes, it leaves the original link in place (with the files you chose not to modify still pointing to it), and then creates a new External object with your new value; the files you chose to change now point to it.

Let's say you have 10 links that all point to a certain external Web page. Then you decide half the links should point to a different page on the site. You can edit that first link in the Reference Inspector and then choose only the five pages you want to change to the new URL from the Change Reference dialog box. GoLive creates a new URL entry and changes five pages to point to it (see Figure 21-39).

TIP:
Use the Edit
Button

URLs are often way too long to fit in the URL field of the External Inspector (see Figure 21-40). Clicking the Edit button brings up a dialog box that allows you to see the entire URL and edit it easily.

Change References. You can select an item in the External tab and bring up the Change References dialog box to choose which reference to point to. This is identical to using the Reference Inspector, but offers a clearer way to see what you're doing (see the "Change References" explanation, earlier in this chapter).

Point & Shoot. You can use Point & Shoot in the In & Out Links palette or Change References dialog box to link to a new URL or address.

Checking Links

GoLive can automatically check whether external links still exist, or whether they've become "cobwebs"—links that no longer bring up pages or sites that no longer exist.

In the External tab, select Check External Links from the Site or contextual menu (see Figure 21-41). Each URL gets a double-arrowed icon in the Status column to indicate that the address is due to be checked. GoLive tests each link, displaying green bug icons to indicate bad links, and checkmarks to note good links.

Once you initiate a check, there isn't much else to be done. The only way to cancel the process is to close the site file. Unfortunately, you can't check only a few URLs; it's check all or nothing.

Figure 21-39
Splitting one
URL into two

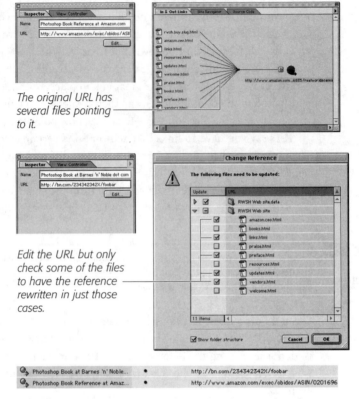

*The original URL has
several files pointing
to it.*

*Edit the URL but only
check some of the files
to have the reference
rewritten in just those
cases.*

*GoLive creates the new object with its new references, but also
leaves the original one in place with unchanged references.*

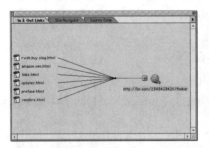

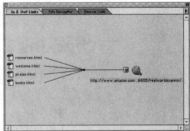

Figure 21-40
Edit URL
dialog box

Use this dialog box to edit or enter longer URLs.

Figure 21-41
Check Links

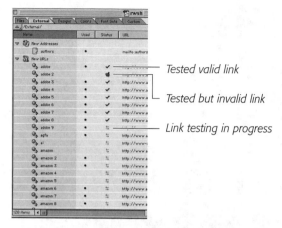

Tested valid link

Tested but invalid link

Link testing in progress

If you have a number of links, the checking can take a while, so you may not see problems immediately; Adobe recommends increasing the memory allotted to GoLive for Macintosh to help avoid problems with larger sites.

If you have a slow connection to the Net, GoLive doesn't take much longer to test links than on a fast connection, because it only has to send a tiny amount of information to validate the link.

TIP:
Tools for Validating Links

Other link checking utilities we've found useful are VSE Link Tester for the Mac (http://www.vse-online.com/) and the free (but somewhat out of date) Xenu's Link Sleuth for Windows (http://home.snafu.de/tilman/xenulink.html).

Right Pane of the Site Window

The Site window has both a left pane (shown as the full window when you open a site file) and a right pane, which you choose to display manually. Click the split-pane icon at the lower-right corner of the screen (see Figure 21-42). The right pane of the Site window contains the FTP and WebDAV tabs, which we discuss in Chapter 23, *Synchronizing Sites*; it also contains the Errors and Extras tabs, which are covered later in this chapter.

The Files and Extras tabs never leave the Site window, but the five other tabs in the left pane (External, Designs, Colors, Fontsets, and Custom) and the three others in the right pane (Errors, FTP, and WebDAV) can be torn off as self-standing windows (see Figure 21-43).

If you drag any of the torn-off tabs back into the Site window, they are put back into place in the same order as their default. If you close a torn-off tab,

Figure 21-42
Right pane of
Site window

Extras tab displayed

Figure 21-43
Tearing off
windows

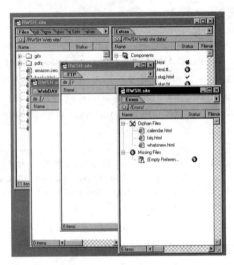

you can bring it back up by selecting its name from the popout menu in the upper-right corner of either pane (see Figure 21-44). You can also restore the default display by selecting Default Configuration from that popout menu.

The Errors tab is a centralized place to troubleshoot a site's file problems, and the Extras tab contains templates, designs, and trash.

Errors

GoLive uses the Errors tab to show problems where files are located—or not located—on the site. Open the split-pane view by pressing the double-arrow icon at the lower-right corner, then click the Errors tab. GoLive lists three kinds of errors there:

Figure 21-44
Window
popout menu

- Missing files, where GoLive can't find the file referred to by a link that's supposed to be in the local site folder

- Orphaned files, where the file referred to is located outside of the site folder on the local hard drive

- Files with illegal names according to the Filename Constraints preferences (discussed earlier in this chapter under "Filename Constraints")

The Errors tab uses the same columns and interface as the Files tab. You can rearrange, resize, and turn columns on and off in the display by dragging and using the View Controller (see Figure 21-45).

Figure 21-45
Errors tab

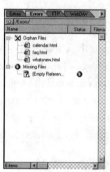

TIP:
Move URL
Left

We recommend moving the URL column to the immediate right of the Name column as it's the piece of information you can use best to troubleshoot problems.

Missing Files

Selecting a file with a question mark next to its name in the Missing Files folder brings up the Error Inspector. You can browse, edit the path, Point & Shoot, or type in a new name to fix the error (see Figure 21-46). You can also bring up the In & Out Links palette, and use Point & Shoot to specify a replacement file or relink to the correct file on your site.

Figure 21-46
Fixing Errors

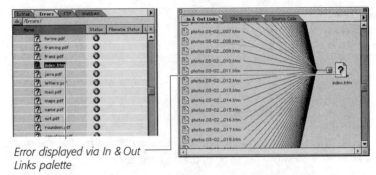

Error displayed via In & Out
Links palette

Use either Change References or the
Error Inspector to link to the correct file.

There's even a third option: select Change References from the Site menu and use that interface, described earlier in the chapter, to update the link.

If you need more information about what link has gone bad, you can use the In & Out Links palette to find files that reference the link. Open one of those files, click the Link Warnings icon, then troll through the page to find what was linking to the missing file (see Figure 21-47). (This is often easier than trying to figure out what a file named "oc8989aa.html" is supposed to contain.)

Figure 21-47
Troubleshooting
bad page links

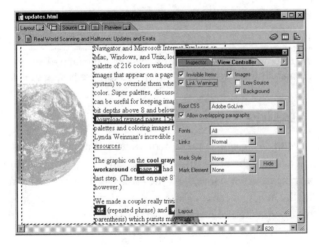

Orphaned Files

Orphaned files are located outside the site folder, and may contain content that you've collected from other sources, such as networked volumes on file servers. However, before you upload the site, you need to make sure that GoLive has incorporated the orphaned file so that it gets properly referenced on the Web—otherwise, users get an error message when they click the link to the orphaned item.

You can choose one of four approaches to correct orphaned files.

Copy them locally. If you simply drag the orphaned file icon into any location in the files list side of the Files tab, GoLive makes a local copy of the file and links it in.

Clean Up Site. The Clean Up Site feature has an option that allows you to copy any external files (into the default "NewFiles" folder in the site) to

Omitting Certain Files

When we link to large files, like PDFs that might be hundreds of kilobytes each, we don't store the file in the local site folder. We store them just on the Web server because we don't want GoLive to re-upload or re-download the file—it's easier to manage on our own. However, not putting in local copies of the files causes GoLive to put every one of them in the Missing Files category of the Errors tab (see Figure 21-48). But there is a way out.

GoLive has a feature called URL Handling (not to be confused with File Mappings or URL Mapping) that lets you specify patterns in file and folders names to ignore any related errors.

For our PDF omission, we go to the Preferences dialog box, and under the General pane, find the URL Handling settings. We add ".pdf" as an item, click OK, and then are prompted (if we have a site file open) to decide whether to apply those changes to all open sites. The answer is usually yes.

By mapping .pdf, the whole list of missing files disappears from the Errors tab, making it easier to understand exactly what's gone wrong with the site. We often map "/cgi-bin/" as well, because the scripts referenced inside GoLive are typically not stored in the local folder, but are on the Web server in that special directory.

TIP:
Smart Omission

A smarter approach might be to select the items we don't want to upload many times, include them in the site, and set their Publish flag to Never in the File Inspector. But we never confessed to being smart, only competent. Anyway, we like to solve every kind of problem, not just stick to a single approach to our methodology.

Figure 21-48
URL Handling

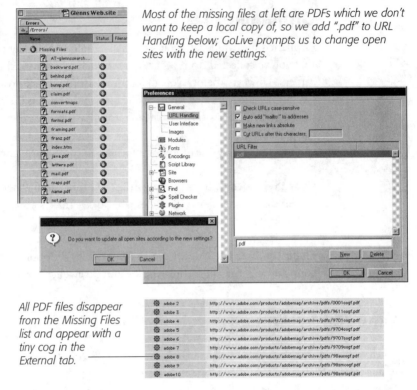

Most of the missing files at left are PDFs which we don't want to keep a local copy of, so we add ".pdf" to URL Handling below; GoLive prompts us to change open sites with the new settings.

All PDF files disappear from the Missing Files list and appear with a tiny cog in the External tab.

correct this problem wherever it appears. It's equivalent to selecting all of the orphaned files and dragging them over, but much simpler. See "Clean Up Site," later in this chapter.

Export Site. You can hold off dealing with this problem until you're ready to transfer the site and use the Export Site feature, which makes a copy of your site. As one of the options, you can specify Export Referenced Files That Are Not Part of the Site; see "Export Site," later in this chapter.

Leave them alone. This only works if you're willing to have broken links on your Web site, though we expect you're probably not.

Extras

Have you found yourself acting somewhat robotic in your Web design and production work, repeating the same activity over and over again with no end in sight (or site)? GoLive offers two site features to relieve tedium caused by a human being having to act like a computer: Stationery and Components, both found in the Extras tab.

TIP:
Designs

The Extras tab also contains the Designs folder, which is the storage location for files used in the Design tab. See Chapter 20, *Prototyping and Mapping*.

TIP:
Site Trash

Although it's not related to mechanical automated workers, the Site Trash folder also lives in the Extras tab. So, for the purpose of consistency and perhaps due to a lack of organizational imagination, we discuss it in this section, as well.

Stationery allows you to label and store specific HTML files as templates that you can use as new, blank pages in the Files tab and the Designs tab. Components are HTML snippets that you insert in Web pages which are managed from a central location. Changes to a Component update all pages on which that Component is placed.

Both Components and Stationeries show up in the Objects palette's Site Extras tab (see Figure 21-49). You can select which of the two you're viewing through a popup menu at the lower right of that tab. Hovering any item in that tab displays the item's name in the lower-left corner of the Objects palette. Components' icons are tiny previews of their contents.

You can save a file in progress directly into the Stationeries or Components folder by selecting either of those folders from the special popup menu in the Save As dialog box (see Figure 21-50).

Figure 21-49
Components
and
Stationeries
folders

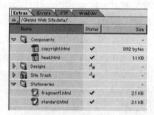

Figure 21-50
Save As special
popup menu

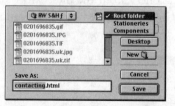

Mac (left) and Windows (right)
position the popup menu differently.

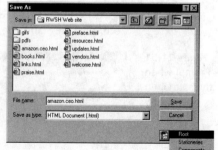

Stationery

Making Stationery is straightforward. Create a template file in GoLive that contains all the elements you want on every page, including Components (described below). You can turn this page into a piece of Stationery by any of these methods:

- Save the file in the Stationeries folder (see above).

- Save the file in the root of the site, and then drag it to the Stationeries folder in the Extras tab. GoLive moves the file, rewrites references, and, on the Mac, changes its icon. (If you Option- or Alt-drag the file, GoLive copies it and turns the copy into stationery.)

- Check the Stationery Pad box in the File Inspector (Mac). (This doesn't move the file, but it does give it Stationery properties, which may not be the best idea.)

Stationery Setting on Desktop (Mac)

The Stationery attribute is set at the file level, so you can examine and change this setting on the Desktop. On the Mac, select the file and choose Get Info from the File menu.

Using Stationery in the Files Tab

When you double-click a Stationery file in the Stationeries folder, GoLive asks you if want to modify the Stationery file itself or create a new document (see Figure 21-51). If you click Create, or if you double-click Stationery that's located in the Files tab, the program opens a new, untitled document window with the name "untitled". GoLive adds a number to the document name if you've opened previous new documents during the same session.

After editing this untitled document, selecting Save or Save As brings up a prompt for a file location and name. After saving the file, it acts just like any other HTML file.

You can also drag Stationery from the Site Extras tab of the Objects palette into the Files tab; GoLive creates a copy of the Stationery called "New from" plus the Stationery's name.

Figure 21-51
Prompt when
trying to open
Stationery

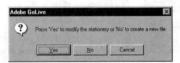

TIP:
Moving
Stationery

If you drag Stationery from its folder to the Files tab, GoLive moves the Stationery file itself, which is not what you want if you mean to create a new document.

Stationery in the Designs Tab

In the Designs tab, with the view set to Navigation Hierarchy, you can drag Stationery either from the Site Extras folder or the Site Extras tab of the Objects palette on top of existing pages. We cover using Stationery in this manner in Chapter 20, *Prototyping and Mapping*.

Components

Components let you reuse the same piece of HTML over and over again while centrally managing the piece through a single editable file. When you edit the Component, every occurrence of that Component throughout a site is automatically updated with the new HTML.

Components can be as small as a single piece of text or a tag, or as large as an entire page including all the appropriate page tags, like the Head tag (see Figure 21-52). Typically, you'd use Components for any kind of element that repeats exactly on every page it appears. You can't use Components to insert, for example, a menu bar with section-based rollovers, unless you devise separate Components for each section. But if you use one menu bar for the entire site that doesn't identify sections, you can certainly include it.

Figure 21-52
Component
preview and
underlying
code

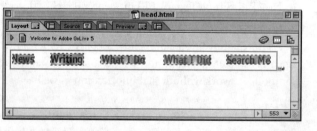

The preview of a Component

```
<html>
    <head>
        <meta content="text/html;charset=ISO-8859-1" http-equiv="content-type">
        <title>Welcome to Adobe GoLive 5</title>
    </head>
    <body>
        <a href="/writing/writing.html"><img src="/images/nav/glenns.navbar.gif"
border="0" width="519" height="37" usemap="#glenns.navbar"><map name="glenns.navbar">
<area coords="420,7,505,24" shape="rect" href="/vanity/searchme.html"><area coords=
"298,8,390,26" shape="rect" href="/vanity/whatidid.html"><area coords="175,9,262,25"
shape="rect" href="/vanity/whatido.html"><area coords="79,6,143,28" shape="rect"
href="/writing/writing.html"><area coords="5,8,47,26" shape="rect" href="/welcome.
html#news"></map></a><br>
    </body>
</html>
```

The Component's raw HTML, including the Html, Head, and Body tags, which GoLive strips off when it inserts the Component into a page

TIP:
Copyright
Component

The best example we can think of for a Component? A copyright statement (see Figure 21-53). Most of the sites we design have a copyright and contact notice at the bottom of every page, no matter how many thousands of pages there are. Using a Component for this enables us to modify the date or contact person once and watch 1,000 pages get rewritten automatically on a particularly large site.

Figure 21-53
Copyright as a
Component

Copyright ©1999 Never Enough Coffee Creations.
Peachpit Press Visual QuickStart Guide logo and
likeness used with permission.

TIP:
JavaScript
References

Because Components are embedded multiple times, you have to reference all the JavaScript that a Component uses through an external link to a JavaScript file rather than embedding every page or embedding in the Component itself. In order to do this, every page on which you use a Component needs to have a reference to a shared JavaScript file; see Chapter 26, *JavaScript*, on how to create this reference.

Creating Components

Since Components are pure HTML, they can be created in two simple ways.

- In the Layout Editor in GoLive, create what you want visually, use the Page Inspector's HTML tab to turn the page into a Component, and save it in the Components folder.

- In the HTML Source Editor in GoLive or in a plain-text editor (such as NotePad, SimpleText, or BBEdit), enter the HTML code directly, and save or drag the file into the Components folder.

As noted above, you can include all of the folderol that a normal HTML page needs, like the Head, Body, Title, and Html tags, but we've found that Components work without that information as well.

Using the Page Inspector to make a Component. You can turn a page you're viewing in the Layout Editor into a Component with the Page Inspector's HTML tab.

1. With the HTML page open and set to the Layout Editor, click the Page icon.

2. Bring up the Page Inspector, and click the HTML tab (see Figure 21-54).

3. Click the Settings to Use Page as a Component button. If the settings are already correct, the button is grayed out.

Figure 21-54
HTML tab

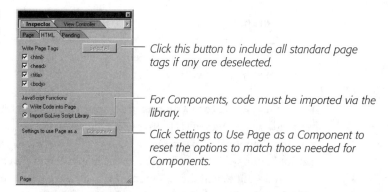

Click this button to include all standard page tags if any are deselected.

For Components, code must be imported via the library.

Click Settings to Use Page as a Component to reset the options to match those needed for Components.

4. Note that Import GoLive Script Library is selected. This is necessary if you use any GoLive Actions on your page; it prevents GoLive from writing the JavaScript libraries into the HTML page you're turning into a Component. This code would otherwise wind up on the individual pages where the Component appears.

Always Use Absolute References

The one real limitation we've run into in creating Components is that because they live outside of your site folder, which contains all of the site's pages and media, references to images and other files might show a full path from the root of your hard drive instead of a relative path.

Components, when inserted into a Web page, may continue to show the local reference to an object instead of a relative reference that works when the page is uploaded to a Web site.

We've gotten around this problem by always enabling Absolute Link for all references in a Component. This ensures that wherever the Component is inserted, the paths to the referenced items work. For each link in the Component, bring up the appropriate Inspector palette, and in the Link tab, click the Absolute Link button. This writes nice, clean HTML that references all files from the root, and never breaks due to a problem with a path.

GoLive 5 changed the checkbox into the Absolute Link button, which is either enabled or not (much like a checkbox being checked or not) on the right side of the URL Getter in any location it appears.

NEW IN 5:
Absolutely
Fabulous

This absolute reference problem was a giant frustration with CyberStudio 3, GoLive 4's predecessor, and many thousands of designers breathed great sighs of relief on seeing the Absolute checkbox that first appeared in GoLive 4.

5. Save the page in the Components folder, making sure to end it with .htm or .html, even though you're not going to load it directly onto a site. With an .htm or .html extension, when you open the file, GoLive lets you edit it visually, even though it's a fragment.

Writing raw HTML for a Component. If you're familiar with HTML, you can type code directly into the HTML Source Editor or a regular text editor and save it in the Components folder. Or, you can create what you need visually in the Layout Editor, switch to the HTML Source Editor, and delete excess HTML.

If you want to edit the Component visually, save it with an .htm or .html extension. But if you just want to edit the text of the Component, save it without an extension or with a .txt extension; this forces GoLive to open the Component in a simple text-editing mode, instead of in a standard page window.

TIP:
HTML
Snippets

Although we prefer to use Components as just snippets of HTML without the surrounding tags for Html, Body, Title, etc., Adobe tech support recommends structuring Components as self-standing pages which you create through the above method.

Adding a Component to a Page

GoLive offers a few approaches to adding Components to a page. In each case, you drag the Component or its placeholder to any insertion point on the page in the Layout Editor.

TIP:
Down in
Front

As with other window overlaps, GoLive won't bring the HTML page to the front if you have the Site window displayed on top. So, before you drag the Component onto a page, arrange your windows so that the part of the page you want to drag onto is visible, or the Components folder is reachable so you can drag from it (see Figure 21-55). Or drag it onto the Select Window button on the Toolbar.

Extras tab. Drag and drop a Component from the Components folder in the Extras tab into the Layout Editor.

Site Extras tab of Objects palette. With Components selected from the popup menu in the lower right of the Site Extras tab of the Objects palette, drag a Component onto the page.

Smart placeholder. Drag the Component icon from the Smart tab of the Objects palette. Use Point & Shoot to connect the placeholder to an item in the Components folder of the Extras tab.

Figure 21-55
Dragging
Components
onto a page

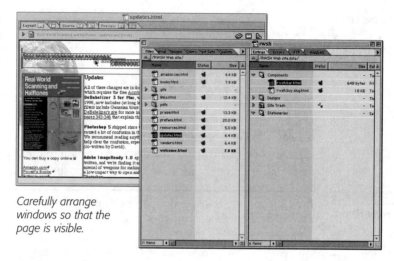

*Carefully arrange
windows so that the
page is visible.*

*Or drag the Component onto the Toolbar's
Select Window button to bring the page to front.*

TIP:
**Pretty
Smart, Eh?**

At first, we were a little perplexed as to why GoLive includes a Component icon on the Smart tab of the Objects palette when all of our Components already exist in the nearby Site Extras tab. After all, who needs a blank Component?

Designers working within large teams, that's who. On big projects, it's not uncommon for one person to build separate pages that reference an object (like a navigation bar) being built by another team member. Using the Smart Component placeholder lets you point to a blank file that later becomes an actual object without having to go back and reassign the link later. As soon as the Component is ready, GoLive can update the entire site to reflect the new element.

Component Code in the Page

Components are inserted distinctively into a page both visually in the Layout Editor and Layout Preview, and textually into the HTML.

Visually, a Component appears as a dotted outline around its contents, with a green triangle in the upper-left corner (see Figure 21-56).

In the underlying HTML, GoLive inserts the contents of the Component surrounded by Csobj open and close tags (see Figure 21-57). The Csobj tag is

Figure 21-56
Component's
visual
indicators

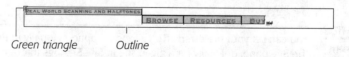

Green triangle   *Outline*

```
<head>
        <csimport user="../../Glenns%20Web%20Site.data/Components/copyright.html"
occur="0">
</csimport>
                <csimport user="../../Glenns%20Web%20Site.data/Components/head.html" occur="0">
</csimport>
        </head>

        <csobj w="433" h="36" t="Component" csref="../../Glenns%20Web%20Site.
data/Components/copyright.html" occur="0">
                <div class="copyright">
                        Copyright &copy;1997-2000 Glenn Fleishman except as noted
otherwise. All rights reserved. For permission to reprint, contact Glenn Fleishman at glenn at
glennf.com. Replace the &quot;at&quot; with an @.</div>
                </csobj>
```

used only by GoLive, and can be omitted when you export or upload pages. It contains a set of attributes that describe the path to the Component, its dimensions, and some other housekeeping information that GoLive requires.

The Csimport tag is inserted in the Head section of the page by GoLive 5 to track all the Components included in an HTML page.

(We introduce a neat trick in Chapter 24, *Importing a Site*, that describes how you can fool GoLive into thinking you've inserted Components throughout a site using Find & Replace to refurbish an older site—or even a newer one that has repeated elements that aren't Components. See "Turning Repeated Elements into Components," in that chapter.)

The Csobj tag commemorates those days, long ago, when GoLive was called GoLive CyberStudio (hence, the item is a "CyberStudio Object"). After Adobe acquired GoLive, Inc., it dropped the product name in favor of the more exciting company moniker.

Because of these extra Csobj and Csimport tags, the resulting HTML can make site validators gag. However, GoLive 5 allows you to strip out these tags when uploading to an FTP or WebDAV server, or when exporting the site into a fresh folder.

1. For FTP, click Upload to Server; for WebDAV, click Synchronize All or Upload Modified Items to Server; for Export, select Export Site from the Site menu's Finder (Mac) or Explorer (Windows) submenu.

2. Click the Strip HTML Code button.

3. Check the Adobe GoLive Elements box. (You can also strip comments, spaces, and linefeeds in most cases without harming the HTML's appearance.)

You can set your preferred HTML stripping option globally in Preferences under the Site pane, or locally for a given site in Site Settings through Upload Settings.

TIP: **Full Astern!**	The only reason not to compact your HTML on uploading to an FTP or WebDAV server is if you have any reason to ever download it back from the server. Very few sites we know modify files on the server themselves; most of the time, files are edited on the local machine that has GoLive or another editing program on it, and uploaded when they're ready to go live (as it were).

Because you've stripped out the special code that allows GoLive to remember that part of the HTML is a Component, you'd have to do some refurbishing to restore files locally from a remote server.

Updating Components

It's quite simple to update any Component (see Figure 21-58). Display the Extras tab and open the Components folder. Double-click any of the Components you've created. Make any changes you want.

When you press Command-S (Mac) or Control-S (Windows) or select Save from the File menu, GoLive reviews its internal database to see which files need to be changed. It then brings up a Change Reference dialog box

Figure 21-58
Updating Components throughout a site

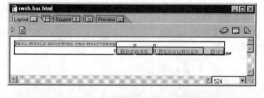

Open an existing Component (above right), edit it (right), and select Save from the File menu.

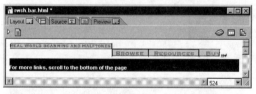

GoLive prompts you to confirm changes to all the files that reference this Component.

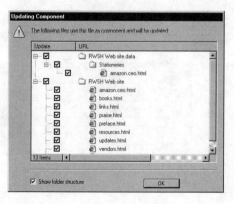

showing all the files that need to be changed. The default is to show the files organized by folders, including any folders in the Extras tab; if you uncheck Show Folder Structure you can see an alphabetical list of items to update.

TIP:
Sort by Update

You can sort by either the URL or Update field in the Change Reference dialog box by clicking the field's name at the top of the box. Sorting by Update allows you to see which items you have or haven't checked.

NEW IN 5:
Files by Folder

Showing files that need to be updated by folder is a new feature that makes it radically simpler to not change files in entire parts of a site. Previously, you were limited to checking or unchecking single files, which is still available as an option.

Select the files to update. You can choose all or none, or select individual files or folders. Click OK, and GoLive shows a progress bar as it updates the files referencing this Component.

TIP:
Synchronize after Updating Components

After updating a Component, you should synchronize your site via FTP or WebDAV, as every page referencing that Component now needs to be transferred to the server. Upload to Server or WebDAV Upload Modified Items both grab the correct files, as GoLive has modified each of them.

Site Trash

When you delete a file from the Files tab or Designs tab of the Site window, GoLive offers a number of configurable options for disposing of that file.

You can have the program toss the file in the Desktop trash (the Mac Trash icon or the Windows Recycle Bin); or, you can keep the trash a little closer by using GoLive's built-in Site Trash folder in the Extras tab of the split-pane (see Figure 21-59). The option of where the deleted files go is set through the Preferences dialog box in the Site pane, in the area marked When Removing Files. If you select Move Them to the Finder Trash (Mac) or System

Figure 21-59
Site Trash

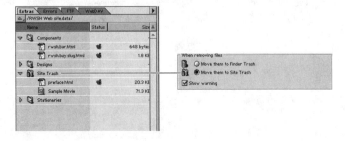

Trash (Windows), GoLive immediately moves files into that location; if you select the other (default) option, Move Them to the Site Trash, the items are stored in the site data folder's Trash folder.

If you uncheck the Show Warning box, files you delete are moved without comment to the appropriate trash. If you are using the Site Trash, right-click (Windows) or Control-click (Mac) the Site Trash folder in the Extras tab, and select Empty Trash from the menu. This doesn't actually empty the trash, but rather moves it to the Desktop trash.

The safety mechanisms built into deletion are noteworthy, as they give you two to four options to say no or recover items before they're gone for good. (Of course, you made a backup, right?)

Managing Media Links

Before GoLive, editing URLs embedded in Acrobat PDFs, QuickTime movies, Flash SWF files, and SVG (Scalable Vector Graphics) files required opening the source files that created the distilled output of the finished files. GoLive allows you to use the same site-management tools that handle URLs embedded in HTML files to update or change URLs embedded in these four media types.

GoLive's management for two of these is set through separate modules: the QuickTime Module for QuickTime, and SWF Module for Flash. PDF and SVG support are built-in as an inherent part of GoLive's imaging model, or the way in which it draws previews. You can enable or disable these modules separately through the Module pane of the Preferences dialog box depending on what media you typically use (see Chapter 25, *Advanced Features*).

TIP:
Only Certain Embedded Management

Although GoLive handles these formats with aplomb, it doesn't manage links embedded in JavaScripts, Java applets, ActiveX controls, external CSS style sheets, and other file types.

TIP:
More on Media

For more information on the QuickTime, PDF, and Flash formats, see Chapter 17, *Media*.

For all four kinds of media, bringing up the In & Out Links palette shows the relationship between all the links embedded in the media files and where they point (see Figure 21-60). You can use the In & Out Links palette's Point & Shoot button to relink any files that are missing or that you want to change.

Figure 21-60
Embedded
Web links in a
PDF

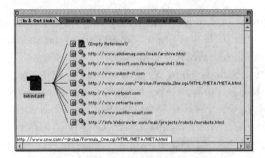

Figure 21-60
Embedded
Web links in a
PDF

QuickTime

QuickTime offers an additional tool for editing URLs. Open the QuickTime movie, select Show Timeline from the Movie menu, and select the HREF Track in the Film Editor. You can now directly edit any URLs embedded in the movie through the HREF Track Inspector (see Figure 21-61).

You can also add HREF tracks to existing QuickTime movies. From the QuickTime tab of the Objects palette, drag an HREF Track icon into the

Figure 21-61
Editing URLs in
QuickTime
movies

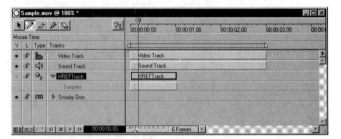

Select the HREFTrack icon in the Timeline Editor and draw an area that corresponds to when the URL should be available; or, select an existing area. Bringing up the HREF Track Inspector (below right) doesn't let you edit the URL. Select the item enclosed beneath it and use the URL Sample Inspector.

Timeline Editor. Chose the Create Sample tool from the Timeline, and draw the location in the time track area at right where the HREF should appear. Selecting the sample brings up the URL Sample Inspector, in which you can specify a URL as a destination.

Sitewide Finding

GoLive's Find feature has three tabs that let you examine usage of given text or HTML throughout a site, and/or make sitewide changes with a click of one button. A fourth tab works to find files in a site. We cover the basics of the Find feature in Chapter 16, *Source Editing*, and more advanced uses in Chapter 25, *Advanced Features*.

The Find & Replace tab in the Find dialog box lets you search for any arbitrary text, whether HTML or text in a document, and replace it in a single file or an entire site, and anywhere in-between.

The Element tab is specific to HTML, and allows you to find and replace, update, or delete any attribute in any HTML tag. This can be useful in targeting individual kinds of tags or attributes. We use the Element tab to great effect in Chapter 22, *Sitewide Sets*, to change colors and font sets throughout a site.

The Site Report tab uncovers errors and other specified items to help debug site problems or determine the usage of certain objects throughout a site.

Find is located in the Edit menu, or by pressing Command-F (Mac) or Control-F (Windows).

Find & Replace

Click the Find & Replace tab, then click the expand control next to the Find in Files checkboxes (see Figure 21-62). The Find & Replace tab now displays controls that allow you to find and replace text in more than one file.

TIP:
Can't Revert

Sitewide Find & Replace is not reversible—you cannot revert to previous copies of the files after performing replaces. This is why we suggest that you always make a backup of your site before making significant sitewide changes. Consult Chapter 19, *Site Management*, for solutions on making backups before proceeding.

The options below control how files are processed.

Find in Files. Once you add files to the file list, checking this box lets you toggle between finding across many files or finding within the file that's currently open and in the frontmost window.

Figure 21-62
Finding in site
in the Find &
Replace tab

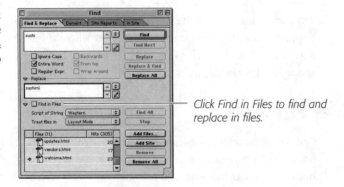

Click Find in Files to find and
replace in files.

Treat Files In. If Treat Files In is set to Source Mode, GoLive examines the underlying HTML of each page. If it's set to Layout Mode, the program looks only at the textual content of the pages, ignoring all HTML formatting.

Setting GoLive to Source Mode can be dangerous unless you're searching for highly specific bits of HTML code, such as searches described in Chapter 24, *Importing a Site*, to clean up the HTML in an old site.

Script of String. If your pages use special encoding for other languages or alphabets and Treat Files In is set to Layout Mode, select the correct script (i.e., language or encoding) before performing searches.

Selecting then Replacing

Your first task is to choose the files you want to search. Either add files one at a time by clicking the Add Files button, or add every HTML file in the frontmost site window by clicking Add Site. You can also drag files from the Find tab into the Find & Replace file list, or drag them from the Desktop into the file list.

Remove files from the list by selecting one or more files and clicking the Remove button. Remove All, naturally, removes all the files from the list. As you add and remove files on the Mac, a counter in the Files heading displays the current number of chosen files (see Figure 21-63).

Finding in Files. Clicking Find All starts the process of scanning through each file; click Stop to halt the operation midway through. If there's one or more matches on the Find term, the number of matches or hits is displayed next to

Figure 21-63
Number of
files in list

Number of selected files

the file name. A counter in the Hits heading shows how many matches were made. An arrow points to each file as it is processed (see Figure 21-64).

You can also use Find to get the first instance, and Find Next to step through each successive instance of a match.

Figure 21-64
Processing the
file and
number of
matches

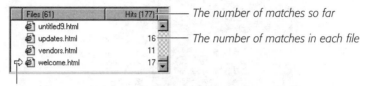

— *The number of matches so far*

— *The number of matches in each file*

The arrow indicates which file is currently in use.

Replacing in Files. Click Replace All, sit back, and watch the results. When GoLive is finished, it will provide a summary of the number of instances changed (see Figure 21-65).

You can step through changes by clicking the Replace button (which replaces but doesn't find the next instance) or clicking the Replace & Find button (which replaces and then finds the next instance), just as you would in an individual file.

Figure 21-65
Number of
replacements

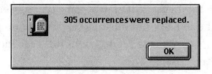

Element

The Element tab is a ridiculously powerful tool that can strip your socks off while you're still wearing your shoes(this is only a small exaggeration). What Element brings to the table, as thoroughly discussed in Chapter 16, *Source Editing*, is the ability to target the contents of HTML tags and make intricate changes. You can find just Font tags where the text color is blue and change them to red, or find every instance of a width attribute in any tag that's set to 100 pixels and change it to 120 pixels.

Element offers a sitewide find-and-replace option that's very similar, but not identical to Find & Replace (see Figure 21-66).

From the file selection dialog at the bottom of the tab, you can either select Files and choose individual files to add via the Add File dialog box; or select Site and choose any open site file from the popup menu. The number of files is shown after the word Files in that column.

Figure 21-66
Element tab

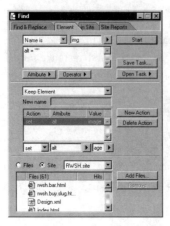

Clicking the Start button causes GoLive to work on each file, and show an arrow pointing at the file currently being modified. The number of matches per file is shown in the hits column next to that file. The overall number of matches is shown after the word Hits in that column.

Site Reports

The Site Reports tab automates a lot of debugging typically necessary to make a site bulletproof. It also helps find missing pieces that you know are somewhere, or it can simply produce a report about the frequency of certain elements or features you've used.

The Site Reports tab searches the entire site without showing specific file-by-file results or allowing you to choose individual files. It has five tabs, corresponding to different aspects of site management.

You can save and load queries, which helps you create complex choices that you don't have to re-enter from scratch each time.

File Info. Three checkboxes let you choose files by file size, download time (based on specific download speeds), and modification or creation dates.

Errors. You can identify several kinds of errors. First, find pages that have something wrong with their title, including the familiar Default Title error which affects potentially hundreds of thousands of pages on the Web. (Search for exactly—without quotes—"title:Welcome to Adobe GoLive" at http://www.av.com/ to see what we mean.)

Second, you can find common image errors. You may want to omit these three attributes from an image, but they speed display and make pages useful for folks who can't or don't want to view images.

Finally, you can tag pages with errors or warnings as determined by GoLive's built-in HTML database in Web Settings.

Site Objects. Site objects allows you to select items that appear in multiple tabs in the Site window: Components, email addresses, fonts and font sets, and colors. Fontset and Site Color correspond to the names of items in the Colors and Font Sets tabs; Font, Name, Value, and Color correspond to individual items that you select or define.

TIP:
Get
References
Used

Before searching on email addresses in the Site Objects tab, remember to switch to the External tab and select Get References Used from the Site menu. This ensures that any email addresses you may have added when editing pages are available in the Containing Addresses popup menu.

Links. You can search for pages with any external links, but oddly not individual links. You can also search for specific extension and protocol types. This is useful if you want to know every page that references a Word document (.doc) or a secure site (https:).

Misc. This last option is fascinating. It's a nice option to be able to see everything that has a navigational relationship away from a file, in part just to make sure that your navigational scheme works.

Site Report Results

Click the Search button to perform a search. The results come up in a window with three tabs offering three views of the results: Files, Navigation, and Structure. The View Controller offers identical options for these three tabs as for the Files tab, and the Designs menu's Navigation View and Links View (except cyclical links), respectively. (The Site Report's Files tab lacks Filename Status, Used, and Locked.)

The Navigation tab is locked in Spotlight mode—explained in Chapter 20, *Prototyping and Mapping*—highlighting the files in the navigational hierarchy of your site that match the criteria in your search. The Structure tab is similar to the Links View found in the Design menu, but it shows just the files that meet your criteria; nothing else.

TIP:
Many Searches,
Many Windows

You can carry out as many searches as you want, and each comes up in its own window.

Selecting files in any of these tabs works just like selecting them in the Site window tabs or Design views they mirror. You can also use contextual menus.

One wrinkle: selected items in any tab may be added to a selection using Remember Selection, just as in a design in the Designs tab. See Chapter 20, *Prototyping and Mapping*, for details on this feature.

Find Files in Site

For truly large sites, you might prefer an option to navigating up and down folders in order to find a specific file or two. The In Site tab of the Find dialog box allows you to do just that (see Figure 21-67).

The menus to the right of Find Item Whose let you define the search by Name or URL, and then by whether a file contains, is (read: is exactly), begins with, or ends with the text you enter below it. The popup menu to the right of that text field shows the last few searches you've performed.

Figure 21-67
Find files in
site

Export Site

While constructing a site, it's easy to wind up with lots of extras as part of the process: extra files that aren't referenced, extra images not found on pages, extra white space characters that help make HTML readable, and so on. Export Site gives you a chance to clean up and simplify without any extra work.

Configuring Export

Select Export Site from the Site menu's Finder submenu (Mac) or Explorer submenu (Windows). A dialog box appears with a number of options in multiple categories that allow you to choose how your HTML files are cleaned up, and how the site is structured (see Figure 21-68).

Hierarchy. Since GoLive maintains its own internal database of files and links within a site, there are a couple options for the exported site's structure. The

Figure 21-68
Export Site

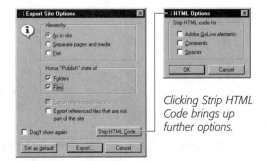

Clicking Strip HTML Code brings up further options.

default is to stick with your current structure (As In Site), but you can also collapse your site in two ways. GoLive automatically rewrites all internal references in the process of exporting.

If you choose Separate Pages and Media, GoLive puts all HTML files into a folder called Pages; everything else on the site goes into a folder called Media. If you check Export Referenced Files That Are Not Part of the Site, GoLive also creates a folder called Other into which it copies files from outside of your site folder referenced in the site. The home page is placed at the same level as the two folders (see Figure 21-69).

TIP:
Choose Your Own Names

GoLive understands that we all have personal preferences. For example, we tend to store graphics in a folder called "images" in our sites, but we know others who use "gifs" or "graphics" instead. You can set the names of the folders that the Separate Pages and Media option creates through the Preferences item in the Edit menu. Click to expand the Site category, and select Folder Names.

You can also select Flat, in which case all of the files in the site, including the home page, are placed in the same folder (see Figure 21-70).

Figure 21-69
Separate pages and media option

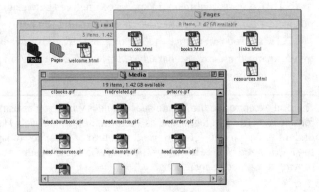

Figure 21-70
Flat option

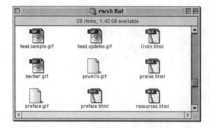

Publish state and references. In Chapter 23, *Synchronizing Sites*, we include an extensive discussion of how you can set and use the Publish state on files to control whether or not they are uploaded to an FTP or WebDAV server when you choose Upload to Server. These same parameters apply here.

If the Publish state of files and folders is set to anything but Always and you check both Folders and Files under Honor "Publish" State Of, the Publish state limits which files are uploaded.

The Export Referenced Files Only checkbox is grayed out if you check the Honor "Publish" State Of boxes, as the Publish state takes precedence.

You can uncheck both Publish state options, and then check Export Referenced Files Only, to export only those files that are part of the site's hierarchy, which can be viewed in the Designs tab's Navigation View. If you uncheck this box, all the site's files are exported.

Strip HTML Code. Clicking the Strip HTML Code button brings up the HTML Options dialog box, which offers some HTML cleaning tools. By checking these items, you can strip out any GoLive-specific tags during export, like those used for inserting Components; comments you've added to annotate your page; and extra spaces, tabs, returns, and linefeeds, collectively known as "white space."

HTML doesn't require extra spaces or linefeeds between items, which are put in just for readability (like when you're using the Source Editor to read raw HTML). You can reduce the size of a page by about five percent or more by removing these excess characters. Browsers don't rely on this spacing to display pages correctly.

TIP:
Important
White Space

The one exception to the "white space" rule is when you're using the Pre tag to format text. The Pre tag, listed as Preformatted in GoLive's Header submenu under the Type menu, lets you use the Return or Enter key to signify the end of the line instead of the HTML tags BR and P. GoLive is clever enough to avoid removing these necessary returns.

TIP:
Global
White Space

The Global tab of the Web Settings dialog (found under the Edit menu or by pressing Command-Shift-Y on the Mac or Control-Shift-Y under Windows) lets you set how GoLive formats HTML for all pages created or modified after you change settings. Thus you can reduce the amount of white space used in your pages and then reformat your site; see Chapter 31, *Web Settings*.

Don't Show Again, Show Options Dialog, Site Specific Settings, and Preferences. As with other dialog boxes in GoLive, checking Don't Show Again allows you to set and use your global preferences for exporting a site without accessing the dialog boxes again. You can also set your preferences in GoLive's Preferences with the Export settings under the Site category; or, by checking Site Specific Settings, you can have export preferences that work just on the current site. The options in both Preferences and Site Settings are identical to those that come up by default when selecting Export Site. However, there's an additional checkbox labeled Show Options Dialog which allows you to display the export options again after checking Don't Show Again.

During and After Export

Click the Export button to start the export process. GoLive first prompts you for a location to save the file in which the exported site is nested. GoLive doesn't copy anything in the site data folder, nor does it copy the site file. Choose a location and a folder name and click OK.

GoLive offers a progress bar that initially reads "Preparing". It provides more information if the operation takes more than a few seconds. The program rewrites and strips the files according to the options you choose in the Export Site Options dialog box.

When GoLive finishes exporting, it pops up a dialog box describing any unusual behavior, such as files that were exported but aren't referenced in the site (see Figure 21-71). Clicking OK dismisses the box; clicking Details creates an HTML file showing any problems plus the options you chose to create the exported site (see Figure 21-72).

Figure 21-71
Export report

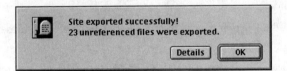

Site exported successfully!
23 unreferenced files were exported.

Details   OK

Figure 21-72
Export details

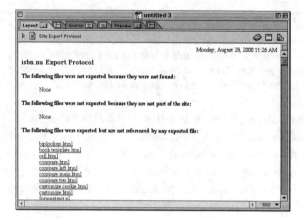

Clean Up Site

Clean Up Site acts like a gardener: it roots out weeds (unused links, colors, email addresses, and font sets), while planting seeds (adding files and objects referenced in the site but not in the site folder). You can control Clean Up Site to a high degree, plucking out just the items that are necessary to keep your site tidy.

NEW IN 5:
Clean Up,
Not Clear

GoLive 4 called Clean Up Site "Clear Site." When we first saw this command, we thought, "Gee whiz, we'd better not accidentally select this! It'll erase (clear) our site!" Clear site was a slight mistranslation from the original intent. In German, the language of GoLive's developers, "klar" can mean "clear" as in "clarified," like, "Is everything clear to you now?" GoLive 5 changed the term, clearing everything up.

The Clean Up Site Options dialog allows you to (see Figure 21-73):

- Rescan the root folder, updating the GoLive site file to reflect any changes you might have made on the Desktop to the files and folders that comprise the local copy of the site. (This is exactly like selecting Rescan from the Site menu or Update from the contextual menu.)

- Add files that are referenced in the site but not located in the site folder, and remove files not referenced in the site but which are located in the site folder.

- Add all elements used in the site that aren't already present, and remove unused ones.

Clean Up Site lets you activate or deactivate the add and remove functions for each kind of behavior described above, on a tab-by-tab basis. That is, you can remove all unused font sets, but leave unused colors, external references, and unreferenced files.

Figure 21-73
Clean Up Site
Options

Clean Up Site's options for adding and removing files are similar to Export Site, except that with Clean Up Site they apply to your current working version of the site stored locally—Export applies only to an exported copy.

Add Used files. By checking Files under Add Used, any files not found in the site folder that are referenced in the site are automatically copied into the site folder, and all references to them are rewritten. Checking Show List of Files to Copy previews and offers a choice of which files to copy over. (This option corresponds to the Export Site's checkbox labeled Export Referenced Files That Are Not Part of the Site.)

Remove unused files. You can automatically remove files that aren't used in the hierarchy of files and links descending from your home page by checking Files under Remove. As with adding used files, checking Show List of Files to Remove lets you preview which files are going to be moved to the trash, and selectively change that list.

Add Used and Remove unused objects. For both the Add Used and Remove Unused areas, GoLive offers items corresponding to three Site window tabs: External, Colors, and Font Sets. These checkboxes correspond exactly to Get …Used and Remove Unused… items under the Site menu in those tabs.

Don't Show Again, Show Options Dialog, Site Specific Settings, and Preferences. As with other dialog boxes in GoLive, checking Don't Show Again allows you to set and use your global preferences for exporting a site without accessing the dialog boxes again. You can also set your preferences in GoLive's Preferences with the Export settings under the Site category; or, by checking Site Specific Settings, you can have export preferences that work just on the current site. The options in both Preferences and Site Settings are identical to those that come up by default when selecting Export Site. However, there's an additional checkbox labeled Show Options Dialog which you can use to display the export options again after checking Don't Show Again.

(Does this paragraph sound familiar? Yes, it's exactly the same as the one we wrote for Export Site; the choices are identical.)

URL Mappings

Sometimes you may have split the content for your site among different servers; for instance, commerce pages may be located on a secure server while the rest of the site uses a normal Web server. (Don't say it's "insecure," as that phrase gives the shakes to those who are nervous about credit cards being stolen.) You might also manage content centrally, but locate it on several intranet Web servers with different names.

Whatever the reason, you don't want to create a separate GoLive site for each project, as the sites share many of the same files, graphics, and pages, and may even link extensively to each other.

The GoLive developers added URL Mappings to allow you to easily manage multiple sites without having to rewrite URLs or have many site files. URL Mappings causes GoLive to address files properly under any given folders in your site.

Take a simple case: you have your secure commerce Web pages in a folder called https and your regular content in a folder called http (see Figure 21-74). These folders both live in the root level of your Web site.

First, you need to set up URL Mappings by bringing up Site Settings and clicking the URL Mappings pane. Click the New button to create a new mapping. Enter the fully qualified URL in the top field; in this case, that's "http://secure.rwsh.com". In the bottom field, use the Browse button to navigate to the folders called https in your site's root. This URL will now be tacked on to the front of any link in that folder; the https part of the path is eliminated.

Now click New again and add the http folder. Type in "http://www.rwsh.com" in the top field and navigate to the http folder in the bottom. Click OK.

You're now ready to link between the two sites in the folder. Create a link, such as the one shown in Figure 21-74, which is a reference to the secure site. You can see in the Text Inspector that the link is correctly made with just the URL plus the page name, as the welcome.html file resides at the top level of the https folder.

Figure 21-74
Linking Web
sites via URL
Mappings

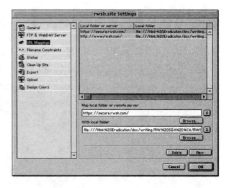

*Set up the http and https folders
to contain your different content
(above). Use URL Mappings under
Site Settings to assign the folders
their fully qualified URLs (right).*

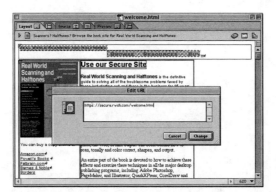

*A link from the regular
site to the secure site
appropriately addresses
the full URL.*

How to upload these sites? Rob Keniger, an Australian GoLive power user who gave us the clarity of mind to understand URL Mapping, noted that on his Web server, he has a "web" folder that contains two folders named (as in this case) http and https. Each of those folders forms the root of the two Web sites; that is, the servers point inside them as the root. This allows him to use GoLive to update both sites simultaneously.

In many cases, however, your content may reside on two different sites, in which case you may need to use the FTP Browser or create multiple FTP server settings and switch between them as you upload files. (It may also behoove you to use Upload Modified Files, which doesn't check the remote files' modification date and time.)

TIP:
Automatic
Mappings

If you check Create URL Mapping for Alias to Folder in the Site pane of the Preferences dialog box, GoLive can automatically build mappings for folder aliases or for your shortcuts between parts of the site. The program prompts you to update all open sites; click OK to add the mappings to the site's settings. This technique can sometimes be easier for existing sites that you're splitting up, or site elements that you're duplicating between multiple sites.

Single File Ahead

Link management is GoLive's single most powerful feature; with control of it, you can maintain sites of hundreds, or even several thousands of pages without breaking a sweat—though you might make the argument for a faster machine despite GoLive's agility. Even the best program needs a little help from the processor.

CHAPTER 22

Sitewide Sets

Consistency may be the hobgoblin of little minds—if you believe Ralph Waldo Emerson—but it's a necessary trait for designers. Keeping track of all the fiddly little bits is the foundation of good Web design.

HTML's built-in color and font support may put the lie to Mr. Emerson. As we noted back in Chapter 8, *Text and Fonts*, and Chapter 10, *Color*, each appearance of a color or set of fonts stands on its own as a separate occurrence. Keeping track of and updating these elements once occupied vast amounts of time for Web page designers and production folks, as they carried out innumerable manual search-and-replaces or used text processors to handle many files.

GoLive provides a central location in the Site window for structuring and viewing font set and color usage. However, it doesn't let you use that central location to change instances of colors and font sets throughout the site. We offer some good workarounds in this chapter that can help. (You can bypass site-management limitations in this regard by using Cascading Style Sheets, but only with 4.0 and later browsers; see the sidebar, "Style Sheets for Pages and Sites," later in this chapter.)

The strength of GoLive's colors and font sets features is the ability to help you deal with handling complex, seemingly arbitrary sets of names and numbers without resorting to pencil, paper, and hand-keying new values everywhere they appear. This ability is especially useful for staying within a designated color palette, particularly when there are several members of a group working on the same site. Our old habit of keeping several pieces of paper with scrawled hex color values is finally waning, thanks to GoLive.

In this chapter, we cover how GoLive approaches centralizing the listing of colors and font sets, how to create new items inside the respective tabs, and some workarounds and solutions for using the Find feature in conjunction with the Colors and Font Sets tab.

Creating and Editing

Colors and font sets each have a dedicated tab in the Site window called, surprisingly enough, Colors and Font Sets. You can use these tabs to view, update, and create colors and font sets.

Both tabs offer similar features, so we'll try to avoid redundancy when explaining them.

TIP:
Font Space Sets

It's not just you—GoLive sometimes calls font sets "fontsets," "font sets," or "fonts," depending on where in the program you are. Whenever you're selecting a range of text and applying a type choice, you're using a font set, whether the set has one member in it or a dozen.

Creating

Let's start with the basics: making new entries in the Colors and Font Sets tabs. You can also group entries into subcategories or hierarchies in each tab.

New Entries

GoLive offers several ways to create new entries. Whichever method you select creates a new entry called "untitled fontset" or "untitled color". If you create several new entries, GoLive adds a number to the subsequent items, as in "untitled color 2".

TIP:
Select the Right Tab

GoLive adds some contextual sensibilities to your actions, so make sure you have the Colors or Font Sets tab selected when you need to work with colors and font sets. If you click the Group icon in the Toolbar, for instance, it creates the appropriate kind of new group depending on which tab is selected. Likewise, only the correct options for the tab you've selected get displayed in the Site menu's New submenu. This may seem like common sense, but we've inadvertently created font sets instead of colors and vice-versa in the heat of production.

What's New in 5

Precious little has changed with font sets or colors in version 5. We have two opposing opinions on this subject: they should have added better management; and they should dump this approach entirely and use these tabs as an interface to CSS management of fonts and colors. See the sidebar, "Style Sheets for Pages and Sites," later in this chapter, for more on these views.

GoLive 5 added contextual menu application of colors and font sets. Select text in a document window and right-click (Windows) or Control-click (Mac) to bring up the contextual menu with Font submenu. To quickly access colors, Control-click a color field (such as in an Inspector or on the Toolbar) for a popup menu of Web-safe colors.

You can create new colors and font sets in one of seven ways.

- From the Site menu, select Color or Font Set from the New submenu

- From the Site tab of the Objects palette, drag a Color or Font Set icon into the appropriate tab

- From the Site tab of the Objects palette, double-click a Color or Font Set icon

- Drag a color swatch from the Color palette directly into the Colors tab (see Figure 22-1)

Figure 22-1
Dragging color
swatch into
Colors tab

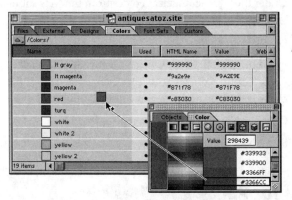

You can drag a color swatch from the Color palette into the Colors tab. GoLive adds the color as an untitled entry.

- Control-click (Mac) or right-click (Windows) and select New Font Set or New Color from the contextual menu

- Create a new color or font set on any page in the site, return to the appropriate tab, and select Get Font Sets Used or Get Colors Used from the Site menu or the contextual menu (see "Extracting," later in this chapter)

- Drag colors or font sets from one Site window to another; you can select items from one site and drag them into the appropriate tab of the other site

You might create a set of colors from scratch in the Colors tab that you're going to use throughout a site, name it distinctly, and then apply it as needed. This is easier than specifying a color each time, or letting GoLive name a color generically—with "untitled"—after you create it (see "Applying," later in this chapter).

New Groups

A group in the Colors or Font Sets tab is simply an enclosing folder that you can name. You can nest groups as deep as you like, putting folder inside folder inside folder. Creating groups can be useful when you're trying to map out where font sets or colors are used in different parts of the site, but this is not a feature we commonly find ourselves using.

TIP:
Inconsistent Group Name
GoLive names groups inconsistently, sometimes calling them folders (as in the Site menu and contextual menu) or groups (in the Objects palette's Site tab). Don't worry; it's always the same thing.

GoLive automatically creates a group called New Fonts or New Colors if you've manipulated or deleted entries and then selected Get Font Sets Used or Get Colors Used (see "Extracting," later).

You can create new groups in five ways.

- Under the Site menu, select Folder from the New submenu.

- From the Site tab of the Objects palette, drag a Font Set Group or Color Group into the tab.

- From the Site tab of the Objects palette, double-click a Font Set Group or Color Group icon. (If you don't click elsewhere in the window, double-clicking the icon again creates a nested group.)

- Click the New Folder icon on the Toolbar.

- Select New Folder from the contextual menu.

Style Sheets for Pages and Sites

Cascading Style Sheets (CSS) allows you to manage colors and fonts in a comprehensive manner, with local, page-wide, and many-page specifications. In fact, any color you could add with the Color attribute or any font you could describe with the Font tag can be described equally well with a CSS style.

It's more work to use CSS because it requires more planning, just as style sheets in a desktop publishing program like InDesign require more work. Just applying colors and fonts is a drag-and-drop procedure. Using CSS requires designing sheets and applying them.

It's clear that CSS will replace local color and font formatting. But it still makes it tricky to manage older sites or to follow specifications that require use of these tags instead of CSS.

CSS support is limited to version 4.0 and later browsers from Microsoft and Netscape, and, to some extent, from other vendors. Also, CSS is not implemented consistently everywhere.

We devote Chapter 29, *Cascading Style Sheets*, to the appropriate occasions to use CSS, and how to use it within GoLive. In the current chapter, we provide solutions for working with about 95 percent of currently used browsers; CSS, on the other hand, works with perhaps 60 to 75 percent of browsers at this writing, depending on the kind of audience for a given site. Keep in mind that current CSS implementations also have drawbacks in reliability and consistency which we discuss in Chapter 29. But don't expect CSS to go away.

Once you've created a group, you can drag any other items from the tab into that group. If you try to drag an item into a group that already contains an item with the same name, GoLive asks you if you want to replace the existing item.

Extracting

GoLive maintains an internal list of font sets and colors in the site file, in the same way it tracks external references and internal links. However, it doesn't automatically update the Colors and Font Sets tabs to display all those items.

When you've made changes to any pages in a site and want to view the current list of active font sets or colors, select Get Colors Used or Get Font Sets Used from the Site menu. GoLive updates the list to add any items not already present. If you're starting from scratch with no colors or font sets listed, GoLive adds them all, and names them just as if you were creating them from scratch: "untitled color", "untitled color 2", and so on.

If you import a site into GoLive, the program automatically scans the site for colors, font sets, links, and external references, and populates all of the tabs in the Site window with "untitled" entries.

GoLive doesn't track colors and font sets by name, so renaming an item doesn't cause GoLive to insert another entry in the Font Sets or Colors tab.

GoLive uses the contents of a color or font set—its stored value, like "Arial,Helvetica,Geneva"—to determine whether or not every font set in the site is already listed. If you edit the value of an object, selecting Get Font Sets Used or Get Colors Used creates a new copy of the object with the original value extracted from the site.

You can also use the Clear Site item in the Site menu, which bundles together a number of site-maintenance features in one fell swoop; we discuss Clear Site in depth in Chapter 21, *Files, Folders, and Links.*

Viewing

You can see which font sets and colors are in use after extracting or creating them by selecting the appropriate tab.

For font sets, GoLive shows the name, whether it's in use in the site, and the full list of fonts in that set.

For colors, GoLive displays the name, whether it's used in the site, the HTML code for the color, the hexadecimal value, and whether it's a Web safe color or not. (For more on these details, see Chapter 10, *Color.*)

In & Out Links palette. Although GoLive lacks global style sheet features for colors and font sets, you can use the In & Out Links palette to display the pages where these objects are used. Selecting a color or font set with the In & Out Links palette displayed shows all HTML files that contain that color or font set (see Figure 22-2).

Figure 22-2
In & Out Links palette's view of links to a color

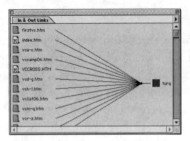

Editing

Editing colors and font sets is simple; it's done through an item-specific Inspector in which you can rename the object or change its value. You can also change the name of a font set or color by clicking its current name in the Font Sets or Colors tab. The item highlights when it's editable, so you can type in a new name or edit the existing one.

TIP:
Renaming Colors and Font Sets

We recommend that you rename colors and font sets to be more descriptive and mnemonic (like "main table cell background color") instead of generic (like "untitled color 17"). GoLive won't touch the name unless you edit its value, so it's a good way to identify for what purpose the color or font set is intended.

Font sets. We introduced the Font Set Editor back in Chapter 8, *Text and Fonts*, and explained its shortcomings and odd design. You would think that in editing font sets in the Font Sets tab you would use the same editor, wouldn't you? Unfortunately, no; we have to introduce yet another Inspector, the Font Set Inspector.

The Font Set Inspector works just like the Font Set Editor and has the same limitations.

The only real difference between the editor and inspector lies in the name. The Font Set Editor calls a font set by the name of the first font in its list; the Font Set Inspector uses the name GoLive gave it, or the set name you provided in the Font Sets tab.

Colors. The Color Inspector includes just two values: the name and a color swatch. You can drag new colors from any tab of the Color palette onto the swatch in the Color Inspector.

Applying

The Font Sets and Colors tabs aren't just useful for seeing what's going on in a site; they can also be used as a source for applying font sets and colors to items on a page. Carefully drag an object from the background without releasing the mouse button, hover over the selected text or the color swatch in an Inspector, and then release (see Figure 22-3). GoLive doesn't bring windows to the front when you're dragging these items onto selections, so you have to play windows gymnastics to display the tab in the background and the HTML page's selection in the foreground. However, you can switch windows by first dragging the font set or color onto the Select Window button on the Toolbar.

Figure 22-3
Dragging colors and font sets onto pages

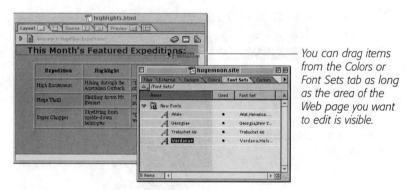

You can drag items from the Colors or Font Sets tab as long as the area of the Web page you want to edit is visible.

Font sets. You can apply font sets by dragging a set from the Font Sets tab onto an HTML page, by selecting one from the Type menu's Font item, or by using the contextual menu's Font item.

If you have a range of text selected, you can drag a font set onto the selected text to apply the new font set (see Figure 22-4).

With or without any text selected, you can choose a font set from the Font submenu under the Type menu or on the contextual menu; font sets listed below the second dividing line are all found in the Font Sets tab (see Figure 22-5).

Site font sets also show up in the popup menus for font specifications when you're creating Cascading Style Sheets; see Chapter 29, *Cascading Style Sheets*, for more on this facet of font sets.

Figure 22-4
Dragging a
font set onto a
selected range
of text

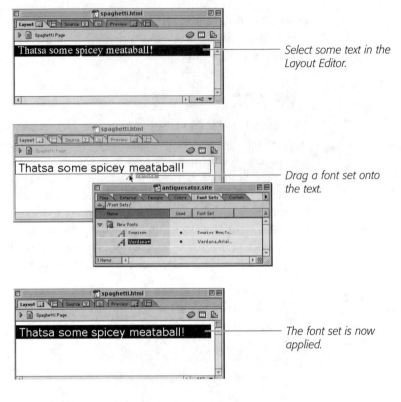

Select some text in the
Layout Editor.

Drag a font set onto
the text.

The font set is now
applied.

Figure 22-5
Font submenu

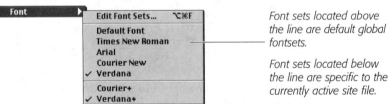

Font sets located above
the line are default global
fontsets.

Font sets located below
the line are specific to the
currently active site file.

Colors. Colors may be applied through many methods. You can:

- Drag a color from the Colors tab onto the Color field in any Inspector.

- Drag a color onto a selection on an HTML page, and GoLive sets the selection to that color.

- Select the color from the Color palette's far right tab, the Site Colors tab, and apply it as you would any other color.

The Site Colors tab displays the name of the current site file in the lower left corner (see Figure 22-6).

Figure 22-6
Color palette
showing site
name

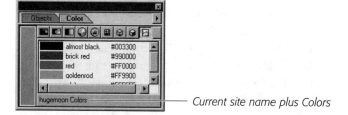

———— *Current site name plus Colors*

Removing Unused

If you want to clean out a cluttered Font Sets or Colors tab after completing a site, select Remove Unused Colors or Removed Unused Font Sets from the Site menu.

If a color or font set you created from scratch in the two tabs has not yet been applied to text or to another object somewhere in the site, don't use this command. Remove Unused deletes every color or font set that isn't applied. If you created those elements to use later, you would have to recreate them.

You can also use the Clear Site command, described in depth in Chapter 21, *Files, Folders, and Links*, to remove unused font sets, colors, links, and other doodads, all at the same time.

Making Sitewide Changes

Since GoLive doesn't provide font set and color management, you have to use workarounds to create the results you want. GoLive does let you create and name font sets and colors, so as long as you never change your mind or your design, you don't need to know these tricks. (Since that's never happened in our experience, you certainly do need to know these tricks.)

Adding. We suggest if you want to apply font sets to ranges of text, use the standard creation and apply processes noted above. There's no simple or even complex way to apply text to certain categories of type (the one exception being the contents of table cells).

Placeholders. One option for making a site manageable is to start out by using a placeholder. Instead of specifying real font names in your font sets, call them "fontset-a", "fontset-b", and so forth. This won't preview badly, as all browsers ignore these unknown fonts and use their default typefaces to display the text.

When you've figured out which fonts you really want to use, you can employ sitewide Find and Replace, described below, to change all instances of your placeholders with real font set names.

Changing. The most typical need for site management is to make a global change that harmonizes all instances of a given item. For instance, let's say you're using two font sets: "Arial,Helvetica,Geneva" and "Geneva,Arial,Helvetica". You decide the latter is more appropriate for your needs than the former, so you simply want to change all instances of "Arial,Helvetica,Geneva" into "Geneva,Arial,Helvetica".

Another case might involve several different font sets, all of which you want to simplify into a single font set that's consistent throughout the site.

Sitewide Find and Replace

To make a sitewide change in a font set or color, use the Find feature's Element tab, accessed from the Edit menu. Since changes made via the Element tab—or the Find & Replace tab, for that matter—are irreversible, make a backup copy of your site as described in Chapter 19, *Site Management*, before proceeding or you'll hear that familiar cartoon ghost voice saying, "yooooooou'll beeeee sorrrrryyyyyy."

Because color settings are attributes (i.e., settings that belong to tags) and font settings are attached to a tag, you must use two different methods to replace colors and font sets.

TIP: More on Find	The Element tab is described in much greater depth in Chapter 21, *Files, Folders, and Links*.
TIP: Saving Tasks	Once you define either replacement routine described here, you can save it as a "task," which you can call up to use later.

Colors

Colors can be stored in the attribute called Color or Bgcolor (for backgrounds in tables and pages), so we need to find and replace both kinds. Follow along in Figure 22-7.

1. Select Find from the Edit menu.

2. Click the Element tab.

3. Click the Site radio button at the bottom of the tab, and make sure your current site is selected.

    If you only need to make these changes on particular pages, click the Files button, then click the Add Files button, and select just the pages you want to change.

Figure 22-7
Replacing
colors using
the Element
tab

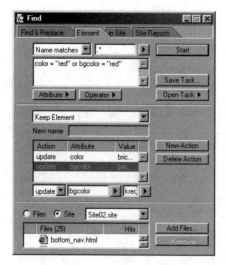

4. From the Name popup menu select Name Matches. Enter ".*" (just a period and an asterisk) in the field to its right (this selects all tags).

5. In the content text area below, enter

   ```
   color = "color name" or bgcolor = "color name"
   ```

   You can find the color name in the Colors tab of the Site window in the column labeled Value. Type this exactly as it appears with straight quotation marks around it.

6. In the next area, select Keep Element from the popup menu.

7. From the action controls below Keep Element, click New Action, and then select Update from the first menu, enter "color" (without quotation marks) in the next field, and enter your new value without quotation marks in the third. Now, click New Action again and enter the same values with "bgcolor" instead of "color".

TIP:

Update, not New

By using the Update item to replace values in HTML tags, you wind up only replacing attributes that exist. This allows you to change both Color and Bgcolor values at the same time, without inserting them where they don't belong.

---

8. Click Start. GoLive warns you that what you're asking it to do is irreversible; click OK.

Font Sets

Follow along in Figure 22-8.

1. Select Find from the Edit menu.

2. Click the Element tab.

3. In the upper left, select Name Is from the popup menu.

4. Next to that menu, select Font from the popup menu, or enter "font" in the text field.

5. Type into the text box below,

    ```
    face = "fontlist"
    ```

    where "fontlist" is replaced with the exact text found in the HTML's Font tag or in the Font Sets tab for that particular font set.

6. From the next segment of the Element tab, select Keep Element from the popup menu.

7. Click the New Action button. Below the Action list, you can set the option. Choose Update from the first menu, Face from the second, and in the third precisely enter the new font set value between quotation marks.

8. Click Start. GoLive warns you that the action cannot be undone; make sure, again, that you've backed up before this step. Click OK to start GoLive processing the activity.

Figure 22-8
Changing font
sets using
Element tab

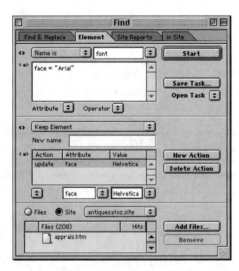

Color Me Fontsettable

Font sets and colors may get a little out of hand, but with some elbow grease they're still manageable—just not site manageable. A hobgoblin may not be man's best friend, but it does keep a Web site under control.

CHAPTER 23

Synchronizing Sites

Trapeze artists may perform their best work without a net, but Webmasters typically work both with the Net and with a net to prevent errors in their work from becoming immediately apparent to their Web site's next visitor.

When you're modifying a site, you're making changes on a local copy stored on your computer's hard drive or a local area network (LAN). Unless you're editing those local files directly, any changes you make have to be synchronized with the remote Web server. Remote, in this case, means any machine other than the one you're working on, whether it's down the hall or across the planet.

The standard method of transferring documents to remote file servers is via File Transfer Protocol, or FTP. Running on everything from ancient mainframes and old minicomputers to recent PCs and futuristic PDAs, FTP is one of the most independent transfer methods available. (If we ever get the ability to store information in chips within our heads, it's even-odds that FTP will be one way we send files to them.)

GoLive has two ways to access remote file systems using FTP. The method you'll probably use the most is embedded inside the Site window's Files tab, and helps you synchronize content between your local copy and remote Web site. The other implementation is a general purpose FTP client, for when you just need to retrieve files via FTP without synchronizing with a GoLive site.

TIP:
Local
Remote

If your Web site server is located on a LAN, you might be able to copy your files to it through a Windows NT shared volume, Samba, an AppleShare file server, NetWare, NFS, or many other programs with trademarked names. However, unlike Dreamweaver, GoLive doesn't offer tools for synchronizing over a LAN. We discuss some solutions for this later in the chapter.

For collaboratively managed Web sites, GoLive also supports WebDAV (Web-based Distributed Authoring and Versioning), a server-based method of checking files in and out, so that anyone using the WebDAV server knows who has the current active file. This prevents people from overwriting updates or getting files out of synchronization.

TIP:
New!
Improved!

WebDAV is pretty new; in fact, we hadn't heard of it until Adobe announced their support for it. The 1.0 release of the module for Apache—the server software used by the vast majority of Web servers on the planet because it's both free and superbly engineered—came while we were finishing the writing of this second edition of the book.

Despite its newness, we have great hopes for WebDAV. It's easier and more reliable to use than FTP, and seems less obscure. WebDAV uses a lot of standards and practices that we're used to from the Web. And, it has that incredible feature of locking files, allowing two or more people to work on a Web site in different locations with different copies of GoLive without overwriting each other's work by accident.

TIP:
Server at
Your Service

We're assuming that you already have access to an FTP or WebDAV server through which you modify your Web site's files. If you don't, it might be wise to get that set up and then return, as both kinds of servers produce obscure status and error messages. It's wise to cultivate a good relationship with your ISP, Information Services department, or Webmaster, since they control the final steps before your site goes live.

How It Works

FTP and WebDAV servers are pieces of software that run on server machines and allow remote users—users not working on a keyboard attached to a machine—to transfer files back and forth from the server machine. The software

What's New in GoLive 5

GoLive 5 added support for WebDAV, a method of allowing multiple people to share access to a group of files by checking them out and in, and having the WebDAV server keep track of file locks and their ownership.

You can now also strip out excess HTML baggage when you upload files to a server just as you can when using the Export feature.

The FTP upload feature now has four—count 'em: four—different modes of uploading: all, incremental, modified items, and selected files. Incremental uploads files in which the local copy is newer than the one on the server; modified uploads files if the local copy has been modified in the interval since GoLive uploaded it last.

The new Network Status display shows network events as they happen—such as the steps that occur when you connect to an FTP server—as well as detailing network errors when things go awry. You can see the actual code exchanged by GoLive and a server, which can help when reporting errors to a system or network administrator.

acts as an intermediary between the server's file system (and the related permissions), and remote users who need to upload and download files. The server might provide access both to hard drives directly connected to it and other storage available over a network or the Internet.

Both FTP and WebDAV require client software—software that runs on your own computer—to communicate with server software. The client interprets messages from the server and handles the sending and receiving of files.

FTP is an old and well-supported standard for exchanging files using rules at the server level to mediate which files a user has access to, including deleting, overwriting, and retrieving. WebDAV has those abilities as well, but adds file locking so that multiple people can edit a group of files at the same time without worrying about whether they have the latest "live" version of the file.

FTP

An FTP server lets you log in, tracks your actions, and handles the transfer of files and other details. The FTP server also protects the server machine on which it runs from unauthorized access, so users can't go messing with files that don't belong to them.

The FTP client talks to the server in a special language that's part of the FTP protocol and allows the two to understand each other. Fortunately, this language is hidden from view most of the time. It usually shows up in error messages, but you don't need to know it to understand what's going on.

FTP clients can be pretty stripped-down, requiring some obscure typed commands, as with the Unix "ftp" command or the similar program found in Windows 98, 2000, and NT as ftp.exe (in Windows\System). But FTP clients can also be highly graphical, hiding all the low-level FTP client/server commands entirely from view.

TIP:
Graphical FTP Software

Some FTP clients for Mac and Windows—like Interarchy for Mac (http://www.stairways.com) and Ipswitch's WS_FTP Pro for Windows (http://www.ip-switch.com/Products/WS_FTP/index.html)—let you access remote files through an interface that resembles the Macintosh or Windows Desktop.

Hopefully, you won't need to use anything but GoLive's FTP clients, but we have found it useful on many occasions to have an easy-to-use FTP program lying around for emergencies and special cases.

Most of what an FTP client accomplishes is sending and receiving files; ditto for the FTP server. The built-in GoLive FTP clients handle that part fine, but they also offer limited control of lower-level settings for file access control.

WebDAV

WebDAV uses the same underlying methods as the Web itself for exchanging files: HTTP (Hypertext Transfer Protocol). This is neither better nor worse than FTP, but it is one fewer thing to worry about for system administrators because they can use the same tools to administer access to a Web site and a WebDAV server. (In fact, plug-ins for existing servers are already available in testing stages.)

A WebDAV server keeps a separate storehouse of information about the files it manages. This includes whether a file is locked or not. WebDAV servers can also store information about when and by whom a file was modified.

Because WebDAV uses the Web itself to transfer files back and forth, user accounts and security are provided in the same way as for a Web site. A Webmaster typically has a tool or a program that lets them create user accounts and passwords.

In future releases of the WebDAV specification, the protocol's promoters plan to add versioning and merging, which would allow a server to keep all revisions of a file (typically as diffs, or the differences between each draft), or allow multiple people to work on a file at the same time and merge the differences.

To read more about WebDAV and find out how to install a server of your own, visit http://www.webdav.org.

Network Status

The Network Status display, introduced in GoLive 5, provides more information about what's happening behind the scenes when you connect to FTP and WebDAV servers. It's only when the network goes down, a server won't let you connect, or some other untoward event occurs that you should need to consult the Network Status window.

To bring up Network Status, select it from the File menu. You can configure what shows up in the display from the Preferences dialog box's Network Status settings under the Network pane (see Figure 23-1).

If you really want to see everything that's happening, check Warnings and Status Messages. The former shows you messages a server sends your client when it doesn't like something but is willing to proceed anyway. Status messages indicate successful activities, like securing a lock or uploading a file.

The icons conform to general standards, showing a stop sign for errors, a yield sign for warnings, and a talking head for status alerts.

Figure 23-1
Network
Status and
preferences

Configure Network Status in the Preferences dialog box (right).

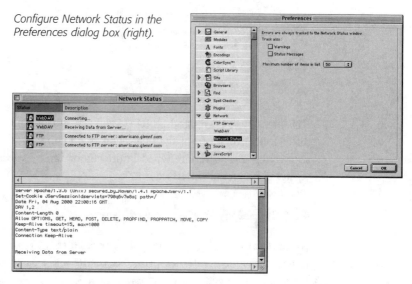

TIP:
Slowdowns

Adobe engineers report that enabling Warnings and Status Messages can substantially slow down file transfer time. Keep these options disabled unless you really need to know what's happening to debug a problem.

Built-In FTP Clients

GoLive's two different methods of working with FTP may seem redundant on the surface, but both offer distinct advantages. The site-based FTP client, accessed through the split-pane view on the right-hand side of the Site window, retains settings for a site. You can use this FTP client to synchronize the site's content on your local hard drive with the files and directories on a remote Web site.

The Site window's FTP settings are displayed by selecting the Settings item from the Site menu (see Figure 23-2), or by clicking the Site Settings button on the Site toolbar, and choosing FTP & WebDAV Server. If you click the FTP Server Connect/Disconnect button on the Site toolbar without entering settings, you are presented with the Settings dialog box set to the FTP pane.

On the other hand, the stand-alone client—called the FTP Browser—lets you easily connect to any FTP server to which you have been granted access, regardless of whether it's associated with a GoLive site file. Since we often find ourselves uploading and downloading files, the FTP Browser can often save us the trouble of launching a separate FTP application. To access the stand-alone

Figure 23-2
FTP Site
Settings

FTP client, type Command-Shift-F (Mac) or Control-Shift-F (Windows), or select FTP Browser from the File menu (see Figure 23-3). The settings for connecting to a server are typed-in directly or can be selected from the favorites popup menu discussed below.

Setting Up a Connection

To connect to any FTP site, you typically need three pieces of information: the FTP server name in Internet form, a username, and a password. You may also have to specify a path to a directory.

Server

The server is the machine that's running FTP software that you connect to in order to change content on your Web site. You need to enter its full name, like "ftp-www.earthlink.net". If you get a DNS error or a "server not found" error, double-check the address.

Figure 23-3
Stand-alone
FTP client

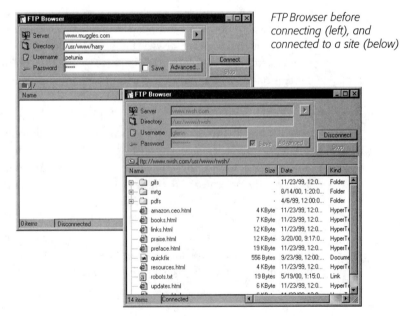

FTP Browser before connecting (left), and connected to a site (below)

Username and Password

A system administrator or ISP should have given you a username or account name and password when you were set up with FTP access. These are typically the same ones you use for email. If you don't have these or get an error when using them, it's time to check back with whomever operates your site's systems.

The username and password allow an FTP server to determine if you have permission to create new files, overwrite old ones, create directories, and perform other file-related tasks (see sidebar, "May I, Please?").

If you don't check Save Password, you'll be prompted during each session for the password the first time you try to connect to the FTP server. After you enter it once, you can connect, disconnect, and reconnect without re-entering it. Closing the Site window or quitting GoLive resets this information, and you'll have to enter the password again on your next use.

TIP:
Anonymous Access

Not all servers require a username or password; some repositories of files offer anonymous FTP access, where you log in as "anonymous" using your e-mail address as a password. However, it's extremely unlikely that you would ever be interacting with Web site content on a WebDAV or FTP server without an account controlling access to the files.

TIP:
Port Value (FTP)

In the site FTP client's settings, if you inadvertently tab into the Port field and overwrite the value, replace it with 21. That's the default value, and is generally what you want it set to.

New in 5:
Saving Passwords (Mac)

Mac OS 9 reintroduced a feature called Keychain that allows you to store passwords securely on your Macintosh by locking them with a passphrase and "strong" encryption. (We can refer you to book-length works on encryption if you're interested.) GoLive 5 takes advantage of this feature, allowing you to store FTP and WebDAV passwords in the Keychain. See Appendix A, Macintosh Issues and Extras.

TIP:
Saving Passwords

We don't recommend you check Save Password on a machine that's not physically secure—other than a Macintosh running Mac OS 9 or later using Keychains; see above. That is, if your machine is used in an environment where others have ready access to it, you're better off entering the password each time. Leaving the password on the machine allows anyone to connect to your live Web site and make changes, including—depending on how the server is configured—deleting all your files. (For many people, this isn't an issue unless you work in a college dorm, have really serious enemies in your company, or have a three-year-old who likes computers.)

Directory

The FTP Directory is the path from the root or top level of the FTP server to
the folder where your Web site files live. This pathway often bears little or no
resemblance to the URL for your Web site. FTP servers can be configured to
hide most directories from users, only letting them have access to a fraction of
the remote files and folders for added security.

Most of the time, you can just enter your account name and password,
leaving Directory blank, and the FTP server automatically brings up the directory for the account. With the FTP Browser, GoLive fills in the Directory
field with the location that the FTP server puts you in. In both clients, the
path displayed at the top of the file list shows that directory (see Figure 23-4).

Figure 23-4
Path to FTP
files

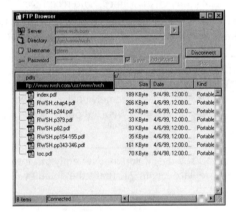 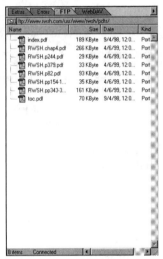

*The same FTP site viewed in the FTP Browser
(above) and in the FTP tab in the Site
window (right).*

ISPs and Directories

Most ISPs configure their FTP servers so that
you don't have to type a long and obscure pathway into the Directory field; they just drop you
into the right location automatically. Some ISPs
set up their internal directories so that your
Web site directory appears as if it's the only directory that the FTP server can reach.

If you use Earthlink's Web service, which
comes with their standard subscriber accounts,
you connect to ftp-www.earthlink.net. If you
enter your user name and password, the Earthlink FTP server drops you into the /webdocs directory. This directory is unique to your
account, and you can't access other directories.

Display Full Paths

The Display Full Paths checkbox in the Site pane of the Preferences dialog box controls whether you see the full path at the top of the Site window's left and right panes. We recommend checking it, as it's another helpful indicator of what's going on while you work.

If you need to enter a directory name, you have to ask the system administrator or Webmaster for the path; it's rarely intuitive, and there's no standard location for where files are found.

Entering a URL

You can paste in a URL, like ftp://water.forchocolate.com/www/nino/pinto/ and GoLive converts it to the correct host and directory format it needs (see Figure 23-5).

Figure 23-5
Pasting URL for conversion

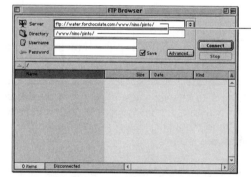

When you paste in ftp://water.forchocolate.com/www/nino/pinto/, GoLive converts it to the necessary format.

Keep in mind that GoLive requires you to enter all paths in the default FTP/Unix format. Each directory is separated by a forward slash (/), even if the remote server is running some flavor of Windows or runs on a Mac. So a Windows NT file path like C:\inetpub\wwwroot\site1\html\ would get entered as /inetpub/wwwroot/site1/html/ as an FTP path.

Advanced Settings

GoLive offers additional options that can help you connect to an FTP server that dislikes the default settings used by all FTP clients. FTP works over TCP/IP, the language of the Internet. TCP/IP uses ports, which are like pigeonholes for mail delivery, to address traffic, with each kind of service (Web, FTP, telnet) having a standard port to handle that protocol.

Getting to Settings

The Site FTP client displays the Port and Use Passive Mode options in Site Settings; in the FTP Browser, click the Advanced button.

FTP service is always initiated from a client to a server via port 21; all FTP servers, by default, expect a note in that slot to initiate an FTP session. Some FTP servers are configured to listen on a different port, however, and you can enter a new value into the Port field.

FTP service uses a variety of ports to handle a session after that first request. The FTP server essentially replies to that note by initiating another connection on a different port. But some local network administrators, for security reasons or just bloodymindedness, may not allow traffic from outside your local network to connect back in.

The Use Passive Mode checkbox allows you to run an FTP session in which the FTP client initiates all traffic. This prevents you from being blocked.

You can set both the port and passive connection on a per-site file basis in Site Settings, on a per-connection basis in FTP Browser, or on a per-Web site basis in the Preferences' Network pane under FTP Server (see Figure 23-6). You can also set the passive mode as a global preference in the Network pane by checking Use Passive Mode.

TIP:
Home Port

You shouldn't have to change the port or use a passive connection unless you're told to by a system administrator or by your ISP or remote Web service provider. See "Troubleshooting," later in this chapter, for advice on this and other problematic connections.

Presets or "Favorites"

Instead of entering information from scratch each time, you can preset information for each Web site you regularly connect to via the FTP Server settings in the Network Pane of GoLive's Preferences dialog box (see Figure 23-7).

Figure 23-6
Setting ports
and passive

Setting port and passive mode in Preferences under the Network pane's FTP settings (left); an identical box pops up when you click Advanced in the FTP Browser (below).

Setting port and passive in Site Settings

Figure 23-7
FTP favorites
preferences

Entering settings for your "favorite" FTP servers makes it easier to later access them through the popup menu on both the FTP Browser and site FTP client's Site Settings (see Figure 23-8).

You can also add items in either FTP client by entering your server information and then selecting Add Current Server from the presets popup menu (also in Figure 23-8).

The FTP Server settings in the Preferences dialog box allow you to set "advanced" properties on a per-Web site basis, such as port and passive mode, discussed above.

Figure 23-8
Selecting and
adding items
to the FTP
favorites
popup menu

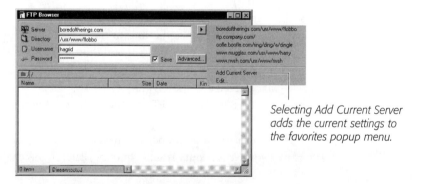

Selecting Add Current Server adds the current settings to the favorites popup menu.

Connecting to the FTP Server

Once you've set up all your parameters, connecting and disconnecting to an FTP server is merely a matter of clicking a button or selecting a menu item.

FTP servers won't let you stay connected indefinitely, but GoLive doesn't provide a warning when the FTP server has booted you off. Most FTP servers disconnect after 10 or 20 minutes of idle time; others may disconnect after hours. If you try to act on files in the FTP window after a disconnect, GoLive displays the error message, "Unexpected Disconnect".

Proxy

Your network administrator may tell you that you have to use a "proxy server" to access FTP and Web servers outside of your local network. If so, you need to set this in the Network pane of the Preferences dialog box. Check the Use FTP Proxy box and enter the values for Host and Port provided by the administrator (see Figure 23-9).

If you're using Mac OS's Internet control panel for your settings and need to configure an FTP proxy, see Appendix A, *Macintosh Issues and Extras.*

Figure 23-9
FTP proxy
settings

Check Use FTP Proxy, and enter
the values provided by your
system administrator.

Connecting

To connect, simply click the Connect button for the FTP Browser, or the FTP Server Connect/Disconnect button on the Site toolbar. For the Site client, click the FTP Server Connect/Disconnect button on the Site toolbar or select Connect from the Site menu's FTP Server submenu. You can also Control-click (Mac) or right-click (Windows) in the window of either the FTP Browser or the Site window's FTP tab and choose Connect from the contextual menu.

If you get an error on connecting that isn't something obvious like "incorrect password," check out "Troubleshooting," later in this chapter.

Disconnecting

To disconnect, click the Disconnect button for the FTP Browser or the FTP Server Connect/Disconnect button on the Site toolbar. For the Site client, click the FTP Server Connect/Disconnect button on the Site toolbar, or select Disconnect from the Site menu's FTP Server submenu. Disconnect is also available on the contextual menu.

Abort

You can abort during the connection process by clicking Stop in the progress dialog, which is labeled Uploading or something similar depending on the action you're carrying out. You can also press Command-period on a Macintosh or the Esc key under Windows to stop the process. (Abort, Command-period, and Escape are also used to stop other FTP behavior in progress.)

Built-In WebDAV Clients

WebDAV servers work similarly to FTP servers, requiring a URL (host and directory path) and a username and password (often, but not always) to access. The WebDAV Browser in the File menu and the WebDAV client used in the WebDAV tab of the Site window work almost identically. Enter settings for the WebDAV Browser at the top of the browser; those for the site-based client are entered via the FTP & WebDAV pane of Site Settings.

TIP: **Déjà Vu All** **Over Again**	You'll hear something familiar in this section on WebDAV clients, as we have liberally copied identical material from the FTP clients section just above. We didn't want to confuse the two by combining the often-different information. So it's not just you—you really may have read the same thing twice with minor changes.

Address

WebDAV uses the Web protocol for sending and retrieving files and file information, so you can simply provide a URL starting with http to indicate the server and directory path to the WebDAV archive. The person giving you access to a WebDAV server needs to give you the full URL, not just a server name, for most purposes. If you get a DNS error or a "server not found" error, double-check the address.

TIP: **Display Full** **Paths**	The Display Full Paths checkbox in the Site pane of the Preferences dialog box controls whether you see the full path at the top of the Site window's left- and right-hand sides. We recommend checking it, as it's another helpful indicator of what's going on while you work.

Username and Password

A WebDAV server typically has its own set of usernames and passwords separate from login permission for a server. This may be confusing, as you might have to maintain multiple accounts for different purposes on the same piece of hardware. A system administrator or Webmaster should be able to sort this out for you, however.

The username and password allow a WebDAV server to determine if you have permission to create new files, lock or unlock files, overwrite old files, create directories, and perform other file-related tasks.

If you don't check Save Password, you'll be prompted during each session for the password the first time you try to connect to the FTP server. After you enter it once, you can connect, disconnect, and reconnect without re-entering it. Closing the Site window or quitting GoLive resets this information, and you'll have to enter the password again on your next use.

TIP:
See FTP Tips on Passwords

See tips above for password advice vis-à-vis GoLive's clients. The advice is the same for FTP and WebDAV.

Authorization

Authorization is typically set to Basic when you need to provide a username and password to log in to a WebDAV server. None can be used when you don't need to provide any username and password.

Presets or "Favorites"

Instead of entering information from scratch each time, you can preset information for each Web site you regularly connect to via the WebDAV settings in the Network pane of GoLive's Preferences dialog box (see Figure 23-10). Entering settings for your "favorite" FTP servers makes it easier to later access them through the popup menu on both the WebDAV Browser and site WebDAV client's Site Settings (see Figure 23-11).

You can also add items in either WebDAV client by entering your server information and then selecting Add Current Server from the presets popup menu (also in Figure 23-12).

Enable Workgroup Support

This option, available only in Site Settings, lets GoLive automatically check files in and out by locking and unlocking them as you download and upload files (see Figure 23-13). This is less tedious than forcing you to choose which

Figure 23-10
WebDAV favorites preferences

Figure 23-11
Accessing
WebDAV
favorites

WebDAV Favorites in Site Settings

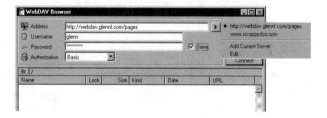

WebDAV Favorites in Preferences

Figure 23-12
Adding current
servers

files to lock and unlock. You may want to lock and unlock individual files for a variety of reasons. But when performing general updates and edits, it's easier to let GoLive handle the whole subject for you.

Connecting to the WebDAV Server

Once you set up all your parameters, connecting and disconnecting to a WebDAV server is merely a matter of clicking a button or selecting a menu item.

TIP:
Booting
You Off

WebDAV servers can be configured to boot you off after a predefined period of time; you can figure out that time period by reading status messages in Network Status; see "Network Status," earlier in this chapter.

Proxy

Your network administrator may tell you that you have to use a "proxy server" to access FTP and Web servers outside of your local network. If so, you need

Figure 23-13
Using
workgroup
support

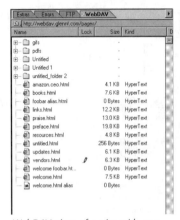

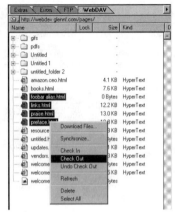

WebDAV view of a site with one
file this user has checked out

Select files and select Check Out
from the contextual menu.

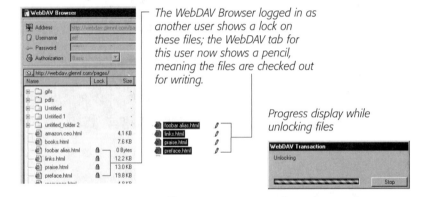

The WebDAV Browser logged in as
another user shows a lock on
these files; the WebDAV tab for
this user now shows a pencil,
meaning the files are checked out
for writing.

Progress display while
unlocking files

to set this in the Network pane of the Preferences dialog box. Check the Use HTTP Proxy box and enter the values for Host and Port provided by the administrator (see Figure 24-9, several pages earlier).

If you're using Mac OS's Internet control panel for your settings and need to configure an HTTP proxy, see Appendix A, *Macintosh Issues and Extras*.

Connecting

To connect, simply click the Connect button for the WebDAV Browser, or the WebDAV Server Connect/Disconnect button on the Site toolbar. For the Site client, click the WebDAV Server Connect/Disconnect button on the Site toolbar or select Connect from the Site menu's WebDAV Server submenu. You can also Control-click (Mac) or right-click (Windows) either the WebDAV Browser or the Site window's WebDAV tab and choose Connect from the contextual menu.

If you get an error on connecting, check out "Troubleshooting," later in this chapter. Small configuration errors in setting up a WebDAV server can disable appropriate login.

Disconnecting

To disconnect, click the Disconnect button for the WebDAV Browser or the WebDAV Server Connect/Disconnect button on the Site toolbar. For the Site client, click the WebDAV Server Connect/Disconnect button on the Site toolbar, or select Disconnect from the Site menu's WebDAV Server submenu. Disconnect is also available on the contextual menu.

Abort

You can abort during the connection process by clicking Stop in the WebDAV Transaction progress dialog (see Figure 24-14). You can also press Command-period on a Macintosh or the Esc key under Windows to stop the process. (Abort, Command-period, and Escape are also used to stop other WebDAV behaviors in progress.)

Figure 23-14
Stopping
WebDAV
transfers

Clicking the Stop button halts the transfer of files via WebDAV.

ISPs and Directories

Because GoLive can't synchronize over a LAN like Macromedia Dreamweaver can, you might think you're out of luck. Not so! It's a trivial matter to set up your own local FTP or Web-DAV server on virtually any computer. Because you're working over a LAN, you won't suffer from bandwidth problems, either.

The trick is that the same machine your Web site lives on, or the file server from which the Web site references its files (such as a network volume on an NT, NetWare, or AppleShare, NFS, or Samba file server) needs to run the FTP or WebDAV server. Then you set up GoLive to communicate with that server.

For the Macintosh, check out NetPresenz, a $75 FTP and Web server (http://www.stairways.com/netpresenz/). For Windows NT or 2000, you can use a built-in FTP server that ships with the software. For Unix, almost every installation comes with wuftpd, a free FTP server.

For WebDAV servers, check out http://webdav.org/projects/, which should list the most current servers available, and see the sidebar, "WebDAV for Apache," below.

Of course, there's some system administration cost associated with this. Someone has to figure out how to appropriately configure the FTP or WebDAV server. But it can provide you LAN-based synchronization that would otherwise be unavailable in GoLive.

WebDAV for Apache

We've really tried to avoid this being a technical manual, but we'd like to provide some information on how to add WebDAV service to an Apache 1.3 server. As of the writing of this book, the 1.0 release of mod_dav (the Apache WebDAV module) has been released and contains most of the basic necessary features for using WebDAV.

(Folks, don't try this at home unless you've compiled software before or have a Linux box and want to experiment with this type of thing. However, any system administrator who has ever compiled Apache should have little or no trouble installing this simple add-on.)

Tell your system administrator to visit http://www.webdav.org/mod_dav/, which is the official home page for the release. Installing mod_dav requires recompiling Apache, which is actually a relatively simple thing to do. Have the sysadmin follow the directions in the Install file that comes with the package. It requires them to separately configure mod_dav and compile it into an existing Apache build directory; this will be make sense to the sysadmin.

After compiling mod_dav and then recompiling Apache to include it properly, the Apache configuration file (often called httpd.conf) needs to be updated. Here is a sample configuration for using WebDAV inside a virtual host. This assumes that the root folder for the Apache server contains a folder named var (owned by the user and group that the server runs as) and conf (containing password and group information).

```
DAVLockDB var/DAVLock
DAVMinTimeout 600
LimitXMLRequestBody 500000
DAVDepthInfinity Off
Alias /pages /usr/www/webdav
<Location /pages>
    DAV On
    AllowOverride None
    Options None
    AuthName WebDAV_Server
    AuthType Basic
    AuthUserFile conf/dav.pass
    AuthGroupFile conf/dav.group
    <Limit PUT POST DELETE \
PROPFIND PROPPATCH MKCOL COPY \
MOVE LOCK UNLOCK> \
require group dav
    </Limit>
</Location>
```

The sysadmin needs to create users in a file called dav.pass in the conf directory using a program that comes with Apache called htpasswd (in Apache's /bin directory). This dav.pass file looks something like (in pure plain text):

```
bill:sad(*&(*f78789
joe:dsffd87*(&(*7d
fred:D*(&(*dfSS&F
```

They then create a plain text file with a regular editing program called dav.group that contains an entry like:

```
dav: bill fred joe
```

That's really the whole formula for setting it up. Only users in that file with those passwords can access that directory (which is set up as a "fake" directory at /pages to make it even harder for someone unauthorized to find).

File Handling

Now that you've connected to a server through FTP or WebDAV, you can manhandle the directory's contents as much as you want—within the constraints set by the system administrator or Webmaster, of course.

FTP servers can separate out several different kinds of file changes. For instance, an FTP server treats deleting, overwriting, creating, and renaming a file as different activities, and can limit different users to varying activities. WebDAV is more lumpy, with users having the ability to write (delete, overwrite, create, or rename) or not, and/or lock or unlock files and directories so that others know whether those files are checked out or not.

The FTP or WebDAV server's configuration for your account establishes how you can act. You may be able to upload files to certain directories of the Web site, for example, but not others. The server might let you delete files in one folder, but not in another.

All of these parameters get defined by the system administrator or Webmaster, so you have to consult with them to apply parameter changes. If you're running your own FTP or WebDAV server, however, you control the means of access, and need only fiddle with settings to make sure you have enough permission to carry out your tasks (see the sidebar, "May I, Please?" later in this chapter).

With the FTP or WebDAV client windows open, you can now examine and manipulate files, folders, and links (see the sidebar, "Aliases, Symbolic Links, and Shortcuts").

Status (FTP Only)

A status field at the bottom of the FTP tab and FTP Browser shows how GoLive is currently interacting with the FTP server (see Figure 23-15). The messages include, "Connecting…", "Connected", "Downloading Files", and other standard behavior. At any point while the status field shows an action in progress, you can click the Stop button to cancel the operation.

Figure 23-15
FTP status

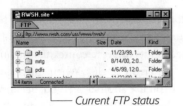

└── *Current FTP status*

Locking (WebDAV Only)

WebDAV allows you to lock files and folders on the WebDAV server so that other users can see who is currently working on a file or directory. It also prevents them from editing the file or folder.

Locking works differently for the WebDAV tab in the Site window depending on whether you have checked the Enable Workgroup Support box in Site Settings. With it unchecked, it works just like the WebDAV Browser; when checked, it has different options for locking and unlocking.

TIP:

Swapping in a Session

You can swap between workgroup support being enabled and disabled by checking or unchecking the Enable Workgroup Support box with a live WebDAV session open in the WebDAV tab.

WebDAV Browser and unchecked Workgroup Support in WebDAV tab. Select any files or folders in any combination and choose Lock or Shared Lock from the contextual menu; this is the only way to lock or unlock an item (see Figure 23-16). You unlock items the same way: select them and select Unlock from the contextual menu.

Force a lock's removal by selecting Reset Lock Status from the contextual menu. This is ill advised unless you're sure the lock is assigned incorrectly.

Figure 23-16
Locking and
unlocking files

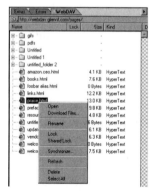

Checked Workgroup Support in WebDAV tab. Files must be checked in and out, not just locked and unlocked. Select any file, files, or folders in any combination and choose Check Out from the contextual menu; this is the only way to check an item out (see Figure 23-17). When you're done working with an item, select Check In; if you use another method, like just copying the file or using Synchronization, the WebDAV server gets confused and may mess up how others can access that file. (The option Undo Check Out reverts to the older file stored on the server and removes the lock.)

Figure 23-17
Workgroup
support for
checking in
and out

GoLive displays an icon for both kinds of lock in the Lock column of the WebDAV Browser or tab (see Figure 23-18). Lock is exclusive; Shared Lock allows others to work on a file while knowing that you've got it checked out as well. If you own an exclusive lock, you see a pencil, indicating you can write the file. An exclusive lock owned by someone else appears as a padlock icon. A shared lock shows up as a two overlapping faces, like a group icon; it also has a pencil with it if you have permission to edit that file.

The lock ownership is shown with detail in the Lock tab of the File Properties Inspector, discussed below.

Figure 23-18
Locked files

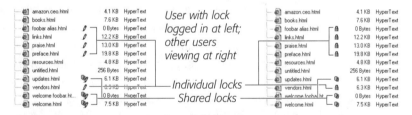

Selection

The FTP and WebDAV clients show you the number of items in the current window just as the count appears in the Files tab (see Chapter 21, *Files, Folders, and Links*). This appears at the bottom left of all clients (see Figure 23-19).

Figure 23-19
Selection
count

Count of selected items

Refreshing

An FTP or WebDAV session can get out sync if changes may be taking place on a server, or if you take our suggestion and use FTP and WebDAV on the same Web server for different purposes. You can refresh the file list in any client window by clicking in the window and selecting Refresh from the Site menu or Update from the contextual menu.

Live Editing

When you double-click any file in the FTP or WebDAV file list, GoLive downloads it to a temporary files location, nesting it inside folders that exactly match the directories in the path to that file via the remote server. GoLive also retrieves any graphics necessary to make the page display correctly and rewrites the links on the page to point to the local temporary storage of those files. (In fact, it's just like the Mac-only Download Page feature under the File menu; see Chapter 18, *Page Specials*.) In the case of WebDAV, the page is automatically locked while it's open so that someone else can't edit it.

TIP:
Temporary Directory for Images

The temporary images directory is set in Preferences in the General pane under Images settings. It's the Import Folder. See Chapter 9, *Images*, for more on this setting.

After making any changes to this file, selecting Save will re-upload it to the same location you downloaded from. The danger with editing files in this manner is that image links are incorrectly rewritten to point to the temporary location; you can keep an eye out for this by using the In & Out Links palette to see the media file links from the page (see Chapter 3, *Palettes and Parts*).

Live editing works with all the clients, and it's a neat trick despite the pitfalls. It combines the advantages of local editing with immediate updating. If you edit a file this way that's part of a site, you can use the Incremental Download item in the FTP Server submenu of the Site menu, or the corresponding button in the Site toolbar, to get the latest version to replace the local hard drive's copy of the file. Or, just drag the file over to the Files tab (see below for more on both options). Or, select the files and choose Download Selection from the FTP Server submenu.

Adding or Uploading

You can add files and folders from the Desktop or the Files tab by dragging them into the client window. The WebDAV clients warn you about overwriting files, while FTP doesn't seem to care, assuming you know what you're doing.

The more sensible way to add files is to use the synchronization features, described later in respective FTP and WebDAV sections. Synchronization ensures that GoLive gives you a realistic and extensive confirmation of all the changes you're about to make. If you don't have permission to create or overwrite files, you get an appropriate error when you attempt it, such as "553 /usr/www/spamalot/guineve.html: Permission denied" (see Figure 23-20).

Figure 23-20
FTP error

Unfortunately, you can't drag aliases or shortcuts into the FTP or WebDAV browsers or tabs and have them appropriately point to another file (see sidebar, "Aliases, Symbolic Links, and Shortcuts," later in this chapter). A system admin with direct access to the Web server file system has to create pointers, whether in Unix or any other operating system.

Downloading

Any file or folder can be downloaded via FTP to your local hard drive by dragging it onto the Desktop or into any open Site window, regardless of which GoLive FTP client you're using. If you drag a folder, all the contents are recursively copied.

If you drag an item into the Files tab of the Site window, and an item with the same name already exists, you'll be asked whether you want to replace it.

When you drag a pointer or link from any WebDAV or FTP client onto the Desktop or into the Files tab, GoLive copies the file that the link on the Web server points to, rather than making a local alias or shortcut to the item. If the link points to a folder, it copies its entire contents.

Creating Folders

In the FTP clients, you click the New Folder icon in the Toolbar to create a new folder. The default name is "folder"; each subsequent folder gets a space and number added to it, like "folder1" and so on. Using the FTP Browser, however, creates folders named "untitled_folder", and increments the names with a space and number, such as "untitled_folder 2".

If you have a folder selected in any client when you add a new folder, GoLive nests the new folder inside the old one. GoLive automatically selects the folder you've just created, so you need to click elsewhere in the browser or tab if you want to create additional empty folders to avoid nesting them.

Using the FTP Browser, if you don't rename the folder and attempt to add an-other one on certain FTP servers, the FTP clients display an error stating that the folder has an illegal character in it. Rename "untitled_folder" to anything else so that the next file created is called "untitled_folder" again, and then it works. This happens because GoLive tries to create a space in the second and subsequent folder names; some servers don't allow spaces in file and folder names.

Moving

You can drag any file in any client window and move it to any folder depth. GoLive doesn't offer the same spring-loaded folder action in these windows as it does in all tabs and windows elsewhere in GoLive, so you will have to click on the folder-expansion icon to display a nested folder or file down more than a single level (see Figure 23-21).

Figure 23-21
Dragging files across folder levels

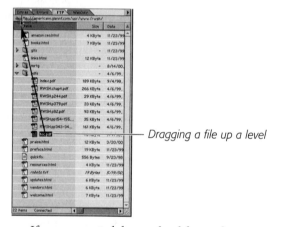

— Dragging a file up a level

If you are nested down a level from where you want to relocate a file, you need to drag that file onto the Path icon first to get to the right level, and then drop the file in the main window of that directory. If you've expanded the folder view and can see the directory level you want to relocate the file to, you just drag the file into the main window (see Figure 23-22).

Technically, FTP servers don't support moving a file. GoLive is actually copying the file to the new location and then deleting it from the old location. Because of FTP restrictions, you may not always be able to move files.

Renaming

You can rename a file in any client by clicking on the file's name. The file's title highlights, and you can type in a new name.

Figure 23-22
Moving a file
into a
subdirectory

TIP:
No Rename
If you don't have renaming permissions on the server, GoLive displays an error.

TIP:
Don't
Rename on
Server

Renaming or moving items on the server is dangerous, because GoLive won't rewrite references to those items as it does when you rename or move files or folders in the file system part of the Files tab. You should only rename or move items on the server when you're trying to fix a problem or move a file or folder to a different name so that you can copy a different version of it to the Web site.

Deleting

Deleting files on a server requires specific permission. If you don't have permission, GoLive displays an error. If you do have permission, GoLive asks you, "Do you really want to delete the selected item(s)?"

TIP:
No Undo
Delete

You cannot revert after deleting a file off the server like you can when you delete a file out of the Files tab, so make sure you're doing the right thing before you click OK. One strategy we've found useful is dragging outdated files into a folder called, predictably enough, "oldfiles". We occasionally go through that folder and toss old items, but having them available for a while ensures that we don't lose any work in case we need to go back a few revisions to restore data.

FTP Inspectors

For viewing detailed properties of items accessed via FTP, GoLive provides three FTP Inspectors, one each for pointers, files, and folders. (If you don't know what a pointer is, see the sidebar, "Aliases, Shortcuts, and Symbolic Links.") These Inspectors are named FTP Link, FTP File, and FTP Folder, respectively (see Figure 23-23).

Figure 23-23
FTP Inspectors

FTP Link Inspector   FTP File Inspector   FTP Folder Inspector

The Inspectors collect details about the items and present them through a consistent interface regardless of whether you're accessing a Macintosh, Windows, Unix, or even a tiny matchbox-sized FTP server on the other end.

All three Inspectors show the modification date of the item, if available, and the URL to reach the item via FTP (also see the sidebar, "Do You Have the Time?"). You can't copy and paste the URL; it's just there for reference.

They also show the permissions "map": who may read, write, and execute the file, folder, or link (see the sidebar, "May I, Please?"). Changing the set of permissions requires you to click the Set Rights button. For folders, you can also change all permissions for every file and folder inside of it, no matter how many levels deep those files and folders are nested, by checking the Recursive box.

Depending on how the FTP server is set up, you may not be able to change permissions at all. If you can't but need to, there's no way to change this in GoLive. You'll need to ask the system administrator responsible for the server to add "chmod" and perhaps "umask" support. (If they don't know what this means, you may just be out of luck.)

TIP:
Execute with Impunity (Unix FTP)

You may wonder why all Web site folders accessed through a Unix FTP server have Execute checked for all three kinds of users. It's an obscure but important attribute; folders that contain items which everyone everywhere can access (whether as read-only or as modifiable items) must be set as executable. It's just one of those things that doesn't make specific sense on the surface, but is required for low-level FTP operations. So don't just uncheck Execute and click Set Rights because it looks wrong, as that will bar all access to the folder.

The FTP Link Inspector also shows the object pointed to in the Pointer field in the form of a URL. The FTP File Inspector reveals the file size of the selected document.

You can change an item's name on the FTP server by changing it in the appropriate FTP Inspector or by clicking the file name and typing a new one. However, making a change in this manner won't rewrite links from other files that point to it.

WebDAV Inspectors

GoLive offers as much information as it can about files and folders stored on a WebDAV server through a single Resource Properties Inspector (see Figure 23-24).

TIP:
Many Servers

Since WebDAV is a protocol, not a product, there are many implementations of it in progress. Many of the features shown in this Inspector may not be populated with some servers and may have excruciating detail with others.

Aliases, Symbolic Links, and Shortcuts

Your mother may have told you that pointing isn't polite, but it is efficient. Every major operating system lets you create multiple pointers to the same document, program, or folder so that you don't have to make multiple copies of the thing itself.

Apple added aliases back in Macintosh System 7 so that users could, for instance, put links to their most common programs and documents in a single place, or get to a specific deeply nested folder without opening window after window. Microsoft added the same functionality starting in Windows 95 through shortcuts. Unix has pretty much always had symbolic links.

What's the difference between aliases, shortcuts, and symbolic links? Not much. They all point to an actual resource and can be moved around and still retain their link to that resource. But they only occupy a few bytes and they don't duplicate the contents of the resource.

The biggest difficulty you'll find with point-

ers is that GoLive, since its 3.x incarnation, always downloads everything found underneath a pointer through its FTP clients. That is, you can't set it to only download the pointer itself, which would logically turn it into an alias or shortcut depending on whether you're running GoLive on a Mac or under Windows. (WebDAV doesn't display pointers, so it's a non-issue.)

When you attempt to upload an alias or shortcut, GoLive turns it into a plain text file on the FTP or WebDAV server, which doesn't serve much of a purpose either; or, it may balk at uploading it at all, saying, "not a plain file."

The FTP and WebDAV protocols don't allow you to make pointers; you have to get a system administrator to make them on the Web site file system.

We provide some strategies for dealing with both shortcomings in the respective "Synchronizing" sections for FTP and WebDAV later in this chapter.

Figure 23-24
Resource
Properties
Inspector

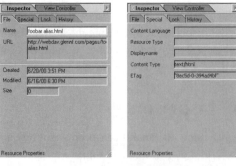

File tab   Special tab

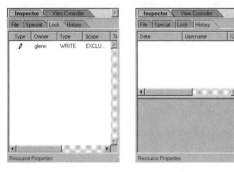

Lock tab   History tab

File. Normal file properties are displayed here, including name, URL, creation and modification datestamps, and size. You can modify the name of the remote file by editing it in the Name field; we don't recommend this, however, as it doesn't update the local file name.

Special. The Special tab offers information that may be stored about a given file, such as the language, resource type, and so on. With the Apache WebDAV server, only Etag (a special, unique property assigned to a file transaction) and content type (the MIME type of the file) appear. (For more on MIME types, see "File Mappings" in Chapter 18, *Page Specials*.)

Lock. This tab shows the current outstanding lock or locks. The properties assigned to a lock include an owner, permissions (such as write), a scope (whether it's shared or exclusive to a single individual), a duration the lock is allowed (which can be "infinite"), and a lock token (used for internal record keeping). If an item has multiple shared locks, they all show up here.

TIP:
XML in
Action
The information shown in this tab is generally stored as part of an XML document. It's a good example of how rich information can be stored in XML instead of requiring complex proprietary databases or other structures. WebDAV servers and clients can both read and write XML, so you don't need to use a particular WebDAV server.

History. This tab should show a list of modifications to a file, but in our testing with the Apache module for WebDAV, this information wasn't retained.

FTP Synchronizing

GoLive includes a simple, powerful set of controls for keeping your local copy of the content and the remote Web site content synchronized over FTP. These features let you synchronize in either direction, and offer some control over what gets uploaded from the local version of the Web site. (Note that synchronization only works with the FTP tab, not the FTP Browser, because you have to have a local set of files to compare.)

TIP:
Your First
Time
The first time you perform an Upload Modified Items with a given site file, GoLive automatically uploads everything even if the remote files have identical modification dates. The reason is explained more fully in the sidebar, "Do You Have the Time." GoLive has to make a record in the site file of the fact that it did synchronize once. There's really no way around this that we've figured out, and Adobe hasn't offered a "pretend everything was uploaded" option yet.

If you use the FTP upload features, only files on your local hard drive that meet certain criteria compared to those on the FTP server are uploaded. There are four options:

- **Upload Modified Items.** GoLive compares the modification date and time of each local file with its counterpart (if any) on the FTP server. If the local file is newer, it uploads it. This operation can take quite a while with larger sites, as GoLive must check the timestamp on every file on the FTP server. You can bypass this check by using Incremental Upload.

TIP:
Harmonizing
Dual
Modifications
If you've edited both the file on the FTP server and in your local copy of the site, GoLive won't harmonize the differences and merge the file. You have to do that yourself, using Microsoft Word's Merge Documents feature or other software. That's why it's wise to always keep track of the latest "live" version of the file, or which copy has been most recently modified.

- **Incremental Upload.** GoLive only uploads files that have been modified in the local site folder since its record of last uploading, but it doesn't check the modification time on the same files stored on the server. This is a way to add missing files quickly.

- **Upload Selection.** Choose some items in the Files tab and invoke this option to upload the selection.

- **Upload All.** We don't fully understand why this option exists, but it's a combination of Export and Upload. GoLive does a full export of the site to a local folder and then uploads the entire site. This could be useful, we guess, if your remote site had become very out of sync and you wanted to simply start from scratch. You could delete the remote site entirely and then select Upload All. However, choosing any of the previous items would seem to do the same thing.

The Incremental Download feature only downloads files from the FTP server that are newer. (The timing issue may be problematic, though; see the sidebar, "Do You Have the Time?") You can also choose files and select Download Selection.

| **TIP:** |
| **Beware** |
| **Downloading** |

Watch out for downloading files if you've used Strip HTML Code—see that eponymous section later in this chapter for more details.

The FTP options are located in the FTP Server submenu of the Site menu as four distinct choices, or as a popup menu in the Site toolbar (see Figure 23-25). You can set one of the four upload options as a default for the Toolbar button.

Getting Set to Synchronize

Before you upload files via FTP for the first time, you should check Site Settings for the FTP tab. Click the Site Settings button or select Settings from the Site menu, and then click FTP & WebDAV Server.

Figure 23-25
FTP upload
options

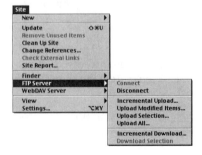

When the correct server information is present and you're ready to upload, select which upload option to use in the Toolbar, and then click the upload buton. You're presented with an Upload Options dialog box with several options.

TIP:
Setting
Defaults

You can set the defaults for the Upload Options through the Upload settings in the Site pane of Preferences. You can also reset these defaults by pressing Set As Default after changing settings in the Upload Options dialog box.

Publish State and References

The two checkboxes for Honor Publish State and Upload Referenced Files Only represent just two separate methods of deciding what to upload, even

May I, Please?

Every computer that lets users access its files remotely has a built-in set of policies that control which users can access and modify files. These policies are called file permissions, and correspond to settings attached to each file (Windows and Unix) or directory (Mac, Windows, and Unix).

For users who haven't had to deal with remote files over a network, file permissions can be intimidating. The Macintosh and Windows systems generally let you read, write, delete, and overwrite all of the files on the local drive; you can lock files in different ways on both with a little effort. But when you share your files or access shared files, there has to be some intermediation so that any user passing by can't destroy your Web site.

File permissions define who owns a particular file or directory, what group (if any) may have special access to it, and how the rest of the world can interact with it. The owner, the group, and the world can each have separate permissions set for access. The owner and

groups are typically set up by user accounts on a system; the owner is a login name for a particular user, while a group contains any number of users and/or other groups, depending on the operating system.

Each platform has slightly different ideas about permissions, but the Mac is most restrictive when used as an FTP server. Unlike Windows NT and Unix and Mac OS X, Mac OS 9 and earlier can't set file permissions for individual files, only for directories (see Table 23-1). GoLive maps this behavior by showing group read and write permissions checked for any file you select and view with the FTP File Inspector. If you try to change the settings and click Set Rights, you get an error: "FTP Error: 404, Parameter Not Accepted."

Unix, on the other hand, not only allows control over all files, but it even uses these access controls to restrict who changes what files when you're working on a keyboard connected directly to the machine.

Table 23-1	GoLive calls it	Owner	Group	Other	Permissions
Permission categories by platform	Mac OS 7 to 9.x	User	Group	Everyone	Folder only
	Mac OS X	User	Group	Everyone	Files/folders
	Windows 98/ME	*	*	*	Folder only
	Windows NT/2000	User	Group	Everybody	Files/folders
	Unix	User	Group	World	Files/folders

* Windows 98/ME supports password-based file sharing and permissions, but FTP servers running under Windows 98/ME may map different permissions settings onto files and folders.

though you can check or uncheck combinations of them (see Figure 23-26). These options are more about deciding what *not* to upload than deciding what gets uploaded.

Figure 23-26
Upload
options

TIP:
Ubiquitous Setting

Every file, folder, and link has a "publish state," which directs GoLive whether or not to upload the object in a file synchronization. You set this state via the Publish popup menu in the File and Folder Inspectors (see Figure 23-27). You can select more than one item at a time without mixing files and folders and set their Publish state through a merged Inspector palette (see Figure 23-28).

The Honor Publish State checkboxes mediate whether files and folders that have Publish set to Never or If Referenced (files)/If Not Empty (folders) get uploaded.

If you check Honor Publish State for Files or Folders, GoLive relies on the Publish flag set for each item, which is set to Always by default. These choices apply only when the file meets the criteria for uploading based on your upload choice, such as local files being newer than on the server.

• If the Publish flag is set to Always, GoLive always uploads the item if the file or folder meets the upload criteria.

• If the flag is set to Never, the item (and its contents, if it's a folder) isn't uploaded.

Figure 23-27
Setting the
Publish state

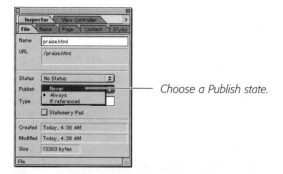

Choose a Publish state.

Figure 23-28
Setting
multiple
Publish states

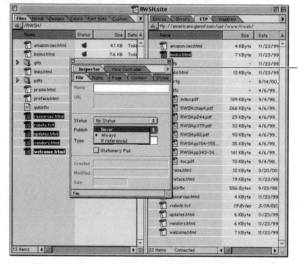

This Inspector
appears when you
have multiple files
or multiple folders
selected, allowing
you to set the
Publish state for all
at once.

- If it's a file and set to If Referenced, GoLive uploads it only if the item appears in the navigation hierarchy; that is, if the item gets referenced from any link that descends from the home page you've defined. You can view the navigation hierarchy via the Navigation View item in the Design menu.

- If it's a folder, and Publish is set to If Not Empty, and the folder has any contents, GoLive creates the folder on the FTP server if one doesn't already exist. However, this option only matters if all the items inside the folder wouldn't upload on their own. GoLive creates any necessary folders for enclosed items that get uploaded.

- If you check either Files or Folders under Honor Publish State, the Upload Referenced Files Only setting is grayed out. (By the way, Windows shows Pages and Groups, which means the same thing, but is an accidental leftover from GoLive 4.)

Do You Have the Time?

When you synchronize files using GoLive's FTP feature set to Upload Modified, you may think you're dealing with absolute time; the files are modified at an exact moment locally or on a Web site, and GoLive just compares those numbers.

Unfortunately, it's more complex. We didn't realize the extent of this problem until we started researching it for the first edition of this book. And, frankly, it's a mess, partly because of the FTP protocol's lack of precision about time.

FTP Time Isn't Your Time. It may come as a surprise that much of the time on the Internet is regulated by time zones. Your email client, for example, makes a quick calculation based on the difference between the time and location a message is sent, and your current time and location.

As a general rule, however, FTP servers don't send the time zone they're in as part of a file listing, nor do they send the seconds after the minute for file modifications. For files older than one year, FTP servers send just the date and year of the file's last modification. (Some FTP software sends more, but the most commonly used Unix servers don't.)

Also, there's no guarantee that the FTP server machine's clock is actually set to atomic-clock time or any other close approximation, and the FTP protocol doesn't include a provision for it to send its current time of day and time zone.

What this adds up to is that if you're working in Oregon and your files are stored on a server in New York, you have a three-hour difference in the modification dates for your files the moment you copy them from your local hard drive to the remote FTP server. The local modifica-tion date and time aren't sent as part of the FTP protocol, either.

So, if we modify a file at 10:22:07 a.m. PDT and copy it to New York over the Internet, assuming the system clock is set right, the modification date on the file server will immediately be set to 1:22:00 p.m. EDT. But the server sends this time as part of the file's listing as just "1:22".

Some servers are set up with a little less-than-attentive care, and they might be set by default to Greenwich Mean Time (GMT), which is eight hours later than Pacific time, and is often the default setting for new Unix servers.

GoLive's Clever Hack. GoLive has a clever workaround. In the site file, it caches the local modification date for any files you copy over to an FTP server during an open connection to the server. That's what it's doing when it displays the "Synchronizing Modification Times" progress bar. So when you copy a file, the time and date you see in the FTP client show as identical to the local file's modification timestamp.

However, if you disconnect and reconnect to the server, close the Site window, or quit GoLive and reopen it, time gets out of joint (thank you, Mr. Shakespeare): the cached value that matches the local file's timestamp is no longer displayed. According to Adobe's technical support staff, the offset is still stored in the site file, but you can't access or see this information.

If you try to synchronize after this, your local file appear older than the server file in the Pacific to Eastern time zone case above. But if GoLive correctly uploaded and stored the time offset, you're still okay. (continued on next page)

(continued from previous page)

Even more subtle is when your files and your server are in the same time zone, but the server's system clock is off, a typical occurrence. Again, GoLive caches the local hard disk modification time, but if the clocks are a few minutes apart, you can run into some baffling problems when using synchronization if you edit and upload a file repeatedly over a few minutes. Typically, GoLive appears to store this information and cope with it correctly, not asking to upload the file again.

But you can get cases in which the time displayed and the actual time may appear off, and yet GoLive refuses to synchronize without providing a clear reason in the Inspectors.

Lots of Improvement. In the first edition of this book, we offered some humble suggestions for fixing this problem. Adobe responded (to general user feedback) by improving how GoLive stores the modification date and time.

It looks to us now like GoLive correctly caches modification timestamps so that you don't wind up with out-of-sync uploads and downloads after GoLive has uploaded the files from your local site at least once. This imposes the burden that each time you create a new site file (perhaps because an old one became corrupted or you're moving the site), GoLive insists on uploading all files. However, this step ensures that GoLive has cached all the modification timestamps and can correctly figure out newer and older files in the future.

With Honor Publish State's settings off and Upload Referenced Files Only checked, GoLive only uploads files that meet the upload criteria and that are in the link hierarchy as described just above. If a new file is in a folder that doesn't exist on the FTP server, this option automatically creates that folder.

Show List of Files to Upload

When either uploading or downloading files, having this option checked shows a list of all the files that are affected. You can then deselect individual files by unchecking them. You can view files by folder or as a flat list omitting folders—which are created as necessary on the FTP server—by unchecking Show Folder Structure (see Figure 23-29). We prefer to view by folder as it's a cleaner organization and we can turn off an entire folder using this method.

TIP:
Unchecking All

If you want to uncheck all files, it's better to uncheck Show Folder Structure, uncheck the box at the top of the list—which unchecks all files—and then check Show Folder Structure again (see Figure 23-30). It sounds complex, but you get used to it, and it's more efficient than unchecking each folder one at a time.

We always leave Show List of Files to Upload checked so we can make sure the right files have been swept up in the net.

Figure 23-29
Flat and
structured
upload

 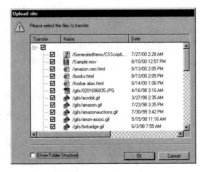

*Structured by folder showing just
necessary items to upload*

Flat list omitting folders

Figure 23-30
Unselecting all
uploads

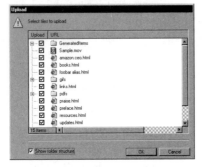 

*1. Show files to upload with Show
Folder Structure checked.*

*2. Uncheck Show Folder Structure and
then uncheck the top Upload box.*

*3. Check Show Folder Structure again,
and now you can choose individual
folders to upload.*

Strip HTML Code

This great feature, added in GoLive 5, lets you apply a filter against your
HTML to strip out extra spaces, GoLive-specific tags and attributes, and embedded comments (see Figure 23-31). This is useful in three respects:

1. It doesn't expose to the world (the world that views source on HTML pages) information you may have inserted in a page for your own reference.

2. It removes GoLive tags, making your HTML that much cleaner (and able to pass validation checks some companies require for their HTML pages).

3. It makes pages slightly smaller, reducing download time by microseconds to seconds for users.

TIP:
Downloading
after
Stripping

The downside of stripping out HTML chunks when uploading is that your remote page no longer matches your local page. If you have to download that page back to your local hard drive, the page may be missing critical Components you use throughout a site; these appear as just regular HTML when the GoLive tags are stripped.

Don't Show Again

Checking this box allows you to bypass the Upload Options dialog box the next time you upload; GoLive follows the settings you've checked or unchecked. If you check this box, you must go to the Preferences dialog box to edit settings for uploading, including forcing GoLive to once again show you the dialog box each time (see Figure 23-32).

Uploading

As noted earlier, there are four ways to upload files via FTP. Choose the most appropriate method from the FTP Server submenu of the Site menu or from the popup menu that emerges from the FTP Upload button to the right of the FTP Server Connect/Discconect button.

If you check Don't Show Again in the Upload Options dialog box, you have to check Show Options Dialog in Preferences to restore it.

GoLive then presents you with the Upload Options dialog box, followed by the file list, as described above.

First Time

The first time you transfer a site to a remote server, GoLive transfers all the files and creates all the directories, essentially initializing the site. As we note earlier, even if all the files are identical on the local hard drive and remote FTP server, GoLive has to synchronize them in order to set up the modification timestamp for each file.

Choosing Files

It's a good idea to choose to upload all files, as GoLive usually figures out which ones are the right ones. If you upload some and not others, you face the problem that some of your links won't work on the live site.

Out of Sync Uploads

If you delete or reorganize your content locally, GoLive can't track these changes and upload them. This means that if you remove a file in the Files tab, it won't be automatically removed from the FTP server when you synchronize.

Similarly, if you move content around, such as transporting all your images from the root level of the Web site to their own folder, GoLive doesn't reshuffle them per your new local arrangement on the FTP server. Instead, it treats the new folder as a new object, and wants to upload it and all the contents.

To fix this problem, you have to delete, rename, or move the corresponding files on the server. Or, you can delete all the items affected, and use the Upload All feature to reinstall a clean copy. This latter solution is easier, but it can take a while if the site is large and you don't have sufficient bandwidth.

If you need to create new pointers, delete old ones, or move existing ones via GoLive—well, you can't. The FTP protocol, as we noted earlier, doesn't have a provision for coping with pointers. You have to ask your system administrator to make these changes on the server itself. (If the system admin is someone other than yourself, ask politely.)

TIP:
Staging Site

To avoid problems that sometimes happen when taking content live, we suggest (if possible) you set up a mirror or "staging" site for help with synchronizing. You can use this location to test the upload and make sure everything worked right. You can then use a stand-alone FTP program to copy the files to the real Web site.

It's possible to set up a staging site to test new content by having a directory pointed to by a separate Web server. Or, you can even nest your test inside a folder on your main Web site. It may sound like a bit of extra work now, but trust us: experience has taught us the value of mirroring sites in progress.

Uploading to Multiple Servers

Updating a site that's split between multiple servers can be tricky, and may involve the use of the URL mapping feature. We discuss this feature and its implications in Chapter 21, *Files, Folders, and Links*.

Exporting

If you want to restructure your site to use a flat organization, such as putting all the media files in one folder and all the pages in another, but keep your local copy intact, you can export your site and then upload those files to the server using the FTP Browser.

Downloading

There are occasions when you have to edit a file on the Web server itself, rather than editing files locally and uploading them. Or, a server might be generating automatic files for you that you need to retrieve.

By clicking Incremental Download in the Site toolbar or selecting that item from the Site menu's FTP Server submenu, you can download all files from the server that were modified more recently than the local copies (see the earlier sidebar, "Do You Have the Time?"). GoLive also downloads any folders and files which aren't found in the local copy of the site.

You can also select one or more items and choose Download Selection from the FTP Server submenu.

TIP:
Overwriting Home Page

In order to overwrite the page you chose as your home page (see Chapter 21, *Folders, Files, and Links*), you must use the Download from Server feature. The workaround is to choose any other file in your site, bring up the File Inspector's Page tab, and check Home Page. You can now download the real home page, and then reverse the process to make it the home page again (see Figure 23-33).

Avoiding Links

The Incremental Download feature tries to download everything that's not present in the local copy, including links or pointers. We haven't figured out a workaround that prevents this behavior, and it can generate an awfully long list of files to review.

The solution, if you have a lot of links or many files nested underneath them, is either to drag specific files you need from the FTP tab to the Files tab, or to uncheck inappropriate items from the files list that appears when you use Incremental Download.

Figure 23-33
Downloading
home page
subterfuge

1. Select another page to substitute as your home page for this subterfuge.

2. Drag the home page from the FTP tab into the Files tab.

3. Reset your home page back to the real McCoy.

Out of Sync Downloads

As noted earlier, GoLive doesn't synchronize file deletions or moves between local and remote copies. So if you have some orphan files on the Web site, the Incremental Download command tries to download these files, as there are no local copies. Either delete these from the Web site, move them, or uncheck them from the files list displayed after you select the command.

WebDAV Synchronizing

Compared to FTP synchronization, WebDAV is a walk in the park. You have fewer options, but it's a lot more visual about what's happening.

Synchronizing, Uploading, Downloading

After you connect to the WebDAV server through one of the methods discussed earlier, you have three options for synchronizing: Synchronize All,

Upload Modified Items, and Download Modified Items. The three buttons in the Site toolbar correspond to these three items; the WebDAV submenu of the Site menu also makes available the same options for items selected in the Files or WebDAV tab.

TIP:
FTP/WebDAV
Combo to
Solve
Permissions

With WebDAV, you can't modify permissions through an Inspector, but you can still get errors when you don't have the right file permissions when you attempt to delete, download, upload, or overwrite files. Sometimes, we set up both an FTP server and a WebDAV server pointing to the same directory: we use the FTP Inspectors to change permissions and WebDAV to handle synchronization.

Choosing any of these options brings up the same dialog box for uploading and downloading (see Figure 23-34). The only difference is that choosing Synchronize All looks for modified files both locally and remotely, while upload and download look on just the local or remote directories, respectively.

Figure 23-34
WebDAV
Synchronize
dialog box

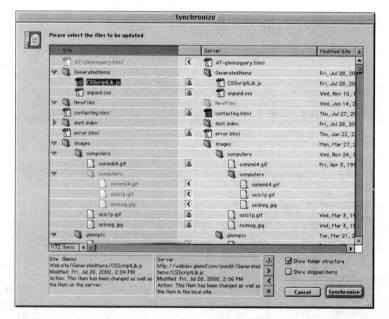

Upload and download actions. This dialog shows a list associating all local and remote files with a clickable icon in the middle between them that indicates the action to take place. There are four possibilities for each file: upload, download, ignore, or delete.

You can click the icon to cycle through any available options, or select one or more files and click the icon in the list below the files list to set the same option for the entire selection.

If you select a folder and click any of the icons at the bottom, any actions you select are applied to all nested files, even though an icon doesn't show up for folders.

Show Folder Structure. If you check this box, the Synchronize dialog box shows you the files organized by folders, including nested folders. Unchecking it shows you the alphabetical listing of all files.

Show Skipped Items. Items that don't need to have an action performed on them, or ones that you manually chose and clicked the Skip button, can be omitted from the file list by checking this box. Unchecking it redisplays them in case you need to make changes to their upload and download behavior as well.

Information. When you select a file, GoLive displays a fair amount of information in two areas at the lower left of the Synchronize window. On the left is information about the local file; on the right, about the remote file. The "Action" describes what GoLive will do.

Errors. Errors are displayed in the Network Status dialog box with a lot of detail—hopefully enough to troubleshoot or report to a sysadmin.

Selecting

You can choose files in either the Files or WebDAV tab and drag them over. GoLive brings up a transfer progress bar and asks you if you're sure you want to copy the files. Often, this involves GoLive first deleting the existing files and replacing them with the ones you want to copy.

TIP:
A Real Drag,
Baby

You can't drag files over if you've checked Enable Workgroup Support in the Site Settings for your site's WebDAV tab. In that mode, GoLive manages all copying.

Exporting

The WebDAV synchronization doesn't allow you to strip HTML code like you can with FTP. To achieve that, export your site using the Export feature and then upload it via the WebDAV Browser. See Chapter 21, *Files, Folders, and Links*, for more information about exporting.

Out of Sync

WebDAV suffers from the same problem as FTP: when you delete files locally, they are not deleted on the WebDAV server; when you move files locally, they aren't moved remotely. The Synchronize dialog box offers the ability to delete files, but this still doesn't synchronize them.

If you wind up out of sync, you may need to delete files remotely and then upload them again from the local directory using Synchronize.

Troubleshooting

Some common problems with FTP and WebDAV that GoLive can't control might plague you. Here are the symptoms, and what you can tell a system administrator to do to fix it.

GoLive passes through errors that the server reports. Many of these are semi-opaque, and provide little information for troubleshooting the problem. However, Network Status can provide quite a lot of information, as you can review it for the actual messages sent back by the server in a transcript of the session.

For a list of all FTP error codes, see the following page at our Web site for reference: http://www.realworldgolive.com/ftpcodes.html. This list is abstracted from the FTP protocol description. A system administrator may want the specific code, so the more information you can provide, the better.

WebDAV's errors are more descriptive, tending to mirror or be identical to those created by a Web server. Anything that doesn't make sense, report to the system administrator.

Connection

Connecting to a server should be straightforward, but there are enough variables to complicate the process.

Wrong username or password. If you enter the wrong username or password for FTP, GoLive should tell you specifically that either the username or password is incorrect. If you think you're using the right information, confirm it with the system admin. We've found that a typical cause for a wrong username or password is incorrect capitalization. Often, it's critical to type a username or password exactly, with the same caps and lower case, as what's provided to you. It's also easy to hit the Caps Lock key by accident, as you can't see what you're typing when you enter the password.

For WebDAV, GoLive fails to provide any warning unless the server balks. We've found that with the way Apache is set up, for instance, you get no warning but you cannot edit any files.

Wrong host name. If you enter the host name incorrectly you should get a DNS error, which means that the domain name you entered with that particular machine or host name doesn't have an Internet address. Double check the information provided and contact the system admin if it persists.

No response from server. The first time you try to connect to a server, if you don't get a response in a reasonable period of time, it might be that the server is down or not reachable from your Internet location. If this persists, contact the system admin with the dates and times you tried to connect.

User not authorized (FTP). Systems often have to be configured to allow users to access them via FTP. Your account may be properly set up, but when you try to connect you get "530: Login failed: user not authorized." The system admin will need to double check his or her settings for your account to confirm you have access.

The server did not send a root resource... (WebDAV). If you connect to a server that isn't running a WebDAV component, you may get this error. Check that you're connecting to the right place.

GoLive can't support server. From your perspective as a user, the server's operating system and type of software are invisible. However, there are dozens (maybe hundreds) of different FTP server software packages, and GoLive only supports the most popular for Unix, Linux, Windows 98/NT, and Macintosh.

The GoLive manual doesn't provide a list of supported servers, but you may get no error—and no connection—when it encounters one that uses a different format from the established standards.

WebDAV is a newer standard with more uniformity and fewer options, so GoLive should support any WebDAV compliant server. However, we're sure quirks will appear.

File List

After GoLive connects to the server, it should quickly display a list of items in the directory you've connected to. If you don't get this list, the problem could be one of the following situations.

Permission problem. The account's directory isn't set up to allow you "read" access, meaning that you can't see the files in them. The system admin must make system changes to make this work for you.

Proxy server or network interference. Networks with firewalls, proxies, or other intermediaries might require you to check Use Passive Mode in order to make an FTP connection work, or you may have to configure a Web or FTP proxy in the Network pane of Preferences. In these cases, you might be able to connect to the server, but it won't download or upload files, and it might not be able to send a file list.

Method Not Allowed (WebDAV). WebDAV servers have to be configured to allow WebDAV access to directories. If the one you attempt to access isn't configured correctly in general or for your username and password, WebDAV offers an error like "PROPFIND / : HTTP/1.1 405 Method Not Allowed". Check with your sysadmin.

Unknown mystery. Sometimes on the Macintosh, we find that we just can't use FTP any longer. Connections get made, but no file lists are ever transferred. Rebooting the Mac through a normal restart from the Finder usually fixes the problem. We haven't found an explanation for this behavior.

Can't drag (WebDAV). If you have Enable Workgroup Support checked in the Site Settings of a site, you can't drag files back and forth between the WebDAV and Files tabs; you must use the synchronization features.

Can't Access Directory or Upload

You may find that there are areas of a site you can't reach via FTP or WebDAV, or certain directories won't allow you to upload files. Both of these problems are permission related, and require the system administrator to change permissions to allow you or your group read, write, and/or execute permission to the appropriate directories.

Upload directive (FTP). Additionally, if you can't upload, many FTP servers require a separate "upload" directive that allows a user to login and upload to specific directories. If the directory isn't specified in that directive, the user can't add, overwrite, delete, or rename files.

Configuration for upload (WebDAV). A WebDAV server has to be configured to allow users to perform each kind of file activity, including adding new files to the directory. This directive might be missing.

Web site is inaccessible (FTP). You may find that Web surfers can't reach files on your Web site. GoLive allows you to change file permissions as long as the FTP server is configured to let you change them. If users can't reach your Web site, make sure the files you've added are set, under the FTP File or FTP Link Inspector, to Read for Other. For folders, both Read and Execute must be checked for others.

If you click Set Rights and get an error, then you will need the system admin to make the permissions changes for you.

For Macintosh Web servers, you only need to set folder permissions via the FTP Folder Inspector to Read and Execute, as files lack separate permission controls.

If you're using WebDAV, you can't change file permissions. This is why we recommend having both FTP and WebDAV access for your sites.

Locked and (Up)loaded

With a mastery of FTP staging and synchronizing in hand, keeping your site up to date involves a minimum of effort and maximum of aplomb.

It's important to remember that even experienced Internet hands find themselves flummoxed facing FTP on occasion, as the number of potential problems in correctly setting up FTP access on a server can be manifold. However, a good network or system administrator can make your part of the job easy: figuring out what goes where and when it needs to get put there.

Importing a Site

If we had chapter subtitles in this book, this chapter's would be "This Old Site." Much like the popular home-fix-it show *This Old House,* this chapter aims to take a perfectly serviceable site that's fallen on hard times, clean it up without radically changing its character, and bring it into the modern age.

Some sites we've worked on started their lives way back in 1995 and have accumulated the equivalent of years of soot and creosote build-up, with ancient tags and old HTML hacks lingering in their crevices. GoLive is an excellent chimney sweep of old sites, brushing away the grime.

However, updating an old site isn't quite as easy as just opening it up in GoLive and creating a site window. In addition to creating the right options in GoLive, you may want to take the opportunity to reorganize the site's files, delete old and orphaned material, clean up outdated or incorrect references, and toss out bad HTML. You'll also want to ditch server-side imagemaps, an outdated method of using images to navigate that adds latency to a Web site.

It's best to approach a site renovation when you first bring a site into GoLive's management. Nail all the problems and make all the corrections in an orgy of find-and-replace actions. You'll be surprised by how much renovation you can do in only a few hours.

Importing

Importing a site is straightforward, but you can save yourself some extra labor and make the process of updating the site easier if you follow this procedure. Let's assume a site is about cardoon growing (see Figure 24-1).

1. Create a folder on your local hard drive called "cardoon project".

2. Create two folders inside this folder: one called "new cardoon site", the other called "old cardoon site".

3. Download or copy your old site into a folder called "cardoon site contents" and create a copy into both the new and old site folders. The intention of this is to keep a backup handy.

4. Open GoLive and select Import from Folder under the File menu's New Site submenu.

5. Select the folder containing the site inside the "new cardoon site" folder. Don't create a new folder, as you've already nested folders correctly.

6. Select your site's existing home page (you can change this later as part of your renovations, if you need to).

7. Click OK. GoLive will now build the site file. For larger sites, this can take some time, and may require you to allocate extra memory to GoLive under the Mac OS or to the system in general in Windows. (See Chapter 1, *Getting Started*.)

Virtually all the site cleanup changes we're going to suggest are not reversible. So, as we suggest in Chapter 19, *Site Management*, you should make backups of your current site folder as you work, to avoid having to return to the beginning after you've made significant progress. Whenever you do a large sitewide change using Find & Replace, for instance, we'd recommend making another site copy just beforehand.

NEW IN 5:
Site File
Backup

GoLive 5 makes a backup of the site file every time you save, as long as you haven't disabled this option in the Site pane of the Preferences dialog box. However, we recommend regularly making a new copy of the site file on your hard drive as you apply the actions suggested in this chapter. This allows you to retreat to a position that still worked even if you have a crash or if the site file becomes corrupted later.

Nothing Up Our Sleeves and...Oops!

Unfortunately, a great trick we used to rewrite sites in GoLive 4 disappeared with the introduction of better features, if you can believe that. Our strategy for such problems as missing quotation marks around attributes in HTML tags was to use Find & Replace to look for and replace a period in every file. This forced GoLive 4 to open each file, make the change (which rewrote the HTML), save it with a preview, and close it.

GoLive 5 is superior in that it both preserves HTML code as a feature (360Code, which prevents scripts written in ASP, PHP3, and other languages from being destroyed by GoLive) and makes Find & Replace changes insanely fast.

GoLive 5 also introduced the Rewrite Source Code option, which rewrites a single page according to the values chosen in Web Settings (see Chapter 16, *Source Editing*). However, you can't apply Rewrite Source Code to an entire site.

We expect that a future version of GoLive will offer a single button to "rewrite site's source code," but until then, you're really stuck with using some of our longer workarounds in this chapter.

Figure 24-1
Setting up
import folders

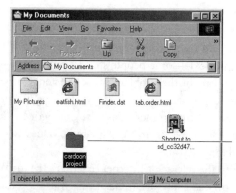

This folder contains the original copy of your site as a backup, and the new, imported copy of the site that you work on in GoLive.

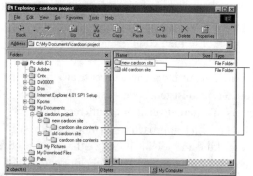

Create two folders, each of which will contain a full copy of the site you're importing.

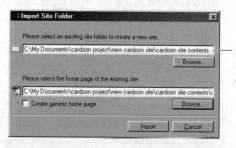

Select the copy of your site that you have placed in the new site folder.

What's New in 5

In the previous edition of this book, we had to offer a huge variety of workarounds to clean up HTML, in part because you had to make sure to select only HTML, not a page's content, when using the Find & Replace tab of the Find feature. The Element tab changes all this.

The Element tab is an HTML-only search-and-replace feature that allows you to specify whether you want to delete, update, or add attributes to specific tags or tags that match a pattern. It can also delete or replace entire tags. This allows you to perform many of the tasks in this chapter with incredible ease and fluency instead of great hackery and kludgery.

Cleaning

Back in the bad, old days, when everyone was writing HTML by hand in NotePad or SimpleText—some people still do, by the way—we wrote some pretty ugly code. Part of the problem was consistency; if you're writing by hand, it's easy to forget elements or do the same thing in a different way each time. Another part of the problem was a lack of rigor by the browsers; you could omit quotation marks around attribute values in HTML tags and Netscape would forgive you.

It wasn't until the release of Internet Explorer (IE) for Windows 2.0 that we discovered how bad a job we'd done. IE was much less forgiving, violating an edict of the Internet: "Be conservative in what you do, liberal in what you accept." However, it was a good wake-up call. (The later versions exercised more of the milk of human coding, and allowed a greater variety of coding errors to go unnoticed.)

Unfortunately, many older pages never heard the alarm go off and contain lingering, terrible, inconsistent code—especially in tables—that can cause unexpected errors in different versions of different browsers.

We have a multistep approach to surmounting these HTML problems by identifying each kind and solving it using either the Find & Replace tab or the Element tab of the Find window. (If you're not comfortable or familiar with these two tabs, we recommend you read up on them in Chapter 16, *Source Editing*. More information on using the Element tab sitewide is in Chapter 21, *Files, Folders, and Links*.)

For each of these examples, we provide the code to put into the appropriate fields. You should select Add Site from the Find & Replace tab or Site from the file selection area at the bottom of the Element tab before making these changes so that they're made consistently across an entire site (see Figure 24-2 for setup guidelines).

TIP:
Review Element Tab

We cover the Element tab thoroughly elsewhere, but it's useful to take a quick review, as the parts of the tab are less well identified than other features in GoLive. The area you select files from, for instance, we call the "file selection area," but there's no label for it on screen.

TIP:
Reparse after Editing

When you've completed any or all of the suggestions in the rest of this chapter, hold down the Option key (Mac) or Control key (Windows) and select Reparse All from the Site menu. This forces GoLive to re-read all the HTML files and rebuild its internal database of links.

Figure 24-2
Setting up Find
features

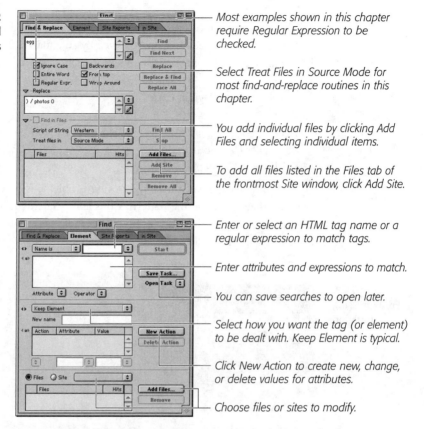

Most examples shown in this chapter
require Regular Expression to be
checked.

Select Treat Files in Source Mode for
most find-and-replace routines in this
chapter.

You add individual files by clicking Add
Files and selecting individual items.

To add all files listed in the Files tab of
the frontmost Site window, click Add Site.

Enter or select an HTML tag name or a
regular expression to match tags.

Enter attributes and expressions to match.

You can save searches to open later.

Select how you want the tag (or element)
to be dealt with. Keep Element is typical.

Click New Action to create new, change,
or delete values for attributes.

Choose files or sites to modify.

Attributes Without Quotation Marks

Early Web browsers didn't always require quotation marks around attributes
in an HTML tag to interpret the tag correctly. This can lead to confusion
when modern browsers read the URL, as certain characters should be surrounded by quotation marks to make it clear that they are part of a value.

The simplest way of making this change sitewide involves regular expression pattern-matching in the Find & Replace tab, described in more depth in
Chapter 25, *Advanced Features* (see Figure 24-3).

TIP:
What's an
Attribute

An attribute is any element that follows the tag's name. For instance, in the expression <img src="/images/joplin.jpg" border="0">, both Border and Src are
attributes of Img. The quotation marks follow the equals sign and fully enclose
their values. Attributes always have a space preceding them, though some of
them don't have values, like the checked or selected attributes for a form checkbox.

This operation finds every instance of a space followed by any text not containing a space or equals sign, followed by an equals sign. The part after the equals sign must not contain a quotation mark, a space, or a close HTML symbol (>).

Check	Regular Expr.
Find	`(\s[^= ]+=)([^" >]+)`
Replace	`\1"\2"`
Treat Files In	Source Mode
Click	Replace All

The only place this feature might cause problems is if you have text in your site that looks like the pattern. Consider a statement like, "You must remember that when x=y, the resultant formula gets changed to q=2xy." The above routine would make the first statement be "x="y"" and the second "q="2xy"".

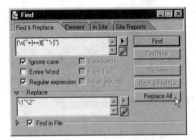

Figure 24-3
Fixing missing quotation marks

Fully Qualified HTTP References

Due to some faulty thinking on the part of some early browsers and our ever-fallible minds, many hypertext references and image source tags in the olden days used the entire site name to reference the object.

That is, we'd write a fully qualified reference like:

```
<a href="http://www.foobard.org/foobard/pages/woof.html">
```

instead of using a relative reference, which would make the site portable and easier to work with, like:

```
<a href="/foobard/pages/woof.html">
```

or even, if the user were viewing another page in the /foobard/pages directory:

```
<a href="woof.html">
```

Using a fully qualified reference means that if you relocate elements, the entire Web site, or even the folder level, you have to rewrite every reference in the site.

GoLive extracts all references like this and lists them in the Site window's External tab. Unfortunately, you can't change an external link into an internal one; GoLive generates a specific error rather than accomplishing the task. But you can use Find & Replace to do it for you.

TIP:
Point & Shoot
External
Changes

You can use Point & Shoot via the In & Out Links palette to change an external link to an internal one (see Figure 24-4).

Figure 24-4
Changing external links to internal links

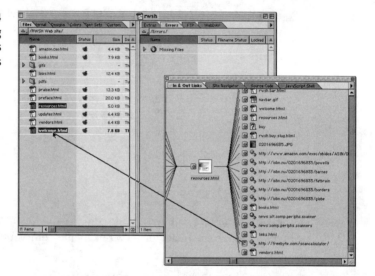

In this next method, we use what GoLive calls Absolute Links, which are actually relative links that specify the root of the Web site (for more on this distinction, read the sidebar "Absolute Versus Relative" in Chapter 21, *Files, Folders, and Links*). If you move files around in GoLive's Site window that are referenced via GoLive Absolute Links, GoLive will rewrite them just like it would any standard relative link.

In the example above, our absolute URL is http://www.foobard.org/foobard/pages/ to reach items on the site; our GoLive replacement URL is just /foobard/pages/ to get to the same location (see Figure 24-5). The following Find & Replace action takes care of the problem.

Uncheck	Regular Expr.
Find	`="http://www.foobard.org/foobard/pages/`
Replace	`="/foobard/pages/`
Click	Replace All

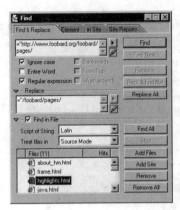

Figure 24-5
Full URL
replacement

Before

```
<LI>For answers to your jousting
questions, visit with <a href=
"http://www.foobard.org/
foobard/pages/joustingexperts.
htm">Jousting with the
Experts</a>.<LI>Feel like
browsing? Check out our
searchable <a href="http://
www.foobard.org/foobard/pages/
calendar/joustsearch.cgi">
Jousting Event Calendar</a>.
```

After

```
<LI>For answers to your jousting questions, visit with <a
href="/foobard/pages/joustingexperts.htm">Jousting with the
Experts</a>. <LI>Feel like browsing? Check out our
searchable <a href="/foobard/pages/calendar/joustsearch.cgi">
Jousting Event Calendar</a>.
```

Subsite Paths

Some early Web servers required an extra directory in the front of the path to your files, so that to get to files for www.ishkabibble.com, your URLs would all look like

```
http://www.ishkabibble.com/ishkabibble/
```

Most servers lack this limitation, and, in fact, we've had to add automatic redirects on our sites so that the server rewrites URLs on the fly to remove this subsite path information. This adds time to processing a Web transaction.

If you no longer need this part of the path, you can easily remove it after following the above steps to clean up quotation marks and full references. Put in your own path for "subsitepath" below, and this will replace all instances (see Figure 24-6).

Uncheck	Regular Expr.
Find	`="/subsitepath/`
Replace	`="/`
Click	Replace All

Figure 24-6
Subsite path
replacement

Before

```
<LI>For answers to your jousting
questions, visit with <a href="
/foobard/pages/joustingexperts.
htm">Jousting with the Experts
</a>.<LI>Feel like browsing?
Check out our searchable <a
href="/foobard/pages/calendar/
joustsearch.cgi">Jousting Event
Calendar</a>.
```

After

```
<LI>For answers to your jousting questions, visit with <a
href="/pages/joustingexperts.htm">Jousting with the Experts
</a>.<LI>Feel like browsing? Check out our searchable <a
href="/pages/calendar/joustsearch.cgi">Jousting Event
Calendar</a>.
```

PageMill Remnant

Just after Adobe shipped the late, sort of lamented PageMill, back in 1995, we started getting reports of a weird attribute that was breaking some weblint (HTML syntax checking) programs. The attribute was Naturalsizeflag. Apparently, PageMill would add this attribute, set to either 0 or 3, for every image source tag in a site.

After some wrangling, it was finally revealed that this attribute was used by PageMill to identify whether an image had been resized within PageMill. If it were set to 3, it was still at its original proportions; otherwise it was set to 0. (GoLive knows this intuitively by reading the contents of the HTML page and comparing the Img tag's dimension attributes with the image's actual dimensions.)

This was the first well-known instance of HTML code that was proprietary to a given visual page editor. The HTML spec has always stated that any tag or attribute that a browser doesn't understand should be ignored, and Adobe tried to take advantage of that concept. (GoLive inserts a Csobj tag and a Csimport header to identify Components, and occasionally inserts other GoLive-specific information that you can strip if you export the site. Components and Export are both discussed in Chapter 21, *Files, Folders, and Links.*)

To get rid of this PageMill tag, use the following procedure in the Element tab (see Figure 24-7).

Attribute   img
Find   naturalsizeflag
Keep Element   selected
Delete attribute   naturalsizeflag
Click   Start

Figure 24-7
Naturalsize
killer

No Background Color or Image

Early HTML lacked any support for a background color or image for a page, so you often find a Body tag all by its lonesome. GoLive doesn't provide a way to set these parameters for a group of pages, so this tip is useful for old and new pages alike (see Figure 24-8).

This will replace any Body tag that contains anything following "body". You can add items like Vlink or other attributes to the basic items listed for Replace below.

Element   body
Find   bgcolor = "" or bgcolor <> ""

To set all backgrounds to white, no background image:

Add attribute
Attribute   bgcolor
Value   #FFFFFF

You can set Find to

bgcolor = "some value"

and change the attribute to update, which changes only the pages that match those parameters.

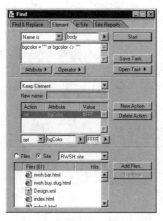

Figure 24-8
Replacing
Body attributes

To set all backgrounds to white with a background image, and with link, text, active, and visited links set to some color:

Set attributes, one for each of these

```
bgcolor       #FFFFFF
background    /gifs/blur.gif
text          black
link          blue
alink         red
vlink         #FF00FF
```

Orphaned Images

You may find yourself with a site full of old images linked to nothing or linked to old pages you no longer use. How to clean out just the images you don't need and keep just the ones in use? Simple: use Export Site (see Figure 24-9).

1. Download the site into a new site file or open the existing site if you've already downloaded it.

2. Make a full copy of the folder as a backup to restore to if necessary.

3. Evaluate which pages are outdated and need to be removed. (There may be none if you've just updated pages with new images over time and left the old ones in place.)

4. Delete those pages (if any). By deleting the pages, you have deleted references to the old images.

5. From the Site menu's Finder (Mac) or Explorer (Windows) submenu, choose Export Site.

6. Uncheck both Publish boxes and check Export Referenced Files Only.

Figure 24-9
Orphan
extraction

1. Download a site (left).
2. Make a backup copy (below).

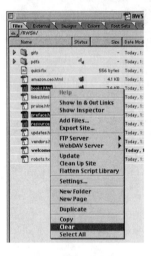

3, 4. Delete old pages (left).
5, 6, 7. Export referenced files (above).
8. Replace site folder with exported one (below left).
9. Rescan site (below middle).
10. Save site file (below right).

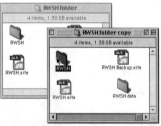

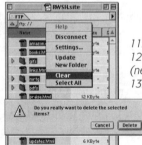

11. Connect via FTP (far left).
12. Delete FTP site contents (near left).
13. Upload All via FTP (below).

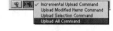

7. Set the Hierarchy value to As in Site so you don't restructure the site. (Although you could do that, too, if you wanted to restructure at the same time.)

8. Replace your site folder with the exported folder, making sure they're named the same, by clicking the Export button.

9. Choose Rescan from the Site menu.

10. Save the site file by choosing Save from the File menu with the Site window foremost.

11. Connect via FTP.

12. Delete all files and folders in the remote server, except ones that your system administrator told you to keep (like aliases or shortcuts to cgi-bin, Architext, etc.).

13. Choose Upload All from the Site toolbar's FTP Upload button (hold the button down to get a popup menu that contains the option), and then click the button again to perform the upload.

The live site now contains just the live HTML and files referenced from them.

Improving

There are many things you can do to improve an old Web site and make it more manageable. This includes updating older features to newer ones, extracting repeated elements to centralize them, and reorganizing the site to be easier to manage.

Replacing Imagemaps

Imagemaps, discussed at length in Chapter 9, *Images*, let a designer set up hot areas of an image on which, if users click, their browsers get directed to a new URL assigned to that area.

Imagemaps date back to the graphical Web Stone Age, but at that time they were handled by the server—and were hence named "server-side" imagemaps. When a user clicked an image that was defined as an imagemap, the browser sent the coordinates of that click to an imagemap program at the server. The server, using this program, examined an imagemap file that contained sets of areas defined as coordinates. If the click landed in a domain (an area defined by a set of coordinates), the server returned a redirection to a new location. If it landed in an undefined area, it would return an error unless there was a default URL set up for the whole image.

Server-side imagemaps add a transaction with the server, plus the processing time for that transaction, which could add several seconds between a click and the new page appearing. It also adds traffic to your Web server.

With Netscape 2, client-side imagemaps gained popularity, meaning that the entire set of map area coordinates would be embedded in an HTML file, and the browser itself would determine whether a domain was clicked on.

TIP:
Keeping Server-side Imagemaps

Older Web pages still have the remnants of server-side imagemaps, and it's not a bad idea to retain them, as probably five percent or less of any given Web audience uses browsers old enough that client-side mapping won't work. This gets discussed below, and in Chapter 9, *Images.*

NEW IN 5:
Imagemap HTML

GoLive 5 shows a small "m" to indicate where a client-side imagemap lives within an HTML page (see Figure 24-10). The imagemap coordinates can be anywhere in the document, or even in some other document, as it's referenced as a URL.

Imagemap code

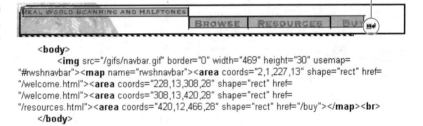

Figure 24-10
M marks the imagemap

```
<body>
    <img src="/gifs/navbar.gif" border="0" width="469" height="30" usemap=
"#rwshnavbar"><map name="rwshnavbar"><area coords="2,1,227,13" shape="rect" href=
"/welcome.html"><area coords="228,13,308,28" shape="rect" href=
"/welcome.html"><area coords="308,13,420,28" shape="rect" href=
"/resources.html"><area coords="420,12,466,28" shape="rect" href="/buy"></map><br>
    </body>
```

This kind of replacement is often substantially trickier than anything we've talked about in this chapter thus far, as we generally find that old files contain lots of variations on a theme, so a single Find & Replace doesn't work.

Here's the procedure we recommend (see Figure 24-11):

1. Go through many files and identify all the places in which an imagemap is used. Collect these instances in HTML and paste them into a text file for reference. These references will look something like this:

    ```
    <A HREF="http://www.foobard.com/cgi-
    bin/htimage/pages/nav.map"><IMG SRC="http://www.foo-
    bard.com/gifs/nav.gif" BORDER="0" ISMAP WIDTH="470"
    HEIGHT="46" ALIGN="BOTTOM"></A>
    ```

2. Create a new imagemap inside GoLive for each of your old ones. You could convert the old server-side imagemap to client-side, or create a map that works for both older and newer browsers; typically, this is not necessary.

Figure 24-11
Turning a
server-side
into a
client-side
imagemap

*The original image
as a server-side
imagemap*

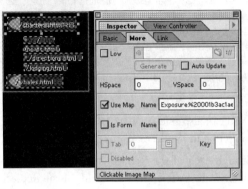

*The image with
client-side regions
defined using the
More tab of the
Image Inspector.*

Before

```
<A HREF="/cgi-bin/htimage/pages/whalenav. map"><IMG SRC="/
gifs/whalenav.gif" BORDER="0" ISMAP WIDTH="133"
HEIGHT="119" ALIGN="BOTTOM"></A>
```

After

```
<img border="1" height="119" width="133" src="../Exposure
%20001.GIF" usemap="#Exposure%20001b3ac1aef"><map name=
"Exposure%20001b3ac1aef"><area href="/whales.html" coords=
"5,93,92,113" shape="rect"><area href="/lodging.html" coords=
"32,76,99,87" shape="rect"><area href="/directions.html"
coords="32,61,123,72" shape="rect"><area href="/boats.html"
coords="31,50,87,58" shape="rect"><area href="/" coords=
"32,36,79,46" shape="rect"><area href="/charters.html"
coords="7,7,113,28" shape="rect"></map>
```

TIP:
**Tool for
Converting
Old Maps**

Rewriting a server-side imagemap into a client-side imagemap is pretty simple, but we've made it even easier by providing a URL where you can paste code from an old-style imagemap into a text box, press Submit, and have the HTML produced for you. The URL is: http://realworldgolive.com/convertmaps.html.

Follow the directions on this page and copy and paste the results into the Replace box, as described below.

3. Switch to the HTML Source Editor after you've tweaked the imagemap to your liking in GoLive, and select everything from the first Img tag that has

the Usemap attribute to the closing </MAP> tag at the end. It will look something like this:

```
<img src="gifs/nav.gif" alt="bottom nav bar" align=
bottom width="470" height="46" usemap="#bottombar"
border="0"><map name="bottombar"><area href="/"
shape="default"><area href="/whatcook/whtscook.htm"
coords="353,1,467,45" shape="rect"><area href=
"/fresh/fresh.htm" coords="245,2,350,43"
shape="rect"><area href="/dearsand/drsandy.htm"
coords="160,2,242,45" shape="rect"></map>
```

Paste the code above into a text file as well, as it will serve as your Replace text. (You can also reference an imagemap in an external file; we discuss how to do that in "Imagemaps" in Chapter 9, *Images.*)

4. Go through each of the iterations of the original imagemap and paste each of them in turn in the Find field. In the Replace field, enter something unique, like [[banana]] that won't appear elsewhere in the site.

   For large sites with lots of inconsistencies, it can literally take hours to fix all the possible combinations; Glenn spent about two hours on this task for a 1,500 page site that used a variant of the same template—almost, but not quite identical—for every page.

5. Now Find: [[banana]] and drop the text you extracted in Step 3 into the Replace field. Press the Replace All button, and you've magically brought your site into the 21st century.

Instead of pasting in imagemaps that all have to be managed individually, you could also create a Component that contains each imagemap and use the technique described next to manage all your imagemaps from a central location.

Turning Repeated Elements into Components

GoLive has a powerful feature called Components that lets you reuse snippets of HTML or parts of a page. We discuss this feature extensively in Chapter 21, *Files, Folders, and Links.* The utility of Components is that you can write the HTML once and apply it to every page you want. Better yet, updating the Components automatically rewrites every page on which they're used throughout the site.

Although GoLive wants you to use the drag-and-drop approach to add Components to a page, we have a trickier method that lets you replace an old site's template with a GoLive equivalent (see Figure 24-12).

1. Identify a repeating element, like a copyright statement, appearing on each page.

2. Create a Component in GoLive, as described in the Chapter 21, *Files, Folders, and Links*, making sure to depress the Absolute Link button for all internal references.

3. Drag this Component onto any page.

4. Select the Component and switch to HTML Source Editor.

5. The HTML that's highlighted will begin with <CSOBJ> and end with </CSOBJ>. This is GoLive's internal tracker for that Component. Copy that text.

TIP:
simport

There's a tag added to the Head section of an HTML page with at least one Component: Csimport. This is a GoLive-specific tag that helps it manage Components. Fortunately, you don't have to create this tag when using this technique. GoLive 5 is backwards compatible with its previous version, and you can hack the code in the way we suggest here.

---

6. In the Find field, use the same technique described under imagemaps above: find every version of the HTML you want to replace with the Component, and replace each piece of HTML with [[banana]] or something unique.

7. Put [[banana]] in the Find field, and paste the CSOBJ copy into the Replace field.

Neat trick, eh? Suddenly all your pages are managed with Components with very little fuss. Remember to Reparse All, or GoLive will act like an aging relative: "Bobby who?"

Adding Alt Tags

Well-designed Web sites include Alt attributes for each image to help people who don't or can't view images to navigate a site. This includes the visually impaired and the bandwidth impaired; it's also just a smarter, more complete way to design a site that works in more circumstances. You can add the Alt attribute through the Image Inspector's Basic tab in the Alt Text field. But if you want to add Alt attributes for every image, we have a sneaky way to get started (see Figure 24-13).

Figure 24-12
Rolling your
own
components
for find and
replace

This is the element we want to repeat on every page. Se
Editor, switch to HTML Source Editor, and carefully copy

Open
docum
Source
text ar
recurri
and sa
Compo

Components
copyright.html
head.html

The newly created com
up in the Palette and in
folder of the Extras tab.

Drag the c
and switch
to drag its
ending with

Iterate through all of the variants
of the HTML you want to replace
with a component, dropping in a
placeholder, like [[banana]].

Now paste [[ban
field, paste the c
in the Replace fi
Replace All.

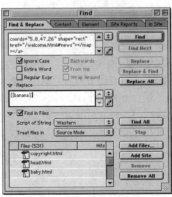

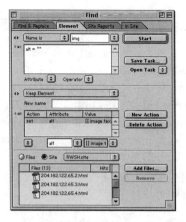

Figure 24-13
Adding
placeholder Alt
attributes

In the Element tab, enter the following information:

Element   `Img`
Find   `alt = ""`
Keep Element
Add Action
Set Attribute `Alt, [[ image text ]]`

Now you can use the Find & Replace tab to search on that text (setting Treat Files In to Source Mode) and go through the entire site adding text as appropriate. Of course, you could instead find the same image throughout the site and add an Alt attribute to it for recurring images (see Figure 24-14).

Element   `Img`
Find   `Src = "exact path to image"`
Keep Element
Add Action
Set Attribute `Alt, text for image`

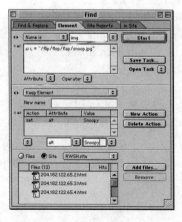

Figure 24-14
Adding Alt
attribute to a
specific image

Renaming Files and Reorganizing Structures

Another ancient problem: indecipherable file names. We often named files briefly to match the pre-Windows 95 naming convention from Microsoft of eight-dot-three names: eight characters, a dot, and then three characters. Or, we got really lazy, and named files "index1.html", "index2.html", and so on.

When faced with hundreds of files named in this fashion, it can be hard to know where to begin. After following the above steps to clean up your HTML, you can use GoLive's Files tab to rename files to more mnemonic names. As you rename them, GoLive prompts you to automatically rewrite all occurrences, of course, throughout the site.

NEW IN 5:
Filename
Constraints

GoLive 5 helps identify filenames that won't work on particular platforms by allowing you specify the target platform you're uploading files to. It then marks any file that's named in a way the platform doesn't support so you can easily rename them.

A related problem of older sites was a lack of planning for the future. Many sites were created in a flat organizational structure, where you could have hundreds or even thousands of files in a single folder. Again, using GoLive's built-in ability to track internal links, create new folders that divvy up the content and drag-and-drop files into the appropriate subdivision.

Fixing Photoshop Web Galleries

Adobe Photoshop added a feature starting with version 5 that lets you take a folder of images (including its subfolders, if you want) and turn them into a simple HTML photo gallery. It resizes the images as appropriate and creates a set of linked HTML pages (see Figure 24-15).

Unfortunately, and bizarrely, Photoshop doesn't insert the image heights and widths. This makes for weird-loading pages, because the browser has to calculate the image size as it loads each image. This slows down the process substantially and is irritating to watch.

To avoid this problem, we use the Find feature's Element tab. Because Photoshop resizes all the thumbnails and larger images to the same pixel dimensions, you only need to figure out what those dimensions are once.

1. Open the index.html page, select the first image, and then select Pixel from the Height and Width popup menus. Make a note of these dimensions; for this example, we assume the height is 100 pixels and the width is 65 pixels.

2. Open the Element tab of the Find feature. Enter these values:

Element	Img
Find	`width = ""`
Keep Element	
Add Action	
Set Attribute	`Height, 100`
Add Action	
Set Attribute	`Width, 65`

3. Choose just the index file in the file list at the bottom of the tab. Click Start, approve the warning, and it fixes that file. Remember to save the file.

    To fix all the individual pages that have the larger images, open the first of them, and repeat the process in step 1 to get the dimensions. Enter the same information as in step 2 with the correct pixel dimensions. Finally, add the entire folder containing the pages to the file list at the bottom of the Element tab.

Figure 24-15
Photoshop
Web Gallery

TIP:
Resize
Button

This works only, of course, for images that are all the same dimensions starting out (such as batches of photos taken with a digital camera). However, even if they're not, you can use the Resize button in the Image Inspector's Basic tab on any images that have been sized other than their correct dimensions. We find it less tedious to click an image, then click the Resize button, than to select Pixel from both Height and Width menus over and over again. Your call, of course!

Brave New World

It's a marvelous thing to wake up in the morning knowing that your site is humming with HTML 4.0 compatibility, ready to take on the next century of HTML. True, not everything on your pages will take full advantage of the latest and greatest features in HTML, but you can have the sleep of the just when a missing quotation mark doesn't wind up derailing your site.

Advanced

PART 4

)-9]*(,[0-9]
[0-9][0-9]?
[a-zA-Z][a-z
[a-zA-Z][a-z
/[a-zA-Z][a-

CHAPTER 25

Advanced Features

GoLive appears to have no end of features, and the more you learn about the program, the more it seems you need—or want—to learn about how to use it more effectively.

In this part of the book, we cover the most difficult-to-learn parts of GoLive, most of which involve a greater knowledge of general Web protocols and standards. GoLive insulates you from the real nitty-gritty, providing a friendly interface that lets you manipulate sophisticated controls behind the scenes. But we'll try to introduce you to the GoLive approach and to show you what's behind the curtain, so you can twist the dials and knobs yourself.

The chapters that follow provide an introduction and an inside look at:

- **JavaScript:** scripting tips using GoLive's tools
- **Animation:** animating objects on a page with Dynamic HTML
- **Actions:** how best to use GoLive's built-in Actions for handling complex coding behavior
- **Cascading Style Sheets:** how to create a single, consistent source for text formatting across a page or an entire site
- **Dynamic Link:** using GoLive's new database-linking tool to hook up data sources for dynamic content creation in a Web site
- **Languages and Scripting:** working with XML, ASP, and other coding languages within GoLive
- **Web Settings:** custom tweaking for more control over underlying HTML and its simulated browser previews when creating pages in GoLive

GoLive's Secret Weapon

This chapter covers a significant advanced feature that doesn't fit neatly into other categories, but certainly goes beyond the kinds of tasks that a user doing page layout and site management might encounter on a regular basis.

We're talking, of course, about regular-expression pattern matching: GoLive's version of a powerful tool for matching patterns in a number of places in the program, including sitewide find and replace.

To the uninitiated, this capability can look like a cat walked across the keyboard and miraculously fixed elements within a page or site; but, in reality, it's one of the most powerful methods for making complex and extensive changes without hand editing.

Regular-Expression Pattern Matching

Regular-expression pattern matching is often found only in the most advanced text editors and word processors, such as BBEdit and Microsoft Word. It's also called "regexp" for short, and known as "grep" (global regular expression pattern matching) in the Unix world.

Regular expressions are wildcard patterns that can match a variety of text that meets their parameters, instead of just an exact set of characters or run of text. For instance, you could find all tags in an HTML file by specifying a pattern that begins with a less-than sign (<), is followed by any text except a greater-than sign (>), and then ends with a greater-than sign.

You can search for or use regular expressions in several places in GoLive: in the Find field of the Find & Replace tab in the Find feature; in the Element tab's Attribute field in the Find feature; in Filename Constraints for legal filenames used in a site; in the Regular Expressions preferences for setting up prefabricated Find patterns; and in the Spell Checker's Pattern Dictionary for ignoring patterns that you don't want to spellcheck, like URLs.

Patterns

Patterns comprise a set of characters that can include typical ones, like letters, numbers, and punctuation that appear in the text you're searching for, and wildcards, which specify special matching patterns. There are five types of wildcards in GoLive:

- Number of characters to be selected by a match
- A range or set of characters to match

- Optional selection that doesn't have to be found to create a positive match
- Start or end of line
- Definite selection

Certain punctuation characters have special meanings in a regular expression to identify groups of characters or other wildcard behavior. These are called reserved characters, as they're reserved for these special purposes. In order to use one of them literally, like a parenthesis in a phrase you want to match, you have to proceed the character with a backslash, or \. So, for instance, if you want to search for "http://www.phlegmatic.com/", you'd enter in the Find field:

```
http\:\/\/www\.phlegmatic\.com\/
```

Although < and > and : don't appear to be reserved characters, we've occasionally found problems searching on them. So just to be on the safe side, we often put a backslash in front of punctuation. GoLive treats backslash plus any character as that character, so adding a backslash doesn't introduce new problems.

Number of Characters

Three symbols control the amount of text selected: the asterisk, the plus sign, and the question mark (*, +, and ?). Let's introduce these first, and then show examples below, under "Pattern," where they make more sense.

Asterisk. An asterisk matches zero or more instances of the preceding character or characters in a pattern.

Plus sign. A plus sign matches one or more instances of the preceding character or characters in a pattern.

Question mark. A question mark makes the preceding character optional. If you precede the question mark with text enclosed in parentheses, the entire text in parentheses is optional.

Ranges

GoLive offers a wide set of character selectors for creating ranges of characters to match. These include selecting any single character, any character in a specified range or set, any character not in a specified range or set, and special selectors that choose all digits, all white space, only returns, and the like.

Period. Entering a period selects any single character. For instance, finding for

```
peters.n
```

matches "peterson" and "petersen" but also "petersbn". To find a run of zero or more instances of any character, you use the very simple expedient of adding an asterisk, as in

```
peters.*
```

which in this example would find "peterson" as well as "petersburg", but it also selects everything to the end of the line. (You need to use negation, below, to limit the number of characters matched.)

Square brackets. You can insert any characters or a range of characters inside square brackets—[and]—to select a range of text that matches only the characters in the square brackets. If you don't put a +, *, or ? after it, it finds just one character that's inside the brackets. Finding for

```
peters[eo]n
```

matches only "peterson" or "petersen".

Negative square brackets. If you put a caret (^) at the start of text inside square brackets, GoLive finds only characters that aren't found in the square brackets. This can be useful for trying to find everything up until a terminator. For instance, if you find for

```
<[^>]+>
```

GoLive matches just the interior of a tag. The "[^>]+" means, "match everything except a greater-than sign," so the pattern matches everything in the interior until it reaches the closing greater-than sign.

If you want to find only whole words that are or start with peters, you could search for everything up until a space; this also matches up to the end of a line for words that end with a hard return:

```
peters[^ ]*
```

Special matches. GoLive also offers a number of special selectors that correspond to any digit, any white space (tab or space characters), any line break, any tab, and many of their negations (see Table 25-1).

Table 25-1 Special matches	Character	Description
	\d	Matches any digit
	\D	Matches anything but a digit (the same as [^\d])
	\w	Matches any alphabetic character, uppercase or lowercase (i.e., A-Z or a-z)
	\W	Matches anything but alphabetic characters (the same as [^\w])
	\s	Matches white space, which in GoLive is just tabs or spaces
	\S	Matches anything but white space (the same as [^\s])
	\r	Used with Find & Replace in the HTML Source Editor, matches line breaks, regardless of platform
	\t	Used with Find & Replace in the HTML Source Editor, matches tabs used for indentation
	\x00 - \xff	For characters that you can't enter from the keyboard, you can enter their base 16 or hexadecimal value to match them. This is rarely needed in GoLive.

Optional Selection

GoLive offers two ways to indicate whether a pattern or range of characters is optional when identifying a match.

Vertical bar. The vertical bar, or |, lets you specify a set of possible matches. For instance, if you wanted to match either the Src or Href attributes in order to change the items they link to, you could find for

```
(HREF|SRC)\=\"
```

You only need to enclose choices in parentheses if there is text before or after the matches that isn't part of what you want to look for. If you wanted to search for Real World Adobe GoLive or Real World Adobe InDesign, you would use parentheses like this

```
Real World Adobe (InDesign|GoLive)
```

Parentheses. If you enclose text in parentheses and follow it by a question mark, the entire bit in parentheses becomes optional. If you want to find any instance of Ezra Stiles College where folks might have forgotten the Ezra, you would search for

```
(Ezra )?Stiles College
```

Start or End of Line

Two special characters help you identify the start or end of a line or filename: the caret (^) for the start of a line or paragraph and the dollar sign ($) for the end of a line or paragraph. This is especially useful with Find & Replace, but it can also be useful when finding the start or end of a complete filename in Filename Constraints.

The use in Find & Replace varies depending on whether you're in the HTML Source Editor (line based) or the Layout Editor (paragraph based) when searching on an individual page, or whether you have the Treat Files In popup menu set to Source Mode or Layout Mode when working on a sitewide operation.

Definite Selection

In the Find & Replace tab, if you surround something by parentheses in the Find field with Regular Expr. checked, you can insert that text in the Replace field by typing a backslash (\) followed by a number indicating that particular parenthetical set's position in the Find field. These are called back references.

For instance, you might want to find every instance of text that matches a URL and want to enclose it in Teletype tags. You wouldn't want to run a separate search for each URL; instead, you can use regular expressions to specify the URL generically and then drop in the matched URL as part of your replacement text.

Although GoLive uses parentheses for three purposes—two of them described under "Optional Selection," earlier in this chapter—any use of them always creates a back reference. So if you're using parentheses to indicate a choice among options, you still have to consider it when counting. For example, changing the start of an absolute reference would look like this in the Find field:

```
(A|IMG) (SRC|HREF)\=\"\~foobar\/
```

In the Replace field, you'd put

```
\1 \2="/~hagar/
```

Find & Replace

You activate regular expressions in the Find & Replace tab by checking the Regular Expr. box (see Figure 25-1). You can then enter patterns into the Field field and replacement values, including back references to any selected patterns.

Figure 25-1
Activating
regular
expressions

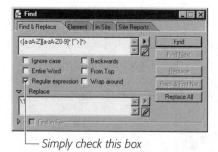

— *Simply check this box*

TIP:
Ignore Case
Applies

Ignore Case still applies to regular expressions, so check or uncheck this as applicable; for HTML tags, you should almost always leave it checked. GoLive creates consistently formatted tags per the settings in the Global tab of Web Settings, so if you're working with a page that hasn't been created by GoLive or had the Rewrite Source Code command applied, Ignore Case is even more important. (See Chapter 16, *Source Editing*, for more on making GoLive rewrite source code).

Prefab Find Regular Expressions

GoLive's developers provide a set of prefabricated regular expressions in the Preferences dialog box's Find pane under Regular Expressions settings (see Figure 25-2). You can select these items from the popup menus to the right of the Find and Replace fields in the Find dialog.

The names that appear in the menus are assigned in the Regular Expressions settings Name column. You can add your own common expressions here, as well.

Figure 25-2
Find pane's
Regular
Expressions
settings

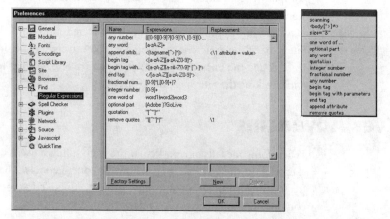

Items in the Regular Expressions settings show up in the popup menus to the right of the Find and Replace fields with the names assigned to them.

Element

The Element tab of the Find feature lets you use regular expressions in just one place: the Attribute field. (You can't, in GoLive 5 at least, pattern match the name or contents of attributes, nor can you replace using patterns matched.) See Chapter 16, *Source Editing*, for more on the Element tab.

Spellchecking

There are some items you don't want GoLive to flag as spelling errors. For instance, GoLive comes with a built-in set of regular expressions that allows its internal spellchecker to ignore anything that looks like a URL. Otherwise, if you included a human-readable URL in the text of your pages, GoLive would flag it as an error. You can also enter more complex technical requirements, or even specific words.

The list is found in the Preferences dialog box under the Spell Checker pane in Regular Expressions. The items here are negative settings, meaning that any pattern you enter is ignored.

Filename Constraints

Filename Constraints is explained fully in Chapter 21, *Files, Folders, and Links*. It lets GoLive easily flag any files that have characters in their names that a given operating system (like MS-DOS or Unix) would find so distasteful that you couldn't upload or transfer the files. You can define your own sets to meet company specifications for file naming, for instance, and use regular expressions to ensure compliance.

The settings for Filename Constraints are found on a global basis in the Site pane of the Preferences dialog box. You can also create site-by-site settings by selecting the Filename Constraints pane in Site Settings for any given site, and checking the Site Specific Settings box.

Ever Advancing

When someone tells us a particular program fulfills a user's every need, we get skeptical. In the case of GoLive, however, our skepticism has been put aside for the time being. Granted, GoLive probably doesn't do everything a designer could want, but it comes pretty darn close.

CHAPTER 26

JavaScript

When you mention the word "programming" to most designers, their eyes glaze over. Programming is something for guys and gals in dark rooms who come into the office at noon or later, and emerge from their hideaways to search for caffeine in the early morning hours. But mention graphical rollovers, form verification, and other nifty tricks that you can carry out in the browser, and the same designers get excited.

JavaScript, a simple scripting language, is a form of programming: defining structured sequences of events that use variable names to control behavior in the browser, thereby adding a lot of low-level, simple interactivity. Luckily, GoLive takes a lot of the sting out of JavaScript by providing tools to help make programming simpler, and predefined routines that involve setting values without messing with the underlying code.

In this chapter, we talk about the programming part of JavaScript, and how GoLive's tools help you write code and debug it. In the next two chapters, we cover animation and GoLive Actions, both of which involve prepackaged JavaScript. Consider this the primer that will help you better understand the whole subject. (If you haven't used JavaScript before, see the sidebar, "Learning JavaScript," before reading the whole chapter.)

Browser Support

Netscape invented JavaScript (originally calling it "LiveScript" before jumping on the Java bandwagon); it has virtually nothing to do with Sun Microsystems' Java programming language aside from marketing hype. Netscape's browsers all support JavaScript to varying degrees.

Microsoft also found JavaScript to be quite useful, adding support for what they call "JScript" since version 3.0 of Internet Explorer. Netscape and Microsoft jointly submitted the JavaScript specification to ECMA, a European technical standards body, to review and maintain as an open standard. You may sometimes run across the strange-sounding name "ECMA Script" which refers to the ratified standard version of JavaScript.

Microsoft also employs JavaScript on the server side—in scripts that run remotely on a Web server to carry out tasks—as one of the scripting languages supported by Active Server Pages (ASP) for server-side scripting. Netscape uses it as well with their server software.

Unfortunately, the JavaScript road has a few potholes. Although it ostensibly works across browsers (Navigator and Internet Explorer) and across platforms (Mac, Windows, and Unix), different browser versions on different platforms support different versions of JavaScript (see Table 26-1).

Learning JavaScript

This chapter isn't intended to teach you JavaScript, but rather to teach you how to use JavaScript most efficiently in GoLive, while taking advantage of GoLive's graphical interface and JavaScript-management features.

If you already know JavaScript, terms like "handler," "procedure," and "variable" shouldn't frighten you. If those terms make you clutch your head and moan, we can recommend some resources for learning JavaScript before getting started.

If you've never touched a programming language before, there are classes and books designed to introduce programming basics using JavaScript's constructs. It's also not a hard language to learn if you've ever written in BASIC, Visual Basic, Fortran, Pascal, or C; you'll pick it up in hours.

JavaScript's popularity has helped create a huge number of excellent books available to help teach yourself the language.

For new users, we recommend *JavaScript for the World Wide Web: Visual QuickStart Guide*, available from—you guessed it!—Peachpit Press. Authors Tom Negrino and Dori Smith assume no previous programming experience on the reader's part. They also include many example scripts that you can use as recipes to put directly into your pages.

Many Web sites also offer excellent tips and tutorials, as well as ready to use cut-and-paste scripts.

- Netscape DevEdge:
  http://devedge.netscape.com/

- Web Review: http://www.webreview.com/

- Developer Shed: http://www.devshed.com/

- Webreference.com:
  http://www.webreference.com

You can find links to these sites and links to buy the book online (or you can buy from your local bookstore, of course) at http://realworldgolive.com/javascript.html.

Table 26-1 Browser support for JavaScript	**Netscape Navigator browser version**	**Platform**	**JavaScript version**
	2.0	PC & Mac	1.0
	3.0	PC & Mac	1.1
	4.0+	PC & Mac	1.2

Microsoft Internet Explorer browser version	**Platform**	**Roughly equivalent JavaScript version**
3.0	PC	1.0
3.1	Mac	1.1
4.0+	PC & Mac	1.1 plus extensions*

* Each platform features slightly different support for this version of JavaScript.

And while both Netscape and Microsoft include JavaScript in their browsers, each has added its own extensions to the standardized version. This mandates testing all your JavaScript scripts in as many different browsers as possible to ensure that they actually work. Many times, we've written simple scripts and watched them break on one browser, even as they work on seven others. It is possible for a skilled scripter to write JavaScript code to work around this problem, so that browsers capable of handling the script simply run it while browsers that can't are unaffected.

Using JavaScript in GoLive

If you've decided to take the plunge and learn JavaScript, or if you're already an experienced scripter, you're all set. GoLive provides excellent support for adding scripts to your pages. There are three typical ways to work with JavaScript in GoLive.

- Using GoLive's built-in JavaScript and DHTML Actions
- Writing scripts by hand using GoLive's Scripts window
- Typing scripts directly into the HTML source code

Why Not Actions?

You may be asking yourself, "Why should I slave away writing my scripts by hand if GoLive can do it for me with Actions?" While GoLive's built-in Actions can save time by giving you drag-and-drop functionality, there are major advantages to rolling your own scripts.

- JavaScript that is written by hand is almost always smaller and more efficient than that created by GoLive's Actions.

- The built-in Actions don't give you many options for dealing with multiple browsers and platforms.

- While there are many useful Actions, there are many more things you can do with JavaScript if you learn how to write it yourself.

- Actions can respond to many user events, but JavaScript itself responds to many more events, which you may want to call on to trigger scripts.

- The code that Actions create is very complex and difficult to edit by hand. If other people have to update and maintain the site without the benefit of

Client-Side Versus Server-Side Scripting

You often hear the terms "client-side" and "server-side" bandied about when talk of scripting languages, Java, and Web server CGI (Common Gateway Interface) scripting comes up.

Client-side scripts are programs run on your computer. That is, the script is downloaded—usually as part of the HTML page, in the case of JavaScript—and then your machine executes the instructions in the program. Generally, this is as simple as a browser monitoring your mouse movements, so that when your mouse passes over an image, the browser executes a program that swaps out a different image while your mouse is hovering. The advantage of client-side programming is speed and flexibility; your machine doesn't need to contact another computer over the Internet or a company's intranet to carry out a task.

In server-side scripting or programming, the software runs remotely on a server. For instance, when you enter data in a form on a browser and then click submit, your browser sends all that data to a server. The server runs a program that examines the data and sends a response back to your server. In a case like this, you're sending data that the server processes and stores or performs some action with, like adding your name to a mailing list.

Where this gets confusing is that JavaScript, Java, and other programming languages can be both client-side and server-side, but not simultaneously. Some servers use JavaScript programs (usually found client-side) to process form submissions. JavaScript is used in some other contexts, too, like validating form entries in Adobe Acrobat, and in writing special modules in GoLive.

Where the action happens is key. In client-side programs, like JavaScript in HTML, your computer executes the program and produces results locally; with server-side programs, you have to send data to a server, have it run a program, and then get fed the response. Often, the bandwidth required to repeatedly pass basic data between a client and server can overshadow the utility of the software existing on the server's machine.

GoLive, the process becomes excruciating. Also, if someone edits the script by hand, GoLive will no longer recognize it as an Action.

- If a page with GoLive Actions is opened in another visual editor, such as Microsoft FrontPage, the JavaScript may be changed and may no longer work properly.

We cover Actions more thoroughly in Chapter 28, *Actions*, where we show you the best way to use these prefab bits.

Adding JavaScript

If you're a JavaScript Jedi Knight, you can simply click the HTML Source Editor tab of the document window and start typing directly into the raw HTML. However, GoLive's built-in scripting environment offers nice features for both the novice and advanced scripter.

Inserting a Script

You can add JavaScripts to either the head or body part of an HTML page. Generally, you insert them in the head part of the page to ensure they load first and are available when event handlers within the body trigger them.

When you add a script in GoLive, the program handles all the housekeeping tasks for you, like inserting a Script tag and comment tags into the HTML to surround the script.

GoLive offers a Scripts window that lets you enter and modify body and head JavaScripts (see Figure 26-1). The Scripts window has a corresponding JavaScript Inspector, discussed at length in this chapter, which lets you choose JavaScript events, objects, and versions.

What about VBScript and ASP?

What about other client-side scripting languages like Microsoft's VBScript? While GoLive doesn't offer direct support for adding VBScripts to your pages, it won't overwrite them or change them should you choose to type them in directly.

The same is true for ASP code. ASP code gets inserted directly into HTML pages, but it is executed by the server when the page is run—the code doesn't get downloaded to the user's machine, just the HTML part of the page.

See Chapter 16, *Source Editing*, for more about ASP support.

Figure 26-1
Script Editor

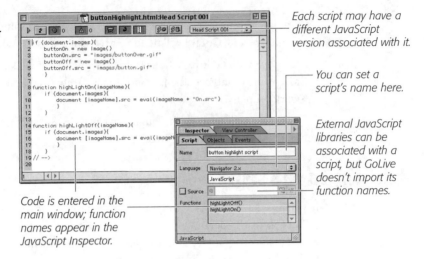

Each script may have a different JavaScript version associated with it.

You can set a script's name here.

External JavaScript libraries can be associated with a script, but GoLive doesn't import its function names.

Code is entered in the main window; function names appear in the JavaScript Inspector.

You can get by with creating a single head script that contains all your JavaScript code. GoLive supports multiple scripts so that you can use different versions of JavaScript in each script, or even different scripting languages, such as Microsoft's JScript.

Adding a head script. Click the JavaScript "coffee bean" button at the top of the Layout Editor to open the Scripts window. Click the New Script Item button to add a new head script. GoLive names it "Head Script 001" by default, but you can modify its name in the JavaScript Inspector.

You can also click the Toggle Head Section triangle in the head part of the Layout Editor, select the newly created JavaScript, and use the Head Script Inspector to name it (see Figure 26-2).

Figure 26-2
Head Script
Inspector used
with the Head
Section

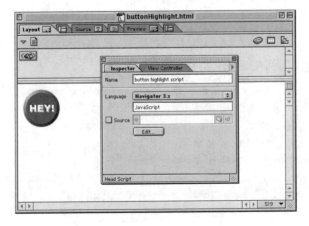

Adding a body script. If, for some reason, you need to insert a JavaScript in the page's body, drag the JavaScript icon from the Basic tab of the Objects palette and drop it anywhere in the body of your page, but preferably before any event handler that needs to use it. The Inspector becomes the Body Script Inspector, and it allows you to name the script and specify a target browser and JavaScript version.

After creating a body script, you can use the Scripts window to edit the script (see Figure 26-3). Select its name from the Select Script menu at the top of the Scripts window.

Figure 26-3
Editing a body
script

A body script can be edited through the Script Editor by double-clicking it.

The script can be named and controlled through the JavaScript Inspector just like a head script.

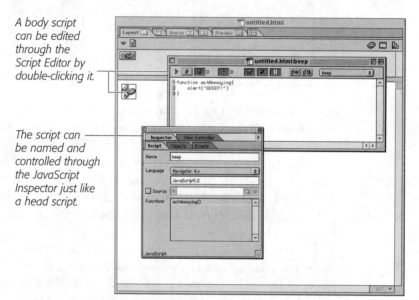

Choosing a Browser and Language Version

When you create a GoLive head or body script, one of the popup menus in the corresponding Inspector is for Language, which lists several browser versions. When you choose one, GoLive automatically places that browser's version or "flavor" of JavaScript in the text box below the menu and adds the same text to the Language attribute of the Script tag. This should prevent a browser that doesn't support the specified level of JavaScript from executing the script.

GoLive tries to help you further by displaying in the JavaScript Inspector's Events and Objects tabs only those items that are supported by the browser version you specified and any later version. So, if you choose to target Navigator 2.0, for example, you don't see the Image object in the object list because that feature was not supported until Navigator 3.0. (See Figure 26-4 for version-specific events.)

Figure 26-4
Events which differ by JavaScript version

Netscape 3 (JavaScript 1.1) events for a submit button at left; Netscape 4 (JavaScript 1.2) events at right.

The JavaScript version control isn't problem-free, though. There are substantial differences among various browsers' definitions of "JavaScript 1.1," or "JScript," especially from platform to platform. Also GoLive's method of blocking browsers still allows errors. If the Script tag says "JavaScript1.2" and the page is viewed in a 3.0 browser, the browser generates a "Function not defined" error when an event handler calls a function, because the browser ignores the head script containing the function, but not the event handler that calls the function.

We prefer adding JavaScript code that checks the browser version and exits without an action if the browser is too old to do what we want it to. You can force GoLive to write a generic JavaScript language setting by deleting the number following JavaScript in the text field below the Language menu (see Figure 26-5). This will allow all browsers that support any version of JavaScript to use event handlers without error, and your script can decide how to cope with them.

Figure 26-5
Setting Language to generic JavaScript

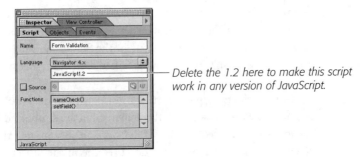

— Delete the 1.2 here to make this script work in any version of JavaScript.

JavaScript Events and the Events Tab

Events are actions initiated by the user, or by JavaScript itself, that occur in the browser window. This includes a mouse click, the browser loading a page, or even the cursor passing over an object (a "mouseover"). All JavaScripts are triggered by events.

For an event to trigger a script, you add an "event handler" that gets inserted into an HTML tag. The Events tab of the JavaScript Inspector displays a hierarchical list of all the HTML objects on the page that can have event handlers attached to them. Clicking the arrows next to these objects displays all the events they support. Clicking the event lets you see a definition of that event; you can enter the name of a JavaScript function in the text box below that gets inserted into the event handler (see Figure 26-6).

The event handler associates a given JavaScript function—a self-contained piece of JavaScript—with an action occurring in connection with an object. For instance, you can specify a graphical rollover by attaching a "mouseover" event handler to a hyperlinked image. When a user moves the cursor over the image, this event handler gets triggered, and calls a JavaScript that swaps out the first image with another image.

You can also drag and drop an event from the Inspector into your code in the Scripts window. GoLive automatically creates a new, empty function, and adds an event handler to the object with a call to the newly created function.

External JavaScripts

If you're going to use the same JavaScript on more than one page, you can put it in a single file instead of repeating it on each Web page.

Create a text file with ".js" (the JavaScript extension that Web servers and browsers recognize) at the end of the file name and place your JavaScripts in it. You can create your JavaScript as a head script to use GoLive's JavaScript syntax and editing tools, then copy and paste the contents of it into the .js file.

To reference that JavaScript file, create a new, blank head script in the Scripts window. Set your language and other options in the JavaScript Inspector. Check the Source box and use the Browse dialog or use Point & Shoot to link to your .js file. GoLive does not show the functions available in this external file; you'll have to make a note of them to enter them into event handlers.

Not all browsers that support JavaScript also support external script files, so be careful to test your pages before creating scripts this way. To bring the script back into the page, copy and paste it from the external file into a blank head script.

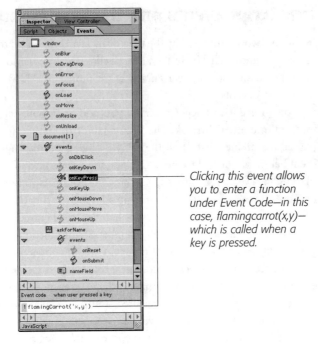

Clicking this event allows you to enter a function under Event Code—in this case, flamingcarrot(x,y)— which is called when a key is pressed.

JavaScript Objects and the Objects Tab

JavaScript views the browser window, the page loaded within it, and everything on the page as a collection of objects that it can retrieve information about and manipulate. This group of objects is referred to as the Document Object Model (DOM), and is structured in a hierarchical tree so that individual objects can be targeted by scripts. Think of the object reference as the item's address within the browser's neighborhood.

The Objects tab of the JavaScript Inspector displays a complete catalog of objects supported by the currently targeted browser—displayed in the same hierarchical order as the DOM—including any properties and methods that can be accessed by scripts (see Figure 26-7).

By expanding the list, you can display any specific object on the page and drag and drop it into the Scripts window to add the object reference to your script. You can choose to reference the object by name (if you've given the object a name within the HTML) or by index number, which GoLive displays. The index number changes as you insert or remove objects that appear earlier than the item in the page.

One reason we suggest appropriately naming form elements, like text-entry boxes, (see Chapter 15, *Forms*), is to use those names in JavaScript. The mnemonic device of having a name associated with a form element makes it easier to conceptualize how you're working with the element, rather than remember that it is element 12 in the form (see Figure 26-8). Also, adding or removing form elements changes the index number; the name stays the same.

Figure 26-7
Document
Object Model
(DOM)

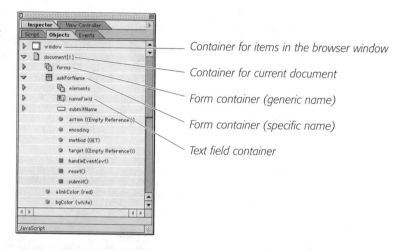

Container for items in the browser window

Container for current document

Form container (generic name)

Form container (specific name)

Text field container

Figure 26-8
Form elements
by number
and name

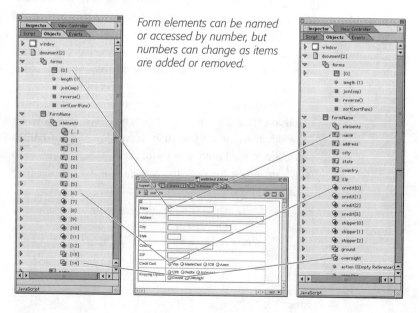

Form elements can be named or accessed by number, but numbers can change as items are added or removed.

Example: The Button Rollover

The best way to illustrate how to take advantage of GoLive's script-editing features is to demonstrate by example. In this case, let's create a version of the popular button highlight or button rollover script. We say "a version" because there are many ways of writing the code to achieve this effect. You can use GoLive's Rollover icon from the Smart tab of the Objects palette to get the same functionality, for example. However, this is the code we've found to be most efficient and easy to maintain.

First, click the "coffee-bean" icon at the top of the Layout Editor to open the Scripts window. Click the New Script Item button (called the Create Script button under Windows) to create a new head script. This first part of the code preloads the button images so they are stored in the browser's cache, ready to appear instantly. This also stores the images as objects that you can use later within functions.

```
if (document.images){
    buttonOn = new Image()
    buttonOn.src = "images/buttonOver.gif"
    buttonOff = new Image()
    buttonOff.src = "images/button.gif"
}
```

Notice we're enclosing this part of the script within an "if" statement. By testing to see if the "images" object exists for this browser, we can determine if the script will run properly. This is a simpler and more foolproof way of making sure the script is blocked from browsers that can't handle it than actually checking the browser version and platform. We include this object-checking step in the functions below for the same reasons.

Now we create two functions to perform the actual switching of the image: one to highlight the button when the cursor enters the image, and one to switch it back when the cursor leaves. We send the name of the image as an argument to the function and store it in "imageName" so the function knows which image on the page to change. Now, we can use these same two functions for any buttons we want to add later.

```
function highLightOn(imageName){
    if (document.images){
        document [imageName].src = eval(imageName + "On.src")
    }
}

function highLightOff(imageName){
    if (document.images){
```

```
document [imageName].src = eval(imageName + "Off.src")
    }
}
```

Be sure to click the Check Syntax button at the top of the Scripts window to make sure you haven't left out any brackets or parentheses.

Finally, we need to add the event handlers to the button image to trigger the functions. First, make sure the image has been set up as a link. Click the Events tab of the JavaScript Inspector and find the link object that holds the URL for the button. We use the link object because the actual image object itself doesn't support mouse events. Click the expansion triangle (Mac) or plus sign (Windows) next to the link object and choose "onMouseOver". Type the function call in the text area below the event list:

```
highLightOn('button')
```

Then call our other function from the "onMouseOut" event handler in the same way.

```
highLightOff('button')
```

That's it! Since GoLive's Layout Preview won't actually display the working JavaScript, click the Show in Browser button to see your script in action.

To add more buttons to the page, just preload the graphics for both button states using the same object-naming convention as the first button: buttonNameOn and buttonNameOff. Be sure to name the buttons within the HTML, then add the event handlers to call the "highLightOn" and "highLightOff" functions, sending the button name as an argument.

Compare the script we just wrote with the code that GoLive creates to accomplish the same thing via an Action (see Figure 26-9).

As you can see, the handwritten script is much shorter and therefore more efficient, and has the added benefit of working in more browsers while avoiding error messages.

Example: Simple Form Validation

Here's a case in which GoLive Actions lack a trigger that you might commonly use to check what a user has entered in a form before the form's contents are sent to the server. This is the "onSubmit" event.

This script checks to make sure the user has filled out a required field when submitting the form. By warning the user before sending the data to the server, you can save the person some time and reduce the load on the server. To keep things simple, we'll use a form with just one field to check (see Figure 26-10).

Figure 26-9
GoLive Action
versus
hand coded
JavaScript

*The Action code
written by GoLive*

Handwritten code

Figure 26-10
Simple form

**Remember
My Name**

As mentioned earlier, to make objects easier to keep track of, don't rely on the less descriptive default index number. Instead, give the form an appropriate name.

Like the button rollover example, this script goes in the Head Section of the page. Click the JavaScript coffee bean icon at the top of the Layout Editor to bring up the Scripts window. Click the New Script Item/Create Script button to create a new header script.

Since this particular script is compatible with any browser that supports even the lowest level of JavaScript, choose Netscape 2.0 as the target browser in the JavaScript Inspector.

Start a new function and give it a name.

```
function nameCheck(){
    if (
```

Use the Objects tab of the JavaScript Inspector to get the object reference for the text field we want to check. Within the Objects list, find the form that contains the text field and click the expansion triangles or plus signs to display the "name" field. Drag and drop the field object "value" reference into the script (see Figure 26-11).

Figure 26-11
Inserting the
property into
the script

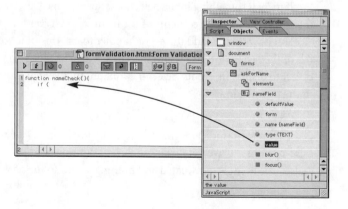

```
function nameCheck(){
    if (document.askForName.nameField.value
```

To check to see if anything has been entered in the "name" field, look to see if the value of the field is empty, indicated by two quotation marks with no space between them. If nothing has been entered, we pop an alert for the user asking them to fill in the form. The script also returns "false," which, for the "onSubmit" handler, keeps the browser from sending the contents to the server (see Figure 26-12).

```
function nameCheck(){
    if (document.askForName.nameField.value == ""){
        alert("Please fill in your name before
            submitting the form")
        return false
    }
    return true
}
```

Figure 26-12
Alert on empty
text field when
submitting

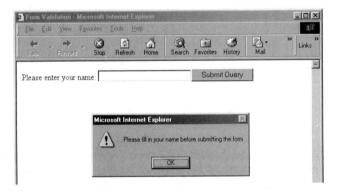

If there is something in the field, the script returns "true," which the browser interprets as "send the contents of the form to the server for processing."

You now need to add the event handler to call this function. In the Events tab of the JavaScript Inspector, click the triangle or plus sign next to the form object to display its events. Select the "onSubmit" event and type the following in the text window.

```
return nameCheck()
```

The "return" indicates that we want the function to give us back a true or false response. If we get "true," the event continues to execute normally; if "false," the event is terminated and nothing is sent to the server.

One more bit of script you need to add ensures there is nothing in the "name" field when the page loads. With some browsers, the first field in a form is automatically given a value of "undefined," which cannot be tested for with a script. So, add another function that makes sure the field is preset to "nothing" (two quotation marks with no space between them).

```
function setField(){
    document.askForName.nameField.value = ""
}
```

Then, call the function with the onLoad event within the Body tag (which is part of the Window object). As before, this happens in the Events tab of the JavaScript Inspector (see Figure 26-13).

```
setField()
```

Again, use the Check Syntax button to check for errors and test the page in multiple browsers to make sure it works properly.

Figure 26-13
Setting a function to prefill a field with a blank when the page loads

Syntax Check

The Scripts window Check Syntax button does not actually institute a bug check. Syntax checking confirms that punctuation and commands all make sense in the context of the programming language. Missing parentheses or quote characters result in a syntax error.

While a syntax check catches many common mistakes, it won't determine whether a script actually runs in a browser. (There is a deep computer science theory called "the halting problem" that describes why it's hard to write a program that can check another program for whether it will actually run or not; checking for proper syntax is as close as you can get most of the time.)

Remember to test in every browser and platform the visitors of your site might be expected to use. For most sites, this means every version of Navigator and Internet Explorer since 3.0, and the Opera browser latest releases.

The Future of JavaScript

Since JavaScript has proven to be so useful and easy to learn, you can be assured that any effort you put into learning to script will not be wasted. In fact, most Web developers now consider knowing JavaScript to be as essential a skill as knowing HTML itself.

As we take a look at Dynamic HTML—which both browser vendors tout as the future of client-side Web development—in the following chapters, you'll see that DHTML is really nothing more than JavaScript combined with the positioning capabilities of Cascading Style Sheets. And, as XML becomes more important, JavaScript will be playing a role there, too.

With its wide support and continuing development, JavaScript isn't going away any time soon.

CHAPTER 27

Animation

It's a rare day when Netscape and Microsoft agree on something—anything—so when both companies decided that Dynamic HTML (or DHTML) would be the wave of the future for Web site design, and they incorporated DHTML features into the 4.0 (and subsequent) versions of their browsers, most designers took a long, hard look. Unfortunately, most came away somewhat frustrated, disappointed, and confused.

DHTML was supposed to be a simple but powerful way to add certain multimedia features to Web pages that would work across platforms, and wouldn't require plug-ins such as Shockwave or Flash, Java, or ActiveX. DHTML would be easy to use; appear and run consistently under Windows, Mac OS, and Unix; and be based on open standards.

But designers' confusion arose from the marketing hype. DHTML sounded like an entirely new animal, when it was actually a patchwork made from many parts, some new and some old. Much like a fax machine was originally the odd union of a slow modem, a cheap scanner, and a bad printer, DHTML joins some new JavaScript features with existing HTML and the object-positioning features of Cascading Style Sheets to create a whole that is a bit greater than its parts.

This realization brought disappointment. The frustration? There were no tools to easily write the extremely complex sequences of JavaScript that provide exact positioning control over time, to move items around or attach animation-like features to a page. Enter GoLive, stage right.

The DHTML Promise

By bringing positioning and scripting together to provide time-based animation controls within the browser, designers gain substantially more control over the layout and interactivity of their pages. DHTML lets a designer specify the absolute position of text and images; provides dynamic control over font size, style, leading, and kerning; and allows the animation of elements on the page by moving them along a path or hiding and showing them. You can even change the size and position of the browser window itself.

This sounds wonderful, and it actually is, but as we saw with JavaScript, there's no such thing as smooth sailing when it comes to Web standards.

First of all, DHTML requires a version 4.0 or later browser to work, and (naturally) Microsoft's and Netscape's versions of DHTML are not the same. Much of Netscape's version relies on the proprietary Layer tag extension to HTML, an extension that Microsoft chose not to implement, and the World Wide Web Consortium (W3C) chose not to ratify as a standard. The W3C opted for the absolute positioning already built into the first Cascading Style Sheets (CSS) version, CSS1 (see Chapter 29, *Cascading Style Sheets*).

TIP: **Ignoring Netscape's Layer Tag**	GoLive's solution for getting around the cross-browser issue is to ignore the Netscape Layer tag completely and employ CSS Div tags to define independently layered page elements, which are represented in GoLive as floating boxes (see Chapter 14, *Floating Boxes*).

Fortunately, both browsers' implementation of DHTML overlap enough that you can often create DHTML that works well in both. GoLive takes advantage of these similarities in its built-in DHTML animation timelines, which is fortunate, since writing DHTML—especially cross-browser animation—can be complex and time consuming.

In Chapter 26, *JavaScript*, we say that writing your own JavaScripts often results in smaller, more efficient pages. However, in the case of DHTML animation, having a WYSIWYG tool that can write the code for you is truly a godsend (and once you take a look at the code required, we're sure you'll agree).

Although folks tend to lump animation and Actions together under the heading of DHTML, we think two distinct kinds of DHTML coexist inside GoLive: animation, in which you're moving objects around a page using floating boxes; and Actions, which are prefab, complex JavaScripts that handle a variety of tasks, like writing a cookie to a browser, or displaying a different image each day of the week.

This chapter covers DHTML animation; Chapter 28 addresses Actions.

Floating Boxes and Time Tracks

GoLive employs two interface elements to let you create and control animation: floating boxes contain the elements you want to animate, and timelines (called time tracks in GoLive) control their speed and timing.

By placing any content—images, text, form elements, even plug-ins or Java applets—into a floating box, GoLive lets you dynamically control the content's visibility and its absolute position within the window. You can also animate the box's content by moving it from point to point or along a path.

You can trigger animation automatically when a page loads, set a timer to delay it, run it once, have it loop, or give control to the viewer through mouse clicks and mouseovers. (For a refresher on floating boxes, see Chapter 14, *Floating Boxes*.)

TIP:

Only 4.0 Browsers Know DHTML

GoLive may do a remarkably good job of dealing with the different implementations of DHTML, but all this slick animation only plays back in the 4.0 and higher browsers. Users with older browsers see nothing. Be sure your audience has a browser advanced enough to display all your hard work before you spend a lot of time and effort building it into all your pages.

Alternatively, you can create two different versions of your pages and use the Browser Switch Action to send viewers to one or the other, based on their browser version (see Chapter 28, *Actions*).

Bring up the Timeline Editor by clicking its icon at the top right of the Layout Editor (see Figure 27-1). When you open the Timeline Editor, all the floating boxes on the page are automatically listed by number in the order you added them to the page. Each floating box has its own time track which allows you to animate each box independently. An arrow next to a time track indicates which floating box is currently selected.

Figure 27-1
Timeline Editor

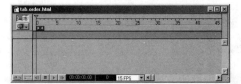

TIP:

Action Track

Above standard time tracks, there's a gray bar, which is the Action Track. This track allows you to choose Actions that are triggered at a given point in time during an animation. The Action Track is explained at the end of this chapter.

The keyframe is the "key" to controlling animation. If you've worked with animation or video-editing applications such as Adobe Live Motion or Premiere, or Macromedia Flash or Director, you're already familiar with the concept of keyframes. If you haven't, keyframes may be a little intimidating at first.

A keyframe is a marker on the time track that tells GoLive where on the page you want your floating box to be at a given time. As you add keyframes and move the box to different locations, GoLive automatically determines the path of the box between keyframes (this is called "tweening" or "interpolation"). The greater the distance between keyframes, the longer it takes the box to move between the two positions. Keyframes can also be used to control more static properties of floating boxes such as visibility and layering order.

Setting Keyframes

Keyframes are set by moving the floating box to a new location and Command-clicking (Mac) or Control-clicking (Windows) the time track at the point in time you want the box to reach that position; or, you can option-drag an existing keyframe to the new time (see Figure 27-2). To change the settings of a keyframe, select it and move the floating box; or go to the Floating Box Inspector to choose new position, visibility, path shape, and/or relative layer depth settings. Dragging keyframes closer together or farther apart lets you change the timing between two keyframes in the animation (see Figure 27-3).

At the top of the Timeline Editor is a time scale with numbers and tickmarks. Each tickmark indicates a frame of animation. By setting the distance between keyframes you can control the number of frames GoLive generates

Figure 27-2
Option-dragging to create a new keyframe

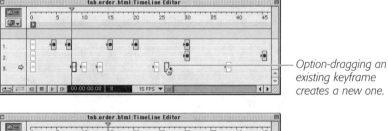

Option-dragging an existing keyframe creates a new one.

Figure 27-3
Changing timing between keyframes

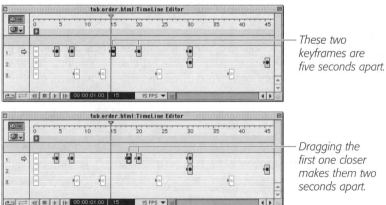

These two keyframes are five seconds apart.

Dragging the first one closer makes them two seconds apart.

between the different locations of a floating box, thus controlling the smoothness of the animation. Setting the number of frames per second in the Frames per Second popup menu at the bottom of the Timeline Editor determines the overall choppiness of the animation; more frames means a smoother performance (see Figure 27-4).

TIP:
Adding Frames Doesn't Affect File Size

Unlike animated GIFs, adding frames to a DHTML animation does not increase the file size of the page by more than literally a few bytes. However, moving images—especially large or multiple images—is very processor intensive. Even if you set the frame rate to 30 frames per second, a viewer using an older computer may only see a choppy animation at 5-10 frames per second. Always try to test animations on a computer that is close to the lowest common denominator of your audience.

Figure 27-4
Frame rate
menu

A few controls in the Floating Box Inspector are used just for animation.

Depth. The Depth field lets you set the layer of a floating box relative to all other floating boxes on the page: the lower the number you enter, the deeper the layer. A floating box with a depth of 1 appears beneath a floating box with a depth of 2 (see Figure 27-5). Each keyframe associated with a floating box can have its own depth setting. This means that you can animate the depth of layers over time, making objects appear first in front of, then behind, other objects.

TIP:
Depth Numbering

The Depth numbers don't have to be sequential. Boxes with depths of 42, 118, and 14321 appear in the same order as if they were numbered 1, 2, and 3.

Visible. The Visible checkbox determines (what else) the visibility of the floating box at any given time during the animation. As with the Depth setting, each keyframe can have its own visibility setting.

TIP:
Start with Invisible Floating Boxes

It is good practice to make all your page's animated floating boxes invisible while the page loads, and then start the animation when the page has finished loading using the Play Scene Action set to be triggered OnLoad (see "Triggering Actions" in Chapter 28, *Actions*). This helps the animation run as smoothly as possible.

Figure 27-5
Changing the
depth of
objects

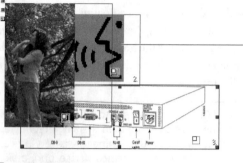

Each of these images is in a separate floating box.

This image has a lower setting in the Depth field than the others.

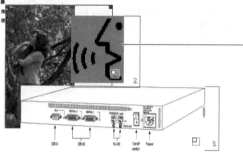

Changing this image's Depth value to be higher than all of the other objects places it (and its floating box) on top.

Figure 27-6
Different types
of animation
paths

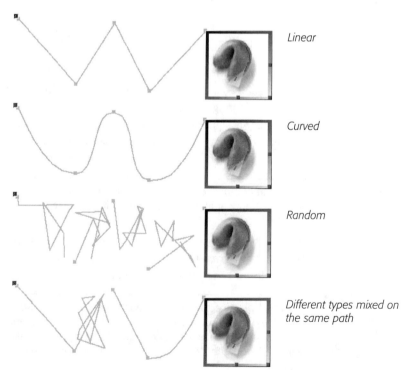

Linear

Curved

Random

Different types mixed on the same path

Animation. The Animation popup menu allows you to select whether the path originating from the keyframe point is sharp and angular (Linear, the default), smooth (Curve), or jittery and shaky (Random). Of course, each keyframe can have its own Animation setting, so your animation path can go from a straight line into a smooth curve into a jitterbug routine (see Figure 27-6).

KeyColor. The KeyColor field lets you change the color of the selected keyframe in the Timeline Editor by dragging a color swatch from the Color palette onto the field. This feature can help you track which keyframes feature specific events, such as changing layering order or when a floating box enters or exits the page.

Record. The Record button lets you create an animation path and all of its keyframes by dragging the floating box along the path you want it to travel. Position the floating box where you want the animation to begin, click the Record button, and drag the box around the page exactly as you want it to animate (see Figure 27-7). When you're done, release the mouse button to stop recording. The animation path appears in the layout and keyframes show up in the Timeline Editor. After recording, you can adjust a recorded animation just like any other by moving or deleting keyframes or selecting keyframes and moving the floating box.

Figure 27-7
Path using
Record

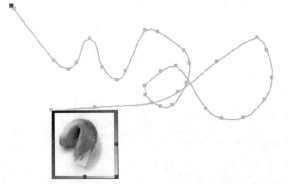

Creating Animations

Building Web elements based on timelines can cause confusion for most traditional Web designers, especially if their primary notion of Web time is the long wait while inadequately optimized Web pages load. So, let's run through a few examples.

For our first exercise, we'll create an animation of a company logo flying in from the left and stopping in the upper-right corner of the page. (If you want to follow along with this example, you can download the two logo elements and the HTML page from http://realworldgolive.com/animation.html.)

1. Add a floating box to your layout by dragging the Floating Box icon from the Basic tab of the Objects palette (see Figure 27-8).

2. Drag the logo—either from an image file, or the Custom tab of the Objects palette—into the floating box. The floating box automatically grows, if necessary, to the dimensions of the image (see Figure 27-9). It doesn't matter where you initially drop the floating box on your page. The position of the top-left corner of the box is always calculated in relation to the upper-left corner of the window.

TIP:
Floating Box Transparency

Since floating boxes are always in front of regular page elements such as text, images, and backgrounds, you may want to make the background of your images in animated floating boxes transparent for a better effect.

Figure 27-8
Inserting a floating box

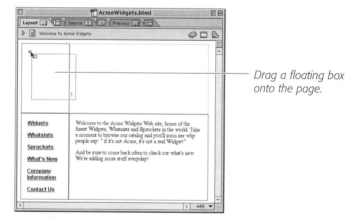

Drag a floating box onto the page.

Figure 27-9
Inserting an image

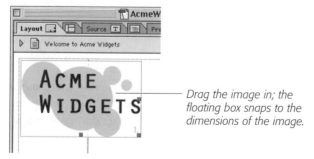

Drag the image in; the floating box snaps to the dimensions of the image.

3. Name the floating box to make it easier to track (see Figure 27-10). GoLive automatically names the floating box "Layer" in the Name field of the Floating Box Inspector. Enter a new name reflecting its contents; in this case, "LogoLayer". (The name must be one word; if not, GoLive pops up an error message and resets the name.)

Figure 27-10
Naming a
floating box

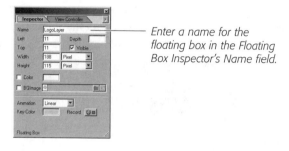

Enter a name for the
floating box in the Floating
Box Inspector's Name field.

TIP:

**Selecting
the Floating
Box**

Sometimes it's tricky to know if you've selected a floating box or the image within it. To ensure that you're selecting the floating box, position the cursor so it is hovering over an edge of the box, then click when the cursor changes into a hand (see Figure 27-11). You know you've selected the box if the Inspector palette changes into the Floating Box Inspector. You can also click the small floating box placeholder icon. If you click in the middle of the box, you select its contents, and could accidentally drag the image out of the box.

Figure 27-11
Selecting a
floating box

The cursor changes into
a hand when you can
drag the floating box.

4. Click the Timeline Editor icon at the top of the Layout Editor. This brings up the Timeline Editor with the floating box already included as the first track with the first keyframe inserted and highlighted (see Figure 27-12).

Figure 27-12
Initial Timeline
Editor view

First keyframe already
inserted and highlighted

5. Select the first keyframe in the LogoLayer track and position the floating box where you want it to appear in the window at the end of the animation. This approach may seem backwards, but it makes it easier to move the logo in a straight line and make it end up where we want it.

6. To add another keyframe, Command-click (Mac) or Control-click (Windows) anywhere in the LogoLayer track, or Option-drag the first keyframe to the point at which you want the animation to end (see Figure 27-13). This creates a keyframe with the logo in exactly the same position as the first keyframe, which is its final position.

Figure 27-13
Ending the
animation

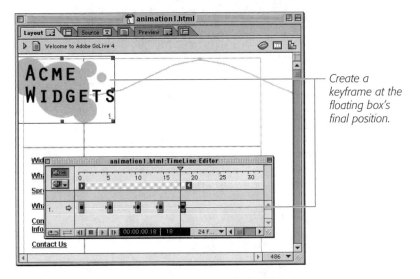

Create a
keyframe at the
floating box's
final position.

Figure 27-14
Starting the
animation off
screen

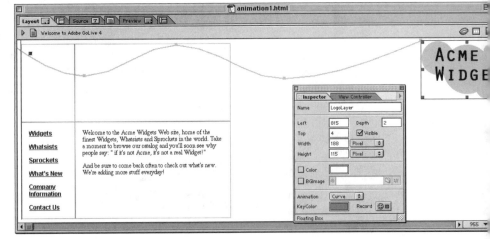

7. Move the logo to its starting point. Make sure the first keyframe is selected—it has a bolder outline when selected—and drag the floating box with the logo far enough to the right so it is beyond the monitor size of most of your audience; 1,000 to 1,200 pixels should be plenty (see Figure 27-14). You can track the pixel location in the Left field of the Floating Box Inspector, or you can directly enter a value there.

    If you move the box by dragging, make sure it's still the same distance from the top of the window as the ending keyframe by clicking each keyframe and checking that each number in the Top field of the Floating Box Inspector is identical.

TIP:

Keyframe Connectors in the Timeline Editor

Notice a light gray line in your layout that connects the first and second keyframe positions. This is the animation path; the squares at the beginning and end indicate keyframes. When we add more keyframes later on, you'll see that each square on the path corresponds with the box's position at that point in time.

These squares are indicators only and cannot be dragged to edit the keyframe data. You can only change keyframe attributes by dragging keyframes within the time track to change timing, clicking them in the time track and dragging the floating box to a new position, or modifying the values in the Floating Box Inspector.

8. Switch to the Layout Preview tab to preview the animation. To make the movement faster or slower, go back to the Layout Editor and drag the final keyframe to the left or right; you can also change the Frames per Second setting to change tempo. Experiment until you like the results.

    The Time display at the bottom of the Timeline Editor tells you how long your animation runs in seconds. Remember, however, that the actual speed and smoothness of the animation depend greatly upon the speed of the viewer's computer.

TIP:

Starting Animations after a Page Loads

By default, GoLive sets up an animation to play when your page loads. However, if you uncheck the Play on Load button, you can use an Action to trigger the start of the animation. We cover this later in "Triggering an Action within an Animation."

Throwing Some Curves

To make our animation a little more interesting, let's add some keyframes.

1. Command-click (Mac) or Control-click (Windows) at several points on the time track.

2. Select each of the new keyframes and move the floating box into the new position to create a zigzag effect as the logo moves across the screen (see Figure 27-15).

Figure 27-15
Inserting
intermediate
keyframes

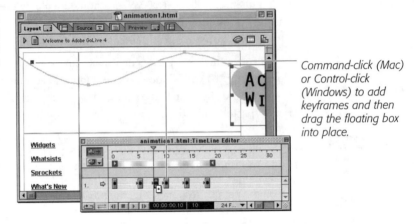

Command-click (Mac)
or Control-click
(Windows) to add
keyframes and then
drag the floating box
into place.

3. When you preview the animation, the logo follows the new zigzag path. (By first setting up a simple linear animation, it only took a few clicks and mouse movements to dramatically alter the logo's path.)

Changing Multiple Keyframes

By default, GoLive sets each new keyframe with linear motion between it and the next keyframe. To make the animation path curve between two points, instead of following a straight line, select the keyframe and choose Curve from the Animation popup menu in the Floating Box Inspector. You can make the entire path curved, or you can mix curved and linear keyframes. This can have some unexpected results, so you may want to experiment a bit to see what works.

Shift-click each keyframe on the floating box's path or drag a marquee around all of the keyframes, then select Curve from the Animation popup menu in the Floating Box Inspector. The animation path should now be curvy instead of straight (see Figure 27-16).

TIP:
Avoid
Random
Motion

The Random option causes the floating box to move in a jittery fashion roughly along the animation path that changes randomly every time the animation plays. We don't recommend this feature (unless that's precisely the effect you're looking for) since you really don't have much control over the effect, and we've experienced intermittent browser incompatibilities.

Figure 27-16
Curvy path

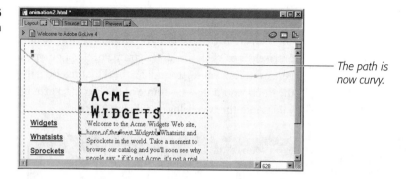

The path is now curvy.

Animating Multiple Elements

Our little logo animation is looking pretty cool now, but what if we want to animate two images independent of each other? To illustrate this idea, let's split the logo into two graphics: the background shape in one file and the type in another. Each new graphic has a transparent background, so the background rectangles won't cover the images below when we move them (see Figure 27-17).

1. Returning to our original bouncing logo animation, select the original logo graphic and replace it with the image containing just the logo's type. Now we have the same animation, but only the logotype bounces into position (see Figure 27-18).

2. To make the background shape drop into position behind the type, add and name a second floating box. This creates a new time track.

Figure 27-17
Logo split into foreground and background

Logo foreground

Logo background

Figure 27-18
Positioning just the logo foreground

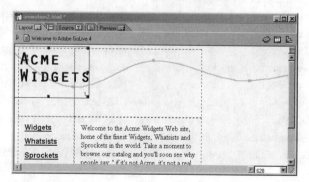

3. Both images share the same dimensions and, when placed on top of one another, are registered exactly. The easiest way to align the two elements precisely is to click the last keyframe of the logotype and write down the Left and Top values found in the Floating Box Inspector. Then click the first—and only—keyframe of the logo background and type the same values into the two fields (see Figure 27-19).

Figure 27-19
Registering
foreground
and
background

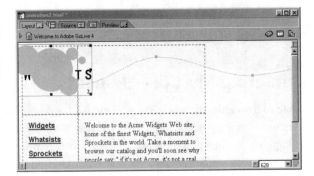

4. Since the background floating box was created last, it is placed in front of the other elements, covering up the logotype box. Move it to the back by setting the Depth value lower than that of the logo box. Remember that

Avoiding Timeline Editor Interface Quirks

There are a few potentially confusing features of the Timeline Editor.

-   The direction the Time Cursor moves—left to right—does not indicate the direction the animated element is moving. For example, in our first animation, the logo moves from right to left while the Time Cursor always moves left to right along the time-elapsed axis.

-   The order of the time tracks in the Timeline Editor does not correspond to the stacking order of the floating boxes, only the order in which they were created. The Floating Box palette doesn't indicate the stacking order either. The only way to

check the stacking order is to select individual keyframes and check the number in the Depth field in the Floating Box Inspector.

-   Selecting a keyframe moves the Time Cursor in the Timeline Editor to that keyframe's location, and it selects the floating box that corresponds to it. But the reverse isn't true; selecting a floating box does not select any keyframe. If you already have a keyframe selected and then click a floating box, the keyframe remains selected and changes in the Floating Box Inspector corresponding to that keyframe, not the floating box you've clicked.

each floating box can be its own layer, so a larger Depth value represents a higher layer, also called the Z-Index.

5. Each keyframe can also have its own depth, with the default being the order in which the floating box was created. Make sure the logotype box is always on top. Select all of its keyframes by Shift-clicking them, then type 2 into the Depth field.

6. Repeat the procedure to set the logo background's floating box to 1.

TIP:

Use Layering to Display Elements

Since keyframes can have independent Depth settings, you can change the depth of a floating box at any time during an animation. This can lead to some interesting effects, such as a moon orbiting a planet using only two graphics and a couple of floating boxes.

Now that the logo background box is behind the logotype, selecting it becomes difficult. This is where the Floating Box palette comes in handy.

1. Choose Floating Boxes from the Window menu to display a small window that lists all the floating boxes on the page by name—another good reason to name your floating boxes mnemonically (see Figure 27-20).

Figure 27-20
Floating Box Controller

Each layer's name is listed, along with an eyeball to show whether it's visible and a pencil to show whether it's editable.

The Controller identifies the number of floating boxes on the page.

2. Click the eye icon next to the logotype box's name in the Floating Boxes palette to make it temporarily invisible, just like Adobe Photoshop's Layers palette. Now we can work with the logo background unencumbered.

TIP:

Invisibility Only Applies to GoLive

Making a floating box invisible or locking it in the Floating Boxes palette has no effect when the animation is run in a browser. This palette is just an organizational tool to help you deal with multiple floating boxes while working on the layout or the animation. To control whether a floating box's contents are hidden or shown when a page loads, use the Visible checkbox in the Floating Box Inspector. Also, since each keyframe can have its own Visible setting (just like the Depth setting), you can make a floating box appear and disappear during an animation.

3. Add a couple more keyframes to the logo background track to animate it. In this case, because we want it to begin moving after the logotype has

stopped, place another keyframe at the same point as the last keyframe of the logotype box.

4. Add one more keyframe about 10 frames later.

5. We want the logo background to begin off the top of the screen, so click the first keyframe and drag its floating box up off the page until it is no longer visible. Make sure that the Left position value is the same as the other keyframes.

6. Drag the second keyframe's floating box offscreen to match the first.

7. Make the logotype visible again and preview the animation.

Animation Scenes

What if you want to animate images separately at different times? For example, can you have one element animate when the page loads and another when the user clicks a button? Or, after running our animation, can we have these same elements move again in an entirely different way on the same page? The answer is yes, with the use of animation scenes.

Think of scenes as somewhat independent time tracks within the same page that can have a set of shared or separate elements, timing, triggers, and Actions. With scenes you can set up and trigger many different animations whenever and however you choose. Let's see how this works by adding a scene to our logo animation.

Setting Up a Second Scene

1. The animation we've already created is called "Scene 1" by default. You can rename this scene if you choose by selecting Rename Scene from the Options menu at the top of the Timeline Editor.

2. Add a new scene by selecting New Scene from the Options Menu and give it a name such as "Click Animation". You see a new time track with both floating boxes listed as tracks, but with no keyframes. Our old animation is still there; use the Scenes menu to switch back to see it (see Figure 27-21).

Figure 27-21
Creating a new
scene

Our old scene, called
LogoScene, is still there.

3. Let's add a little animation that plays when the viewer clicks the logo. To create the animation path this time, we use Record to build a path to match how we move the background image. In Scene 1, select the last keyframe to view both logo graphics in their final positions, then switch back to the Click Animation scene.

4. As before, make the logotype temporarily invisible using the eye icon in the Floating Box palette.

5. To start recording, select the first keyframe of the logo background track and click the Record button in the Floating Box Inspector.

6. Drag the background floating box to create the animation path; in this case we'll move it in a circle and return it to where it started.

7. Release the floating box to stop recording. GoLive creates a new animation path and a bunch of keyframes (see Figure 27-22).

Figure 27-22
Recorded path
in new scene

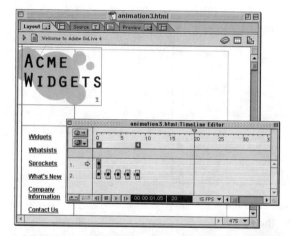

8. Preview the animation. The Record operation creates normal keyframes, so you can adjust movement or timing just like any other animation.

One adjustment you may want to make is to check the position of the last keyframe to ensure it's the same as the first keyframe, leaving the image back in registration with the logotype. You may also want to delete excess keyframes, as Record creates more than are strictly needed—the more keyframes, the more browser computation.

Using an Action to Trigger the Second Scene

Now we have two scenes using the same images that both play when the page loads. This obviously creates a conflict, so we need to make the second scene play when the viewer clicks the logo. To do this, we add an Action to play the scene onClick and attach it to the logotype image. (We add the Action to the logotype and not to the logo background, even though that is the graphic that animates, because the logo background can't be clicked when it's behind the logotype.)

1. Make sure you turn off Play on Load for the Click Animation scene at the top of the time track.

2. Select the logotype graphic inside the floating box and add a link to it, but don't worry about linking it to anything. (You can't attach an Action to a floating box, and you must have a link in order to attach an Action.)

3. Open the Actions palette and add a Mouse Click trigger.

4. Choose Play Scene from the Multimedia submenu of the Action menu.

5. From the Action configuration options that appear in the Actions palette, choose Click Animation from the Scenes popup (see Figure 27-23). (Actions are covered in depth in the next chapter.)

Figure 27-23
Selecting an
Action for a
Mouse Click
trigger

6. When you preview the page in a browser you should see the logo animate in the window as before and stop. When you click the logo, the background image should wiggle in a circle back to where it started.

Triggering an Action within an Animation

We've just used an Action to trigger an animation, but you can also use an animation to trigger an Action by using the Action Track, the gray bar at the top of the Timeline Editor. Assign an Action to a point in time by Command-clicking (Mac) or Control-clicking (Windows) the Action Track at the point in time that you want the Action to be triggered (see Figure 27-24).

To demonstrate, instead of using a Mouse Click to trigger the Click Animation scene, let's make the first scene trigger the next when the first is done playing (see Figure 27-25).

Figure 27-24
Using the
Action Track

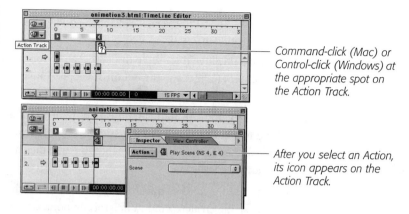

Command-click (Mac) or
Control-click (Windows) at
the appropriate spot on
the Action Track.

After you select an Action,
its icon appears on the
Action Track.

Figure 27-25
Triggering a
scene via the
Action Track

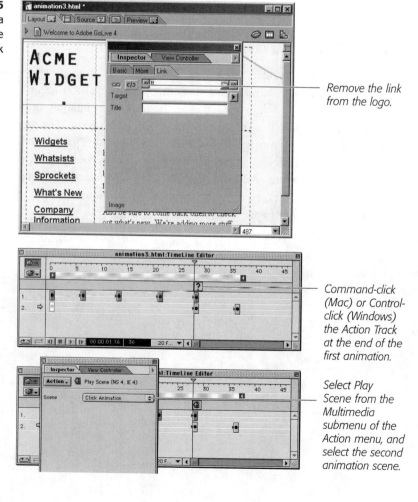

Remove the link
from the logo.

Command-click
(Mac) or Control-
click (Windows)
the Action Track
at the end of the
first animation.

Select Play
Scene from the
Multimedia
submenu of the
Action menu, and
select the second
animation scene.

1. Remove the link from the logotype image, which automatically eliminates the Action attached to it.

2. With the Timeline Editor set to display Scene 1, Command-click (Mac) or Control-click (Windows) the Action Track just above the last keyframe of the first scene. The Action Inspector appears.

3. Choose Play Scene from the Actions popup menu under the Multimedia submenu and choose Click Animation from the Scene popup. When the page loads, the first animation sequence runs and then it triggers the second scene automatically.

You can use the Actions track to trigger any of the other Actions as well, such as displaying an alert window at a certain point or playing a sound each time the animation loops.

The Hard Truth

As we said in Chapter 26, *JavaScript*, if you are a savvy scripter, you can write code by hand that is much more compact and efficient. But even if you are savvy enough to hand code, the DHTML animation scripting is complicated enough that the time and effort GoLive saves you is worth the extra overhead.

Although GoLive makes it easy to create DHTML animations, try not to go nuts adding lots of animation all over your pages unless you know that your audience employs a fast network connection. If done in moderation—a little bit here, a little bit there—DHTML animations can add style and impact to your pages.

CHAPTER 28

Actions

Back in the JavaScript chapter, we provided some persuasive reasons why you should hand code your scripts whenever possible. Now we're contradicting ourselves by advising you to consider GoLive's built-in Actions: prefabricated powerful JavaScript and DHTML behaviors that require no programming whatsoever.

What's the incongruity here? It's simple. Scripts created "by hand" offer more flexibility and control, and are almost always smaller, more efficient, and carry out their tasks faster than Actions. In addition, Actions are almost impossible to modify or update without using GoLive; if multiple people are maintaining a site, multiple copies of the software are needed. You can't get by, for instance, with one person using BBEdit, another using Dreamweaver, and the rest using GoLive.

But if you're in a hurry and want to assemble prototype pages; if learning anything more complicated than point-and-click might fill your brain with things you don't really want to learn; or if you're in charge of updating your site and you have complete control over which applications to use—then Actions (and related Smart Objects) make it quick and easy to add functionality and special effects with drag-and-drop ease.

Actions are prefabricated sets of JavaScript and Cascading Style Sheets settings (otherwise known as DHTML—or Dynamic HTML—when they involve animation) that allow you to just plug in values and let GoLive write and modify the code. Your interface with an Action is through the Actions palette, which activates whenever you select an item that can have an Action attached to it. This palette provides you with all the necessary fields and menus to enter numbers, text, or other values specific to each Action.

TIP:
Action Inspectors

For Head Actions, Body Actions, and Actions found on the Timeline Editor's Action Track, the old standby Inspector palette (in the form of the Action Inspector) handles configuring Actions.

GoLive comes with a few dozen Actions that encompass a whole range of activities; a few examples include writing a cookie to a user's browser, handling conditions (like "if such-and-such happens, then do this other thing"), and forcing a page to load as the only thing in a window if it finds itself as part of a frameset.

Adobe has also made additional Actions available free for downloading, and set up an area on their Web site as an Actions exchange for independent developers. See http://realworldgolive.com for links to that material.

In this chapter, we also talk about Smart Objects, which are like simpler-to-use Actions you insert to include the date or time at which the page was last updated, or redirect users if they're not using a browser you require. Smart Objects also provide GoLive containers for placing Actions in the Head or body section of an HTML page.

Most GoLive Actions only work properly in Netscape and Microsoft's 4.0 (or later) browser releases. You can see each Action's compatible browsers next to the Action's name in the palette you've selected it from (the Actions palette or Inspector palette, depending on context). GoLive automatically writes the code so the JavaScript is hidden from browsers that can't run it. However, this means that users with older browsers see nothing, rather than alternate content which could be displayed if the script were written by an experienced scripter.

The only option GoLive provides for dealing with browser incompatibility is a Browser Detection Action that lets you divert users with older browsers to an alternate page. This solution is useful, but it means you must maintain multiple versions for each page containing Actions, adding extra complexity to your site.

If any of the JavaScript code that GoLive Actions create is modified by hand or by editing the file in another visual editor, GoLive no longer recognizes it as an Action and you can't edit it using the Actions palette.

Smart Objects

We need to introduce Smart Objects before we talk about GoLive's Actions, as some Smart Objects are required to use Actions properly. Smart Objects are special GoLive elements. They insert or control internal objects (like date-and timestamps); act as a container for Actions not connected to a link in the Head section or body; and offer special options that regular Actions couldn't include, such as automatically redirecting a browser to another page based on the browser's platform and version. GoLive groups these items together for no particular reason, except that they don't really belong anywhere else, and you might use them in tandem quite often.

To add these objects to a page, click the Smart tab of the Objects palette and drag a Smart Object icon into the Layout Editor's body or Head section where you want it to appear. The inspector changes to the name of the Smart Object and allows you to set its parameters.

TIP:
Smart Object Compatibility

Unlike the Actions palette, the Smart Object Inspector does not indicate which browsers the Smart Object works with, so it's critical to test them with multiple browsers.

Internal Objects

GoLive uses two Smart Objects to act as containers for content that the program updates. Neither of them uses JavaScript, nor are they really Actions.

Modified Date. Modified Date inserts the date and/or time that the document was last edited into a specific location on a page. It's not JavaScript or an Action, but a placeholder that GoLive uses to identify where to insert static text into the HTML each time the page is opened and saved. (To update the timestamp, just open the page; GoLive makes the change.)

You can select one of several formats for the date or time, and choose a language/country style from a popup menu (see Figure 28-1).

This Smart Object cannot be accessed or used by other Smart Objects or Actions; it's really just text that GoLive inserts each time you update the page. Unlike a JavaScript (or an Action described later) that can display the current date and time, Modified Date is plain old HTML in a wrapper.

Figure 28-1
Modified Date
Smart Object

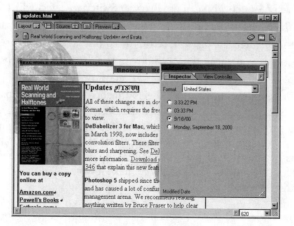

Component. The Component Smart Object is a placeholder for inserting a component, a centrally-managed template for a fragment of a page. We cover components and this placeholder thoroughly in Chapter 21, *Files, Folders, and Links*.

Smart Photoshop, Illustrator, and LiveMotion Smart Objects. The Smart Objects for Photoshop, Illustrator, and LiveMotion let you embed links to native files for these three programs. (You must have the software packages installed for these icons to appear.) Modifying the element causes your computer to open the creating applications, make the changes, save it, and reload it in GoLive. For a full explanation, see Chapter 9, *Images*.

Page Actions

The page-based Action Smart Objects are dissected later in this chapter in "Triggering Actions." The Body Action and Head Action allow you to insert an Action directly into the Head section or body of a page to trigger Actions based on activity (mouse movement, key presses, etc.) in the browser window.

Standard Actions

Browser Switch, Rollover, and URL Popup are essentially identical to any Action in the Actions palette. But limitations in the nature of Actions themselves required these special Smart Objects to work more closely with the innards of GoLive.

Browser Switch. You can use Browser Switch to detect which browser is loading the page (see Figure 28-2). The Smart Object can automatically redirect a user to an alternate page based on the combination of browser, platform, and version. If you check the Auto box in the Browser Switch Inspector, GoLive writes the JavaScript code to redirect any browser that can't handle the Actions, animations, or style sheets attached to the current page.

TIP:
Handling Older Browsers

Browser Switch is the only option to display different content for users with older browsers, if you are not writing JavaScript yourself by hand. Also, 2.0 and older browsers on all platforms ignore the Browser Switch because they don't support the JavaScript necessary to make it work.

Figure 28-2
Browser
Switch Smart
Object

Rollover. Rollover is a simple way to create a button that changes its content based on a user action (see Figure 28-3). You can specify a default image (labeled Main), an image that displays when the user has the cursor over the image (Over), and an image that displays when the user clicks the image (Click). JavaScript code swaps out the image displayed in the browser for another graphic when the specified mouse event occurs.

Figure 28-3
Rollover Smart
Object

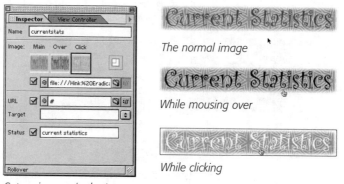

The normal image

While mousing over

While clicking

Set up images in the Inspector.

To use Rollover, create two or three images that have identical dimensions. (The browser scales the images to fit if they are not the same dimensions, but this may break the Smart Object in some browsers.) Click the buttons labeled Main, Over, and Click in the Rollover Inspector to define the appropriate image for each action.

You can specify a URL for the button to link to when clicked, or Actions for it to trigger. The Rollover Inspector also provides a place to enter a message that appears at the bottom of the browser window in the status field: check the Status box in the Inspector, and enter your text.

You can create these same effects with Actions as well, but since using this one Smart Object can take the place of up to five or six Actions per button, it can be much easier to use and set up.

URL Popup. The URL Popup Smart Object provides an easy way to include a popular Web site feature in which selecting an item from a popup menu instantly loads a new page upon release of the mouse button (see Figure 28-4). You can use the URLPopup Inspector (yes, the Inspector's name lacks a space) to enter a list of pages or sites, including locations in your own site. The Target box at the bottom of the Inspector enables you to select whether the new page is loaded in its own new window, or whether it interacts within an existing frameset.

If a user has JavaScript disabled or is using an old browser, selecting an item from the popup menu has no effect; GoLive doesn't include a "Go" button or other submit button coupled with a CGI script that would provide an alternative for older browsers to use this method.

Figure 28-4
URL Popup
Smart Object

Triggering Actions

Since Actions are made up of JavaScript code, they must be triggered by specific events, such as a mouse click or a page loading. Let's walk through the different categories of event handlers and discuss how to apply them. To apply some of the Actions discussed later, you use items found in the Objects palette's Smart tab.

Event handlers are attached in one of three general ways: to a page, to text and image links, and to the Timeline Editor's Action Track. Page-based event handlers trigger Actions from browser-window activity, like loading a page. Text and image link event handlers respond to user activities, such as moving the cursor over an image. Action Track triggers are integrated with the Dynamic HTML (DHTML) Timeline Editor, discussed in Chapter 27, *Animation.* A few JavaScript events available in browsers aren't supported by GoLive Actions.

Page Event Handlers

GoLive offers four ways of triggering Actions to respond to browser-window activity.

- **OnLoad:** when the entire contents of the page have finished loading in the browser window. This is handy for triggering a behavior only when the computer is at rest and has all its resources available.

- **OnUnload:** when the browser begins to access another page. Many adult Web sites use this technique to bring up another window, sometimes in endless succession, to keep users from ever escaping their sites. (Kind of like a Roach Motel with ads for pay-per-view channels.)

- **OnParse:** when the script is read by the browser, but before the rest of the page has loaded. This event handler lets you immediately trigger a behavior, which is useful on longer page loads.

- **OnCall:** when a specific function is called by name. This method allows you to trigger Actions stored in the Head section from anywhere in the page without having to write custom function calls.

You can use these events to trigger any arbitrary Action by inserting a Head Action or Body Action from the Smart tab of the Objects palette.

Drag the Head Action icon to the Head section of the Layout Editor. In the Action Inspector you can choose one of the four events described above, and then select a particular Action and configure it (see Figure 28-5).

Figure 28-5
Configuring a
Head Action

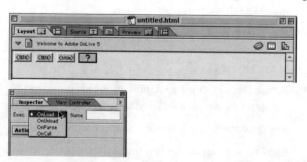

For example, if you want to use one of these triggers to insert text into the body of a page, drag a Body Action into the appropriate location in the page's body. In the Body Action Inspector, select Document Write from the Action menu's Message submenu (see Figure 28-6); we describe how to configure Document Write in "Message Actions," later in this chapter.

Figure 28-6
Writing text
into a page

Text and Image Link Event Handlers

Text and Image events are things users do that can be detected and "handled" by any range of text, image, or area of an imagemap that has a hyperlink attached to it.

- **Mouse Click:** the mouse button is pressed and released over the object the Action is attached to.

- **Mouse Enter:** the cursor moves over the object the Action is attached to (known as "mouseover" in JavaScript).

- **Mouse Exit:** the cursor leaves the object the Action is attached to (known as "mouseout" in JavaScript).

- **Double Click:** the mouse button is quickly pressed and released twice over the object the Action is attached to.

- **Mouse Down:** when the mouse button is pressed and held over the object the Action is attached to, as if the user were dragging; this is the first half of the Mouse Click.

- **Mouse Up:** when the mouse button, already pressed and held, is released over the object the Action is attached to; this is the second half of the Mouse Click.

- **Key Down:** when any key on the keyboard is pressed.

- **Key Press:** when any key on the keyboard is pressed or held down.

- **Key Up:** when any key on the keyboard is released.

To attach an Action to a linked image, text, or imagemap area, select the object and bring up the Actions palette (see Figure 28-7). A scrolling list of valid events appears under Events. Select the event that is to trigger the Action, click the New Action button (which looks like a page with the corner turned up), and choose the Action you want the event to trigger from the Action popup menu. Finally, set its options.

Figure 28-7
Attaching an
Action

*Select an object and
add a link.*

*Choose an event,
such as Mouse Enter.*

*Click the New Action
button.*

*Choose an Action
from the popup
menu, such as
Open Window.*

*Configure
the Action's
options.*

You can add multiple events to a link object, and each event can trigger more than one Action. The order that Actions are executed is set by the order you add them to the event handler. A bullet appears next to each event handler to which an Action is assigned.

Each area on an imagemap can have its own set of event handlers associated with it (see Figure 28-8).

Figure 28-8
An imagemap
with many
Actions

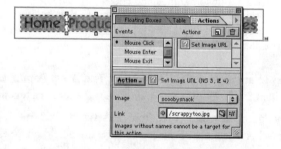

TIP:

**Pounding
Away**

You can get around the limitation of needing a link to assign an Action by linking the text, image, or imagemap region to just the pound-sign (#) character. This tells the browser to link to the current page; when the user clicks the link, the Action is triggered, but a new page isn't loaded. Leaving the link set to "(Empty Reference!)" also works, but causes a link warning.

Form Element Event Handlers

Some form elements, such as text boxes, buttons, check boxes, radio buttons, popup menus—even the Form object itself, or the container surrounding form elements—can detect certain events. Some of these events are unique to form elements, and others overlap text and image handlers. The Actions palette shows these events contextually for whatever form element is selected; the form elements for each type of handler are listed in parentheses following the handler name.

TIP:
JavaScript Alternatives

You can access these handlers via the JavaScript Inspector's Events tab, too. In GoLive 4, this was the only way; in 5, you have the choice. We're very happy they added these handlers to their graphical Actions approach, as it means you don't have to be a rocket scientist (or JavaScript programmer) to use these triggers now.

- **Form Submit (Form object):** This handler triggers when the user clicks the submit button in a form, but before the information is sent to the server.

- **Form Reset (Form object):** Ditto for the reset button.

- **Mouse Click (Submit, Reset, Radio Button, Check Box):** Clicking any of these four form elements both affects the element (the submit and reset buttons look "depressed," the radio button is selected, or the box is checked) and triggers an Action.

TIP:
Checking for Checks

We use the Mouse Click handler in some forms we work on to ensure that an exclusive choice was made. Radio buttons require that one of the group of buttons is checked. But sometimes, the choice isn't one or the other, but none, or just one. Using the Mouse Click handler lets us pop up an alert if someone attempts to select both checkboxes, but does nothing if neither or just one remains checked.

- **Text Change (Text Field, Password, Text Area, Popup, List Box):** Select an item from a popup menu, or change the text in a text field or area.

- **Key Focus, Key Blur (Text Field, Password, Text Area):** Key Focus triggers when the cursor is placed in these three field types; Key Blur triggers when the cursor leaves the field. Under Windows (any browser) or IE 5 or later for Mac, focus and blur occur as you tab from field to field. See Chapter 15, *Forms*, for a fuller explanation of these two terms.

- **Mouse Up, Mouse Down (Submit, Reset):** see these items in "Text and Image Link Event Handlers," earlier in the chapter.

- **Key Down, Key Up (Text Area):** see these items in "Text and Image Link Event Handlers," above.

Action Track Event Handlers

Actions within an animation are triggered by a timing event controlled by the Action's position in time on the Action Track in the Timeline Editor. See Chapter 27, *Animation*, for details on triggering Actions within animations.

Unsupported Actions

If you know JavaScript well, you may have noticed that several JavaScript events are not listed above, including onFocus, onBlur, onError, and onSelect. The built-in GoLive Actions lack support for these events, or only support them for certain items. For example, you can trigger an Action with onFocus attached to a text box in a form, but not with a window or frame. If you want to use them to trigger activities, you have to write the code yourself, inserting the triggers in the HTML Source Editor.

Configuring Actions

All Actions and their options are configured through the Actions palette, or the Action Inspector if you are using a Smart Object or the Action Track of the Timeline Editor. Each Action has its own set of text fields, popup menus, and buttons which set its parameters.

TIP:
Finding Actions

Some Actions are found only in the Smart tab of the Objects palette. These Smart Objects are a motley collection of Actions, GoLive features, and place-holders, which we explain in "Smart Objects," earlier in this chapter.

While GoLive makes it easy to apply and configure individual Actions—and the online manual explains every last Action in excellent detail—the tricky part is learning how Actions can interact to combine them to build more complex functionality.

First, we take a look at all the available Actions, discussing what they do and the best ways to use them. Then, we show examples of GoLive gene splicing: using multiple Actions together and setting them up to add some serious capabilities to your pages.

Actions are categorized in GoLive by what they accomplish or the kinds of objects they work with. Getters retrieve something, such as a floating box position or a form value; Link Actions work with links or the contents of pages.

TIP:
ActionsPlus

Even though ActionsPlus occurs first on the Action menu, we discuss it almost last. The Actions in this submenu are extras, even though they ship with the program, and don't all fit into one category.

Getters Actions

Getters gather information from the user via HTML forms and store that information in a page-based variable or a browser-stored cookie. Getters also let you detect the position of a floating box within the browser window.

Get Floating Box Position. When triggered by an event, this Action returns the current top-left corner coordinates in pixels of the specified floating box. It can be used with Condition or Idle Actions to trigger an Action when an animated floating box moves to a certain position.

Get Form Value. Get Form Value retrieves the value or contents of a specific form element (numbers entered in a text box, the chosen item from a popup menu, etc.) within a specific form.

Field Entry Indicator

GoLive displays an icon next to many of the fields in an Actions palette; click the icon to change the kind of data you enter into the field (see Figure 28-9).

When the red "C" is displayed (the default), you generally type into the field to set the

Figure 28-9
Field entry indicators

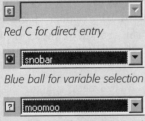

Red C for direct entry

Blue ball for variable selection

Green box with question mark for onCall Action selection

Action target or value. With some Actions, you can also use Point & Shoot to set the value, or even select a value from a popup menu.

With the blue ball displayed, GoLive provides a popup list of variables defined on the page that contain compatible values, such as a variable set to a URL for a field that requires a URL. This variable might be read from a cookie, for instance, passed from a previous time the user was on the page.

When the question mark in a green box appears, select an Action from a menu listing all the currently specified Actions. You must first select and configure other Actions before this option is available. Use this option when you have other actions set to execute "OnCall".

TIP:
Value Plus
Action Equals
Behavior

Get Form Value is only useful when combined with another Action that does something to the value, such as write it to a cookie, or modify the value of some other form element. As of this writing, there is no such behavior available. Consult our Web site (realworldgolive.com) for updates on this issue.

Image Actions

The Image Actions let you control the display of images on the page; they also let you change images via user events or other Actions.

Preload Image. This Action loads an image into the browser's cache so it can be displayed quickly when called for by another Action. It's usually used in the Head section to preload hand-coded button rollovers.

Random Image. Random Image randomly switches among three different images. It can be used to randomize a rollover, or, when placed in-line with the Inline Action Smart Object and triggered by onParse, it can be used to randomize the look of the page or the display of banner ads. When it is used to randomly change an existing image on the page, all three images must have the same dimensions or the browser distorts the new image to fit the original graphic's area. The base image must be hyperlinked for the randomizing to work, but this link doesn't have to connect to anything; you can leave it set to "(Empty Reference!)".

Set Image URL. As one of our most requested explanations, we've devoted a sidebar to this Action; see "Set Image URL Tutorial."

Set Image URL Tutorial

Set Image URL allows you to use any trigger on any link—whether an image or a text hyperlink—to display an image. You can choose Mouse Click, Mouse Enter, or any of the other triggers to associate this Action. When a user performs the appropriate action or clicks, the Action loads an image into an existing location on the page: it substitutes a new image specified in the Action. It might have been better named Substitute Image instead of Set Image URL.

The images you substitute should be the same size as the original image. (Internet Explorer can automatically display the image at its own dimensions, but Netscape Navigator lacks this ability.)

continues on next page

Set Image URL Tutorial *continued*

To start with, create a set of links and an image (or images) that you're going to swap out with other pictures. In this example, we created a simple set of text links that swap out photos from a trip into the space at right. We use a floating box to hold the image.

The image we start with is a simple white-only GIF to create a blank space. In the Image Inspector, name the image and set up its dimensions. In the Basic tab, set Height and Width to the pixel dimensions that all the images share (see Figure 28-10). This allows the substituted images to retain their correct dimensions when loaded.

In the More tab, name the image by entering any text into the Name field next to the Is Form checkbox (see Figure 28-11). This Name field's location is a bit misleading. Although you can name a button that's used to submit a form, this identification information is also required for other tasks to pick out a specific image.

Next, choose any link on the page, and bring up the Actions palette. In this case, we're using Mouse Enter to trigger the Action, so that as a user sweeps his or her mouse over the link, the image comes up. (For a more sophisticated approach, you could load a thumbnail for Mouse Enter and the full resolution image only on Mouse Click.) For Mouse Out, we plop back the original white image, so that when someone is off the link, the image is no longer displayed.

Select Mouse Enter and click the New Action button. From the Action menu, select Set Image URL from the Image submenu. You can then select the image you originally named above to serve as the one that gets swapped out, and select the image to be swapped into its place (see Figure 28-12). Select Mouse Exit, and follow the same instructions to put the white-only GIF back in its place.

Repeat this for each link. It's important to remember to select the image from the popup menu each time; it's easy to forget, and GoLive doesn't care if it's not selected. However, the JavaScript generates an error on loading into a browser if you fail to select the image name.

If you'd like to go one level more technical, you could use another Action to preload all the images you're going to swap in. This wouldn't delay the page load, but it would speed up the swap process, since the browser would have cached all the images.

From the Smart tab of the Objects palette, drag the Head Action icon into the Head section of the page. Select the Preload Image Action from the Action menu's Image submenu. Point & Shoot, enter the name of, or Browse to the first image you're swapping in (see Figure 28-13). Repeat for each additional image. (You can copy and paste the Head Action so you don't have to drag it from the palette and reselect the Preload Image Action over and over again.)

There you have it: very simple, very straightforward, and a good building block for a more dynamic page (see Figure 28-14). For an example of Set Image URL in action, see http://realworldgolive.com/setimageurl/. You could use this with images, creating small thumbnails, each of which loads an image. You can have multiple images on a page, each with its own name, which get swapped out. You can also assign Actions to mapped areas in an imagemap, and use those areas as triggers.

Figure 28-10
Fixing image
size

Figure 28-11
Naming image

*Set the Width and Height values
to the shared pixel dimensions.*

Figure 28-12
Swapping out
image

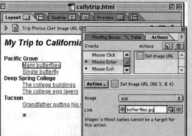

Figure 28-13
Inserting Head
Action

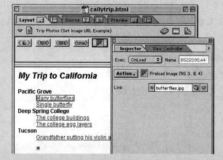

Figure 28-14
The final page

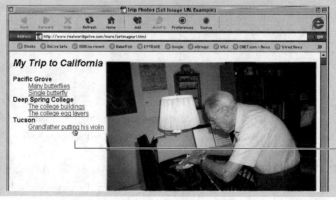

*Mousing
over a link
displays the
appropriate
image at
right.*

Link Actions

These Actions control links within a page and the contents of the browser window or frameset.

Go Last Page. This Action reads the browser history—or which pages the user has visited—and sends a user to the one previously viewed, creating a true Back button.

Goto Link. When triggered, this Action sends the user to a specified URL, either local or external. It can be used in the Actions track of an animation to send the user to another page at a specific point in time along the Timetrack.

Navigate History. You can use Navigate History to create a link that takes the user forward or backward within the browser history; it can also jump more than one page at a time.

Open Window. This Action lets you open a new browser window, specify the HTML page to display in the window, specify the name of the window in the titlebar, and declare its size and whether to display scroll bars, menu bar, directory buttons, status bar, toolbar, location field, and resize handles (see Figure 28-15).

Figure 28-15
Popping up a customized window

Message Actions

These Actions let you communicate directly with users through HTML within the page, the text in the status bar, and dialog boxes.

Document Write. Used with the Inline Action Smart Object, this Action allows you to display customized HTML when the page loads. It is used inline and triggered when parsed because HTML cannot be written to the page once it has finished loading. The HTML displayed may come from a variable, another Action, or text you type into the Actions palette yourself.

Open Alert Window. This Action opens a dialog box displaying a message, which the user can dismiss by clicking the OK button. Since every browser displays this dialog box differently, the only control you have over how it looks is the text contents (see Figure 28-16).

Figure 28-16
Alert window

IE for Macintosh alert

Netscape for Windows alert

Set Status. The Set Status Action lets you create a message at the bottom of the browser window in the status bar (see Figure 28-17). It's usually used in conjunction with the Mouse Enter event attached to a button to give the visitor a better idea of where the link takes them.

Figure 28-17
Status display

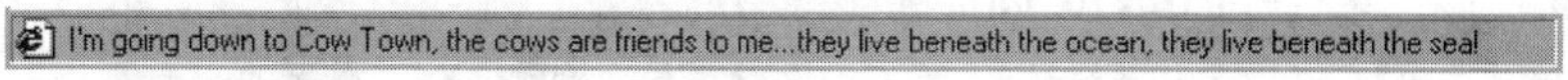

I'm going down to Cow Town, the cows are friends to me...they live beneath the ocean, they live beneath the sea!

Multimedia Actions

The Multimedia Actions deal with controlling floating boxes and animation (see Chapter 27, *Animation*).

Drag Floating Box. This Action lets a user drag a specified floating box. Unfortunately, the box's outline and contents are not visible while it is being dragged.

Flip Move. When triggered, Flip Move moves a floating box from one absolute position to another; when triggered again, the box moves back to original position.

Move By. When triggered, Move By moves a floating box a specified distance from its last position.

Move To. When triggered, this Action moves a floating box to an absolute position in the browser window from wherever it is on the page.

Play Scene. This Action triggers a DHTML animation timeline. For instance, you might want an animation to play when a user clicks a button that reads "play animation." (There's an example of using this in Chapter 27, *Animation.*)

Play Sound. This Action directs a specified plug-in to play a sound. The plug-in must have the ability to respond to JavaScript; check the plug-in's documentation to find out if it is compatible or not.

ShowHide. ShowHide toggles a floating box's visibility, changing its state from visible to invisible, or vice-versa.

Stop Complete. This Action stops all DHTML animation currently running on the page. It's polite to give the viewer the option to stop animation on a page, to keep it from transitioning from entertaining to annoying. Or, you can stop an animation automatically after a certain time has passed using the Condition Action.

Stop Scene. You can choose to stop a specific DHTML animation scene with this Action.

Stop Sound. This Action directs a specified plug-in to stop playing sound. The plug-in must support JavaScript events; see Play Sound above.

Wipe Transition. Wipe Transition lets you use a "wipe" style of transition when hiding or showing a floating box. It's used with the ShowHide Action.

Others Actions

The Others Actions mostly act on the browser window itself.

Netscape CSS Fix. A Netscape 4 bug causes pages to lose most of their Cascading Style Sheet (CSS) formatting information when the window is resized. This occurs because Netscape reparses the page's HTML when the window is resized, without taking into account CSS. To be safe you should add Netscape CSS Fix to every page that includes Style Sheets.

Resize Window. This Action changes the size of the current window.

Scroll Down, Scroll Left, Scroll Right, and Scroll Up. This set of Actions scrolls the window down, left, right, or up by an amount in pixels at a speed you specify.

Set BackColor. Set BackColor changes the current window's background color. You can't change the background image using this Action, but you can use a floating box as a background and change it using the Set Image URL Action (see sidebar, "Set Image URL Tutorial," earlier in the chapter).

Specials Actions

There are always things that don't fit into a neat category. The Specials Actions relate to grouping and referencing other Actions.

Action Group. The Action Group is a container that lets you group a set of Actions to be triggered together.

Call Action. You may want to place an Action in the Head section so that it loads first, but then trigger it later at a specific time via some other behavior in the body section.

If you select OnCall as the handler for a Head Action, you can also name that Action (see Figure 28-18). Then, you can select that Action by name from the Call Action's popup menu with the red C or green box with a question mark showing.

Figure 28-18
Calling a
Head Action

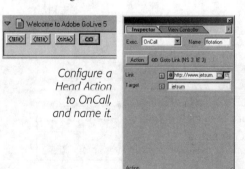

Configure a
Head Action
to OnCall,
and name it.

Choose that Head Action from
the Call Action's popup menu.

Call Function. For hand-coded JavaScripts, use Call Function to trigger a function within a custom-coded JavaScript. This feature allows you to write custom functions using the JavaScript editor for behavior not available in an Action, while integrating this custom feature with Actions to speed up the development process.

Condition. This Action tests to see if two floating boxes are intersecting (such as when an animation is playing), if a specified key is being pressed, if a certain amount of time has passed, or if a variable matches a value such as true or false (see Figure 28-19). You can trigger one Action if the condition is true and a different Action—or no Action at all—if the condition is false.

Figure 28-19
Condition
example

Declare a variable in the Head section with onLoad set.

Configure an item on the page, such as this checkbox, that changes the variable's value.

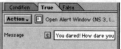

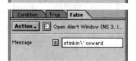

Set up a condition to check whether the box was checked or not.

The results of truth

The results of falsehood

Idle. When placed in the Head section of the Layout Editor, the Idle Action can be set to wait either until two floating boxes are intersecting (usually used with the Drag Floating Box Action) or a specified amount of time has passed.

You can specify an Action to trigger when the condition has occurred, as well as an Action to trigger over and over again if the condition is false. You can also set the Idle Action to continue even after the condition has been met, or stop after the first time it tests true. However, you cannot stop the Idle Action once it is set in motion; you have to wait until the condition is met and then only if you previously set it to stop. Once stopped, it can be restarted using Call Action.

The Condition Action and the Idle action differ in how they search for behavior to trigger their events. The Condition Action is triggered directly when you test whether something is true or false in the moment. The Idle Action runs continuously in the background for a limited range of behaviors, and, only when a condition is met, can it trigger an Action.

Intersection, Key Compare, Timeout. These three Specials Actions can only be invoked from the Idle Action; they're sort of sub-Action Actions.

Intersection lets you make an event become true when two floating boxes cross paths. Key Compare becomes true if a given key is pressed. Timeout lets a specified amount of time pass, and then declares itself true.

Variables

A variable is a container that lets you store text or numbers for use in other Actions. For example, you can ask a visitor what his or her favorite color is and store it as a variable using the Get Form Value Action. Then you can use that variable to change the background color of the page using the Set Back Color Action. In order to use a variable, you must first create and name it using the Declare Variable Action.

One shortcoming of variables is that the browser can't remember them from page to page; they only work within Actions called on the same page that the variable was created or modified. One way around this limitation is to store the variable's value in a cookie, a small bit of text that a Web server or JavaScript can ask a browser to store on the user's hard drive. Cookies can be named and can contain up to 4,096 characters of alphanumeric data (letters, numbers, and punctuation).

You can also assign an expiration date to a cookie, so that you can retrieve the stored value or update it for a fixed period of time. That might be an hour from when you set it, a week later, or even 10 years later (though the odds that someone will be using the same browser in 10 years is too small to measure even with the most advanced computers). If you do not give the cookie an expiration date, it lasts only as long as the browser is open and running. When you quit the browser or reboot your machine, the cookie is deleted.

Cookies are stored for a specific site, and a browser reveals a cookie only when it returns to a page at the site for which the cookie was originally stored. Most cookies are set to be available on every page in the site. You update cookies by writing new values to them, which replace any value stored.

TIP:
**Finding
These
Actions**

The first six Actions are in the Variables submenu; the last two in the ActionsPlus submenu. ActionsPlus is described just below in more depth.

Declare Variable. This Action creates a new variable; it can be stored in an existing cookie using Write Cookie.

Init Variable. Set the initial value of a variable with Init Variable.

Read Cookie. Get information stored in a cookie specified by name with Read Cookie.

Set Variable. Store a value in a variable with this Action.

Test Variable. You can only use Test Variable within the Idle Action. With Test Variable, you can determine whether one of your variables meets, exceeds, or doesn't match a given value, and then behave accordingly.

Write Cookie. Write Cookie creates a cookie on the user's computer with a name and expiration time (in hours) that you specify. It also lets you specify which pages on the site the browser reveals the cookie to; most of the time, you should set this to "/" to let the cookie be revealed on any page on the site.

Delete Cookie. To get rid of a cookie, use Delete Cookie (under the ActionsPlus submenu). It sets the cookie's expiration date to the current time.

Visitor Cookie. You can use Visitor Cookie from the ActionsPlus submenu to mark that a user has been to your site. After the first visit, the Action reads the cookie that notes that the user has been there before, and redirects the browser to another page that you choose. This lets you display a welcoming splash screen to first time visitors, and then take them directly to the real main page when they come back.

ActionsPlus

ActionsPlus was a set of extra Actions that appeared after GoLive 4 shipped; you had to manually install them into GoLive. GoLive 5 preinstalls them. The Actions here are a jumble of different types of functionality such as slide shows, frame management and timed events, but most can be characterized as fairly complex, single-purpose widgets.

(These Actions are listed out of alphabetical order to better group them by function; you'll find the two cookie-related ones above, under "Variables," where their explanation belongs.)

Daily Redirect. When you want to direct users to a page based on the day of the week, use Daily Redirect. It can be applied to the header to display a different page every time a user loads the page, or to a link object to change the link daily.

Daily Image URL. This Action changes an image based on the day of the week.

Time Redirect. This action redirects the user to a different HTML page based on the time of day on the user's computer.

Force Frame. If another site attempts to link to an individual page on your site that is normally viewed within a frameset, this Action loads the enclosing frameset with the linked page in the correct frame. This Action helps you put a page back into context when a user follows a link to the contents of a frame, such as from a search engine results page.

Search engines, like Excite or Lycos, often index the pages that make up a framed page, but you don't want users to load that sub-page without the rest of the framed content. If your site navigation or even a company name exists in its own frame, as is common, the user would have no way to get to the rest of your site.

Kill Frame. If another site attempts to hijack your page and display it within their own frameset, this Action reloads the current page in a frameless browser window.

Target Two Frames. Target Two Frames allows one link to change pages in two different frames at the same time. For example, if you have a frame that contains a navigation bar listing options as well as a frame that contains some actual content, like one of the items in the navigation bar, you might want to design it so that the navigation bar presents different options when the user moves to a different section of the site. With this Action, the user can click a link and the Action can change both the navigation bar frame and the content frame.

Password. Password allows you to protect pages on your site by using an encrypted password hidden in the JavaScript. Although the password is encrypted, this control doesn't prevent a slightly knowledgeable person from getting past it, because JavaScript can be turned off and this protection can be bypassed.

Target Remote. Used with the Open Window Action, this Action allows a user to click a link in one named window and have changes appear in another named window.

Confirm Link. This Action opens a dialog box with OK and Cancel buttons as well as any message you want to display. If the user clicks OK, the browser continues on to the linked page. This allows you to ask users a yes or no question, such as, "Are you sure you want to leave this site?" and give them the option of canceling the link.

Slide Show. This Action creates a slide show that a user can move through by clicking a button image or text link. All the graphics must have the same dimensions or the browser distorts them to fit the area of the first image.

Slide Show Auto. You can run a slide show through its images automatically using this Action. As with Slide Show, all the graphics must have the same dimensions or the browser distorts them to fit.

Slide Show Auto Stop. You can use this Action along with the Slide Show Auto Action to let the visitor pause and continue the slide show. This Action can be attached to a button image or text link.

Even More Actions Plus

Creative minds don't stop ticking, and even after GoLive 5.0 shipped, Adobe kept working away. The set of actions known as GL5 Actions Plus (to distinguish them from the GoLive 4 ActionsPlus set described above) can be downloaded for free from http://www.adobe.com/products/golive/actions/main.html. (These

Actions may show up in a folder called TransmitMedia instead of GL5 Actions
Plus; that's the name of the firm that developed them.)

TIP:
New and
Exciting
Actions at
the Exchange

Watch that URL, which Adobe has dubbed the ActionsXchange, for new Actions
and links to other sites providing free and commercial Actions. Matt Ridley's site
(MattRidley.com), for instance, features an awesome set of "charityware"
Actions. He was the author of many of the ActionsPlus set, too.

TIP:
Installing
GL5 Actions
Plus

After downloading and decompressing these Actions, drag the entire folder into
a deeply nested folder: GoLive application folder, Modules, JScripts, Actions.
Quit GoLive if it's running; the next time you run, you'll find these Actions in the
popup menu of the Actions palette and related Inspectors.

CloseWindow. You'd think that a) this is an obvious one and, b) it's too simple to include, but without it, you're sunk if you aren't a JavaScript coder.

FieldValidator. This Action practically pays for GoLive. Typically, writing
JavaScript to validate the contents of a field takes a lot of patience and testing.
Having all the options in one place helps a lot, and means that anyone can use
form validation with little fuss.

   The options are pretty straightforward, letting you confirm whether a
field has the right kind of information in it, including whether a credit card
number conforms to the formula that credit card companies use to make up
numbers. (Yes, there is a system.) You can alert users if the value doesn't meet
your needs when they tab or move out of the field.

FloatLayer. Coolo-beanos: lock a floating box in place when the rest of the
page scrolls.

MouseFollow. The documents say, "Floating layer will follow mouse movement
on-screen." Creepy? Cool? Annoying? All of the above, depending on its use.

OpenWindowPrompt. This is a nifty tool for debugging and testing sites by
prompting the visitor for a window height and width. Most users don't need
this capability, so it's really intended for us designers.

pdfRedirect, svgRedirect, swfRedirect. These three Actions form a troika of
plug-in detection. If the visitor's browser lacks the appropriate plug-in (PDF,
SVG for Scalable Vector Graphics, or Flash for SWF format files), you can
redirect them to a page that explains why they can't view the page they tried to

load. Or berate them for not having all the plug-ins installed on their machine! These should be added to Head Actions set to onLoad so that they appropriately intercept the visitor before the page loads.

RedirectPrompt. We don't quite know what to make of this. This Action lets you ask a user which of up to five choices they'd like to be redirected to upon triggering the Action. You can also choose to use a cookie to remember their choice. Now tell us: what would you use this for? (Honest, we want to know. Tell us at authors@realworldgolive.com. Depending on the number of responses, we'll put them up on the realworldgolive.com Web site.)

ScrollStatus. This implements one of the most-requested features of all time, or so we think. A few years ago, some brilliant mind figured out how to scroll stuff through the status field using JavaScript; this Action makes it simple, and offers choices for speed and direction. Use with care; it might annoy your visitors.

SearchEngine. It's hard to express our limitless joy at this feature. This allows you to create a custom search form on any of several major search engines with an option to have the results pop up into their own window. You can use your own search string, too. (We'd recommend checking on this Action frequently, as search engines change their formats all the time, and we'd guess this needs to be updated by the developers when that happens.)

SlideNewWindow. Almost identical to the standard Open Window Action, SlideNewWindow centers a new window in the screen through a sliding behavior. You have to try it to understand it.

TimesVisited. This Action requires users to accept a cookie to track how many times they've been to that page. It updates the count, and allows you to display messages to the user based on their first and subsequent visits.

WorldClock. This little Action inserts the current time and date in clock format using the visitor's computer's own time. So if their clock is off, this display is off. You can use GMT offset to show the time anywhere in the world.

If you want to have the time inserted into a form element (like a text field), make sure you've named your form and the field. Then check the Form Field box and enter the name of the form and field into Form Name and Field Name fields.

Checking Status Bar shows the time in the status bar of the browser.

Combining Actions

Actions don't do much by themselves; creating a variable or retrieving the position of a floating box may be interesting, but it certainly isn't useful unless you apply that information. The trick to unlocking the power of Actions is to create a group that works together to accomplish a task. Here are three examples to get you started thinking about how to use Actions for real-world solutions. (Download the source materials for these examples from http://realworldgolive/actions.html.)

Rotating Banner Ads

Actions used: *Idle/Timeout, Random Image*

This first example randomly changes an image on the page—in this case a banner ad—at set time intervals.

At the top of your example page, place a banner ad that you want to be randomly replaced. For the Actions to work, the image has to have a name; select the image and enter "bannerAd" in the Name field next to the Is Form checkbox in the Image Inspector's More tab (see Figure 28-20).

This Action needs to start running as soon as the page loads, so insert a Head Action, and bring up the Action Inspector (see Figure 28-21).

Figure 28-20
Naming the image

Figure 28-21
Action Inspector for Head Action

Choose OnLoad from the Exec menu to trigger the Action as soon as the entire page has downloaded. Select Idle from the Action menu under the Specials submenu. We want the banner to change every 30 seconds, so make sure Exit Idle If Condition Returns "True" is not checked, and, in the Condition tab, choose Timeout from the Specials submenu of the Action menu. There is only one option to set for Timeout, the length of time to wait in seconds; enter 30 in the Timeout field (see Figure 28-22).

Figure 28-22
Setting Idle conditions

After 30 seconds, the Idle Action triggers the Action specified in the True tab. Select the True tab and then choose Random Image from the Image submenu of the Action menu. Since you named the banner ad earlier, you can select it in the Base Image menu to target it. All that's left to do now is to specify graphics for the three random image slots (see Figure 28-23).

Figure 28-23
Filling out the random slots

Save the page and preview it in a browser. If all went as planned, the banner should now change to one of three randomly chosen ads every 30 seconds. Because the images are chosen at random, you might see the same one twice in a row; be patient if it doesn't change after 30 seconds (or change the interval to a shorter period to preview the changes).

Open a Remote Control Subwindow

Actions used: *Open Window, Target Remote*

This example opens a small subwindow with a menu bar that functions like a remote control, so that when you click a button in the subwindow the browser loads a new page in the main window.

First, create a new page with menu buttons to be linked to other pages on your site. Don't link the buttons just yet (see Figure 28-24).

Figure 28-24
A page with
menu buttons

Add a link or button to your main page layout—for this example, add a text link—that you want visitors to click to open the remote-control window. You could also place this Action in the Head section with an OnLoad trigger to automatically open the second window when the page loads.

Select the link and open the Actions palette. Choose Mouse Click from the Events list and click the New Action button. Choose Open Window from the Action menu's Link submenu. Name the new window "remote" in the Target field and make it 100 by 200 pixels. Uncheck all the display options so that only the status bar is displayed (see Figure 28-25).

Figure 28-25
Setting up the
new window

Use Point & Shoot navigation or browse to the menu buttons page created earlier to use it as the link page that is displayed in the new window.

To make the buttons in the remote control window functional, open the menu buttons page you created earlier. Select the first button and make it a link. Open the Actions palette, if is isn't already open, add a Mouse Click, and select Target Remote from the Action menu's ActionsPlus submenu.

The Target Remote action automatically targets the original window that opened our new subwindow, so just link to the page we want to display. In this example, we link to "rotatingBanner.html" (see Figure 28-26). As you can see from the options in the Inspector palette, if the original page contained frames we could also target a frame within that frameset.

Figure 28-26
Linking to the
page in the
main window

Repeat this last operation with the rest of the menu buttons on the remote control page, then test your new creation in several browsers to see how it works (see Figure 28-27).

Figure 28-27
Testing remote
control

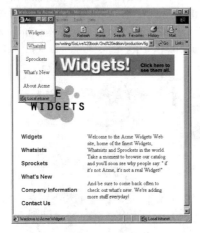

Storing Information in a Cookie

Actions used: *Declare Variable, Init Variable, Write Cookie, Set Variable, Read Cookie, Set BackColor, Condition, Document Write*

To demonstrate how to get information into a cookie and read it out again later on other pages, create a page named askcolor.html that prompts users to choose between two colors. On the next page, we use Actions to set the background to the color they chose, as well as insert the color name in the page itself.

Let's start with the page where the visitor makes their choice. Drag a Head Action icon from the Smart tab into the page's Head section. In the Action Inspector, choose Declare Variable from the Variables submenu of the Action menu (see Figure 28-28). Give the variable the name "color", set the Type to

String (to indicate we are storing text in the variable), and, in the Cookie field, type "colorPref". This last parameter doesn't actually create the cookie, but it does indicate which cookie ends up storing this variable's contents. Finally, choose OnParse from the Exec menu so the variable is created as soon as the browser reads this Action.

Next, we want to put a default value into the variable, so drag another Head Action into the Head section, and choose Init Variable from the Variables submenu (see Figure 28-29). Set Exec to OnParse, choose "color" (the name of the variable we just created) from the Variable menu, and type "nothing" into the value field. Now, when the browser reads these Actions, we have a variable named "color" which contains the word "nothing".

Let's store this default value in a cookie in case the visitor decides not to choose a color. Drag yet another Head Action into the Head section, and set Exec to OnParse (see Figure 28-30). Choose Write Cookie from the Variables submenu and give it the name "colorPref". Because we also filled in the Cookie field on our "color" variable with the same name, the Write Cookie Action automatically links up with that variable and stores its contents in a cookie named "colorPref".

Figure 28-28
Setting up
Declare
Variable

Figure 28-29
Setting up Init
Variable

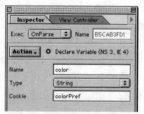

Figure 28-30
Setting up
Write Cookie

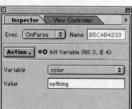

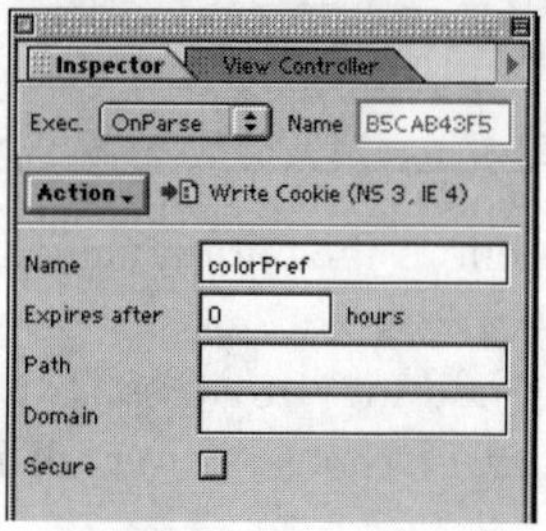

With these three Actions set up in the Head section, we can now build a form from which the user chooses a color (see Figure 28-31). Add a Form object from the Forms tab of the Objects palette to the body of the page. In the Form object, enter some text, such as "Which color do you prefer?" Add a paragraph break and drag in a Submit Button icon from the Forms tab. In the Form Button Inspector, choose Normal as the button type. Check the Label box and enter "blue" for the button label.

Figure 28-31
Making a color choosing form

We need to add three Actions to the Mouse Click event for this button, so bring up the Actions palette, and, with the submit button selected, add the first Mouse Click event by clicking the New Action button (see Figure 28-32). Choose Set Variable from the Variables submenu, and choose "color" from the Variable menu, which should be the only choice. In this case we give the variable the value "blue" since that is the button the user is clicking.

Figure 28-32
Three mouse click Actions to handle the color choice

Add another Mouse Click event to the button named blue, and choose Write Cookie. Just like before, type in "colorPref" for the name. This causes the word "blue" to overwrite the "nothing" we stored in the colorPref cookie earlier. For our last Mouse Click event, choose Goto Link from the Link submenu and enter the URL of our next page (in this case "showcolor.html") in the Link field.

Let's take a shortcut in adding a second button to the form. Select the Blue button and copy it (see Figure 28-33). Type a space after the existing button, and select Paste from the Edit menu. Select the second button and change its label in the Form Button Inspector to "red". Now we just have to make one change to this new button's Actions to store a different value in our colorPref cookie. Select the Red button with the Actions palette visible. In the Set Variable options, change the Value field from "blue" to "red". Now we can move on to the next page where we read the cookie and use the information we stored in it.

Figure 28-33
Configuring the second button

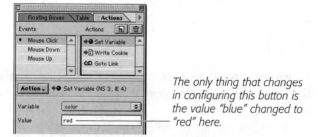

The only thing that changes in configuring this button is the value "blue" changed to "red" here.

Create a new page and save it as "showcolor.html". Just as we did before, add two Head Action objects to the page to declare a variable named color and a cookie named "colorPref"; set it to "nothing", or just copy and paste the first two Head Actions from the askcolor.html page.

Next, add another Head Action and choose Read Cookie from the Variables submenu (see Figure 28-34). We assign it the name "colorPref" so that the browser can retrieve the cookie we stored earlier and place its contents (in this case either "blue" or "red") in the variable "color". Make sure all three of these Actions are set to Execute OnParse.

Figure 28-34
Adding Read Cookie

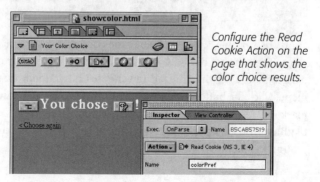

Configure the Read Cookie Action on the page that shows the color choice results.

Lastly, we add two more Actions to the Head section (see Figure 28-35). For both, choose Set BackColor from the Others submenu and set Exec to OnCall, since we trigger them later using another Action. Name the first one "BkgBlue", and set the color to whatever blue you like; name the second Action "BkgRed", and set its color to your favorite red.

Figure 28-35
Setting
BackColor

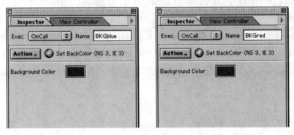

The two options for color results which are called from a conditional Action

We can now test to see what the user actually chose on the previous page. Drag a Body Action object onto the page, and choose Condition from the Specials submenu in the Body Action Inspector (see Figure 28-36). In the Condition tab, choose Test Variable from Variables and set Variable to "color" (it should be the only choice). We know that the value we got from the cookie and stored in the color variable is either "blue" or "red", so to test to see if the user chose blue, enter "blue" into the Value field, and set Operation to Equal.

Figure 28-36
Conditional
color setting

If the variable "color" is "blue", the condition tests true. In that case, we want to call the Set BackColor Action to change the background color of the page to blue. Click the True tab and choose Call Action from the Specials submenu. Click the button next to Action until it is a green square with a question mark in it (see sidebar, "Field Entry Indicator," earlier in this chapter). Choose BkgBlue from the popup to target the Head Action that changes the background to blue.

We're assuming that if the color is not blue, it's red, so in the False tab (because true is blue), we can trigger a different Action. Choose Call Action, but this time set Action to "BkgRed".

Let's do one more thing with our cookie contents before testing these pages. In the body of showcolor.html, enter the words "You chose", add a space, and drag in another Body Action object (see Figure 28-37). In the Body Action Inspector choose Document Write from the Message submenu and click the little button next to HTML until it is a blue ball. By choosing "color" from the popup menu, the browser inserts the word stored in the variable "color" into that spot on the page.

Figure 28-37
Showing what
the user chose

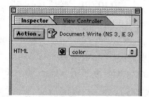

Let's test. Load askcolor.html into a browser, and click on either the Blue or Red button. If everything is configured correctly you should go to the showcolor page and it should have the background color of your choice, as well as tell you at the top of the page "You chose blue" or "You chose red" (see Figure 28-38).

Figure 28-38
The results of
choosing

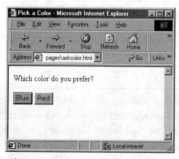

Choose a color.   *The color you chose.*

Shifting Scripts to an External Library File

For a change of pace, let's finish up with a discussion of where GoLive sticks all the JavaScript necessary to handle Actions, Smart Objects, and DHTML animations. By default, GoLive stores all this JavaScript in the Head section of each page on which any of the objects or animations appear. Though convenient, this is wasteful, because if you use the same behavior on multiple pages, a visitor to your site has to load that code several times.

GoLive offers the option to externalize all this JavaScript in a separate file that a visitor's browser loads just once when they reach any page referencing it. After that, it holds it in its local cache, speeding up the time to handle any Actions or other routines.

You can externalize the code of a particular page in your site, or a Component that contains elements requiring GoLive's JavaScript library. (This doesn't work for a single page; only for pages or elements in a site.) Open the page or Component, click the Page icon at the top of the Layout Editor, and then choose the HTML tab in the Page Inspector.

You can select one of two options under JavaScript Functions. The default, Write Code into Page, leaves all the JavaScript in the page's Head section. Choosing Import GoLive Script Library removes all code necessary for the page or Component's Actions, animations, and Smart Objects, leaving behind only some page-specific parameters.

GoLive adds a link from the page to a file called, by default, CSScriptLib.js, which it places into a folder in the root level of your site called GeneratedItems.

The changes are applied as soon as you choose any of these options, and made permanent when you save the page.

TIP:
Library Privileges

GoLive automatically restricts access to the external code to browsers that support JavaScript 1.2 or higher, so even if the Actions you've used are compatible with some 3.0 browsers, the scripts are hidden from them. These days, only a very small percentage of users (maybe as low as 2 to 3 percent) use 3.0 or earlier browsers.

TIP:
Setting Library Import Globally

The Script Library pane of the Preferences dialog box lets you set your global preference for Write Code in Page and Import GoLive Script Library. This pane also contains the default name and folder location of your script library, which you can modify. Changing any of these settings only affects pages created subsequently; existing pages have to be modified by hand via the HTML tab of the Page Inspector.

TIP:
Handwritten Libraries

GoLive's Script Library doesn't contain any JavaScript you added by hand or via the JavaScript Editor into a page. We recommend creating your own, separate JavaScript library file for your own reusable routines. Name it with ".js" at the end; consult Chapter 26, *JavaScript*, for more details.

TIP:
Flat as Flounder

There's another trick to improve this option further: Flatten Script Library. Available only via the contextual menu in the Files tab, this option scans all files that use GoLive's JavaScript library and rewrites that external file to contain only the exact JavaScript needed for the site. You have to perform this operation every time you edit any page on the site, and then re-upload the JavaScript library to your site.

TIP:
Rebuilding Better, Stronger, Faster

The Rebuild button in the Script Library pane of Preferences doesn't rebuild existing pages in a site. It rebuilds the master list of Actions that show up in the Inspector palette's Actions tab after you add a new Action to the appropriate folder.

Building Action-Packed Web Sites

Actions offer enormous help by bundling so many complex features into a few relatively simple-to-use tools. Although Actions don't solve every problem or provide an interface to every possible need, they're comprehensive enough to let non-programmers build sophisticated sites, and to let programmers quickly prototype new features without expending the effort to hand code advanced functionality.

Cascading Style Sheets

Early Web designers found frustration in many aspects of HTML's inflexibility. One of the biggest annoyances was having to apply specifications individually to every piece of text to make it look a certain way. Even today, color, font, and style attributes get applied over and over again.

Cascading Style Sheets (CSS) provides a neat end-run around this problem. It allows designers to define their specifications once, in a style sheet, and then apply those specifications to text anywhere on a page or site. Updating the style sheet's source specifications changes the appearance of any text tagged with that style sheet the next time the text is viewed in a browser, or, immediately in GoLive's Layout Editor; the code surrounding the text is left untouched.

CSS helps tease out the tangled mess of HTML by taking formatting attributes—including color, typography, alignment, and page positioning—out of individual HTML tags. Before CSS, you had to figure out which tags took which properties; with CSS, every tag can take every property. This allows you to put a background image or color behind a block of text as easily as behind an entire page. The consistency and large set of features make CSS a terrific replacement for HTML's spotty support for formatting.

GoLive can handle virtually every CSS formatting feature, including positioning, font specification, borders, colors, and other, more esoteric, options. GoLive even uses CSS to control floating boxes (see Chapter 14, *Floating Boxes*), and as part of its Dynamic HTML Animation features, described in Chapter 27, *Animation*.

At the end of this chapter, we offer tips for making changes in raw CSS in the HTML Source Editor so you can add codes and features that GoLive does not yet support. If you already understand how style sheets and CSS work, feel free to skip "Style Sheets Backgrounder," and go straight to "Previewing in GoLive."

TIP:
CSS1 and CSS2

CSS is a specification proposed by the World Wide Web Consortium (http://www.w3c.org) on which each Web browser puts its own spin. The first formal spec was called CSS1, and the second spec, CSS2, is in wide circulation; CSS3 is starting to make the rounds as of this writing. Many browsers have picked and chosen from CSS2 features, which we discuss a bit in "Advanced CSS," later in this chapter. GoLive generally provides CSS1 features, but in cases where the feature described is part of CSS2, we make note of it. The development of CSS3 by the consortium is already underway, with some interesting twists that may not show up for years in browsers.

What's New in 5

Most of the CSS changes from GoLive 4 to 5 improve the way in which you view and apply internal and external style sheets.

You can now apply external style sheets to multiple pages by selecting the pages in the Files tab of the Site window and using the Styles tab of the File Inspector to add external references.

Internal selectors and external style sheets are now organized in separate folders in the same pane of the Style Sheet Editor. You can have multiple internal style sheets in the Head section of a page, and the Style Sheet Editor displays them each in a separate folder. The Head section now displays an icon for each style sheet reference (internal or external); double-clicking it brings up the Style Sheet Editor.

Undo actually works with reversing style deletion. You can now delete styles by selecting them in the Style Sheet Editor and pressing the Delete key; but selecting Undo returns them. The new History palette also lets you revert deletions.

Style Sheets Backgrounder

If you've never used the style sheet features in a word processor or desktop-publishing program, the concept of creating a single definition for text specifications might be foreign. Here's a little background to give you context on their origins and uses.

Ancient Times

Before the digital imaging age, designers could type up a list of specifications—on a typewriter, even—for text they needed typeset for a project, such as a book or brochure. They would write out these "style sheets" defining the font, style, size, paragraph spacing, and other characteristics on a piece of paper with numbers assigned to each style. When a typesetter saw a circled numeral 1, for instance, he or she would refer back to style sheet 1 and carry out its specifications.

This concept carried over into early word processors and page-layout programs like Microsoft Word and Aldus PageMaker. In every program, the concept is the same: you define the style sheet once in a central location, like a style sheet editor or dialog box, and then select pieces of text and apply a style. The program keeps track of which pieces of text are tagged with which styles.

Changing any part of the style definition updates all occurrences of text tagged with that style in a single document for local styles, or across many documents that link to the same set of external style sheets (see Figure 29-1).

Figure 29-1
Changing
elements of
styles in
QuarkXPress

A chapter of a book set up with styles   *The same text with changes to the styles; the names are the same, but the settings are different.*

HTML and Style Sheets

After a few years of wrestling with hand-coding type specifications, CSS arrived with a great cheer, as it provides style sheets that control text formatting like style sheets in DTP programs, combined with page geometry features that have a DTP feel to them.

CSS defines typographic specifications for ranges of HTML, including color, size, character and line spacing, and font face; and absolute positioning, borders, margins, and other spacing controls for chunks of HTML that display text, images, and other objects.

CSS also defines the interaction between adjacent blocks of HTML to control overlap or text wrapping. You can package these specifications into a style sheet which is applied via generic or special HTML tags and attributes to different types of text and HTML selections.

You can also base one CSS on another, inheriting all its definitions and adding or changing selected ones. This is where the *cascading* part of CSS comes in, as you can modify style sheets that underlie many other style sheets. The display of the text is based on specifications that cascade through the style sheets, from the first parent style down to the last child, which is actually applied to the text. (CSS also includes user settings and browser defaults as part of this cascade, although not all browsers currently define local settings as CSS styles. This issue is discussed in "Advanced CSS," later in this chapter.)

The main difference between the DTP approach and CSS is that in a page-layout program, changing the style results in predictable, consistent changes every time you view the document, because a single company wrote the style sheet format and the system that previews text on screen. With CSS, as with all HTML-based type specs, the browser controls the display. So, depending on the browser, its version, the platform, and certain choices the user might have made, text defined by a CSS can display differently from browser to browser.

However, it's a large step in the right direction, and it enables a previously impossible level of typographic specification and sophistication that can improve Web site design.

Previewing Style Sheets

The giddy thrill of creating style sheets can give way to a bit of regret if you haven't done a thorough job of reviewing which properties and features work in standard browsers, or haven't tested your style sheets with extensive previewing. So before we show you the GoLive approach to CSS, allow us to offer a few words on planning and previewing your work.

CSS Resources

Our favorite CSS resource online is WebReference.com's set of tutorials by the incredibly talented youth Stephanos Piperoglou: a Greek native attending an English university writing for Americans (and the rest of the world)! See http://www.webreference.com/html/.

You can also read about various aspects of CSS, including troubleshooting and coding tips, in articles written mostly by Eric Meyer on WebReview.com at http://style.webreview.com, plus the mother of all CSS compatibility charts, the Master List. The list shows every aspect of CSS from selector types to individual specifica-

tions and the level of support in each major browser release by platform. Eric also has a book out from O'Reilly & Associates called *Cascading Style Sheets: The Definitive Guide.* Visit http://realworldgolive.com/resources.html to buy the book online.

If you'd like to wade through a somewhat dry, but thoroughly comprehensive, view of the ideal version of the specification, you can read the actual CSS specification at http://www.w3.org/TR/REC-CSS1. The CSS1 specification is the one currently implemented in some partial form by all the 4.0 browsers.

As we suggest often in this book and in this chapter, despite GoLive's generally excellent preview simulations of browsers, there's really no reliable way to tell how a feature—especially a CSS property—works in an actual browser. In this regard, GoLive's failing is in being too good. All browsers are "broken" in some regard: a programming mistake or design choice makes combinations of tags work inconsistently; tables are a notable example of broken behavior, in which small, insignificant changes in tags cause a table to work or not.

GoLive implements all its previewing features consistently, using a structured framework, so a feature that works inconsistently in the actual browser shows up correctly in GoLive. (We don't want to be the ones to ask the GoLive engineers to purposely break their software; do you?)

Targeting Browsers

Before you ever design a style sheet, you have to make hard decisions about which browsers you plan to support with your site. You face three primary options.

Simple CSS Coding

CSS has a very simple structure for defining the name of a style sheet and its properties within HTML:

```
selector { property: value }
```

The selector is the name of the style, which also defines what text gets selected by it. The property is an attribute, such as font size or width of a rule; the value is, well, the value, defined in units appropriate to the property. (Selectors, properties, and values are described in more detail in "Creating Style Sheets," later in this chapter.)

You can have many properties in the same definition, separated by semicolons:

```
EM.figures { color: olive; font-style:
italic; font-variant: small-caps }
```

Because older browsers don't support CSS, GoLive and other programs must hide style sheet code from these older browsers, just as with JavaScript and other scripting languages.

GoLive inserts the style information into the head portion of an HTML page. A typical example looks like this:

```
<html>
 <head>
  <title>An Average Page</title>
  <style type="text/css"
  media="screen"><!--
    #headings { color: olive;
      font-style : italic;
      font-variant: small-caps }
    h1 { font-family:
      "Times New Roman", Georgia,
      Times; text-indent: 1pt }
--></style>
 </head>
 <body>
  <h1>How do you solve a problem
  like <span id="headings">
  Maria</span>?</h1>
 </body>
</html>
```

- Support all browsers and use no advanced features. In this case, you can exit this chapter (and this part of the book), since JavaScript, many CSS features, and even frames require you to abandon some part of the audience, even if it's a small percentage of users.

- Support all browsers by providing alternatives to advanced features. You can code CSS into a site that uses all tag selectors (explained later in this chapter) so a browser lacking CSS support falls back to using normal HTML tags, like H1, to display headings and body copy.

- Support only newer, CSS-capable browsers. In the previous version of this book, we didn't recommend this. However, by mid-2000, the vast majority of users on the Net browse with either Netscape or Internet Explorer 4.0 or later, or use other browsers, such as Opera or iCab, that support a significant number of CSS specifications. You're still cutting out part of your audience, but those folks increasingly can't visit many Web sites comfortably, anyway. So unless you have a particular segment of old-browser users, this may be a reasonable option.

A middle road is to use advanced features as appropriate, but use tag selectors as much as you can. This approach leads to a site that looks just fine in a non-CSS-capable browser, but which could look spectacular (or at least great) in a CSS-compliant browser.

Previewing in GoLive

GoLive can preview an enormous number of the CSS properties it allows you to set. It also previews some features that you have to hand code. (These distinctions are discussed in more detail later, but it's worth knowing now what these settings do before you launch into building style sheets.)

Root CSS menu. You can simulate different browsers by selecting them from the Root CSS popup menu of the View Controller palette. These simulations combine the defaults GoLive has encoded for each of the browser versions.

TIP:
GoLive's Default Browser Assumptions

If you want to examine GoLive's assumptions about browser defaults, select Web Settings from the Edit menu and click the CSS tab. Select one of the browsers in the list, and bring up the Root Style Sheet Inspector. Though you can't edit any of the settings, clicking the Source tab shows you each default that GoLive has set for each tag. This approach lets Adobe easily add new browsers' defaults without recoding the whole program. (For more information, see Chapter 31, *Web Settings*.)

(A tip within a tip: choosing one of the formatting options for the text that makes up CSS styles, described later in this chapter, sets the readability of the items in the Source tab of the Root Style Sheet Inspector. Select Pretty 2, for instance, click the XML tab and then the CSS tab, and you can more easily read the options set in the Source tab.)

Allow Overlapping Paragraphs. Checking Allow Overlapping Paragraphs lets GoLive preview negative margin values, so blocks that may cross each other are correctly displayed.

Mark menus. The Mark Style menu displays any defined classes or IDs; the Mark Element menu shows the A and Body tags by default, but also any tags which have been turned into selectors and applied to any text in the document. Selecting an item from either menu highlights its occurrence throughout the document. Clicking Hide resets both Mark menus to None.

Links menu. Selecting Active or Visited previews the look of links while being selected or after being visited. This is nominally a CSS issue because you can also set the active and visited color in the Body tag (through the Page Inspector's Page tab).

Previewing in Real Browsers

You know you have to do it, but many designers resist: preview your pages in multiple browsers to ensure that the CSS specifications are doing what you hoped and not flowing text off the screen, compressing it beyond legibility, or otherwise impairing the page.

We recommend testing every page of a site on the Macintosh (still at least 15 percent of traffic to most sites) and under Windows in multiple browsers. From our testing, it doesn't seem to matter what version of Windows (95 through present) or Mac OS (version 8 through present) you're running.

The minimally acceptable test bed at this writing includes Windows and Mac machines with few fonts installed (just the defaults, if possible, for best previewing effect) running the last or latest release of:

- Windows
  Internet Explorer 4, 5, 5.5; Netscape Navigator 4, 4.5, 6

- Macintosh
  Internet Explorer 4.5 5; Netscape Navigator 4, 4.6; iCab (beta release)

TIP:
Mac IE 5
Fully
Compatible

Microsoft claims that Macintosh Internet Explorer 5 is fully compliant with all current CSS specifications (CSS1 and CSS2) and Eric Meyer's Master List of compatibility at Web Review appears to confirm this. So if you want to test styles in the most ideal of all possible circumstances, use that version on that platform. At this writing, Windows IE lagged in CSS compliance.

If newer browsers have appeared, add them to the list. If you want to ensure less compatibility or are sure your users are running newer browsers, you can omit everything but the latest versions of each, reducing your test bed to six browsers instead of 12.

Creating Style Sheets

CSS has two distinct parts: creation and management of the styles themselves, and application of those styles to text or HTML ranges. We address the first part in this section, and the second in "Applying Style Sheets," later in this chapter.

GoLive Tools

It's easy to create CSS specifications in GoLive, as the program puts a friendly interface on top of a truly enormous number of choices and specifications. It's not quite an interactive editor, but it's structured just like you'd define a style sheet in a DTP program. You work primarily with two tools: the Style Sheet Editor and the CSS Selector Inspector.

TIP:
Live CSS
Preview

Create a new, blank page, and enter some sample text on it that's representative of what you'll be using the styles for. Create new empty CSS styles and name them. Where necessary, apply the styles to the text on the page (with classes and IDs; see "Applying Styles," later in this chapter).

As you edit the style's specifications in the CSS Selector Inspector, the type on your test page immediately displays the effects of the changes (see Figure 29-2).

Both tools let you specify an extensive, seemingly boundless set of CSS specifications; we talk about an end-run around its limitations for certain kinds of special, browser-specific, and advanced tags later in this chapter in "Advanced CSS."

Style Sheet Editor

CSS specifications have their own editor in GoLive, reachable by clicking the Cascading Style Sheets button—the ziggurat-like stairstepped icon at the top right of the Layout Editor. This action opens the Style Sheet Editor, which handles style sheets just for that page.

Figure 29-2
Live CSS
preview

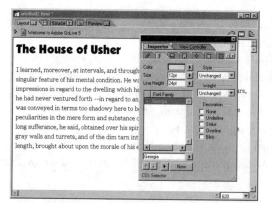

*As you edit in
the CSS Selector
Inspector palette,
changes appear
on the page.*

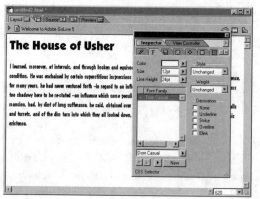

TIP:
**Head of the
Class**

If you like having multiple ways to perform every action—and who doesn't?—here's a second way to bring up the Style Sheet Editor: open the Head section of a document and double-click the stairstepped icon that appears there (see Figure 29-3). You might have multiple ziggurats if you have multiple sets of style sheets or local and external style sheets.

Figure 29-3
Accessing style
sheets from
Head section

You can also create a standalone set of style sheets in its own file that can be referenced from one or more HTML files on your site; select Style Sheet Document from the New Special submenu of the File menu. This is a convenient way to create a site-wide, intranet-wide, or Internet-wide set of shared formatting.

Viewing styles. Styles are sorted in the Style Sheet Editor first by ID, class, and element—corresponding to the order in which they're applied to items in a document—and then alphabetically.

Viewing options can be set in the View Controller, or by bringing up the contextual menu in the Style Sheet Editor, and selecting from the View sub-menu. By default, the Folder for Sections and Show Prefixes options are

Using Import to Link Style Sheets

A different method of linking external style sheets is via the import method, which is not used by GoLive, but which it supports for compatibility—as long as you leave the code alone when editing the Head sections of pages in the Layout Editor.

GoLive's method of linking an external style sheet uses the Link tag, which can also be used for embedding fonts and other external objects. For example:

```
<link href="/shared/standard.css"
rel="stylesheet" media="screen"
title="Shared Sheet">
```

This is standard enough, and all the browsers that support CSS also allow you to reference external style sheets with Link. The difference between import and Link is that import statements are embedded inside a style definition.

```
<STYLE><!-
@import url(http://w3c.org/styles/
core-set.css);
-></STYLE>
```

Import's advantage over Link is that because it's nested inside the Style tag container, it can import a set of styles that have import statements in them, too. You can also put more than one import statement in a style definition. So styles can import other styles, which themselves can import styles, ad infinitum. This lets you create a powerful hierarchy of nested styles for especially complex interlocked sets of documents, such as technical documents that are part of a series of similar, but not identical, documents.

Without the import feature, each page would have to use Link separately to connect to multiple external style sheets. And you'd have to spend some amount of time managing those Link statements, including updating all of them if a single file name changed.

Import statements work like Link statements: the order in which they appear in an HTML file controls precedence. The earlier they appear, the lower their precedence; see "Cascading," later in this chapter.

GoLive won't let you create import statements, but if you have a file that contains them, GoLive reads the styles and leaves them alone. Import statements show up as style sheet icons in the Head section, but don't try to edit them through the Inspector, as GoLive displays the entire import statement as the name of a CSS class selector.

checked. Unchecking Folder for Sections removes the folder display separating internal and external style sheets.

Folder for Selectors lets you add faux folders to enclose tags, classes, and IDs, so that you can collapse their display and make items in the editor easier to sift through.

Prefixes removes the "#" or "." before IDs and classes, since they're already identified by the type of icon appearing before each style.

TIP:
Internal and External Style Sheet Editors

The difference between the Style Sheet Editor that you use with editing styles located inside an HTML page and the editor that handles external style sheet files is twofold. The name in their respective title bars is different—the page-specific editor has the file name plus ": Style Sheet," while the standalone document displays only its filename—and the page-specific editor has a folder for Internal and External style sheets (see Figure 29-4). Using external style sheets is discussed under "Cascading," later in this chapter. In all other ways, they work identically.

Figure 29-4
Internal and external folders and editors

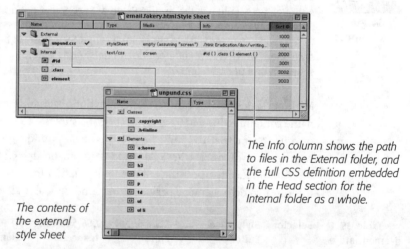

The contents of the external style sheet

The Info column shows the path to files in the External folder, and the full CSS definition embedded in the Head section for the Internal folder as a whole.

Adding styles. You add styles based on their type (see "Style Sheet Selectors," below) by clicking the New Element Selector, New ID Selector, and New Class Selector buttons in the CSS Toolbar (see Figure 29-5). You can also add selector options using the contextual menu.

Creating a new style brings up the CSS Selector Inspector. New tags, IDs, and class selectors are named "element", "#id", and ".class", by default. When you click the buttons repeatedly, new items are created with incremented numbers following the default name, like ".class2".

Figure 29-5
Adding styles

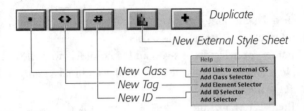

Duplicate

New External Style Sheet

New Class — Add Link to external CSS
New Tag — Add Class Selector
Add Element Selector
New ID — Add ID Selector
Add Selector ▶

Importing styles. You can also import the entire contents of style sheets. This is different from using an external style sheet, which merely references another file. The external style sheet stays intact and separate, and can be linked from many files. Importing style sheets copies the entire contents of a CSS style sheet as local styles.

From the File menu's Import submenu, select External Style Sheet. This option is also available in the Style Sheet Editor by selecting Import External CSS from the contextual menu.

TIP:
When to
Import

Although you could use the Import External Style Sheet option to set the styles for each page you're working on, it's far more efficient (and less labor-intensive) to reference an external style sheet. Importing CSS is best for building a master style sheet from several different documents, or as a quick way to apply style sheets in one or two pages.

Naming styles. Styles can be named anything alphanumeric; that is, any name containing just letters and numbers. Be sure not to include any spaces or other characters. IDs must be preceded by a pound sign, which GoLive requires that you insert (they're not added automatically). GoLive does, however, automatically insert the required punctuation for classes (a period, in this case), so do not enter a period in the name (see Table 29-1).

Table 29-1
Nomenclature
for CSS in
palettes and
editors

Selector	Style Sheet Editor convention	Style Sheet Editor example	CSS Selector Inspector example	HTML example
Tag	No brackets	H1	H1	H1 { bold }
Class	Leading period	.fridges	fridges	.fridges { font-style: italic }
ID	Leading pound-sign	#aquaman	#aquaman	#aquaman { border-top: 1pt dotted aqua }

TIP:
**Changing
Selector
Types**

You can change a Class to an ID by adding a pound sign at the beginning of the name. You can change a tag to a Class by inserting a period, or to an ID by inserting a pound sign. Finally, a tag can become a Class by changing the pound sign to a period, or a tag by removing the pound sign.

These changes only appear in the selector's icon in the CSS Selector Inspector when you click somewhere else in the editor to deselect the current selector. The change shows up immediately in the Style Sheet Editor.

If you're truly obsessed, switch to the HTML Source Editor to directly edit the names of selectors. When you return to Layout Editor, GoLive correctly re-interprets the names.

Duplicating existing styles. Select a style in the Style Sheets Editor and click the Duplicate button in the Toolbar to create an exact copy of an existing style. This method is far preferable to making a similar style from scratch.

Deleting styles. Select the style you want to delete and press the Delete key, or select Clear from the Edit menu.

NEW IN 5:
**Undoable
Delete**

Undo is quite powerful in GoLive 5; you can even undo the deletion of a style sheet. This feature is especially important as GoLive doesn't prompt you to confirm deletions. You can also use the History palette to step backwards through deletions.

Creating selectors that GoLive doesn't support. GoLive allows you to name styles with identifiers that contain extended selections as described in "Style Sheet Selectors" and "Advanced CSS." Generally, these kinds of selectors start with a tag, so create a new tag and, in the Name field of the CSS Selector Inspector, enter the entire selector. (For instance, "H1.extended UL LI" is perfectly legal in GoLive, even though the program can't preview its effect.)

Linking external style sheets. Click the New Style Sheet File icon, shaped like the stairstepped CSS icon in the CSS Toolbar. Or select Add Link to External CSS from the contextual menu. Either action adds an icon to the External folder of the Style Sheet Editor and brings up the External Style Sheet Inspector, which lets you choose a file to link to (see Figure 29-6).

Figure 29-6
Adding
external style
sheets

NEW IN 5:
**Adding
External
Style Sheets
in the Site
Window**

In the Files tab of the Site window, you can select one or more files and then use the Styles tab of the File Inspector to link in external style sheets (see Figure 29-7). This beats the method required in GoLive 4 of opening every file and repeating the process.

Figure 29-7
Using the
Styles tab

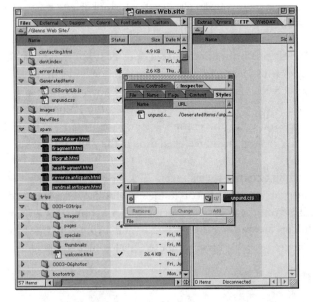

Selecting one or more files and then adding the style sheet through the Styles tab of the File Inspector links that style sheet to the whole selection at once.

Relation, although you can edit it, should remain set to the default "stylesheet". Media is a simple reference which might someday be used by software that's customized depending on what device you're using. The default is "screen," but "wireless device" and other options might be appropriate in the future. Title can be anything you want, but it's not a required field.

If you link more than one external style sheet, you can change their order—and thereby the precedence of the properties of style sheets embedded in the external file—by clicking the up and down Move arrows in the External Style Sheet Inspector. The closer to the top of the list the external style sheet appears, the lower its precedence. (For more on this subject, see "Cascading," later in this chapter.)

Clicking the Open button opens the external file for editing using the Style Sheets Editor, as long as it has a .css extension to the file name.

Exporting style sheets. You can export your local styles to an external style sheet by selecting Internal Style Sheet from the File menu's Export submenu; or, by selecting Export Internal CSS from the contextual menu in the Style Sheet Editor.

Editing external style sheets. Although you can use the Style Sheet Editor combined with the CSS Selector Inspector to edit individual styles, GoLive also offers Edit Source Code in the contextual menu for the Style Sheet Editor. This lets you edit the code directly as if you were viewing the style sheet as a text file (see Figure 29-8). You can also edit it via the Source Code palette (see Figure 29-9).

Figure 29-8
Edit Source
Code option

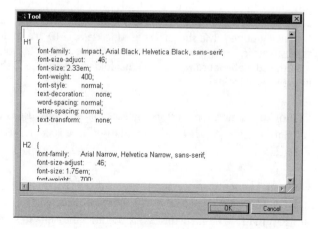

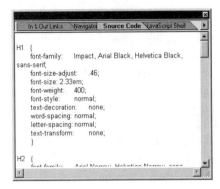

Figure 29-9
Editing via the
Source Code
palette

CSS Selector Inspector

Creating a new style through the Style Sheets Editor and selecting it activates the CSS Selector Inspector, your window into the vast specification arena for CSS.

The Basic tab of this inspector allows you to name your style sheet. It also provides a preview of how the actual code of the style sheet definition will appear in your HTML code or external CSS file. A full breakout of each tab of the CSS Selector Inspector is explained in "Style Sheet Specifications," later in this chapter.

Style Sheet Selectors

CSS categorizes style sheets by how they get applied to HTML. GoLive breaks these into three categories: element, class, and ID. Each of these types is a selector, the method by which text in the document is "selected."

NEW IN 5:
Reorganization

GoLive 4 grouped style sheets by type: tag, class, or ID. It also displayed external style sheets in a separate tab of the Style Sheets Editor. In GoLive 5, CSS styles are arrayed alphabetically in an Internal folder; external style sheets are located in the External folder.

You can name these selectors anything that contains just letters and numbers (alphanumerics). Spaces and punctuation have specific, reserved meanings in selectors.

Element. Element selectors apply to specific HTML tags, whether they're real, like a Heading 3 (H3) or teletype (TT) tag, or invented, like <SPAGHETTINI> or <RAVIOLI>. The element selector modifies the element's default appearance if one is built into the browser that's displaying the page.

TIP:
Inventing Elements

Invented elements generally work, as most browsers ignore tags they don't understand. But it makes more sense to use classes to define your own categories, unless you have specific reasons to roll your own.

Using elements is the most conservative course, since browsers that don't support CSS use the browser's defaults for the tag; those that support CSS show the style sheets' specifications. Omit the < and > in a element name.

Class. Classes are like the French Club in high school: anyone can join the group whether they're a freshman, sophomore, junior, or senior. After defining a class, you can plug the class into any kind of tag and the text selected by that tag inherits the properties of that class.

Classes are preceded by a period (such as ".mynewfriend"). You can combine tags and classes, and have a class that only applies to a given tag. This can be useful for creating a CSS that still works with a non-CSS browser; you can use H2, for instance, for similar levels of information, while using the class to format some H2s differently than others.

TIP:
Contextual Selectors

CSS supports selectors that use nested tags and classes, so you can define something as particular as "an unnumbered list element beneath another unnumbered list element in a paragraph that belongs to the paragraph class 'f1.'" This would be written simply as "P.f1 UL LI UL LI"; pretty elegant, eh? GoLive doesn't preview this behavior, but you can name a tag with a contextual selector and GoLive leaves it alone. This subject is discussed in greater depth in "Advanced CSS," later in this chapter.

ID. IDs are uniquely numbered and can be used only once in a document. GoLive currently only lets you define IDs; you have to edit the HTML to apply them. When you define an ID, precede its name with a pound sign (#). (If you delete the pound sign in the name, GoLive changes the selector to a tag selector.)

TIP:
IDs in External Style Sheets

If you use external style sheets, everything in every document is uniquely numbered to avoid potentially erratic behavior. (It's possible that some browsers would let you use the same ID for items on different pages, but you're better off using a class for that kind of shared behavior.)

Style Sheet Specifications

Of the more than 50 CSS properties you can apply to text selections and blocks, GoLive lets you specify almost all of them through popup menus or field values. However, GoLive can't preview all of the choices it offers for selection or specification.

TIP:
Preview in Browsers for Best Results

Although GoLive previews many effects, we recommend that you use GoLive just for coding style sheets. Rely on actual browsers to determine whether the effects or styles you're applying actually look the way you want them to.

As mentioned earlier in the chapter, Eric Meyer's Master List at Web-review.com is your best resource for determining which features to use to achieve maximum compatibility with the platforms and browsers expected to display your pages.

CSS Model

CSS's inline and block definitions closely match the character and paragraph styles of DTP programs like Adobe InDesign and QuarkXPress. This parallel is helpful if you've used those programs.

Character styles get applied to any range of text, and typically include just font formatting. Paragraph styles include leading (the vertical space from one line of type to the next), rules (borders around the text), background shades, margins, and vertical space above and below the paragraph (see Figure 29-10). CSS differentiates between inline elements and block elements.

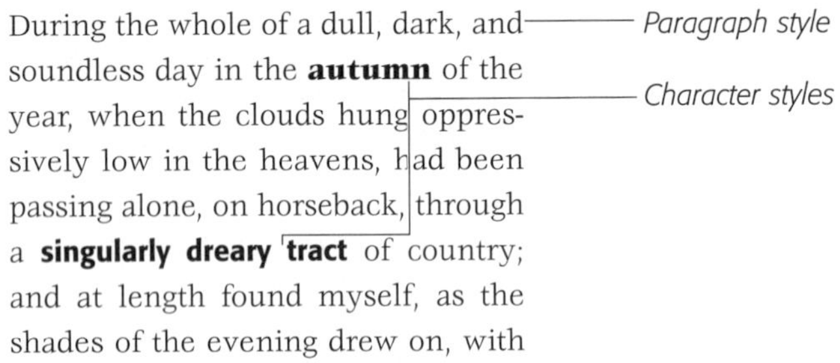

Figure 29-10
Paragraph and character styles

During the whole of a dull, dark, and ——— *Paragraph style*
soundless day in the **autumn** of the
year, when the clouds hung oppres- ——— *Character styles*
sively low in the heavens, had been
passing alone, on horseback, through
a **singularly dreary tract** of country;
and at length found myself, as the
shades of the evening drew on, with

An inline element is one that doesn't have a line break before and after it, such as the B (bold) tag. It refers to properties that can affect ranges of HTML without affecting surrounding formatting.

A block element creates a break in sequence with the HTML above and below it, such as the P (paragraph) tag.

HTML offers ways to create inline and block elements when using selectors that aren't based on the type of element you want to apply. The Span tag creates an inline range of text; the Div tag creates a super-block of text that can encompass one or more paragraphs (see Figure 29-11).

Because properties by their definition apply to inline or block elements (or both), you can often write a single style that works for both inline and block elements; the block properties are ignored when the style is used with an inline selector.

Figure 29-11
Span versus
Div

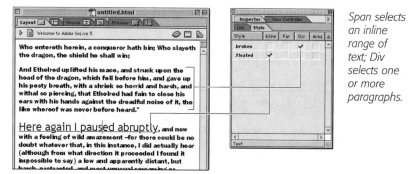

*Span selects
an inline
range of
text; Div
selects one
or more
paragraphs.*

CSS Specifications

GoLive lets you set most CSS specifications directly through the CSS Selector Inspector. Many of the specs are self-explanatory, such as type size or weight.

The CSS Selector Inspector has six kinds of settings:

- **Measurement.** For font size or line spacing, enter a number with a measurement (such a "1 px" for one pixel). You can also just enter a number, then select a measurement unit from the popup menu next to the field. To reset the field value to empty, select Unchanged from the popup menu.

- **Color.** Select a standard color from the popup menu or use the Color palette to drag in a swatch.

- **Popup selection.** Some options list only a few defined choices in a popup menu next to the specification's name. For instance, Float can only be set to Left, Right, or None.

- **Image reference.** A background for the area selected by this style or a list background can be chosen via the URL Getter. The Style Sheet Editor displays the status of any links in a style sheet, showing a green bug for bad links and a checkmark if all the files exist. (See Chapter 21, *Files, Folders, and Links* for a complete explanation of these icons.)

- **Font tab.** The Decoration checkboxes and Font Family list don't conform to the rest of the interface. Clicking New adds items to the Font Family list; the arrows rearrange order; and pressing Delete with one or more items selected removes the fonts. The checkboxes under Decoration set the style of type.

- **Other properties.** You can add properties that aren't part of GoLive's repertoire by using the Other Properties list in the List & Others tab. If you've defined properties like this, they show up in this tab for editing.

We've broken down the kinds of specs into major categories for ease of reference.

TIP:
Each
Specification's
Meaning

For more information about each of these specifications, it's best to refer to one of our CSS resources, as we could devote 50 pages to how the specifications work, and that seems excessive in a book about GoLive!

TIP:
Previewing
the CSS
Definition

GoLive shows the definition of the style sheet as it gets written in the Basics tab; it includes any hand tweaking you've done in the HTML Source Editor. Although you can't edit or copy the text in this preview, it's nice to see all the parameters in one place (see Figure 29-12).

Figure 29-12
Text Selector

Units

CSS uses several standard units for measuring items; GoLive supports all these through appropriate popup menus in the CSS Selector Inspector.

Point, pica, inch, cm, and mm. These five units are absolutes. Traditionally, as well as in the CSS specification, there are 12 points to a pica, and six picas to the inch; therefore a point is $\frac{1}{12}$-inch and a pica is $\frac{1}{6}$-inch. Inches are inches. A centimeter (cm) is 10 times as large as a millimeter (mm); there are 2.54 centimeters to an inch.

Absolute units appear limited to two decimal places to the right of the decimal point, which in any unit is more precise than is even possible to display. GoLive truncates further digits; it doesn't round them up.

Point, pica, and inch are abbreviated "pt", "pc", and "in" in any measurement field.

TIP:
Unit Conversions

If you select point, pica, pixel, inch, cm, or mm as your measurement unit and enter a value, you can then select a different unit from the popup menu and GoLive automatically converts one unit into terms of another. GoLive somehow stores extra precision for each number, as you can freely convert back and forth without encountering rounding or changes in the original value.

TIP:
Inches Aren't Always Inches

Note that selecting these absolute units doesn't guarantee absolute results. Since Web pages are viewed on thousands of different computer and monitor configurations, an inch viewed at one resolution is different than an inch viewed at another resolution. At best, these measurements are relative guides.

Pixel. You can specify items in absolute pixels, abbreviated as "px" in a measurement field, which is the unit that can be used most reliably on a computer screen, since screens are measured in pixels.

TIP:
Ideal Pixels

The CSS specification notes that browser developers should consider implementing the pixel measurement using a standard reference pixel so that the same measurement on different monitors would have the same pixel height regardless of the monitor's pitch, or the number of pixels per inch on screen. Most monitors display between 80 and 90 pixels per inch.

TIP:
Higher DPI

IE for Macintosh 5 allows you to adjust the default ppi in its Preferences under Languages & Fonts. The default for this version is 96 dpi (really ppi), which freaked out a lot of Mac users, as it made the screen display much larger for a lot of sites. However, it's just the default. If you use CSS at all, it overrides IE's dpi setting.

Em and ex. An em and an ex are relative measures based on the height of the capital letter M (for em) and the lower-case x (for ex) in the font, style, and type size defined or inherited in the style sheet.

TIP:
Not Your Grandfather's Em

The em measurement in CSS may confuse typographers and desktop publishers who are used to the traditional definition of an em that dates back to the last century, if not longer: the width, not height, of a capital letter M. The typographer's name for the CSS em unit would be "cap height," while the ex would be "x-height."

Percentage. If you specify percentage, the question becomes, "Percentage of what?" The percentage is always in terms of another defined unit in the same style sheet, or of an inherited default. Each property that allows percentage as a unit also defines what property the percentage is based on.

In the case of line height, for instance, percentage is based on the text size. If you define H1 as using a font size of 24 points, you can define a line height of 125 percent, which a CSS-compliant browser calculates as 30 points (24 multiplied by 1.25).

Other relative measures (100, XX-Large, Larger, Lighter, Bolder, etc.). CSS uses several relative measures for font size, line thickness, and other specifications that rely heavily on the browser to figure out what's meant. For instance, you can set a font's size to XX-Large, but a browser has to figure out what the current size is and what's relatively extra-extra large by comparison.

Different browsers map these relative measurements to different aspects, so you're counting on testing and luck to get what you want if you use these kinds of measurements.

Auto. Selecting this option, where available, rescales the given specification to fit the space in question. So, a border set to Auto causes the border to be displayed and to span the width of whatever block it's applied to.

Normal. Where Normal is available as an option, CSS defaults to a standard specification. This option is more typically used to reset a value in a cascade. So if the style sheet that has more precedence in a cascade says that the line height should be 100 points, selecting Normal resets the item to the default without requiring you to enter an exact number.

Typography. CSS lets you define characteristics of type, including character-specific attributes (font name, color, and size) and paragraph- and range-based settings (line spacing, spacing between letters, and vertical and horizontal alignment). GoLive splits the categories into the CSS Selector Inspector's Font and Text tabs.

Font characteristics are, by their nature, inline properties, while some of the items found in the Text tab have an effect on blocks, like alignment. The Font Family list requires a little extra explanation.

The Font Family specifications work just like the Font tag's Face attribute discussed in Chapter 22, *Sitewide Sets*. Clicking the New button adds a blank entry. You can type in a font from scratch, select a system font (i.e., one installed on your machine) from the popup menu to the right, or select a font set from the popup menu next to the New button (see Figure 29-13). If you select a font set, GoLive inserts each member of the font set in order into the Font Family list.

Figure 29-13
Choosing a
font or font set

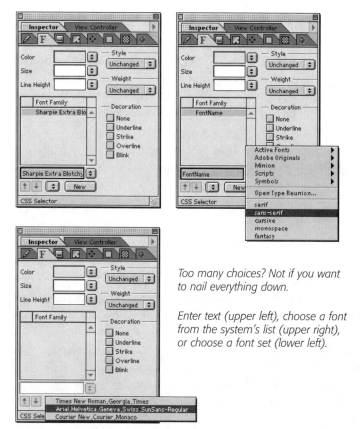

*Too many choices? Not if you want
to nail everything down.*

*Enter text (upper left), choose a font
from the system's list (upper right),
or choose a font set (lower left).*

TIP:
**Rearranging
Fonts**

The arrow buttons allow you to rearrange the items in the Font Family list into a
new cascade. Select a font in the list, and click the up or down arrow repeatedly
to move into the correct order.

TIP:
**Making Type
the Same on
All Platforms**

The same typeface with the same defaults in the same browsers display at varying
sizes on different browsers. You can use an absolute pixel measurement to set
type to a real size that will always use the same number of pixels, regardless of
platform. Set the Size property to a pixel value in the Font tab.

For the world's best explanation of this problem and other solutions, see
Geoff Duncan's TidBITS article, "Why Windows Web Pages Have Tiny Text" at
http://db.tidbits.com/getbits.acgi?tbart=05284, which we've excerpted in large
part in Chapter 8, *Text and Fonts.*

Borders, fills, and spacing. CSS offers substantial control over the borders and spaces surrounding a block. The CSS model breaks down a block into several areas, each of which has its own control in the Block and Border tabs of the CSS Selector Inspector (see Figure 29-14). Select the bottom-most item for Margin and Padding in the Block tab to set the specifications identically for all four sides of that part of the object model (see Figure 29-15).

Embedding Fonts in GoLive

Type choices on the Web are typically limited to the typefaces that users have installed on their browsers. Site designers would like to reference real fonts (i.e., PostScript and TrueType printer fonts) that would be downloaded as needed to a user's machine. Perhaps GoLive or another utility would examine the faces used in a Web site and create custom packages that the pages referenced.

Unfortunately, all of this is currently in limbo. Two competing systems for font embedding in Web pages exist: OpenType, supported by Adobe and Microsoft, and TrueDoc, a creation of Netscape and the Bitstream font foundry. Both systems allow a browser to download outline fonts, whether subsets of full fonts or the entire font, and use them to locally render type precisely as specified by a designer.

We don't want to sound like partisans of Adobe, even though we're writing a book about Adobe software, but it's clear that TrueDoc will fall by the wayside unless America Online, which acquired Netscape, has some peculiar font agenda they want to push as part of their battle against Microsoft's hegemony.

TrueDoc is supported by just Netscape's 4.03 (Windows) and 4.05 (Mac) and later. It can work on Internet Explorer, but requires an ActiveX plug-in. OpenType works on 4.0 and later versions of Internet Explorer for Mac and Windows. But with IE at a 75 percent or higher usage share, and with both Adobe and Microsoft behind it, it seems likely to prevail.

GoLive doesn't directly support using either TrueDoc or OpenType. It requires third party programs to even create the files you need to embed. And then you have to edit your HTML directly to include the appropriate references.

If you've somehow talked yourself into using this technology, you can add font specifications via CSS for the Adobe and Microsoft OpenType format.

If you really want to add references to OpenType font files via GoLive, use the List & Others tab of the CSS Selector Inspector for an existing style. Add a property named "fontface" with a value that is the exact name of the embedded font package; the software that creates embeddable fonts can help with this.

For more on TrueDoc, consult www.truedoc.com. For more on OpenType, Microsoft maintains the most up-to-date resources at http://www.microsoft.com/typography/default.asp. We've put a copy of an article Glenn wrote for the late, lamented *Adobe Magazine* about the subject at http://realworldgolive/embedding.html, and we'll post updates and tutorials if anyone actually bothers to continue developing this useful technology.

Figure 29-14
CSS model
and GoLive
controls

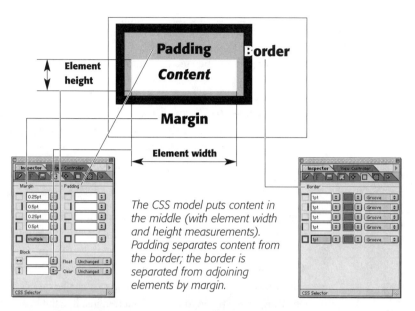

The CSS model puts content in the middle (with element width and height measurements). Padding separates content from the border; the border is separated from adjoining elements by margin.

Figure 29-15
Setting all four
sides

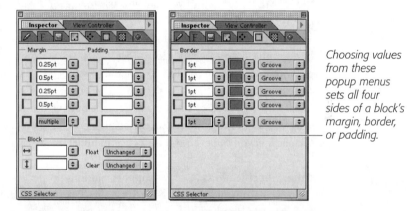

Choosing values from these popup menus sets all four sides of a block's margin, border, or padding.

Two controls are particularly useful for controlling text flow: Float and Clear. Float allows you to set a block as a run-around element, so text flows around it to the right or left. Clear modifies a floating block, so that text to the right or left starts flowing only at the vertical bottom of the box.

The Position tab has two additional block-display features: Overflow and Visibility. The Overflow options set how a block behaves when its contents overflow its container. Visibility allows a block's contents to be hidden or displayed. Both features are part of CSS2, so the level of support among browsers will vary.

TIP:
Float and
Clear

Float and Clear are equivalent to the Align attribute for the Img tag, and the Clear attribute for the P and BR tags. Because all items related to formatting are eventually going to be steamrolled out of HTML proper, CSS takes the place of a lot of attributes in current HTML tags.

Positioning. With CSS, you can specify an exact position on a page relative to the upper-left corner of the browser window. Many of the controls in the Position tab are identical, or nearly so, to those in the Floating Box Inspector. The Z-Index field, for instance, corresponds to the Floating Box Inspector's Layer field.

Clipping. Clipping, found in the Position tab, is part of the CSS2 specification and controls how much overlap is displayed between adjacent, conflicting blocks.

Background. You can control the background of a block or the entire page, including offsetting elements from the upper left. CSS allows you to set a repeating image through the URL Getter, just like the Background attribute of the HTML Body tag, but you can also use images and colors to set the background of blocks.

A very cool CSS addition to background is the Attach feature: you can set a background image to be Fixed so that as you scroll down a page, the background is static in the window. This actually works on some current browsers!

Lists. If you're tired of boring list element bullets, use list specifications in the List & Others tab to perk up the display, providing better control over the formatting; you can even choose a custom bullet image via the URL Getter.

Other Specifications. GoLive supports adding properties that it currently doesn't offer through its List & Others tab. Click the New button, then enter the property name and its value. This feature doesn't work for properties without values, as it insists on putting a colon at the end of the property name, even when the value is empty.

This is a simple way to add CSS2 properties, as appropriate, without having to code by hand.

Cascading

The CSS cascade allows you to apply more than one selector to the same tags or classes as well as more than one style sheet that contains the same selector. The rules of cascading define how conflicts are resolved.

For instance, let's say you have an external style sheet with an H1 selector that defines all Heading 1's as dark blue, 36-point Helvetica; an internal style sheet that defines H1 as 24-point (but has nothing to say about color font face); and another internal style sheet called H1.nimby that defines a 1-pt. border. For HTML that looks like:

```
<H1 class="nimby">Not In My Bike's Yoke</H1>
```

CSS's cascade rules would take the color and font face from the external style sheet, let the internal H1 selector override the size (setting it to 24 points), and put a 1-pt. border around it.

CSS has two distinct kinds of cascades:

- A general-to-specific set of rules that controls how the properties of one selector override those of another selector, preferring the more specific selector

- A set of rules about precedence that resolves which specifications get applied or overriden for identical selectors or selectors that include the same HTML based on a clearly defined hierarchy of style sheets in internal, external, and browser-based style sheets

General to specific. CSS defines selectors in terms of how specific they are; there's even a little formula, with more technical detail than you may ever need to know, that you can use to calculate specificity (see sidebar, "The Specificity Formula").

The Specificity Formula

We expect you won't need this information except for complex sets of interlocked documents or style sheets; nonetheless, we're here to serve you, so here goes.

An ID is worth 100 points. Classes are worth 10 points each. Tag selectors are worth a single point each. The higher the number, the higher the precedence of the selector, meaning that any conflicting information in it will override anything with lower precedence.

Here are the examples modified from the CSS1 specification:

Tag	ID	Class	Tag	Specificity
LI	0	0	1	1
UL LI	0	0	2	2
UL OL LI	0	0	3	3
LI.red	0	1	1	11
UL OL LI.red	0	1	3	13
#x34y	1	0	0	100

Typically, a more specific selector overrides properties in a more general selector. So you might define some characteristics for EM, but any properties in EM UL LI (a list element in an unnumbered list set inside an EM tag) override those in EM because they are more specific. For example, if you define a type face as Bodoni Poster in the EM selector, and Bembo Book in the EM UL LI selector, the nested text would be set to Bembo Book.

Classes are always more specific than tags, and IDs are the most specific of all. Combining classes, tags, and IDs can create a complex set of overrides. If you start to develop style sheets that require this level of control, we suggest you learn the spec inside and out, especially the specificity formula.

Precedence. More commonly, you encounter issues of precedence and hierarchy in how rules get interpreted. In the current CSS model, a browser has built-in style sheets that reflect the browser developer's assumptions. For instance, all the heading styles may be defined using certain fonts that are always found on an operating system.

The browser's styles are overridden by a user's browser preferences (also called the reader's preferences), which represent the next level up in the hierarchy. A user might choose, for instance, to use a font on their system, like Garamond, to display body copy. However, an author's styles—the author being the person who wrote the CSS style sheets in a Web page—override a user's styles except in special cases.

External style sheets have lower precedence than ones embedded in a Web page, and the order in which external style sheets are listed controls their precedence: the earlier a style sheet appears (or higher in the HTML document), the lower the precedence.

You can adjust this precedence in the External tab of the Style Sheet Editor by selecting an external reference and using the arrows to adjust its position up or down. External style sheets linked via the import command must be rearranged by hand in the HTML to adjust their order of precedence.

All external style sheets linked using the GoLive method or the Link tag are lower in precedence than any file linked via the import method.

! important. There's one way to assure precedence, which is to use the "! important" override, which GoLive doesn't support or preview. If you insert "! important" after any property's value, that value overrides all other values for that property based on the cascade.

For instance,

```
H1 { color: olive ! important }
```

in an external style sheet overrides

```
H1 { color: aqua }
```

in an internal style sheet. If more than one conflicting style uses "! important" for the same property, the general-to-specific and precedence cascade rules determine which "! important" is more important.

TIP:
**In CSS,
Readers
Come First**

CSS2 uses the "! important" tag to let a reader or user override an author's definitions, the converse of the current version. This lets readers really have their way when they want it.

Applying Style Sheets

So far, it may seem as if setting up style sheets is a chore…and sometimes it can be. But the reward comes when it's time to apply them to text on your page, which is a breeze.

You can only apply classes to ranges of text. IDs must be inserted by hand in the current release. Element selectors correspond directly to tags, so text defined by tags is automatically updated in the Layout Editor to reflect the style definitions.

Applying Classes

GoLive applies classes to text through the Style tab of the Text Inspector. GoLive divides elements into four categories, each of which has its own column heading. Each class, including classes that are subsets of tags, has four checkboxes to the right of its name (see Figure 29-16).

Figure 29-16
Applying class
styles

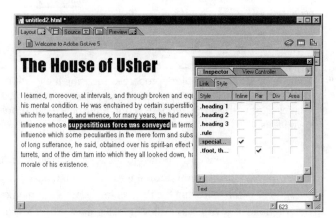

Hovering over a checkbox adds a green plus sign to the cursor; clicking puts a checkmark in the box. To remove the setting, hover over the box again, and notice that the cursor has a red minus sign; click to remove the checkmark.

You can apply multiple settings to the same text, checking one or more of the element categories. If you select more than one paragraph at a time or text that has different settings applied, the checkboxes display a hyphen or dash to indicate multiple settings.

Inline. Inline corresponds exactly to inline elements. GoLive uses the Span tag to insert class selectors used as an inline element. Because the Span tag has no other purpose, it won't cause any other changes to the HTML.

To apply an Inline element, select a range of text before checking the Inline box (see Figure 29-17).

Figure 29-17
Applying an
inline style

Text selected and Inline style applied

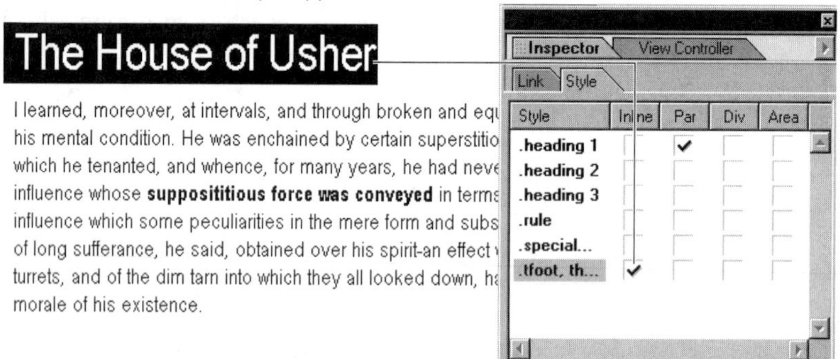

```
<span class="tfoot,thead">
The House of Usher</span>
```

Resulting HTML

TIP:
Block That
Class!

If you apply a class with block properties set using the Inline checkbox, the CSS spec says that the block properties are supposed to be ignored by the browser. However, as with all CSS properties and principles, each browser may have its own ideas.

Par. The Par element corresponds to the P, or paragraph, HTML tag. You can either place your insertion point anywhere in a paragraph, or select multiple paragraphs before checking the Par box for a class. Each paragraph in the selection becomes its own separate block (see Figure 29-18). This could work well for vertical spacing and other paragraph-specific attributes that affect type flow.

Figure 29-18
Par and Div
styles

*Par checked for selection, applying
block style to each paragraph*

*Div checked for selection, applying
block style around entire selection*

Div. Unlike the Par element, the Div, or division, element creates just one set of Div tags around the entire set of selected paragraphs or other block units.

This creates one large block, and block properties, like borders and margins, get applied around the entire division (also see Figure 29-18, above).

TIP:

**Floating
Boxes Took
Over My
Style!**

If you use absolute positioning with the Visibility attribute set to Visible in a style sheet selected by an ID, then apply that style to text with the Div element, beware: switch modes between HTML Source Editor and Layout Editor, or close and open the file, and GoLive turns your unsuspecting text into a floating box with its own ID (see Figure 29-19)! This is a highly specific set of actions you have to take, but, still, GoLive eats your style.

It's unclear whether this is a feature or a bug in the HTML parser, or something entirely different. What we do know is that once your text becomes a floating box, you can apply "local" positioning to it that gets stored as part of the ID definition, not as part of the class definition.

Figure 29-19
Floating box
takeover of
absolute
positioning
area.

*Absolute positioning
applied in a style to
a specific block.*

*After switching to HTML
Source Editor and back to
Layout Editor, the block
has become a floating box
with the text pasted in.*

Area. The Area element sets the Class attribute for the Body tag if the text insertion point is in plain text; the entire page is affected by the Body tag, of course. If the cursor is in a table cell, the Area element affects just the cell, modifying the TD or TH tag for the cell.

Applying IDs

Applying IDs is fairly easy, even though it has to be done by hand. GoLive neither tracks nor allows you to apply them directly, but it does appropriately preview any element with an ID applied.

1. Select the text or block to apply an ID to.

2. Switch to the HTML Source Editor.

3. Omitting the leading pound sign (#) in the name of the ID, apply the ID to the text in one of three ways:

    a. If the text you want is entirely surrounded by opening and closing HTML tags, insert the ID into the opening tag.

        ```
        <H1 ID="flooby">Town of Flooby Nooby</H1>
        ```

    b. If the text is a range inside a paragraph, use a set of Span tags.

        ```
        The first time I heard of <SPAN ID="flooby">the Town
        of Flooby Nooby</SPAN>, I was in the Caspian Sea.
        ```

    c. If you want to create a block covering more than one set of block tags (like P or UL), surround the range with a set of Div tags.

        ```
        <DIV ID="flooby">Lots of paraphenalia<P>here to
        think<P>about.<P></DIV>
        ```

4. Switch back to the Layout Editor to preview your IDs.

Advanced CSS

GoLive, in our experience, is the leading bi-platform CSS editor, providing a truly useful and straightforward interface to CSS complexity.

There are two kinds of features we lump into "Advanced CSS": those that require more detail in the selector part of the CSS (the part that defines which tags, classes, IDs, or other characters a style sheet gets applied to), and those that are part of the style sheet definition itself.

Complex Selectors

CSS offers even more specificity and complexity in selectors than are available for preview and full support in GoLive. You can enter all these selectors in the Name field of the CSS Selector Inspector, even though GoLive won't preview them.

Specificity. Selectors can be nested fairly deeply, so you can specify, for instance, that bold type in a list element of an unnumbered list inside a particular class gets such-and-such properties. You'd write that as:

```
.classname UL LI B
```

That selector won't affect italic formatting in the same nested location. This specificity has a complex set of rules that affects which properties override others; this is explained earlier in the chapter, in "Cascading."

Mix-and-match. You can mix tags, selectors, and IDs with amazing aplomb. So, for instance, you can define a selector that affects only the ID #Z27 inside an H1. This would be distinct from ID #Z27 by itself, or ID #Z27 for an unnumbered list element:

```
H1#Z27
#Z27
UL LI#Z27
```

Multiple selectors. All the properties of a selector don't have to appear in the same, single definition, so you can set multiple selectors to have the same property by separating them with commas, and then applying specifics after that.

```
H1, P.barge, EM UL LI LI { font-size: 13 px }
H1 { color: fuchsia }
```

Pseudo-Selectors

The CSS spec provides for what it calls "pseudo-selectors": items that don't really fit the selector mode, but rather directly modify parts of the browser display. This allows the spec to be a little more flexible about certain aspects of the browser interface.

NEW IN 5:
Adding Pseudo-Selectors

In the Style Sheet Editor, you can select one of several anchor-related pseudo-selectors from the Add Selector submenu of the contextual menu.

Anchor-related. A special class of selectors work with the A or anchor tag: active, link, and visited. These selectors allow you to override the built-in browser behavior, which typically turn an active link (one that's being clicked on) purple, a regular link blue, and a visited address red.

Using the syntax A plus a colon plus active, link, or visited, you can specify a variety of inline type effects.

For instance, the following would make all links on a page display in italic regardless of other properties:

```
A:link { font-style: italic }
```

Paragraph-related. CSS defines a few DTP-like characteristics that allow you to provide special treatment on the first character of a paragraph (a drop cap) and the first line of a paragraph.

Use P:first-letter to select the first character, and P:first-line to—surprise!—select the first line.

Browser-Specific Features

Here's a shocker: some browser makers have added features that aren't part of any CSS spec or are currently only supported by a given browser release or platform.

Internet Explorer

Several of the IE-specific tags are cribbed from CSS2, so other browsers may be expected to offer them in time.

A:hover. This selector offers a simple rollover function. Whenever the cursor passes over any hyperlink, the browser changes the type to reflect the properties defined for it. You can even light up the entire area in a different color. (See http://www.webreference.com/dhtml/diner/hover/hover2.html for some incredibly neat examples.)

Display. The display property supports four possible values: none, block, inline, and list-item. None suppresses display—actually deletes it from the screen—of any enclosed HTML. Combined with a relatively simple JavaScript, this property can provide a way to have click-down menus on a single HTML page. Clicking a triangle, for instance, toggles whether the text below that item gets displayed or not.

Cursor. The cursor property changes the shape of the cursor into a specified value when the cursor passes over the item that has the property attached to it. The possible values are quite extensive: hand (the little, um, "famous mouse" hand), crosshair, default (normal cursor), move (four direction cursor), text (the I-beam), wait (watch or hourglass), and help.

There is also a set of "resize" cursors (e-resize, ne-resize, nw-resize, n-resize, se-resize, sw-resize, s-resize, and w-resize) that corresponds to the compass point being used for resizing.

Designing with Style

Repetition is tedious. Repetition is tedious. Repetition is…okay, you get the point. We like using style sheets to avoid tedious repetition of repetitive tedium. It lets us not only control the look of our pages with more specificity, but with remarkably little work as well. For designers working on a Web site in teams, the ability to set central styles that work over an internal network or the Internet can provide a sense of continuity and consistency that many Web sites lack or spend an enormous amount of effort keeping track of.

CHAPTER 30

Dynamic Link

GoLive gives Web designers several tools to make pages visually dynamic: Go-Live Actions, DHTML animation, and browser plug-ins. But, up until early 2000, using GoLive to add dynamic content that would pull information from a database via a server required you to hand-code perl or ASPs (Active Server Pages), depending on your platform and preference.

Adobe wanted to make GoLive the center of all Web design and management activities, and so Adobe built a powerful technology into the program that allows you to interact directly with a database with the same drag-and-drop ease with which you can add Actions to a page.

Dynamic Link is Adobe's solution. This GoLive module allows you to build and maintain complex sites much more efficiently by linking to a database that may store some, most, or all of your site's content. This can give users access to hundreds or thousands of pages of information, while you create and maintain a few template pages.

When you need to change or add more data, you simply edit the database, which you can do directly using the database's own software, or via another set of database administration Web pages. The information can then be made available instantly to site visitors—no more tedious HTML page editing!

And since the layout and visual appearance of the content is controlled by a few template pages, when you want to change how the content is displayed, you edit the templates—not individual pages. This is an improvement over Components, even, which still require GoLive to rewrite pages and then upload to the server to make them available.

Not all sites need to be database-driven. Good candidates for this treatment include product catalogs, press release archives, employee bios, and current job listings; that is, any set of information that has multiple items with similar characteristics.

Though the Dynamic Link interface is quite simple and easy to use, a few caveats remain:

1. It does not create the database for you, which means you have to own the appropriate database software and know how to use it before you can do anything with Dynamic Link. (More on databases later in the chapter.)

2. Dynamic Link currently works just with Microsoft ASPs, which run on Microsoft's own Web server software, or on other servers using Chili!Soft's ASP software (see "ASP Support" in Chapter 32, *Languages and Scripting*, for more on ASP.)

TIP:
More
Methods of
Linking

At the time this book went to press, Adobe was promising more extensive support for other server-scripting languages; watch our Web site at http://real-worldgolive.com/dlink.html for details.

3. When you use the visual Dynamic Link tool, you are limited to a narrow subset of ASP capabilities: basically getting data out of and into a database, and displaying it within a Web page. Just like JavaScript, there are many more actions that ASPs can carry out which are only possible with hand-coding.

4. Dynamic Link uses a feature of ASP to reference external files so that your HTML files stay small. This feature, server-side include, works much like external JavaScript libraries. The routines that GoLive stores in these included files handle much of the actual work of moving the data into and out of the database. However, the code in the included files is neither short nor simple, and it can be very difficult to decipher it if you later want to hand-code additional functionality or troubleshoot an error.

Although this chapter focuses on using Dynamic Link with ASPs, the general techniques described here should apply to interacting with other database solutions as they become available.

ASP Workflow

ASPs interact with a Web server (typically, Microsoft's Internet Information Server or IIS) to process information on the server and interact with databases (see Figure 30-1). ASPs work like JavaScript; in fact, you can write ASPs using JavaScript, although Microsoft's VBScript is more commonly used.

An ASP comprises two parts: scripts, and the HTML template that the scripts act on. (In many cases, the HTML template may contain an entire page

Figure 30-1
Information flowing from browser to server to browser

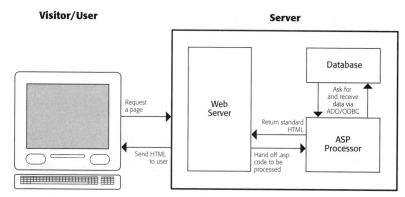

that the user's browser receives without modification.) The script part of the ASP isn't carried out by the browser, like JavaScript; instead, the scripts are processed by the server before being sent to the user. The user never sees the script; the server sends just the HTML portion of the page. And, because the browser doesn't have to deal with the code, you don't have to rely on every visitor to your site having a browser with a certain kind of support.

The server knows a requested page has ASP code in it because the file name ends with an extension of ".asp" instead of ".html".

Dynamic Link: One Tool Among Many

Jeff and Glenn went to the Macworld Expo in San Francisco in January 2000 to meet users and hang out at the Adobe booth. We learned a lot from the experience, including the fact that Dynamic Link, which had been released in a beta version at that point, was confusing the heck out of users.

One fellow had flown in from across the country to get answers to questions about linking databases to the Web via GoLive and Dynamic Link. Unfortunately, he didn't know exactly what a database was, how to set up a server, or how to write scripts. He assumed that the software was a package that would do all that for him.

We heard similar tales repeatedly throughout the event, and continue to hear them as of the publication of this book. Although people are itching for a single overall solution, Dynamic Link is merely one piece in a chain of parts linking data to Web visitors; it's not an entire system.

As time passes, you will see more databases and database connectors that come with GoLive tools built-in; in fact, before GoLive 5 had even shipped, developers such as Blue World Communications had announced support for it.

But remember that regardless of how WYSI-WIG and spiffy Dynamic Link or other tools may be, you still have to fit them all together into an unbroken chain that conveys information. This is always easier said than done, and it often requires expertise beyond what you can pick up from a manual or Web page.

Installing Dynamic Link

Adobe requires you to carry out several steps to add Dynamic Link support in GoLive (see Figure 30-2). Some of these steps happen inside GoLive itself; others, on the server that contains the database gateway software and ASP-supporting server.

Figure 30-2
Installing
Dynamic Link
parts

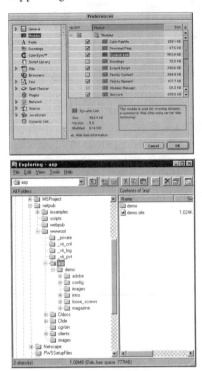

Turn the module on.

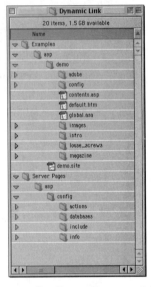

Copy the files to the server (left) from the GoLive application folder (above).

Turning on the GoLive Module

The Dynamic Link module comes pre-installed with GoLive 5, but it is turned off by default. To turn it on, open Preferences, select the Modules pane, and check the box next to Dynamic Link. You have to quit GoLive and launch it again to activate Dynamic Link.

Server Requirements

If you are building your site on a Mac, you need to have access to a Windows NT Server running IIS 3.0 or later, or a PC running Windows 98 or NT and Microsoft Personal Web Server (PWS). If you are building your site on a

Windows PC, you can run either IIS or PWS on your own machine, and install the appropriate GoLive files locally; or, you can use a remote server.

TIP:
Unix and ASP

As noted above and elsewhere in this book, ASP support is not limited to Microsoft servers, but our examples and most people's use of ASP tends to involve Windows. For more information on using ASP with Unix, see Chili!Soft's site at http://www.chilisoft.com/.

Installing Special ASP Files

Adobe ships its own ASP files to handle database access via your Web server. These files are found nested in the GoLive application folder inside the Dynamic Link folder. The two folders are Server Pages and Examples, both of which contain a folder called "asp".

We recommend that you use a two-server system—separate development and production (or "live") servers—if at all possible. These two servers can co-exist on the same hardware; the point is that one is exposed to the rest of the world, and the other is used to test new development before letting people use it.

If you follow this arrangement, copy the "asp" folder from the Examples folder onto your development server, and the "asp" folder from the Server Pages folder onto your live production server. The Examples "asp" folder contains some sample files, databases, and troubleshooting tools you can use for testing. (You want to use the files from the Server Pages folder on your production server to avoid potential security issues.)

These files should wind up in the wwwroot folder if you're running IIS, or whatever the root folder of your Web server is. This is the point from which, as you know from building sites in GoLive, the server starts looking for files, folders, and subdirectories when you enter a URL.

Who Your "Friends" Are

Dynamic Link provides a method of preventing unauthorized users from messing with your files via a file called "friends.asp". This file is found in both "asp" folders, nested in the config folder's include folder. When you open this file—either in GoLive or a text editor, as it's plain text—you see instructions on how to add your workstation IP (Internet Protocol) number both to allow you access and keep your pages secure.

Make sure after you edit this page that it uses Windows line-break characters (see sidebar, "ASPs Need Windows Line Endings," earlier in this chapter).

Testing Setup

Once all the GoLive ASP files are installed on the server, and the Dynamic Link Module is turned on, you can test to make sure everything is set up correctly. Open a Web browser and enter the URL or IP address of the server you installed the Examples folder files on, followed by the path to the "troubleshooting.asp" file. This should be something like:

```
http://www.yourdomainname.com/asp/demo/config/info/
troubleshooting.asp
```

or

```
http://192.168.0.100/asp/demo/config/info/troubleshooting.asp
```

This displays a diagnostic of your server setup and whether or not everything is installed and configured properly. If there are problems, it should also give you some hints on fixing them.

Building a Database

Before you can work with Dynamic Link, you must create a database and add some data to it.

TIP:
Microsoft Access

For our examples, we use Microsoft Access, which is one of the most common and easy to use databases out there. Other databases that work with Dynamic Link include Oracle's and Microsoft SQL Server. The module also interacts via ActiveX Data Objects (ADO) and Open Database Connectivity (ODBC), Microsoft technologies that provide a conduit through which database software can share their contents with other programs and Web servers. FileMaker Pro supports ODBC via additional driver software.

ASPs Need Windows Line Endings

One crucial, yet obscure requirement of ASPs is that all ASP files must contain Windows-style line endings. As we note in the next chapter, *Web Settings*, the Unix, Mac, and Windows operating systems each use different characters to signal a hard return at the end of a line.

If you're using the Macintosh version of GoLive, be sure to set the Line Break Character in Web Settings's Global tab to Windows (CR/LF) before creating any Dynamic pages. (This bit us, preventing us from testing Dynamic Link for a while, until we figured it out.)

The ASP files that ship with the Mac version of GoLive have Mac line endings (for reasons that escape us). To fix these files, make the Web Settings change first. Then open each file, select Rewrite Source Code from the Special menu, and save each file (see Figure 30-3). If you find yourself getting odd, undefined server errors when you start testing your dynamic pages, using the wrong line break characters may very well be the culprit.

Figure 30-3
Fixing line
endings

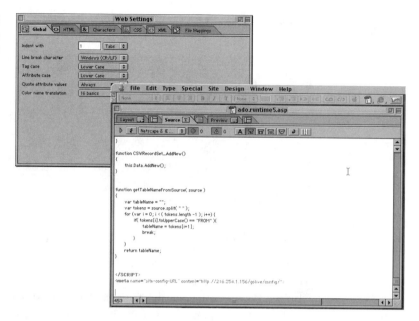

Parts of a Database

Databases consist of tables of information; each table usually contains data about a single subject (see Figure 30-4). A table is divided into columns and rows, like a spreadsheet. An entire row is called a record and contains all the information in that table about a single entry.

Within a record are fields, each of which contains one type of information about the entry, such as a phone number, a price, or a name. Usually, you configure the table so that each record has an automatically assigned unique ID number as the record's first field. When you later retrieve information from that table, you can tell the database exactly which entry or entries you want. This unique ID must be designated the Primary Key for the table.

TIP:
Database
Keys

A database key is what makes a record unique. For instance, in a customer table in a database, each record contains a customer name, address, and other information. However, more than one customer may have the same name; a unique ID helps "key" that record differently, so you can tell the difference between Bob Smith in Omaha and Bob Smith in Pistascataquawamesett.

Other tables might use a text key to contain a number of entries that correspond to the same name. For instance, if you frequently sorted customers by city, you might have a table that uses the city name as the key or unique identifier, and multiple customer IDs would appear in each record.

Figure 30-4 Database tables

Products : Table

ProductID	Name	Type	Category	Description	Price	ImageURL
1		Front Door	Doors	Guaranteed to keep pesky salesmen at bay.	$300.00	images/doors/OS17006.JF
2		Old Wooden Door	Doors	The colonial look for the dignified family.	$250.00	images/doors/OS17010.JF
3		Old Wooden Door	Doors	Rustic but serviceable. Be sure to check out our	$225.00	images/doors/OS17016.JF
4		Door to Room	Doors	Shhh! Studious students studying inside.	$85.00	images/doors/OS17019.JF
5		Church Door	Doors	The doorway to salvation.	$450.00	images/doors/OS17050.JF
8		Sash Window	Windows	Comes with a 14 page operation manual.	$95.00	images/windows/OS17093
9		House Window	Windows	Twelve separate glass panes are extra insurance	$110.00	images/windows/OS17100
10		House Window	Windows	Perfect for the cat.	$130.00	images/windows/OS17102
11		Hatchet	Hammers	Great for pounding in railroad spikes (but watch o	$25.00	images/hammers/OS1002
12		Hammer	Hammers	Precision made by the same factory that brought	$12.00	images/hammers/OS1003
13		Black Hammer	Hammers	Boink! Boink! Boink!	$10.00	images/hammers/OS1008
14		Silver Hammer	Hammers	The handle unscrews to reveal a Chinese puzzle-l	$10.00	images/hammers/OS1011
15		Ax	Hammers	Spook your enemies. Family and friends, too.	$40.00	images/hammers/OS1610
16		Rubber Mallet	Hammers	Perfect for wooden pegs. Not recommended for t	$8.00	images/hammers/OS1610
17		Claw Hammer with Tape a	Hammers	Never lose your grip again.	$18.00	images/hammers/OS1610
18		Ball Peen Hammer	Hammers	Ideally balanced for juggling during the lunch brea	$10.00	images/hammers/OS1610
19		Stone Hammer	Hammers	A classic design copied from cave paintings.	$17.00	images/hammers/OS1610
20		Scissors	Pliers	Doubles as a nostril hair trimmer for the daring.	$8.00	images/pliers/OS10044.JF
21		Pliers	Pliers	Complete with a set of exchangeable handle colo	$8.00	images/pliers/OS10045.JF
22		Scissors	Pliers	Springy for life.	$14.00	images/pliers/OS10043.JF
23		Vice Grip	Pliers	No lug nut will ever escape again with this iron gri	$12.00	images/pliers/OS10112.JF
24		Metal Pliers	Pliers	Hot coal anyone?	$6.00	images/pliers/OS16081.JF
25		Slip Joint Pliers	Pliers	The time tested model for the traditionalist.	$8.00	images/pliers/OS16082.JF
26		Rib Joint Pliers	Pliers	Eeeeeeextra wide to accommodate all shapes an	$10.00	images/pliers/OS16083.JF
27	Crocodile	Handsaw	Saw Blades	Tapered like a crocodile's snout.	$15.00	images/saw_blades/OS16
28	Steel Too	Saw Blade	Saw Blades	Cuts through tin and toilet paper with equal ease.	$42.00	images/saw_blades/OS16
29	Chomper	Circular Saw Blade	Saw Blades	Old chomper; big boards only please!	$28.00	images/saw_blades/OS16

Record: 1 of 31

Creating a Flower Catalog

For an example, we'll create a simple, one-table database for a flower catalog with information on all of Flora's Flowers arrangements (see Figure 30-5). (You can download this database and supporting ASP files to follow along with from http://realworldgolive.com/dlink.html.) This database remains nice and simple because, even though Dynamic Link can deal with multiple tables, it doesn't support relational tables. (Relational tables have records which reference records in other tables by name or number.)

Each record in the Arrangements table has a field for a unique item ID number, a flower name, a description, height, a thumbnail image, a full-size image, and a price. The images are stored in the database as file paths, because databases typically only contain text and numbers. That is, no pure "data." (You'll see how we use these file paths to display the actual images a little later.)

Figure 30-5 FlorasFlowers database arrangements table

Arrangements : Table

arrID	name	price	description	photoSmall	photoBig
1	Spring Orchids	$30.00	Yellow tulips and sprays of pink orchids in a very modern and dramatic arrangement.	images/Arr01-2.jpg	images/Arr01.jpg
2	Sunshine in a Basket	$20.00	Sunny yellow sunflowers and daisys in a reusable wicker basket with a charming carrying	images/Arr02-2.jpg	images/Arr02.jpg
3	Pretty in Pink	$20.00	Carnations, daisys and snap dragons all in shades of pink spill out of a square basket.	images/Arr03-2.jpg	images/Arr03.jpg
4	Romantic Roses	$15.00	Three long-stem red roses with baby's breath and fern leaves, all dressed up with a red ribbon	images/Arr04-2.jpg	images/Arr04.jpg
5	Pop Art	$20.00	A bouquet of intensly colored daisys bursting from a cobalt blue glass vase.	images/Arr05-2.jpg	images/Arr05.jpg
6	Iris Bouquet	$20.00	Elegant and architectural purple irises arranged in an asian-style graphite ceramic vase.	images/Arr06-2.jpg	images/Arr06.jpg
7	Fresh as a Daisy	$10.00	What could be more cheerful than two dozen fresh-picked white daisys presented in a pink	images/Arr07-2.jpg	images/Arr07.jpg
8	Springtime Spray	$25.00	A variety of flowers highlighted by fresias and daisys in springtime pastels arranged in a bright	images/Arr08-2.jpg	images/Arr08.jpg
9	Carnation Bouquet	$10.00	Pink carnations with baby's breath and fern leaves will seem to last for ever in this white	images/Arr09-2.jpg	images/Arr09.jpg
10	Single Red Rose	$10.00	Nothing is more elegant than this single long-stem red rose in a clear glass bud vase	images/Arr10-2.jpg	images/Ar10.jpg

Record: 10 of 15

Configuring the Server

For our example, let's build a simple, browseable catalog of our flower arrangements. Before making pages, we need to upload the FlorasFlowers.mdb database to the databases folder in the config folder on the server (see Figure 30-6). Since we are using an Access database, that is all we have to do to make it available to Dynamic Link. Other databases, such as Microsoft SQL Server or FileMaker Pro, a few more steps are required before they can be connected.

Figure 30-6
Database file
on server

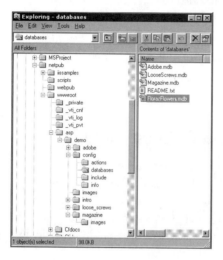

Start building the catalog by creating a main catalog page layout just like you would a normal static page with tables, text, and images. Add dummy copy and images as placeholders for the content that comes from the database later.

When the layout appears as you like it, select the Dynamic Link palette from the Window menu. Currently the only format you can choose is ASP/VBScript. You can check the box to keep a copy of the original HTML page if you like, then click Make Dynamic.

If this if the first Dynamic page you've created, you see a message saying there was an error connecting to the server and GoLive is switching to off-line mode. Don't panic yet; we just need to tell Dynamic Link where our server files are.

At the top of the Content Sources tab, type in the address of the config folder on the server. This is something like:

```
http://www.yourdomainname.com/asp/demo/config/
```

or

```
http://192.168.0.100/asp/demo/config/
```

Or, if you are using Microsoft Personal Web Server on your local machine for development, it reads:

```
http://127.0.0.1/asp/demo/config/
```

If you still get an error message after typing in the address and path to your config folder:

- Make sure the address for your server is correct.

- Ensure that you added your IP address to the friends.asp folder (see "Who Your 'Friends' Are," earlier in the chapter).

- Check that your line breaks on all the server files are set to Windows format (see the sidebar, "ASPs Need Windows Line Endings," earlier).

- Recheck troubleshooting.asp to see if there is anything missing or not working on the server.

Setting Up a Catalog Page

After making a connection to the server, you can start creating connections to the database itself and placing data into record sets. GoLive calls these sets "content sources." In the Content Sources tab of the Dynamic Link palette click New. In the New Content Source dialog box that appears, enter "arrangements" as the content source in the Description field. Database Query is selected by default for Type.

Select a database from the popup menu. In our example, choose Floras-Flowers, and then select the Arrangements table. All the field names in the Arrangements table should now appear below the name (see Figure 30-7).

Figure 30-7
Field names for FlorasFlowers

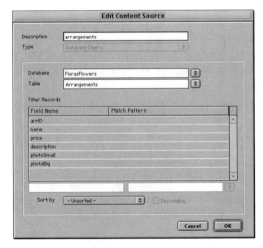

Sorting

We talk about Match Pattern later in this chapter, but let's take a look at the Sort By menu at the bottom of the dialog box. This menu lets you choose the order for sorting information retrieved from the database. For example, if we want to display the arrangements alphabetically by name we would choose "name" in the Sort by menu. And if we wanted them listed by highest price to lowest we would choose "price", and then click the Descending checkbox to reverse the low-to-high default. Click OK and return to the Dynamic Link palette, and you now see the "arrangements" table as content source with all of its fields listed.

Dynamic Table Setup

As you can see from our layout, we have several bits of content displayed from fields in the database's table (see Figure 30-8). In the main content area, we want to list arrangements with their title, price, and a small photo. Since we want these grouped by arrangement, we have to generate a dynamic table in which each row displays data from a single record. In our static Web page layout, we add a table with three rows and two columns containing placeholder content for three arrangements.

Figure 30-8
Example
template

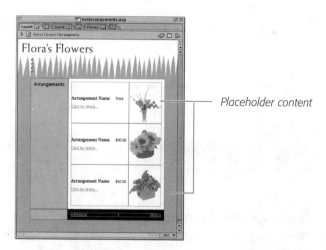

Placeholder content

To create dynamic data bindings, select the first arrangement's name, and then check the box next to the "name" field in the Dynamic Link palette (see Figure 30-9). Next, repeat this action with the price by linking it to the "price" field, followed by linking the small photo to the "photoSmall" field.

Figure 30-9
Making data
bindings

Figure 30-9
Making data
bindings

TIP:
**Highlighting
Bindings**

Dynamic Link automatically draws a green border which highlights bound (linked) objects as you create them (see Figure 30-10). You can turn this highlighting on and off by clicking the gear icon in the top-right corner of the Dynamic Link palette. If the highlighting is red, that indicates a bad link to the Content Source, just like the bad link warning for hypertext links.

Figure 30-10
Highlighted
objects

Filtering and Formatting Data

There is one extra step to display the price in dollars and cents: filtering and formatting the data. Again, select the price in the first row and click the Binding Details tab (see Figure 30-11). For each binding, we can structure the data before it is displayed. This can include ensuring text is correctly formatted for HTML. Or, you can take a raw date and time, and display it in a friendlier format. In this example, we want to choose Format Currency from the VBScript submenu.

Figure 30-11
Filtering and
formatting
content

Making a Link Dynamic

For the "Click for details…" link in the template, select the link, and choose the Binding Details tab of the Dynamic Link palette. Checking the Link Action box causes GoLive to make this link display dynamic content on another page or change the content displayed on the current page. In our example, we want to take visitors to a larger photo and more information on the selected flower arrangement when they click the link. Choose Show Details of Current Record, and make sure "arrangements" is selected as the content source (see Figure 30-12).

Figure 30-12
Setting up
dynamic
content

The two photo fields contain just the path to the image. Dynamic Link expects this and replaces the "src" parameter with the text from the database. Make sure the image path you put in the database is either relative from this page, or absolute from the server root.

TIP:
Dynamic
Images

One thing to remember when creating images for dynamic pages and adding placeholders for them on a page: the height and width of the images aren't dynamic, just the source parameters of the Img tag. The dimensions of the placeholder graphics are the height and width that are used for all of the dynamic images.

Choosing Records

Since this is going to be a dynamic table, we only link the content in the first row; Dynamic Link takes care of adding and populating all the other rows. But, first, we have to add some binding information.

Select the table and click Binding Details in the Dynamic Link palette. Check Replace Rows, and choose "arrangements" as the content source. Click the Preview tab in the document window to preview content (see Figure 30-13).

The page now displays every record from the database table—which creates a really long list, especially when we start adding more arrangements. So how about just displaying three items at a time? Go back to the Binding Details tab, select the Records/Page radio button and enter 3 for three records per page (see Figure 30-14). Now, when we check Preview, only the first three items from the table appear.

Figure 30-13
Previewing the
work so far

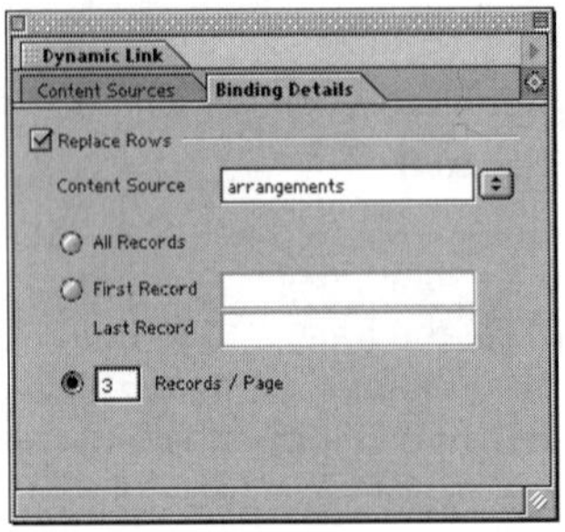

Figure 30-14
Minimizing
record display

Linking Back and Forth

But what about all the other flowers? This is where our next and previous links at the bottom of the layout come in. First, select the Next link and click the Binding Details tab. Check Link Action again, but this time choose Show Next Record from the menu (see Figure 30-15). Normally this option would only show the next single record in our Content Source, but Dynamic Link knows that we've chosen to display three records per page earlier, so it now displays the next three records automatically. Finish up by selecting the Previous link and binding it to Show Previous Record in the Link Action Menu.

Figure 30-15
Next and
previous
records

Testing the Results

Now to test this last functionality, we have to save the page and upload it to the server. Next, enter its address in a browser, making sure you type ".asp" at the end and not ".html". Now if everything is set up and configured correctly, we should be able to page through all our records three at a time by clicking Next and Previous.

When we are at the beginning of the records there is no Previous button (see Figure 30-16). Likewise, when we reach the end of the record set the Next button disappears. This is Dynamic Link taking care of us behind the scenes; otherwise, we would get an error message if we clicked on the Next Link and there was nothing more to display. Pretty cool.

Creating a "Details" Page

In our example, we need to create a new page to display detail information. Like above, you need to build a new page layout to show the larger photo and description information for one flower arrangement using whatever HTML elements you want (see Figure 30-17).

Next, make the page dynamic by clicking the Make Dynamic button on the Dynamic Link palette. We also need to create a new Content source: click

Figure 30-16
Appropriate
navigation
buttons

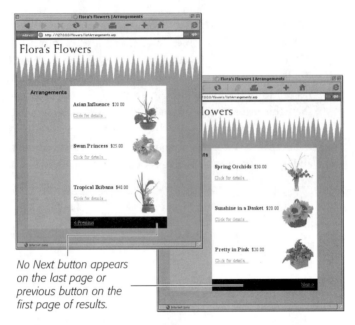

*No Next button appears
on the last page or
previous button on the
first page of results.*

Figure 30-17
Details page
template

the New button and give it the description "detail", since we're displaying detail info for one arrangement. Just like before, choose the FlorasFlowers database and the "arrangements" table. But this content source has one difference: we are using the Filter Records area to make sure only information about the arrangement the visitor chose displays.

Passing Variables

How does the server know which arrangement the user clicked on so it displays the right content when we only have one details page for the entire catalog? When the user clicked the "Click for details" link, the server received more information than just the URL for the next page. Dynamic Link automatically added a URL parameter to the address. It looks like this:

```
http://www.servername.com/details.asp?dino=dinosaur&
daughter=pebbles
```

The question mark after the file name tells the server that everything that follows is not part of the address of the page, but a set of one or more variable names with paired values. These values are passed to the script that runs on the page.

In the case of this URL, we have a variable named "dino" containing a value of "dinosaur", and a variable named "daughter" containing the word "pebbles". Dynamic Link makes use of the URL parameter to tell the next page which arrangement the user chose.

Choosing and Formatting the Data

To complete the action started on the main page, we add a filter to the Content Source in our detail page. Select the field name "arrID", which is the primary key field for this table; from the popup menu at bottom right, choose Match URL parameter [name]. One other filter choice that you may use frequently with Dynamic Link is Match Form Field [name]. This makes use of any information sent to the server from a previous page if this page were the target action of a form.

Since we only display data from one record, we don't make any of the tables dynamic. Just select the content placeholders—in this case the arrangement name, the large photo, the description, and the price—and link them to the Content Source fields just like the previous page. Make sure to add the Format Currency filter to the "Price" binding.

Finishing Up

That's it for this page. But before we test, make sure you link the "Click for details" link in the first table row of the main catalog page to our new details page.

Upload both the just-edited main page and the new details page, and test them in the browser by typing the address of the main page. Now, when you click the "details" link, you should be taken to the details page, where you see just the information and large photo for the arrangement we selected.

Updating and Adding to the Database

Dynamic link can also build pages that let us maintain our database using any browser. Actually, we only need to create one page that lets us add new flower arrangements, as well as edit the information of existing ones (follow along in Figure 30-18).

Start by creating another new page layout, but, this time, we build a form with fields for all the database fields we want to update or add to. Once again, make the page dynamic in the Dynamic Link palette and create a new content source. Give it the description "arrangements", and then choose the FlorasFlowers database and the Arrangements table. Click OK.

Drag a Form object onto the page and, in the Form Inspector, link the Action field to the current page. When you save the page, Dynamic Link replaces this URL with a link to one of its own configuration files.

Now, we link the form fields themselves to the database fields to display the content as editable text. Link the text field next to "Name" to the "name" field in the Content Sources tab and the text area next to "Description" to the "description" field. Continue down the form, linking form items to database fields.

At the end of the form, select the submit button and click the Binding Details tab of the Dynamic Link palette. Check the Action box, and choose Update Record from the Database submenu.

We can now see a record from the database and update it, but we need a way to get to other records. Simple: we can add Next and Previous buttons just like on our main catalog page. Select the "Previous" link and, under Binding Details, give it a Link Action of Show Previous Record. Then, select the "Next" link and give it a Link Action of Show Next Record.

Adding a new record is just as easy. Select the New link and, under the Binding Details tab, give it a Link Action of Show Empty Record. Choose "arrangements" as the content source. When the user clicks this link, the page reloads with all the form fields empty, ready to type in information for a new arrangement.

To make it a little easier, we can let the user know how many records there are in the table they are editing, and which record they are viewing. Select the number "2" in the text "2 of 11" and, in the Binding Details tab, bind it to the "arrangements" content source. However, for the field, choose Record Number at the bottom of the menu. Next, select the "11" and bind it to "arrangements", and then choose Record Count as the field. These two field choices are data that Dynamic Link keeps track of and updates automatically.

Figure 30-18
Database
administration
*(continued on
next page)*

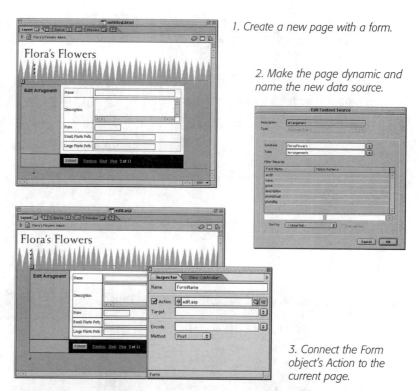

1. Create a new page with a form.

2. Make the page dynamic and
name the new data source.

3. Connect the Form
object's Action to the
current page.

4. Link the form fields to the database fields.

5. Select Submit, and use the Binding Details
tab to choose Update Record.

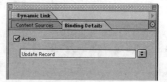

6. Show next and previous items.

Figure 30-18
Database
administration
*(continued
from previous
page)*

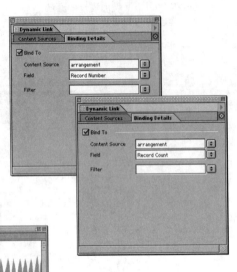

7. Create a link that adds an empty record.

*8. Link to show the current
record number out of total
records (e.g., "5 of 12").*

*The completed record
entry and updater page*

E-commerce Capabilities

In the manual, Adobe touts Dynamic Link's capabilities in creating e-commerce sites. In reality, there is both more and less to this story.

There's more, in that you need to install and set up the Microsoft Commerce software on the server on top of all the other software required for Dynamic Link, as well as set up the database to conform to the Commerce Server's needs.

There's less, in that Dynamic Link does nothing to help you with some of the key function-

ality of sites that sell goods online, such as credit-card processing, robust security, shipping, and order tracking.

That said, Dynamic Link can be a quick and easy way to set up prototype functionality for an e-commerce site with a catalog, shopping cart, and checkout pages. Just make sure you have an experienced Web developer or two available to either finish the job, or recreate the programming of the site in a more robust fashion.

Save the page and upload it to the server for testing. When you load it into the browser you should see all the data from the first record populating the form fields, and the text at the bottom of the page should read "1 of 15" (or however many records are currently in the database table). That record number text should change to "2 of 15" when you click the "Next" button. Try editing the text of one of the records and click the submit button. The page reloads with the new data. Also, try adding a new arrangement with the "New" link. You can verify the changes to the database by opening it and checking the fields in the table.

Future Dynamism

Dynamic Link as shipped with GoLive 5.0 marks a great step forward for integrating database-driven information with drag-and-drop page and site management. The next steps, which may be announced by the time you read this, will allow you more choices for databases, more methods of linking, and more help with making it all work.

CHAPTER 31

Web Settings

Web Settings is GoLive's unsung hero. It stores all the program's assumptions about how tags work so that as you build pages visually, you get a nice, clean preview. When you switch to the Layout Preview, the browser preview options listed in the Root menu of the Layout View Controller are all based on Web Settings for each browser.

GoLive uses Web Settings to store all the rules governing tags, including how they are written (their syntax), how they interact with other tags, which browsers they work on, and how they display in the HTML Source Editor.

Other WYSIWYG Web tools have similar embedded properties, but GoLive is unique in building an extensible system that you can access directly as an advanced user. By opening up the behind-the-scenes processes, GoLive gives you the ability to customize how it writes and displays HTML and to add new tags as the HTML standard is updated. This way, you're not beholden to a product's update cycle to add some of the compatibility you need.

Web Settings can also be used:

- To reset some of GoLive's HTML writing defaults

- To define new defaults for some HTML objects that GoLive creates on pages

- As an HTML and character encoding reference

- To add browser-dependent, proprietary, or non-standard tags

- To add new special characters or "entities"

- To view examples of special characters

- To control what applications open which files in the Files and Designs tabs of Site windows

Web Settings Doesn't...

GoLive limits the kinds of changes to program behavior you can make by altering elements in Web Settings. You cannot change or add interface items to menus, Inspector palettes, or the Objects palette. (You can use the Software Developer's Kit for some of that. Consult Adobe's online help.) If you add an attribute to an existing tag, you don't have access to it through the Inspector palette. However, the new tag or attribute appears as an option in the HTML Outline Editor (see Figure 31-1).

Any new HTML tags or special characters added to Web Settings aren't previewable by GoLive, either in the Layout Editor or the Layout Preview. Also, GoLive can't automatically detect the browser compatibility of new tags added to Web Settings, so if you want GoLive to be able to display warnings for the new tags using its HTML syntax checker, you must gather and set compatibility information yourself.

Figure 31-1
New attributes available in the Outline Editor

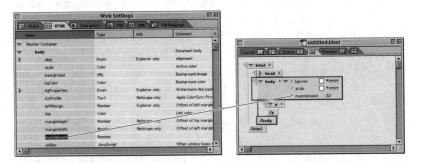

What's New in GoLive 5

In GoLive 4, Web Settings was called the Web Database and appeared in the Special menu. It now appears more appropriately in the Edit menu near Preferences. Otherwise, the differences are cosmetic. The contents of Web Settings are almost identical in form and function to the GoLive 4 Web Database, but now won't confuse users into thinking that GoLive includes a built-in method of using information from databases.

The formatting previews that were within the Web Database window are now separate: select the Global tab and bring up the Source Code palette to see a preview of some sample text being affected by any changes you make in the Global tab. Likewise, the CSS tab's style sheets are now formatted in the Root Style Sheet Inspector's Source tab.

The File Mappings tab has been moved to Web Settings where it makes more sense than its previous home as a preference.

TIP:
**Previewing
Output**

If you open the Source Code palette, you can preview the effects of the changes you make to formatting specifications in the Global and CSS tabs' settings on a sample bit of HTML (see Figure 31-2). You can edit this preview, either by pasting in your own text, or editing material that's already there.

The Global tab affects all the preview (and HTML writing) of all tags and attributes; the CSS tab controls just the CSS definitions in the Head section of the HTML and the preview in the Root Style Sheet Inspector's Source tab.

Figure 31-2
Previewing
formatting in
the Global and
CSS tabs

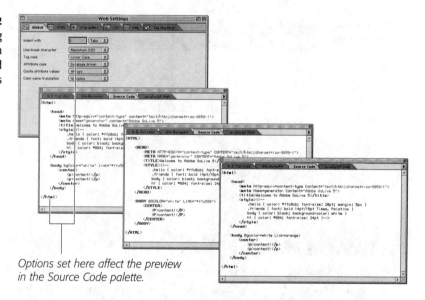

*Options set here affect the preview
in the Source Code palette.*

*Changing the Output option updates the preview
in the Root Style Sheet Inspector's Source tab.*

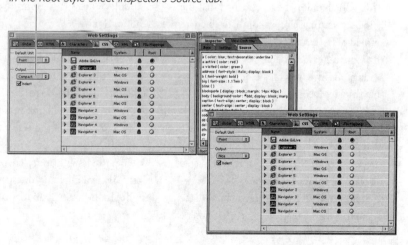

Global Tab

When you open Web Settings for the first time, you see the Global tab. Here, GoLive organizes most of its HTML-writing preferences regardless of whether they're single HTML pages or part of a site (see Figure 31-3). These settings affect the way GoLive writes source HTML code, not how the browser displays the page.

Figure 31-3
Global tab

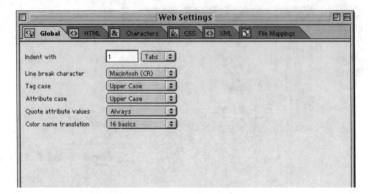

A Word of Warning

While it's commendable that GoLive offers access to its inner workings, this power doesn't come without grave responsibility. Before you dive into Web Settings and begin changing settings with wild abandon, be forewarned that the existing tag settings closely conform to currently ratified HTML standards. If you alter the tags, their attributes, enumerations, or compatibility settings, GoLive may create non-standard code that displays incorrectly in browsers.

Also, GoLive uses Web Settings when checking your code for errors. If the tags have been changed to non-standard settings, the syntax checker accepts them as correct and may fail to display important warnings.

However, you can easily revert back to factory defaults if you've made changes that don't work

out. Just throw away GoLive's Web Settings folder or any of its subfolders after quitting the program. On both Mac and Windows, the folder is found in the GoLive application folder's Modules folder. The next time you run the application, GoLive creates a new Web Settings folder with the factory settings.

Mac users, don't be fooled by the Import Old Web Settings Database contextual menu item that appears in the HTML and Characters tabs. As far as we can tell, the option isn't wired to work with the application in GoLive 4 or 5. The Import feature appears to be a way to update Web Settings with more current information, but this capability and the specifications aren't found in the manual or elsewhere.

HTML Formatting

Most of the settings in the Global tab affect only the appearance of HTML in the HTML Source Editor, to make reading and editing the code easier.

Break Text. Checking this box automatically adds a line break in the HTML after the number of characters you specify. Browsers ignore line breaks, except when used in conjunction with the Pre (preformatted) tag.

Indent With. GoLive "nests" HTML, using tabs or spaces to make it more readable by applying a structure based on the blocks and elements. Table rows, for instance, are nested inside Table tags; cells are nested inside rows. You can turn this function off by setting the value to 0 (zero), or have GoLive use spaces instead of tabs.

Line Break Character. The line break character is the symbol or symbols that each of the three major platforms—Macintosh, Windows, and Unix—considers a signal for the end of a line. Don't ask why each platform decided on a different symbol; line-break envy? GoLive tells you which platform corresponds to which signal as part of the popup values. Using Macintosh line endings puts in a carriage return, or ASCII 13; Unix uses a line feed, ASCII 10, to signal the end; and Windows is gluttonous and uses both.

TIP:
Targeting Platforms Endings

If you're creating pages in GoLive for Web serving or editing on another platform—often the case—choosing the line-ending style for that platform can prevent line break characters from becoming visible in the local text editor; and from being ignored, thereby turning the entire page into a single, way-too-long-to-edit line of text. (FTP programs should convert line breaks to the destination platform, so this problem may only occur when copying files on a network or onto disks, or emailing them elsewhere.)

Applying Changes Globally

Changes in the Global tab don't affect pages in GoLive retroactively, even though they're program-wide settings. Instead, you have to open each file, select Rewrite Source Code from the Special menu, and then save the file for the HTML to be updated.

The one workaround we found for GoLive 4 was to use the Find feature's Find & Replace tab to find and replace the same item that occurs in every file. This procedure used to force GoLive to open, modify, and save every file in a site, resulting in entirely rewritten HTML. However, GoLive 5's 360Code feature—which modifies HTML only when you specify it—stops GoLive from rewriting the source HTML when it makes global changes. We haven't figured out a new way around this yet. Watch the realworldgolive.com Web site for tips.

Tag Case, Attribute Case. The tag and attribute case affect capitalization. There's no technical reason to set them any specific way, as browsers ignore capitalization in tags and attributes. Some people prefer tags to appear in all caps, for example, to distinguish them from the rest of the text. (Older browsers were less forgiving, and this could cause a problem; but that's mostly pre-1996 browsers. Future versions of HTML may require tags to be all lower case, though.)

If you set these options to Database Driven, then capitalization for tags and attributes is set by whatever values are built into the Web Settings's HTML settings. This allows you to spot certain tags more easily when editing source code; for example, you could have all lowercase tags except for table-related tags, which could be uppercase for easy identification.

Quote Attribute Values. This setting adds quotation marks around values like image height and width. For the highest level of compatibility, set this option to Always.

Color Name Translation. GoLive can turn the hexadecimal values used to specify colors into sensible names like "red" and "white." Some browsers recognize only 16 common names, while Netscape has named many more. Although this option makes it easier to identify a color in the HTML code if it's named, you're likely to avoid compatibility snafus if you set this to Do Not.

HTML Tab

The HTML tab organizes all of GoLive's assumptions, preferences, defaults, and compatibility settings for tags—and their legal attributes and attribute values—in one convenient, easy-to-browse location. You can use the HTML tab in three primary ways:

- As a reference to the properties and syntax of existing tags
- To add new tags that Adobe hasn't yet added to GoLive or that the designers chose to exclude to increase compatibility
- To modify some of GoLive's defaults when creating certain new objects

Examining Tags

The HTML tab can organize all the tags and characters logically by where they are used in the page structure or alphabetically by the tags' names. You can opt to view the entries as Structured (by category) or Flat (all tags listed alphabetically) by selecting the appropriate button on the Web Settings View Controller. Or, with the HTML tab open, bring up the contextual menu and highlight Flat Structure under the View submenu; highlight it again to toggle the setting.

TIP:
Alphabetical Tabs

Pressing the Tab key advances through the list of tags alphabetically. In the Structured view, this can look chaotic as the selection moves among categories; the Flat view is more sensible for selecting tags using this method.

The HTML tab uses several Web Settings Inspector palettes that assist with viewing and editing HTML tags. To understand the Inspectors, we need to quickly cover the structure of an HTML tag, whether in GoLive or in the HTML specification.

HTML Syntax and Web Settings Inspectors

An HTML tag has a name, like H1 or Img. Each property in a tag, like the height in pixels of an image, is an attribute. Each attribute may have enumerations, each of which is a legal or accepted (in other words, understood by a browser) value for that particular attribute. For instance, an enumerated attribute for Table is align; it can take the values center, char, decimal, justify, left, and right. Most attributes do not have specific enumerations, but can take a required value type, like a color value, number in some unit (pixels, inches, percentage, etc.), or URL (see Figure 31-4).

Expanding the view under a tag shows its attributes; expanding enumerations under attributes show the attribute's legal enumerations, when they exist. Using the Inspectors, you can view substantial detail about a tag's preview in GoLive, its nature and function in HTML, and how the tag gets structured and interpreted by GoLive.

Figure 31-4
Tag structure

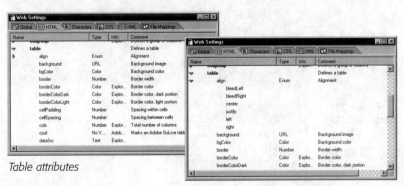

Table attributes

The Table tag's Align enumerations

Web Settings Element Inspector. Selecting a tag from the HTML tab brings up the Web Settings Element Inspector, which includes naming and structure, output preview, and compatibility tabs (see Figure 31-5).

Web Settings Attribute Inspector. Selecting any tag's attribute brings up the Web Settings Attribute Inspector, through which the attribute's values are defined, as well as its compatibility and necessity; many attributes are optional (see Figure 31-6).

Web Settings Enum Inspector. If the attribute has only one set of allowed values—an enumerated list—you can drill down another level and select any enumeration to see the Web Settings Enum Inspector, which merely shows its name and compatibility (see Figure 31-7).

Figure 31-5
Web Settings
Element
Inspector

Figure 31-6
Web Settings
Attribute
Inspector

Figure 31-7
Web Settings
Enum
Inspector

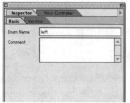

Basic Inspector Settings

The Web Settings Inspectors' Basic tabs access the most general characteristics of tags, attributes, and enumerations.

Basic tab basics. The Basic tab for each Web Settings Inspector contains the name of the item and whether it's a tag, attribute, or enumeration. Generally, the Comment field is filled out just for tags, and contains a brief description of the tag's function.

The Tag and Attribute Inspectors offer additional options in their Basic tabs; the Enumeration Inspector has just the Name and Comment fields.

Web Settings Element Inspector. This Inspector's Basic tab has three additional items: Structure, Content, and End Tag menus.

The Structure menu defines a tag's nature in terms of its contents. (See Chapter 29, *Cascading Style Sheets*, for more on block and inline elements.)

- **Block:** any tag that spans paragraphs or other block elements.
- **Inline Visible:** applies to tags that a browser interprets in order to insert content in their place, like the HL (horizontal line) tag.
- **Inline Invisible:** tags that affect their contents, such as the H1 (heading 1) tag.
- **Inline Container:** can both insert content in their place and contain formatted text or other details. The Applet tag for inserting Java applets is an example of this mixed element.
- **Inline Killer:** used only with the BR tag. The BR (line break) tag is a special case, whether in HTML or in the CSS specification, as it "kills" or ends a line.

The Content menu defines whether GoLive should remove what it considers extraneous information in a tag. Set to Normal, GoLive cleans up the tag and its contents (if a container) per standard rules.

- The Get All Spaces option preserves extra white space, which is needed in the Pre (preformatted) tag, primarily.
- Core Text leaves the tag and its contents alone to prevent any changes to the syntax of unusual tags. The Noedit tag, for instance, is set to Core Text to prevent GoLive from even attempting to rewrite its HTML.

The End Tag menu corresponds to whether the tag is a container, which requires both an opening and closing tag. Set to None, GoLive doesn't write an end tag; set to Required, it always does.

The two Optional menu items are a matter of fine distinction. Some tags don't require an end tag, but it's useful to insert one for consistency or for some specific browser support. If the End Tag is set to "Optional (Do Not Write)", it means that the person who defined the tag wanted to note it could have an end tag, even though GoLive doesn't write it. "Optional (Write)" is identical to Required in function; this may also avoid errors in HTML validation. (The Attribute option is left as an exercise for the reader, as it is not explained in documentation or through testing.)

Web Settings Attribute Inspector. This Inspector's Basic tab features three additional items. The Attribute Is menu has three values that fit into two categories. The Required and Optional settings control whether GoLive writes the tag or not, and whether the syntax checker marks an error if a required attribute is missing. The third option, Alternate, allows an attribute to be missing in raw HTML and not tagged as an error, although GoLive writes the attribute if you create the tag through its interface.

Value Type defines the legal contents of an attribute. The options are relatively self-explanatory. If Enumeration is selected, GoLive has a set of finite possible values for an attribute.

Create This Attribute provides a default value for GoLive to use when inserting the attribute, such as a default border of one for tables. We discuss using this item under "Changing GoLive HTML Defaults," later in this chapter.

TIP:
Filling in
Empty
Attributes

Create This Attribute is also useful while creating and editing tags, as it allows you to preview a tag's contents by setting the attribute's value. When you drag and drop the tag into the Source Code palette's sample HTML, the tag is fleshed out with both required attributes and any attributes for which you used Create This Attribute.

However, if you've done this as a test for previewing, remember to uncheck the box before leaving the HTML tab to avoid making this your default.

Output Tab

The Output tab appears only in the Web Settings Element Inspector, and controls how GoLive previews a tag in the HTML Source Editor. The tab displays a greeked preview of the HTML formatting.

The Inside and Outside settings are both active if the tag is defined as requiring an end tag. Inside formats the space between the opening and closing tags; Outside formats the space before and after the set of tags.

Setting Inside and Outside to Small provides the simplest formatting, ensuring that each tag is on a line by itself with minimal space before and after. Setting both (or just Inside for standalone tags) to None runs the tags solid in the HTML without any line breaks.

Checking Indent Content indents the tag's contents. For nested blocks of HTML tags, indentation can help aid legibility if the HTML needs to be viewed in its raw state.

Version Tab

The Version tab reveals the GoLive developers' analysis of which tags, attributes, and enumerations are valid in each browser release and HTML specification.

GoLive uses the settings in the Version tab to allow its HTML syntax checking to interpret correctly whether a given tag, attribute, or enumeration is supported by the browser or browsers against which it is checking. (See Chapter 16, *Source Editing.*)

Version settings don't affect how HTML is written in GoLive, nor do they change preferences or settings in browsers loaded on your machine. These settings do correspond exactly with the list of available browsers and specifications shown in the Preferences dialog box's Browser Sets preference under the Source panel.

Major browsers. The browser releases include three generic releases of Internet Explorer and Netscape Navigator each (2.x, 3.x, and a combination of 4.x and 5.x). These are not platform-specific to Mac, Windows, and Unix, despite some differences in implementation in each browser.

HTML specs. GoLive also includes three HTML specifications: HTML 2.0, 3.2, and 4.0. As these specifications tend to either be recommendations for browser developers or documentation of features implemented in earlier browsers, it's more useful as a reference to know which specification a tag appeared in.

As of this writing, the HTML 4.0 spec has been largely but not entirely implemented in the latest versions of Internet Explorer and Netscape Navigator. The Version tab becomes extremely useful in this case, allowing you to determine whether a tag is supported only by HTML 4.0 and not by any of the most popular browsers. It's also a good way to double-check whether you unintentionally used an HTML 4.0 feature in GoLive, which is easy to do.

TIP:
Moving Target

HTML 4 has been kicking around as a final recommendation for years now, but browser makers have focused on other issues. Most HTML 4 features have found their way into browsers, but there hasn't been a concerted effort—as with Cascading Style Sheets—to release a totally compliant browser.

New browsers and specs. The Version tab only shows major browser and specification releases as of mid-2000. GoLive differentiates between the 4.0 and 4.5 releases of Internet Explorer for the Mac, 5.0 and 5.5 version of Windows IE, or 4.0 and 4.5 or 4.7 versions of Netscape Navigator under Windows and Mac.

TIP:
Importing Browsers

If Adobe releases Web Settings for newer browsers, you should be able to find them on the Adobe site (or linked from our Web site at http://realworldgo-live.com) and import them into your version of the program. As we went to press, GoLive 5 contained root styles for everything but IE 5.5 for Windows (which Adobe seems to lump together with 5.0) and the beta release of Netscape Navigator 6.

Can Have Any Attribute. Checking this box suppresses error messages in the syntax checker if attributes exist for a tag that aren't defined in the HTML tab. This is useful for hand-coded HTML that contains nonstandard attributes necessary for particular Web sites or Web server applications.

Adding HTML Tags

Tired of that old, boring HTML? Want to invent some new, exciting HTML? Now you can! Not that it'll work in any browser, but that hasn't stopped anyone yet. But, you might ask, why would I want to add new HTML items?

You may need to add tags to support local uses, like tags used to control database or Web server functionality (but ignored by browsers). Or, you might be relying on a tag or enumeration that none of the major browsers or releases known to GoLive currently support. Or, you might disagree with the GoLive developers' choices about which names or attributes to assign to tags and want to add others.

Whatever your reasons, GoLive's Web Settings makes adding new HTML characteristics a straightforward process through clicking and selecting items from menus.

Creating New Items

The Web Settings toolbar provides the necessary buttons for inserting new HTML items, and offers contextual choices depending on what you have select-ed. The contextual menu offers the same (appropriately contextual) choices.

Once you add any of the items discussed in this section, the appropriate Web Settings Inspector, including the Web Settings Section Inspector—which we haven't mentioned yet because it's only used to modify section names—allows you to modify any of the settings from the defaults.

New Section. With the HTML tab set to view as Structured, clicking the New Section button creates a new division under which you can organize tags. The Web Settings Section Inspector allows you to name the section and describe it (see Figure 31-8).

Figure 31-8
Adding a new
section

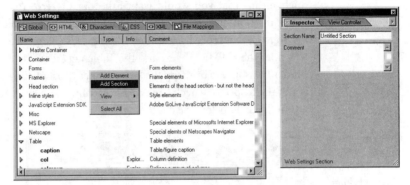

New Element. Clicking the New Element button creates an untitled tag.

New Attribute. With a tag selected, clicking the New Attribute button adds an untitled attribute. You can click this button as many times as you want to create more attributes.

New Enumeration. If you set Value Type in the Web Settings Attribute Inspector to Enumeration, the New Enumeration button activates. Clicking it one or more times creates enumeration entries that correspond to the attribute you selected.

New Character. The New Character button (titled New Enumeration under Windows, but sharing the ampersand (&) symbol) works only when you're working in the Web Settings Characters tab, and defines the ISO codes and other information for new characters (see "Characters Tab" later in this chapter).

Duplicate. The Duplicate button (also the same as selecting Duplicate from the Edit menu) creates an exact copy of any tag, attribute, or enumeration.

Changing GoLive HTML Defaults

As you now understand, GoLive creates HTML tags on pages as objects that are defined in the HTML tab of Web Settings. Changing elements of these objects can change some, but not all, of GoLive's default behavior for inserting new HTML-based items.

Table Border to Zero

As an example, let's look at the Table tag. When you add a table to a page, GoLive automatically gives it a border with a width of one pixel.

However, suppose that you only use tables as structure for your pages, which means that you would want a border of zero. You could manually change the Border field to "0" in the Table Inspector for every new table, but why go to all that repetitive trouble? Instead, let's change Web Settings.

Under the HTML tab, expand the Table tag (see Figure 31-9). Select the "border" attribute to bring up the Web Settings Attribute Inspector. At the bottom of the Inspector, check Create This Attribute and enter "0" (the numeral zero) in the field below the checkbox.

Figure 31-9
Setting default
to zero for
image border

Characters Tab

HTML itself supports only a limited set of characters and punctuation, and therefore has to use a special method to encode characters that aren't part of that set. It does this using entities, or characters given names that are mnemonics for their content. This also frees HTML from relying on the character encoding of a specific platform; no two platforms use the same character code to generate an E with a grave accent over it (è), for example.

A browser interprets the entity and replaces it onscreen with the appropriate character from its local character set. An entity is signaled by an initial ampersand and terminated by a semicolon; for example, "©" is the code for ©, the copyright symbol.

HTML displays all the special characters in the Characters tab. This set of characters includes most everything in the ISO 8859-1 character set, also known as ISOLatin1 to desktop publishers. The ISO standard reflects standard Roman character sets represented by American and European languages.

You can see a list of all entities, ISO 8859-1 and HTML 3.2, at http://www.w3.org/TR/REC-html32.html.

GoLive also includes a few special characters defined as entities as part of the HTML 3.2 specification, like the greater-than sign (>) and less-than sign (<). These are so-called reserved characters; they have a meaning in the syntax of HTML, so if you want to use the actual character, you have to use an entity that represents it.

Organization. GoLive can organize the tab by the character's name (Flat view) or into three categories (Structured view): Basics, Characters, and General Punctuation.

Character details. The Characters tab shows several details about each entity: its name, the character produced, its Mac and ISO 8859-1 character code, and a comment that describes the entity.

Web Settings Entity Inspector. This Inspector includes all the information in the general list and provides the hexadecimal values for the ISO and Mac character codes. It also shows a preview of the character that the entity represents. Making the Inspector larger creates a larger preview (see Figure 31-10).

Figure 31-10
Web Settings
Entity
Inspector

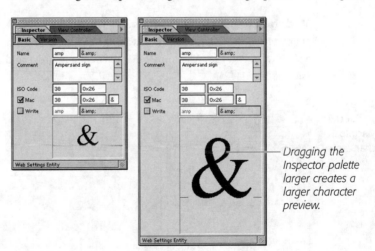

Dragging the Inspector palette larger creates a larger character preview.

Adding Characters

If you're working with non-Western alphabets, you may need to add characters or an entire set into the Characters tab, but it's unlikely you will ever need to add other characters, as new characters need to be supported directly in the browser. Nonetheless, you can easily add new characters to GoLive by selecting New Character (New Enumeration under Windows) from the Web Settings toolbar.

Clicking the New Character button creates an untitled entry. Define the character by providing its entity name, which GoLive assumes is the name that gets inserted inside HTML. If you want to name the character differently from its entity value, enter the name in the Name field, and then check the Write box. Enter the entity value in that field, and the preview appears to its right (see Figure 31-11).

Figure 31-11
Setting the entity's name separately from its HTML value

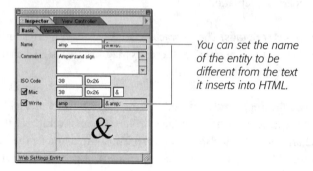

You can set the name of the entity to be different from the text it inserts into HTML.

Macintosh display. Both Windows and Mac versions of GoLive show the ISO character code for most entities, so the Macintosh version of GoLive must also have an entry for Macintosh character code in order to display it correctly (see Figure 31-12).

Figure 31-12
Special Macintosh characters

Adding sections. If you add new kinds of characters, you might also want to create new sections under which to organize them. Click the New Section button on the Web Settings toolbar, then use the Web Settings Section Inspector to name it and add a comment describing it.

Tweakery. GoLive uses an XML-structured document to store all its entity information. If you wanted, you could add characters directly through this document, called "entities.dctd" and found in GoLive's application folder under Modules, Web Settings, HTML. However, given that GoLive reads and writes to this document to generate the contents of the Characters tab and to insert entities into HTML, we'd recommend against tweaking the file, unless you're truly insane (or just very determined).

CSS Tab

Contrary to what you might expect, this tab doesn't allow you to define or change CSS properties, like font size. Instead, the CSS tab has two distinct purposes: to enable the Layout Preview to simulate a variety of appearances based on the built-in CSS styles in major browsers, and to set program-wide preferences related to CSS styles.

Browser Preview Settings

The CSS tab provides insight into the way GoLive creates previews of pages in different browsers on different platforms through the Layout Preview's Layout View Controller. On the right of the tab, GoLive lists, by browser/platform pairs, the sets of assumptions that GoLive's designers have encoded about the default CSS browser style sheets for several major browser releases. Consult Chapter 29, *Cascading Style Sheets*, for more information about defining, applying, and previewing CSS styles.

GoLive has 11 sets of built-in CSS browser style sheets:

- Adobe GoLive: the standard GoLive preview

- Internet Explorer 3, 4, and 5 for Windows and Mac (six sets)

- Navigator 3 and 4 for Windows and Mac (four sets)

TIP:
Windows Preview

Because the Windows version of GoLive uses Internet Explorer to provide the Layout Preview, the difference between selecting Adobe GoLive and Explorer 5 from the Root CSS menu of the Layout View Controller is nonexistent, even if you're using a newer version of IE.

NEW IN 5:
The Fat Lady Sang

GoLive 4 features a CSS browser set for Opera, a commercial browser seen as a full-featured and compact (small download, small memory footprint) alternative to Internet Explorer and Netscape Navigator. This support was dropped in GoLive 5, possibly due to the small installed base of Opera. A site Glenn runs had 77 visits from an Opera browser out of 70,000 total visits. For more information about Opera, see http://www.operasoftware.com.

These browser-based style sheets correspond to items in the View Controller's Root CSS popup menu when you view HTML pages in Layout Preview (see Figure 31-13).

You can change the default for what the Layout View Controller shows as its Root CSS style sheet by selecting the Root radio button next to your preferred browser (see Figure 31-14). Adobe GoLive is the default Root setting.

Figure 31-13
Root CSS
menu in View
Controller

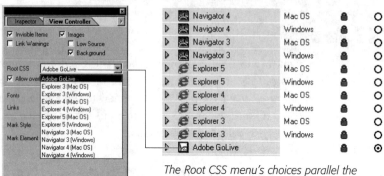

The Root CSS menu's choices parallel the entries in the CSS tab.

Figure 31-14
Setting default
root browser
set

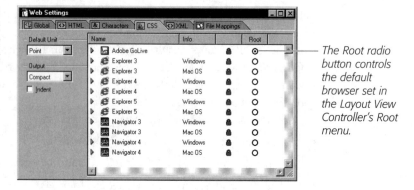

The Root radio button controls the default browser set in the Layout View Controller's Root menu.

Settings

Selecting any browser set brings up the Root Style Sheet Inspector. For built-in styles, you can view, but not edit, settings. The Lock icon provides a visual reminder for these sets; new sets you create have a pencil next to them, showing they're "writable."

Basic tab. The Basic tab displays a browser set's name, operating system, and any comments. These items are all for reference and do not have any bearing on how GoLive creates a preview.

Settings tab. Each browser and platform includes a built-in idea of what the screen density or pixels per inch are. It uses this information to create appropriate sizes of text; we discuss this in depth under "Units" in Chapter 29, *Cascading Style Sheets*. Windows monitors are typically set to 96 dpi, while Mac monitors are set to 72 dpi.

Gamma controls the relative darkness curve, which is dependent on the platform you're on. Windows generally displays images with a higher gamma, which makes darker colors even darkers than on the Macintosh. (See Chapter 9, *Images*, for more about gamma.) The Can Handle Stylesheets checkbox toggles between whether a browser supports style sheets or not. Can Handle Images is checked for all default browsers; a browser like the Unix "lynx" would be an example of one which can't, as it is a terminal-based, text-only browser.

The six checkboxes labeled Does Create Virtual Body Element, Can Handle Inline Border, Inline Applies Inline Properties to Block, Inline Applies Block Properties to Block, Block Applies Inline Properties to Table, Body Applies Inline Properties to Table describe pretty accurately the level and consistency of CSS support for various properties taken as a whole.

Source tab. The Source tab lists all the styles and their properties as they would be inserted into the Head part of an HTML page. This list cannot be edited directly.

TIP:
Controlling Source Preview

The CSS tab's formatting settings control how the preview in the Source tab is formatted.

Adding New Sets

GoLive offers the flexibility to create new sets as new browsers and browser versions become available.

To create a new browser set, select any existing browser set and click the Duplicate button in the Web Settings toolbar or choose it from the contextual menu. You can't create a new, empty set, but must duplicate an existing one.

After duplicating a set, use the CSS Style Sheet Inspector to manipulate any of the set-related preferences. To edit individual tags in the set, expand the set's view and select any tag. The familiar CSS Selector Inspector appears, and all the standard options explained in Chapter 29, *Cascading Style Sheets*, are available.

If you need to add new tags, click the New Element Selector button in the toolbar. To delete tags, select the tag and press the Delete key, or choose Clear from the Edit menu.

TIP:
Locked Sets

GoLive has write-protected—hence the lock symbol—these built-in style sheets to prevent changes to core browser previews. However, you can duplicate them and create your own.

If you feel an inherent need to tinker, you can edit the XML-based definitions for this part of Web Settings. To do so, head to the Modules folder in the application folder. Look inside the Web Settings folder for the Browser folder; inside that is the Default folder. Each CSS set for each browser has its own XML file here. User sets are stored in the User folder at the same level as the Default folder.

CSS Settings

Preferences for each different kind of content are found in an area relating to that content. The CSS tab includes several settings that control how CSS styles are used and written in any subsequently created or previewed page.

Default Unit. When defining or modifying styles in the CSS Selector Inspector, the Default Unit setting controls which default unit to display in the popup menu by default for any CSS property that uses a unit-based measurement.

Output. The Output menu in the CSS tab controls both the Source Sample preview and all HTML output of CSS definitions (see Figure 31-15). As with all HTML, white space is optional in most cases.

The first two Output options, Compressed and Compact, are two variations on tight packing. Compressed removes all extraneous spaces; Compact leaves a few in to keep it legible.

Pretty 1, Pretty 2, and Pretty 3 are variations on vertical spacing, indents, and whether the closing bracket appears on a line by itself. Nice is yet another variation on this theme that uses a little less vertical space.

If you uncheck the Indent box, all indents for the Output menu style are measured from a flush left start.

Figure 31-15
CSS formatting
in HTML

Compressed

```
.newclass{color:olive;font-weight:bold;font-size:11px;font-
family:Arial,Geneva;text-align:center}
```

Compact

```
.newclass { color: olive; font-weight: bold; font-size: 11px;
font-family: Arial, Geneva; text-align: center }
```

Pretty 1 & 2 (vertical space varies)

```
.newclass {
   color: olive;
   font-weight: bold;
   font-size: 11px;
   font-family: Arial, Geneva;
   text-align: center }
```

Pretty 3

```
.newclass {
   color: olive;
   font-weight: bold;
   font-size: 11px;
   font-family: Arial, Geneva;
   text-align: center
   }
```

Nice

```
.newclass {
   color:        olive;
   font-weight: bold;
   font-size:    11px;
   font-family: Arial, Geneva;
   text-align:   center }
```

File Mappings

File Mappings control which applications open which files. This tool is useful throughout the program when you need to open a file for editing, especially in the Files tab. In GoLive 4, File Mappings controls were embedded deeply in Preferences; in GoLive 5, they're more accessible.

However, because of the utility of File Mappings, we've discussed this tab fully earlier in the book, in Chapter 18, *Page Specials*.

Other Tabs

You might notice an XML or WebObjects tab in Web Settings. These tabs appear by turning Modules on and off; we discuss these extra tags and their corresponding Modules in Chapter 32, *Languages and Scripting*.

Give It a Try

By giving users access to some of the "guts" of the application, GoLive opens the door to creative and useful customization unavailable in any other programs. Of course, freedom brings responsibility, as abusing Web Settings can backfire on you and cause GoLive to create bad HTML without you necessarily realizing it. But don't be afraid to get under the hood and tinker; you can always revert to factory settings even after disassembling the machine.

CHAPTER 32

Languages and Scripting

Web development these days isn't just about writing fancy (yet clean and nimble) HTML code. Your viewers now expect rich, interactive pages and personalization features. Now that the Internet can be viewed using an ever wider assortment of devices, it's important for Web publishers to be multi-lingual in order to write code that can be understood and rendered correctly by desktop PCs, PDAs, and cell phones.

You can add interactivity using Java applets (which are cross-platform) and ActiveX controls (a Microsoft technology that, oddly enough, can be read primarily on Windows browsers). GoLive also offers significant support for embedding and working with three other kinds of advanced Web features: XML, a content-encoding standard; WebObjects, a powerful tool for running applications on Web sites; and ASP, Microsoft's solution for putting scripts into Web pages.

Java Applets and Objects

Before getting into the nitty gritty of GoLive's tools for configuring Java and W3CObjects (as the GoLive manual refers to them), let's identify what these distinct technologies represent:

- The Java programming language was developed by Sun Microsystems to be platform independent. Small Java "applets" (which provide a range of functions from groovy animation to database mining) can run on any compatible browser across most platforms. When hooking a Java applet into a GoLive page, look for a file with a .class extension (which compiles Java's bytecode).

- Objects, or W3CObject controls, refer to executable, object-oriented "controls" such as Microsoft's ActiveX. Unlike Java, these items must be developed and compiled for a specific platform; so far, that's mostly Windows. An out-growth of Microsoft's Object Linking and Embedding (OLE) technologies, ActiveX controls can be inserted into Web pages to offer new features. The "critical upgrades" function in Windows 98 that scans your local hard drive and downloads appropriate Windows patches is an example. The main difference from Java is that ActiveX controls can also interact with a wide range of programming languages and applications (including, of course, those created by Microsoft).

GoLive, for the most part, treats these two media objects much like it does plug-ins and images. Simply drag either the Java Applet or Object icon from the Objects palette into the Layout Editor, and the appropriate Inspector is called up. The Basic tabs of the two Inspectors are similar, but with a few important differences at least on the Mac side (outlined below); the Windows version of the Object Inspector adds buttons to the bottom of the Basic tab that let you create and configure a control (se e Figure 32-1).

Figure 32-1
Basic tab of Java Applet and Object Inspectors

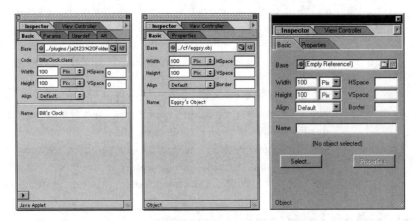

- In the Base field, type or navigate to the location of the applet or object. In GoLive for Windows, click the Select button to bring up the Insert Object dialog box, from which you can add or create an object or ActiveX control (detailed in the "Object Inspector Specifics" section, later in this chapter).

- Type values in the Width and Height fields; you can also choose between a fixed pixel or percentage measurement using the popup menus.

- In the HSpace and VSpace fields, you can add blank space (in pixels) surrounding the object; in the Object Inspector, you can also add a border.

- The Align popup menu offers you the usual attributes for placing your object.

- Type a unique identifier in the Name field.

You can further modify these objects and applets by adding attributes via the Properties tab of the Object Inspector and the Params tab of the Java Applet Inspector. Click the New button, then enter the attribute in the Property (Object) or Name (Java) field and its value in the Value field. Be sure to click New when you add an attribute to avoid typing over the attribute you just set (see Figure 32-2).

Figure 32-2
Params tab of
Java Applet
and Object
Inspectors

Java Applet Inspector Specifics

In the Alt Text field of the Alt tab, you can add a plain text message that displays when a user disables the browser's Java functionality and then loads the page.

To format a rich HTML message containing formatting or images, check Show Alternative HTML. A text box appears within the Java Applet placeholder. Like Alt Text, it displays when Java is turned off or is not supported by the user's browser; however, you can use HTML code to format the message's appearance.

Click within the box and type or paste your code, or drag tag icons from the Objects palette. If you supply a notation in the Alt Text field and a rich HTML message, they both appear in a browser that's not showing Java.

TIP:
**Press to
Play (Mac)**

You can preview a Java applet within the Layout Editor by selecting the placeholder item, and then clicking the play button that appears in the bottom-left corner of the Java Applet Inspector tabs.

TIP:
Java Display Bug

If you switch to another editor within the GoLive document window, then return to the Layout Editor, the Java Applet placeholder returns to its normal icon. Check the Show Alternative HTML again to display the work you've already done, then add more if needed (see Figure 32-3).

Figure 32-3
Displaying alternative HTML for Java

Normal Java Applet tag icon    *Java Applet tag icon with Show Alternative HTML checked*

TIP:
Userdef Java files (Mac only)

If you created a Java applet using a definition file, click the Userdef tab to display its operators. The Userdef tab does not appear in GoLive 5 for Windows.

Object Inspector Specifics

On the Mac, you can only specify the location of an object using the Base field on the Object Inspector's Basic tab. However, the Windows version of GoLive offers a more direct route—due largely to the fact that ActiveX is first and foremost a Windows standard—via the Select button at the bottom of the Basic tab. In fact, you must use this route to add ActiveX controls and objects.

Clicking the Select button or double-clicking the Object placeholder icon brings up the Insert Object dialog box, which gives you three options: Create Control, Create from File, and Create New (see Figure 32-4). If you want to

Figure 32-4
Windows Insert Object dialog box

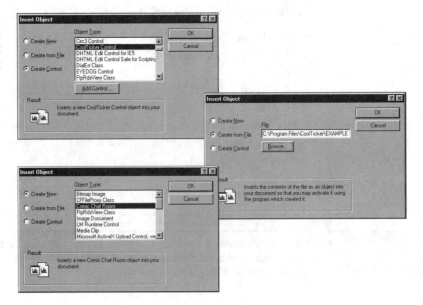

add an ActiveX control, choose Create Control, scroll through the list of controls available on your system, and choose an appropriate control type. Choosing Create New allows you to begin from scratch, while choosing Create from File loads an object into your page.

After adding a control or object, you can configure it by adding attributes on the Properties tab. Some ActiveX controls also allow you to open a Properties dialog box associated directly with the control; the Properties button on the Basic tab becomes active if this is the case (see Figure 32-5).

Figure 32-5
Configuring
ActiveX control
properties

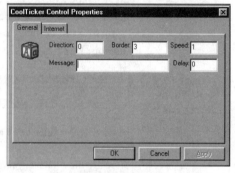

If the Properties button doesn't become active, you can configure attributes on the Properties tab.

ASP Support

Active Server Pages (ASPs) have programming code embedded in an HTML page. When a user requests a page, the server looks through the page on the local hard drive, finds ASP code (if any), and executes it. The server might take any kind of action as a result of ASP code, including just feeding out the HTML part of the page, modifying parts of the HTML (like dropping in custom information), setting a cookie on the user's browser, or redirecting the user to another page on the site or the Web. This makes it easy for a Webmaster or site developer to put programs and pages in the same file, rather than requiring lots of server configuration or perl scripts.

TIP:
Microsoft Among Others

The ASP scripting language and technology was developed by Microsoft for use with their Web server, Internet Information Server (IIS); it can be added on to other platforms and servers via products like Chili!Soft ASP (www.chilisoft.com).

GoLive takes a hands-off approach to all this ASP business. You can read ASP code and write it back to a file, as well as work with any number of other codes and proprietary languages (JScript, VBScript, Visual Basic, etc.) that are used in Web pages. You just can't do it visually with fancy icons and helpful Inspectors.

If you open a file with ASP code in it, GoLive uses a placeholder icon to indicate where the code exists and the Special Item Inspector (formerly the Foreign Item Inspector) allows you to edit it (see Figure 32-6) You can also edit ASP code directly in the HTML Source Editor, Source Code palette, or HTML Outline Editor (see Figure 32-7).

By the way, GoLive doesn't preview or execute ASP code; you have to upload your files to a server that supports ASP to test it directly.

Figure 32-6
ASP in the
Layout Editor

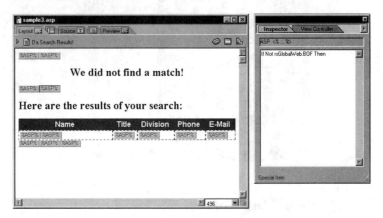

Figure 32-7
ASP in the
Outline Editor

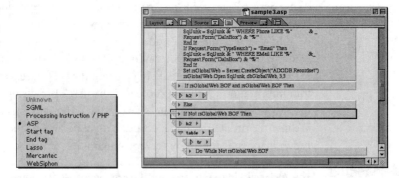

XML

XML (or eXtensible Markup Language) is the greatest thing since spatially divided grain-based baked food products—or so its proponents maintain. Based on SGML (Standard Generalized Markup Language), XML is a human-readable, machine-understandable, general syntax for describing hierarchical data that lets users define and tag discrete categories of information using simple text labels.

Huh?

In other words, XML is customizable (i.e., "extensible") code that looks and reads like you do, but there's no implication built into the format that describes how the data should look (as in HTML). Instead, it just describes what the data consists of. For instance, <H3> in HTML always means a heading level 3, and virtually all browsers interpret it as such—it has a fixed meaning that defines both the content and its display (bold and a font size of about 14 points). Whereas, in XML, you might define a headline in some fashion, like <BOOKTITLE>, but that definition wouldn't inherently describe its output, just that the enclosed information was, in this case, a book's title. (It could also be the name of a type of flower, because the tag's name is entirely arbitrary; but it's not likely.)

Instead of relying on (and conforming to) the fixed code of HTML from which each browser or other interpreting software has to decipher what P and A Href mean, you could create your own XML language (or "vocabulary") that describes the data that's being presented (rather than telling the browser how to present it). Thus, a file might start:

```
<booktitle>Real World Scanning and Halftones</booktitle>
<price currency="us">29.95</price>
<pagecount>464</pagecount>
```

The idea is that a database can write this kind of output using agreed-upon names for items. Any kind of information could be structured using tags, and any kind of display program (a browser or word processor) or interpreter (like a database or a price-comparison engine or whatever) would be able to process or display information in a document using definitions identical to those in the program that created the document.

This function allows many different programs (from standard Web browsers to mobile phone microbrowsers) to access the same data without using proprietary formats, making it easier to exchange rich information across systems and to reuse the same information in many different places without rewriting it for each purpose.

It also means that more advanced browsers or other systems could read HTML files and use embedded XML tags that describe the actual data in those files to provide better kinds of information, or a wider variety of displays. For instance, all bookstores could use a shared vocabulary for describing book content like price, name, authors, and so on. A price-comparison engine could be built into a browser that would extract this information without a lot of tedious pattern recognition—it would just see <PRICE> and go from there.

To create your own XML language, you would create a Document Type Definition (DTD), which defines the elements, structure, and behavior for this vocabulary. (In fact, HTML is redefined as XML in the form of a DTD.)

TIP:
More XML
Information

We really can't teach you XML in a few pages, but we can point you in the right directions for learning more about it. The World Wide Web Consortium (W3C) offers extensive documentation, examples, and other information at its Web site at http://www.w3.org/. A great starting point for learning about XML is http://www.w3.org/XML/1999/XML-in-10-points.

XML in GoLive

So how does XML work with GoLive? Well, though it doesn't exactly support XML, GoLive does allow it to be used without a hassle.

In Web Settings, click the XML tab to view available XML tags and definitions. The structure of Inspectors associated with this tab is similar to the HTML and Characters tabs. Click a DTD group file (with a .dtd extension) to reveal the XML DTD Inspector; click the directory triangle to open up a list of elements. Select a bold element to view the XML DTD Element Inspector, then go one more level down, select an attribute and view the XML DTD Attribute Inspector (see Figure 32-8).

Figure 32-8
XML Tab's file
structure

XML tab of Web Database

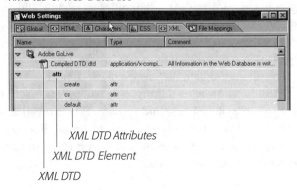

XML DTD Attributes

XML DTD Element

XML DTD

Click the Compiled DTD.dtd file icon in Web Settings to learn an interesting little fact about GoLive and XML: GoLive's underlying code database—parameters for HTML, XML, CSS—is written in XML (see Figure 32-9). Very clever, Mr. Bond!

Figure 32-9
XML DTD
Inspector

The Web Settings toolbar is inactive while in the XML tab; you must use contextual menus instead. You can't make an addition to one of the three GoLive XML DTDs, although you can Clear or Delete an item. But you can bring in your own DTD by choosing Import DTD. GoLive automatically deposits this text-formatted file in a folder titled Imported within the XML folder. This folder doesn't appear in Web Settings.

Condensation

TIP: You can't import a .cdtd file—only .dtd files; when a DTD is imported, GoLive creates a condensed companion .cdtd file directly from the source DTD.

XML DTD Inspector

In the XML tab of Web Settings, select one of the DTD files; this causes the XML DTD Inspector to display general information about this vocabulary file (see Figure 32-9, above). The Name field displays the file's title, but is uneditable.

Type a brief description of this DTD file in the Description field. If you're configuring an imported DTD file, the MIME Type, Extensions, and Kind fields are blank. (When viewing a default GoLive DTD, these fields are filled in and MIME Type is inactive.) To give your DTD file a proper MIME Type, enter "application/x-compiled-dtd" in the field.

XML DTD Element Inspector

Much like the Web Settings Element Inspector, the XML DTD Element Inspector displays the name of the XML element and allows you to type a brief note in the Comment/Description field.

However, that's about it for the Basic tab. Is Document Root is unchecked; it is only checked for the element that previously has been selected as the root (marked as Master in the Type column of the Web Settings XML tab). In the case of GoLive's Compiled DTD.dtd file, the Compiled element is selected as the root. For DTD files that have been imported, this option is checked and inactive if an element has been selected as the root. However, you can check this option on another element, and checking it switches the root to that item.

Click the Output tab to configure how the tag displays within the XML code; this tab functions just like the Web Settings Element Inspector's Output tab (see Figure 32-10).

Figure 32-10
XML DTD
Element
Inspector

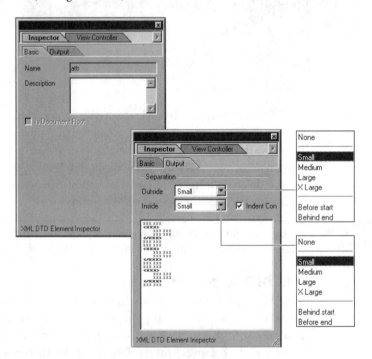

XML DTD Attribute Inspector

Toggle a triangle to the left of an XML element to reveal its list of attributes; the Inspector then switches to become the XML DTD Attribute Inspector. Again, you find the Name field inactive and a Comment/Description box ready for a brief description (if not already supplied). The Attribute Is and Value Type popup menus are inactive and don't seem to become active for editing. And while the Default field is active for you to type in, its popup button menu only brings up options for a few attributes (see Figure 32-11).

Figure 32-11
XML DTD
Attribute
Inspector

XML Item and Foreign Item Inspectors

If you want to see what an XML file looks like, double-click a DTD file outside of GoLive. If you open a file with a .dtd extension (for instance, Compiled DTD.dtd), you see a gaggle of foreign item tag icons. Select one of the tags to bring up the Special Item Inspector (see Figure 32-12).

Figure 32-12
Viewing
DTD file

However, if you open a file with either an .xml or .cdtd extension (such as the Compiled DTD.cdtd), the Layout Editor view becomes structured much like the Outline Editor (see Figure 32-13). Selecting an item brings up the XML Item Inspector, from which you can assign a name to the element, edit attributes and values, and add or delete attribute/value pairings from the list. The Settings tab, however, only reminds you that because this tag was not marked as plain text, it can't be edited (see Figure 32-14).

Figure 32-13
Viewing
XML file

Figure 32-14
XML Item
Inspector

If editing in the Outline Editor, use items from the Special menu to add new elements and attributes, or click the New Element button from the Web Settings Toolbar (see Figure 32-15).

Figure 32-15
Viewing XML
in Outline
Editor

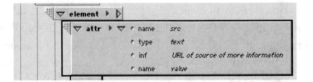

WebObjects

The GoLive printed manual doesn't mention WebObjects at all, and online help tells you to consult the documentation that comes with WebObjects itself. We intend to follow suit—no offense to any of you WebObjects users, which is an elite (read: fairly small but truly devoted) group. WebObjects is a system that integrates database information and the World Wide Web fairly efficiently and seamlessly, allowing ordinary users to manipulate and retrieve information between a database and a Web server handling user transactions without a lot of messy coding. This system was developed by NeXT Computer, later acquired by Apple Computer. (For a great example of a site built and maintained with WebObjects, visit the Apple Store at http://store.apple.com.)

GoLive offers tight integration of WebObjects controllers and its Layout Editor. If you turn on WebObjects in the Modules pane of the Preferences dialog box—and we only recommend you do if you actually use a WebObjects server—GoLive adds an additional tab to the Web Settings dialog, the Document window, and the Objects palette (see Figure 32-16).

If you're a WebObjects user, all these controls and options make great sense, and you're probably ecstatic to see them. For the rest of us, it's important to just leave the WebObjects Module turned off to keep memory usage low.

¿Habla Usted Java…ActiveX…XML? ¡Sí!

As Web publishing continues to mature and become more robust, we need to continue to push the envelope with XML and object-oriented programming languages such as Java and ActiveX. While it's still necessary to create applets and controls using other resources, GoLive 5 continues to make it easy to quickly add these objects to your pages as well as write XML.

Figure 32-16
Various and
sundry
WebObject
items

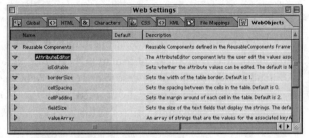

Web Settings WebObjects tab

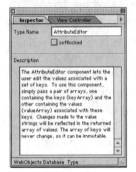

WebObjects Database
Type Inspector

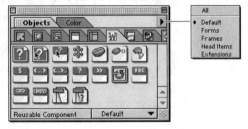

WebObjects tab in Objects Palette tab

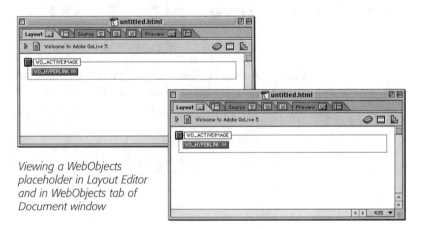

Viewing a WebObjects
placeholder in Layout Editor
and in WebObjects tab of
Document window

Appendixes & Index

APPENDIX A

Macintosh Issues & Extras

Even though GoLive appeared first on the Macintosh (as versions of GoLive CyberStudio, the product's previous name), Adobe has done a fairly seamless job of making sure the Macintosh and Windows versions of the product are in parity. GoLive 5 brought a lot of dangling feature differences into sync across platforms, making it hard to tell which machine you're on without examining the scrollbars or other minor interface elements.

TIP:
Site File Compatibility

Starting with GoLive 5, the Macintosh and Windows site files are entirely compatible, which means you can exchange them across platforms and open them on either without requiring any conversion. You can share sites on a networked drive that both Macs and PCs can access, and use just a single site file to manage the site.

Most of the Macintosh-only features in GoLive relate to operating system details, not functionality in the program itself. That is, GoLive taps into some items that the Mac OS has built into it or that you extend the Mac OS to support, rather than GoLive for Macintosh having some kind of site-mapping view not found on Windows.

- **File details.** The Mac stores extra information with each file, such as the program that created it and a label in the Finder (on the Desktop) that GoLive maps to a Windows-compatible setting.

- **Mac OS 8.5 and later specials.** With Mac OS 8.5, Apple introduced a couple extras that programs could take advantage of: an extended file selection dialog box for opening and saving files, and a method of changing the appearance of all interface elements to be consistent throughout all applications. (Don't worry; you can turn these features off if you don't like them.)

- **Mac OS 9 and later specials.** Mac OS 9 introduced (or rather, reintroduced) the Keychain for storing passwords securely on your computer.

- **Mac OS X and later.** Mac OS X was shipping in a public beta when we put this book to press. Check our Web site for updates.

- **Search engine simulation.** GoLive taps into Apple's built-in search-engine technology in its Find by Content Module to provide a simulation of what an Internet search engine might come up with when indexing your pages.

- **ColorSync.** Apple offers a system-level color management system called ColorSync that, ideally, lets you scan, edit, view, and output images in a variety of programs, on a variety of machines, with some semblance of color consistency and tonality.

- **Internet control panel.** The Macintosh version of GoLive can leverage a set of common Internet settings (formerly called Internet Config) modified and stored in the Internet control panel in Mac OS 9 and later. This includes file mappings for files opened via GoLive or downloaded via FTP, and preferences for configuring proxy servers.

- **AppleScript.** The Mac OS has a built-in scripting language that lets you control a lot of the functions of the Finder and various AppleScript-savvy programs. GoLive supports AppleScript in its HTML Source Editor view; you can use AppleScript to automate certain tasks.

File Features

GoLive inserts Macintosh-specific differences in a few of the Inspector palettes used to examine files.

Finder Label

The Finder label can be set up on the Macintosh Desktop. From the Edit menu, select the Labels tab of the Preferences dialog box (see Figure A-1).

You have seven possible labels preset to some generic names like "Essential" and "Project 1", which can be renamed to something meaningful to you. The color may also be changed by clicking the color swatch next to the name. The order in which the items appear in the Labels tab affects the sorting order in the Finder when you sort the view by Label.

Labels may be assigned in the Finder by selecting one or more items and selecting a label from the Label item in the popup contextual menu (see Figure A-2).

Figure A-1
Setting Label
color and text

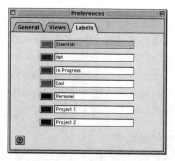

Figure A-2
Label
contextual
menu

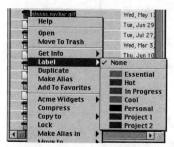

In GoLive 4, the Finder Label was available in three places to set or view items by those labels. This was out of sync with the Windows version, which didn't sport a Label setting. Both Mac and Windows versions of GoLive did support a Status label, which seemed redundant on the Macintosh.

GoLive 5 got this back into shape by using the Status label exclusively. On the Macintosh, Status includes all the choices of the Label colors and names. Under Windows, the standard set of Macintosh labels is available; you can also define new ones on a site-by-site basis.

Type and Creator

When you create or import HTML files from many sources, you can wind up with funky icons on the Macintosh Desktop and in the Site window's Files tab. Worse, double-clicking the file opens it in Microsoft Word, BBEdit, or SimpleText. GoLive provides a simple way to fix this problem.

The Macintosh stores two pieces of information with every file: its creator and its type. The creator and type are four-character codes that correspond to the program which created the file and the type of file it is. Each application on the Macintosh has a unique creator code so that every file knows exactly to which program it belongs. Each application can define any number of its own types so that the application knows what kind of file it's looking at—TIFF, GIF, JPEG for an image-editing program, etc.

Select a file in the Files tab in the Site window and bring up the File Inspector's File tab. The two fields labeled Type and Creator correspond to the Finder's type and creator. To change an HTML file so that it thinks it was created by GoLive, make sure Type is set to "TEXT" and creator is set to "GoMk" (case is important). As soon as you press Return or switch to another field, the icon in the Files tab changes immediately to the GoLive icon (see Figure A-3).

Figure A-3
Changing Creator code to fix program association

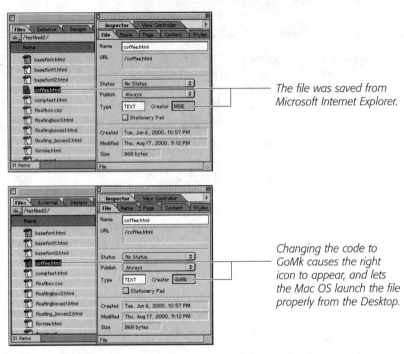

The file was saved from Microsoft Internet Explorer.

Changing the code to GoMk causes the right icon to appear, and lets the Mac OS launch the file properly from the Desktop.

TIP:
Creator Type Batch Utility

CTC (change-creator-type) is a freeware program that lets you batch process a set of files to change their creator or type to something else. You can download it from http://www.imagemontage.com/Docs/CTC.html

Mac OS 8.5 and Later Specials

Apple added two significant user-interface changes in Mac OS 8.5 and subsequent systems that (supposedly) improve a user's ability to find files and to change the appearance of the system. We're not the biggest fans of either, as the former chews more processing power while delivering less performance, and the latter doesn't always result in a consistent appearance.

GoLive controls both of these 8.5 additions in the Preferences dialog box under the General pane in the User Interface settings. The two top boxes on the Mac are Appearance Theme Savvy and Use Navigation Services.

Appearance Theme Savvy

In the Appearance control panel, Apple lets you choose a "theme" that affects the color and kind of windows, icons, and other doodads that the Desktop and standard applications use (see Figure A-4). The trick is that the applications have to be "appearance aware": that is, they have to know how to read and use the settings.

Figure A-4
Appearance
control panel

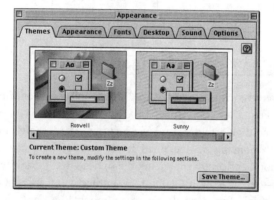

If you uncheck Appearance Themes Savvy, GoLive uses default settings for all its interface elements. If you check it, it picks up the settings in the Appearance control panel.

Use Navigation Services

Navigation Services was introduced by Apple to improve how users navigate through their hard drives and other resources when trying to open and save files, and select destination folders. Unfortunately, the current incarnation seems more confusing, and it's certainly more time-consuming. For some reason, the feature takes a substantial amount of time to bring up the dialog box (not just in GoLive).

With Use Navigation Services checked, the dialog box has been enhanced with extra popup menus: Shortcuts, Favorites, and Recent (see Figure A-5). Shortcuts points to all the currently mounted drives and removable cartridges and disks (like CD-ROMs and Jaz disks), and lets you connect to network resources. Favorites contains a list of all the files you've designated as Favorites; you can add and remove files from the Favorites menu itself. Recent shows folders and files accessed most recently, segregated into folders at the top, files at the bottom.

Figure A-5
Navigation
Services

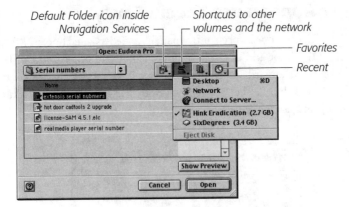

Default Folder icon inside
Navigation Services —

Shortcuts to other
— volumes and the network

Favorites

Recent

We recommend unchecking Use Navigation Services and, instead, installing Default Folder, available from St. Clair Software at http://www.stclairsoft.com/DefaultFolder/index.html (see Figure A-6). It's shareware, and we think it's worth ponying up the small fee to register it. It can also work with Navigation Services by enhancing the options and flexibility of the built-in features—see its icon in Figure A-5—but we prefer using it on its own. (In fact, we think Apple should just have bought the rights and used Default Folder instead of Navigation Services.)

Figure A-6
Default Folder

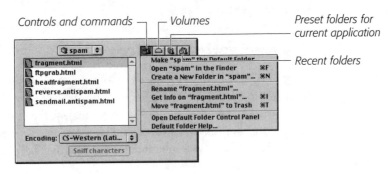

Controls and commands — — Volumes

Preset folders for
— current application

Recent folders

Mac OS 9.0 and Later Specials

In GoLive 5, Adobe nicely added support for Mac OS 9's Keychain feature. The Keychain allows you to store commonly used passwords in a single managed interface that is only accessible after you type in a passphrase to unlock it (see Figure A-7). The Keychain is handy; instead of storing passwords in lots of insecure locations that someone could, potentially, snag from your machine, passwords are stored centrally in an encrypted format and only accessed as needed by programs.

Figure A-7
Keychain
access

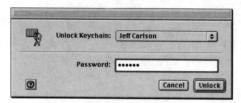

You can use the Keychain quite simply. In the Preferences dialog's Network pane, make sure Use System Keychain for Passwords is checked. You can choose to automatically add passwords to the Keychain by unchecking the Ask Before Adding Passwords box below the main preference.

To modify passwords stored in the Keychain, select the Keychain Access control panel. GoLive passwords appear with a GoLive icon next to them, but Apple lists them just as "Internet passwords" under the Kind column. You can also delete and edit passwords here.

Find by Content

GoLive uses built-in Apple technology to create a simulation of Internet search engine indexing and matching, like that done by AltaVista or Google. The Find by Content Module for the Macintosh contains the necessary bits and pieces; it is not loaded by default. (See Chapter 4, *Preferences and Customizing*, for details on loading Modules.)

This simulation doesn't claim to match how search engines really perform indexes and searches, but it certainly gives you a little insight into how your pages are structured and what words you're using. It's a good tool for making some decisions about what's important to have on a page.

If you have the Find by Content Module loaded and have a Site window as the frontmost window, bringing up the Find dialog box reveals an extra tab: Search in Site Index. Select this tab, and click Build Index to create a word-based index of all of the HTML files on the site. You can click Update Index if you've built it previously and don't have Auto Update checked; if you check Auto Update, the index gets newly updated every time you save.

Searching is straightforward: enter some keywords and click Search (see Figure A-8). Select an Encoding if you have text in a language other than that selected in the popup menu. If multiple sites are open at once, you can select them from the Site menu; closing a Site window removes it from the menu.

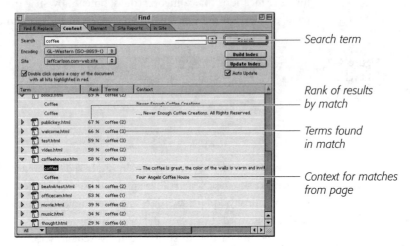

Search term

Rank of results
by match

Terms found
in match

Context for matches
from page

Checking the Double Click Opens… box provides some visual feedback by highlighting any matched words in red in a new document window if you double click a match (see Figure A-9). (It's titled "Matches in…" followed by the HTML file name so that the formatting can overwrite the file's content without making that change in the source file itself.)

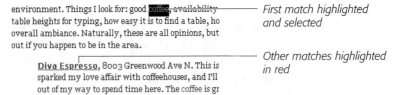

First match highlighted
and selected

Other matches highlighted
in red

The results in the Search in Site Index tab are scored by an algorithm that assigns percentages to how close the file is to containing the keywords in the form they appear. There must be other, undocumented factors at work, since two files containing the same words get scored differently, perhaps based on the proximity of the words and their frequency. (This mystery is fine, because it parallels the mystery of how Internet search engines rank results.)

Clicking the triangle (Mac) or plus sign (Windows) next to a file match displays all the occurrences of search words in that document, including a few words of context.

Please note that the Find by Content module doesn't add site searching to your Web site; it only works locally inside GoLive as a simulation. To add Web site searches, you have to install special software like Excite for Web Servers (EWS) that scans files' contents and creates a searchable index on the Web server itself.

ColorSync

ColorSync, as noted above, tries to provide consistent color across machines, programs, devices (scanners, monitors, and printers), and platforms. It eliminates the variables and differences between systems and devices so that you're looking at the closest approximation to a standard image as possible.

Because Apple has announced its intention to extend ColorSync onto Windows, and because Microsoft built ColorSync support into the Macintosh version of Internet Explorer starting way back in version 4.5, we've opted to write about ColorSync in Chapter 9, *Images*. We believe that in future updates of GoLive and Windows, ColorSync will be either an integral part or a simple add-on, but we aren't exactly holding our breath. In either case, we aren't gung-ho about its use on the Web yet. But see Chapter 9 for more on this subject, including updating and installing ColorSync in GoLive for Macintosh.

Internet Control Panel

The Internet control panel began its life as Internet Config, a helpful Internet settings utility written and given away by Peter N. Lewis and Quinn "the Eskimo" to the Internet community. Their goal was to standardize the location and nature of Internet preferences—for email addresses, mail servers, etc.—and file mappings.

It worked; most programs adopted its settings, then Apple took over the public domain software lock, stock, and barrel by turning it into the Internet control panel. Many thanks are owed to Peter and Quinn for their selfless act that actually made things better.

TIP:
Old Systems

If you're using GoLive on Mac OS 8.6, you can download Internet Config as a standalone utility from a variety of sources, including the "official" home page, which hasn't been updated since 1998, the last time Peter and Quinn were working on the project.: http://www.stairways.com/ic/. Everything noted here applies to the older version except where some of the settings are located.

The Internet control panel gets used in two ways in Macintosh GoLive: to supplement and manage file mappings for opening files directly from GoLive and to set up proxy server settings for environments.

File Mappings

In Chapter 18, *Page Specials*, we talk about File Mapping: GoLive's built-in ability to know which applications should open which files when you double-click them in the Files or Site tab, or select and open them directly from a page.

GoLive for Mac offers an additional feature: you can tie in a list of file extensions, MIME types, and programs associated with them from the Internet control panel.

Most Internet files have their type determined in part by their file extension: a three- or four-letter code after a period or dot at the end of their name. Windows users have handled extensions for years; filenames, even under Windows NT, ME and 2000, still require a three-letter extension to let Windows know what program created and/or should open a given file.

Under Windows, the extension is the only clue to a file's creating application. The extension gets mapped to an application that can open and edit the file through the Windows Registry, a kind of low-level database of program information. The Registry contains a single association for each extension.

If you install Photoshop, CorelDraw, and PhotoImpact one after another, TIFF files you double-click will only open in PhotoImpact, the last one to install its entries in the Registry.

The Internet control panel brings some of the management features of the Registry without any of the craziness. It comes with a number of mappings built in for standard Internet programs.

TIP:
Accessing Internet Control Panel's File Mappings

The default view of the Internet control panel is designed not to frighten small children and dogs, and therefore hides the file mappings. From the Edit menu, select User Mode, then choose Advanced or Administration from the resulting dialog box; the latter allows you to lock settings and protect them with a password. Click OK, and an Advanced tab appears; one of the panes at left is File Mapping.

In the File Mapping tab of Web Settings (available under the Edit menu), checking Use Internet control panel instantly imports all the Internet settings (see Figure A-10). In fact, it instantly overwrites any customized settings you might have applied, so beware. (You can apply settings via the Internet control panel itself and then, when you import, those settings are brought in as well.)

Figure A-10
Internet
control panel's
File Mapping
settings

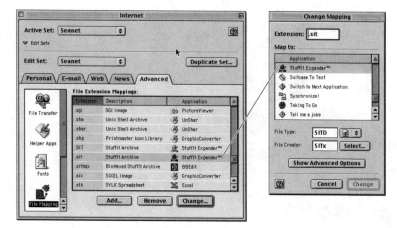

If, for some reason, you think you made a mistake by using the Internet control panel settings, uncheck Use Internet Control Panel and GoLive reverts to its built-in settings.

TIP:
Odd
Programs

The Internet control panel specifies default programs for lots and lots of extensions that you've probably never heard of. It also lists programs you certainly don't have installed on your machine. But these settings are only invoked if a file with the appropriate extension is encountered. Even then, if you don't have the application, GoLive prompts you or tries to open with the most likely application depending on what other software you have installed.

Proxy Servers

GoLive also relies on the Internet control panel as an option for linking to a proxy server. If you don't know what a proxy server is and you've never had anything to do with one, you can ignore this section entirely. But if you work in an institution or corporation, your Web requests may have to go through an indirect method. A proxy server generally sits on your local or corporate network; it receives requests from browsers or FTP clients inside the network, goes out on the Internet to retrieve the requests pages or items, then sends them back to the machine that requested them.

GoLive for Macintosh can import your proxy settings from the Internet control panel in the Network pane of Preferences (see Figure A-11). Clicking Import Now brings the current settings in, but checking Use Always keeps the settings current whenever you change them in the Internet control panel and then launch GoLive.

You can click the Internet control panel icon to set your proxy addresses and features and then return to GoLive to see them applied.

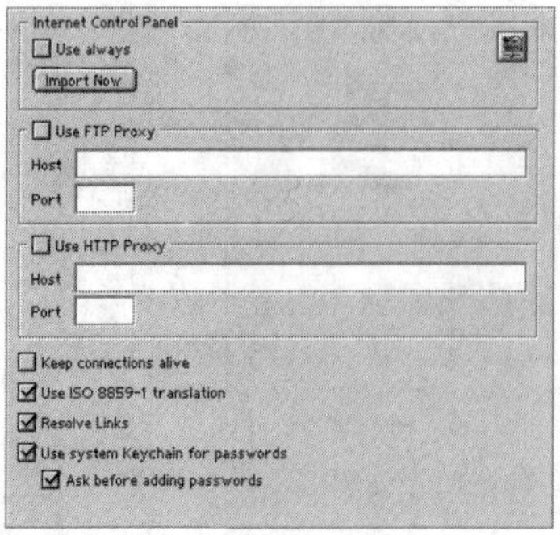

Figure A-11
Proxy settings

AppleScript

Apple offers a simple scripting language that most Macintosh users barely notice. It's an easy-to-learn programming language, but it is programming, and it's not for every user. However, for automating behavior that requires some flexibility or conditionality, AppleScript can create entire publishing and production systems that wildly extend the abilities of ordinary programs.

Many publishing companies combine AppleScript and QuarkXPress to create a system that allows them to automate workflow from word-processing files through to final laid-out pages.

GoLive offers control only over items in the HTML Source Editor, but it does provide tools to allow you to select, insert, and format text according to HTML specifications, as well as create and name documents.

The reference provided by Adobe in the GoLive manual is extensive and specific enough to avoid repetition here. You can also find much of the same detail built into GoLive's internal AppleScript dictionary definitions. Find the program called Script Editor that should have been installed along with your system. (If it's not on your hard drive, you need to go back and reinstall Apple-Script from your Mac OS disk or download it from http://www.apple-script.com/.)

Run Script Editor and select Open Dictionary from the File menu. Then select the GoLive application itself, and the Script Editor displays the reference of events that GoLive knows how to work with (see Figure A-12).

A couple ideas for using AppleScript include:

• Scripting FileMaker Pro to create output that's used along with a template to create static HTML pages with content extracted from a database. Combined with Anarchie (http://www.stairways.com), another AppleScript-able program, you could set up a system that, on demand, created new pages and uploaded them to your Web site via FTP.

- Creating a standalone AppleScript that prompted for a folder location and then performed a find-and-replace operation on every HTML file in the folder to fix standard HTML problems described in Chapter 24, *Importing a Site*.

For more details on AppleScript, consult Apple's site at http://www.applescript.com/, or buy Danny Goodman's AppleScript Handbook, the definitive book on the subject; these links are also found at http://realworldgolive.com.

Figure A-12
GoLive
AppleScript
dictionary

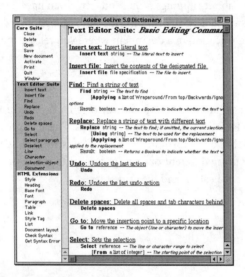

Text Clippings

Another of the Mac OS's varying methods for storing snippets of text (like the Scrapbook and Stickies utilities) is the clippings feature. Simply select a block of text and drag it to the Desktop to create a new read-only file containing that text, which the Finder can open directly without the aid of a third-party word processor (see Figure A-13).

Figure A-13
Text clippings

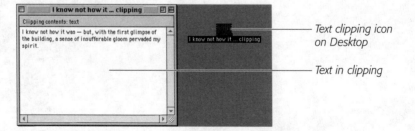

Text clipping icon on Desktop

Text in clipping

One advantage to creating text clippings is the easy availability of frequently used text. But you could also use them as temporary storage for information that can't all fit on the Clipboard at once. Clippings also retain most of the basic formatting applied to the original text, such as font, bold, italics, and underlines, without requiring you to create a new file with a word processor.

Once you've created a clipping file, you can copy its contents by opening the file and selecting Copy from the Edit menu (or pressing Command-C). But what's nice about clippings is that you don't even have to open them to get to their text: simply drag the clipping file onto an open window; the text will be placed at the location in a document where you release the clipping file.

Core Apple

GoLive has shed most of its Macintosh origins by synchronizing features between the Macintosh and Windows versions. These improvements make it easier to work back and forth between platforms, and allow teams of people that might be using different operating systems to more seamlessly function with the same application and the same files.

APPENDIX B

Windows Issues & Extras

In the first edition of this book, this appendix didn't exist. And, yes, we got some flak for it from Windows users who thought we were slighting them. (For the record, everything in both editions of the book was tested on both platforms multiple times to make sure we got it right.)

But the folks who complained to us failed to note one important fact: GoLive for Macintosh supports a bunch of Apple technology (ColorSync, Keychain, Find by Content, etc.), while GoLive for Windows doesn't. It doesn't because, um, Windows doesn't have corresponding technology that's useful for managing Web sites.

Okay, here come the phone calls and letters, right? We use Windows all the time, in versions from 95 to 2000, NT to ME, as well as m-o-u-s-e.

It's not that Windows isn't great or that it doesn't support everything or that it doesn't work. It does: it's terrific. It handles fonts, files, FTP, etc.

But it lacks system-level color-management support ; it doesn't have an indexing system for simulating search engine results that GoLive can tie into; its system-level password support doesn't have hooks to store FTP and WebDAV passwords; its file information is in the extension, not stored somewhere else. (There is the Windows Registry, but that's a Pandora's box; there's no reason why a user should ever touch the Registry directly.)

Windows does have a scripting system to automate tasks (like AppleScript on the Mac), but unfortunately the current release doesn't support VBScript. (Maybe in a future release.)

We're just vamping here to fill up space. Can you tell?

Look, we'll make you a deal: check our site at http://realworldgolive.com/windows.html from time to time, or subscribe to our updates mailing list. If anything changes, we'll let you know.

Index

This index is also available free of charge as a downloadable Acrobat PDF (Portable Document Format) file for searching and printing at: http://realworldgolive.com/rwgl5index.html.

Keep in Touch!

We improve our books by listening to readers, so stay in touch! Your feedback is valuable, and as you read through this book, you'll see many mentions of questions from readers that we answer in this edition, or suggestions provided by you all that we try to incorporate. We try to answer all the email we get, although a prompt answer isn't always possible.

We'd also recommend you hop on our moderated email list, which you can subscribe to via http://realworldgolive.com. This list is full of sophisticated GoLive users who share their questions and solutions for using the program to create their designs. The same is true of the Adobe Forums, where tech support and fellow users help out (http://www.adobe.com/support/forums/main.html).

Here's how to reach us:

Snail mail:
7300 E. Green Lake Dr. N., Suite 200
Seattle, WA 98115-5304
Fax (206) 528-2999

Email
authors@realworldgolive.com

—*Jeff Carlson, Never Enough Coffee Creations, http://necoffee.com*
& Glenn Fleishman, Unsolicited Pundit, http://glennf.com